T0345004

NBER Macroeconomics Annual 2017

NBER Macroeconomics Annual 2017

Edited by
Martin Eichenbaum and Jonathan A. Parker

The University of Chicago Press
Chicago and London

NBER Macroeconomics Annual 2017, Number 32

Published annually by The University of Chicago Press.

Standing orders
To place a standing order for this book series, please address your request to The University of Chicago Press, Chicago Distribution Center, Attn. Standing Orders/Customer Service, 11030 S. Langley Avenue, Chicago, IL 60628. Telephone toll free in the U.S. and Canada: 1-800-621-2736; or 1-773-702-7000. Fax toll free in the U.S. and Canada: 1-800-621-8476; or 1-773-702-7212.

Single-copy orders
In the U.K. and Europe: Order from your local bookseller or direct from The University of Chicago Press, c/o John Wiley Ltd. Distribution Center, 1 Oldlands Way, Bognor Regis, West Sussex PO22 9SA, UK. Telephone 01243 779777 or Fax 01243 820250. E-mail: cs-books@wiley.co.uk

In the U.S., Canada, and the rest of the world: Order from your local bookseller or direct from The University of Chicago Press, Chicago Distribution Center, 11030 S. Langley Avenue, Chicago, IL 60628. Telephone toll free in the U.S. and Canada: 1-800-621-2736; or 1-773-702-7000. Fax toll free in the U.S. and Canada: 1-800-621-8476; or 1-773-702-7212.

Special orders
University of Chicago Press books may be purchased at quantity discounts for business or promotional use. For information, please write to Sales Department—Special Sales, The University of Chicago Press, 1427 E. 60th Street, Chicago, IL 60637 USA or telephone 1-773-702-7723.

This book was printed and bound in the United States of America.

ISSN: 0889-3365
ISBN-13: 978-0-226-57766-1 (hc.:alk.paper)
ISBN-13: 978-0-226-57797-5 (e-book)

10 9 8 7 6 5 4 3 2 1

Relation of the Directors to the Work and Publications of the NBER

1. The object of the NBER is to ascertain and present to the economics profession, and to the public more generally, important economic facts and their interpretation in a scientific manner without policy recommendations. The Board of Directors is charged with the responsibility of ensuring that the work of the NBER is carried on in strict conformity with this object.

2. The President shall establish an internal review process to ensure that book manuscripts proposed for publication DO NOT contain policy recommendations. This shall apply both to the proceedings of conferences and to manuscripts by a single author or by one or more co-authors but shall not apply to authors of comments at NBER conferences who are not NBER affiliates.

3. No book manuscript reporting research shall be published by the NBER until the President has sent to each member of the Board a notice that a manuscript is recommended for publication and that in the President's opinion it is suitable for publication in accordance with the above principles of the NBER. Such notification will include a table of contents and an abstract or summary of the manuscript's content, a list of contributors if applicable, and a response form for use by Directors who desire a copy of the manuscript for review. Each manuscript shall contain a summary drawing attention to the nature and treatment of the problem studied and the main conclusions reached.

4. No volume shall be published until forty-five days have elapsed from the above notification of intention to publish it. During this period a copy shall be sent to any Director requesting it, and if any Director objects to publication on the grounds that the manuscript contains policy recommendations, the objection will be presented to the author(s) or editor(s). In case of dispute, all members of the Board shall be notified,

and the President shall appoint an ad hoc committee of the Board to decide the matter; thirty days additional shall be granted for this purpose.

5. The President shall present annually to the Board a report describing the internal manuscript review process, any objections made by Directors before publication or by anyone after publication, any disputes about such matters, and how they were handled.

6. Publications of the NBER issued for informational purposes concerning the work of the Bureau, or issued to inform the public of the activities at the Bureau, including but not limited to the NBER Digest and Reporter, shall be consistent with the object stated in paragraph 1. They shall contain a specific disclaimer noting that they have not passed through the review procedures required in this resolution. The Executive Committee of the Board is charged with the review of all such publications from time to time.

7. NBER working papers and manuscripts distributed on the Bureau's web site are not deemed to be publications for the purpose of this resolution, but they shall be consistent with the object stated in paragraph 1. Working papers shall contain a specific disclaimer noting that they have not passed through the review procedures required in this resolution. The NBER's web site shall contain a similar disclaimer. The President shall establish an internal review process to ensure that the working papers and the web site do not contain policy recommendations, and shall report annually to the Board on this process and any concerns raised in connection with it.

8. Unless otherwise determined by the Board or exempted by the terms of paragraphs 6 and 7, a copy of this resolution shall be printed in each NBER publication as described in paragraph 2 above.

Contents

Editorial

Martin Eichenbaum, *Northwestern University and NBER*
Jonathan A. Parker, *MIT and NBER*

The NBER's 32nd Annual Conference on Macroeconomics brought together leading scholars to present, discuss, and debate six research papers on central issues in contemporary macroeconomics. In addition, Olivier Blanchard, former Chief Economist at the International Monetary Fund, delivered a thought-provoking talk after dinner on whether current models of macroeconomic fluctuations focus on the central distortions underlying business cycles. Finally, we had a special panel session on the economic implications of changes in financial regulation featuring three experts in this area: Lisa Emsbo-Mattingly, Director of Research in Global Asset Allocation at Fidelity Investments and former President of the National Association for Business Economics; Karen Dynan of Harvard and a former Assistant Secretary for Domestic Policy at the US Treasury Department; and Jeremy Stein of Harvard and former board member at the Board of Governors of the Federal Reserve System. Video recordings of the presentations of the papers, summaries of the papers by the authors, the after-dinner speech, and the lunchtime panel discussion are all accessible on the NBER Annual Conference on Macroeconomics web page (http://www.nber.org/macroannualconference2017/macroannual2017.html). We hope that these videos make a useful complement to this volume and make the content of the conference more widely accessible.

This conference volume contains edited versions of the six papers presented at the conference, each followed by two written discussions by leading scholars and a summary of the debates that followed each paper. A final chapter contains a paper by Olivier Blanchard based on his speech at the conference.

The first paper in this year's volume is a significant methodological step forward in non-representative-agent macroeconomics as well as a contribution to the study of the dynamics of national consumption expenditures. "When Inequality Matters for Macro and Macro Matters for Inequality" by SeHyoun Ahn, Greg Kaplan, Benjamin Moll, Thomas Winberry, and Christian Wolf introduces a general methodology for solving macroeconomic models with heterogeneous agents in which the state space includes a high-dimensional distribution. The current approach to the solution of such models is the canonical Krusell and Smith (1998) approach, which approximates this distribution by a few moments and solves for optimal individual behavior when individuals only have information on these moments rather than on the complete distribution. In practice, in nearly all applications, the first moment suffices in the sense that the agent's welfare gain to using more moments in the information set of its optimization problem is trivial. This (quasi) result, known as "quasi aggregation," is widely used, widely cited, and sometimes misunderstood. While aggregate quantities are largely sufficient for prediction, the dynamics of aggregate quantities are often significantly different from those in the equivalent representative agent economy. And as a result, the response to shocks, and so the effects of policy, may be very different.

The paper presents a novel alternative method for the solution of these models that allows agents' optimal policy rules to depend on a large number of state variables, such as the distribution of wealth in the economy. The essence of the method is to approximate the evolution of the aggregate economy, including the distribution, as a linear system and use dimension-reduction methods to reduce complexity even further. Together, these two steps make solving for the equilibrium very rapid. In addition, provided the time intervals in the discrete approximation are taken to be "small enough," convergence of the economy back to its steady state from any point is accurately measured (it would be exact in the continuous time limit with a continuous sample path). Accompanying the paper, the authors have made toolboxes available to implement the methods of the paper in general models. One discussant refers to the method as a "weapon of mass creation." While the method is quite rapid even for large dimensional state spaces, it does not yet permit nonlinearized initial responses to any given disturbance (that is, the method relies on certainty equivalence to aggregate shocks).

The paper develops two examples of incomplete markets economies in which individual consumer's consumption choices are not linear in own wealth. So that the distribution of wealth in the economy is necessary to describe the state of the economy. Applying the paper's methods, these examples show how, in one case, the presence of heterogeneity significantly alters the dynamics of the economy and how, in the other case, one can track the impact of a macroeconomic shock on the complex distribution of wealth in the economy.

Turning to our next paper, a central feature of the post-financial crisis macroeconomic environment is the coexistence of low, nonvolatile inflation rates, near-zero short-term interest rates, and an explosion in monetary aggregates. John H. Cochrane's paper, "Michelson-Morley, Fisher, and Occam: The Radical Implications of Stable Quiet Inflation at the Zero Bound," is a provocative treatise that focuses on the questions: What class of macro models most naturally explains these observations and what are the implications for monetary policy? The recent US experience of low levels of inflation along with the explosion of monetary aggregates is evidence inconsistent with canonical monetarism. Dispatching the standard New Keynesian model is harder work. The standard, rational expectations New Keynesian model predicts that under an interest rate peg, the equilibrium is indeterminate and gives rise to the possibility of sunspot volatility. If the recent experience constitutes an interest rate peg, then the fact that inflation was quite smooth is evidence against the standard New Keynesian model. In contrast, the paper argues that the New Keynesian model merged with the fiscal theory of the price level is consistent with these postcrisis facts.

The paper then draws out the implications of the fiscal theory for current monetary policy issues. First, what happens to inflation if central banks raise interest rates? The first-order answer to this question is neo-Fisherian: higher interest rates lead to higher inflation except under very special assumptions. Second, the paper assesses the implications for the stance of monetary policy and the view that monetary policy should be normalized, that is, interest rates should be raised closer to their precrisis levels.

Not surprisingly, the paper led to spirited discussions. The first discussant called into question the premise that low postcrisis interest rates should be thought of as an interest rate peg. The second discussant questioned whether New Keynesian models have difficulty generating a decline in inflation after a policy-induced rise in the nominal interest rate. A lot of discussion also focused on the fiscal theory of the price level more generally, and whether it robustly leads to a determinate price level or accounts for ongoing low inflation rates in the face of a pronounced rise in public debt.

Our third paper turns to the topic of the US financial crisis and Great Recession. Both followed the subprime meltdown, leading the media and many observers to infer that the subprime crisis caused the financial crisis and Great Recession. This paper, "Dynamics of Housing Debt in the Recent Boom and Great Recession" by Manuel Adelino, Antoinette Schoar, and Felipe Severino, asks about the deeper causes of this lending boom. Much research has confirmed that the expansion of mortgage borrowing and the rise and collapse in house prices was, if not the main cause of, at least a major propagator and amplifier of the Great Recession. But was the lending boom driven by relaxation of credit provision to low-income and low-credit-score households, or was it instead a widespread expansion of collateralized lending based on ex post incorrect expectations of the value of housing as collateral?

The paper shows that the house price boom, the expansion of mortgage debt, and the following wave of defaults was not a subprime phenomenon. Rather, it was spread across the distribution of incomes and house values in the United States. More specifically, the paper uses detailed microdata on mortgages to show that the evolution of borrowing, subsequent defaults, debt-to-income ratios, and loan-to-value ratios were similar across the income distribution throughout the boom and bust. This paper thus adds to the research of Adelino, Schoar, and Severino (2016), Foote, Loewenstein, and Willen (2016), Mian and Sufi (2016), and Albanesi, DeGiorgi, and Nosal (2017) that shows that there was no major dislocation of credit and shift in defaults toward low-income households.

The paper and the written discussions place the evidence from the paper in the context of some of the leading general equilibrium models that have attempted to explain the Great Recession through a housing channel. The evidence in the paper is consistent with the expectations view. But it is also consistent with any theory based on a broad-based expansion in borrowing by US households followed by widespread defaults.

Recent research has documented that the United States and many other countries experienced large increases in income inequality over the past several decades. Further, across countries, those with greater inequality have lower social mobility. This stylized fact is referred to as the Great Gatsby curve. The question tackled by our fourth paper, "Understanding the Great Gatsby Curve" by Steven Durlauf and Ananth Seshadri, is: Do increases in inequality cause lower levels of economic mobility or opportunity? The paper brings both a structural model and a battery of empirical evidence to argue that the answer to this question is yes. A significant body of research supports the idea that nonmarket, neighborhood characteristics are important determinants of child outcomes through such channels as education, role models, and social learning.

Good neighborhood characteristics come from high-skill or high-income neighbors (through, e.g., taxes). So positive assortative matching can be privately optimal. The paper builds a model in which this positive assortative matching implies that greater income inequality reduces income mobility and so propagates through time. In the model, households select into neighborhoods, neighborhoods are a critical ingredient in the development of skills by children, and, through positive associative matching, greater individual-level inequality leads to more inequality across neighborhoods. A critical assumption is that borrowing constraints prohibit parents from borrowing against their children's income to increase the quality of the neighborhood they live in to raise their children's income. Thus, increases in inequality at a point in time increase differences across neighborhoods, which in turn reduces mobility across generations and leads to further increases in inequality. Through this dynamic, the model generates a cross-sectional Great Gatsby curve. But it also provides a worrisome picture of the future. Recent increases in inequality may lead to still larger increases in the future through more unequal distribution of opportunity. The paper also presents evidence regarding the critical elements of the model, including estimating a reduced-form Great Gatsby curve and investigating the role of neighborhood in intergenerational mobility in the United States.

The discussion extends the paper's analysis of existing evidence. In particular, it notes that greater inequality could lead to greater redistribution. But existing evidence suggests that the reverse is true: greater inequality leads to less redistribution. The discussion also analyzes the empirical analysis and places the theory in the literature using a simplified, unifying model.

Since the rational expectations revolution, macroeconomic research has mainly focused on rational expectations equilibria in which the probability distributions that agents perceive correspond to the actual probability distributions that govern the dynamics of the model economy. Based on revealed preference data alone, beliefs and utility functions are not separately identified. Rational expectations equilibria is an assumption that separates the two. An alternative approach is to consider evidence besides that revealed by behavior. Our fifth paper, "Survey

Measurement of Probabilistic Macroeconomic Expectations: Progress and Promise" by Charles F. Manski, discusses the history and current state of the direct measurement of beliefs through the use of surveys.

The paper reviews and evaluates the main criticisms of the use of survey expectations. Many issues relate to problems with survey measurement more generally, and on most of these issues, significant progress has been achieved. As an example, the paper discusses in detail survey measures of inflation expectations, which, among survey-based expectation measures, have been used the most for research in macroeconomics. The two main surveys of inflation expectations use two different approaches: questions that ask for point predictions and questions that ask for probabilities of different outcomes to construct more of the distribution. The paper discusses how the different approaches have different implications for what one infers about expected inflation. Even with the progress that has been made, the paper notes several open questions about survey measures, such as whether responses themselves conflate utility and probability.

The paper also analyzes the question of how the data from expectations surveys can be used. Should such data be viewed as informative or taken as literally true? The paper shows that expectations are extremely useful for predicting behavior, but that they are likely measured with significant error so that it is not yet clear how best to incorporate them directly into analysis of choice. Among other topics, the discussions take up this issue and propose building a model of survey response errors to improve inference and modeling based on the survey responses.

The paper concludes by discussing future uses of survey data. The most promising use is probably in the development of structural models of belief formation. In part due to the availability of more survey-based measures of subjective expectations, some recent macroeconomic models deviate from rational expectations and employ alternative models of expectations formation. The paper argues that survey expectations can provide some discipline for these exercises. Without additional data on expectations, beliefs and other aspects of models are not separately identified. In keeping with the centrality of the topic, the paper brought out a lively debate at the conference, much of which is reproduced after the written discussions.

The final paper in the volume, "Credit Market Freezes" by Efraim Benmelech and Nittai K. Bergman, analyzes a central feature of financial crises: large declines in debt issuance and the evaporation of market liquidity. The paper's first contribution is to collect and present data on bond issuance during the period surrounding the 1873, 1929, and 2008–2009 financial crises, and to show that there was a substantial decline in bond issuance during and after the onset of these crises.

The second contribution is to try and discriminate between two different explanations of why credit market liquidity declines so much during financial crises using evidence from the cross section of bonds in each crisis. If credit markets freeze because frictions like asymmetric information and adverse selection in bond markets rise, then bond illiquidity should rise as bond values decline. Alternatively, if the crisis makes beliefs more homogenous, then as the dispersion of beliefs about the common value of a given bond declines, there will be less trading and so less liquidity in the crisis, subject to certain caveats about the distribution of endowments among bond participants. Thus, if credit markets freeze because beliefs about common value become more homogeneous, then bond liquidity should be lower for bonds about which there is more agreement.

The paper finds that measures of illiquidity, like bid-ask spreads, rise the most for bonds whose market value decline the most relative to face value. This finding supports an asymmetric information or adverse-selection-based theory of credit market freezes. Additionally, using different proxies for belief dispersion in markets, the paper finds that illiquidity and dispersion in beliefs both rise during financial crises. This finding is inconsistent with liquidity differences being caused by differences in belief dispersion. The paper concludes with a discussion of the implications of the empirical findings for the efficacy of monetary policy during financial crises.

The first discussant raised questions about whether the empirical findings in the paper provide a convincing test of the particular theory of asymmetric information and adverse selection that the paper emphasizes. The discussion presents an alternative framework with adverse selection and reputation that can account for the paper's findings; the credit market equilibrium is typically efficient and abrupt collapses in trade volume are not a sign of poorly functioning markets. The second discussant raised the same questions and argued that there are a number of models that have similar predictions and for which the policy implications are quite different. Among other topics, the general discussion considered what evidence could distinguish among different theories of illiquidity spikes during financial crises.

The final chapter in this volume is an edited version of the after-dinner speech by Olivier Blanchard, a longtime MIT faculty member and NBER affiliate, a former editor of the *NBER Macroeconomics Annual*, one of the authors in the inaugural issue, and more recently, chief economist at the International Monetary Fund for seven eventful years that included the US financial crisis and the European sovereign debt crisis. The theme of the talk was that macroeconomic research is far from over. Economic models simplify the real world so that we can understand much of how it works. The most strenuous debates in macroeconomics have always involved *how* we simplify. The after-dinner speech first suggested that the key distortions that we currently focus on in models of business cycles may not be the central ones, and as a result we may need a new core model for economic fluctuations. Second, and more tentatively, the talk proposed a set of ingredients for a new core model.

The talk sets out the intellectual history that has led us to the New Keynesian synthesis that lies behind most models used in academic research and by central banks today, and focuses on the distortions that arise from price stickiness (and monopolistic competition). But there are other distortions, such as those arising from wage stickiness, credit frictions, frictions in the banking sector, and liquidity. There are also now rigorously founded behavioral frictions such as limited attention. These frictions may be as critical as nominal rigidities, or even provide a foundation for nominal rigidities as well as other distortions in the economy. The talk sketches a first pass at the ingredients that Blanchard sees as critical for a new generation of dynamic stochastic general equilibrium models. Like many other after-dinner talks at the Annual Conference on Macroeconomics, Blanchard's provocative ideas led to a vigorous debate after the talk.

As in previous years, the editors posted and distributed a call for proposals in the spring and summer prior to the conference, and some of the papers in this volume were selected from proposals submitted in response to this call. Other papers are commissioned on central and topical areas in macroeconomics. Both are done in consultation with the advisory board, who we thank for their input and support of both the conference and the published volume.

The authors and the editors would like to take this opportunity to thank Jim Poterba and the National Bureau of Economic Research for their continued support for the *NBER Macroeconomics Annual* and the associated conference. We would also like to thank the NBER conference staff, particularly Rob Shannon, for his continued excellent organization and support. We want to thank the advisory board for their assistance in evaluating papers and suggesting topics. We would also like to thank the NBER Public Information staff, and Charlie Radin in particular, for producing the high-quality multimedia content. Financial assistance from the National Science Foundation is gratefully acknowledged. Daniel Green and Gideon Bornstein provided invaluable help in preparing the summaries of the discussions. And last, but far from least, we are grateful to Helena Fitz-Patrick for her invaluable assistance in editing and publishing the volume.

Endnote

For acknowledgments, sources of research support, and disclosure of the authors' material financial relationships, if any, please see http://www.nber.org/chapters/c13906.ack.

References (also appear in the papers)

Adelino, Manuel, Antoinette Schoar, and Felipe Severino. 2016. "Loan Originations and Defaults in the Mortgage Crisis: The Role of the Middle Class." *Review of Financial Studies* 29 (7): 1635–70.
Albanesi, Stefania, Giacamo DeGiorgi, and Jaromic Nosal. 2017. "Credit Growth and the Financial Crisis: A New Narrative." Working paper.
Foote, Christopher L., Lara Loewenstein, and Paul S. Willen. 2016. "Cross-Sectional Patterns of Mortgage Debt during the Housing Boom: Evidence and Implications." NBER Working Paper no. 22985, Cambridge, MA.
Mian, Atif, and Amir Sufi. 2009. "The Consequences of Mortgage Credit Expansion: Evidence from the US Mortgage Default Crisis." *Quarterly Journal of Economics* 124 (4): 1449–96.
———. 2016. "Household Debt and Defaults from 2000 to 2010: The Credit Supply View." Working paper.

Abstracts

1 When Inequality Matters for Macro and Macro Matters for Inequality
SeHyoun Ahn, Greg Kaplan, Benjamin Moll, Thomas Winberry, and Christian Wolf

We develop an efficient and easy-to-use computational method for solving a wide class of general equilibrium heterogeneous agent models with aggregate shocks together with an open source suite of codes that implement our algorithms in an easy-to-use toolbox. Our method extends standard linearization techniques and is designed to work in cases when inequality matters for the dynamics of macroeconomic aggregates. We present two applications that analyze a two-asset incomplete markets model parameterized to match the distribution of income, wealth, and marginal propensities to consume. First, we show that our model is consistent with two key features of aggregate consumption dynamics that are difficult to match with representative agent models: (1) the sensitivity of aggregate consumption to predictable changes in aggregate income, and (2) the relative smoothness of aggregate consumption. Second, we extend the model to feature capital-skill complementarity and show how factor-specific productivity shocks shape dynamics of income and consumption inequality.

2 Michelson-Morley, Fisher, and Occam: The Radical Implications of Stable Quiet Inflation at the Zero Bound
John H. Cochrane

The long period of quiet inflation at near-zero interest rates, with large quantitative easing, suggests that core monetary doctrines are wrong. It suggests that inflation can be stable and determinate at the zero bound, and by extension under passive policy including a nominal interest rate peg, and that arbitrary amounts of interest-paying reserves are not inflationary. Of the known alternatives, the New Keynesian model merged with the fiscal theory of the price level is the only simple economic model consistent with this interpretation of the facts.

I explore two implications of this conclusion. First, what happens if central banks raise interest rates? Inflation stability implies that higher nominal interest rates will eventually result in higher inflation. But can higher interest rates temporarily reduce inflation? Yes, but only by a novel mechanism that depends crucially on fiscal policy. Second, what are the implications for monetary policy and the urgency to "normalize"? Inflation stability implies that low-interest-rate monetary policy is, perhaps unintentionally, benign, producing a stable Friedman-optimal quantity of money, that a large interest-paying balance sheet can be maintained indefinitely. The fiscal anchoring required by this interpretation of the data responds to discount rates, however, and may not be as strong as it appears.

3   Dynamics of Housing Debt in the Recent Boom and Great Recession
Manuel Adelino, Antoinette Schoar, and Felipe Severino

This paper documents a number of key facts about the evolution of mortgage debt, homeownership, debt burden, and subsequent delinquency during the recent housing boom and Great Recession. We show that the mortgage expansion was shared across the entire income distribution; that is, the flow and stock of debt rose across all income groups (except for the top 5%). The mortgage expansion was especially pronounced in areas with increased house prices, and the speed at which houses turned over (churn) in these areas went up significantly. However, the average loan-to-value ratios (LTV) at origination did not increase over the boom period. While homeownership rates increased for the middle- and upper-income households, there was no increase in homeownership for the lowest income groups. Finally, default rates postcrisis went up predominantly in areas with large house price drops, especially for high-income and high-FICO borrowers. These results are consistent with a view that the run-up in mortgage debt over the precrisis period was driven by rising home values and expectations of increasing prices.

4 Understanding the Great Gatsby Curve
Steven N. Durlauf and Ananth Seshadri

The Great Gatsby Curve, the observation that for OECD countries greater cross-sectional income inequality is associated with lower mobility, has become a prominent part of scholarly and policy discussions because of its implications for the relationship between inequality of outcomes and inequality of opportunities. We explore this relationship by focusing on evidence and interpretation of an intertemporal Gatsby Curve for the United States. We consider inequality/mobility relationships that are derived from nonlinearities in the transmission process of income from parents to children and the relationship that is derived from the effects of inequality of socioeconomic segregation, which then affects children. Empirical evidence for the mechanisms we identify is strong. We find modest reduced-form evidence and structural evidence of an intertemporal Gatsby Curve for the United States as mediated by social influences.

5 Survey Measurement of Probabilistic Macroeconomic Expectations: Progress and Promise
Charles F. Manski

Economists commonly suppose that persons have probabilistic expectations for uncertain events, yet empirical research measuring expectations was long rare. The inhibition against collection of expectations data has gradually lessened, generating a substantial body of recent evidence on the expectations of broad populations. This paper first summarizes the history leading to development of the modern literature and overviews its main concerns. I then describe research on three subjects that should be of direct concern to macroeconomists: expectations of equity returns, inflation expectations, and professional macroeconomic forecasters. I also describe work that questions the assumption that persons have well-defined probabilistic expectations and communicate them accurately in surveys. Finally, I consider the evolution of thinking about expectations formation in macroeconomic policy analysis. I favorably observe the increasing willingness of theorists to study alternatives to rational expectations assumptions, but I express concern that models of expectations formation will proliferate in the absence of empirical research to discipline thinking. To make progress,

I urge measurement and analysis of the revisions to expectations that agents make following occurrence of unanticipated shocks.

6   Credit Market Freezes

Efraim Benmelech and Nittai K. Bergman

Credit market freezes in which debt issuance declines dramatically and market liquidity evaporates are typically observed during financial crises. In the financial crisis of 2008–2009, the structured credit market froze, issuance of corporate bonds declined, and secondary credit markets became highly illiquid. In this paper, we analyze liquidity in bond markets during financial crises and compare two main theories of liquidity in markets: (1) asymmetric information and adverse selection, and (2) heterogenous beliefs. Analyzing the 1873 financial crisis as well as the 2008–2009 crisis, we find that when bond value deteriorates, bond illiquidity increases, consistent with an adverse-selection model of the information sensitivity of debt contracts. While we show that the adverse-selection model of debt liquidity explains a large portion of the rise in illiquidity, we find little support for the hypothesis that opinion dispersion explains illiquidity in financial crises.

1

When Inequality Matters for Macro and Macro Matters for Inequality

SeHyoun Ahn, *Princeton University*
Greg Kaplan, *University of Chicago and NBER*
Benjamin Moll, *Princeton University, CEPR, and NBER*
Thomas Winberry, *Chicago Booth and NBER*
Christian Wolf, *Princeton University*

I. Introduction

Over the last 30 years, tremendous progress has been made in developing models that reproduce salient features of the rich heterogeneity in income, wealth, and consumption behavior across households that is routinely observed in microdata. These heterogeneous agent models often deliver strikingly different implications of monetary and fiscal policies than do representative agent models, and allow us to study the distributional implications of these policies across households.[1] In principle, this class of models can therefore incorporate the rich interaction between inequality and the macroeconomy that characterizes our world: on the one hand, inequality shapes macroeconomic aggregates; on the other hand, macroeconomic shocks and policies also affect inequality.

Despite providing a framework for thinking about these important issues, heterogeneous agent models are not yet part of policymakers' toolboxes for evaluating the macroeconomic and distributional consequences of their proposed policies. Instead, most quantitative analyses of the macroeconomy, particularly in central banks and other policy institutions, still employ representative agent models. Applied macroeconomists tend to make two excuses for this abstraction. First, they argue that the computational difficulties involved in solving and analyzing heterogeneous agent models render their use intractable, especially compared to the ease with which they can analyze representative agent models using software packages like Dynare. Second, there is a perception among macroeconomists that models that incorporate realistic heterogeneity are unnecessarily complicated because they generate only limited additional explanatory power for aggregate phenomena. Part of this perception stems from the seminal work of Krusell and Smith (1998), who found that the business cycle properties of aggregates in a baseline heterogeneous agent model are virtually indistinguishable from those in the representative agent counterpart.[2]

Our paper's main message is that both of these excuses are less valid than commonly thought. To this end, we make two contributions. First, we develop an efficient and easy-to-use computational method for solving a wide class of general equilibrium heterogeneous agent macro models with aggregate shocks, thereby invalidating the first excuse. Importantly, our method also applies in environments that violate what Krusell and Smith (1998) have termed "approximate aggregation," that is, that macroeconomic aggregates can be well described using only the mean of the wealth distribution.

Second, we use the method to analyze the time series behavior of a rich two-asset heterogeneous agent model parameterized to match the distribution of income, wealth, and marginal propensities to consume (MPCs) in the microdata. We show that the model is consistent with two features of the time series of aggregate consumption that have proven to be a challenge for representative agent models: consumption responds to predictable changes in income, but at the same time is substantially less volatile than realized income. We then demonstrate how a quantitatively plausible heterogeneous agent economy such as ours can be useful in understanding the distributional consequences of aggregate shocks, thus paving the way for a complete analysis of the transmission of shocks to inequality. These results invalidate the second excuse: not only does macro matter for inequality, but inequality also matters for macro. We therefore view an important part of the future of macroeconomics as the study of distributions—the representative-agent shortcut may both miss a large part of the story (the distributional implications) and get the small remaining part wrong (the implications for aggregates).

In Section II, we introduce our computational methodology, which extends standard linearization techniques, routinely used to solve representative agent models, to the heterogeneous agent context.[3] For pedagogical reasons, we describe our methods in the context of the Krusell and Smith (1998) model, but the methods are applicable much more broadly. We first solve for the stationary equilibrium of the model *without* aggregate shocks (but with idiosyncratic shocks) using a global nonlinear approximation. We use the finite difference method of Achdou et al. (2015) but, in principle, other methods can be used as well. This approximation gives a discretized representation of the model's stationary equilibrium, which includes a nondegenerate distribution of agents over their individual state variables. We then compute a first-order Taylor expansion of the discretized model *with* aggregate shocks around the stationary equilibrium. This results in a large, but linear, system of stochastic differential equations, which we solve using standard solution techniques. Although our solution method relies on linearization with respect to the economy's aggregate state variables, it preserves important nonlinearities at the micro level. In particular, the response of macroeconomic aggregates to aggregate shocks may depend on the distribution of households across idiosyncratic states because of heterogeneity in the response to the shock across the distribution.

Our solution method is both faster and more accurate than existing methods. Of the five solution methods for the Krusell and Smith (1998) model included in the *Journal of Economic Dynamics and Control* comparison project (Den Haan 2010), the fastest takes around seven minutes to solve. With the same calibration our model takes around a quarter of a second to solve. The most accurate method in the comparison project has a maximum aggregate policy rule error of 0.16% (Den Haan's [2010] preferred accuracy metric). With a standard deviation of productivity shocks that is comparable to the Den Haan, Judd, and Julliard (2010) calibration, the maximum aggregate policy rule error using our method is 0.05%. Since our methodology uses a linear approximation with respect to aggregate shocks, the accuracy worsens as the standard deviation of shocks increases.[4]

However, the most important advantage of our method is not its speed or accuracy for solving the Krusell and Smith (1998) model. Rather, it is the potential for solving much larger models in which approximate aggregation does not hold and existing methods are infeasible. An example is the two-asset model of Kaplan, Moll, and Violante (2016), where the presence of three individual state variables renders the resulting linear system so large that it is numerically impossible to solve. In order to be able to handle larger models such as this, in Section III we develop a model-free reduction method to reduce the dimensionality of the system of linear stochastic differential equations that characterizes the equilibrium. Our method generalizes Krusell and Smith's (1998) insight that only a small subset of the information contained in the cross-sectional distribution of agents across idiosyncratic states is required to accurately forecast the variables that agents need to know in order to solve their decision problems. Krusell and Smith's (1998) procedure posits a set of moments that capture this information based on economic intuition, and verifies its accuracy ex post using a forecast-error metric; our method instead leverages advances in engineering to allow the computer to identify the necessary information in a completely model-free way.[5]

To make these methods as accessible as possible, and to encourage the use of heterogeneous agent models among researchers and policymakers, we are publishing an open-source suite of codes that implement our algorithms in an easy-to-use toolbox.[6] Users of the codes provide just two inputs: (1) a function that evaluates the discretized equilibrium conditions, and (2) the solution to the stationary equilibrium *without* aggregate shocks. Our toolbox then solves for the equilibrium of the corresponding economy *with* aggregate shocks—linearizes the model, reduces the dimensionality, solves the system of stochastic differential equations, and produces impulse responses.[7]

In Sections V and VI, we use our toolbox to solve a two-asset heterogeneous agent economy inspired by Kaplan and Violante (2014) and Kaplan et al. (2016) in which households can save in liquid and illiquid assets. In equilibrium, illiquid assets earn a higher return than liquid assets because they are subject to a transaction cost. This economy naturally generates "wealthy hand-to-mouth" households—households who endogenously choose to hold all their wealth as illiquid assets and to set their consumption equal to their disposable income. Such households have high MPCs in line with empirical evidence presented in Johnson, Parker, and Souleles (2006), Parker et al. (2013), and Fagereng, Holm, and Natvik (2016). Because of the two-asset structure and the presence of the wealthy hand-to-mouth, the parameterized model can match key features of the joint distribution of household portfolios and MPCs—properties that one-asset models have difficulty in replicating.[8] Matching these features of the data leads to a failure of approximate aggregation, which together with the model's size, render it an ideal setting to illustrate the power of our methods. To the best of our knowledge, this model cannot be solved using any existing methods.

In our first application (Sec. V) we show that inequality can matter for macro aggregates. We demonstrate that the response of aggregate consumption to an aggregate productivity shock is larger and more transitory than in either the corresponding representative agent or one-asset heterogeneous agent economies, whereas a shock to productivity *growth* is substantially smaller and more persistent in the two-asset economy than in either the corresponding representative agent or one-asset heterogeneous agent economies. Matching the wealth distribution, in particular the consumption share of hand-to-mouth households, drives these findings since hand-to-mouth households are limited in their ability to immediately increase consumption in response to higher future income growth, their impact consumption response is weaker, and their lagged consumption response is stronger than the response of non-hand-to-mouth households. An implication of these individual-level consumption dynamics is that the two-asset model outperforms the representative agent models in terms of its ability to match the smoothness and sensitivity of aggregate consumption.[9] Jointly matching these two features of aggregate consumption dynamics has posed a challenge for many benchmark models in the literature (Campbell and Mankiw 1989, Christiano 1989, and Ludvigson and Michaelides 2001).

In our second application (Sec. VI) we show that macro shocks can additionally matter for inequality, resulting in rich interactions between inequality and the macroeconomy. To clearly highlight how quantitatively realistic heterogeneous agent economies such as ours can be useful in understanding the distributional consequences of aggregate shocks, in Section VI we relax the typical assumption in incomplete market models that the cross-sectional distribution of labor income is exogenous. We adopt a nested constant elasticity of substitution (CES) production function with capital-skill complementarity as in Krusell et al. (2000), in which high-skilled workers are more complementary with capital in production than are low-skilled workers. First, we show how a negative shock to the productivity of unskilled labor generates a recession that disproportionately hurts low-skilled workers, thus also leading to an increase in income and consumption inequality. Second, we show how a positive shock to the productivity of capital generates a boom that disproportionately benefits high-skilled workers, thus leading to an increase in income and consumption inequality. The response of aggregate consumption to both of these aggregate shocks differs dramatically from that in the representative agent counterpart, thereby providing a striking counterexample to the main result of Krusell and Smith (1998). These findings illustrate how different aggregate shocks shape the dynamics of inequality and may generate rich interactions between inequality and macroeconomic aggregates.

II.   Linearizing Heterogeneous Agent Models

We present our computational method in two steps. First, in this section we describe our approach to linearizing heterogeneous agent models.

Second, in Section III we describe our model-free reduction method for reducing the size of the linearized system. We separate the two steps because the reduction step is only necessary for large models.

We describe our method in the context of the Krusell and Smith (1998) model. This model is a natural expository tool because it is well known and substantially simpler than the two-asset model in Section V. As we show in Section V, our method is applicable to a broad class of models.

Continuous Time. We present our method in continuous time. While discrete time poses no conceptual difficulty (in fact, Campbell [1998], Dotsey, King, and Wolman [1999], Veracierto [2002], and Reiter [2009] originally proposed this general approach in discrete time), working in continuous time has three key numerical advantages that we heavily exploit.

First, it is easier to capture occasionally binding constraints and inaction in continuous time than in discrete time. For example, the borrowing constraint in the Krusell and Smith (1998) model below is absorbed into a simple boundary condition on the value function and therefore the first-order condition for consumption holds with equality everywhere in the interior of the state space. Occasionally binding constraints and inaction are often included in heterogeneous agent models in order to match features of microdata.

Second, first-order conditions characterizing optimal policy functions typically have a simpler structure than in discrete time and can often be solved by hand.

Third, and most importantly in practice, continuous time naturally generates sparsity in the matrices characterizing the model's equilibrium conditions. Intuitively, continuously moving state variables like wealth only drift an infinitesimal amount in an infinitesimal unit of time, and therefore a typical approximation that discretizes the state space has the feature that households reach only states that directly neighbor the current state. Our two-asset model in Section V is so large that sparsity is necessary to store and manipulate these matrices.[10]

A.   Model Description

Environment

There is a continuum of households with fixed mass indexed by $j \in [0, 1]$ who have preferences represented by the expected utility function

$$\mathbb{E}_0 \int_0^\infty e^{-\rho t} \frac{c_{jt}^{1-\theta}}{1-\theta} \, dt,$$

where ρ is the rate of time preference and θ is the coefficient of relative risk aversion. At each instant t, a household's idiosyncratic labor productivity is $z_{jt} \in \{z_L, z_H\}$ with $z_L < z_H$. Households switch between the two values for labor productivity according to a Poisson process with arrival rates λ_L and λ_H.[11] The aggregate supply of efficiency units of labor is exogenous and constant and denoted by $\bar{N} = \int_0^1 z_{jt} dj$. A household with labor productivity z_{jt} earns labor income $w_t z_{jt}$. Markets are incomplete; households can only trade in productive capital a_{jt} subject to the borrowing constraint $a_{jt} \geq 0$.

There is a representative firm that has access to the Cobb-Douglas production function

$$Y_t = e^{Z_t} K_t^\alpha N_t^{1-\alpha},$$

where Z_t is (the logarithm of) aggregate productivity, K_t is aggregate capital, and N_t is aggregate labor. The logarithm of aggregate productivity follows the Ornstein-Uhlenbeck process

$$dZ_t = -\eta Z_t dt + \sigma dW_t, \tag{1}$$

where dW_t is the innovation to a standard Brownian motion, η is the rate of mean reversion, and σ captures the size of innovations.[12]

Equilibrium

In equilibrium, household decisions depend on individual state variables specific to a particular household, and aggregate state variables, which are common to all households. The individual state variables are capital holdings a and idiosyncratic labor productivity z. The aggregate state variables are aggregate productivity Z_t and the cross-sectional distribution of households over their individual state variables, $g_t(a, z)$.

For notational convenience, we denote the dependence of a given equilibrium object on a particular realization of the aggregate state $(g_t(a, z), Z_t)$ with a subscript t. That is, we use time-dependent notation with respect to those aggregate states. In contrast, we use recursive notation with respect to the idiosyncratic states (a, z). This notation anticipates our solution method that linearizes with respect to the aggregate states but not the idiosyncratic states.[13] An equilibrium of the model is characterized by the following equations:

$$\rho v_t(a, z) = \max_{c} u(c) + \partial_a v_t(a, z)(w_t z + r_t a - c)$$
$$+ \lambda_z(v_t(a, z') - v_t(a, z)) + \frac{1}{dt} \mathbb{E}_t[dv_t(a, z)], \quad a \geq 0 \tag{2}$$

$$\frac{dg_t(a, z)}{dt} = -\partial_a[s_t(a, z)g_t(a, z)] - \lambda_z g_t(a, z) + \lambda_{z'} g_t(a, z'), \tag{3}$$

$$dZ_t = -\eta Z_t dt + \sigma dW_t, \tag{4}$$

$$w_t = (1 - \alpha)e^{Z_t} K_t^{\alpha} \bar{N}^{-\alpha}, \tag{5}$$

$$r_t = \alpha e^{Z_t} K_t^{\alpha-1} \bar{N}^{1-\alpha} - \delta, \tag{6}$$

$$K_t = \int ag_t(a, z)dadz. \tag{7}$$

Here $s_t(a, z) = w_t z + r_t a - c_t(a, z)$ is the optimal saving policy function corresponding to the household optimization problem (2) and here and elsewhere $(1/dt)\mathbb{E}_t[dv_t]$ is short-hand notation for $\lim_{s \downarrow 0} \mathbb{E}_t[v_{t+s} - v_t]/s$.

For detailed derivations of these equations, see Achdou et al. (2015). The household's Hamilton-Jacobi-Bellman equation (2) is the continuous-time analog of the discrete-time Bellman equation. The flow value of a household's lifetime utility is given by the sum of four terms: the flow utility of consumption, the marginal value of savings, the expected change due to idiosyncratic productivity shocks, and the expected change due to aggregate productivity shocks. Due to our use of time-dependent notation with respect to aggregate states, $\mathbb{E}_t$ denotes the conditional expectation with respect to aggregate states only.[14] The Kolmogorov Forward equation (3) describes the evolution of the distribution over time. The flow change in the mass of households at a given point in the state space is determined by their savings behavior and idiosyncratic productivity shocks. Equation (4) describes the evolution of aggregate productivity. Finally, equations (5), (6), and (7) define prices given the aggregate state.

We define a *steady state* as an equilibrium with constant aggregate productivity $Z_t = 0$ and a time-invariant distribution $g(a, z)$. The steady-state system is given by

$$\rho v(a, z) = \max_{c} u(c) + \partial_a v(a, z)(wz + ra - c)$$
$$+ \lambda_z(v(a, z') - v(a, z)), \quad a \geq 0 \tag{8}$$

$$0 = -\partial_a[s(a, z)g(a, z)] - \lambda_z g(a, z) + \lambda_{z'} g(a, z'), \tag{9}$$

$$w = (1 - \alpha)K^{\alpha}\bar{N}^{-\alpha}, \tag{10}$$

$$r = \alpha K^{\alpha-1}\bar{N}^{1-\alpha} - \delta, \tag{11}$$

$$K = \int a g(a, z) da dz. \tag{12}$$

B.   Linearization Procedure

Our linearization procedure consists of three steps. First, we solve for the steady state of the model without aggregate shocks, but with idiosyncratic shocks. Second, we take a first-order Taylor expansion of the equilibrium conditions around the steady state, yielding a linear system of stochastic differential equations. Third, we solve the linear system using standard techniques. Conceptually, each of these steps is a straightforward extension of standard linearization techniques to the heterogeneous agent context. However, the size of heterogeneous agent models leads to a number of computational challenges which we address.

Step 1: Approximate Steady State. Because households face idiosyncratic uncertainty, the steady-state value function varies over individual state variables $v(a, z)$, and there is a nondegenerate stationary distribution of households $g(a, z)$. To numerically approximate these functions we must represent them in a finite-dimensional way. We use a nonlinear approximation in order to retain the rich nonlinearities and heterogeneity at the individual level. In principle, any approximation method can be used in this step; we use the finite difference methods outlined in Achdou et al. (2015) because they are fast, accurate, and robust.

We approximate the value function and distribution over a discretized grid of asset holdings $\mathbf{a} = (a_1 = 0, a_2, \ldots, a_I)^{\mathsf{T}}$. Denote the value function and distribution along this discrete grid using the vectors $\mathbf{v} = (v(a_1, z_L), \ldots, v(a_I, z_H))^{\mathsf{T}}$ and $\mathbf{g} = (g(a_1, z_L), \ldots, g(a_I, z_H))^{\mathsf{T}}$; both $\mathbf{v}$ and $\mathbf{g}$ are of dimension $N \times 1$ where $N = 2I$ is the total number of grid points in the individual state space. We solve the steady-state versions of equations (2) and (3) at each point on this grid, approximating the partial derivatives using finite differences. Achdou et al. (2015) show that if the finite difference approximation is chosen correctly, the discretized steady state is the solution to the following system of matrix equations:

$$\rho \mathbf{v} = \mathbf{u}(\mathbf{v}) + \mathbf{A}(\mathbf{v}; \mathbf{p})\mathbf{v}$$
$$0 = \mathbf{A}(\mathbf{v}; \mathbf{p})^{\mathsf{T}}\mathbf{g} \tag{13}$$
$$\mathbf{p} = \mathbf{F}(\mathbf{g}).$$

The first equation is the approximated steady-state HJB equation (8) for each point on the discretized grid, expressed in our vector notation. The vector $\mathbf{u}(\mathbf{v})$ is the maximized utility function over the grid and the matrix multiplication $\mathbf{A}(\mathbf{v}; \mathbf{p})\mathbf{v}$ captures the remaining terms in equation (8). The second equation is the discretized version of the steady-state Kolmogorov Forward equation (9). The transition matrix $\mathbf{A}(\mathbf{v}; \mathbf{p})$ is simply the transpose of the matrix from the discretized HJB equation because it encodes how households move around the individual state space. Finally, the third equation defines the prices $\mathbf{p} = (r, w)^{\mathrm{T}}$ as a function of aggregate capital through the distribution $\mathbf{g}$.[15]

Since $\mathbf{v}$ and $\mathbf{g}$ each have N entries, the total system has $2N + 2$ equations in $2N + 2$ unknowns. In simple models like this one, highly accurate solutions can be obtained with as little as $N = 200$ grid points (i.e., $I = 100$ asset grid points together with the two income states); however, in more complicated models, such as the two-asset model in Section V, N can easily grow into the tens of thousands. Exploiting the sparsity of the transition matrix $\mathbf{A}(\mathbf{v}; \mathbf{p})$ is necessary to even represent the steady state of such large models.

Step 2: Linearize Equilibrium Conditions. The second step of our method is to compute a first-order Taylor expansion of the model's discretized equilibrium conditions around steady state. With aggregate shocks, the discretized equilibrium is characterized by

$$\rho \mathbf{v}_t = \mathbf{u}(\mathbf{v}_t) + \mathbf{A}(\mathbf{v}_t; \mathbf{p}_t)\mathbf{v}_t + \frac{1}{\mathrm{d}t}\, \mathbb{E}_t \mathrm{d}\mathbf{v}_t \qquad (14)$$

$$\frac{\mathrm{d}\mathbf{g}_t}{\mathrm{d}t} = \mathbf{A}(\mathbf{v}_t; \mathbf{p}_t)^{\mathrm{T}}\mathbf{g}_t$$

$$\mathrm{d}Z_t = -\eta Z_t \mathrm{d}t + \sigma \mathrm{d}W_t$$

$$\mathbf{p}_t = \mathbf{F}(\mathbf{g}_t; Z_t).$$

The system (14) is a nonlinear system of $2N + 3$ stochastic differential equations in $2N + 3$ variables (the $2N + 2$ variables from the steady state, plus aggregate productivity Z_t). Shocks to TFP Z_t induce fluctuations in marginal products and therefore prices $\mathbf{p}_t = \mathbf{F}(\mathbf{g}_t; Z_t)$. Fluctuations in prices in turn induce fluctuations in households' decisions and therefore in $\mathbf{v}_t$ and the transition matrix $\mathbf{A}(\mathbf{v}_t; \mathbf{p}_t)$.[16] Fluctuations in the transition matrix then induce fluctuations in the distribution of households $\mathbf{g}_t$.

The key insight is that this large-dimensional system of stochastic differential equations has exactly the same structure as more standard representative agent models that are normally solved by means of linearization methods. To make this point, the "Fully Recursive Formulation of Krussell-Smith (1998)" section of the appendix relates the system (14) to the real business cycle (RBC) model. The discretized value function points $\mathbf{v}_t$ are jump variables, like aggregate consumption C_t in the RBC model. The discretized distribution points $\mathbf{g}_t$ are endogenous state variables, like aggregate capital K_t in the RBC model. TFP Z_t is an exogenous state variable. Finally, the wage and real interest rate are statically defined variables, just as in the Krusell and Smith (1998) model.

As already anticipated, we exploit this analogy and solve the nonlinear system (14) by linearizing it around the steady state. Since the dimension of the system is large, it is impossible to compute derivatives by hand. We use a recently developed technique called automatic (or algorithmic) differentiation that is fast and accurate up to machine precision. It dominates finite differences in terms of accuracy and symbolic differentiation in terms of speed. Automatic differentiation exploits the fact that the computer represents any function as the composition of various elementary functions such as addition, multiplication, or exponentiation, which have known derivatives. It builds the derivative of the original function by iteratively applying the chain rule. This allows automatic differentiation to exploit the sparsity of the transition matrix $\mathbf{A}(\mathbf{v}_t; \mathbf{p}_t)$ when taking derivatives, which is essential for numerical feasibility in large models.[17]

The first-order Taylor expansion of equation (14) can be written as:[18]

$$\mathbb{E}_t \begin{bmatrix} d\hat{\mathbf{v}}_t \\ d\hat{\mathbf{g}}_t \\ dZ_t \\ 0 \end{bmatrix} = \begin{bmatrix} \mathbf{B}_{vv} & 0 & 0 & \mathbf{B}_{vp} \\ \mathbf{B}_{gv} & \mathbf{B}_{gg} & 0 & \mathbf{B}_{gp} \\ 0 & 0 & -\eta & 0 \\ 0 & \mathbf{B}_{pg} & \mathbf{B}_{pZ} & -\mathbf{I} \end{bmatrix} \begin{bmatrix} \hat{\mathbf{v}}_t \\ \hat{\mathbf{g}}_t \\ Z_t \\ \hat{\mathbf{p}}_t \end{bmatrix} dt. \qquad (15)$$

The variables in the system, $\hat{\mathbf{v}}_t$, $\hat{\mathbf{g}}_t$, Z_t, and $\hat{\mathbf{p}}_t$, are expressed as deviations from their steady-state values, and the matrix is composed of the derivatives of the equilibrium conditions evaluated at steady state. Since the pricing equations are static, the fourth row of this matrix equation only has nonzero entries on the right-hand side.[19] It is convenient to plug the pricing equations $\hat{\mathbf{p}}_t = \mathbf{B}_{pg}\hat{\mathbf{g}}_t + \mathbf{B}_{pZ}Z_t$ into the remaining equations of the system, yielding

$$\mathbb{E}_t \begin{bmatrix} d\hat{\mathbf{v}}_t \\ d\hat{\mathbf{g}}_t \\ dZ_t \end{bmatrix} = \underbrace{\begin{bmatrix} \mathbf{B}_{vv} & \mathbf{B}_{vp}\mathbf{B}_{pg} & \mathbf{B}_{vp}\mathbf{B}_{pZ} \\ \mathbf{B}_{gv} & \mathbf{B}_{gg}+\mathbf{B}_{gp}\mathbf{B}_{pg} & \mathbf{B}_{gp}\mathbf{B}_{pZ} \\ 0 & 0 & -\eta \end{bmatrix}}_{\mathbf{B}} \begin{bmatrix} \hat{\mathbf{v}}_t \\ \hat{\mathbf{g}}_t \\ Z_t \end{bmatrix} dt. \qquad (16)$$

Step 3: Solve Linear System. The final step of our method is to solve the linear system of stochastic differential equations (16). Following standard practice, we perform a Schur decomposition of the matrix $\mathbf{B}$ to identify the stable and unstable roots of the system. If the Blanchard and Kahn (1980) condition holds, that is, the number of stable roots equals the number of state variables $\hat{\mathbf{g}}_t$ and Z_t, then we can compute the solution:

$$\hat{\mathbf{v}}_t = \mathbf{D}_{vg}\hat{\mathbf{g}}_t + \mathbf{D}_{vZ}Z_t,$$

$$\frac{d\hat{\mathbf{g}}_t}{dt} = (\mathbf{B}_{gg} + \mathbf{B}_{gp}\mathbf{B}_{pg} + \mathbf{B}_{gv}\mathbf{D}_{vg})\hat{\mathbf{g}}_t + (\mathbf{B}_{gp}\mathbf{B}_{pZ} + \mathbf{B}_{gv}\mathbf{D}_{vZ})Z_t, \qquad (17)$$

$$dZ_t = -\eta Z_t dt + \sigma dW_t,$$

$$\hat{\mathbf{p}}_t = \mathbf{B}_{pg}\hat{\mathbf{g}}_t + \mathbf{B}_{pZ}Z_t.$$

The first line of equation (17) sets the control variables $\hat{\mathbf{v}}_t$ as functions of the state variables $\hat{\mathbf{g}}_t$ and Z_t, that is, the matrices $\mathbf{D}_{vg}$ and $\mathbf{D}_{vZ}$ characterize the optimal decision rules as a function of aggregate states. The second line plugs that solution into the system (16) to compute the evolution of the distribution. The third line is the stochastic process for the aggregate productivity shock, and the fourth line is the definition of prices $\hat{\mathbf{p}}_t$.

C.   What Does Linearization Capture and What Does It Lose?

Our method uses a mix of nonlinear approximation with respect to individual state variables, and linear approximation with respect to aggregate state variables. Concretely, from the first line of equation (17), the approximated solution for the value function is of the form

$$v_t(a_i, z_j) = v(a_i, z_j) + \sum_{k=1}^{I}\sum_{\ell=1}^{2}\mathbf{D}_{vg}[i, j; k, l](g_t(a_k, z_\ell) - g(a_k, z_\ell)) + \mathbf{D}_{vZ}[i, j]Z_t, \quad (18)$$

where $\mathbf{D}_{vg}[i, j; k, l]$ and $\mathbf{D}_{vZ}[i, j]$ denote the relevant elements of $\mathbf{D}_{vg}$ and $\mathbf{D}_{vZ}$, and $v(a, z)$ and $g(a, z)$ are the steady-state value function and distribution. Given the value function $v_t(a_i, z_j)$, optimal consumption at different points of the income and wealth distribution is then given by

$$c_t(a_i, z_j) = (\partial_a v_t(a_i, z_j))^{-1/\theta}. \qquad (19)$$

Certainty Equivalence. Expressions (18) and (19) show that our solution features *certainty equivalence* with respect to aggregate shocks; the standard deviation σ of aggregate TFP Z_t does not enter households' decision rules.[20] This is a generic feature of all linearization techniques.

However, our solution does *not* feature certainty equivalence with respect to idiosyncratic shocks because the distribution of idiosyncratic shocks enters the HJB equation (2), as well as its linearized counterpart in equation (16) directly. A corollary of this is that our method *does* capture the effect of aggregate uncertainty to the extent that aggregate shocks affect the distribution of idiosyncratic shocks. For example, Bloom et al. (2014) and Bayer et al. (2015) study the effect of "uncertainty shocks" that result in an increase in the dispersion of idiosyncratic shocks and can be captured by our method.[21]

Our solution method may instead be less suitable for various asset-pricing applications in which the direct effect of aggregate uncertainty on individual decision rules is key. In future work we hope to encompass such applications by extending our first-order perturbation method to higher orders, or by allowing the decision rules to depend nonlinearly on relevant low-dimensional aggregate state variables (but not the high-dimensional distribution). Yet another strategy could be to assume that individuals are averse to ambiguity so that risk premia survive linearization (Ilut and Schneider 2014).

Distributional Dependence of Aggregates. A common motivation for studying heterogeneous agent models is that the response of macroeconomic aggregates to aggregate shocks may depend on the distribution of idiosyncratic states. For example, different joint distributions of income and wealth $g(a, z)$ can result in different impulse responses of aggregates to the same aggregate shock. Our solution method preserves such *distributional dependence*.

To fix ideas, consider the impulse response of aggregate consumption C_t to a productivity shock Z_t, starting from the steady-state distribution $g(a, z)$. First consider the response of initial aggregate consumption C_0 only. We compute the impact effect of the shock on the initial value function $v_0(a, z)$ and initial consumption $c_0(a, z)$ from equations (18) and (19). Integrate this over households to get aggregate consumption

$$C_0 = \int c_0(a, z)g(a, z)dadz \approx \sum_{i=1}^{I}\sum_{j=1}^{2} c_0(a_i, z_j)g(a_i, z_j)\Delta a \Delta z.$$

The impulse response of C_0 depends on the initial distribution $g_0(a, z)$ because the elasticities of individual consumption $c_0(a, z)$ with respect to the aggregate shock Z_0 are different for individuals with different levels of income and/or wealth. These individual elasticities are then aggregated according to the initial distribution. Therefore, the effect of the shock depends on the initial distribution $g_0(a, z)$.

To see this even more clearly, it is useful to briefly work with the continuous rather than discretized value and consumption policy functions. Analogous to equation (18), we can write the initial value function response as $\hat{v}_0(a, z) = \mathbf{D}_{vZ}(a, z)Z_0$ where $\mathbf{D}_{vZ}(a, z)$ are the elements of $\mathbf{D}_{vZ}$ in (17) and where we have used the fact that the initial distribution does not move (i.e., $\hat{g}_0(a, z) = 0$) by virtue of g being a state variable. We can use this to show that the deviation of initial consumption from steady state satisfies $\hat{c}_0(a, z) = \mathbf{D}_{cZ}(a, z)Z_0$ where $\mathbf{D}_{cZ}(a, z)$ captures the responsiveness of consumption to the aggregate shock.[22] The impulse response of initial aggregate consumption is then

$$\hat{C}_0 = \int \mathbf{D}_{cZ}(a, z)g(a, z)dadz \times Z_0. \tag{20}$$

It depends on the steady-state distribution $g(a, z)$ since the responsiveness of individual consumption to the aggregate shock $\mathbf{D}_{cZ}(a, z)$ differs across (a, z).

Size and Sign Dependence. Another question of interest is whether our economy features size or sign dependence, that is, whether it responds nonlinearly to aggregate shocks of different sizes or asymmetrically to positive and negative shocks.[23] In contrast to state dependence, our linearization method eliminates any potential sign and size dependence. This can again be seen clearly from the impulse response of initial aggregate consumption in equation (20), which is linear in the aggregate shock Z_0. This immediately rules out size and sign dependence in the response of aggregate consumption to the aggregate shock.[24]

In future work, we hope to make progress on relaxing this feature of our solution method. Extending our first-order perturbation method to higher orders would again help in this regard. Another idea is to leverage the linear model solution together with parts of the full nonlinear model to simulate the model in a way that preserves these nonlinearities. In particular, one could use the fully nonlinear Kolmogorov Forward equation in (14) instead of the linearized version in equation (16) to solve for the path of the distribution for times $t > 0$: $dg_t / dt = \mathbf{A}(\mathbf{v}_t; \mathbf{p}_t)^{\mathsf{T}}\mathbf{g}_t$. This procedure allows us to preserve *size dependence* after the initial impact $t > 0$ because larger shocks potentially induce nonproportional movements in the individual state space, and therefore different distributional dynamics going forward.[25]

Small versus Large Aggregate Shocks. Another generic feature of linearization techniques is that the linearized solution is expected to be a good approximation to the true nonlinear solution for small aggregate shocks and less so for large ones. Section II.D documents that our approximate dynamics of the distribution is accurate for the typical calibration of TFP shocks in the Krusell and Smith (1998) model, but breaks down for very large shocks.[26]

D.   Performance of Linearization in Krusell-Smith Model

In order to compare the performance of our method to previous work, we solve the model under the parameterization of the JEDC comparison project (Den Haan et al. 2010). A unit of time is one quarter. We set the rate of time preference $\rho = 0.01$ and the coefficient of relative risk aversion $\theta = 1$. Capital depreciates at rate $\delta = 0.025$ per quarter and the capital share is $\alpha = 0.36$. We set the levels of idiosyncratic labor productivity z_L and z_H following Den Haan et al. (2010).

One difference between our model and Den Haan et al. (2010) is that we assume aggregate productivity follows the continuous-time, continuous-state Ornstein-Uhlenbeck process (1) rather than the discrete-time, two-state Markov chain in Den Haan et al. (2010). To remain as consistent with Den Haan et al.'s (2010) calibration as possible, we choose the approximate quarterly persistence corr$(\log Z_{t+1}, \log Z_t) = e^{-\eta} \approx 1 - \eta = 0.75$ and the volatility of innovations $\sigma = 0.007$ to match the standard deviation and autocorrelation of Den Haan et al.'s (2010) two-state process.[27]

In our approximation we set the size of the individual asset grid $I = 100$, ranging from $a_1 = 0$ to $a_I = 100$. Together with the two values for idiosyncratic productivity, the total number of grid points is $N = 200$ and the total size of the dynamic system (16) is 400.[28]

Table 1 shows that our linearization method solves the Krusell and Smith (1998) model in approximately one-quarter of one second. In contrast, the fastest algorithm documented in the comparison project by Den Haan (2010) takes over seven minutes to solve the model—more than 1,500 times slower than our method (see table 2 in Den Haan [2010]).[29] In Section III, we solve the model in approximately 0.1 seconds using our model-free reduction method.

Accuracy of Linearization. The key restriction that our method imposes is linearity with respect to the aggregate state variables Z_t and $\hat{g}_t$.

Table 1
Run Time for Solving Krusell-Smith Model

	Full Model
Steady state	0.082 sec
Derivatives	0.021 sec
Linear system	0.14 sec
Simulate IRF	0.024 sec
Total	**0.27 sec**

Notes: Time to solve Krusell-Smith model once on Mac-Book Pro 2016 laptop with 3.3 GHz processor and 16 GB RAM, using Matlab R2016b and our code toolbox. "Steady state" reports time to compute steady state. "Derivatives" reports time to compute derivatives of discretized equilibrium conditions. "Linear system" reports time to solve system of linear differential equations. "Simulate IRF" reports time to simulate impulse responses reported in figure 1. "Total" is the sum of all these tasks.

We evaluate the accuracy of this approximation using the error metric suggested by Den Haan (2010). The Den Haan error metric compares the dynamics of the aggregate capital stock under two simulations of the model for $T = 10{,}000$ periods. The first simulation computes the path of aggregate capital K_t from our linearized solution (17). The second simulation computes the path of aggregate capital K_t^* from simulating the model using the nonlinear dynamics (3) as discussed in Section II.C. We then compare the maximum log difference between the two series,

$$\varepsilon^{DH} = 100 \times \max_{t \in [0,T]} \left| \log K_t - \log K_t^* \right|.$$

Den Haan originally proposed this metric to compute the accuracy of the forecasting rule in the Krusell and Smith (1998) algorithm; in our method, the linearized dynamics of the distribution $\mathbf{g}_t$ are analogous to the forecasting rule.

When the standard deviation of productivity shocks is 0.7%, our method gives a maximum percentage error $\varepsilon^{DH} = 0.049\%$, implying that households in our model make small errors in forecasting the distribution. Our method is three times as accurate as the Krusell and Smith (1998) method, which is the most accurate algorithm in Den Haan (2010), and gives $\varepsilon^{DH} = 0.16\%$. Table 2 shows that, since our method is locally

Table 2
Maximum Den Haan Error in %

Std. Dev. Productivity Shocks (%)	Maximum Den Haan Error (%)
.01	0.000
.1	0.001
.7	0.049
1.0	0.118
5.0	3.282

Notes: Maximum percentage error in accuracy check suggested by Den Haan (2010). The error is the percentage difference between the time series of aggregate capital under our linearized solution and a nonlinear simulation of the model, as described in the main text. The third row denotes the calibrated value $\sigma = 0.007$.

accurate, its accuracy decreases in the size of the shocks σ. However, with the size of aggregate shocks in the baseline calibration, it provides exceptional accuracy.

III. Model Reduction

Solving the linear system (16) is extremely efficient because the Krusell and Smith (1998) model is relatively small. However, the required matrix decomposition becomes prohibitively expensive in larger models like the two-asset model that we will study in Section V. We must therefore reduce the size of the system to solve these more general models. Furthermore, even in smaller models like Krusell and Smith (1998), model reduction makes likelihood-based estimation feasible by reducing the size of the associated filtering problem.[30]

In this section, we develop a model-free reduction method to reduce the size of the linear system while preserving accuracy. Our approach projects the high-dimensional distribution $\hat{\mathbf{g}}_t$ and value function $\hat{\mathbf{v}}_t$ onto low-dimensional subspaces and solves the resulting low-dimensional system. The main challenge is reducing the distribution, which we discuss in Sections III.A, III.B, and III.C. Section III.D describes how we reduce the value function. Section III.E puts the two together to solve the reduced model and describes the numerical implementation. Finally, Section III.F shows that our reduction method performs well in the Krusell and Smith (1998) model.

In order to simplify notation, for the remainder of this section we use

$\mathbf{v}_t$, $\mathbf{g}_t$ and $\mathbf{p}_t$ to denote the *deviations from steady state* in the value function, distribution, and prices. In Section II, we had denoted these objects using $\hat{\mathbf{v}}_t$, $\hat{\mathbf{g}}_t$ and $\hat{\mathbf{p}}_t$. This change of notation applies to Section III only, and we will remind the reader whenever this change could cause confusion.

A. Overview of Distribution Reduction

The basic insight that we exploit is that only a small subset of the information in $\mathbf{g}_t$ is necessary to accurately forecast the path of prices $\mathbf{p}_t$. In fact, in the discrete-time version of this model, Krusell and Smith (1998) show that just the mean of the asset distribution $\mathbf{g}_t$ is sufficient to forecast $\mathbf{p}_t$ according to a forecast-error metric. However, the success of their reduction strategy relies on the economic properties of the model, so it is not obvious how to generalize it to other environments. We use a set of tools from the engineering literature known as *model reduction* to generalize Krusell and Smith's (1998) insight in a model-free way, allowing the computer to compute the features of the distribution that are necessary to accurately forecast $\mathbf{p}_t$.[31]

It is important to note that the vector $\mathbf{p}_t$ does not need to literally consist of prices; it is simply the vector of objects we wish to accurately describe. In practice, we often also include other variables of interest, such as aggregate consumption or output, to ensure that the reduced model accurately describes their dynamics as well.

The Distribution Reduction Problem

We say that the distribution *exactly reduces* if there exists a k_S-dimensional time-invariant subspace S with $k_S \ll N$ such that, for all distributions $\mathbf{g}_t$ that occur in equilibrium,

$$\mathbf{g}_t = \gamma_{1t}\mathbf{x}_1 + \gamma_{2t}\mathbf{x}_2 + \dots + \gamma_{k_St}\mathbf{x}_{k_S},$$

where $\mathbf{X}_S = [\mathbf{x}_1, \dots, \mathbf{x}_{k_S}] \in \mathbb{R}^{N \times k_S}$ is a basis for the subspace S and $\gamma_{1t}, \dots, \gamma_{k_St}$ are scalars. If we knew the time-invariant basis $\mathbf{X}_S$, we could decrease the dimensionality of the problem by tracking only the k_S-dimensional vector of coefficients γ_t.

Typically exact reduction as described above does not hold, so we instead must estimate a *trial basis* $\mathbf{X} = [\mathbf{x}_1, \dots, \mathbf{x}_k] \in \mathbb{R}^{N \times k}$ such that the distribution *approximately reduces*, that is,

$$\mathbf{g}_t \approx \gamma_{1t}\mathbf{x}_1 + \gamma_{2t}\mathbf{x}_2 + \dots + \gamma_{kt}\mathbf{x}_k,$$

or, in matrix form, $\mathbf{g}_t \approx \mathbf{X}\gamma_t$. Denote the resulting approximation of the distribution by $\tilde{\mathbf{g}}_t = \mathbf{X}\gamma_t$ and the approximate prices by $\tilde{\mathbf{p}}_t = \mathbf{B}_{pg}\tilde{\mathbf{g}}_t + \mathbf{B}_{pZ}Z_t$.

Our model maps directly into the prototypical problem considered by the model reduction literature if the decision rules are exogenous, that is, the matrices $\mathbf{D}_{vg}$ and $\mathbf{D}_{vZ}$ in equation (17) are exogenously given.[32] This case assumes away a crucial part of the economics we are interested in studying, but nevertheless has pedagogical use in connecting to the existing literature. In this case, using the second and fourth equations of (17) and recalling our convention in this section to drop hats from variables, our dynamical system becomes

$$\frac{d\mathbf{g}_t}{dt} = \mathbf{C}_{gg}\mathbf{g}_t + \mathbf{C}_{gZ}Z_t \tag{21}$$

$$\mathbf{p}_t = \mathbf{B}_{pg}\mathbf{g}_t + \mathbf{B}_{pZ}Z_t,$$

where $\mathbf{C}_{gg} = \mathbf{B}_{gg} + \mathbf{B}_{gp}\mathbf{B}_{pg} + \mathbf{B}_{gv}\mathbf{D}_{vg}$ and $\mathbf{C}_{gZ} = \mathbf{B}_{gp}\mathbf{B}_{pZ} + \mathbf{B}_{gv}\mathbf{D}_{vZ}$. This system maps a low-dimensional vector of "inputs" (aggregate productivity Z_t) into a low-dimensional vector of "outputs" (prices $\mathbf{p}_t$), intermediated through the high-dimensional distribution $\mathbf{g}_t$.[33] The model reduction literature provides an off-the-shelf set of tools to replace the high-dimensional "intermediating variable" $\mathbf{g}_t$ with a low-dimensional approximation γ_t while preserving the mapping from inputs to outputs.

Of course, our economic model is more complicated than this special case because the distribution reduction feeds back into agents' decisions through the endogenous value function $\mathbf{v}_t$. It is helpful to restate the system with endogenous $\mathbf{v}_t$ in a form closer to that in the model-reduction literature:

$$\begin{bmatrix} \mathbb{E}_t[d\mathbf{v}_t] \\ d\mathbf{g}_t \end{bmatrix} = \begin{bmatrix} \mathbf{B}_{vv} & \mathbf{B}_{vp}\mathbf{B}_{pg} \\ \mathbf{B}_{gv} & \mathbf{B}_{gg}+\mathbf{B}_{gp}\mathbf{B}_{pg} \end{bmatrix} \begin{bmatrix} \mathbf{v}_t \\ \mathbf{g}_t \end{bmatrix} dt + \begin{bmatrix} \mathbf{B}_{vp}\mathbf{B}_{pZ} \\ \mathbf{B}_{gp}\mathbf{B}_{pZ} \end{bmatrix} Z_t dt \tag{22}$$

$$\mathbf{p}_t = \mathbf{B}_{pg}\mathbf{g}_t + \mathbf{B}_{pZ}Z_t,$$

given the exogenous stochastic process for productivity (4). This system still maps the low-dimensional input Z_t into the low-dimensional output $\mathbf{p}_t$. However, the intermediating variables are now both the distribution $\mathbf{g}_t$ and the forward-looking decisions $\mathbf{v}_t$.

Deriving the Reduced System Given Basis $\mathbf{X}$

Model reduction involves two related tasks: first, given a trial basis $\mathbf{X}$, we must compute the dynamics of the reduced system in terms of the distribution coefficients γ_t; and second, we must choose the basis $\mathbf{X}$ itself. In this subsection, we complete the first step of characterizing the reduced system given a basis $\mathbf{X}$, which is substantially easier than the second step of choosing the basis. Sections III.B and III.C discuss how we choose the basis.

Mathematically, we project the distribution $\mathbf{g}_t$ onto the subspace spanned by the basis $\mathbf{X} \in \mathbb{R}^{N \times k}$. Write the requirement that $\mathbf{g}_t \approx \mathbf{X}\gamma_t$ as

$$\mathbf{g}_t = \mathbf{X}\gamma_t + \varepsilon_t, \tag{23}$$

where $\varepsilon_t \in \mathbb{R}^N$ is a residual. The formulation (23) is a standard linear regression in which the distribution $\mathbf{g}_t$ is the dependent variable, the basis vectors $\mathbf{X}$ are the independent variables, and the coefficients γ_t are to be estimated.

Just as in ordinary least squares, we can estimate the projection coefficients γ_t by imposing the orthogonality condition $\mathbf{X}^T\varepsilon_t = 0$, giving the familiar formula

$$\gamma_t = (\mathbf{X}^T\mathbf{X})^{-1}\mathbf{X}^T\mathbf{g}_t. \tag{24}$$

A sensible basis will be orthonormal, so that $(\mathbf{X}^T\mathbf{X})^{-1} = \mathbf{I}$, further simplifying equation (24) to $\gamma_t = \mathbf{X}^T\mathbf{g}_t$.[34] We can compute the evolution of this coefficient vector by differentiating equation (24) with respect to time and using equation (23) to get

$$\frac{d\gamma_t}{dt} = \mathbf{X}^T\frac{d\mathbf{g}_t}{dt} = \mathbf{X}^T\mathbf{B}_{gv}\mathbf{v}_t + \mathbf{X}^T(\mathbf{B}_{gg} + \mathbf{B}_{gp}\mathbf{B}_{pg})(\mathbf{X}\gamma_t + \varepsilon_t) + \mathbf{X}^T\mathbf{B}_{gp}\mathbf{B}_{pg}Z_t$$

$$\approx \mathbf{X}^T\mathbf{B}_{gv}\mathbf{v}_t + \mathbf{X}^T(\mathbf{B}_{gg} + \mathbf{B}_{gp}\mathbf{B}_{pg})\mathbf{X}\gamma_t + \mathbf{X}^T\mathbf{B}_{gp}\mathbf{B}_{pg}Z_t.$$

The hope is that the residuals ε_t are small, and so the last approximation is good. Assuming this is the case, we have the reduced version of equation (22)

$$\begin{bmatrix} \mathbb{E}_t[d\mathbf{v}_t] \\ d\gamma_t \end{bmatrix} = \begin{bmatrix} \mathbf{B}_{vv} & \mathbf{B}_{vp}\mathbf{B}_{pg}\mathbf{X} \\ \mathbf{X}^T\mathbf{B}_{gv} & \mathbf{X}^T(\mathbf{B}_{gg} + \mathbf{B}_{gp}\mathbf{B}_{pg})\mathbf{X} \end{bmatrix} \begin{bmatrix} \mathbf{v}_t \\ \gamma_t \end{bmatrix} dt + \begin{bmatrix} \mathbf{B}_{vp}\mathbf{B}_{pZ} \\ \mathbf{X}^T\mathbf{B}_{gp}\mathbf{B}_{pZ} \end{bmatrix} Z_t dt, \tag{25}$$

$$\tilde{\mathbf{p}}_t = \mathbf{B}_{pg}\mathbf{X}\gamma_t + \mathbf{B}_{pZ}Z_t.$$

Summing up, assuming we have the basis $\mathbf{X}$, this projection procedure takes us from the system of differential equations involving the

N-dimensional vector $\mathbf{g}_t$ in equation (22) to a system involving only the k-dimensional vector γ_t in equation (25).[35]

B. Choosing the Basis $\mathbf{X}$ with Exogenous Decision Rules

We now turn to choosing a good basis $\mathbf{X}$. In this section we explain how to choose a basis in a model with exogenous decision rules, allowing us to use preexisting tools from the model reduction literature. In Section III.C we extend the strategy to the case with endogenous decision rules.

Mechanically increasing the size of the basis $\mathbf{X}$ will improve the approximation of the distribution $\mathbf{g}_t$; in the limit where $\mathbf{X}$ spans $\mathbb{R}^N$, we will not reduce the distribution at all. The goal of the model reduction literature is to provide a good approximation of the mapping from inputs Z_t to outputs $\mathbf{p}_t$ with as small a basis $\mathbf{X}$ as possible. We operationalize the notion of a "good approximation" by matching the impulse response function of $\mathbf{p}_t$ to a shock to Z_t up to a specified order k.[36]

Choosing the Basis in a Simplified Deterministic Model

To transparently motivate our choice of basis $\mathbf{X}$, we begin with a simplified version of the system (21). In particular, we make two simplifying assumptions. First, we assume that there are no aggregate shocks, so that $Z_t = 0$ for all t. This allows us to focus on deterministic transition paths starting from an exogenously given initial distribution $\mathbf{g}_0$; because certainty equivalence with respect to aggregate shocks holds in our linear setting, these transition paths are intimately related to impulse responses driven by shocks to Z_t. Our second simplifying assumption is that $\mathbf{p}_t = p_t$ is a scalar. This emphasizes that the price vector we are trying to approximate is a low-dimensional object. Under these assumptions, we obtain the following simplified version of the system (21)

$$\frac{d\mathbf{g}_t}{dt} = \mathbf{C}_{gg}\mathbf{g}_t \tag{26}$$

$$p_t = \mathbf{b}_{pg}\mathbf{g}_t,$$

where $\mathbf{b}_{pg}$ is a $1 \times N$ vector. The reduced version of this system is

$$\frac{d\gamma_t}{dt} = \mathbf{X}^{\mathsf{T}}\mathbf{C}_{gg}\mathbf{X}\gamma_t \tag{27}$$

$$\tilde{p}_t = \mathbf{b}_{pg}\mathbf{X}\gamma_t,$$

where $\tilde{p}_t$ denotes the reduced path of prices. Since the system (26) is linear, it has a simple solution. The solution of the first equation is $\mathbf{g}_t = e^{\mathbf{C}_{gg}t}\mathbf{g}_0$ where $e^{\mathbf{C}_{gg}t}$ is a matrix exponential. Hence

$$p_t = \mathbf{b}_{pg}e^{\mathbf{C}_{gg}t}\mathbf{g}_0. \tag{28}$$

Similarly, we can derive an analogous solution for the reduced prices which satisfy equation (27)

$$\tilde{p}_t = \mathbf{b}_{pg}\mathbf{X}e^{\mathbf{X}^{\mathsf{T}}\mathbf{C}_{gg}\mathbf{X}t}\gamma_0. \tag{29}$$

The goal is then to choose $\mathbf{X}$ such that p_t in equation (28) is "close" to $\tilde{p}_t$ in equation (29). The key idea is to choose $\mathbf{X}$ such that the kth-order Taylor-series approximation of p_t in equation (28) around $t = 0$ *exactly matches* that of $\tilde{p}_t$ in equation (29).

The Taylor-series approximation of the time path of prices (28) around $t = 0$ is[37]

$$p_t \approx \mathbf{b}_{pg}\left[\mathbf{I} + \mathbf{C}_{gg}t + \frac{1}{2}\mathbf{C}_{gg}^2 t^2 + \ldots + \tfrac{1}{(k-1)!}\mathbf{C}_{gg}^{k-1}t^{k-1}\right]\mathbf{g}_0, \tag{30}$$

where we have used that $e^{\mathbf{C}_{gg}t} \approx \mathbf{I} + \mathbf{C}_{gg}t + (1/2)\mathbf{C}_{gg}^2 t^2 + \ldots$. Similarly, the Taylor-series approximation of reduced prices is

$$\tilde{p}_t \approx \mathbf{b}_{pg}\mathbf{X}\left[\mathbf{I} + (\mathbf{X}^{\mathsf{T}}\mathbf{C}_{gg}\mathbf{X})t + \frac{1}{2}(\mathbf{X}^{\mathsf{T}}\mathbf{C}_{gg}\mathbf{X})^2 t + \ldots + \tfrac{1}{(k-1)!}(\mathbf{X}^{\mathsf{T}}\mathbf{C}_{gg}\mathbf{X})^{k-1}t^{k-1}\right]\gamma_0. \tag{31}$$

We want to choose $\mathbf{X}$ so that the first k terms of the two Taylor-series expansions are identical. With $\gamma_0 = \mathbf{X}^{\mathsf{T}}\mathbf{g}_0$, this means that we require $\mathbf{b}_{pg} = \mathbf{b}_{pg}\mathbf{X}\mathbf{X}^{\mathsf{T}}$, $\mathbf{b}_{pg}\mathbf{C}_{gg} = \mathbf{b}_{pg}\mathbf{X}\mathbf{X}^{\mathsf{T}}\mathbf{C}_{gg}\mathbf{X}\mathbf{X}^{\mathsf{T}}$, and so on. If γ_t has the same dimensionality as $\mathbf{g}_t$ ($k = N$, i.e., we are not reducing the distribution at all), then $\mathbf{X}$ has to be orthogonal, that is, $\mathbf{X}\mathbf{X}^{\mathsf{T}} = \mathbf{I}$, and the conclusion trivially follows. But once we have proper reduction this equality does not hold, and the problem of Taylor-series coefficient matching becomes nontrivial. Fortunately, the model reduction literature gives us a systematic way for choosing $\mathbf{X}$ such that equation (30) matches equation (31). This systematic way builds upon what is known as the order-k *observability matrix* of the system (26):[38]

$$\mathcal{O}(\mathbf{b}_{pg}, \mathbf{C}_{gg}) := \begin{bmatrix} \mathbf{b}_{pg} \\ \mathbf{b}_{pg}\mathbf{C}_{gg} \\ \mathbf{b}_{pg}\mathbf{C}_{gg}^2 \\ \vdots \\ \mathbf{b}_{pg}\mathbf{C}_{gg}^{k-1} \end{bmatrix}. \tag{32}$$

It turns out that if the basis $\mathbf{X}$ spans the subspace generated by the transpose of the observability matrix $\mathcal{O}(\mathbf{b}_{pg}, \mathbf{C}_{gg})$, then the kth-order Taylor-series approximation of reduced prices (31) exactly matches that of unreduced prices (30), even though it only uses information on the reduced state vector γ_t. Showing this just requires a few lines of algebra, which we present in the appendix section "Deterministic Model."

To gain some intuition why the observability matrix (32) makes an appearance, note that the Taylor-series approximation (30) can be written more compactly using matrix notation as

$$p_t \approx \left[1, t, \tfrac{1}{2}\,t^2, ..., \tfrac{1}{(k-1)!}\,t^{k-1}\right] \mathcal{O}(\mathbf{b}_{pg}, \mathbf{C}_{gg})\mathbf{g}_0.$$

Related, $\mathcal{O}(\mathbf{b}_{pg}, \mathbf{C}_{gg})\mathbf{g}_t$ is simply the vector of time derivatives of p_t, that is, $\dot{p}_t$, $\ddot{p}_t$ and so on (see endnote 37).

Choosing the Basis in the Stochastic Model

The deterministic case makes clear that the observability matrix $\mathcal{O}(\mathbf{b}_{pg}, \mathbf{C}_{gg})$ plays a key role in model reduction. The logic of this simple case carries through the stochastic model, but the full derivation is more involved and details can be found in the appendix section "Model Reduction and Proof of Proposition 1." Because the model is now stochastic, the correct notion of "matching the path of prices" is to match the impulse response function of prices.

Proposition 1.   *Consider the stochastic model with exogenous decision rules (21). Let $\mathbf{X}$ be a basis that spans the subspace generated by the observability matrix $\mathcal{O}(\mathbf{b}_{pg}, \mathbf{C}_{gg})^\mathsf{T}$ with $\mathbf{C}_{gg} = \mathbf{B}_{gg} + \mathbf{B}_{gp}\mathbf{b}_{pg} + \mathbf{B}_{gv}\mathbf{D}_{vg}$. Then the impulse response function of prices $\tilde{p}_t$ to an aggregate productivity shock Z_t in the reduced model equals the impulse response function of prices p_t in the unreduced model up to order k.*

Proof.   See appendix section "Stochastic Model: Proof of Proposition 1."

The impulse response function in the stochastic model combines the impact effect of an aggregate shock Z_t together with the transition back to steady state. We do not reduce the exogenous state variable Z_t, so the reduced model captures the impact effect of a shock exactly. The role of the observability matrix is to approximate the transition back to steady state analogously to the deterministic case.

Finally, note that in this section we have assumed p_t is a scalar to emphasize that it is a low-dimensional object. In general $\mathbf{p}_t$ is an $\ell \times 1$ vector. One can extend the argument above to show that the correct basis $\mathbf{X}$ spans the subspace generated by $\mathcal{O}(\mathbf{B}_{pg}, \mathbf{C}_{gg})^\mathsf{T}$ for $\mathbf{C}_{gg} = \mathbf{B}_{gg} + \mathbf{B}_{gp}\mathbf{B}_{pg} +$

$\mathbf{B}_{gv}\mathbf{D}_{vg}$ where now $\mathbf{B}_{pg}$ is an $\ell \times N$ matrix. Matching impulse-response functions of $\mathbf{p}_t$ up to order k requires matching ℓk terms in the corresponding Taylor-series approximation, and hence the observability matrix $\mathcal{O}(\mathbf{B}_{pg}, \mathbf{C}_{gg})$ is now of dimension $k_g \times N$, where $k_g = \ell k < N$.

C. Choosing the Basis **X** with Endogenous Decision Rules

Section III.B shows that if decision rules $\mathbf{D}_{vg}$ are exogenously given, then choosing the basis **X** to span the subspace generated by $\mathcal{O}(\mathbf{B}_{pg}, \mathbf{C}_{gg})^{\mathrm{T}}$ guarantees that the impulse response of the reduced price $\tilde{p}_t$ matches the unreduced model up to a pre-specified order k. However, when decision rules are endogenous, the choice of basis impacts agents' decisions and therefore the evolution of the distribution. In this case, the results of Section III.B do not apply.

However, the choice of basis in Section III.B was only dictated by the concern of *efficiently* approximating the distribution with as small a basis as possible; it is always possible to improve *accuracy* by adding additional orthogonal basis vectors. In fact, in the finite limit when $k = N$, any linearly independent basis spans all of $\mathbb{R}^N$ so the distribution is not reduced at all and the reduced model is vacuously accurate. Therefore, setting the basis **X** to the subspace generated by $\mathcal{O}(\mathbf{B}_{pg}, \mathbf{B}_{gg} + \mathbf{B}_{gp}\mathbf{B}_{pg})^{\mathrm{T}}$, that is, ignoring feedback from individuals' decisions to the distribution by effectively setting $\mathbf{D}_{vg} = 0$, will not be efficient but may still be accurate. In practice, we have found in both the simple Krusell and Smith (1998) model and the two-asset model in Section V that this choice leads to accurate solutions for high enough order k of the observability matrix.

In cases where choosing the basis to span the subspace $\mathcal{O}(\mathbf{B}_{pg}, \mathbf{B}_{gg} + \mathbf{B}_{gp}\mathbf{B}_{pg})^{\mathrm{T}}$ is not accurate even for as high an order k as numerically feasible, we suggest an iterative procedure. First, we solve the reduced model (25) based on the inaccurate basis choice for the subspace $\mathcal{O}(\mathbf{B}_{pg}, \mathbf{B}_{gg} + \mathbf{B}_{gp}\mathbf{B}_{pg})^{\mathrm{T}}$. This yields decision rules $\mathbf{D}_{v\gamma}$ defining a mapping from the reduced distribution γ_t to the value function. We then use these to construct an approximation to the true decision rules $\mathbf{D}_{vg}$ (which map the full distribution to the value function), that is, $\widetilde{\mathbf{D}}_{vg} = \mathbf{D}_{v\gamma}\mathbf{X}^{\mathrm{T}}$.[39] Next we choose a new basis of the subspace generated by $\mathcal{O}(\mathbf{B}_{pg}, \mathbf{B}_{gg} + \mathbf{B}_{gg} + \mathbf{B}_{gp}\mathbf{B}_{pg} + \mathbf{B}_{gv}\widetilde{\mathbf{D}}_{vg})^{\mathrm{T}}$ and solve the model again based on the new reduction. If the second reduction gives an accurate solution, we are done; if not, we continue the iteration. Although we have no theoretical guarantee that this iteration will converge, in practice we have found that it does.

Choosing k and Internal Consistency with Endogenous Decision Rules.
A key practical step in reducing the distribution is choosing the order of
the observability matrix k, which determines the size of the basis $\mathbf{X}$. With
exogenous decision rules, we showed that a basis of order k implies that
the path of reduced prices $\tilde{p}_t$ matches the k-th order Taylor expansion of
the path of true prices p_t, providing a natural metric for assessing accuracy.[40] However, this logic does not carry through with endogenous decision rules, leaving unclear what exactly a basis of order k captures.

In the finite limit when $k = N$, any linearly independent basis spans
all of $\mathbb{R}^N$ so the distribution is not reduced at all and the reduced model
is vacuously accurate. Hence, a natural procedure is to increase k until
the dynamics of reduced prices converge. In practice, this convergence
is often monotonic. However, we cannot prove convergence is always
monotonic, still leaving open the question of what exactly the reduced
model captures for a given order k.

We suggest an *internal consistency* metric to assess the extent to which
the reduced model satisfies the model's equilibrium conditions. The
spirit of our internal consistency check is similar to Krusell and Smith's
(1998) R^2 forecast-error metric and Den Haan's (2010) accuracy measure
discussed in Section II: If agents make decisions based on the price path
implied by the reduced distribution, but we aggregate those decisions
against the true full distribution, do the prices generated by the true
distribution match the forecasts?

Concretely, our internal consistency check consists of three steps.
First, we compute households' decisions based on the reduced distribu-
tion, $\tilde{\mathbf{v}}_t = \mathbf{D}_{v\gamma}\gamma_t$. Second, we use these decisions to simulate the nonlinear dynamics of the full distribution $\mathbf{g}_t^*$—not the reduced version γ_t—
and its implied prices p_t^* for a given path of aggregate shocks Z_t

$$\mathbf{p}_t^* = \mathbf{B}_{pg}\mathbf{g}_t^* + \mathbf{B}_{pZ}Z_t$$

$$\frac{d\mathbf{g}_t^*}{dt} = \mathbf{A}(\tilde{\mathbf{v}}_t, \mathbf{p}_t^*)\mathbf{g}_t^*,$$

where $\mathbf{A}(\tilde{\mathbf{v}}_t, p_t^*)$ is the nonlinear transition matrix implied by the decision rules $\tilde{\mathbf{v}}_t$ and price p_t^*. The third step of our internal accuracy check
is to assess the extent to which the dynamics of p_t^* matches the dynam-
ics implied by the reduced system $\tilde{p}_t$. If the two paths are close, households in the reduced model could not significantly improve their forecasts by using additional information about the distribution. Once
again, we compare the maximum log deviation of the two paths

$$\varepsilon = \max_i \max_{t \geq 0} \left| \log \tilde{p}_{it} - \log p_{it}^* \right|,$$

where i denotes an entry in the price vector.

Computing the Basis X. Following the discussion above, we choose the basis $\mathbf{X}$ to span the subspace generated by $\mathcal{O}(\mathbf{B}_{pg}, \mathbf{B}_{gg} + \mathbf{B}_{gp}\mathbf{B}_{pg})^T$. However, using $\mathcal{O}(\mathbf{B}_{pg}, \mathbf{B}_{gg} + \mathbf{B}_{gp}\mathbf{B}_{pg})^T$ directly is numerically unstable due to approximate multicollinearity; as in standard regression, high-degree standard polynomials are nearly collinear due to the fact that, for large k, $\mathbf{B}_{pg}(\mathbf{B}_{gg} + \mathbf{B}_{gp}\mathbf{B}_{pg})^{k-2} \approx \mathbf{B}_{pg}(\mathbf{B}_{gg} + \mathbf{B}_{gp}\mathbf{B}_{pg})^{k-1}$, leaving the necessary projection of the distribution onto $\mathbf{X}$ numerically intractable.

We overcome this challenge by relying on a *Krylov subspace method*, an equivalent but more numerically stable class of methods.[41] For any $N \times N$ matrix $\mathbf{A}$ and $N \times 1$ vector $\mathbf{b}$, the order-k Krylov subspace is

$$\mathcal{K}_k(\mathbf{A}, \mathbf{b}) = span\left(\{\mathbf{b}, \mathbf{Ab}, \mathbf{A}^2\mathbf{b}, ..., \mathbf{A}^{k-1}\mathbf{b}\}\right).$$

From this definition it can be seen that the subspace spanned by the columns of $\mathcal{O}(\mathbf{B}_{pg}, \mathbf{B}_{gg} + \mathbf{B}_{gp}\mathbf{B}_{pg})^T$ is simply the order-k Krylov subspace generated by $(\mathbf{B}_{gg} + \mathbf{B}_{gp}\mathbf{B}_{pg})^T$ and $\mathbf{B}_{pg}^T$, that is, $\mathcal{K}_k(\mathbf{B}_{gg}^T + \mathbf{B}_{gp}^T\mathbf{B}_{pg}^T, \mathbf{B}_{pg}^T)$. Therefore, the projection of $\mathbf{g}_t$ on $\mathcal{O}(\mathbf{B}_{pg}, \mathbf{B}_{gg} + \mathbf{B}_{gp}\mathbf{B}_{pg})^T$ is equivalent to the projection of $\mathbf{g}_t$ onto this Krylov subspace.

There are many methods for projecting onto Krylov subspaces in the literature. One important feature of all these methods is that they take advantage of the sparsity of the underlying matrices.[42] We have found that one particular method, *deflated block Arnoldi iteration*, is a robust procedure. Deflated block Arnoldi iteration has two advantages for our application. First, it is a stable procedure to orthogonalize the columns of the basis $\mathbf{X}$ and eliminate the approximate multicollinearity. Second, the *deflation* component handles multicollinearity that can arise even with nondeflated block Arnoldi iteration.

D. Value Function Reduction

After reducing the dimensionality of the distribution $\mathbf{g}_t$, we are left with a system of dimension $N + k_g$ with $k_g \ll N$ (recall $k_g = \ell \times k$ where ℓ is the number of prices and k is the order of the approximation according to which the basis $\mathbf{X}$ is chosen). Although this is considerably smaller than the original system, which was of size $2N$, it is still large because it contains N equations for the value function—one for each point in the individual state space. In complex models, this leaves the linear system too large for matrix decomposition methods to be feasible.[43]

We therefore also reduce the dimensionality of the distribution $\mathbf{v}_t$. Just like in our method for reducing the distribution $\mathbf{g}_t$, we project the (deviation from steady state of the) value function $\mathbf{v}_t$ onto a lower-dimensional subspace. As before, an important question is how to choose the basis for this projection. We choose it by appealing to the theory for approximating smooth functions and approximate $\mathbf{v}_t$ using splines. In most models, the value function is sufficiently smooth that a low-dimensional spline provides an accurate approximation. In particular, any spline approximation can be written as the projection

$$\mathbf{v}_t \approx \mathbf{X}_v \nu_t,$$

where $\mathbf{X}_v$ is an $N \times k_v$ matrix defining the spline knot points and ν_t are the k_v coefficients at those knot points.[44] Given this linear projection the coefficients are given by $\nu_t = (\mathbf{X}_v^\mathsf{T} \mathbf{X}_v)^{-1} \mathbf{X}_v^\mathsf{T} \mathbf{v}_t = \mathbf{X}_v^\mathsf{T} \mathbf{v}_t$, where we have used that we typically choose an orthonormal $\mathbf{X}_v$ so that $\mathbf{X}_v^\mathsf{T} \mathbf{X}_v = \mathbf{I}$.

It is worth emphasizing the symmetry with our distribution-reduction method, the projection (23). In order to do so we add a g-subscript to the basis in the distribution reduction for the remainder of the paper and write equation (23) as $\mathbf{g}_t \approx \mathbf{X}_g \gamma_t$. Hence from now on $\mathbf{X}_g$ denotes the basis in the reduction of the distribution $\mathbf{g}_t$ and $\mathbf{X}_v$ denotes the basis in the reduction of the value function $\mathbf{v}_t$. It is also important to note that we are approximating the deviation of the value function from its steady-state value, not the value function itself (the reader should recall our convention in the present section to drop hat superscripts from variables that are in deviation from steady state for notational simplicity).

We have found that nonuniformly spaced quadratic splines work well for three reasons. First, the nonuniform spacing can be used to place more knots in regions of the state space with high curvature, allowing for an efficient dimensionality reduction. Second, the quadratic spline preserves monotonicity and concavity between knot points, which is important in computing first-order conditions. Third, and related, the local nature of splines implies that they avoid creating spurious oscillations at the edges of the state space (Runge's phenomenon), which often occurs with global approximations like high-degree polynomials.

It is also important to note the difference between approximating the deviations of the value function from steady state using quadratic splines—which we do—versus solving for the steady-state value using quadratic splines—which we do not do. The finite difference method we use to compute the steady state does not impose that the value function is everywhere differentiable, which is potentially important for capturing the effects of nonconvexities. However, after having computed the steady-state value functions, it is typically the case that they have kinks at a finite number of points and are well approximated by smooth functions between these points. It is then straightforward to fit quadratic splines between the points of nondifferentiability.

E. Putting It All Together: A Numerical Toolbox

Summarizing the previous sections, we have projected the distribution g_t onto the subspace spanned by X_g and the value function v_t onto the subspace spanned by X_v. Now we simply need to keep track of the $k_v \times 1$ coefficient vector v_t for the value function and the $k_g \times 1$ coefficient vector γ_t for the distribution. Because knowledge of these coefficients is sufficient to reconstruct the full value function and distribution, we will also sometimes refer to v_t as the reduced value function and to γ_t as the reduced distribution. Our original system (16) is now reduced to

$$
\mathbb{E}_t \begin{bmatrix} dv_t \\ d\gamma_t \\ dZ_t \end{bmatrix} = \begin{bmatrix} X_v^T B_{vv} X_v & X_v^T B_{vp} B_{pg} X_g & X_v^T B_{vp} B_{pZ} \\ X_g^T B_{gv} X_v & X_g^T (B_{gg} + B_{gp} B_{pg}) X_g & X_g^T B_{gp} B_{pZ} \\ 0 & 0 & -\eta \end{bmatrix} \begin{bmatrix} v_t \\ \gamma_t \\ Z_t \end{bmatrix} dt. \quad (33)
$$

We have provided a numerical toolbox implementing the key steps in our computational method at the github page associated with this project.[45] Broadly, the user provides two files: one that solves for the steady state and another that evaluates the model's equilibrium conditions. Our toolbox then implements the following algorithm (we here revert back to denoting deviations from steady state with hat superscripts):

1. Compute the steady state values of v, g and p.

2. Compute a first-order Taylor expansion of the equilibrium conditions (14) around steady state using automatic differentiation, yielding the system (16) in terms of deviations from steady state $\hat{v}_t$, $\hat{g}_t$, $\hat{p}_t$ and Z_t.

3. If necessary, reduce the model, yielding the system (33) in terms of (v_t, γ_t, Z_t).
    (a) Distribution reduction: compute the basis $X_g = \mathcal{O}(B_{pg}, B_{gg} + B_{gp} B_{pg})^T$ using deflated Arnoldi iteration and project $\hat{g}_t$ on X_g to obtain the reduced distribution γ_t.
    (b) Value function reduction: compute the spline basis X_v and project $\hat{v}_t$ on X_v to obtain the reduced value function v_t.

4. Solve the system (16) or, if reduced, (33).

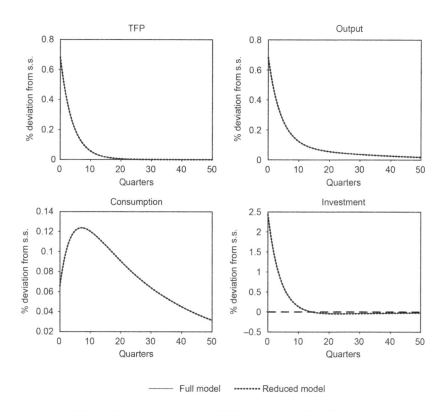

Fig. 1.   Impulse responses to TFP shock in Krusell-Smith model

Note: Impulse responses to an instantaneous positive unit standard deviation size shock (Dirac delta function) to aggregate TFP. We simulate the model by discretizing the time dimension with step size $dt = 0.1$. "Full model" refers to model solved without model reduction and "reduced model" with reduction, using $k_g = 2$ (forecasting $\ell = 5$ objects, of which two are linearly independent, with a $k = 1$-order Taylor-series approximation) and $k_v = 24$.

5. Simulate the system to compute impulse responses and time-series statistics.

F.   Model Reduction in Krusell-Smith Model

The Krusell and Smith (1998) model is a useful environment for evaluating our model-reduction methodology because it is possible to solve the full unreduced model as a benchmark. We are able to substantially reduce the size of the system: projecting the distribution on an observability matrix of order $k = 1$ and approximating the value function at 24 spline knot points provides an extremely accurate approximation of the model's dynamics.[46] Figure 1 shows that the impulse responses of key

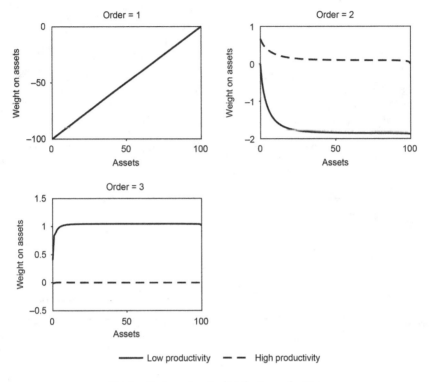

Fig. 2. Basis vectors in distribution reduction

Note: The columns of $\mathbf{X}_g = \mathcal{O}(\mathbf{B}_{pg}, \mathbf{B}_{gg} + \mathbf{B}_{gp}\mathbf{B}_{pg})^{\mathrm{T}}$, here displayed for the capital stock, up to order $k = 4$. These correspond to the basis vectors in the approximated distribution $\mathbf{g}_t \approx \gamma_{1t}\mathbf{x}_{g,1} + \cdots + \gamma_{4t}\mathbf{x}_{g,4}$.

aggregate variables in the reduced model are almost exactly identical to the full, unreduced model, despite approximating the $N = 400$ dimensional dynamic system with a 30-dimensional system.[47]

The fact that we can reduce the distribution with an observability matrix of order $k = 1$ is consistent with Krusell and Smith's (1998) finding of "approximate aggregation" using a computationally distinct procedure and accuracy measure. In fact, as figure 2 shows, a $k = 1$ order approximation of the distribution returns precisely the mean. The top left panel of the figure plots the basis vector associated with $k = 1$, split into two 100-dimensional vectors corresponding to the two values for idiosyncratic productivity. It shows that indeed the first basis vector $\mathbf{x}_{g,1} = \left[\begin{smallmatrix} a \\ a \end{smallmatrix}\right]$, implying that $\gamma_t = \mathbf{x}_{g,1}^{\mathrm{T}}\mathbf{g}_t = \left[\begin{smallmatrix} a \\ a \end{smallmatrix}\right]^{\mathrm{T}}\mathbf{g}_t = \hat{K}_t$, the (deviation from steady state of the) mean of the distribution. The remaining panels plot

Table 3
Run Time for Solving Krusell-Smith Model

	Full Model	Reduced Model
Steady state	0.082 sec	0.082 sec
Derivatives	0.021 sec	0.021 sec
Dim reduction	×	0.007 sec
Linear system	0.14 sec	0.002 sec
Simulate IRF	0.024 sec	0.003 sec
Total	**0.267 sec**	**0.116 sec**

Notes: Time to solve Krusell-Smith model once on MacBook Pro 2016 laptop with 3.3 GHz processor and 16 GB RAM, using Matlab R2016b and our code toolbox. "Full model" refers to solving model without model reduction and "reduced model" with reduction, using $k_g = 1$ and $k_v = 12$. "Steady state" reports time to compute steady state. "Derivatives" reports time to compute derivatives of discretized equilibrium conditions. "Dim reduction" reports time to compute both the distribution and value function reduction. "Linear system" reports time to solve system of linear differential equations. "Simulate IRF" reports time to simulate impulse responses reported in figure 1. "Total" is the sum of all these tasks.

the higher-order elements of $\mathbf{X}_g$, which quickly converge to constants that do not add information to the approximation. Hence, our model-free reduction method confirms Krusell and Smith's (1998) approximate aggregation result in this simple model.

With or without dimensionality reduction, our method solves and simulates the model in less than 0.3 seconds. Table 3 reports the running time of using our Matlab code suite on a desktop PC. Although reduction is not necessary to solve this simple model, it nevertheless reduces running time by more than 50% and takes approximately 0.1 seconds.[48] In the two-asset model in Section V, model reduction is necessary to even solve the model.

Our internal consistency check confirms the fact that the distribution reduction is accurate; the maximum log deviation is 0.065%, which is twice as small as the most accurate algorithm in the JEDC comparison (Den Haan 2010). Recall that the maximum log deviation in the unreduced model is 0.049%, capturing the error due to linearization. Hence, the additional error due to our model reduction is extremely small. Figure 3 plots the two series for a random 400-quarter period of simulation and shows that the two series are extremely close to each other.[49]

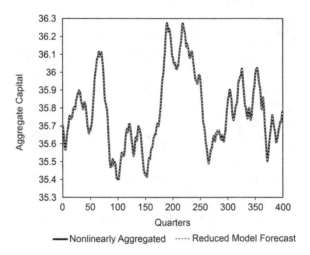

Fig. 3. Internal consistency check

Note: Two series for aggregate capital that enter the internal consistency check ε. "Reduced model forecast" computes the path $\bar{K}_t$ implied by the reduced linear model. "Nonlinear model forecast" computes the path K_t^* from updating the distribution according to the nonlinear KFE (3).

IV.   Two-Asset Incomplete Markets Model

While the Krusell and Smith (1998) model is a useful pedagogical tool for explaining our computational method, it does not reproduce key features of the distribution of household-level income, wealth, and consumption in the microdata. In this section, we apply our method to solve a two-asset incomplete markets model in the spirit of Kaplan and Violante (2014) and Kaplan et al. (2016), which is explicitly parameterized to match key features of these distributions. Accurately reproducing these features leads to a failure of approximate aggregation, which together with the model's size, render it an ideal setting to illustrate the power of our method. In Sections V and VI, we use the model to illustrate a rich interaction between inequality and macroeconomic dynamics.

A.   Model

The household side of the model is a simplified version of Kaplan et al. (2016), so we refer the interested reader to that paper for full details. The firm side follows the standard real business cycle model with aggregate productivity shocks.

Environment

Households. There is a unit mass of households indexed by $j \in [0, 1]$. At each instant of time, households hold liquid assets b_{jt}, illiquid assets a_{jt}, and have labor productivity z_{jt}. Households die with an exogenous Poisson intensity ζ and upon death give birth to an offspring with zero wealth $a_{jt} = b_{jt} = 0$ and labor productivity drawn from its ergodic distribution. There are perfect annuity markets, implying that the wealth of deceased households is distributed to other households in proportion to their asset holdings.[50] Each household has preferences over consumption c_{jt} represented by the expected utility function

$$\mathbb{E}_0 \int_0^\infty e^{-(\rho+\zeta)t} \log c_{jt} dt.$$

A household with labor productivity z_{jt} earns labor income $w_t z_{jt}$ and pays a linear income tax at rate τ. Each household also receives a constant lump-sum transfer from the government, T. Labor productivity follows a discrete-state Poisson process, taking values from the set $z_{jt} \in \{z_1, ..., z_J\}$. Households switch from state z to state z' with Poisson intensity $\lambda_{zz'}$.

The liquid asset b_{jt} pays a rate of return r_t^b. Households can borrow in liquid assets up to an exogenous limit $\underline{b}$. The interest rate on borrowing is $r_t^b = r_t^b + \kappa$ where $\kappa > 0$ is a wedge between borrowing and lending rates. Define $r_t^b(b_t)$ to be the interest-rate function that takes both of these cases into account.

The illiquid asset a_{jt} pays a rate of return r_t^a. It is illiquid in the sense that households must pay a flow cost $\chi(d_{jt}, a_{jt})$ to transfer assets at rate d_{jt} from the illiquid to the liquid account. The transaction cost function is given by[51]

$$\chi(d, a) = \chi_0 |d| + \chi_1 \left|\frac{d}{a}\right|^{\chi_2} a.$$

The linear component $\chi_0 > 0$ generates inaction in households' optimal deposit decisions. The convex component ($\chi_1 > 0$, $\chi_2 > 1$) ensures that deposit rates d / a are finite, so that households' asset holdings never jump. Scaling the convex term by illiquid assets a ensures that marginal transaction costs $\chi_d(d, a)$ are homogeneous of degree zero in the deposit rate d / a, which implies that the marginal cost depends on the fraction of illiquid assets transacted rather than the raw size of the transaction. The laws of motion for liquid and illiquid assets are

$$\frac{db_{jt}}{dt} = (1 - \tau)we^{z_{jt}} + T + r_t^b(b_{jt})b_{jt} - \chi(d_{jt}, a_{jt}) - c_{jt} - d_{jt}$$

$$\frac{da_{jt}}{dt} = r_t^a a_{jt} + d_{jt}.$$

Firms. There is a representative firm with the Cobb-Douglas production function

$$Y_t = e^{Z_t} K_t^\alpha \bar{L}^{1-\alpha},$$

where as before Z_t is the logarithm of aggregate productivity, K_t is aggregate capital, and $\bar{L}$ is aggregate labor supply, which is constant by assumption. The logarithm of aggregate productivity again follows the Ornstein-Uhlenbeck process

$$dZ_t = -\eta Z_t dt + \sigma dW_t,$$

where dW_t is the innovation to a standard Brownian motion, η is the rate of mean reversion, and σ captures the size of innovations.

Government. There is a government that balances its budget each period. Since the labor tax rate τ and lump-sum transfer rate T are constant, we assume that government spending G_t adjusts each period to satisfy the government budget constraint

$$\int_0^1 \tau w_t z_{jt} dj = G_t + \int_0^1 T dj. \tag{34}$$

Government spending G_t is not valued by households.

Asset Market Clearing. The aggregate capital stock is the total amount of illiquid assets in the economy,

$$K_t = \int_0^1 a_{jt} dj.$$

The market for capital is competitive, so the return on the illiquid asset r_t^a is simply the rental rate of capital.

The supply of liquid assets is fixed exogenously at $B_t = B^*$, where B^* is the steady-state demand for liquid assets given $r_b^* = 0.005$ (discussed below). For simplicity, we assume that interest payments on the liquid assets come from outside the economy.

Equilibrium

The household-level state variables are illiquid asset holdings a, liquid asset holdings b, and labor productivity z. The aggregate state variables are aggregate productivity Z_t and the cross-sectional distribution of households over their individual states $g_t(a, b, z)$. As in Section II, we denote an equilibrium object conditional on a particular realization of the aggregate state $(g_t(a, b, z), Z_t)$ with a subscript t.

Households. The household's Hamilton-Jacobi-Bellman equation is given by

$$(\rho + \zeta)v_t(a,b,z) = \max_{c,d} \log c$$

$$+ \partial_b v_t(a,b,z)(T + (1 - \tau)w_t e^z + r_t^b(b)b - \chi(d,a) - c - d)$$

$$+ \partial_a v_t(a,b,z)(r_t^a a + d) \tag{35}$$

$$+ \sum_{z'} \lambda_{zz'}(v_t(a,b,z') - v_t(a,b,z)) + \frac{1}{dt}\mathbb{E}_t[dv_t(a,b,z)].$$

The cross-sectional distribution $g_t(a, b, z)$ satisfies the Kolmogorov Forward equation

$$\frac{dg_t(a, b, z)}{dt} = -\partial_a(s_t^a(a, b, z)g_t(a, b, z)) - \partial_b(s_t^b(a, b, z)g_t(a, b, z))$$

$$- \sum_{z'} \lambda_{zz'} g_t(a, b, z) + \sum_{z'} \lambda_{z'z} g_t(a, b, z) \tag{36}$$

$$- \zeta g_t(a, b, z) + \zeta \delta(a)\delta(b)g^*(z),$$

where s_t^a and s_t^b are the optimal drifts in illiquid and liquid assets implied by equation (35), $g^*(z)$ is the ergodic distribution of z, and δ is the Dirac delta function with $\delta(a)\delta(b)$ capturing birth at $a = b = 0$.

Firms. The equilibrium conditions for the production side are the firm optimality conditions, together with the process for aggregate productivity:

$$r_t^a = \alpha e^{Z_t} K_t^{\alpha-1} \bar{L}^{1-\alpha} - \delta$$

$$w_t = (1 - \alpha)e^{Z_t} K_t^{\alpha} \bar{L}^{-\alpha}$$

$$dZ_t = -\eta Z_t dt + \sigma dW_t.$$

Market Clearing. Capital market clearing is given by

$$K_t = \int ag_t(a, b, z)dadbdz.$$

Liquid asset market clearing is given by

$$B = \int b g_t(a, b, z) \mathrm{d}a \mathrm{d}b \mathrm{d}z.$$

Given these conditions, as well as the government budget constraint (34), the market for output clears by Walras's law.

B.   Calibration

We calibrate the steady state of the model without aggregate shocks to match key features of the cross-sectional distributions of household income and balance sheets. Our calibration closely follows Kaplan et al. (2016).

Exogenously Set Parameters. We choose the quarterly death rate $\zeta = 1 /$ 180 so that households live 45 years on average. We set the tax rate $\tau =$ 30% and set the lump-sum transfer T to 10% of steady-state output. Given our labor productivity process, this policy implies that in steady state around 35% of households receive a net transfer from the government, consistent with the Congressional Budget Office (2013). We interpret borrowing in the liquid asset as unsecured credit and therefore set the borrowing limit $\underline{b}$ at one times average quarterly labor income.

We set the capital share in production $\alpha = 0.4$ and the annual depreciation rate on capital $\delta = 0.075$. With an equilibrium steady-state ratio of capital to annual output of 3.0 (see below) this implies an annual return on illiquid assets r^a of 5.8%.

Labor Productivity Shocks. Following Kaplan et al. (2016), we assume that the discrete-state process for labor productivity is a discretized version of the following continuous-state process. The logarithm of idiosyncratic labor productivity is the sum of two independent components

$$\log z_{jt} = z_{1,jt} + z_{2,jt}, \tag{37}$$

where each process follows the jump-drift process

$$\mathrm{d}z_{i,jt} = -\beta_i z_{i,jt} \mathrm{d}t + \mathrm{d}J_{i,jt}. \tag{38}$$

Jumps arrive for component i at Poisson arrival rate λ_i. Conditional on a jump, a new log-earnings state $z_{c,it}$ is drawn from a normal distribution with mean zero and variance σ_i^2. Between jumps, the process drifts toward zero at rate β_i.[52] The parameters σ_i govern the size of the shocks, the parameters β_i govern the persistence of the shocks, and the parameters λ_i govern the frequency of their arrival.

Table 4
Targeted Labor Income Moments

Moment	Data	Model Estimated	Model Discretized
Variance: Annual log earns	0.70	0.70	0.76
Variance: 1 yr. change	0.23	0.23	0.21
Variance: 5 yr. change	0.46	0.46	0.46
Kurtosis: 1 yr. change	17.8	16.5	17.3
Kurtosis: 5 yr. change	11.6	12.1	10.9
Frac. 1 yr. change < 10%	0.54	0.56	0.64
Frac. 1 yr. change < 20%	0.71	0.67	0.70
Frac. 1 yr. change < 50%	0.86	0.85	0.86

Note: Moments of the earning process targeted in the calibration. "Data" refers to SSAA data on male earnings from Guvenen et al. (2015). "Model Estimated" refers to the continuous process (37) and (38). "Model Discretized" refers to discrete Poisson approximation of the process used in model computation.

Jump-drift processes of this form are closely related to discrete-time AR(1) processes, with the modification that shocks arrive at random, rather than deterministic, dates. Allowing for the random arrival of shocks is important for matching the leptokurtic nature of annual income growth rates, which we discuss below. It is also important for matching observed household portfolio choices of liquid and illiquid assets. If the majority of earnings shocks are transitory and frequent (high β, high λ), households would accumulate a buffer stock of liquid assets to self-insure. On the other hand, if earnings shocks are persistent and infrequent (low β, low λ), households would prefer to save in high-return illiquid assets and pay the transaction costs to rebalance their portfolio when shocks occur.

Recent work by Guvenen et al. (2015) shows that changes in annual labor income are extremely leptokurtic, meaning that most absolute annual income changes are small but a small number are very large. We use the extent of this leptokurtosis, together with standard moments on the variance of log earnings and log earnings growth rates, to estimate the parameters of the earnings process (37) and (38). The moments we match, together with the fit of the estimated model, are shown in table 4.

The estimated parameters in table 5 indicate that the two jump-drift processes can be broadly interpreted as a transitory and a persistent component. The transitory component ($j = 1$) arrives on average once every three years and has a half-life of around one quarter. The persistent component ($j = 2$) arrives on average once every 38 years and has a

Table 5
Estimated Labor Income Process

Parameter		Component $j = 1$	Component $j = 2$
Arrival rate	λ_j	0.080	0.007
Mean reversion	β_j	0.761	0.009
Std. deviation of innovations	σ_j	1.74	1.53

Note: Parameters of the income process (37) and (38) estimated to match the moments in table 4. The $j = 1$ component arrives on average once every three years with half-life approximately one quarter. The $j = 2$ component arrives once every 38 years with half-life approximately 18 years.

half-life of around 18 years. In the context of an infinite-horizon model, the persistent component can be interpreted as a "career shock." We discretize the continuous process (38) using 10 points for the persistent component and 3 points for the transitory component. The fit of the discretized process for the targeted moments is shown in table 4.

Adjustment Costs and Discount Factor. The five remaining parameters on the household side of the model—the discount rate ρ, the borrowing wedge κ, and the parameters of the adjustment cost function χ_0, χ_1, and χ_2—jointly determine the incentives of households to accumulate liquid and illiquid assets. We choose these parameters to match five moments of household balance sheets from the Survey of Consumer Finances 2004: the mean of the illiquid and liquid wealth distributions, the fraction of poor hand-to-mouth households (with $b = 0$ and $a = 0$), the fraction of wealthy hand-to-mouth households (with $b = 0$ and $a > 0$), and the fraction of households with negative assets. We match mean illiquid and liquid wealth so that the model is consistent with the aggregate wealth in the US economy. We match the fraction of hand-to-mouth households because these households have higher than average marginal propensities to consume. See Kaplan et al. (2016) for details on the classification of liquid and illiquid assets.

Table 6 shows that our calibrated model matches these five moments well. The implied annual discount rate is 5.8% annually and the annual borrowing wedge is 8.1% annually. Figure 4 plots the calibrated adjustment cost function together with the steady-state distribution of quarterly deposits. The transaction cost is less than 1% of the transaction for small transactions and rises to around 10% of the transaction for a quarterly transaction that is 2% of illiquid assets. The function

Table 6
Targeted Wealth Distribution Moments

	Target	Model
Mean illiquid assets (multiple of annual GDP)	3.000	3.000
Mean liquid assets (multiple of annual GDP)	0.375	0.375
Frac. with $b = 0$ and $a = 0$	0.100	0.105
Frac. with $b = 0$ and $a > 0$	0.200	0.172
Frac. with $b < 0$	0.150	0.135

Note: Moments of asset distribution targeted in calibration.
Data source: SCF 2004. Liquid assets are revolving consumer debt, deposits, corporate bonds, and government bonds. Illiquid assets are net housing, net durables, corporate equity, and private equity.

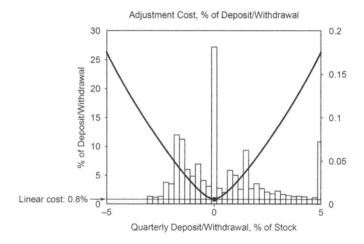

Fig. 4. Calibrated adjustment cost function
Note: Solid line plots adjustment costs as a fraction of the amount being transacted d, $\chi(d, a)/d$, where $\chi(d, a) = \chi_0|d| + \chi_1|d/a|^{\chi_2} a$. Histogram displays the steady-state distribution of deposit rates d/a.

has a kink at $d = 0$, which generates a mass of households who neither deposit nor withdraw.

The calibrated distributions of liquid and illiquid wealth are displayed in figure 5. Approximately 28% are hand-to-mouth households (i.e., have zero liquid wealth) and another 14% have negative liquid wealth. Roughly two-thirds of the hand-to-mouth households are "wealthy hand-to-mouth," that is, have positive illiquid assets, while the remaining one-third are "poor hand-to-mouth, that is, have zero illiquid assets. Both distributions are extremely skewed; 3% of house-

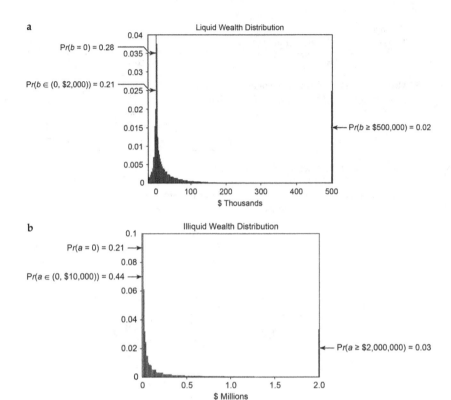

Fig. 5.   Liquid and illiquid wealth distribution in steady state; panel (a) liquid assets *b*, panel (b) illiquid assets *a*.

Note: Steady-state distributions of liquid and illiquid wealth in the calibrated model.

holds have more than $2,000,000 in illiquid assets and the top 10% hold 85% of total illiquid wealth in the economy.

The presence of hand-to-mouth households generates a distribution of marginal propensities to consume in line with empirical evidence. The average quarterly MPC out of a $500 cash windfall is 22.5%, in line with the empirical estimates of Johnson et al. (2006) and Parker et al. (2013). The average number is composed of high MPCs for hand-to-mouth households (around 0.4) and small MPCs for non-hand-to-mouth households. This bimodality can be seen in figure 6, panel (a), and is consistent with recent work by Fagereng et al. (2016).[53] Figure 6, panel (b), shows that only households with zero (or very negative) liquid wealth have substantial MPCs, even for households with positive illiquid assets.

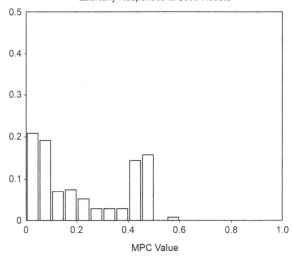

a   Quarterly Responses to $500 Rebate

MPC Value

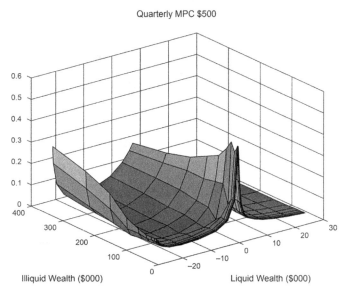

b   Quarterly MPC $500

Illiquid Wealth ($000)   Liquid Wealth ($000)

Fig. 6. Heterogeneity in MPCs across households; panel (a) distribution in steady state, panel (b) MPC function.

Note: Quarterly MPCs out of a $500 windfall in steady state. The MPC over a period τ is $MPC_\tau(a, b, z) = \partial C_\tau(a, b, z) / \partial b$, where $C_\tau(a, b, z) = \mathbb{E}[\int_0^\tau c(a_t, b_t, z_t)dt \mid a_0 = a, b_0 = b, z_0 = z]$.

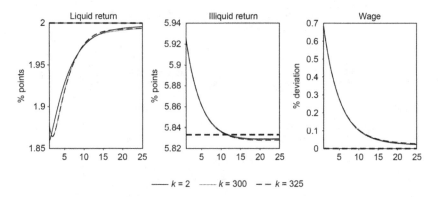

$$— k = 2 \quad \cdots k = 300 \quad -- k = 325$$

Fig. 7. Impulse responses for different orders of distribution reduction

Notes: Impulse responses to an instantaneous positive unit standard deviation size shock (Dirac delta function) to aggregate TFP. Note that "$k = 2$" corresponds to distribution reduction based on an order 2 observability matrix, "$k = 300$" corresponds to distribution reduction based on an order 300 observability matrix, and "$k = 325$" corresponds to distribution reduction based on an order 325 observability matrix. We simulate the model by discretizing the time dimension with step size $dt = 0.1$.

Aggregate Shocks. As in Section II, we set the rate of mean reversion of aggregate productivity shocks ε to ensure that their quarterly autocorrelation $e^{-\eta} \approx 1 - \eta = 0.75$, and we set the volatility of innovations $\sigma = 0.007$.

C. Performance of Computational Method

Our discretization of the individual state space (a, b, z) contains $N = 60{,}000$ points, implying that the total unreduced dynamic system contains more than 120,000 equations in 120,000 variables.[54] We reduce the value function $\hat{\mathbf{v}}_t$ using the spline approximation discussed in Section III.D, bringing the size of the value function down from $N = 60{,}000$ gridpoints to $k_v = 2{,}145$ knot points.

Failure of Approximate Aggregation. We reduce the distribution $\hat{\mathbf{g}}_t$ using a $k = 300$ order observability matrix to form the basis $\mathbf{X}$. In the finite limit where k is equal to the size of the unreduced state space, the reduced model converges to the true unreduced model. Figure 7 shows that the impulse responses of the three prices in the model—the liquid return, the illiquid return, and the wage—appear to have converged by $k = 300$.

The fact that the distribution reduction step requires $k > 1$ suggests that "approximate aggregation" does not hold in the two-asset model.[55]

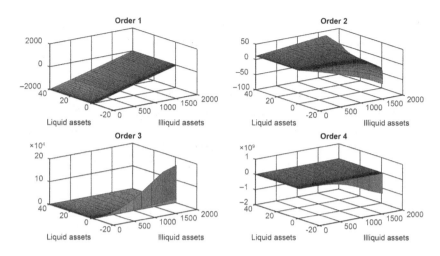

Fig. 8. Basis vectors for approximating distribution in two-asset model

Note: Columns of the observability matrix $\mathcal{O}(\mathbf{B}_{pg}, \mathbf{B}_{gg} + \mathbf{B}_{gp}\mathbf{B}_{pg})^{\mathsf{T}}$ corresponding to aggregate capital K_t. The four panels plot the first four columns of the observability matrix over liquid and illiquid assets conditional on the median realization of labor productivity z.

Figure 7 shows that using $k = 2$ provides a poor approximation of the model's dynamics, particularly for the liquid return r_t^b. This result suggests that approximating the distribution with a small number of moments using Krusell and Smith's (1998) procedure would be infeasible in this model.[56]

There are two main reasons why approximate aggregation does not hold in the two-asset model. First, recall that the reason for approximate aggregation in the Krusell and Smith (1998) model is that consumption functions are approximately linear in wealth, except for hand-to-mouth households near the borrowing constraint. However, in the one-asset model these households do not contribute very much to the aggregate capital stock (by virtue of holding very little capital) and hence their consumption dynamics are not important for the dynamics of aggregate capital. In contrast, in the two-asset model, there are a substantial number of wealthy hand-to-mouth households who have both highly nonlinear consumption functions (by virtue of holding very little liquid wealth) and constitute a nontrivial contribution to the dynamics of aggregate capital (by virtue of holding substantial quantities of illiquid wealth).

Consistent with this intuition, the basis $\mathbf{X}$ of our distribution reduction places weight on regions of the state space that have a significant fraction of hand-to-mouth households. Figure 8 plots the first four column vectors of the observability matrix associated with forecasting the aggregate capital stock K_t.[57] Each panel plots a given column of the matrix over liquid and illiquid assets, conditional on the median realization of labor productivity z. The first column captures exactly the mean of the illiquid asset distribution, which corresponds to aggregate capital. The next three columns focus on regions of the state space in which households have low liquid assets—and so are hand-to-mouth households—as well as high illiquid assets—and so contribute substantially to aggregate capital.

The second reason why approximate aggregation breaks down in the two-asset model is that households must track the liquid return r_t^b in addition to the aggregate capital stock K_t.[58] The dynamics of r_t^b feature stronger distributional dependence than the dynamics of K_t because the liquid asset is in fixed supply B^*; an increase in savings in one region of the state space must be met with a decrease in savings elsewhere in the state space. Indeed, figure 7 shows that the liquid return is the most poorly approximated variable in a $k = 2$ order approximation.[59]

Run Time. Our numerical toolbox solves and simulates the two-asset model in 4 minutes, 46 seconds. Table 7 decomposes the total run time into various tasks and shows that over two-thirds of the time is spent in the model-reduction step. In order to illustrate how the method scales with k, table 7 also reports the run time for a smaller $k = 150$ order observability matrix. With this smaller approximation of the distribution, the total run time falls to 2 minutes, 28 seconds.

D. Impulse Response to TFP Shock Z_t

Figure 9 plots the impulse responses of aggregate output and consumption to a positive aggregate productivity shock Z_t. Higher productivity directly increases output Y_t through the production function. It also increases the return on capital r_t^a, which encourages capital accumulation and further increases output over time. The marginal product of labor also rises, increasing the real wage w_t. Both of these price increases lead to an increase in household income.

The increase in household income has differential effects on the consumption of hand-to-mouth and non-hand-to-mouth households. Non-hand-to-mouth households respond primarily to the change in their

Table 7
Run Time for Solving Two-Asset Model

	$k = 300$	$k = 150$
Steady state	56.64 sec	56.64 sec
Derivatives	13.97 sec	13.97 sec
Dim reduction	199.71 sec	67.48 sec
Linear system	12.89 sec	7.70 sec
Simulate IRF	3.03 sec	2.31 sec
Total	**286.24 sec**	**148.10 sec**

Notes: Time to solve the two-asset model on a Mac-Book Pro 2016 laptop with 3.3 GHz processor and 16 GB RAM, using Matlab R2016b and our code tool-box; k refers to order of the observability matrix used to compute basis **X**. "Steady state" reports time to compute steady state. "Derivatives" reports time to compute derivatives of discretized equilibrium conditions. "Dim reduction" reports time to compute both the distribution and value function reduction. "Linear system" reports time to solve system of linear differential equations. "Simulate IRF" reports time to simulate impulse responses reported. "Total" is the sum of all these tasks.

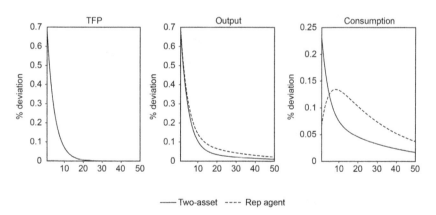

Fig. 9. Aggregate impulse responses to aggregate productivity shock Z_t

Notes: Impulse responses to an instantaneous positive unit standard deviation size shock (Dirac delta function) to aggregate TFP. "Two-asset" refers to the two-asset model developed in Section IV.A. "Representative agent" refers to the representative agent version of the model, in which the households are replaced by a representative household who can only save in aggregate capital; see appendix section "Representative Agent and Spender-Saver Models" for details. We simulate the model by discretizing the time dimension with step size $dt = 0.1$ using an implicit updating scheme.

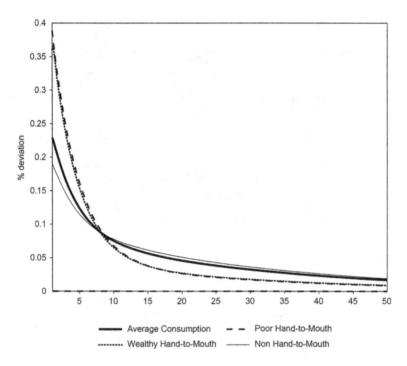

Fig. 10. Consumption response by hand-to-mouth status

Notes: Impulse responses to an instantaneous positive unit standard deviation size shock (Dirac delta function) to aggregate TFP. "Wealthy hand-to-mouth" refers to households with $b = 0$ and $a > 0$. "Poor hand-to-mouth" refers to households with $b = 0$ and $a = 0$. "Average consumption" is aggregate consumption. "Non-hand-to-mouth" is computed as the residual. We simulate the model by discretizing the time dimension with step size $dt = 0.1$ using an implicit updating scheme.

permanent income. The change in permanent income is relatively small (because the productivity shock Z_t is transitory) but is persistent (because of the dynamics of the capital stock). In contrast, hand-to-mouth households respond primarily to the change in their *current income.* The change in current income is larger than the change in permanent income and is less persistent. Consistent with this logic, figure 10 shows that the consumption of the hand-to-mouth households responds twice as much as average consumption upon impact, but dies out more quickly. Due to the presence of these hand-to-mouth households, the impulse response of aggregate consumption to a productivity shock is very different in the two-asset model compared with a representative agent model.

V. Aggregate Consumption Dynamics in Two-Asset Model

In this section, we use the two-asset model developed in Section IV to illustrate how inequality shapes the dynamics of macroeconomic aggregates. Specifically, we show that although the model is parameterized to match *household-level* data, it also matches key features of the joint dynamics of *aggregate* consumption and income.

A. Model with Growth Rate Shocks

Following a long line of work in the consumption dynamics literature, such as Campbell and Mankiw (1989), we compare the predictions of our model to data on aggregate consumption and aggregate income *growth*. However, the Ornstein-Uhlenbeck process for aggregate productivity we have been working with so far implies that aggregate income growth is negatively autocorrelated, which is at odds with the data. Therefore, we modify the shock process so that aggregate productivity *growth*, rather than the level, follows an Ornstein-Uhlenbeck process. In addition, we assume that the liquid interest rate r_t^b is fixed at its steady-state value $r_b^* = 0.005$ and that the liquid-asset supply adjusts perfectly elastically at this price, as in a small open economomy. This simplifying assumption ensures that the only time-varying interest rate is the return on capital, making the comparison with representative agent models more transparent. Both of these modifications apply to this section only.

Production and Aggregate Shock Process. The production function with growth rate shocks is

$$Y_t = K_t^\alpha \left(Q_t \bar{L} \right)^{1-\alpha},$$

where Q_t is aggregate productivity. Aggregate productivity growth follows the process

$$\mathrm{d} \log Q_t = Z_t \mathrm{d}t$$

$$\mathrm{d}Z_t = -\eta Z_t \mathrm{d}t + \sigma \mathrm{d}W_t,$$

where $\mathrm{d}W_t$ is an innovation to a standard Brownian motion. Hence, aggregate productivity growth is subject to the Ornstein-Uhlenbeck process Z_t.

Table 8
Targeted Moments of Real GDP Growth

	Data	Model
$\sigma(\Delta \log Y_t)$	0.89	0.89
$\text{Corr}(\Delta \log Y_t, \Delta \log Y_{t-2})$	0.21	0.20

Note: Targeted moments of per capita real GDP growth, 1953:Q1—2016:Q2.

Given the other calibrated parameters from Section IV, we choose the parameters of the TFP growth process Z_t so that equilibrium dynamics of aggregate income growth $\Delta \log Y_t$ match two key features of the data: the standard deviation of income growth $\sigma(\Delta \log Y_t)$ and the second-order autocorrelation of income growth $\text{Corr}(\Delta \log Y_t, \Delta \log Y_{t-2})$.[60] These moments in the data and the model's fit are reported in table 8.

Model Computation. Many equilibrium objects in the model are nonstationary due to the nonstationarity of aggregate productivity Q_t. We cannot directly apply our computational methodology in this setting, which relies on approximating the model's dynamics around a stationary equilibrium. Therefore, we detrend the model to express the equilibrium in terms of stationary objects; for details, see the appendix section "Detrending the Nonstationary Model."

B. Comparison to the Data

We focus our analysis on two sets of facts about the joint dynamics of aggregate consumption and income. The first set of facts, known as *sensitivity*, describes how aggregate consumption growth co-moves with predictable changes in aggregate income growth. The second set of facts, known as *smoothness*, refers to the extent of the time-series variation in aggregate consumption growth.

Sensitivity. We present several measures of sensitivity in the top panel of table 9. These measures all compute how predictable changes in income pass through to changes in consumption, but differ in two key respects. The first two measures of sensitivity are coefficients from ordinary least squares regressions, whereas the second two measures are coefficients from instrumental variables regressions. The second and fourth measures include real interest rates in the conditioning set,

Table 9
Joint Dynamics of Consumption and Income

			Models	
	Data	Two-Asset	Rep Agent	Sp-Sa
Sensitivity to Income				
$\Delta \log C_t = \beta_0 + \beta_1 \Delta \log Y_{t-2} + \varepsilon_t$	0.12	0.14	0.12	0.16
	(0.03)			
$\Delta \log C_t = \beta_0 + \beta_1 \Delta \log Y_{t-2} + \beta_2 r_{t-2} + \varepsilon_t$	0.12	0.09	0.04	0.11
	(0.03)			
IV($\Delta \log C_t$ on $\Delta \log Y_t$ | $\Delta \log Y_{t-2}$)	0.55	0.70	0.54	0.78
	(0.15)			
Campbell-Mankiw IV	0.49	0.40	0.004	0.50
	(0.15)			(calibrated)
Smoothness				
$\sigma(\Delta\log C_t)/\sigma(\Delta\log Y_t)$	0.52	0.70	0.80	0.70
Corr($\Delta\log C_t$, $\Delta\log C_{t-2}$)	0.33	0.24	0.16	0.27

Notes: Measures of sensitivity of aggregate consumption to income and the smoothness of aggregate consumption. In the data, aggregate consumption C_t is measured as the sum of real nondurable plus durable services, per capita, and aggregate income Y_t is real GDP per capita. Both series are quarterly 1953:Q1–2016:Q2. "Rep agent" refers to the representative agent model described in the appendix section "Representative Agent and Spender-Saver Models." "Two-asset" refers to the full two-asset model. "Sp-Sa" refers to the spender-saver model described in the appendix section "Representative Agent and Spender-Saver Models." "$\Delta \log C_t = \beta_0 + \beta_1 \Delta \log Y_{t-2} + \varepsilon_t$" refers to β_1 in the regression. "$\Delta \log C_t = \beta_0 + \beta_1 \Delta \log Y_{t-2} + \beta_2 r_{t-2} + \varepsilon_t$" refers to the coefficient β_1 in the regression. "IV($\Delta \log C_t$ on $\Delta \log Y_t$ \| $\Delta \log Y_{t-2}$)" refers to β_1 in the instrumental variables regression $\Delta \log C_t = \beta_0 + \beta_1 \Delta \log Y_t + \varepsilon_t$, using $\Delta \log Y_{t-2}$ to instrument for $\Delta \log Y_t$. "Campbell-Mankiw IV" refers to the β_1 in the instrumental variables regression $\Delta \log C_t = \beta_0 + \beta_1 \Delta \log Y_t + \beta_2 r_t + \varepsilon_t$, using $\Delta \log Y_{t-2}$, $\Delta \log Y_{t-3}$, $\Delta \log Y_{t-4}$, r_{t-2}, r_{t-3}, and r_{t-4} to instrument for the right-hand side. We time-aggregate our continuous time model to the quarterly frequency by computing the simple average within a quarter.

whereas the first and third measures do not. We present this range of measures to represent the range of approaches in the existing literature.

We measure aggregate income growth as the quarterly change in log real GDP per capita during the period 1953:Q1 to 2016:Q2. We measure aggregate consumption growth as the quarterly change in log real nondurables plus durable services consumption per capita during the same period. Finally, we measure the real interest rate as the real return on 90-day Treasury bills, adjusted for realized inflation.

In the data, all measures of sensitivity indicate that a substantial portion of aggregate income growth passes through to consumption growth. Consistent with the arguments in Campbell and Mankiw (1989) and Ludvigson and Michaelides (2001), among others, the representative agent model generates too little sensitivity once we condition on the real interest rate.[61] In contrast, the two-asset heterogeneous agent model generates substantial sensitivity of consumption growth to predictable changes in income growth.

Sensitivity in the two-asset model is driven by the presence of hand-to-mouth consumers who do not smooth their consumption over time. In the representative agent model, consumption jumps upon impact of the growth shock Z_t because permanent income immediately jumps to a new level. However, in the two-asset model, consumption of hand-to-mouth households jumps less upon impact—because the change in current income is smaller than the change in permanent income—but is more persistent. The persistence generates autocorrelation in consumption that allows the model to match the fact that consumption responds even to predictable changes in income.

Table 9 also reports the predictions of a simple spender-saver model in the spirit of Campbell and Mankiw (1989). It extends the representative agent model to include an exogenous fraction λ of households who are permanently hand-to-mouth. We calibrate the fraction of spenders λ to match the Campbell-Mankiw IV measure of consumption sensitivity. This reverse-engineered model is also consistent with the degree of sensitivity in the data by construction. In contrast, our two-asset model has only been parameterized to match microlevel behavior, not aggregate sensitivity.

Smoothness. We present two measures of smoothness in the bottom panel of table 9. The first is the standard deviation of consumption growth relative to the standard deviation of income growth. In the data, consumption growth is about half as volatile as income growth. The second measure of smoothness is the second-order autocorrelation of consumption growth.

The two-asset heterogeneous agent model, the representative agent model, and the spender-saver model all overpredict the volatility of consumption growth relative to income growth. Consistent with the degree of sensitivity discussed above, both the two-asset model and the spender-saver model generate significant autocorrelation of consumption growth.

VI.   Business Cycle Dynamics of Inequality

The previous section explored how inequality shapes the joint dynamics of aggregate consumption and income. In this section, we briefly explore how aggregate shocks themselves shape the dynamics of inequality across households. However, with the Cobb-Douglas production function we have used so far, the distribution of labor income is given exogenously by the distribution of labor productivity shocks z. Therefore, we first extend the production side of the economy to include high- and low-skill workers, which are not perfect substitutes with each other or with capital. We then explore the effects of shock to the productivity of unskilled labor, and a shock to the productivity of capital. By construction, this shock has differential effects across workers, generating substantial movements in income and consumption inequality. In addition, the resulting dynamics of aggregate variables are different from the representative agent counterpart of the model.

A.   Model with Imperfect Substitutability among Workers

Following Krusell et al. (2000), we modify the production function to feature two types of workers and capital-skill complementarity.

Production Structure. The production function is

$$Y_t = \left[\mu(Z_t^U U_t)^\sigma + (1 - \mu)\left(\lambda(Z_t^K K_t)^\rho + (1 - \lambda)S_t^\rho\right)^{\frac{\sigma}{\rho}} \right]^{\frac{1}{\sigma}}, \tag{39}$$

where Z_t^U is an unskilled labor-specific productivity shock, Z_t^K is capital-specific productivity shock, U_t is the amount of unskilled labor, and S_t is the amount of skilled labor (all described in more detail below). The elasticity of substitution between unskilled labor and capital, which is equal to the elasticity between unskilled and skilled labor, is $1/(1 - \sigma)$. The elasticity of substitution between skilled labor and capital is $1/(1 - \rho)$. If, as in our calibration, $\sigma > \rho$, high-skill workers are complementary with capital.[62]

We posit a simple mapping from labor productivity z into skill. Recall that we modeled the logarithm of labor productivity as the sum of two components, $\log z = z_1 + z_2$. We estimated that z_1 is a transitory component and z_2 is a persistent component. With our estimated parameters, shocks to the persistent component arrive on average once every 38 years. Hence, a natural interpretation of the persistent component in an infinite-horizon model is a "career shock." We therefore map workers into skills based on the realization of the persistent component—we label the top 50% of workers as high-skill and the bottom 50% as low-skill.

We assume that both aggregate productivity shocks follow the Ornstein-Uhlenbeck process

$$d \log Z_t^U = -\eta_U \log Z_t^U dt + \sigma_U dW_t^U$$

$$d \log Z_t^K = -\eta_K \log Z_t^K dt + \sigma_K dW_t^K.$$

where η_U and η_K control the rate of mean reversion and σ_U and σ_K control the size of innovations.

Calibration. We set the elasticities of substitution in production to the estimated values in Krusell et al. (2000): $\sigma = 0.401$ and $\rho = -.495$. Since $\sigma > \rho$, the production function features capital-skill complementarity, that is, capital-specific productivity shocks disproportionately favor skilled labor.

Given the values for these elasticities, and all the other calibrated parameters from Section IV.B, we choose the factor shares μ and λ to match two steady-state targets. First, we target a steady-state labor share of 60%, as in Section IV.B. Second, we target a steady-state skill premium—the ratio of the average skilled worker's earnings to the average unskilled worker's earnings—of 1.97, which is the value of the college skill premium reported in Acemoglu and Autor (2011). This yields $\mu = 0.52$ and $\lambda = 0.86$.

We set the process for the unskilled-labor productivity shock to be equivalent to our factor-neutral productivity shock process in the case of Cobb-Douglas production. Therefore, as in Section IV.B, we set the rate of mean reversion to $\eta_U = 0.25$. We set the standard deviation of innovations σ_U so that they generate the same impact effect on output as the factor-neutral shocks in Section IV.B.

B.   Inequality Dynamics Following Unskilled Labor-Specific Shock

Figure 11 plots the impulse responses of key features of the distribution of income across households. The wage rate of unskilled workers falls fives times more than the wage rate of skilled workers, due to the fact that the shock directly affects the marginal product of unskilled workers and these workers are not perfect substitutes for skilled workers. Hence, the dispersion of pretax labor income across households increases by nearly 0.2% and the 90–10 percentile ratio increases by nearly 1%.[63]

Figure 12 plots the impulse responses of features of the distribution of consumption across workers. The average consumption of low-skill workers falls more than twice the amount of high-skill workers. This

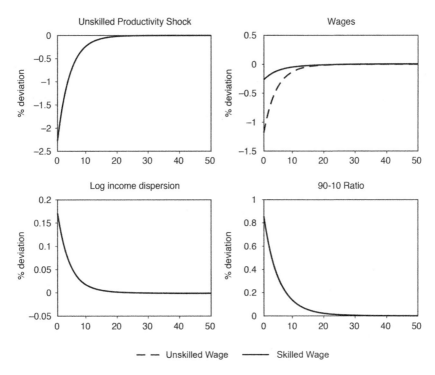

Fig. 11.   Impulse responses to unskilled labor-specific productivity shock

Notes: Impulse responses to an instantaneous positive unit standard deviation size shock (Dirac delta function) to unskilled labor-specific productivity. "Unskilled wage" is the wage rate per efficiency unit of labor for unskilled workers. "Skilled wage" is the wage rate per efficiency unit of labor for skilled workers. "Log income dispersion" is the cross-sectional standard deviation of log pretax labor income across households. "90-10 Ratio" is the ratio of the 90th percentile of pretax labor income to the 10th percentile. We simulate the model by discretizing the time dimension with step size $dt = 0.1$ using an implicit updating scheme.

differential effect reflects the combination of two forces. First, the shock decreases unskilled workers' wages more than skilled workers, so the permanent income of unskilled workers is lower. Second, unskilled workers are over 30% more likely to be hand-to-mouth, making them more sensitive to changes in income.

C.   *Aggregate Dynamics Following Unskilled-Labor Specific Shock*

Figure 13 plots the impulse responses of aggregate output and consumption following the unskilled-specific shock, and compares the responses to the representative agent version of the model. Although the

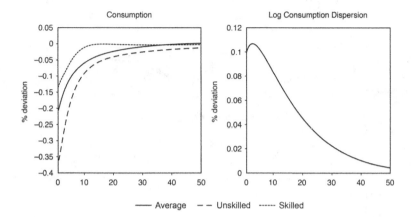

Fig. 12. Impulse responses to unskilled labor-specific productivity shock

Notes: Impulse responses to an instantaneous negative unit standard deviation size shock (Dirac delta function) to unskilled labor-specific productivity. "Unskilled" is the average consumption of unskilled workers. "Skilled" is the average consumption of skilled workers. "Average" is aggregate consumption. "Log consumption dispersion" is the cross-sectional standard deviation of log consumption across households. We simulate the model by discretizing the time dimension with step size dt = 0.1 using an implicit updating scheme.

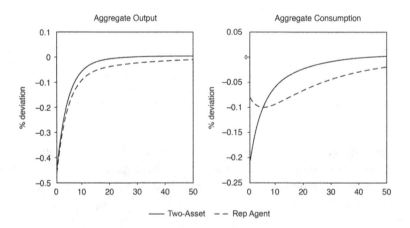

Fig. 13. Impulse responses to unskilled labor-specific productivity shock

Notes: Impulse responses to an instantaneous negative unit standard deviation size shock (Dirac delta function) to unskilled labor-specific productivity. "Two-asset" refers to the two-asset model. "Rep agent" refers to the representative agent version of the model, described in the appendix section "Representative Agent and Spender-Saver Models." We simulate the model by discretizing the time dimension with step size dt = 0.1 using an implicit updating scheme.

output responses are very similar across the two models, the trough in consumption is more than twice as low in the two-asset model than in the representative agent model.

The severity of the consumption response in the two-asset model reflects the combination of two forces. First, the two-asset model features a substantial fraction of hand-to-mouth households that respond more strongly to income changes than the representative household. The presence of hand-to-mouth households also changes the consumption response to factor-neutral shocks, as discussed in Section IV. Second, the unskilled labor-specific shock is concentrated among low-skill workers who are more likely to be hand-to-mouth. This concentration is absent in the factor-neutral shock case, and in that case, the difference between the two-asset and representative agent models is 25% smaller. Hence, the fact that the unskilled labor-specific shock is concentrated among a particular region of the distribution shapes aggregate business cycle dynamics of the model.

D.   Inequality Dynamics Following Capital-Specific Shock

We close this section with a brief example to show that, due to capital-specific complementarity, a shock to capital-specific productivity Z_t^K can generate dynamics of income inequality. We set the rate of mean reversion $\eta_K = 0.25$ and calibrate the standard deviation of innovations σ_K so that it generates the same impact effect on output as the factor-neutral shocks in Section IV.B.

Figure 14 shows that the capital shock increases labor income inequality. The left panel shows that high-skill wages increase by more than low-skill wages due to capital-skill complementarity; in response to the capital-specific shock, the representative firm substitutes toward skilled labor. Hence, the dispersion of labor income across households increases as well.

VII.   Conclusion

Our paper's main message is that two of the most common excuses that macroeconomists make for employing representative agent models are less valid than commonly thought. First, we develop an efficient and easy-to-use computational method for solving a wide class of general equilibrium heterogeneous agent macro models with aggregate shocks, thereby invalidating the excuse that these models are subject to extreme

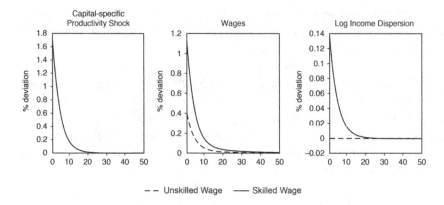

Fig. 14. Impulse responses to capital-specific productivity shock

Notes: Impulse responses to an instantaneous positive unit standard deviation size shock (Dirac delta function) to capital-specific productivity. "Unskilled wage" is the wage rate per efficiency unit of labor for unskilled workers. "Skilled wage" is the wage rate per efficiency unit of labor for skilled workers. "Log income dispersion" is the cross-sectional standard deviation of log pretax labor income across households. We simulate the model by discretizing the time dimension with step size $dt = 0.1$ using an implicit updating scheme.

computational difficulties. Second, our results in Sections V and VI show that inequality may matter greatly for the dynamics of standard macroeconomic aggregates. These results invalidate the excuse that heterogeneous agent models are unnecessarily complicated because they generate only limited additional explanatory power for aggregate phenomena.

Due to its speed, our method opens up the door to estimating macroeconomic models in which distributions play an important role with microdata. Existing attempts to bring macroeconomic models to the data typically use either only aggregate time series to discipline aggregate dynamics (in the case of representative agent models), or they use cross-sectional microdata at a given point in time to discipline a stationary equilibrium without aggregate shocks (in the case of heterogeneous agent models). Instead, future research should use *microdata capturing distributional dynamics over time*, that is, panel data or repeated cross sections. An important hurdle in this endeavor is that microdata, especially from surveys, are often inconsistent with national accounts data on macroeconomic aggregates (see, e.g., Deaton 2005). Attempts to produce time series on distributional variables that capture 100% of national income like the Distributional National Accounts of Piketty, Saez, and Zucman (2016) are welcome in this regard.

Appendix

Fully Recursive Formulation of Krusell-Smith (1998)

When writing the equilibrium conditions (2) to (7), we used recursive notation with respect to the idiosyncratic states (a, z), but time-dependent notation with respect to the aggregate states (g, Z). For completeness, this appendix shows how to write the corresponding equations using fully recursive notation, and how to obtain the hybrid-notation conditions in the main text from the equations using fully recursive notation. In mathematics terminology, the problem we study is a Mean Field Game (MFG). The fully recursive version is what Cardaliaguet et al. (2015) term the "Master equation for Mean Field Games with common noise" whereas the hybrid-notation system (2) to (7) corresponds to their "MFG system with common noise."

To this end, define the wage and interest rate as functions of the state variables (g, Z)

$$w(g, Z) = (1 - \alpha)e^Z K(g)^\alpha, \tag{A1}$$

$$r(g, Z) = \alpha e^Z K(g)^{\alpha-1} - \delta, \tag{A2}$$

$$where \ \ K(g) = \int ag(a, z)dadz \tag{A3}$$

is the aggregate capital stock as a function of the distribution and where the normalize aggregate labor supply to one. Furthermore, define the "Kolmogorov Forward operator" $\mathcal{K}_Z$ that operates on distributions g as

$$(\mathcal{K}_Z g)(a, z) := - \partial_a[s(a, z, g, Z)g(a, z)] - \lambda_z g(a, z) + \lambda_{z'} g(a, z')$$

where $s(a, z, g, Z)$ is the optimal saving policy function (determined below). This operator maps distribution functions g into time derivatives of that distribution. Using this tool one can, for example, write the Kolmogorov Forward equation (3) compactly as

$$\frac{dg_t(a, z)}{dt} = (\mathcal{K}_Z g_t)(a, z).$$

With this machinery in hand, the fully recursive, infinite-dimensional HJB equation is:

$$\begin{aligned}
\rho V(a, z, g, Z) = \max_c \ &u(c) + \partial_a V(a, z, g, Z)(w(g, Z)z + r(g, Z)a - c) \\
&+ \lambda_z(V(a, z', g, Z) - V(a, z, g, Z)) \\
&+ \partial_Z V(a, z, g, Z)(-\eta Z) + \frac{1}{2}\partial_{ZZ}V(a, z, g, Z)\sigma^2 \\
&+ \int \frac{\delta V(a, z, g, Z)}{\delta g(a, z)}(\mathcal{K}_Z g)(a, z)dadz.
\end{aligned} \tag{A4}$$

The first and second lines in this infinite-dimensional HJB equation capture the evolution of the *idiosyncratic* states (a, z) (just like in equation (2)). The third and fourth lines capture the evolution of the *aggregate* states (g, Z). The third line captures the evolution of aggregate TFP Z with standard "Ito's Formula terms" involving the first and second derivatives of the value function with respect to Z. The fourth line captures the evolution of the distribution g. Since g is a function, it involves the functional derivative of V with respect to g at point (a, z), which we denote by $\delta V / \delta g(a, z)$. The equilibrium in fully recursive notation is then characterized by (A4) together with (A1), (A2), and (A3).

To understand the last term in (A4), assume momentarily that the distribution is an N-dimensional vector $\mathbf{g} = (g_1, \ldots, g_N)$ rather than a function (i.e., an infinite-dimensional object). Then the HJB equation would be

$$\rho V(a, z, \mathbf{g}, Z) = \max_{c} u(c) + \partial_a V(a, z, \mathbf{g}, Z)(w(\mathbf{g}, Z)z + r(\mathbf{g}, Z)a - c)$$

$$+ \lambda_z(V(a, z', \mathbf{g}, Z) - V(a, z, \mathbf{g}, Z))$$

$$+ \partial_Z V(a, z, \mathbf{g}, Z)(-\eta Z) + \frac{1}{2} \partial_{ZZ} V(a, z, \mathbf{g}, Z)\sigma^2$$

$$+ \sum_{i=1}^{N} \frac{\partial V(a, z, \mathbf{g}, Z)}{\partial g_i} \dot{g}_i.$$

Since a functional derivative $\delta V / \delta g(a, z)$ is the natural generalization of the partial derivative $\partial V / \partial g_i$ to the infinite-dimensional case, if g is a function rather than a vector we get (A4).

The equilibrium conditions (2) to (7) in the main text can be obtained from this system by evaluating "along the characteristic" (g_t, Z_t) that satisfies equations (3) and (4). In particular, the value function $v_t(a, z)$ in equation (2) is obtained from evaluating (A4) at (g_t, Z_t), that is,

$$v_t(a, z) = V(a, z, g_t, Z_t).$$

In particular, by Ito's Formula

$$dv_t(a, z) = \left(\partial_Z V(a, z, g_t, Z_t)(-\eta Z_t) + \frac{1}{2} \partial_{ZZ} V(a, z, g_t, Z_t)\sigma^2 \right) dt$$

$$+ \sigma\, \partial_Z V(a, z, g_t, Z_t) dW_t$$

$$+ \int \frac{\delta V(a, z, g_t, Z_t)}{\delta g_t(a, z)} (K_Z g_t)(a, z) da dz\; dt$$

and hence using that $\mathbb{E}_t[dW_t] = 0$

$$\frac{1}{dt} \mathbb{E}_t[dv_t(a, z)] = \partial_z V(a, z, g_t, Z_t)(-\eta Z_t) + \frac{1}{2} \partial_{zz} V(a, z, g_t, Z_t)\sigma^2$$

$$+ \int \frac{\delta V(a, z, g_t, Z_t)}{\delta g_t(a, z)} (\mathcal{K}_z g_t)(a, z)dadz.$$

Similarly, the prices and capital stock in equations (5) to (7) are obtained by evaluating (A1) to (A3) at (g_t, Z_t), that is,

$$w_t = w(g_t, Z_t), \quad r_t = r(g_t, Z_t), \quad K_t = K(g_t).$$

Connection to Linearization of Representative Agent Models

This appendix develops the relationship between our linearization of heterogeneous agent models and standard linearization of representative agent business cycle models. For illustration, consider a simple real business cycle model. As in our heterogeneous agent models in the main text, the equilibrium of this representative agent model is characterized by a forward-looking equation for controls, a backward-looking equation for the endogenous state, several static relations, and an evolution equation for the exogenous state.

Defining the representative household's marginal utility $\Lambda_t := C_t^{-\gamma}$, the equilibrium conditions can be written as

$$\frac{1}{dt} \mathbb{E}_t[d\Lambda_t] = (\rho - r_t)\Lambda_t \qquad (A5)$$

$$\frac{dK_t}{dt} = w_t + r_t K_t - C_t$$

$$dZ_t = -\eta Z_t dt + \sigma dW_t$$

$$r_t = \alpha e^{Z_t} K_t^{\alpha-1} - \delta$$

$$w_t = (1 - \alpha)e^{Z_t} K_t^{\alpha}$$

and where $C_t = \Lambda_t^{-1/\gamma}$. The first equation is the Euler equation. Marginal utility Λ_t is the single control variable; we could have alternatively written the Euler equation in terms of consumption C_t, but working with marginal utility is more convenient. The second equation is the evolution of the aggregate capital stock, which is the single endogenous state variable. The third equation is the stochastic process for aggregate productivity, which is the exogenous state variable. The last two equations define equilibrium prices.

The equilibrium conditions (14) of the simple Krusell and Smith (1998) model have the same structure as the representative agent model above. The discretized value function $\mathbf{v}_t$ is the endogenous control vector, analogous to marginal utility Λ_t (or aggregate consumption C_t) in the representative agent model. The distribution $\mathbf{g}_t$ is the endogenous state variable, analogous to aggregate capital K_t. Finally, TFP Z_t is the exogenous state variable, just as in the representative agent model.

The representative agent model's equilibrium conditions can be linearized and the resulting linear system solved exactly as the heterogeneous agent model in the main text. Let hatted variables denote deviations from steady state. Then we have the control variable $\widehat{\Lambda}_t$, the endogenous state $\widehat{K}_t$, the exogenous state Z_t, and the prices $\hat{\mathbf{p}}_t = (\hat{r}_t, \widehat{w}_t)$. We can thus write

$$
\mathbb{E}_t \begin{bmatrix} d\widehat{\Lambda}_t \\ d\widehat{K}_t \\ dZ_t \\ 0 \end{bmatrix} = \begin{bmatrix} \mathbf{B}_{\Lambda\Lambda} & 0 & 0 & \mathbf{B}_{\Lambda p} \\ \mathbf{B}_{K\Lambda} & \mathbf{B}_{KK} & 0 & \mathbf{B}_{Kp} \\ 0 & 0 & -\eta & 0 \\ 0 & \mathbf{B}_{pK} & \mathbf{B}_{pZ} & -\mathbf{I} \end{bmatrix} \begin{bmatrix} \widehat{\Lambda}_t \\ \widehat{K}_t \\ Z_t \\ \hat{\mathbf{p}}_t \end{bmatrix} dt.
$$

Note that our linearized heterogeneous agent model (15) has the same form as this system.

Model Reduction and Proof of Proposition 1

This appendix proves the results cited in the main text regarding our distribution reduction method. We also show that, in discrete time, our approach corresponds to matching the first k periods of the impulse response function.

A. Deterministic Model

As in the main text, consider first the simplified model (26) that we briefly restate here:

$$
\dot{\mathbf{g}}_t = \mathbf{C}_{gg}\mathbf{g}_t,
$$

$$
p_t = \mathbf{b}_{pg}\mathbf{g}_t.
$$

Solving this for p_t gives

$$
p_t = \mathbf{b}_{pg}e^{\mathbf{C}_{gg}t}\mathbf{g}_0
$$

$$
= \mathbf{b}_{pg}\left[\mathbf{I} + \mathbf{C}_{gg}t + \frac{1}{2}\mathbf{C}_{gg}^2 t^2 + \frac{1}{6}\mathbf{C}_{gg}^3 t^3 + \ldots\right]\mathbf{g}_0.
$$

We consider a reduced model obtained by means of *projection*. That is, we project the distribution $\mathbf{g}_t$ on a lower-dimensional space, and then analyze the dynamics of the corresponding reduced system. Of course, all that ultimately matters for the dynamics of the reduced system is that projection space itself, and not the particular basis chosen for the purpose of projection. Thus, for ease of presentation, in the main text we consider a semi-orthogonal basis $\mathbf{X}^T$, that is, a matrix $\mathbf{X}$ that satisfies $\mathbf{X}^T\mathbf{X} = \mathbf{I}$. Under this assumption, the reduced distribution is given by $\gamma_t = (\mathbf{X}^T\mathbf{X})^{-1}\mathbf{X}^T\mathbf{g}_t = \mathbf{X}^T\mathbf{g}_t$. For the proofs in this appendix, however, it will turn out to be more convenient to work with a nonnormalized (non-semi-orthogonal) basis. Specifically, we consider a pair of matrices $\mathbf{V}$, $\mathbf{W}^T$ such that $\mathbf{W}^T\mathbf{V} = \mathbf{I}$. This formulation nests our analysis from the main text with $\mathbf{X} = \mathbf{V}$ and $\mathbf{X}^T = \mathbf{W}^T$.

We then approximate the distribution $\mathbf{g}_t$ through $\gamma_t = (\mathbf{W}^T\mathbf{V})^{-1}\mathbf{W}^T\mathbf{g}_t = \mathbf{W}^T\mathbf{g}_t$. Conversely, up to projection error, we have that $\mathbf{g}_t = \mathbf{V}\gamma_t$.[64] Differentiating with respect to time thus gives the reduced-system dynamics

$$\dot{\gamma}_t = \mathbf{W}^T\mathbf{C}_{gg}\mathbf{V}\gamma_t$$

$$\tilde{p}_t = \mathbf{b}_{pg}\mathbf{V}\gamma_t.$$

Note that, with $\mathbf{V} = \mathbf{X}$, $\mathbf{W}^T = \mathbf{X}^T$, this system simply collapses to the formulation in the main text. From here, we then get

$$\tilde{p}_t = \mathbf{b}_{pg}\mathbf{V}e^{(\mathbf{W}^T\mathbf{C}_{gg}\mathbf{V})t}\mathbf{W}^T\mathbf{g}_0$$

$$= \mathbf{b}_{pg}\mathbf{V}\left[\mathbf{I} + (\mathbf{W}^T\mathbf{C}_{gg}\mathbf{V})t + \frac{1}{2}(\mathbf{W}^T\mathbf{C}_{gg}\mathbf{V})^2t^2 + \frac{1}{6}(\mathbf{W}^T\mathbf{C}_{gg}\mathbf{V})^3t^3 + \ldots\right]\mathbf{W}^T\mathbf{g}_0.$$

We choose the projection matrices $\mathbf{V}$, $\mathbf{W}^T$ to ensure that the dynamics of the reduced $\tilde{p}_t$ match as closely as possible those of the unreduced p_t. Following insights from the model reduction literature, we take this to mean that Taylor-series expansions of p_t and $\tilde{p}_t$ around $t = 0$ share the first k expansion coefficients. As argued before, the dynamics of the system—and so these expansion coefficients—do not depend on the projection matrices $\mathbf{V}$, $\mathbf{W}^T$ themselves, but only on the subspaces associated with them.[65] It is in this sense that we can first focus on general $\mathbf{V}$, $\mathbf{W}^T$, and then simply conclude that all results will extend to semi-orthogonal matrices $\mathbf{X}$ that span the same subspace of $\mathbb{R}^N$. To match the first k expansion coefficients, it is useful to consider what is known as the order-k observability matrix $\mathcal{O}(\mathbf{b}_{pg}, \mathbf{C}_{gg})$:

$$\mathcal{O}(\mathbf{b}_{pg}, \mathbf{C}_{gg}) := \begin{bmatrix} \mathbf{b}_{pg} \\ \mathbf{b}_{pg}\mathbf{C}_{gg} \\ \mathbf{b}_{pg}(\mathbf{C}_{gg})^2 \\ \vdots \\ \mathbf{b}_{pg}(\mathbf{C}_{gg})^{k-1} \end{bmatrix}.$$

We propose to consider the pair $\mathbf{V}$, $\mathbf{W}^\mathsf{T}$ with $\mathbf{W}^\mathsf{T} = \mathcal{O}(\mathbf{b}_{pg}, \mathbf{C}_{gg})$ and $\mathbf{V}$ chosen such that $\mathbf{W}^\mathsf{T}\mathbf{V} = \mathbf{I}$. To see that this works, let us consider each term separately in the Taylor-series expansions derived above. In all of the following, $\mathbf{e}_i$ denotes the ith standard unit vector and $\mathbf{W}_i^\mathsf{T}$ denotes the ith submatrix of $\mathbf{W}^\mathsf{T}$ (corresponding to $\mathbf{b}_{pg}(\mathbf{C}_{gg})^{i-1}$). First of all we have

$$\mathbf{b}_{pg}\mathbf{V}\mathbf{W}^\mathsf{T} = \mathbf{W}_1^\mathsf{T}\mathbf{V}\mathbf{W}^\mathsf{T}$$

$$= \mathbf{e}_1\mathbf{W}^\mathsf{T} = \mathbf{W}_1^\mathsf{T} = \mathbf{b}_{pg}$$

where we have used the fact that, by construction, $\mathbf{W}^\mathsf{T}\mathbf{V} = \mathbf{I}$. Next we have

$$\mathbf{b}_{pg}\mathbf{V}\mathbf{W}^\mathsf{T}\mathbf{C}_{gg}\mathbf{V}\mathbf{W}^\mathsf{T} = \mathbf{W}_1^\mathsf{T}\mathbf{V}\mathbf{W}^\mathsf{T}\mathbf{C}_{gg}\mathbf{V}\mathbf{W}^\mathsf{T}$$

$$= \mathbf{W}_2^\mathsf{T}\mathbf{V}\mathbf{W}^\mathsf{T} = \mathbf{e}_2\mathbf{W}^\mathsf{T} = \mathbf{W}_2^\mathsf{T} = \mathbf{b}_{pg}\mathbf{C}_{gg}$$

where again we have used that $\mathbf{W}^\mathsf{T}\mathbf{V} = \mathbf{I}$, together with the definition of $\mathbf{W}^\mathsf{T}$. All higher-order terms then follow analogously. Putting things together in the notation of the main text, we see that picking $\mathbf{X}^\mathsf{T}$ to be a semi-orthogonal basis of the space spanned by $\mathcal{O}(\mathbf{b}_{pg}, \mathbf{C}_{gg})$ is sufficient to ensure that the Taylor-series expansion coefficients are matched.

Stochastic Model: Proof of Proposition 1

Solving out prices and the decision rules for the controls v_t, we get the system

$$\dot{\mathbf{g}}_t = \underbrace{(\mathbf{B}_{gg} + \mathbf{B}_{gp}\mathbf{b}_{pg} + \mathbf{B}_{gv}\mathbf{D}_{vg})}_{\mathbf{C}_{gg}}\mathbf{g}_t + \underbrace{(\mathbf{B}_{gv}\mathbf{D}_{vZ})}_{\mathbf{C}_{gZ}}Z_t$$

$$p_t = \mathbf{b}_{pg}\mathbf{g}_t + \mathbf{b}_{pZ}Z_t.$$

The dynamics of this stochastic system are characterized by the impulse response function

$$h(t) = \mathbf{b}_{pg}e^{\mathbf{C}_{gg}t}\mathbf{C}_{gZ} + \delta(t)\mathbf{b}_{pZ}$$

where $\delta(t)$ is the Dirac delta function. This impulse response function induces the following dynamic behavior:

$$p_t = \underbrace{\mathbf{b}_{pg}e^{\mathbf{C}_{gg}t}\mathbf{g}_0}_{\text{det.part}} + \underbrace{\int_0^t h(t-s)Z_s ds}_{\text{stoch.part}}.$$

As before, we consider the projection $\gamma_t = \mathbf{W}^T \mathbf{g}_t$ and (up to projection error) $\mathbf{g}_t = \mathbf{V}\gamma_t$. This gives

$$\dot{\gamma}_t = \mathbf{W}^T \mathbf{C}_{gg}\mathbf{V}\gamma_t + \mathbf{W}^T \mathbf{C}_{gZ}Z_t$$

$$\tilde{p}_t = \mathbf{b}_{pg}\mathbf{V}\gamma_t + \mathbf{b}_{pZ}Z_t.$$

This model induces the impulse response function

$$\tilde{h}(t) = \mathbf{b}_{pg}\mathbf{V}e^{(\mathbf{W}^T \mathbf{C}_{gg}\mathbf{V})t}\mathbf{W}^T \mathbf{C}_{gZ} + \delta(t)\mathbf{b}_{pZ}$$

and so the dynamics

$$\tilde{p}_t = \mathbf{b}_{pg}\mathbf{V}e^{(\mathbf{W}^T \mathbf{C}_{gg}\mathbf{V})t}\mathbf{W}^T \mathbf{g}_0 + \int_0^t \tilde{h}(t-s)Z_s ds.$$

We now proceed exactly as before and consider the order-k observability matrix $\mathcal{O}(\mathbf{b}_{pg}, \mathbf{C}_{gg})$:

$$\mathcal{O}(\mathbf{b}_{pg}, \mathbf{C}_{gg}) := \begin{bmatrix} \mathbf{b}_{pg} \\ \mathbf{b}_{pg}\mathbf{C}_{gg} \\ \mathbf{b}_{pg}(\mathbf{C}_{gg})^2 \\ \vdots \\ \mathbf{b}_{pg}(\mathbf{C}_{gg})^{k-1} \end{bmatrix}.$$

We again set $\mathbf{W}^T$ and $\mathbf{V}$ such that $\mathbf{W}^T = \mathcal{O}(\mathbf{b}_{pg}, \mathbf{C}_{gg})$ and $\mathbf{W}^T\mathbf{V} = \mathbf{I}$. Showing that all terms in the deterministic part are matched is exactly analogous to the argument given above. For the stochastic part, we also do not need to change much. The impact impulse response $\mathbf{b}_{pZ}$ is matched irrespective of the choice of projection matrix. Next we have

$$\mathbf{b}_{pg}\mathbf{V}\mathbf{W}^T \mathbf{C}_{gZ} = \mathbf{W}_1^T \mathbf{V}\mathbf{W}^T \mathbf{C}_{gZ}$$

$$= \mathbf{e}_1 \mathbf{W}^T \mathbf{C}_{gZ} = \mathbf{W}_1^T \mathbf{C}_{gZ} = \mathbf{b}_{pg}\mathbf{C}_{gZ}.$$

As before, we exploit the definition of $\mathbf{W}^T$ as well as the fact that $\mathbf{W}^T\mathbf{V} = \mathbf{I}$. And finally,

$$\mathbf{b}_{pg}\mathbf{VW}^{\mathsf{T}}\mathbf{C}_{gg}\mathbf{VW}^{\mathsf{T}}\mathbf{C}_{gZ} = \mathbf{W}_1^{\mathsf{T}}\mathbf{VW}^{\mathsf{T}}\mathbf{C}_{gg}\mathbf{VW}^{\mathsf{T}}\mathbf{C}_{gZ}$$

$$= \mathbf{W}_2^{\mathsf{T}}\mathbf{VW}^{\mathsf{T}}\mathbf{C}_{gZ} = \mathbf{e}_2\mathbf{W}^{\mathsf{T}}\mathbf{C}_{gZ}$$

$$= \mathbf{W}_2^{\mathsf{T}}\mathbf{C}_{gZ} = \mathbf{b}_{pg}\mathbf{C}_{gg}\mathbf{C}_{gZ}$$

again exactly analogous to the derivation for the deterministic part above. We are thus matching both the deterministic and the stochastic part of the dynamics up to order k in a Taylor-series expansion around time $t = 0$. Finally, returning to the notation of the main body of the text, we see that letting $\mathbf{X}^{\mathsf{T}}$ be a semi-orthogonal basis of the space spanned by $\mathcal{O}(\mathbf{b}_{pg}, \mathbf{C}_{gg})$ is again sufficient for the impulse-response matching.

Discrete Time

As we have seen, in continuous time, our model-reduction procedure ensures that the coefficients of a Taylor-series expansion around $t = 0$ are matched. In discrete time, this procedure guarantees that we match the first k periods of the impulse response functions. The stochastic discrete-time model is

$$\mathbf{g}_t = \mathbf{C}_{gg}\mathbf{g}_{t-1} + \mathbf{C}_{gZ}Z_t$$

$$p_t = \mathbf{b}_{pg}\mathbf{g}_{t-1} + \mathbf{b}_{pZ}Z_t.$$

The impulse responses of this system are $\mathbf{b}_{pZ}$ on impact and $\mathbf{b}_{pg}\mathbf{C}_{gg}^{h-1}\mathbf{C}_{gZ}$ for horizons $h = 1, 2,$. As before, we consider the reduced system

$$\gamma_t = \mathbf{W}^{\mathsf{T}}\mathbf{C}_{gg}\mathbf{V}\gamma_{t-1} + \mathbf{W}^{\mathsf{T}}\mathbf{C}_{gZ}Z_t$$

$$p_t = \mathbf{b}_{pg}\mathbf{V}\gamma_{t-1} + \mathbf{b}_{pZ}Z_t.$$

Equality of the induced impulse responses for impact $h = 0$ is immediate. For all higher horizons, we proceed exactly as before and show that

$$\mathbf{b}_{pg}\mathbf{VW}^{\mathsf{T}}\mathbf{C}_{gz} = \mathbf{b}_{pg}\mathbf{C}_{gz}$$

as well as

$$\mathbf{b}_{pg}\mathbf{VW}^{\mathsf{T}}\mathbf{C}_{gg}\mathbf{VW}^{\mathsf{T}}\mathbf{C}_{gz} = \mathbf{b}_{pg}\mathbf{C}_{gg}\mathbf{C}_{gz}.$$

Detrending the Nonstationary Model

Many equilibrium objects in the version of the model described in Section V are nonstationary. In this appendix, we develop a normalized version of the equilibrium involving only stationary objects. In addition to the production side of the model described in the main text, we make three modifications to the two-asset model in the presence of nonstationary shocks. First, the borrowing constraint for liquid assets is $b > \underline{b}Q_t$, where Q_t is the level of aggregate productivity. Second, the transaction cost for accessing the illiquid account is now $\chi(d, a)Q_t$. Third, the lump-sum transfer from the government is now TQ_t.

The equilibrium of this model can be equivalently represented by a set of normalized objects $\hat{v}_t(\hat{a}, \hat{b}, z)$, $g_t(\hat{a}, \hat{b}, z)$, $\hat{K}_t$, r_t^a, $\hat{w}_t$, r_t^b, and Z_t such that

1. *Transformed HJB*: $\hat{v}_t(\hat{a}, \hat{b}, z)$ solves

$$(\rho + \zeta - (1 - \theta)Z_t)\hat{v}_t(\hat{a}, \hat{b}, z) = \max_{\hat{c}, d} \frac{\hat{c}^{1-\theta}}{1 - \theta} \tag{A6}$$

$$+ \partial_{\hat{b}}\hat{v}_t(\hat{a}, \hat{b}, z)(T + (1 - \tau)\hat{w}_t e^z + r_t^b(\hat{b})\hat{b} - \chi(\hat{d}, \hat{a}) - \hat{c} - \hat{d} - \hat{b}Z_t)$$

$$+ \partial_{\hat{a}}\hat{v}_t(\hat{a}, \hat{b}, z)(r_t^a\hat{a} + \hat{d} - \hat{a}Z_t) + \sum_{z'}\lambda_{zz'}(\hat{v}_t(\hat{a}, \hat{b}, z') - \hat{v}_t(\hat{a}, \hat{b}, z))$$

$$+ \frac{1}{dt}\mathbb{E}_t[d\hat{v}_t(\hat{a}, \hat{b}, z)].$$

The fact that TFP growth is permanent changes the effective discount factor in the households' HJB equation.

2. *Transformed KFE*: $g_t(\hat{a}, \hat{b}, z)$ evolves according to

$$\frac{dg_t(\hat{a}, \hat{b}, z)}{dt} = -\partial_{\hat{a}}(s_t^a(\hat{a}, \hat{b}, z)g_t(\hat{a}, \hat{b}, z)) - \partial_{\hat{b}}(s_t^b(\hat{a}, \hat{b}, z)g_t(\hat{a}, \hat{b}, z)) \tag{A7}$$

$$- \sum_{z'}\lambda_{zz'}g_t(\hat{a}, \hat{b}, z) + \sum_{z'}\lambda_{z'z}g_t(\hat{a}, \hat{b}, z)$$

$$- \zeta g_t(\hat{a}, \hat{b}, z) + \zeta\delta(\hat{a})\delta(\hat{b})g^*(z), \quad \text{where}$$

$$s_t^b(\hat{a}, \hat{b}, z) = T + (1 - \tau)\hat{w}_t e^z + r_t^b(\hat{b})\hat{b} - \chi(\hat{d}, \hat{a}) - \hat{c} - \hat{d} - \hat{b}Z_t \quad \text{and}$$

$$s_t^a(\hat{a}, \hat{b}, z) = r_t^a\hat{a} + \hat{d} - \hat{a}Z_t.$$

Permanent TFP shocks change the effective depreciation rate of assets.

3. *Transformed firm conditions*: r_t^a, $\hat{w}_t$, and Z_t satisfy

$$r_t^a = \alpha\hat{K}_t^{\alpha-1}\bar{L}^{1-\alpha} - \delta$$

$$\hat{w}_t = (1 - \alpha)\hat{K}_t^{\alpha}\bar{L}^{-\alpha}$$

$$dZ_t = -\nu Z_t dt + \sigma dW_t.$$

4. *Transformed asset market clearing conditions*

$$B^* = \int \hat{b} g_t(\hat{a}, \hat{b}, z) d\hat{b} d\hat{a} dz$$

$$\hat{K}_t = \int \hat{a} g_t(\hat{a}, \hat{b}, z) d\hat{b} d\hat{a} dz.$$

To derive this normalized equilibrium, we detrend the model's original equilibrium objects by aggregate productivity Q_t. Almost all variables in the model naturally scale with the level of productivity Q_t; for any such variable x_t, let $\hat{x}_t = x_t / Q_t$ denote its detrended version. The one exception to this scheme is the households' value function $v_t(a, b, z)$, which scales with $Q_t^{1-\theta}$.

HJB Equation. First define an intermediate detrended value function $\tilde{v}_t(a, b, z) = v_t(a, b, z) / Q_t^{1-\theta}$. Divide both sides of the HJB (35) by $Q_t^{1-\theta}$ to get

$$(\rho + \zeta)\tilde{v}_t(a, b, z) = \max_{c,d} \frac{\hat{c}^{1-\theta}}{1-\theta} \tag{A8}$$

$$+ \partial_b \tilde{v}_t(a, b, z)(TQ_t + (1-\tau)w_t e^z + r_t^b(b)b - \chi(d, a)Q_t - c - d)$$

$$+ \partial_a \tilde{v}_t(a, b, z)(r_t^a a + d) + \sum_{z'} \lambda_{zz'}(\tilde{v}_t(a, b, z') - \tilde{v}_t(a, b, z))$$

$$+ \frac{1}{Q_t^{1-\theta}} \times \frac{1}{dt}\mathbb{E}_t[dv_t(a, b, z)].$$

Next, to replace the $(1 / dt)\mathbb{E}_t[dv_t(a, b, z)]$ term, note that by the chain rule

$$\frac{d}{dt}\tilde{v}_t(a, b, z) = \frac{(d / dt)v_t(a, b, z)}{Q_t^{1-\theta}} + (\theta - 1)\frac{d \log Q_t}{dt}\tilde{v}_t(a, b, z),$$

which implies that

$$\frac{1}{Q_t^{1-\theta}} \times \frac{1}{dt}\mathbb{E}_t[dv_t(a, b, z)] = \frac{1}{dt}\mathbb{E}_t[d\hat{v}_t(a, b, z)] + (1-\theta)\frac{d \log Q_t}{dt}\hat{v}_t(a, b, z).$$

Plug this back into equation (A8) and rearrange to get

$$\left(\rho + \zeta + (\theta - 1)\frac{d \log Q_t}{dt}\right)\tilde{v}_t(a, b, z) = \max_{c,d} \frac{\hat{c}^{1-\theta}}{1-\theta} \tag{A9}$$

$$+ \partial_b \tilde{v}_t(a, b, z)(TQ_t + (1-\tau)w_t e^z + r_t^b(b)b - \chi(d, a)Q_t$$

$$- c - d) + \partial_a \tilde{v}_t(a, b, z)(r_t^a a + d)$$

$$+ \sum_{z'} \lambda_{zz'}(\tilde{v}_t(a, b, z') - \tilde{v}_t(a, b, z)) + \frac{1}{dt}\mathbb{E}_t[d\tilde{v}_t(a, b, z)].$$

The formulation in equation (A9) is still not stationary because there are permanent changes in the state variables a and b, the wage w_t, and the transaction cost on the right-hand side. To address this, we characterize the value function in terms of $\hat{a}$ and $\hat{b}$, rather than a and b themselves. Define the final detrended value function $\hat{v}_t(\hat{a}, \hat{b}, z)$ as $\hat{v}_t(\hat{a}, \hat{b}, z) = \tilde{v}_t(a, b, z)$.

We guess that this function $\hat{v}_t(\hat{a}, \hat{b}, z)$ does not depend on the nonstationary variable Q_t and now verify that indeed it does not. Note that

$$\partial_b \tilde{v}_t(a, b, z) = \partial_b \hat{v}_t\left(\frac{a}{Q_t}, \frac{b}{Q_t}, z\right) = \frac{1}{Q_t} \partial_{\hat{b}} \hat{v}_t(\hat{a}, \hat{b}, z),$$

$$\partial_a \tilde{v}_t(a, b, z) = \partial_a \hat{v}_t\left(\frac{a}{Q_t}, \frac{b}{Q_t}, z\right) = \frac{1}{Q_t} \partial_{\hat{a}} \hat{v}_t(\hat{a}, \hat{b}, z),$$

$$\frac{1}{dt} \mathbb{E}_t[d\tilde{v}_t(a, b, z)] = \frac{1}{dt} \mathbb{E}_t\left[d\hat{v}_t\left(\frac{a}{Q_t}, \frac{b}{Q_t}, z\right)\right]$$

$$= \frac{1}{dt} \mathbb{E}_t\left[d\hat{v}_t\left(\hat{a}, \hat{b}, z\right)\right] - \partial_{\hat{a}} \hat{v}_t(\hat{a}, \hat{b}, z)\hat{a}\frac{d \log Q_t}{dt}$$

$$- \partial_{\hat{b}} \hat{v}_t(\hat{a}, \hat{b}, z)\hat{b}\frac{d \log Q_t}{dt}.$$

These equations then imply

$$\partial_b \tilde{v}_t(a, b, z)(TQ_t + (1 - \tau)w_t e^z + r_t^b(b)b - \chi(d, a)Q_t - c - d)$$

$$= \partial_{\hat{b}} \hat{v}_t(\hat{a}, \hat{b}, z)(T + (1 - \tau)\hat{w}_t e^z + r_t^b(\hat{b})\hat{b} - \chi(\hat{d}, \hat{a}) - \hat{c} - \hat{d})$$

and that

$$\partial_a \tilde{v}_t(a, b, z)(r_t^a a + d) = \partial_{\hat{a}} \hat{v}_t(\hat{a}, \hat{b}, z)(r_t^a \hat{a} + \hat{d}).$$

Putting all these results together, and using the definition $d \log Q_t / dt = Z_t$, we get the final detrended HJB equation (A6).

KFE. The cross-sectional distribution of households over $\hat{a}, \hat{b}, z$ is stationary. We will directly construct the KFE for the distribution over this space. Analogously to equation (36), this is given by

$$\frac{dg_t(\hat{a}, \hat{b}, z)}{dt} = - \partial_{\hat{a}}(\dot{\hat{a}}_t(a, b, z)g_t(\hat{a}, \hat{b}, z)) - \partial_{\hat{b}}(\dot{\hat{b}}_t(a, b, z)g_t(\hat{a}, \hat{b}, z))$$

$$- \sum_{z'} \lambda_{zz'} g_t(\hat{a}, \hat{b}, z) + \sum_{z'} \lambda_{z'z} g_t(\hat{a}, \hat{b}, z)$$

$$- \zeta g_t(\hat{a}, \hat{b}, z) + \zeta \delta(\hat{a})\delta(\hat{b})g^*(z).$$

The modified HJB (A6) gives the evolution $\dot{a}$ / Q_t = $r_t^a\hat{a} + \hat{d}$. Note that by the product rule,

$$\dot{\hat{a}}_t = \frac{\dot{a}_t}{Q_t} - \frac{d \log Q_t}{dt}\hat{a}_t,$$

so that $\dot{\hat{a}}_t = r_t^a\hat{a} + \hat{d} - (d \log Q_t / dt)\hat{a}$. Using this result, and the analogous one for $\hat{b}_t$, we get the detrended KFE (A7).

Other Equilibrium Conditions. Detrending the remaining equilibrium conditions is simple:

$$r_t^a = \alpha\hat{K}_t^{\alpha-1}\overline{L}^{1-\alpha} - \delta$$

$$\hat{w}_t = (1 - \alpha)\hat{K}_t^{\alpha}\overline{L}^{-\alpha}$$

$$dZ_t = -\nu Z_t dt + \sigma dW_t.$$

Representative Agent and Spender-Saver Models

Representative Agent. The representative agent model is identical to the RBC model described in the appendix section "Connection to Linearization of Representative Agent Models."

Spender-Saver. The spender-saver model extends the household side of the representative agent model above to two types of households. First, there is a fraction λ of hand-to-mouth households who simply consume their income each period. Second, the remaining fraction $1 - \lambda$ of households make an optimal consumption-savings decision like in the representative agent model.

Endnotes

We thank Chris Carroll, Chris Sims, Jonathan Parker, Bruce Preston, Stephen Terry, and our discussant John Stachurski for useful comments. Paymon Khorrami provided excellent research assistance. The Matlab toolbox referred to in the paper is currently available at https://github.com/gregkaplan/phact. Author email addresses: Ahn (sehyouna@princeton.edu), Kaplan (gkaplan@uchicago.edu), Moll (moll@princeton.edu), Winberry (Thomas.Winberry@chicagobooth.edu), and Wolf (ckwolf@princeton.edu). For acknowledgments, sources of research support, and disclosure of the authors' material financial relationships, if any, please see http://www.nber.org/chapters/c13927.ack.
    1. For examples studying fiscal policy, see McKay and Reis (2013) and Kaplan and Violante (2014); for monetary policy, see McKay, Nakamura, and Steinsson (2015), Auclert (2014), and Kaplan et al. (2016).
    2. More precisely, in Krusell and Smith's (1998) baseline model, which is a heterogeneous agent version of a standard Real Business Cycle (RBC) model with inelastic labor

supply, the effects of technology shocks on aggregate output, consumption, and investment are indistinguishable from those in the RBC model. Lucas (2003) succinctly captures many macroeconomists' view when he summarizes Krusell and Smith's findings as follows: "For determining the behavior of aggregates, they discovered, realistically modeled household heterogeneity just does not matter very much. For individual behavior and welfare, of course, heterogeneity is everything." Interestingly, there is a discrepancy between this perception and the results in Krusell and Smith (1998): they show that an extension of their baseline model with preference heterogeneity, thereby implying a more realistic wealth distribution, "features aggregate time series that depart significantly from permanent income behavior."

3. As we discuss in more detail below, the use of linearization to solve heterogeneous agent economies is not new. Our method builds on the ideas of Dotsey et al. (1999), Campbell (1998), Veracierto (2002), and Reiter (2009), and is related to Preston and Roca (2007). In contrast to these contributions, we cast our linearization method in continuous time. While discrete time poses no conceptual difficulty, working in continuous time has a number of numerical advantages that we heavily exploit.

4. See table 16 of Den Haan (2010). See Section II for a description of this error metric and how we compare our continuous-state, continuous-time productivity process with the two-state, discrete-time productivity process in Den Haan (2010).

5. More precisely, we apply tools from the so-called *model reduction* literature, in particular Amsallem and Farhat (2011) and Antoulas (2005).

We build on Reiter (2010), who first applied these ideas to reduce the dimensionality of linearized heterogeneous agent models in economics.

6. The codes are initially available as a Matlab toolbox at https://github.com/gregkaplan/phact, but we hope to make them available in other languages in future releases. Also see the Heterogeneous Agent Resource and toolKit (HARK) by Carroll et al. (2016) (available at https://github.com/econ-ark/HARK) for another project that shares our aim of encouraging the use of heterogeneous agent models among researchers and policymakers by making computations easier and faster.

7. We describe our methodology in the context of incomplete markets models with heterogeneous households, but the toolbox is applicable for a much broader class of models. Essentially any high-dimensional model in which equilibrium objects are a smooth function of aggregate states can be handled with the linearization methods.

8. One-asset heterogeneous agent models, in the spirit of Aiyagari (1994) and Krusell and Smith (1998), endogenize the fraction of hand-to-mouth households with a simple borrowing constraint. Standard calibrations of these models that match the aggregate capital-income ratio feature far too few high-MPC households relative to the data. In contrast when these models are calibrated to only *liquid* wealth, they are better able to match the distribution of MPCs in the data. Such economies, however, grossly understate the level of aggregate capital, and so are ill suited to general equilibrium settings. They also miss almost the entire wealth distribution, so that they are of limited use in studying the effects of macro shocks on inequality.

9. "Sensitivity" is a term used to describe how aggregate consumption responds more to predictable changes in aggregate income than implied by benchmark representative agent economies. "Smoothness" is a term used to describe how aggregate consumption growth is less volatile, relative to aggregate income growth, than implied by benchmark representative agent economies.

10. As Reiter (2010) notes in his discussion of a related method "For reasons of computational efficiency, the transition matrix [. . .] should be sparse. With more than 10,000 state variables, a dense [transition matrix] might not even fit into computer memory. Economically this means that, from any given individual state today (a given level of capital, for example), there is only a small set of states tomorrow that the agent can reach with positive probability. The level of sparsity is usually a function of the time period. A model at monthly frequency will probably be sparser, and therefore easier to handle, than a model at annual frequency." We take this logic a step further by working with a continuous-time model. As Reiter's discussion makes clear, discrete-time models can also generate sparsity in particular cases. However, this will happen either in models with

very short time periods (as suggested by Reiter), which are known to be difficult to solve because the discount factor of households is close to one, or the resulting matrices will be sparse but with a considerably higher *bandwidth* or *density* than in the matrices generated by a continuous-time model. A low bandwidth is important for efficiently solving sparse linear systems.

11. The assumption that idiosyncratic shocks follow a Poisson process is for simplicity of exposition; the method can also handle diffusion or jump-diffusion shock processes.

12. This process is the analog of an AR(1) process in discrete time.

13. The "Fully Recursive Formulation of Krussell-Smith (1998)" section of the appendix writes the equilibrium conditions using fully recursive conditions and shows how to obtain the system here by evaluating these conditions "along the characteristic" $(g_t(a, z), Z_t)$.

14. The borrowing constraint only affects equation (2) through the boundary condition $u'(w_t z_i) \geq \partial_a v_i(0, z)$ for $i = L, H$. We impose this condition in our numerical computations, but for the ease of exposition suppress the notation here.

15. The fact that prices are an explicit function of the distribution is a special feature of the Krusell and Smith (1998) model. In general, market-clearing conditions take the form $F(v, g, p) = 0$. Our solution method also handles this more general case.

16. We have written the price vector p_t as a function of the state vector to easily exposit our methodology in a way that directly extends to models with more general market-clearing conditions (see endnote 15). However, this approach is not necessary in the Krusell and Smith (1998) model because we can simply substitute the expression for prices directly into the households' budget constraint and hence the matrix $A(v_t; p_t)$.

17. To the best of our knowledge, there is no existing open-source automatic differentiation package for Matlab that exploits sparsity. We therefore wrote our own package for the computational toolbox.

18. To arrive at equation (15), we first rearrange equation (14) so that all time derivatives are on the left-hand side. We then take the expectation of the entire system and use the fact that the expectation of a Brownian increment is zero, $\mathbb{E}_t[dW_t] = 0$, to write equation (14) compactly without the stochastic term as

$$\mathbb{E}_t \begin{bmatrix} d v_t \\ d g_t \\ d Z_t \\ 0 \end{bmatrix} = \begin{bmatrix} u(v_t; p_t) + A(v_t; p_t) v_t - \rho v_t \\ A(v_t; p_t)^T g_t \\ -\eta Z_t \\ F(g_t; Z_t) - p_t \end{bmatrix} dt.$$

Finally, we linearize this system to arrive at equation (15). Note that this compact notation loses the information contained in the stochastic term dW_t. However, since we linearize the system this is without loss of generality—as we discuss later, linearized systems feature certainty equivalence.

19. The special structure of the matrix B involving zeros is particular to the Krusell and Smith (1998) model and can be relaxed. In addition, the fact that we can express prices as a static function of $\hat{g}_t$ and Z_t is a special feature of the model; more generally, the equilibrium prices are only defined implicitly by a set of market-clearing conditions.

20. Note that σ does not enter the matrix B characterizing the linearized system (16) and therefore also does not enter the matrices characterizing the optimal decision rules D_{vg} and D_{vZ}.

21. McKay (2017) studies time-varying idiosyncratic uncertainty on aggregate consumption dynamics. Terry (2017) studies how well discrete-time relatives of our method capture time variation in the dispersion of productivity shocks in a heterogeneous firm model.

22. In particular $D_{cZ}(a, z) = (\partial_a v(a, z))^{-(1/\theta)-1} \partial_a D_{vZ}(a, z)$. To see this note that

$$\hat{c}_0(a, z) = (\partial_a v(a, z))^{-(1/\theta)-1} \partial_a \hat{v}_0(a, z) = (\partial_a v(a, z))^{-(1/\theta)-1} \partial_a D_{vZ}(a, z) Z_0 := D_{cZ}(a, z) Z_0.$$

23. Note that this is separate from the state dependence we just discussed, which is concerned with how the distribution may affect the *linear* dynamics of the system.

24. Note that expression (20) only holds at $t = 0$. At times $t > 0$, the distribution also moves $\hat{g}_t(a, z) \neq 0$. The generalization of equation (20) to $t > 0$ is $\hat{C}_t \approx \int \hat{c}_t(a, z) g(a, z) da\,dz + \int c(a, z) \hat{g}_t(a, z) da\,dz$. Since both $\hat{c}_t(a, z)$ and $\hat{g}_t(a, z)$ will be linear in Z_t, so will be $\hat{C}_t$, again ruling out size and sign dependence.

25. An open question is under what conditions this procedure would be consistent with our use of linear approximations to solve the model. One possible scenario is as follows: even though the time path for the distribution might differ substantially when computed using the nonlinear Kolmogorov Forward equation, the time path for prices may still be well approximated by the linearized solution. Hence, the error in the HJB equation from using the linearized prices may be small.

26. Related, our linearization method obviously rules out nonlinear amplification effects that result in a bimodal ergodic distribution of aggregate states as in He and Krishnamurthy (2013) and Brunnermeier and Sannikov (2014).

27. Another difference is that Den Haan et al. (2010) allow the process for idiosyncratic shocks to depend on the aggregate state. We set our idiosyncratic shock process to match the average transition probabilities in Den Haan et al. (2010). We have solved the model with time-varying transition probabilities and obtained quantitatively similar results. Details are available from the authors upon request.

28. In this calculation, we have dropped one grid point from the distribution using the restriction that the distribution integrates to one. Hence there are $N = 200$ equations for $\hat{\mathbf{v}}_t$, $N - 1 = 199$ equations for $\hat{g}_t$, and one equation for Z_t.

29. As discussed by Den Haan (2010), there is one algorithm (Penal) that "is even faster, but this algorithm does not solve the actual [Krusell-Smith] model specified."

30. Mongey and Williams (2016) use a discrete-time relative of our method without model reduction to estimate a small heterogeneous firm model. Winberry (2016) provides an alternative parametric approach for reducing the distribution and also uses it to estimate a small heterogeneous firm model.

31. The following material is based on lecture notes by Amsallem and Farhat (2011), which in turn build on a book by Antoulas (2005). Lectures 3 and 7 by Amsallem and Farhat (2011) and chapters 1 and 11 in Antoulas (2005) are particularly relevant. All lecture notes for Amsallem and Farhat (2011) are available online at https://web.stanford. edu/group/frg/course_work/CME345/ and the book by Antoulas (2005) is available for free at http://epubs.siam.org/doi/book/10.1137/1.9780898718713. Also see Reiter (2010), who applies related ideas from the model reduction literature in order to reduce the dimensionality of a linearized discrete-time heterogeneous agent model.

32. Exogenous decision rules usually relate the value function to prices, that is, $\mathbf{v}_t = \mathbf{D}_{vp}\mathbf{p}_t$. But prices $\mathbf{p}_t = \mathbf{B}_{pg}\mathbf{g}_t + \mathbf{B}_{pZ}Z_t$ in turn depend on the distribution $\mathbf{g}_t$ and productivity Z_t. Hence, so do the decision rules: $\mathbf{v}_t = \mathbf{D}_{vg}\mathbf{g}_t + \mathbf{D}_{vZ}Z_t$, with $\mathbf{D}_{vg} = \mathbf{D}_{vp}\mathbf{B}_{pg}$ and $\mathbf{D}_{vZ} = \mathbf{D}_{vp}\mathbf{D}_{pZ}$.

33. The system (21) is called a *linear time invariant (LTI) system*; Z_t is an *input* into the system and $\mathbf{p}_t$ is an *output*. If both inputs and outputs are scalars, the system is called a *single-input-single-output (SISO) system*. If both inputs and outputs are vectors, it is called a *multiple-input-multiple-output (MIMO) system*. Instead of assuming that decision rules are exogenous, we could have assumed that there is no feedback from individuals' decisions to the distribution $\mathbf{B}_{gv} = 0$. In that case the system (16) again becomes a backward-looking system of the LTI form (21), now with $\mathbf{C}_{gg} = \mathbf{B}_{gg} + \mathbf{B}_{gp}\mathbf{B}_{pg}$ and $\mathbf{C}_{gZ} = \mathbf{B}_{gp}\mathbf{B}_{pZ}$ $\mathbf{C}_{gZ} = \mathbf{B}_{gp}\mathbf{B}_{pZ}$.

34. The assumption that $\mathbf{X}$ is orthonormal is not necessary to derive our results, but makes the exposition transparent. Appendix section "Model Reduction and Proof of Proposition 1" derives our results using nonnormalized projection matrices.

35. The model reduction literature also presents alternatives to our "least squares" approach to computing the coefficients γ_t. In particular, one can also estimate γ_t using what amounts to an instrumental variables strategy: one can define a second subspace spanned by the columns of some matrix $\mathbf{Z}$ and impose the orthogonality condition $\mathbf{Z}^T\varepsilon_t = 0$. This yields an alternative estimate $\gamma_t = (\mathbf{Z}^T\mathbf{X})^{-1}\mathbf{Z}^T\mathbf{g}_t$. Mathematically, this is called an *oblique projection* (as opposed to an orthogonal projection) of $\mathbf{g}_t$ onto the k-dimensional subspace spanned by the columns $\mathbf{X}$ along the kernel of $\mathbf{Z}^T$. See Amsallem and Farhat (2011, lecture 3) and Antoulas (2005) for more detail on oblique projections.

36. Our approach for choosing the basis **X** is a simplified version of what the model reduction literature calls "moment matching." See Amsallem and Farhat (2011, lecture 7) and Antoulas (2005, chapter 11). It is also the continuous-time analogue of what Reiter (2010) terms "conditional expectation approach" (see his Section 3.2.2).

37. In this simple deterministic model, equation (30) can also be derived in a simpler fashion: the Taylor-series approximation around $t = 0$ is $p_t \approx p_0 + \dot{p}_0 t + (1/2)\ddot{p}_0 t^2 + \ldots + [1 / (k-1)!]p_0^{(k-1)}t^{k-1}$. This is equivalent to equation (30) because the derivatives are given by $\dot{p}_t = \mathbf{b}_{pg}\dot{\mathbf{g}}_t = \mathbf{b}_{pg}\mathbf{C}_{gg}\mathbf{g}_t$, $\ddot{p}_t = \mathbf{b}_{pg}\mathbf{C}_{gg}^2\mathbf{g}_t$ and so on. This strategy no longer works in the full model with aggregate productivity shocks. In contrast, the derivation in terms of the matrix exponential $e^{\mathbf{C}_{gg}t}$ can be easily extended to the stochastic case.

38. Observability of a dynamical system is an important concept in control theory introduced by Rudolf Kalman, the inventor of the Kalman filter. It is a measure of how well a system's states (here $\mathbf{g}_t$) can be inferred from knowledge of its outputs (here p_t). For systems like ours observability can be directly inferred from the observability matrix $\mathcal{O}(\mathbf{b}_{pg}, \mathbf{C}_{gg})$ with $k = N$. Note that some texts refer only to $\mathcal{O}(\mathbf{b}_{pg}, \mathbf{C}_{gg})$ with $k = N$ as "observability matrix" and to the matrix with $k < N$ as "partial observability matrix."

39. Recall from equation (24) that the projection of $\mathbf{g}_t$ onto **X** defines the reduced distribution as $\gamma_t = \mathbf{X}^\mathsf{T}\mathbf{g}_t$. Hence the optimal decision rule can be written as $\tilde{\mathbf{v}}_t = \mathbf{D}_{v\gamma}\gamma_t = \mathbf{D}_{v\gamma}\mathbf{X}^\mathsf{T}\mathbf{g}_t = \tilde{\mathbf{D}}_{vg}\mathbf{g}_t$ where $\tilde{\mathbf{D}}_{vg} = \mathbf{D}_{v\gamma}\mathbf{X}^\mathsf{T}$.

40. Recall that in general p_t includes both prices and other observables of interest to the researcher.

41. See Antoulas (2005, chapter 11) and Amsallem and Farhat (2011, lecture 7).

42. Even though $\mathbf{B}_{gg}$ is sparse and $\mathbf{B}_{gp}$ and $\mathbf{B}_{pg}$ are only $\ell \times N$, the matrix $\mathbf{B}_{gg} + \mathbf{B}_{gp}\mathbf{B}_{pg}$ that actually enters the system (22) is $N \times N$ and not sparse (because $\mathbf{B}_{gp}\mathbf{B}_{pg}$ is $N \times N$ and not sparse). In the two-asset model in Section V, $N = 60,000$, and even storing this matrix is not feasible. Fortunately it is never actually necessary to compute this full matrix; instead, it is only necessary to compute $\mathbf{B}_{pg}(\mathbf{B}_{gg} + \mathbf{B}_{gp}\mathbf{B}_{pg})$, which involves the action of $\mathbf{B}_{gp}\mathbf{B}_{pg}$ on a thin $\ell \times N$ matrix $\mathbf{B}_{pg}$ and can be computed as $(\mathbf{B}_{pg}\mathbf{B}_{gp})\mathbf{B}_{pg}$.

43. One way to overcome this challenge is to use sparse matrix methods to find just the k eigenvalues associated with the stable eigenvectors. This is much faster than computing the full matrix decomposition necessary to obtain the full set of eigenvectors. However, it is slower than the approach we pursue in this subsection.

44. Note that, in general, the number of coefficients is different from the number of knot points.

45. Currently at: https://github.com/gregkaplan/phact.

46. More precisely, we choose the observability matrix so as to forecast $\ell = 5$ equilibrium objects (namely the wage and the interest rate, plus the three equilibrium aggregates we are most interested in: aggregate output, consumption, investment) to order $k = 1$ resulting in a reduced distribution γ_t of dimension $k_g = \ell \times k = 5$, and we approximate the value function at 12 spline knot points in the wealth dimension resulting in a reduced value function v_t of dimension $k_v = 2 \times 12 = 24$.

47. There are $k_v = 12 \times 2 = 24$ points for the value function, $k_g = k \times \ell = 1 \times 5 = 5$ points for the distribution because we are tracking five elements of the $\mathbf{p}_t$ vector, and 1 point for TFP Z_t.

48. Recall that the fastest algorithm in the JEDC comparison (Den Haan 2010) is more than 7 minutes, or 3,500 times longer.

49. Den Haan (2010) refers to this type of figure as the "fundamental accuracy plot."

50. We implement perfect annuity markets by making an adjustment to the asset returns faced by households. In order to save on notation, we do not explicitly display these adjustments here, so throughout asset returns should be interpreted as inclusive of annuity payments.

51. Because the transaction cost at $a = 0$ is infinite, in computations we replace the term a with $\max\{\underline{a}, a\}$, where the threshold $\underline{a} > 0$ is a small value (2% of quarterly GDP per household, which is around $500). This guarantees that costs remain finite even for households with $a = 0$.

52. See Kaplan et al. (2016) for a formal description of these processes.

53. Fagereng et al. (2016) study consumption responses to lottery winnings using Norwegian administrative data. They find that MPCs are high for households with nearly zero liquid assets, even if the household has positive illiquid assets.

54. The two-asset model is so much larger than the simple Krusell and Smith (1998) model because the individual state space is three-dimensional. To ensure an accurate approximation of the steady state, we use 30 grid points for labor productivity, 40 points for the illiquid asset, and 50 points for the liquid asset. The total number of grid points is therefore $N = 30 \times 40 \times 50 = 60,000$.

55. Recall that $k = 1$ does provide an accurate approximation in the simple Krusell and Smith (1998) model.

56. As discussed in Section III.C, with endogenous decision rules our method does not necessarily provide the most efficient choice of basis $\mathbf{X}$. It is possible that by following the iterative procedure outlined in that section, one could obtain an accurate reduced model with $k < 300$.

57. Recall that our basis $\mathbf{X}$ spans the subspace generated by the columns of the observability matrix.

58. Note that the aggregate capital stock is sufficient to compute the wage w_t and illiquid return r_t^a.

59. We have also computed a version of the model in which we drop the liquid asset market clearing condition, and instead assume that the liquid return r_t^b is fixed and that the bond supply adjusts perfectly elastically to meet the demand. In this version of the model, a $k = 100$ order observability matrix appears sufficient to reduce the distribution.

60. We match the second-order autocorrelation, rather than the first, due to potential time aggregation issues, as discussed in Campbell and Mankiw (1989).

61. In the special case of the representative agent model in which the interest rate is constant and income growth is a random walk, these sensitivity measures are exactly zero. The representative agent version of our model does not satisfy this special case, generating nonzero measures of sensitivity.

62. Krusell et al. (2000) assume that only equipment capital features capital-skill complementarity, while structures capital has unitary elasticity of substitution. We omit structures capital for simplicity.

63. Recall that with Cobb-Douglas the dispersion of pretax labor income is constant.

64. Formally, $\Pi := \mathbf{VW}^T$ is a projection, and we have that $\Pi \mathbf{g}_t = \mathbf{V}\gamma_t$.

65. For a detailed discussion of this, see Amsallem and Farhat (2011, lecture 7). The intuition is that, for the dynamics of a reduced system, only the *space* on which we project the large-dimensional state variable matters. A sketch of the formal argument goes as follows: $\mathbf{V}$ and $\mathbf{X}$ are bases of the same space, so there exists an invertible matrix $\mathbf{Z}$ such that $\mathbf{VZ} = \mathbf{X}$, so $\mathbf{Z}^{-1} = \mathbf{X}^T\mathbf{V}$ and $\mathbf{Z} = (\mathbf{X}^T\mathbf{V})^{-1}$. Similarly, there exists an invertible matrix $\tilde{\mathbf{Z}}$ such that $\tilde{\mathbf{Z}}\mathbf{W}^T = \mathbf{X}^T$, so $\tilde{\mathbf{Z}}^{-1} = \mathbf{W}^T\mathbf{X}$ and $\tilde{\mathbf{Z}} = (\mathbf{W}^T\mathbf{X})^{-1}$. But $\mathbf{W}^T\mathbf{X} = \mathbf{W}^T\mathbf{VZ} = \mathbf{Z}$, so $\tilde{\mathbf{Z}} = \mathbf{Z}^{-1}$. Then $\mathbf{VW}^T = \mathbf{XZ}^{-1}\mathbf{W}^T = \mathbf{X}\tilde{\mathbf{Z}}\mathbf{W}^T = \mathbf{XX}^T$ and the projections are identical.

References

Acemoglu, D., and D. Autor. 2011. "Skills, Tasks, and Technologies: Implications for Employment and Earnings." *Handbook of Labor Economics* 4:1043–171.

Achdou, Y., J. Han, J-M. Lasry, P-L. Lions, and B. Moll. 2017. "Income and Wealth Distribution in Macroeconomics: A Continuous-Time Approach." NBER Working Paper no. 23732, Cambridge, MA.

Aiyagari, S. R. 1994. "Uninsured Idiosyncratic Risk and Aggregate Saving." *Quarterly Journal of Economics* 109 (3): 659–84.

Amsallem, D., and C. Farhat. 2011. Lecture Notes for CME 345: Model Reduction. https://web.stanford.edu/group/frg/course_work/CME345/.

Antoulas, A. 2005. *Approximation of Large-Scale Dynamical Systems (Advances in Design and Control)*. Philadelphia: Society for Industrial and Applied Mathematics.

Auclert, A. 2014. "Monetary Policy and the Redistribution Channel." Technical Report, Massachusetts Institute of Technology.

Bayer, C., R. Luetticke, L. Pham-Dao, and V. Tjaden. 2015. "Precautionary Savings, Illiquid Assets, and the Aggregate Consequences of Shocks to Household Income Risk." Technical Report, University of Bonn.

Blanchard, O. J., and C. M. Kahn. 1980. "The Solution of Linear Difference Models under Rational Expectations." *Econometrica* 48 (5): 1305–11.

Bloom, N., M. Floetotto, N. Jaimovich, I. Saporta-Eksten, and S. Terry. 2014. "Really Uncertain Business Cycles." Center for Economic Studies Paper no. CES-WP-14-18, US Census Bureau.

Brunnermeier, M. K., and Y. Sannikov. 2014. "A Macroeconomic Model with a Financial Sector." *American Economic Review* 104 (2): 379–421.

Campbell, J. 1998. "Entry, Exit, Embodied Technology, and Business Cycles. *Review of Economic Dynamics* 1 (2): 371–408.

Campbell, J. Y., and N. G. Mankiw. 1989. "Consumption, Income and Interest Rates: Reinterpreting the Time Series Evidence." In *NBER Macroeconomics Annual 1989*, vol. 4, ed. Jonathan A. Parker and Michael Woodford, 185–216. Chicago: University of Chicago Press.

Cardaliaguet, P., F. Delarue, J.-M. Lasry, and P.-L. Lions (2015): "The master equation and the convergence problem in mean field games," ArXiv e-prints.

Carroll, C., M. White, N. Palmer, D. Low, and A. Kaufman. 2016. Heterogenous Agents Resources & toolKit. https://github.com/econ-ark/HARK.

Christiano, L. 1989. Comment on "Consumption, Income and Interest Rates: Reinterpreting the Time Series Evidence." In *NBER Macroeconomics Annual 1989*, vol. 4, ed. Jonathan A. Parker and Michael Woodford, 216–33. Chicago: University of Chicago Press.

Congressional Budget Office. 2013. "The Distribution of Federal Spending and Taxes in 2006." Technical Report, Washington, DC, United States Congress.

Deaton, A. 2005. "Measuring Poverty in a Growing World (or Measuring Growth in a Poor World)." *Review of Economics and Statistics* 87 (1): 1–19.

Den Haan, W. J. 2010. "Comparison of Solutions to the Incomplete Markets Model with Aggregate Uncertainty." *Journal of Economic Dynamics and Control* 34 (1): 4–27.

Den Haan, W., K. Judd, and M. Julliard. 2010. "Computational Suite of Models with Heterogeneous Agents: Incomplete Markets and Aggregate Uncertainty." *Journal of Economic Dynamics and Control* 34 (1): 1–3.

Dotsey, M., R. King, and A. Wolman. 1999. "State-Dependent Pricing and the General Equilibrium Dynamics of Money and Output." *Quarterly Journal of Economics* 114 (2): 655–90.

Fagereng, A., M. B. Holm, and G. J. Natvik. 2016. "MPC Heterogeneity and Household Balance Sheets." Discussion Paper, Statistics Norway.

Guvenen, F., F. Karahan, S. Ozkan, and J. Song. 2015. "What Do Data on Millions of US Workers Reveal about Life-Cycle Earnings Risk?" NBER Working Paper no. 20913, Cambridge, MA.

He, Z., and A. Krishnamurthy. 2013. "Intermediary Asset Pricing." *American Economic Review* 103 (2): 732–70.

Ilut, C. L., and M. Schneider. 2014. "Ambiguous Business Cycles." *American Economic Review* 104 (8): 2368–99.

Johnson, D. S., J. A. Parker, and N. S. Souleles. 2006. "Household Expenditure and the Income Tax Rebates of 2001." *American Economic Review* 96 (5): 1589–610.

Kaplan, G., B. Moll, and G. L. Violante. 2016. "Monetary Policy According to HANK." Working Paper no. 1602, Council on Economic Policies.

Kaplan, G., and G. L. Violante. 2014. "A Model of the Consumption Response to Fiscal Stimulus Payments." *Econometrica* 82 (4): 1199–239.

Krusell, P., L. Ohanian, V. Rios-Rull, and G. Violante. 2000. "Capital-Skill Complementarity and Inequality: A Macroeconomic Analysis." *Econometrica* 68:1029–53.

Krusell, P., and A. A. Smith. 1998. "Income and Wealth Heterogeneity in the Macroeconomy." *Journal of Political Economy* 106 (5): 867–96.

Lucas, R. E. 2003. "Macroeconomic Priorities." *American Economic Review* 93 (1): 1–14.

Ludvigson, S. C., and A. Michaelides. 2001. "Does Buffer-Stock Saving Explain the Smoothness and Excess Sensitivity of Consumption?" *American Economic Review* 91 (3): 631–47.

McKay, A. 2017. "Time-Varying Idiosyncratic Risk and Aggregate Consumption Dynamics." Technical Report, Boston University.

McKay, A., E. Nakamura, and J. Steinsson. 2016. "The Power of Forward Guidance Revisited." *American Economic Review* 106 (10): 3133–3158.

McKay, A., and R. Reis. 2016. "The Role of Automatic Stabilizers in the US Business Cycle." *Econometrica* 84: 141–194.

Mongey, S., and J. Williams. 2016. "Firm Dispersion and Business Cycles: Estimating Aggregate Shocks Using Panel Data." Working Paper, New York University.

Parker, J. A., N. S. Souleles, D. S. Johnson, and R. McClelland. 2013. "Consumer Spending and the Economic Stimulus Payments of 2008." *American Economic Review* 103 (6): 2530–53.

Piketty, T., E. Saez, and G. Zucman. 2016. "Distributional National Accounts: Methods and Estimates for the United States." NBER Working Paper no. 22945, Cambridge, MA.

Preston, B., and M. Roca. 2007. "Incomplete Markets, Heterogeneity and Macroeconomic Dynamics." NBER Working Paper no. 13260, Cambridge, MA.

Reiter, M. 2009. "Solving Heterogeneous-Agent Models by Projection and Perturbation." *Journal of Economic Dynamics and Control* 33 (3): 649–65.

———. 2010. "Approximate and Almost-Exact Aggregation in Dynamic Stochastic Heterogeneous-Agent Models." Economics Series no. 258, Institute for Advanced Studies.

Terry, S. 2017. "Alternative Methods for Solving Heterogeneous Firm Models." *Journal of Money, Credit, and Banking* 49 (6): 1081–1111.

Veracierto, M. 2002. "Plant Level Irreversible Investment and Equilibrium Business Cycles." *American Economic Review* 92:181–97.

Winberry, T. 2016. "A Toolbox for Solving and Estimating Heterogeneous Agent Macro Models" Working Paper, University of Chicago.

Comment

Christopher D. Carroll, *Johns Hopkins University and NBER*
Edmund Crawley, *Johns Hopkins University*

What's Wrong with Macroeconomics, and Can This Paper Fix It?

For roughly 30 years leading up to the Great Recession, the attention of much of the macroeconomics profession was focused on constructing models in which a single representative agent made optimizing choices that determined the economy's endogenous dynamics. By a curious (and regrettable) convention, a shorthand term to distinguish such models from their predecessors was to describe them as having "microfoundations."

Larry Summers (2011) clearly had such models in mind when he summed up his experience at the National Economic Council in the Obama administration: "I would have to say that the vast edifice in both its new Keynesian variety and its new classical variety of attempting to place micro foundations under macroeconomics was not something that informed the policy-making process in any important way." While Summers's wording was impolite, his view that the new generation of macroeconomic models had little useful to say in the crisis was widely shared among policymakers who were called upon to make difficult decisions at that time.

After thinking things over, a number of such policymakers including Fed Chair Janet Yellen (2016), former IMF Chief Economist Olivier Blanchard (2016), ECB Governing Board Member Benoit Coeure (2013), and Bank of England Chief Economist Andy Haldane (2016) have recently suggested that incorporating the right kinds of microeconomic heterogeneity into benchmark macro models would make a major contribution to improving both their performance and their credibility.

Below, we will suggest that the way to heed this call is to construct models with what we will call "serious" microfoundations (to distinguish them from the models Summers was criticizing, whose claim to be "microfounded" rests on grounds other than matching the pertinent microeconomic evidence). The paper by Ahn et al. is an important step in the construction of this new class of models because the main obstacle to a "seriously" microfounded macroeconomics has long been the mathematical and computational difficulty of solving models with enough heterogeneity (of right kind). Building on the pioneering work of Reiter (2009, 2010), Ahn and colleagues describe a methodology and provide a toolkit that promises to vastly expand the scope of questions that can be addressed by models with such heterogeneity. Providing a toolkit is a key step: arguably much of the reason for the ubiquity of RA models is the creation of the DYNARE toolkit, which vastly simplified construction of such models.[1]

The paper provides an exhaustive description of its methodological advances, so our discussion will focus on two other questions: Why (and how) serious microfoundations might matter for macroeconomic questions, and the related question of how best to do "quantitative theory" using tools like those the authors provide.[2]

Why "Serious" Heterogeneity Matters for Macroeconomics

A.   What is "Serious" Heterogeneity?

A recent paper by Auclert (2015) distills a key insight from the heterogeneous agents (HA) macroeconomics literature: Auclert produces a reasonably general model with heterogeneous and microconomically optimizing consumers in which, for some questions, the aggregate marginal propensity to consume (MPC—henceforth, $\bar{\kappa}$) is a "sufficient statistic" for most of what a macroeconomist might need to know about the economy's response to certain kinds of shocks.

One interpretation of Auclert is that the "representative agent" (RA) macroeconomics literature has been handicapped since its origin by the convention that the appropriate target to "represent" is the aggregate wealth-to-income ratio. A standard optimizing consumer with a wealth-to-income ratio of 3 or 4 will inevitably have a value of κ closer to 0.03 than to Milton Friedman's (1963) estimate of $\bar{\kappa} \approx 0.33$ (which has held up well in subsequent research—see below); so to the extent that Auclert's insight generalizes, any model calibrated to match aggregate wealth will badly misrepresent the key "sufficient statistic" required for obtaining the right answer to at least some questions.

Auclert's paper makes it plausible that many macroeconomic questions might be better studied using a "Representative-$\bar{\kappa}$" (for short, "Rκ") model whose single optimizing agent has a target level of wealth at which the MPC matches empirical measures of $\bar{\kappa}$. (Such models have long been available in the "buffer-stock saving" literature [Deaton 1991; Carroll 1997] explicitly targeted an MPC of 0.4), but were viewed as having little to say about macroeconomics because they made no effort to match aggregate wealth.)

Auclert's paper nevertheless demonstrates that there are many kinds of macroeconomic shocks for which $\bar{\kappa}$ is *not* a sufficient statistic—most prominently (for monetary policy analysis), the effects of interest rate movements. While it is a good guess that an Rκ model might do better on many such questions than standard RA models, it would take a long time to rework the bulk of the RA literature as an Rκ literature, and that reworked literature might uncover deficiencies in the Rκ model just as serious as those of the RA model.

If the HA literature to which Ahn et al. makes a major methodological contribution succeeds (as we think it ultimately will), workhorse macroeconomic models in the future will dispense altogether with the convenient fiction that the behavior of a single agent can capture everything important about the macroeconomy (whether calibrated to match aggregate wealth or $\bar{\kappa}$).

Of course, households are heterogeneous in an almost unlimited number of ways; in order to be useful, or even feasible, the HA literature will need to make judicious choices about which kinds of heterogeneity are important for macroeconomic analysis and which can be safely ignored. The long history of what has worked (and what has not) in the HA literature leads us to the view that a model qualifies as having a serious treatment of heterogeneity (by which we mean that it captures the dimensions of heterogeneity that both theory and evidence suggest matter for macroeconomic outcomes) if it:

1. Matches the microeconomic evidence on the dynamics of household-level income (see motivation below).

2. Produces, as an equilibrium outcome, distributions of wealth and income that match key data on the level and joint distribution of wealth and income, *particularly for consumers who the model says should have a high* κ.

3. Generates a $\bar{\kappa}$ that is at least roughly consistent with the vast and diverse microeconomic literature attempting to estimate that object.[3]

The applications of the authors' methodology here, and some previous work by some of them, are among the first examples of models that do a colorable job of satisfying all our criteria of seriousness, and are at the same time capable of being used to simulate and study macroeconomic dynamics. The Ahn et al. paper achieves these goals (at least partially) by following Kaplan and Violante (2014) in assuming that even for many wealthy consumers, illiquid assets are largely inaccessible for consumption-smoothing purposes (though the paper makes an important advance over Kaplan and Violante [2014] by incorporating empirically calibrated [and large] transitory shocks to income).

Another, much simpler way to achieve all of these goals is to violate the taboo established by Stigler and Becker (1977), and enforced with remarkable rigor in macroeconomics until recently (though not microeconomics),[4] against allowing ex ante heterogeneity in preferences across consumers. Krusell and Smith (1998) broke the taboo, but did not match either $\bar{\kappa}$ or the distribution of wealth. Carroll et al. (forthcoming) (and, following them, Krueger, Mitman, and Perri's [forthcoming] chapter in the *Handbook of Macroeconomics*) show that all of our proposed elements of seriousness can be satisfied by allowing a modest difference in time preference rates (or optimism/pessimism about future growth, or persistent differences in rates of return, or other forms of preference or belief heterogeneity) across consumers, avoiding the complexity associated with modeling the interplay between liquid and illiquid assets.

B. Implications for Monetary and Fiscal Policy

While macroeconomists address an enormous range of topics, analysis of most questions partakes strongly of answers to some related question about either monetary or fiscal policy. We will therefore assess the importance of serious heterogeneity by asking how its incorporation might change our view of the operation of fiscal and monetary policy, compared to a standard off-the-shelf representative agent New Keynesian (RANK) model of the type that was in 2008, and today still is, widely used at central banks and other policy institutions.

Fiscal Policy

Unless modified to incorporate heterogeneity, such a model would typically imply that a fiscal stimulus payment of the kind implemented by

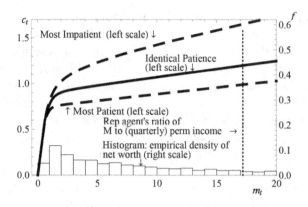

Fig. 1. Empirical wealth distribution and consumption functions of patient and impatient agents.

the Bush administration in 2008 (to choose a particularly clean example) would generate extra spending over the subsequent year (an MPC)[5] of only around 0.02 to 0.03 cents on the dollar (even leaving aside the Ricardian Equivalence proposition, which would further attenuate any extra spending).

Broda and Parker (2014), Parker et al. (2013), and a number of other papers find estimates of the MPC out of this stimulus payment that are at least an order of magnitude larger than would be implied by a RANK model. This finding is consistent with a large body of microeconomic evidence spanning the entire interval over which economists have been attempting to estimate the MPC, from Friedman (1957) to Fagereng, Holm, and Natvik (2017), using data of many kinds and from many places and applying to many populations; broadly speaking, estimates of the MPC typically lie somewhere in the range of 0.2 to 0.7.

An illustration of the reason for our earlier proposition that seriousness requires matching the wealth distribution *particularly for high-κ consumers* is captured intuitively in a figure from Carroll et al., which overlays the empirical distribution of wealth from the US *Survey of Consumer Finances* with the consumption functions that characterize the optimal solution to different kinds of consumers' optimal consumption plans.

The steeper of the two consumption functions in figure 1 corresponds to the most "impatient" category of consumer in the model; such consumers, in our model's equilibrium, constitute the great majority of the people with low levels of wealth.[6] The figure shows that the *optimal* MPC (that is, the MPC that is the optimal solution of their standard dynamic stochastic optimization problem) is exceptionally high for people with low levels of wealth.

A defender of the current approach to RANK modeling *status quo* might object that, with much less work, the high average MPC can be adequately captured by adding to the RANK model some "rule-of-thumb" consumers á la Campbell and Mankiw's (1989) *Macro Annual* paper (a "CM model"). This brings us back to Auclert: his work shows that $\bar{\kappa}$ is a sufficient statistic *if that $\bar{\kappa}$ reflects the decisions of optimizing consumers*. The logic of his argument implies that a model that achieves a high $\bar{\kappa}$ by combining nonoptimizing rule-of-thumb consumers with very wealthy "perfect foresight" consumers has no theoretical claim to provide good answers to questions about dynamic macroeconomic questions.

A pertinent illustration of this point comes from a comparison of the implications of the Rκ and the CM models for the role of uncertainty over the business cycle, which a growing literature suggests is of first-order importance. An optimizing consumer whose κ is 0.33 is one whose primary motivation for holding any wealth at all is as a buffer against uncertainty. When uncertainty rises, that consumer should respond with a sharp cut in spending in order to build the bigger buffer stock appropriate for the greater degree of uncertainty. In contrast, the CM rule-of-thumb consumers do not respond at all to uncertainty, and the CM model's wealthy consumers' optimal response would be quite small, even if they were to take uncertainty into account in their optimization problem.

Monetary Policy

Monetary policy operates via the central bank's control over nominal (and, given the sluggishness of inflation, real) interest rates. The mechanism by which interest rates affect behavior is therefore the substance of a model's theory of how monetary policy works.

By this standard, RANK models do not have a credible theory of the operation of monetary policy. Interest rates are hypothesized to affect consumption mainly via the intertemporal substitution channel: when interest rates rise unexpectedly, consumption ought to drop instantly and sharply in response. The failure of consumption to behave in this manner was recognized in perhaps the first attempt at a structural model of how monetary policy works, by Rotemberg and Woodford (1997) in the *Macro Annual* 20 years ago, and remains a core problem;

as Blanchard (2016) recently put it, "[The RANK model's] implications with respect to the role of interest rates in twisting the path of consumption, are strongly at odds with the empirical evidence." Rotemberg and Woodford's (1997) solution was simply to hardwire a one-year lag into the response of consumption to interest rates, which they invited readers to think of as a crude way to capture the existence of predetermined and unalterable spending plans. The subsequent literature has adopted subtler expedients, with the most common solution today being the incorporation of habit formation in the utility function of the representative agent.

The habit formation solution has (at least) two problems: there is essentially no microeconomic evidence for the existence of habits (a fact that has held up robustly since Deaton [1992] articulated it, strongly reinforced by Dynan [2000] and subsequent work), and the introduction of habits substantially further undermines the ability of the model to match the empirical evidence on the MPC. (Consumers with habits might have an MPC as low as 1%.)

Recent work by Kaplan, Moll, and Violante (2016) shows that a model with heterogeneous agents provides a major improvement on the benchmark RA model. In a model like the one in Ahn et al., but which also includes a New Keynesian production function, Kaplan et al. (2016) find that only about 15% of the response of consumption to interest rates is attributable to the (not very credible) intertemporal substitution channel that is essentially the only mechanism for interest rate effects in RANK models.

In sum, serious treatment of heterogeneity deeply changes our understanding of the operation of both fiscal and monetary policy, and by implication much of the rest of macroeconomics.

How to Do Quantitative Theory

The history of the HA macro literature motivates the seriousness criteria we formulated above; different strands of the literature have focused on different elements of seriousness, but (in addition to the computational challenges) part of the reason HA models have been compelling enough to convert the representative macroeconomist to the HA approach is that until recently each previous effort failed in some crucial *quantitative* way.

Numerical solutions to models with heterogeneous agents facing uninsurable idiosyncratic risks have been available at least since Zeldes

(1989), and efforts to calibrate such models to empirical measurements of household income dynamics have proliferated since the first such effort by Carroll (1992). The first efforts to construct such a model whose interest rate was consistent with the model-generated aggregate capital-to-output ratio (the most basic definition of a steady-state "general equilibrium") were papers by Hubbard, Skinner, and Zeldes (1994, 1995). Aiyagari (1994) produced a much simpler GE model without a life cycle and with an implausible income process, but which did not require a supercomputer to solve (and thus was much more feasible to build upon).

Aiyagari was focused on the quantitative magnitude of the precautionary saving induced by uninsurable idiosyncratic risks; he found that, when calibrated as he had done, such risks increased the wealth-to-income ratio by only a few percentage points, leading to a natural interpretation that the introduction of idiosyncratic risk made little quantitative difference to macroeconomic outcomes.

These papers failed the seriousness criteria above partly because they did not even attempt to match the degree of inequality in the distribution of wealth. As we now know, many of the quantitative answers obtained from such models (e.g., about $\bar{\kappa}$) change drastically when income dynamics and wealth inequality are both matched. Furthermore, none of these papers could really be used for questions at the heart of macroeconomics involving macroeconomic dynamics.

The first of the major contributions of Krusell and Smith (1998) was to introduce a method for solving dynamic versions HA models. But, as in Aiyagari (1994), the wealth distribution in the benchmark version of their model was concentrated around the representative agent's wealth, and the dynamics of their benchmark model differed little from those of a corresponding representative agent model; as a result, many readers reached the conclusion that Krusell and Smith (1998) had confirmed that heterogeneity did not matter.

That was not the message the authors had intended, and neglected their second major contribution, which was to begin to explore how adding heterogeneity beyond that induced by income shocks might improve the model's fit to the empirical wealth distribution. While this was a major advance in seriousness (as above), even their dynastic model greatly understated the degree of wealth inequality; in particular, it produced very few consumers at low levels of wealth where the κ is high, and as a result it generated a $\bar{\kappa}$ that was only modestly higher than in the RA model (see Carroll et al., forthcoming). Consequently, even their dynastic model did not have implications profoundly different from those of the corresponding RA model.

The point of this history is that the extent to which heterogeneity matters is a profoundly quantitative question, and answering it credibly turns out to require getting right the quantities that are the key inputs to the model. This history motivates our seriousness criteria above, and leads us back now to discussion of Ahn et al.

A.   Consumption and Income Dynamics

Income Dynamics in Continuous Time

Friedman (1957) famously proposed that income has two components: transitory and permanent. A very large subsequent literature, including work with administrative data from the IRS (DeBacker et al. 2013) and the Social Security Administration (Sabelhaus and Song 2010) and work by one of the authors (Kaplan 2012), has found that Friedman's characterization remains quite a good one, though perhaps the long-lasting shocks that arrive annually are not completely permanent (DeBacker et al. [2013] and Kaplan [2012] estimate the AR(1) coefficient of the persistent component to be 0.97 or 0.98 instead of 1.0).

Being reminded of Friedman's framework helps in thinking through the treatment of income dynamics in Ahn et al. The authors attribute their fantastic increase in computing speed to their use of continuous-time computational tools drawn from the engineering literature. Unfortunately, there is no neat analogue in continuous time to Friedmanian transitory shocks; the authors argue that their model captures transitory and persistent (nearly permanent) shocks by the Poisson arrival of their z_1 and z_2 shocks that decay (with perfect predictability, unless another Poisson shock arrives) according to the continuous-time equivalent of an AR(1). (The authors call this a "jump-drift" process, but because "drift" seems both random and directionless, we will call it a "jump-decay" process.)

By matching some moments from Guvenen et al. (2015), they calibrate the "transitory" shock z_1 to arrive approximately once every three years and have a half life of about a quarter, while the "persistent" shock z_2 arrives approximately once every 38 years and has a half life of 18 years.

These extreme intervals between shocks (especially the persistent shocks) appear to result from a mismatch between their assumption that income shocks are lognormal and the enormous kurtosis of annual income shocks estimated by Guvenen et al.

Guvenen et al. describe their own findings as the nail in the coffin of the assumption that income shocks are lognormal. Ahn and colleague's calibration shows that, in principle, it is possible to generate Guvenen et al.-sized kurtosis in annual data from a process driven by lognormally distributed jump-decay shocks, but to accomplish that goal it is necessary for the shocks to be very large and very rare. (A permanent shock that arrives once every 38 years would typically happen at most once in a working lifetime.) In a way, the fact that calibrating lognormal shocks to the Guvenen et al. data violates other facts that we know from many other data sources (but that Ahn and colleagues do not try to match), is just a confirmation of Guvenen et al.'s claim that shocks cannot be lognormal.

Another concern is that it is unclear what sort of event the authors' transitory shock might represent. The discrete-time equivalent of their continuous-time model would be, for example, to treat the arrival of the 2008 $600 stimulus checks as though what had actually happened was an increment of roughly $35 to the consumer's weekly paycheck in the first week, $33 in the second week, and so on forever (for a sequence whose PDV adds up to $600). We are certain that Friedman's description of transitory shocks is a much better representation of the 2008 stimulus check than the jump-decay representation, and also feel sure that it is a much better representation of most other transitory movements in income. Indeed, we have been unable to think of any real-world shocks that resemble their process.

Of course, in principle, their solution methods are able to handle any arbitrary calibration of the transitory AR(1) process. If, for example, the specification of the shock were chosen so that, say, 90% of the mass of the stimulus payments got paid out in the first week, that would be almost equivalent to a Friedmanian shock.[7] Our guess would be that their framework can handle an AR(1) decay that is fast enough to satisfy any reasonable person, but it would be nice to know if that guess is right—particularly in light of our earlier point that credibility about results in quantitative theory models requires credible quantification of the inputs to those models.

In fact, it seems likely that the authors could capture reasonably well a Friedmanian process like that used by most of the prior HA macro literature (including Kaplan 2012); certainly, they could get a lot closer than they are now to previous models' calibrations that have been closely tied to the large literature on income dynamics. Bearing in mind the lesson from the history of the HA literature that calibrational assumptions matter profoundly for quantitative conclusions, some caution is warranted in the interpretation of all of their quantitative results.

What Is "the MPC" out of a Transitory Shock?

Another concern about the authors' calibration is that the right way to compute something that can be designated as "the MPC" out of one of their z_1 transitory shocks is not so obvious.

Since, in continuous time, both income and consumption are flow variables, only when the flow has been integrated over some finite interval does it become possible to speak of a marginal propensity to consume over that interval. Hence our explicit earlier definition above of κ as the amount of extra spending *over the subsequent year* induced by the arrival of a transitory shock. Concretely, then, the MPC over one period (between t and $t + 1$) out of a lump-sum Friedmanian transitory shock of size $x at date t would be

$$\kappa = \frac{\int_t^{t+1}(c_\tau - c_\tau^*)\,d\tau}{x} \tag{1}$$

where c_τ^* is the consumption that would have occurred in the absence of the shock.

Indeed, this is the method used for calculating what the authors report as the MPC in the paper, despite the fact that Friedmanian shocks are not what is expected by the consumers in the model. (Thus their MPC is calculated as the consequence of what has recently come to be referred to as "an MIT shock.")

If the authors wanted to calculate the "MPC out of a transitory shock" for the model-consistent transitory shocks that their consumers experience, the numerator would be the same as in the equation above, but they would have (at least) two choices for the denominator. The first would be to integrate the flow of transitory income over the same interval that applies to consumption:

$$x_a = \int_t^{t+1} z_{1,\tau}\,d\tau. \tag{2}$$

The other is to use the entire PDV of the shock as the denominator,

$$x_b = \int_t^{\infty} z_{1,\tau}\,d\tau. \tag{3}$$

If virtually all of the transitory shock has arrived by the beginning of period $t + 1$, the two measures will be almost the same. But at the quarterly frequency, their transitory shock's flow has only fallen by half, so there is a great deal more income that has yet to reach the consumer.

So, unless the AR(1) coefficient is quite small (and theirs is not), there can be a substantial difference between the MPC out of a Friedman transitory shock and the MPC out of their transitory shock.

What we are less sure of is how much the discrepancy matters; there are circumstances under which their shock would have effects virtually identical to those of the Friedman shock. In the certainty-equivalent (CEQ) or the perfect foresight (PF) formulations of the permanent income hypothesis, consumption is a function of the PDV of income, without regard to income's timing. But, what this means is that the circumstances in which their shock is equivalent to a Friedman shock are basically the circumstances under which their model most closely resembles the CEQ/PF model. Thus, to some degree, the more different their model is from the CEQ/PF model, the less plausible is their treatment of transitory shocks, and the only way to get around this trade-off is to make the AR(1) decay speed very rapid.

Excess Sensitivity and Excess Smoothness

The authors use their two-asset model to see how well it can match the empirical phenomena of excess sensitivity and excess smoothness.

It is not clear that the results from the two-asset model are an overall improvement on existing models (see table 9); the most striking result is their model's Campbell-Mankiw coefficient of 0.98. This contrasts with essentially 0.00 for the representative agent model and 0.49 in the data. The authors account for this large coefficient by the existence of hand-to-mouth consumers who do not smooth their consumption over time. However, the quarterly MPC in their model is 22%. A naive estimate of the Campbell-Mankiw coefficient in their model might then be 0.22 in a similar way that the saver-spender model with 50% hand-to-mouth consumers leads to a Campbell-Mankiw coefficient of 0.5. Exactly why this is not so is worthy of further investigation. We believe that the coefficient may be very sensitive to two unconventional ways in which the model is calibrated.

First, they model income *growth* as an AR(1). Campbell and Deaton (1989) pointed out long ago that if income *growth* follows an AR(1), then permanent income goes up more than one-to-one with an unexpected increase in income, and therefore in a CEQ model, consumption would be expected to increase by more than the change in current income.

Unfortunately, our short macro time series are not very informative about the nature of the income process, particularly in the long run (see Stock 1991). The ratio of the volatility of consumption to the volatility of income (another statistic reported in the paper) should be highly sensitive to the exact assumption about the income-growth process, and we suspect the Campbell-Mankiw coefficient is likely to be similarly sensitive; so, we are doubtful that their 0.98 Campbell-Mankiw coefficient would be robust to alternative choices of income-growth processes.

Second, in order to make comparison with the one-asset models more straightforward, the authors assume that the supply of the liquid asset is elastic. Implicitly, it is as though the liquid asset freely trades as in a small open economy, but there are strict capital controls on the illiquid asset. We have not succeed in thinking this through completely, but are concerned that this may open up large differences between the two interest rates upon arrival of a positive TFP shock. In turn, that might result in many more consumers hitting their borrowing constraint in order to invest at the higher interest rate available in the illiquid asset. A bit more investigation into the exact mechanism here, along with some empirical work as to whether it is reasonable, would help us understand whether the high Campbell-Mankiw coefficient in the model should be taken seriously.

B.   A Note on the Failure of Approximate Aggregation

The computational methods presented in the paper are particularly applicable for models where "approximate aggregation" (per Krusell and Smith) fails. This is important to their model's solution because the failure of approximate aggregation in the authors' two-asset model is extreme. While the Krusell-Smith algorithm needs just one state variable to retrieve the path of wages and interest rates to a very high degree of accuracy, the authors find that 300 or more dimensions are required for their two-asset model.

Of course, for showing off their toolkit's powers, a model that is not easily represented by a small basis is ideal. But as economists, we would like to understand what is driving the dynamics of our models. The high dimensionality of the two-asset model implies that small changes in particular parts of the distribution can significantly alter the path of prices, particularly of the liquid asset; it would be a formidable challenge to obtain some intuition for the mechanisms involved. A related problem is that, if even economists have trouble understanding

the mechanics of the model, the assumption that all consumers understand it perfectly (as required by their rational expectations solution
method) is far more questionable than when the economy's dynamics
are relatively simple.

A possible resolution of this puzzle is that the basis that the authors
make available to their algorithm is inefficient. The motivation for the
basis comes from matching the first k terms of the Taylor series for the
impulse response of prices around the time of impact (see equations
[30] and [31]). For an exogenous decision rule, the basis is chosen to
be an exact match. For endogenous decisions rules (such as those in
economic models), the basis is chosen by ignoring the feedback from
individuals' decisions to the distribution. While this means the terms
of the Taylor series are no longer exactly matched, the hope is that the
assumption may be approximately true and the resulting basis will nevertheless allow for a large reduction in dimension. Figure 7 shows the
impulse response for different orders of distribution reduction. If the
first k terms of the Taylor expansion were well approximated, we would
expect that the impulse response would be accurate for small values
of t, deteriorating as the time from impact increases. This is indeed the
case for the illiquid return and wage impulse responses. The $k = 2$ approximation to the impulse response for the liquid asset, on the other
hand, is most inaccurate for small values of t. This suggests the failure
of approximate aggregation may be as much due to having chosen an
inefficient basis as to the underlying economic structure.

The authors suggest an iterative procedure to improve the efficiency
of the basis in cases where the degree of dimension reduction in the
basic algorithm is still not enough to make the model numerically tractable. It should be possible to use the same algorithm to find an efficient
basis that accurately matches the first k terms of the impulse response
Taylor expansion. Replicating figure 7 with this new basis should match
the liquid return well for small values of t and it would be interesting to
know how well it does for larger values of t. It is our guess that finding
a better basis would not only improve the computational performance
of their algorithm, but also might shed light on the economic forces
driving the model.

Conclusion

This paper comes at a good time. A critical mass of policymakers and
academics seems to have been convinced by the events of the Great

Recession that the incorporation of serious heterogeneity will be essential to the creation of a new generation of macroeconomic models that will be more useful than existing benchmark models (and more credible because of their correspondence with microeconomic evidence). And, prior work in the HA literature has converged on something like a consensus about the kinds of heterogeneity that will be needed.

This paper offers tools that promise to help remove the chief barrier to the construction of such models, which is the computational bottleneck that has profoundly restricted the extent to which models including serious heterogeneity could be used to perform general-purpose macroeconomic analysis. As with any new tool, the immediate agenda is to confirm that the tool works for problems whose solution is well known, to build a bridge between what is known now and what will be possible in the future. The authors have done that already with the canonical Krusell-Smith model, and we are confident that, with some adjustment to its calibration choices, it will be possible to show that the model can be used to obtain essentially the same results that other papers in the existing literature have obtained, but several orders of magnitude faster. Once that is done, the floodgates will be open for a new generation of general-purpose macro models that will truly deserve to be called "microfounded."

Endnotes

Contact: ccarroll@jhu.edu, Department of Economics, 590 Wyman Hall, Johns Hopkins University, Baltimore, MD 21218, http://econ.jhu.edu/people/ccarroll, and National Bureau of Economic Research. Contact: edmundcrawley@gmail.com, Department of Economics, Johns Hopkins University, Baltimore, MD 21218. For acknowledgments, sources of research support, and disclosure of the authors' material financial relationships, if any, please see http://www.nber.org/chapters/c13928.ack.

1. The first author is PI on a Sloan Foundation grant funding a comprehensive effort to construct a general-purpose toolkit for heterogeneous agent macroeconomics—and other computational economics topics—(available at econ-ark.orghttp://econ-ark.org), with the aim of becoming the DYNARE for heterogeneous agents models; incorporation of the Ahn et al. tools is on the agenda for the econ-ark.org team.

2. We endorse most of the points they make about how macro can matter for inequality, but will leave them undiscussed because this is the NBER Macro Annual and not the NBER Inequality Annual.

3. A more ambitious goal would be to match the distribution of κ across households, but measuring κ at the level of individual households presents such formidable challenges that constructing a population distribution had never even been attempted until national registry data became available very recently; see Fagereng et al. (2017) for the first effort we know of.

4. Microeconomists have ignored the injunction; in his Nobel lecture, for example, and a number of other places, Heckman (2001) has repeatedly argued that measuring and accounting for such heterogeneity is perhaps the central task for microeconomics.

5. Here and henceforth, quantitative statements about "the MPC" will mean the amount of extra spending that will occur over the next year in consequence of an unanticipated "windfall" shock to income that is not expected to be reversed.

6. That model matches the data on the wealth distribution at the bottom well, so there is no need to superimpose a third element in the figure.

7. The limit of this approach would be a Dirac δ function that would cause the level of liquid assets to jump discretely; this would result in a Friedman shock, and so presumably at some sufficiently extreme point their computational method would break down.

References

Aiyagari, S. R. 1994. "Uninsured Idiosyncratic Risk and Aggregate Saving." *Quarterly Journal of Economics* 109:659–84.

Auclert, A. 2015. "Monetary Policy and the Redistribution Channel." Unpublished manuscript.

Blanchard, O. 2016. "Do DSGE Models Have a Future?" Technical Report, Petersen Institute for International Economics. https://piie.com/system/files/documents/pb16-11.pdf

Broda, C., and J. A. Parker. 2014. "The Economic Stimulus Payments of 2008 and the Aggregate Demand for Consumption." *Journal of Monetary Economics* 68:S20–36.

Campbell, J., and A. Deaton. 1989. "Why is Consumption So Smooth?" *Review of Economic Studies* 56 (3): 357–73.

Campbell, J. Y., and N. G. Mankiw. 1989. "Consumption, Income, and Interest Rates: Reinterpreting the Time-Series Evidence." In *NBER Macroeconomics Annual 1989*, ed. O. J. Blanchard and S. Fischer, 185–216. Cambridge, MA: MIT Press.

Carroll, C. D. 1992. "The Buffer-Stock Theory of Saving: Some Macroeconomic Evidence." *Brookings Papers on Economic Activity* 1992 (2): 61–156.

———. 1997. "Buffer-Stock Saving and the Life Cycle/Permanent Income Hypothesis." *Quarterly Journal of Economics*, 107 (1): 1–56.

Carroll, C. D., J. Slacalek, K. Tokuoka, and M. N. White. 2017. "The Distribution of Wealth and the Marginal Propensity to Consume." *Quantitative Economics* 8 (3): 977–1020.

Coeure, B. 2013. "The Relevance of Household-Level Data for Monetary Policy and Financial Stability Analysis." Unpublished manuscript.

Deaton, A. S. 1991. "Saving and Liquidity Constraints." *Econometrica* 59:1221–48.

———. 1992. *Understanding Consumption*. New York: Oxford University Press.

DeBacker, J., B. Heim, V. Panousi, S. Ramnath, and I. Vidangos. 2013. "Rising Inequality: Transitory or Persistent? New Evidence from a Panel of US Tax Returns." *Brookings Papers on Economic Activity* Spring:67–122.

Dynan, K. E. 2000. "Habit Formation in Consumer Preferences: Evidence from Panel Data. *American Economic Review* 90 (3): 391–406.

Fagereng, A., M. B. Holm, and G. J. Natvik. 2017. "MPC Heterogeneity and Household Balance Sheets." Unpublished manuscript.

Friedman, M. A. 1957. *A Theory of the Consumption Function*. Princeton, NJ: Princeton University Press.

———. 1963. "Windfalls, the 'Horizon,' and Related Concepts in the Permanent Income Hypothesis." In *Measurement in Economics*, ed. C. Christ, 1–28. Palo Alto, CA: Stanford University Press.

Guvenen, F., F. Karahan, S. Ozkan, and J. Song. 2015. "What do Data on Millions of US Workers Reveal about Life-Cycle Earnings Risk?" NBER Working Paper no. 20913, Cambridge, MA.

Haldane, A. 2016. "The Dappled World." Technical Report, Bank of England. http://www.bankofengland.co.uk/publications/Pages/speeches/2016/937.aspx.

Heckman, J. J. 2001. "Micro Data, Heterogeneity, and the Evaluation of Public Policy: Nobel Lecture." *Journal of Political Economy* 109 (4):673–748.

Hubbard, R. G., J. S. Skinner, and S. P. Zeldes. 1994. "The Importance of Precautionary Motives for Explaining Individual and Aggregate Saving." *Carnegie-Rochester Conference Series on Public Policy* 40:59–126.

———. 1995. "Precautionary Saving and Social Insurance." *Journal of Political Economy* 103:330–99.

Kaplan, G. 2012. "Inequality and the Life Cycle." *Quantitative Economics* 3 (3): 471–525.

Kaplan, G., B. Moll, and G. L. Violante. 2016. "Monetary Policy According to HANK." Working Paper no. 21897, Cambridge, MA.

Kaplan, G., and G. L. Violante. 2014. "A Model of the Consumption Response to Fiscal Stimulus Payments." *Econometrica* 82 (4): 1199–239.

Krueger, D., K. Mitman, and F. Perri. Forthcoming. "Macroeconomics and Heterogeneity, Including Inequality." *Handbook of Macroeconomics*.

Krusell, P., and A. A. Smith. 1998. "Income and Wealth Heterogeneity in the Macroeconomy." *Journal of Political Economy* 106 (5): 867–96.

Parker, J. A., N. S. Souleles, D. S. Johnson, and R. McClelland. 2013. "Consumer Spending and the Economic Stimulus Payments of 2008." *American Economic Review* 103 (6): 2530–53.

Reiter, M. 2009. "Solving Heterogeneous-Agent Models by Projection and Perturbation." *Journal of Economic Dynamics and Control* 33 (3): 649–65.

———. 2010. "Approximate and Almost-Exact Aggregation in Dynamic Stochastic Heterogeneous-Agent Models." Technical Report no. 258, Institute for Advanced Studies.

Rotemberg, J. J., and M. Woodford. 1997. "An Optimization-Based Econometric Model for the Evaluation of Monetary Policy." In *NBER Macroeconomics Annual 1997*, vol. 12, ed. B. S. Bernanke and J. J. Rotemberg, 297–346. Cambridge, MA: MIT Press.

Sabelhaus, J., and J. Song. 2010. "The Great Moderation in Micro Labor Earnings." *Journal of Monetary Economics* 57 (4): 391–403.

Stigler, G. J., and G. S. Becker. 1977. "De Gustibus Non Est Disputandum." *American Economic Review* 67 (2): 76–90.

Stock, J. 1991. "Confidence Intervals for the Largest Autoregressive Root in US Macroeconomic Time Series." *Journal of Monetary Economics* 28 (3): 435–59.

Summers, L. H. 2011. "Larry Summers and Martin Wolf on New Economic Thinking." Interview, *Financial Times*, April 8. http://larrysummers.com/commentary/speeches/brenton-woods-speech/.

Yellen, J. 2016. "Macroeconomic Research after the Crisis." Available at: https://www.federalreserve.gov/newsevents/speech/yellen20161014a.htm.

Zeldes, S. P. 1989. "Optimal Consumption with Stochastic Income: Deviations from Certainty Equivalence." *Quarterly Journal of Economics* 104 (2): 275–98.

Comment

Per Krusell, Institute for International Economic Studies and NBER

Introduction

The authors of the present paper have embarked on a very ambitious, in my view very important, and, I hope, very successful agenda, which is to provide a rather general toolbox for solving (and, ultimately, estimating) interesting macroeconomic models with heterogeneity. The basic challenge in solving dynamic macroeconomic models, in comparison with dynamic models from, say, the natural sciences, is that the economy's particles—our consumers and firms—are forward-looking. An economic outcome today will therefore depend on the outcome in the future, not only under fully rational expectations, but as long as there is some degree of rationality in forward-looking. If a long time horizon is considered, these economic models then amount to a high-dimensional fixed-point problem. This challenge has been faced and handled in the representative-agent macroeconomic literature, but it becomes a formidable hurdle in a heterogeneous-agent model. If the natural state variable is a distribution, say, of wealth—and hence a whole function, that is, a very high-dimensional object—then the mapping between the present and the future (in fact, all future periods) may not be feasible to solve for. However, a variety of methods have been proposed and successfully implemented recently and there is now widespread optimism that a large set of macroeconomic models with heterogeneous agents can be solved and studied. The present paper by Ahn et al. is an important contribution in this endeavor.

My overall evaluation of the Ahn et al. paper is very positive, and partly for this reason I will first take the opportunity here to reflect on the literature a little. Hopefully this will explain on a somewhat deeper level why I like this agenda so much: why it is not just "cool" to work on these rich, yet somehow tractable, models. It will also help answer some questions about the paper: Are the proposed methods needed? Do they provide a useful direction for future research? Are they general enough? and so on. In part, my text will be a discussion about methodology in a somewhat broad sense and, in part, it will discuss computational methods. I will then make some more targeted comments on the present project and paper. I will make quite a few comments on how Ahn et al. relates to my own work with Tony Smith, but I feel this should not be too heavy an imposition on the reader as Ahn et al. comments on our work in many ways.

The Meandering Macroeconomic Modeling

It is hard to define the starting point of modern macroeconomic theory— whereby "modern" refers to the use of models where the microeconomic structure is clearly spelled out, on the basis of which welfare statements, and therefore meaningful policy comparisons, can be made, and so on—but some of the very earliest and most influential papers featured both heterogeneity among economic decision makers and prominent frictions. An example is Lucas's (1972) "Expectations and the Neutrality of Money." From that perspective, are we perhaps now back where we started? The Ahn et al. paper, which is most definitely on the research frontier, does emphasize the need to analyze models with precisely these ingredients, in contrast with the representative-agent framework that has been quite dominant in macroeconomics both for analyzing long-run and short-run questions. As a matter of fact, we are not even back to where Lucas started in the sense that the majority of papers written today, not to mention the policy-oriented models used in central banks and elsewhere, still feature no heterogeneity (or at least very limited heterogeneity). Frictions, on the other hand, are probably present in most papers today. But how should we interpret the meandering path of macroeconomic research since Lucas's seminal paper?

Two key ingredients in the development of modern macroeconomics must be emphasized in this context. One is our need to understand mechanisms and the second is quantitative theory. I make this distinction in order to more clearly underline the usefulness of work along the lines of the Ahn et al. paper.

A. Mechanism Inspection

I see Lucas's paper as a mechanism inspection study: the idea was to understand the conditions under which systematic monetary policy could affect output, and he constructed a transparent counterexample to conventional wisdom. Though in some ways quite complex, this model explained the challenges of monetary policy in a rational-agent world. The logic was (and still is) impressive and the profession learned a lot from it. The examination of mechanisms often arises as a result of the perceived macroeconomic needs such as: What could possibly have explained stagflation in the 1970s or the recent Great Recession? Certainly the Great Recession has given heterogeneous-agent modeling a new push forward in some key ways that I will return to below. The need to understand mechanisms continues and an important part of the key papers in this literature precisely thus lay bare new mechanisms (e.g., there are a number of important papers on credit-market frictions of this sort). In the enterprise of examining mechanisms in macroeconomics, the representative-agent model was used a fair amount, but it was also common, and often necessary, as in Lucas's early paper, to consider heterogeneity. The reason is that there has been an increasing interest in studying various forms of market imperfections. In turn, frictions tend to generate different outcomes for different people. As I will argue below, the methods proposed by Ahn et al. have the potential to contribute greatly to our understanding of mechanisms.

B. Quantitative Theory

The second ingredient arises from our aim to understand the broad macroeconomic developments and to offer policy advice: for this we need make quantitative statements in macroeconomics. That is, we need to compare, or simply juxtapose, mechanisms: Among different mechanisms, which have quantitative bite and how do the mechanisms interact? Here I personally view Kydland and Prescott's (1982) work as pivotal in that they gave the "quantitative theory" agenda the first real push forward.[1] Up to that point, structural estimation proved challenging in a number of ways, and it is not until relatively recently that we have experienced a significant increase in formal estimation methods using nonlinear models (and nonlinear solution methods for these models). However, by insisting on a nonlinear model solution,

Kydland and Prescott's work also meant that the main framework became a representative-agent model: it was computationally feasible to study this model, but not necessarily (early on, at least) models with much heterogeneity.[2] The Kydland-Prescott project—quantitative RBC theory—generated a very large literature, especially if one includes the New Keynesian frameworks that were to be built on top of their framework, introducing pricing frictions of a variety of sorts. With heterogeneity in prices across firms, there was renewed pressure to save on state variables and, hence, the representative-consumer model almost became a must.

C.   Developments

Both these ingredients have developed fast since Lucas's work and in some ways these two approaches are beginning to have significant overlap. At this overlap, the methods proposed in the current paper can become very productive.

. . . in mechanism inspection. . .

In terms of the further developments, first, the inspection of mechanisms has expanded and visited a great number of interesting topics. Most of these studies are, like Lucas's study, entirely analytical, but an increasing number of papers examine mechanisms using numerical methods: they produce model solutions and study them in the model laboratory. The theoretical mechanism literature has also produced material for the quantitative theory-minded macroeconomists to work on, that is, to attempt to quantify and include in their models. It should be emphasized that this is often easier said than done because the hallmark of the quantitative theory approach, at least as I define it, is to introduce new theoretical modules in such a way that any new parameters are subject to quantitative discipline. That might mean that they can be estimated directly or inferred in separate studies (in the best-case scenario, just borrowed from empirical microeconomic studies). This procedure imposes a quantitative discipline on the work that has been very productive, I think, but it has often been difficult to implement for many of the theoretical mechanisms explored. One reason for this is that the frictions in focus often involve features in the microeconomic setting that are hard to quantify, such as the nature of binding constraints for households, private information, or commitment problems in private contracts.

One of the key challenges going forward is precisely to come up with ways to restrict models with heterogeneity and frictions to match observables. A very successful example here is the empirical work underlying the calibration of the first application in Ahn et al.: the study imposes as discipline to match the distribution of marginal propensities to consume as inferred from the studies by Johnson, Parker, and Souleles (2006) and later related papers. More studies of this kind now begin to emerge and they can be of great help in bringing the heterogeneity-and-frictions work into the truly quantitative realm.[3] In short, in the many studies of frictions, we have come to deeply appreciate the potential relevance of heterogeneity, both ex ante and ex post, for understanding the macroeconomy, but the key word here is "potential": whether heterogeneity/frictions in any given context is crucial or not is a quantitative issue.

The numerically based approach to studying macroeconomic theory by Ahn et al. also offers many opportunities to discover new mechanism simply by "playing around with and trying to understand" models. The idea here is simply that the model is a laboratory and that models can sometimes produce big surprises and, in fact, ultimately tell us things about the real world. When an interesting pattern is found with this approach, one would then simplify and try to focus on the key reason for the pattern and often it is possible to arrive at an entirely analytical setting this way, even though it started with a numerical method applied to a complex model. There is obviously no predictably successful path forward here along these lines, but I would nevertheless applaud and encourage work of this sort using methods like those put forth here.

. . . and in quantitative theory

The quantitative-theory approach has proceeded in different ways. A common way has been to begin by *posing a question*, then construct a model—typically based on one or more well-understood mechanisms—that can answer the question, assign parameter values (using calibration/ estimation), and then obtain a quantitative answer. This is the approach Kydland and Prescott themselves have argued most strongly for. Early examples of this approach that are relevant to the present paper are Huggett's (1993) paper examining the role of market incompleteness for the risk-free rate puzzle, and Aiyagari (1994) focusing on quantitative role for precautionary saving in aggregate capital formation: both use fundamentally nonlinear heterogeneous-agent models. With reference to the Great Recession, an increasing number of papers look at how fiscal and monetary "multipliers" might become significantly larger if heterogeneity is taken into account (and change over time in response to movements in aggregate variables as well as inequality).

Another important development within quantitative theory has been to examine the *robustness of models* to a priori reasonable extensions. A way of thinking about this approach is that the researcher incorporates more realism into a known/often used model by including additional plausibly quantitatively important features. In fact, one perspective on the heterogeneous-agents literature is that it simply asks: Are the early representative-agent models that form the core of our business-cycle toolbox sensitive to the introduction of consumer (or firm) heterogeneity? That is, do the answers to commonly asked questions change only marginally when reasonable amounts of heterogeneity are introduced? The present paper provides methods that obviously suit this approach very well. I will offer some "ideas" for work along these lines in the conclusions.

My own papers with Tony Smith on Aiyagari models with aggregate shocks (e.g., Krusell and Smith [1997, 1998], the latter of which is discussed in detail by Ahn et al.) are an example of both the robustness and the question-posing approaches. The purpose of the project was to try to provide a framework that would allow a lot of interesting questions to be asked. In particular, we addressed the price of risk/equity premium in the 1997 paper and consumption-output correlations in the 1998 paper. At the same time, these papers clearly also begin the agenda of examining robustness of the representative-agent model to what I would argue is an eminently plausible and very rich set of generalizations. The paper is also an example of how one can obtain a mechanism insight, in that we found that *approximate aggregation*—near independence of equilibrium aggregates on anything but the mean of the asset distribution as the economy experiences aggregate shocks—holds in a set of models. We learned a lot from examining the roots of approximate aggregations. The Ahn et al. paper adds another computational tool to our arsenal of heterogeneous-agent model solvers, and I think that it can ultimately generate many new insights about how our models work and, by extension, how our economies work.

The Methods Offered in This Paper

Turning specifically to what the present paper adds, its aim is clearly to provide fast and accurate methods for solving heterogeneous-agent macro models with aggregate shocks (suitable particularly for business-cycle analysis). It analyzes two example economies, mostly for illustration, and although I find them interesting in their own right I will not comment on them more than marginally. Relative to the earlier literature on model solving, the key components to be emphasized here are that the authors use (a) continuous time, (b) linearization of "aggregate objects" (laws of motion for distribution, value function, etc.), and (c) reduction techniques for describing the high-dimensional objects approximated in an efficient way.

Continuous time appears to offer some improvements in computation speed, as argued in Achdou et al. (2015), in part at least because the optimization problem is made simpler—this insight is useful particularly for the solution of the stationary equilibrium. My main worry about continuous-time methods is that I find them a little less intuitive for teaching, especially when they involve stochastics. For advanced students and researchers, this difficulty should not be a problem, but for making methods broadly available I still feel that discrete time offers much easier intuition. My own recommendation for macroeconomics students would be initial learning (of both theory and numerical methods) based on discrete time and then investments in continuous-time theory and numerical methods later on.

Linearization is obviously very convenient whenever applicable. The linearization approach has been pursued before but, as far as I am aware, the first fully and successfully implemented linearization-based model for solving heterogeneous-agent models was provided by Michael Reiter (2009, 2010).[4] Reiter's method, like the present one, proceeds in two main steps: (1) solve for the stationary equilibrium with nonlinear methods and obtain, in particular, agents' nonlinear decision rules; and (2) describe the distribution and decision rules by a finite set of parameters and then linearize the model with respect to these parameters. For example, in Reiter's model, one can imagine a decision rule for saving as a function of cash on hand; this function would typically have a kink below which the borrowing constraint binds. This function is thus fully nonlinear and the question is then how this function moves over time in response to aggregate shocks (and in response to movements in a set of aggregate variables, more generally). Thus, we can imagine a parametric description of the nonlinear equation—for example, with one parameter equal to the wealth level at which the borrowing constraint just binds and a number of other parameters fitting a spline to the rest of the function—and then the equilibrium conditions can be used to provide a linearization of these parameters with respect to the aggregate moments (which will include moments of the joint distribution of wealth and income). Conceptually, the method is rather straightforward and the challenge is how to implement it. For example, the continuous-time approach makes it more convenient to work with value functions than with decision rules. In addition, Ahn et al. use an arguably better way of parameterizing the distribution than does Reiter.

One challenge in the implementation is that the set of parameters needed to describe the linear system is large, and this is where the reduction techniques the authors offer are used. Here, they borrow from Antoulas (2005) and they discuss in great detail in the paper how reduction is applied to distributions as well as value functions. The approach here is to rely on an automatized, and efficient, method. The resulting reduction is therefore not necessarily immediately suggestive of intuition. On the one hand, an intuition-based approach would be easier to grasp. What Tony and I did here was to describe the distribution with a set of moments, perhaps augmented with a statistic indicating the fraction of agents for whom the borrowing constraint binds; here, there is clear intuition backing up why the first moment will matter and at least some intuition for the higher orders. On the other hand, our intuition often misses important mechanisms, and it may be that an automatized procedure can indicate a key mechanism that needs to be "discovered"; here, I think, the reduction method Ahn and colleagues use offers opportunities for discovery. That is, it might be productive in any given application—and they offer two in this paper—to try to understand the particular result of the reduction. I think the authors could have worked more on this. It would be great with an example where we learn about the deep mechanisms of the model from scrutinizing the reduction results.

The speed and accuracy are discussed in some detail in the paper. In speed, linearization makes great strides forward. In terms of accuracy, a basic challenge, of course is that it is hard to assess without access to the exact solution of the model. The paper focuses on Den Haan's (2010) metric, which is a version of one of the measures Tony and I used. In our work, the key aim was to provide a robust algorithm and to document approximate aggregation for the set of models we examined there. In the present paper, the aim is also to show how cases where approximate aggregation does not hold can be solved.

A.   What the Ahn et al. Method Can and Cannot (Yet?) Do

The authors discuss in some detail what their linearization technique cannot handle. First, because it features certainty equivalence, it cannot address how higher moments of the aggregate shocks influence the economy: by definition, they do not influence the economy (a feature of all linearization techniques). This means, for example, that asset-price analysis is not possible (for assets contingent on an aggregate, stochastic state) and that welfare-cost-of-cycles calculations cannot be performed. An extension of the method to a second-order approximation is briefly discussed, but it is clearly only in the planning stages.[5] In Krusell and Smith (1997), we successfully used our nonlinear method and approximate aggregation to solve a portfolio-choice model with endogenous asset prices; this computational approach can, in principle, be readily applied to asset-pricing applications. In Krusell et al. (2009), we studied the welfare costs of business cycles in an Aiyagari model, also using a setting with approximate aggregation. When approximate aggregation fails one needs to find ways of summarizing what other distributional statistics matter for prices. Here I think a combined Ahn et al. and Krusell and Smith (1997, 1998) approach offers some promise in that the reduction technique can yield insights into how to restrict the set of endogenous aggregate moments, and then the nonlinear Krusell and Smith (1997) model solution can be used to compute the equilibrium.

Second, the Ahn et al. method does not allow aggregate nonlinearities to be well captured. For example, positive and negative shocks may have different effects on the economy if the economic model is sufficiently nonlinear. Again, higher-order approximations as an extension to the current approach are possible to develop in principle, but they will likely not be available any time soon. It is an open question how, for example, New Keynesian settings with zero-lower-bound regions can be addressed with Ahn et al. As a related aside, it would have been interesting to have seen the Ahn et al. approach applied to a Calvo-based price stickiness model where the linearization is produced around a steady state with positive inflation, and hence there is a distribution of firms with different prices.

B.   Other Challenges

My 1998 paper with Tony has done very well in terms of impact and citations—I think I speak for the two of us when I say that we are more than happy—but it may nevertheless be useful to mention some challenges we have experienced, as they may apply to the Ahn et al. paper as well.

First and foremost, many references to Krusell and Smith (1998) use the paper as a red flag: we need to avoid heterogeneous-agent computation since it is so challenging. As such, the typical reference would read something like "in this paper we simplify to avoid the mess of truly heterogeneous agents; for a mess, see Krusell and Smith (1998)." I fear that the Ahn et al. paper, despite its ambition to produce a "canned" and, hence, easy-to-use method, might face the same difficulty. To understand the Ahn et al. methods in detail is much more challenging than to understand our method—they require, and use, quite a bit more advanced mathematics—and hence all of those researchers would feel a need to understand the methods needed to go through significant investments before using Ahn et al.'s method.

Here, although I just emphasized that Ahn et al. is in some ways a more challenging method, my answer to whether we should avoid challenging modeling is a resounding "No." I just do not think that our profession can afford laziness or rely on the belief that mere elegant modeling can suffice. By the arguments I give above, quantitative theory is an indispensable part of our knowledge base and it often requires numerical methods. As economic researchers, we cannot hope to produce the same exactness in our models as the natural scientists often can in their modeling, but to simply abstract from factors that are arguably important and could be taken into account does not appear to be defensible. Still, this remains an ongoing battle and I can only hope that Ahn et al.'s work will help push our profession in the right direction!

A number of papers have also been produced in order to show how the Krusell and Smith (1998) method are inadequate/can be improved upon, typically because of a hunch that more than the first moment is necessary in the approximation. So far, the finding in this respect has been that it is hard to find reasonably calibrated model examples where approximate aggregation does not apply. Of course there are exceptions, and the first application in Ahn et al. is a solid and very interesting example of this kind. In the wealthy hand-to-mouth models, the borrowing constraint binds, or is close to binding, not just for the very poorest (who have little wealth and hence, at least, are not crucial for the determination of aggregate saving) but for a very large part of the population. Hence, there can be significant dispersion in the marginal propensities to save among people.[6] So when approximate aggregation does not hold, how difficult is the model-solving challenge? Papers with the aim of finding cases where approximate aggregation does not hold also argue that, under these circumstances, other methods than the one proposed in Krusell and Smith (1998) are needed. This is not at all clear: the method we proposed was rather general. Higher moments can be readily included in (or are really a part of) our algorithm toward better and better accuracy, and it would be interesting to see comparisons between using our approach here and the given proposed alternative.[7]

In the case of the present paper, it appears in the wealthy hand-to-mouth case that our method would not do well because the reduction outcome produces something very far from just the mean capital holdings. At the same time, a comparison between Ahn et al. and our algorithm based on adding more moments would have been interesting to see explicitly in the paper. One could add judiciously chosen other distributional statistics here to capture as well as possible the heterogeneity in marginal propensities. Another way to improve accuracy that the paper could have commented on or compared to uses the idea to expand the set of statistics to include past periods' endogenous variables, such as prices or aggregate quantities; this approach was followed by Storesletten, Telmer, and Yaron (2007). Unless the distribution moves drastically from period to period, such a method might fare very well, even in the hand-to-mouth case.

Third, there has been a presumption in the literature that the distribution does not matter in the determination of aggregates, that is, that if one is only interested in predicting, or understanding aggregate variables, heterogeneous-agent models are not helpful (Ahn and colleagues discuss this issue briefly). Already in Krusell and Smith (1997, 1998) we made clear that this is not correct. For example, in the 1998 paper we show that a model with discount-factor heterogeneity gives consumption-output dynamics that are very different from those of the corresponding representative-agent model; rather, the dynamics are very similar to the Campbell-Mankiw 1989 model where a fraction of the agents is hand-to-mouth and the remainder "standard" permanent-income consumers. Fortunately, I think the Ahn et al. paper will not have to face this challenge since there appears to be a broad realization in the literature now that the heterogeneous-agent model has much to add. In particular, models where many agents are significantly affected by borrowing constraints display a great variety of marginal propensities to consume and work, and then the distribution of income and wealth can matter greatly and lead to very different aggregate dynamics.

Such models have, in particular, been examined from the perspective of understanding the Great Recession. In addition, the responses to policy in such models can be very different (see, for the example of fiscal multipliers, Brinca et al. [2015]).

C. Are Canned Packages Useful?

A number of canned packages have been produced and successfully applied in the business-cycle literature. Will the Ahn et al. package be the equivalent of Dynare or the Uhlig Toolkit for heterogeneous-agent macro? That would be great, but I can see some challenges here too. One reason why Tony and I did not provide an easy-to-use package building on our methods (relying on Matlab, not FORTRAN) is that we perceived the heterogeneous-agent literature as being at its early stages and not yet ripe for "mass creation." But perhaps it is now? As I have argued above, I think having more people learn the methods and extend the models will also be a learning opportunity: we will expand the understanding of these models further.

I am also of the belief that some of the most interesting model developments benefit greatly from, and may even sometimes necessitate, truly tailor-made numerical methods. That is, some analytical insights may be needed to simplify computation. Perhaps this belief is based on the fact that I am not interested in computational methods per se, but rather in models and their relation to reality: computational methods are simply a means to an end, and sometimes this end is best attained with appropriately designed methods that are not of general value and therefore not worth canning.

Going Forward

Let me finally and very briefly discuss a few interesting avenues for future research on heterogeneous-agent research. I find models of explicit information asymmetries and commitment problems—and therefrom induced constraints on market trades—very promising, but I will refrain from commenting on those here since the Ahn et al. approach is perhaps not directly applicable to that class (though I am sure it can be). Rather, I will comment on some forms of heterogeneity and frictions that seem useful to study more carefully in the short run.

One observation is that the literature so far has entertained very limited kinds of heterogeneity. The focal case has been to assume identical preferences among agents that belong to the Gorman class, so that aggregation would be exact under complete markets, and then incomplete markets with respect to stochastic productivity/employment outcomes. There are two obvious ways to depart from this case. One is to consider preferences that are not of the Gorman form. One of the most commonly used utility function over consumption and leisure in the business-cycle literature is $u(c, l) = \log c - \psi h^{[1+(1/\theta)]} / [1 + (1 / \theta)]$. This function is consistent with balanced growth but is not in the Gorman class, and in an economy where all agents have such preferences wealth inequality would influence aggregates even under complete markets: marginal propensities to work and consume out of wealth would differ across people. Another way to depart from the standard case is to allow outright preference heterogeneity. As for this case, many researchers seem reluctant to consider discount-factor heterogeneity, but my view is that heterogeneity should be the rule rather than the exception, not just for productivity but also for preferences, including the consumption-leisure preferences. For examples, in recent work, we look at a complete-markets model as a first step toward understanding labor supply decisions across people, and here we both consider non-Gorman preferences a number of dimensions of heterogeneity captured through differences in the effort cost of working (a parameter in the utility function; see Boppart, Krusell, and Olsson [2017]). Heterogeneity in risk aversion is another avenue barely considered in the literature (Guvenen's [2006] paper is an early exception). When it comes to housing and, more generally, durable-goods preferences—as many recent papers consider these choices—it is very natural to take the view that preferences are in the non-Gorman class and that there is additional heterogeneity. In these cases, even under complete markets, our understanding of how such economies behave is quite limited and, in my view, limiting from the perspective of analyzing policy.

The Ahn et al. paper also asks, in its title, when macro matters for inequality. This is another interesting topic that is only beginning to attract attention. The paper's second application is an interesting avenue toward a deeper understanding of income inequality and, more generally, the data Piketty (2014) and related papers unveil scream for explanations. Hubmer, Krusell, and Smith (2017) look at a straightforward application of the Aiyagari setting applied to the US context and its recorded macroeconomic developments (in particular, policy changes) to see how much of the movements in wealth inequality can be accounted for. That paper abstracts from aggregate uncertainty. Looking at how inequality evolves over the business cycle (and comparing models from this perspective) appears feasible with the new wealth of data.

A related, and in my view not yet sufficiently explored, issue is whether there are useful models "in between" the representative-agent setting and the full heterogeneous-agent models considered by Ahn et al. The Campbell and Mankiw paper is a case in point: some analytical insights can be gained from looking at such a setting and the multiple discount factor model in Krusell and Smith (1998) almost generates this model in reduced form. Similarly, capitalist-worker models could be found to behave quite similarly to models with much richer heterogeneity.[8] The nice thing about two-agent models is that they are readily analyzable using Dynare and thus immediately accessible to a very broad set of applied researchers.

As the theme of his dinner speech at the conference, Olivier Blanchard asked about what frictions are key for business-cycle modeling. This is a million-dollar question, and the heterogeneous-agent literature discussed here has so far only considered a few. Olivier Blanchard proposed that (limited versions of) bounded rationality needed to be explored, and I generally concur, though it seems far too early to pinpoint which forms of bounds on rationality are most promising. An example of a form of bounded rationality is proposed recently in Rozsypal and Schlafmann (2017), who argue based on data from the Michigan survey that individuals' forecasts of their own future income feature a statistically and economically significant "persistence bias," that is, temporary shocks are expected to last longer than they actually last. Rozsypal and Schlafmann then show that it is straightforward to incorporate this feature into an Aiyagari-style model and that this model's aggregate behavior changes under these alternative assumptions. With carefully modeled and empirically grounded departures from rationality, our models' implications may change importantly. Interestingly in this context, our motivation for formulating the model in Krusell and Smith (1998) was in fact the notion that forecasts did not have to be literally perfect to be taken seriously in modeling the world, and I very much maintain this view.

Finally, there are indications that frictions and heterogeneity often interact in crucial ways. Already in our review paper in the 2006 Econometric Society volume, Tony Smith and I pointed to this phenomenon and provided some two-period examples. I think the subsequent literature has underscored this point and that the really promising paths forward in this literature involve interaction between frictions and heterogeneity.

Conclusions

Lucas was probably ahead of his time by more than economists realized when he wrote his 1972 paper: his model featured several of the components that are the most intensively researched today. Still, my view is that macroeconomic research has come a long way the 45 years that have passed since Lucas's paper, especially in its quantitative focus. The paper by Ahn et al. is an impressive testament to this statement, and I really hope that it will become a weapon of mass creation.

Endnotes

For acknowledgments, sources of research support, and disclosure of the author's material financial relationships, if any, please see http://www.nber.org/chapters/c13929.ack.
1. The push for quantitative theory, in my view, was at least as important for macroeconomics as the RBC model in itself.
2. In addition, Gorman aggregation holds in many of the frameworks they studied, so at least from the perspective of aggregation across wealth levels of different consumers, nothing was lost from using the representative-agent construct.
3. See, for example, Cesarini et al. (2016) and Fagereng et al. (2016).
4. Early approaches were provided by, among others, Jeff Campbell, Hess Chung (2007), Stefan Krieger (1999), and Marcelo Veracierto; a current parallel approach can be found in David Childers's (2017) job-market paper.
5. One might need more than a second-order approximation to study cases with low-probability disaster shocks.
6. It would be interesting to see a similar model applied toward understanding the equity premium.
7. Our general algorithm is described in detail in Krusell and Smith (1998) and also implemented with higher moments there.
8. For a hunch in this direction in the context of a New Keynesian model, see Broer et al. (2017).

References

Boppart, T., P. Krusell, and J. Olsson. 2017. "Labor Supply in the Long Run: Who Will Work?" Working paper.
Brinca, P., H. Holter, P. Krusell, and L. Malafry. 2015. "Fiscal Multipliers in the 21st Century." *Journal of Monetary Economics* 77:53–69.
Broer, T., N.-J. Harbo Hansen, P. Krusell, and E. Öberg. 2017. "The New Keynesian Transmission Mechanism: A Heterogeneous-Agent Perspective." CEPR Discussion Paper no. 11382, Centre for Economic Policy Research.
Cesarini, D., E. Lindqvist, M. Notowidigdo, and R. Östling. 2016. "The Effect of Wealth on Individual and Household Labor Supply: Evidence from Swedish Lotteries." Working paper.
Childers, D. 2017. "On the Solution and Application of Rational Expectations Models with Function Valued States." Working paper.
Chung, H. 2007. "Perturbation Methods for Heterogeneous Agent DSGE Models." Working paper.

Fagereng, A., M. B. Holm, and G. J. Natvik. 2016. "MPC Heterogeneity and Household Balance Sheets." Discussion Paper, Statistics Norway.

Guvenen, F. 2006. "Reconciling Conflicting Evidence on the Elasticity of Intertemporal Substitution: A Macroeconomic Perspective." *Journal of Monetary Economics* 53 (7): 1451–72.

Hubmer, J., P. Krusell, and A. Smith, Jr. 2017. "The Historical Evolution of the Wealth Distribution: A Quantitative-Theoretic Investigation." Working paper.

Huggett, M. 1993. "The Risk-Free Rate in Heterogeneous-Agent Incomplete-Insurance Economies." *Journal of Economic Dynamics and Control* 17 (5): 953–69.

Krieger, S. 1999. "Bankruptcy Costs, Financial Constraints and the Business Cycle." Working paper.

Krusell, P., T. Mukoyama, A. Sahin, and A. Smith, Jr. 2009. "Revisiting the Welfare Effects of Eliminating Business Cycles." *Review of Economic Dynamics* 12 (3): 393–402.

Krusell, P., and A. Smith, Jr. 1997. "Income and Wealth Heterogeneity, Portfolio Choice, and Equilibrium Asset Returns." *Macroeconomic Dynamics* 1 (2): 387–422.

———. 1998. "Income and Wealth Heterogeneity in the Macroeconomy." *Journal of Political Economy* 106 (5): 867–96.

Kydland, F., and E. Prescott. 1982. "Time to Build and Aggregate Fluctuations." *Econometrica* 1345–70.

Lucas, Robert E. 1972. "Expectations and the Neutrality of Money." *Journal of Economic Theory* 4 (2): 103–24.

Piketty, T. 2014. *Capital in the 21st Century*. Cambridge, MA: Harvard University Press.

Reiter, M., 2009. "Solving heterogeneous-agent models by projection and perturbation." *Journal of Economic Dynamics and Control* 33 (3), 649–665 .

Reiter, M., 2010. "Approximate and almost-exact aggregation in dynamic stochastic heterogeneous-agent models." IHS WP 259.

Rozsypal, F., and K. Schlafmann. 2017. "Overpersistence Bias in Individual Income Expectations and its Aggregate Implications." Working paper.

Storesletten, K., C. Telmer, and A. Yaron. 2007. "Asset Pricing with Idiosyncratic Risk and Overlapping Generations." *Review of Economic Dynamics* 10 (4): 519–48.

Discussion

Given the methodological focus of the paper, the ensuing discussion was at times fairly technical. Lars Hansen asked the authors whether the paper's methodology can accommodate nonlinear models; for example, models with nonlinearity at the aggregate level such as He and Krishnamurthy (2013) and Brunnermier and Sannikov (2016). Later, Robert Hall followed up on Hansen's question stating that the two big challenges in macroeconomics are heterogeneity and asset pricing. He argued that for a model to match asset prices, it would need to be highly nonlinear so that states that occur with low probability and are associated with high marginal utility of consumption would affect asset prices. The authors responded that while their model can accommodate some degree of nonlinearity using higher-order approximations, their method does not extend to highly nonlinear models.

Gianluca Violante asked what key variables households in the model use to predict future prices. Specifically, he wondered whether including the measure of wealthy hand-to-mouth households, in addition to the aggregate level of capital, as a predictor of future prices improves the accuracy of prediction significantly. The authors answered that their benchmark model requires 300 state variables to properly predict future prices. They indicated that when limiting the number of state variables to 200 the impulse response functions change significantly, hinting that the inclusion of the measure of wealthy hand-to-mouth households on its own would not help in accurately predicting future prices. They did, however, point out that many of the 300 state variables used to predict future prices are related to regions in the distribution capturing wealthy liquidity-constrained agents.

Jon Steinsson noted that the current bottleneck in solving heterogeneous-agent models with aggregate fluctuations is keeping track of enough state variables so that households can accurately predict future prices. As the authors' methodology can accommodate a much larger number of state variables than the existing literature, Steinsson asked what is the remaining bottleneck in solving these types of models. The authors responded that their methodology requires linearization at the aggregate level, and that the reduction techniques they take advantage of would not work when the number of prices in the economy is arbitrarily large.

Ricardo Reis expressed enthusiasm for the authors' research agenda. Studying quantitative models with heterogeneous agents extends the scope of data that can be matched to macroeconomic models, as it allows estimating models not only using aggregate variables but also taking advantage of microdata now abundantly available. Reis had three comments regarding the authors' methodology. First, he shared his concern about the state-reduction techniques used, arguing that he had personally found such techniques to be fast, yet not robust. Second, he asked whether the authors' algorithm is also able to calculate the likelihood function quickly enough to conduct inference. The algorithm quickly computes impulse responses by enlarging the state space to keep track of distributions, but to build the likelihood would then usually require using the Kalman smoother, which can be painfully slow with a state vector with hundreds of variables. Finally, he noted that in the standard New Keynesian model a second-order approximation is needed to study welfare implications, as explained in Rotemberg and Woodford (1997). Reis therefore wondered whether the authors can approximate the model to a second order to analyze welfare.

The authors first said they believe the most value added of their paper is in the reduction techniques used, and that they are confident the techniques they currently take advantage of are robust. They have said they are aware of the challenges of estimating the model using likelihood techniques and are currently thinking about how to deal with those issues. Regarding welfare, the authors responded that their model is not fully linear, as the solution to the individual agents' problem is global. They believe most of the welfare implications concern redistribution across agents within the economy, which their model fully captures. In addition, they can use second-order approximations to capture additional welfare consequences at the aggregate level.

Following Reis's comments, Alisdair McKay asked the authors when their methods are applicable. He said that he had tried their methodology in a model featuring uncertainty shocks, but that it had not worked.

He noted that while we have a good understanding of under what conditions linearization works well in a representative agent framework, we do not know in which cases the linear approximation is accurate when the model features heterogeneous agents. He suggested adding a measure to the toolbox that will report the error due to the linear approximation. The authors agreed that would be a useful tool and would consider adding it to their toolbox.

Regarding welfare implications, Larry Christiano pointed out that monetary policy is at its core highly redistributive. A decrease in interest rates results in higher wages for workers, which induce them to work harder, and lower rents for capital owners. For that reason, there is potential for the distribution to play an important role in the monetary transmission mechanism.

John Cochrane stated that while heterogeneous agent models are obviously important for studying inequality, he expressed his doubts about the importance of the distribution of agents in the economy for the laws of motion of aggregate variables. In his view, he explained, the defining theme of macroeconomics is the study of aggregates, and it is not clear that distributional state variables are needed to understand the stochastic processes of aggregates. In response to Cochrane, Andrew Caplin said he intuitively believes in findings that are micro founded. He suggested estimating two models on a subsample of historical data, a representative-agent model estimated using only aggregate variables and the authors' model estimated using both aggregate variables and the microdata. He said that by comparing out-of-sample predictions of the two models for aggregate variables, the authors can hopefully show that their model fits the data better.

The authors responded by affirming their belief that modeling heterogeneous agents is important for studying distribution objects such as inequality, which they believe is an important topic in macroeconomics in its own right. They further disagreed with Cochrane's suggestion that distributional considerations may not be important for aggregate dynamics. The authors do think the distribution of agents matters for the behavior of aggregate variables. In response to Caplin's comment, the authors said they do not think such exercise would be insightful as it would simply be a test of which model is better at forecasting. They said that their model is not intended for forecasting aggregate variables, but rather for understanding how the distribution of agents is affected and affects macroeconomic dynamics in the presence of aggregate shocks. Jonathan Parker added that by simply doing a forecasting exercise using aggregate variables only, one might miss macroeconomic dynamics that result from the decisions of the different agents in the economy. This misspecification may lead to wrong conclusions regarding the macroeconomic effects of different policies. Parker also raised the point that if a model is too complex it becomes a black box.

In addition to his previous comment, Cochrane indicated his satisfaction with the authors' model as a means to illustrate their methodological contribution. He advocated putting less emphasis on the resolution of the correlation puzzle between consumption and income. He argued this correlation may be spurious, due to the way the BLS collects consumption data. Even if this correlation is positive, he continued, Campbell and Mankiw (1989) have shown how introducing agents who follow a rule-of-thumb for their consumption decision can reconcile this fact. Instead, he suggested the authors should frame their results as microfoundations for rule-of-thumb agents, and not as a resolution to the puzzle. The authors said that the main goal of their paper is indeed not to obtain the positive correlation between consumption and income, but rather to provide new methodology that allows us to study models that were not computationally feasible to solve in the past.

2

Michelson-Morley, Fisher, and Occam: The Radical Implications of Stable Quiet Inflation at the Zero Bound

John H. Cochrane, *Stanford University and NBER*

I. Summary and Overview

For nearly a decade in the United States, the United Kingdom, and Europe, and three decades in Japan, short-term interest rates have been stuck near zero. In the last decade, central banks also embarked on immense open-market operations. US quantitative easing (QE) raised bank reserves from $10 billion on the eve of the crisis in August 2008 to $2,759 billion in August 2014.

The economy's response to this important experiment in monetary policy has been silence. Inflation is stable, and if anything, less volatile than before. There is no visually apparent difference in macroeconomic dynamics in the near-zero-rate, large-reserves state than before.

Existing theories of inflation make sharp predictions about this circumstance: Old Keynesian models, characterized by adaptive expectations, and in use throughout the policy world, predict that inflation is unstable when interest rates do not respond adequately to inflation, ($\phi < 1$ in $i_t = \phi\pi_t$) and so they predict a deflation spiral at the zero bound. It did not happen. Much monetarist thought, $MV = PY$ with V "stable" in the long run, predicts that a massive increase in reserves must lead to galloping inflation. It did not happen.

New Keynesian models, featuring rational expectations, predict that inflation is stable at the zero bound, and more generally under passive policy. Unless one adds frictions, those models also predict that quantitative easing operations are irrelevant. The observed inflation stability is thus a big feather in the New Keynesian cap. But standard New Keynesian models predict that inflation becomes indeterminate when interest rates do not or cannot move in response to inflation. These models have multiple self-confirming equilibria and can jump from one to the other equilibrium. Therefore, New Keynesian models predict greater inflation and output volatility at the zero bound. These models also predict a menagerie of policy paradoxes: productivity improvements are bad, promises further in the future have larger effects today, and reducing price stickiness makes matters worse, without limit.

This is a Michelson-Morley[1] moment for monetary policy. We observe a decisive experiment, in which previously hard-to-distinguish theories clearly predict large outcomes. That experiment yields a null result, which invalidates those theories.

Now, any theory, especially in economics, invites rescue by epicycles. Perhaps inflation really is unstable, but artful quantitative easing just offset the deflation vortex. Or perhaps wages are much "stickier" than we thought, or money is taking a long time to leak from reserves to broader aggregates, so we just need to wait a bit more for unstable inflation to show itself. Perhaps a peg really does lead to indeterminacy and sunspots, but expectations about active ($\phi > 1$) monetary policy in the far future takes the place of current Taylor-rule responses to select equilibria. Perhaps we have experienced the proverbial seven years of bad luck, and Japan twenty, so that expectations always featured a quick escape from stuck interest rates. Perhaps the Earth drags the ether along with it.

Occam responds: perhaps. Or, perhaps one should take seriously the simplest answer: perhaps inflation can be stable and determinate under passive monetary policy, including an interest rate peg, and with arbitrarily large interest-bearing reserves. Classic contrary doctrines were simply wrong.

We are not left, as Michelson and Morley were, with a puzzle—a set of facts that existing theories cannot account for. Adding the fiscal theory of the price level to the standard rational-expectations framework, including New Keynesian price stickiness, we obtain a simple economic model in which inflation can be stable and determinate under passive policy, zero bound, or even a peg, and despite arbitrary quantitative easing. It predicts no spiral, and it is consistent with no additional volatility at the zero bound. The model also has a smooth frictionless limit, and resolves New Keynesian policy paradoxes.

What does this experience, and theoretical interpretation, imply about monetary policy going forward?

First, if inflation is stable at the zero bound, and by extension under an interest rate peg, then it follows that were the central bank to raise interest rates and leave them there, without fiscal shocks, then inflation must eventually *rise*. This reversal of the usual sign of monetary policy has become known as the "neo-Fisherian" hypothesis.

Stability and this form of long-run neutrality are linked, which merits treating them together. If $i_t = r_t + E_t\pi_{t+1}$ is a stable steady state, meaning that once r_t, unaffected by inflation in the long run, settles down, an interest rate peg i will draw inflation π toward it, then raising i and keeping it there must eventually raise π (as long as fiscal policy can and does support the value of government debt, whether "actively" or "passively"). Whether one can accept the long-run neutrality helps to digest stability. Whether the data speak loudly enough on stability illuminates long-run neutrality.

Stable models have this form of long-run neutrality. Both the standard New Keynesian model and its extension with fiscal theory are stable, and in both cases a prolonged interest rate rise raises inflation. The models differ only on determinacy, equilibrium selection, and hence the immediate response to shocks and their predictions for volatility at the zero bound.

A long-run positive sign is entwined with the standard New Keynesian equilibrium-selection scheme as well. In the standard New Keynesian model, when the Federal Reserve (Fed) reacts ($\phi > 1$) by raising interest rates more than one-for-one with inflation, this reaction *raises* subsequent inflation. Inflation then spirals off to infinity, unless the economy jumps to one specific saddle-path equilibrium. This mechanism requires that persistently higher interest rates raise inflation. If persistently higher interest rates eventually lowered inflation, then the path with initially higher inflation would not be ruled out, and the system would remain indeterminate, with multiple stable equilibria.

In sum, stability implies long-run neutrality, and both flavors of the New Keynesian model have stability and long-run neutrality.

However, higher interest rates might still *temporarily* lower inflation before eventually raising inflation. I investigate what minimal set of ingredients it takes to produce a negative short-run impact of interest rates on inflation.

This quest has a larger goal. We do not have a simple economic baseline model that produces a negative response of inflation to a rise in interest rates in our world of interest rate targets and abundant excess reserves. If there is a short-run negative relationship, what is its basic economic nature?

The natural starting place in this quest is the simple frictionless Fisherian model, $i_t = r + E_t\pi_{t+1}$. A rise in interest rates i produces an immediate and permanent rise in expected inflation. In the search for a temporary negative sign, I add to this basic frictionless model New Keynesian pricing frictions, backward-looking Phillips curves, and monetary frictions. These ingredients robustly fail to produce the short-run negative sign. Even the standard active money ($\phi > 1$) New Keynesian solutions are Fisherian. You cannot truthfully explain, say, to an undergraduate or policymaker, that higher interest rates produce lower inflation because prices are sticky, or because lower money supply drives up rates and down prices, and our fancy models build on this basic intuition.

One fiscal-theory variation can robustly and simply produce the desired temporary negative sign. If we add long-term debt, then a rise in interest rates can produce a temporary inflation decline. Higher nominal rates lower the nominal present value of long-term debt; absent any change in expected surpluses, the price level must fall to restore the real present value of the debt. That works, but it is a rather dramatically novel mechanism relative to all standard economic stories and policy discussions. It also remains long-run Fisherian. Protracted interest rate rises eventually raise, not lower, inflation. It cannot give the traditional account of the 1980s.

We are left with a logical conundrum: either (a) the world really is Fisherian, higher interest rates raise inflation in both short and long run; (b) more complex ingredients, including frictions or irrationalities, are *necessary* as well as sufficient to deliver the negative sign, so this hallowed belief relies on those complex ingredients; or (c) the negative sign ultimately relies on the fiscal theory story involving long-term debt—and has nothing to do with any of the mechanisms commonly alluded for it.

The first view is not as crazy as it seems. The vector autoregression (VAR) evidence for the traditional sign, reviewed below, is weak. Perhaps the persistent "price puzzle" was trying to tell us something for all these decades. Correlations are of little use, as interest rates and inflation move closely together under either theoretical view, at least away from the zero bound. The second view accepts this paper's charge that there is no alternative *simple economic* model behind a negative sign, so that additional complications or frictions are *necessary* to produce it. Either the second or third view rather deeply changes the nature of monetary policy economics.

The second set of policy issues: Is it important for central banks to promptly raise nominal rates and reduce the size of their balance sheets?

Should central banks return to rationing non-interest-bearing reserves, and conducting interest rate policy by conventional open-market operations? Is it important to swiftly return to active $\phi > 1$ policy rules?

The experience of stable inflation at near-zero interest rates, and this theoretical interpretation, says that we *can* instead live the Friedman optimal quantity of money forever—a large quantity of interest-bearing reserves, low or zero interest rates, with corresponding low inflation or even slight deflation.

Whether we *should* do so requires listing (here) and quantifying (eventually) trade-offs. A steady nominal rate means that variations in the real rate will be, but also must be, accompanied by inverse variations in inflation, which in a sticky-price context can cause output variation. If the Fed can diagnose "natural" real-rate variation, then moving the nominal rate can stabilize inflation. Many arguments for more activist policy, such as offsetting shocks, remain valid. The argument that without activism inflation will spiral off or become indeterminate is denied, but that is not the only argument for activism. Actual and optimal interest rate policy may not end up looking that different, rising in booms and with inflation, and falling in bad times, as natural real interest rates plausibly have that pattern.

On the other hand, stability and determinacy open additional possibilities. For example, the Fed could simply target the spread between indexed and nonindexed bonds, and let the level of interest rates vary arbitrarily to market forces. Expected inflation and, with stable fiscal policy, actual inflation will follow.

I address a wide range of common fiscal-theory objections. Among others: How can the fiscal theory be consistent with low inflation, given huge debts and ongoing deficits? Fortunately, the fiscal theory does not predict a tight linkage between current debts, deficits, and inflation. Discount rates matter as well, and discount rates for government debt are very low. What about other pegs, which did fall apart? Answer: fiscal policy fell apart.

That last observation leads to a final warning. My careful hedging, that an interest rate peg *can* be stable, refers to the necessary fiscal foundations. If fiscal foundations evaporate, that theory warns, and harsh experience reminds us, so can our benign moment of subdued and quiet inflation. Contrariwise, lowering inflation in countries that are experiencing high inflation, along with fiscal and credibility problems, is not a simple matter of lowering interest rates. Without a commitment to the duration of low rates, and without solving the underlying fiscal problems, that strategy will blow up again as it has often in the past.

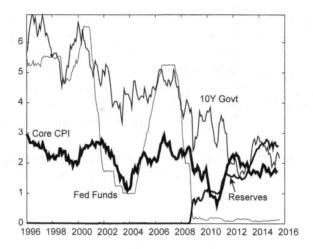

Fig. 1. Recent US experience

Note: Core CPI (percent change from a year earlier), federal funds rate (percent), total reserves (trillions), and 10 year Treasury rate (percent).

II. Michelson-Morley

The first part of this paper documents the facts of stable and quiet (opposite of volatile) inflation at the zero bound, the predictions of standard models that inflation should be unstable or volatile at the zero bound, and how the New Keynesian plus fiscal theory model is consistent with stability and quiet.

A. Nothing Happened

Figure 1 presents the last 20 years of interest rates, inflation, and reserves in the United States.

The federal funds rate follows its familiar cyclical pattern, until it hits essentially zero in 2008 and stays there. In 2008–2009, the severity of the recession and low inflation required sharply negative interest rates, in most observers' eyes and in most specifications of a Taylor rule. The "zero bound" was binding. If you see data only up to the bottom of inflation in late 2010, and if you view inflation as unstable under passive monetary policy, fear of a "deflation spiral" is natural and justified.

But the spiral never happened. Despite interest rates stuck near zero, inflation rebounded with about the same pattern as it did following the

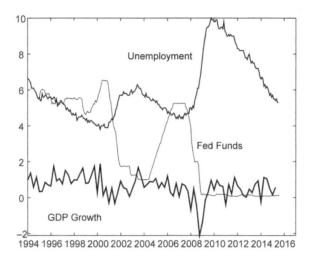

Fig. 2. US federal funds rate, unemployment rate, and real GDP growth rate

previous two much milder recessions, then resumed its gradual 20-year downward trend.

After 2012, when the financial crisis and deep recession receded, inflation volatility appears *lower* than it was before 2009, when interest rates could "actively" stabilize inflation, not higher as predicted by New Keynesian models. More generally, the zero bound does not seem to be an important state variable for stability, determinacy, or any other aspect of inflation dynamics.

The Fed increased bank reserves, from about $10 billion to nearly $3,000 billion, in three quantitative-easing (QE) operations, as shown in figure 1. Once again, nothing visible happened. QE2 is associated with a rise in inflation, but QE1 and QE3 are associated with a decline. And the rise in inflation coincided with QE2 mirrors the QE-free rise coming out of the much milder 2001 recession.

QE2 and QE3 were supposed to lower long-term interest rates. To the eye, the 20-year downward trend in long-term rates is essentially unaffected by QE. Long-term interest rates rose coincident with QE2 and QE3 purchases.

Figure 2 plots the unemployment rate and gross domestic product (GDP) growth rate. Together with figure 1, these figures also show no visible difference in macroeconomic dynamics in and out of the zero rate/QE state, and in particular no increased volatility at the zero bound. Yes, there was a bigger shock in 2008. But the unemployment recovery looks, if anything, a bit faster than previous recessions. Output growth, though too low in most opinions, is if anything less volatile than before.

Figure 3 tells a similar but longer story for Japan. Japanese interest rates declined swiftly in the early 1990s, and essentially hit zero in 1995. Again, armed with the traditional theory, and seeing data up to the bottom of inflation in 2001, or again in late 2010, predicting a deflation "spiral" is natural. But again, it never happened. Despite large fiscal stimulus and quantitative-easing operations, Japanese interest rates stuck at zero with slight deflation for nearly two decades. The 10-year government bond rate never budged from its steady downward trend.

The bottom panel of figure 3 repeats the story for Europe. Here the spread of low rates and slight deflation is even stronger than in the United States.

Both Japan and Europe diverge from the United States in the last few years, with less inflation and lower interest rates. But are Japanese and European inflation lower despite their lower or even negative interest rates, or because of them?

B. Theories

Old Keynesian models predict that inflation is unstable at the zero bound, as it is under passive policy or an interest rate peg. The Taylor rule stabilizes an otherwise unstable economy, but when the Taylor rule cannot operate, inflation will spiral out of control. (I use "zero bound" as a shorthand. The fact that interest rates were .25% above or below zero is not important to this discussion. The key point is that interest rates no longer move more than one-for-one with inflation in the downward direction.)

New Keynesian models predict that inflation is stable at the zero bound, as it is under passive policy or an interest rate peg. However, New Keynesian models are indeterminate at the zero bound. There are many equilibria, and the economy can jump between them following "sunspots" or "self-confirming expectations." Thus, the zero bound, passive interest rate policy, or an interest rate peg lead to extra inflation volatility. In these models, an interest rate rule that responds to off-equilibrium inflation more than one-for-one destabilizes an otherwise stable economy. The economy is then assumed to jump to the one remaining nonexplosive equilibrium. Destabilization removes local indeterminacies. But when this "active" rule cannot operate, sunspot volatility breaks out.

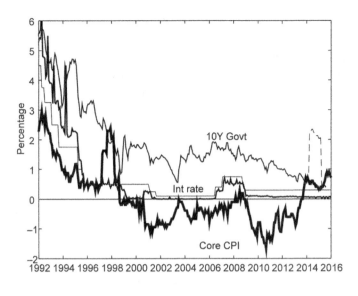

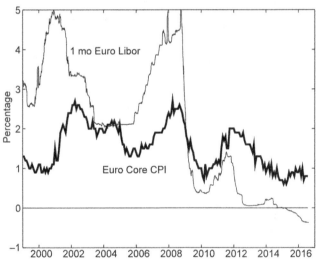

Fig. 3. Japan and Europe

Note: Top panel: discount rate, call rate, core CPI, and 10-year government bond yield in Japan. The dashed line presents the raw CPI data. Thick line adjusts the CPI for the consumption tax by forcing the April 2014 CPI rise to equal the rise in March 2014. Bottom panel: Europe.

The key distinction between the Old and New Keynesian models is rational versus adaptive expectations.

The fiscal theory of the price level adds an "active" fiscal policy to the New Keynesian model. Rather than assume that Congress will raise or lower taxes or spending to pay off any multiple-equilibrium, inflation-induced change in the real value of government debt, we assume that people expect less than perfect adjustment. Now unexpected inflation is determined by the change in present value of primary surpluses. If there is no change in volatility of that present value at and away from the zero bound, then there is no change in the volatility of unexpected inflation. Thus, adding the fiscal theory of the price level to the sticky-price, rational-expectations New Keynesian framework, we have a theory that is both stable and determinate at the zero bound, and therefore consistent with the low volatility of inflation.

The three models are hard to tell apart in normal times, when the Taylor rule or active New Keynesian policy can operate. Interest rates and inflation all move up and down together in all three views. In normal times, the standard active-money, New Keynesian view and the fiscal-theory view are observationally equivalent (Cochrane 1998, 2011b). That is why a long zero bound is such an important experiment.

Since these points are known, though perhaps underappreciated due to the technical complexity of realistic models, the pedagogical model here maximizes simplicity and transparency rather than realism or generality.

C. A Simple Model

Consider a Fisher equation, a Phillips curve, a static investment/saving (IS) curve, and a Taylor rule for monetary policy:

$$i_t = r_t + \pi_t^e \quad \text{Fisher} \tag{1}$$

$$\pi_t = \pi_t^e + \kappa x_t \quad \text{Phillips} \tag{2}$$

$$x_t = -\sigma(r_t - r^* - v_t^r) \quad \text{IS} \tag{3}$$

$$i_t = \max[r^* + \pi^* + \phi(\pi_t - \pi^*) + v_t^i, 0]. \quad \text{Taylor} \tag{4}$$

Here i is the nominal interest rate, r is the real interest rate, π is inflation, π^* is the inflation target, r^* is the natural rate, π^e is expected inflation, x is the output gap, v^i is a monetary policy disturbance, and we can call v^r

a "natural rate" disturbance. By specifying a static IS equation, without the usual term $E_t x_{t+1}$ on the right-hand side, we can solve the model trivially. The same points hold in more general and realistic models.

Eliminating x and r, we reduce the model to the solution of a single equation in π:

$$i_t = \max[r^* + \pi^* + \phi(\pi_t - \pi^*) + v_t^i, 0] = -\frac{1}{\sigma\kappa}\pi_t + \left(1 + \frac{1}{\sigma\kappa}\right)\pi_t^e + r^* + v_t^r, \quad (5)$$

or

$$(1 + \phi\sigma\kappa)(\pi_t - \pi^*) = (1 + \sigma\kappa)(\pi_t^e - \pi^*) + \sigma\kappa(v_t^r - v_t^i) \quad (6)$$

when we ignore the zero bound, or when the interest rate is positive, that is, when

$$i_t > 0 \leftrightarrow r^* + \pi^* + \phi(\pi_t - \pi^*) + v_t^i > 0, \quad (7)$$

and

$$\pi_t = (1 + \sigma\kappa)\pi_t^e + \sigma\kappa(r^* + v_t^r) \quad (8)$$

when the zero bound binds, and equation (7) does not hold. Equation (8) is the same solution as obtains from equation (6) if the Taylor rule chooses to be unresponsive, and chooses a zero interest rate, but there is no bound forcing such choices, that is, with $\phi = 0$, and $v_t^i = -(r^* + \pi^*)$.

By substituting $\pi_t^e = \pi_{t-1}$ or $\pi_t^e = E_t\pi_{t+1}$, we recover adaptive versus rational expectations versions of the model.

D. Old Keynesian

Old Keynesian models, including much monetarist thought such as Friedman (1968), specify adaptive expectations, $\pi_t^e = \pi_{t-1}$. Substituting that specification in equation (6) we obtain

$$(\pi_t - \pi^*) = \frac{1 + \sigma\kappa}{1 + \phi\sigma\kappa}(\pi_{t-1} - \pi^*) + \frac{\sigma\kappa}{1 + \phi\sigma\kappa}(v_t^r - v_t^i). \quad (9)$$

For $\phi < 1$, or at a peg $\phi = 0$, the dynamics of this system are *unstable* and *determinate*. The coefficient on lagged inflation is above one. There is only one solution.

In this model, the Taylor rule stabilizes an otherwise unstable economy. Raising ϕ to a value greater than one, the coefficient on lagged inflation becomes less than one. But if the Taylor rule cannot or does not act, inflation will spiral away.

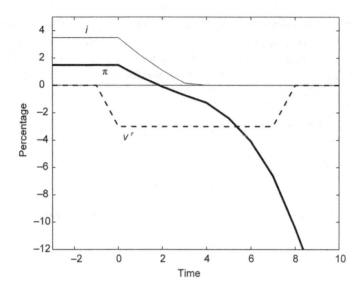

Fig. 4. Old Keynesian spiral at the zero bound

If $\phi > 1$ but the economy hits the zero bound, then equation (8) takes over, in this case

$$\pi_t = (1 + \sigma\kappa)\pi_{t-1} + \sigma\kappa(r^* + v_t^r). \tag{10}$$

Now the coefficient on π_{t-1} is greater than one, and a deflation spiral can set in. (Equation [10] is the same as equation [9] at $\phi = 0$, $v_t^i = -(r^* + \pi^*)$.)

Figure 4 illustrates a typical Old Keynesian spiral prediction. The economy starts at the steady state, $i = i^* = 2\%$, $\pi = \pi^* = 2\%$. The figure then considers a 3-percentage-point decline in the natural rate v^r. I simulate equations (9) and (10) forward. With the new −3% real rate, the economy needs to find a steady state in which inflation rises 3 percentage points relative to the interest rate. Indeed interest rates fall more than inflation, starting to produce a lower real rate. But soon the interest rate can fall no more; we switch to equation (10) dynamics, and then deflation spirals out of control. Once in the trap, deflation keeps spiraling even though the natural rate shock ends.

E. New Keynesian

The New Keynesian tradition instead uses rational expectations: $\pi_t^e = E_t\pi_{t+1}$. Substituting this specification into equation (6), we obtain

$$E_t(\pi_{t+1} - \pi^*) = \frac{1 + \phi\sigma\kappa}{1 + \sigma\kappa}(\pi_t - \pi^*) + \frac{\sigma\kappa}{1 + \sigma\kappa}(v_t^i - v_t^r). \qquad (11)$$

For $\phi < 1$, the coefficient on π_t is less than one, so this model is *stable* all on its own, even under an interest rate peg $\phi = 0$ or at the zero bound. Adaptive, backward-looking expectations make price dynamics unstable, like driving a car by looking in the rearview mirror. Rational, forward-looking expectations make price dynamics stable, as when drivers look forward and veer back on the road without outside help. The New Keynesian model thus reverses the hallowed doctrine—the first item in the Friedman (1968) list of what monetary policy cannot do—that interest rate pegs are unstable.

However, the New Keynesian model with $\phi < 1$ is *indeterminate*. It only ties down expected inflation $E_t\pi_{t+1}$, where the Old Keynesian model ties down actual inflation. To the solutions of this model we can add any expectational error, δ_{t+1}, such that $E_t\delta_{t+1} = 0$, and then write the model's solutions as

$$(\pi_{t+1} - \pi^*) = \frac{1 + \sigma\kappa\phi}{1 + \sigma\kappa}(\pi_t - \pi^*) + \frac{\sigma\kappa}{1 + \sigma\kappa}(v_t^i - v_t^r) + \delta_{t+1}. \qquad (12)$$

The δ shocks that index multiple equilibria are "sunspots," or "multiple self-confirming equilibria." In the usual causal interpretation of the equations, small changes in expectations about the future $E_t\pi_{t+j}$ induce jumps between equilibria π_t. Passive policy, a peg or the zero bound, induce inflation *volatility*.

In this model, an active policy $\phi > 1$ induces *instability* into an otherwise *stable* model, in order to try to render it locally *determinate*—to select a particular choice of $\{\delta_{t+1}\}$. For $\phi > 1$, expected inflation diverges for all values of inflation π_t other than

$$\pi_t - \pi^* = -\frac{\sigma\kappa}{1 + \sigma\kappa}\sum_{j=0}^{\infty}\left(\frac{1 + \sigma\kappa}{1 + \sigma\kappa\phi}\right)^{j+1} E_t(v_{t+j}^i - v_{t+j}^r). \qquad (13)$$

Equivalently, taking $E_t - E_{t-1}$,

$$\delta_t = -\frac{\sigma\kappa}{1 + \sigma\kappa}\sum_{j=0}^{\infty}\left(\frac{1 + \sigma\kappa}{1 + \sigma\kappa\phi}\right)^{j+1}(E_t - E_{t-1})(v_{t+j}^i - v_{t+j}^r). \qquad (14)$$

The economy jumps by an expectational error δ_t just enough so that expected inflation does not explode.

This method of inducing determinacy is not entirely uncontroversial (Cochrane 2011b). That controversy is one motivation to look for an-

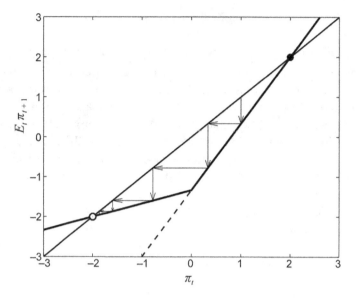

Fig. 5. The zero bound in a New Keynesian model
Note: The kinked line expresses the equilibrium condition (15). The straight line is the 45-degree line. The two dots express the two steady states. The left-hand one is the stable indeterminate "liquidity trap" state. The right-hand steady state is the unstable determinate state. Arrows indicate dynamics. The dashed line shows the policy rule in the absence of the zero bound. The parameters are $\phi = 2$, $\pi^* = 2\%$, $r = 2\%$, $\sigma\kappa = 2$.

other theory. But that controversy is not central here. If we have passive policy or a peg $\phi < 1$, we are back to the conclusion of equation (12): stability—no spirals—but indeterminacy leading to volatility.

New Keynesian models also predict multiplicity and thus inflation volatility at the zero bound. The dynamics switch to

$$E_t\pi_{t+1} = \frac{1}{1 + \sigma\kappa}\,\pi_t - \frac{\sigma\kappa}{1 + \sigma\kappa}(r + v_t^r) \tag{15}$$

at the bound. (These $i = 0$ dynamics are also the same as equation [11] with $\phi = 0$, $v^i = -(\pi^* + r^*)$.)

Figure 5 illustrates the model with a zero bound. The kinked line expresses the equilibrium conditions of equations (11)–(15). As a result of the zero bound, there are two steady states, represented by dots. The arrows represent the dynamics. The right-hand steady state is the conventional "active" equilibrium. This is unstable and hence locally determinate. Any other equilibrium spirals away. However, the presence of the zero bound means that interest rates i cannot move downward more than one-for-one with inflation forever. Therefore, there is a second, stable, "liquidity trap" steady state, with $i = 0$ at the left.

The zero-bound steady state is indeterminate as well as stable. The model does not pin down $\pi_{t+1} - E_t\pi_{t+1}$, so inflation can always jump away from this steady state. Such jumps are expected to revert back to the liquidity trap steady state, so the rule in these models that one throws out explosive equilibria cannot eliminate them.

As a result of the potential extra sunspot volatility of inflation, authors such as Benhabib, Schmitt-Grohé, and Uribe (2002) view the liquidity trap state as a problem, and devote great effort to additional policy prescriptions that governments might adopt to avoid it, despite the fact that absent volatility that steady state would improve welfare. Zero interest rates are the Friedman-optimal quantity of money after all, and low inflation reduces the distortions of sticky prices.

The alternative equilibrium shown by arrows in figure 5 starts away from the zero bound. This equilibrium reminds us that the zero bound is an attractive state for any value of inflation below the active equilibrium on the right. In particular, even sunspot jumps that raise inflation and temporarily relax the zero bound do not allow the economy to escape the trap. And small downward jumps out of the rightmost "active" steady state now converge to the zero bound as well.

In figure 5, the slide to a liquidity trap can happen all on its own. However, as in the Old Keynesian models, shocks can move us there as well. I discuss this mechanism below.

(These points can be made most simply without pricing frictions, as in Benhabib et al. 2002. If we merge the policy rule [4] with the frictionless Fisher equation

$$i_t = r + E_t\pi_{t+1}$$

then inflation dynamics follow

$$E_t\pi_{t+1} = \max[\phi(\pi_t - \pi^*) + \pi^*, -r].$$

The frictionless version leads to the same analysis as in figure 4, but with a horizontal line to the left of the kink. Benhabib et al. 2002 also use the fully nonlinear model, but in this range it is visually indistinguishable from the linearization.)

F. Fiscal Theory of the Price Level

To show how the fiscal theory of the price level enters this kind of model in the simplest way, I specify one-period or floating-rate debt. Then the government-debt valuation equation stating that the real value of nominal debt equals the present value of primary (net of interest) surpluses reads

$$\frac{B_{t-1}}{P_t} = E_t\sum_{j=0}^{\infty} M_{t,t+j}s_{t+j} = E_t\sum_{j=0}^{\infty}\frac{1}{R_{t,t+j}}s_{t+j} = E_t\sum_{j=0}^{\infty}\beta^j s_{t+j}. \quad (16)$$

Here, B_{t-1} is the face value of one-period debt, issued at $t-1$ and coming due at t, P_t is the price level, and s_t is the real primary surplus. In the first equality, we discount the future with a general stochastic discount factor M. In the second equality, we discount the future with the ex post real rate of return on government debt. Either of these statements is valid in general; the latter ex post as well. The third version specializes to a constant real interest rate with $\beta = 1/(1 + r)$.

In general, real interest rate variation affects the present value of surpluses on the right-hand side of equation (16). Models with sticky prices imply variation in real interest rates. I argue below that such real interest rate variation is of first-order importance to understand data, experience, and policy via the fiscal theory. However, the stability and determinacy points are not affected by long-term debt or real rate variation, so I specify constant real rates and short-term debt to make basic points here, then generalize at a cost in algebra below.

Moving the index forward one period, multiplying and dividing equation (16) by P_t and taking innovations,

$$\frac{B_t}{P_t}(E_{t+1} - E_t)\left(\frac{P_t}{P_{t+1}}\right) = (E_{t+1} - E_t)\sum_{j=0}^{\infty}\beta^j s_{t+1+j}. \quad (17)$$

In this simple setup, *unexpected inflation is determined by innovations to the expected present value of surpluses.*

Indeterminacy is the inability of the standard New Keynesian model to nail down unexpected inflation with passive policy $\phi < 1$, because we can always add any unexpected shock δ to the solution as in equation (12). Equation (17) shows that the fiscal theory of the price level solves the indeterminacy problem. Unexpected inflation or disinflation revalues outstanding government debt, which requires changes in discounted future surpluses. If people do not expect, say, that an unexpected deflation will be met by more taxes or less spending to finance a windfall to bondholders, then the bondholders try to get rid of overvalued bonds, which raises aggregate demand and hence keeps the price level from falling in the first place.

In sum, the fiscal theory of the price level merged with the New Keynesian model says that at the zero bound, as under an interest rate peg passive $\phi < 1$ policy, inflation is *stable* and *determinate*. If there is no change in the volatility of fiscal expectations or their discount rate, there is no change in the volatility of unexpected inflation at the zero bound.

The central bank is far from powerless in the fiscal theory. In this simple frictionless model, the Fed, by setting in interest rate target i_t will set expected inflation $i_t = r + E_t \pi_{t+1}$. Expectations of discounted fiscal policy then select which value of unexpected inflation $\pi_{t+1} - E_t \pi_{t+1}$ occurs. Monetary policy—setting of interest rate targets—remains the central determinant of the path of expected inflation. Stable fiscal policy expectations just cut down on unexpected inflation volatility. (Cochrane 2014b explains how the Fed and Treasury can target the nominal interest rate in this model, even with no nominal rigidities, no monetary frictions, and no open market operations, by varying the interest the Fed pays on reserves.)

Below, I describe how to integrate fiscal theory with the New Keynesian model with sticky prices. Again, the fiscal theory ends up just choosing equilibria, and does not alter the equilibrium dynamics. However, time-varying real interest rates now contribute to a time-varying discount rate in the government debt present value relation, so just which equilibrium gets picked is a bit different than in this constant-interest-rate, present-value calculation.

Equation (16) *holds* in all models. One cannot "test the fiscal theory" by testing whether this equation holds, and the standard New Keynesian model does not operate aloof from fiscal foundations. In the standard New Keynesian model one assumes that the Treasury always adjusts surpluses s_t ex post to validate equation (16) for whatever price level emerges by the Fed's equilibrium-selection policies. That assumption means the equation now determines surpluses rather than the price level. But the equation still holds. All unexpected inflations and deflations correspond to changes in expected fiscal policy in both models. If people do not expect Congress and the Treasury to follow "passive" policy, for example raising taxes or cutting spending to validate an disinflation-induced present to bondholders, then the unexpected disinflation will not happen.

G. *Language*

The language used to describe dynamic properties of economic models varies, and I can dispel some remaining confusion by being explicit about my language choices.

I use the words "stable" and "unstable" in their classic engineering sense, to refer to the dynamic properties of the underlying dynamic system. A scalar system $z_{t+1} = Az_t + \varepsilon_{t+1}$ is stable if $|A| < 1$ and unstable if $|A| > 1$. Authors often use "stable" to mean the opposite of "volatile," which I term "quiet," but stability and volatility are distinct concepts. A stable system with large shocks can display lots of volatility.

I use the word "determinate" to mean that an economic model only has one equilibrium. Determinacy is also distinct from volatility and stability, all frequently confused no matter how one names them.

A harder case concerns expectational models with roots greater than one, and a variable that can jump, $E_t(z_{t+1}) = Az_t + v_t$, $|A| > 1$. I continue to use the word "unstable" to describe their dynamics. However, if one rules out explosions and solves forward, $z_t = E_t\sum_{j=0}^{\infty}A^{-(j+1)}v_{t+j}$, then one could justifiably call the equilibrium path of $\{z_t\}$ "stable" since it always jumps just enough to forestall explosions, and samples show future z expected to revert back after a shock. This behavior is sometimes called "saddle-path stable." I use the term "stationary" to describe this property of *equilibrium* paths, using the word "stable" or "unstable" to describe the properties of the dynamic system, A. The "stability" of a forward-looking system that jumps to offset instability is qualitatively different from that of a system with backward-looking dynamics and no jump variables, in which economic forces slowly push the system back to equilibrium.

The standard three-equation New Keynesian model with passive $\phi < 1$ monetary policy has dynamics of the form $E_t(z_{t+1}) = Az_t + v_t$ in which one eigenvalue of A is greater than one and unstable, and the other is less than one and stable. One could call such a model "mixed," or develop additional language to describe the relative number of unstable eigenvalues and expectational equations. However, in this case, we uncontroversially solve the unstable eigenvalue forward, using the real transversality condition, and uniquely determining one eigenvector linear combination of variables. Then, the other linear combination follows a scalar $E_t(z_{t+1}) = Az_t + v_t$ with $A < 1$. I use the language "stable" versus "unstable" and "determinate" versus "indeterminate" to describe the remaining linear combination of variables.

I use the word "policy rule" rather than "Taylor rule" to describe $i_t = \phi \pi_t$ with $\phi > 1$ in New Keynesian models. The latter is really a misnomer. Taylor's rule stabilizes an unstable determinate model to bring unstable inflation under control (see Taylor 1993, 1999). In New Keynesian models, the rule operates to turn a stable model into an unstable one and produce local determinacy, which is an entirely different function.

The "active" and "passive" terminology to describe $\phi > 1$ versus $\phi < 1$ in monetary policy, and surpluses that do not versus do move exactly enough to validate any inflation that comes along in fiscal policy, comes from Leeper (1991).

I use the word "disturbance" rather than "shock" and roman letters v rather than greek ε as a reminder that "disturbances" can be serially correlated, where "shocks" are unpredictable.

I refer to unstable dynamics such as graphed in figure 3 as a "spiral," but a downward price-level jump followed by recovery, produced by some New Keynesian zero-bound models such as Werning (2011) or Cochrane (2017) as a "jump." (See the top panel of figure 19 for an example.) Some authors use the same word for both. I think this confuses the quite different dynamics of New and Old Keynesian models.

H.   Monetarism and QE

Monetarist thought took a back seat during the interest-rate targeting period starting in 1982. It largely disappeared from academia, but remains a powerful strain of thought in policy circles and commentary. When Japan hit zero interest rates in the 1990s, monetarist ideas came back quickly in the form of "helicopter money." Ben Bernanke advocated the view most prominently, among other alternative policies (see the review and fascinating discussion in Ball 2016). Monetarist ideas remain a force behind the analysis of QE (quantitative easing).

Quantitative easing has two parts: the Fed buys bonds or other assets, and issues reserves. Here I consider the question whether larger reserve supply is inflationary. In traditional monetarist thought, whether the increase in the M of $MV = PY$ stems from the Fed buying short-term Treasuries, long-term Treasuries, mortgage-backed securities, or from buying nothing—from helicopter drops, or changes in reserve requirements allowing more inside money—makes no difference.

Much of the current QE discussion takes on a diametrically opposite view: the liabilities (reserves) are irrelevant, but QE works by affecting the term and credit spreads in long-term interest rates in segmented bond markets. The asset purchases matter, not the reserve issues. Whether or not QE lowered long-term rates by as much as 0.5% via this mechanism, for how long, and whether such rate declines in segmented markets had a stimulative effect, is really unrelated to the big issues of inflation stability and determinacy that matter here, so I ignore this question.

Helicopter money combines increased money with a fiscal expansion. From a fiscal theoretic point of view, that such an expansion could cause inflation is not a surprise. In this section, therefore, I only consider increases in reserves accompanied by asset purchases, and hence no direct implied fiscal expansion (ignoring also the Fed's assumption of credit and term risk in asset purchases).

In standard New Keynesian models (before adding extra frictions, see Woodford 2012), QE has no inflationary effect.

In classic monetarist thought, the zero bound is not an important constraint on monetary policy. Yes, the Fed can then no longer control the quantity of money implicitly via an interest rate target. But nothing stops the Fed from buying bonds and issuing reservers at a zero interest rate and letting $MV = PY$ do its work—as, a monetarist might add, it should have been doing all along anyway.

The behavior of velocity, equivalently of money demand, at zero interest rates is the central issue. Monetarist thought emphasizes the idea that velocity is "stable," at least in the long run. Even at zero interest rates, or with interest-paying reserves, or in the puzzling situation that reserves pay even more than treasuries, and even if velocity V decreases somewhat temporarily when M increases, velocity will soon bounce back and persistently more M will lead to more PY.

The contrary view is that at zero interest rates, or when money pays market interest, money and short-term bonds become perfect substitutes. Velocity becomes a correspondence, not a function of interest rates. $MV = PY$ becomes $V = PY/M$; velocity passively adjusts to whatever split of debt between money and reserves the Fed chooses. The financial system is perfectly happy to hold arbitrary amounts of reserves in place of short-term treasuries. Open-market operations have no more effect on spending than open-change operations, in which the Fed trades two $10 bills for each $20.

This issue was central to the monetarist versus Keynesian debates of the 1950s and 1960s. Keynesians thought that at the zero rates of the Great Depression, money and bonds were perfect substitutes, so monetary policy could do nothing, and advocated fiscal stimulus instead.

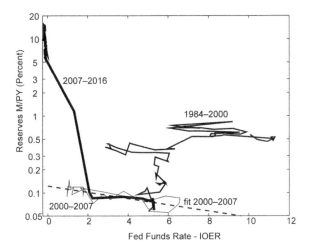

Fig. 6. Reserves versus opportunity cost

Note: Y axis: Total reserves (Fred series WRESBAL) at end of quarter divided by nominal GDP; log scale. X axis: Effective federal funds rate (Fred FF) less interest on excess reserves (Federal Reserve website policy rates). Sample 1984:1-2016:2. Line fit by OLS 2000:1–2006:4.

Monetarists held that additional money, even at zero rates, would be stimulative; the Fed's failure to provide additional money was the great policy error of that decade.

In the postwar era of positive interest rates, with zero interest on reserves, there was really no way to tell these views apart. Now there is, and the experiment is nearly as decisive as the stability of an interest rate peg.

Figure 1 already demonstrates no visible time-series relationship between the massive increase in reserves and inflation. Figure 6 presents a more traditional picture of reserves, scaled by nominal GDP, as a function of their opportunity cost, the difference between the effective Federal Funds rate (the rate at which banks can lend out reserves) and the interest on excess reserves at the Fed. You see a steady decline in reserves from 1980 to 2000, as fewer bank liabilities required reserves and banks became better at avoiding excess reserves. You also see a negatively sloped curve in the periodic recessions. Following tradition, I'll just call this plot a "demand curve" without further ado. I fit the dashed line to the 2000–2007 period, and it gives a conventional semi-elasticity log(reserves/PY) = constant −0.094 (interest rate). If one extends the line to the vertical axis, it suggests that reserve demand should top out at

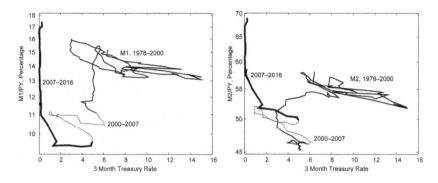

Fig. 7.   M/PY versus three-month Treasury bill rate, using M1 and M2

about 0.12% of GDP, and if reserve velocity is stable, further increases should lead to increases in nominal GDP.

What does reserve demand do at zero opportunity cost? As figure 6 shows, we have now run this out-of-sample experiment on a grand scale—note the numbers on the log scale y-axis. Reserves increased by two orders of magnitude—from 0.1% of GDP to 15% of GDP—with no visible effect on inflation or nominal GDP.

The answer seems unavoidable: reserve demand is a correspondence when reserves pay market interest rates, reserves and short-term debt are perfect substitutes, there is no tendency for velocity to revert to some stable previous value, and arbitrary quantities of zero-cost reserves do not cause inflation. The massive size of the experiment avoids conventional objections—perhaps there was a contemporaneous velocity shock such as those alleged to move money demand in the 1980s; perhaps nominal GDP would have fallen had the Fed not increased reserves, and so on.

One may object that reserves are not the relevant M in MV = PY. Figure 7 presents M1 and M2 as percentages of nominal GDP PY, versus the three-month Treasury-bill rate. (Since many components of these aggregates pay interest, the three-month Treasury-bill rate is not a good measure of their opportunity costs, but I am both following tradition and keeping it simple.) Each aggregate increased since 2007, but less, proportionally, than reserves increased. M1 increased from about 9% of GDP to almost 18%, a bit less than doubling—but not rising by a factor of 100. M2 increased from 50% of GDP to almost 70% of GDP, "only" a 60% rise. Currency (not shown) rose from 5.9% of GDP to 7.5%, a 30% increase.

These are still substantial increases, which if velocity were stable should result in equiproportionate rises in nominal income, and eventually the price level.

But even making these plots grants too much. How much inflation a monetarist view predicts for the recent period is beside the point. The question for us is whether arbitrary amounts of *reserves*, exchanged for short-term treasuries, cause any inflation; whether open-market operations or QE operations affect inflation. Even if one believes that $M2 \times V = PY$ (say), and one claims that a monetarist view does not predict inflation in the current period because reserves did not leak in to M2, that fact only verifies that arbitrary quantities of *reserves* are not inflationary, precisely because they do not leak into M2. That leakage is a central part of the transmission mechanism, and it is not transmitting. When banks are holding trillions of dollars of excess reserves, the money multiplier ceases to operate. So, to argue there is no inflation because M2 did not rise much is precisely to admit that arbitrary quantities of interest-bearing reserves, corresponding to arbitrarily lower quantities of interest-bearing treasuries, are not inflationary.

Figure 6 really only makes a secondary point: What would happen if reserves *were* to leak to larger increases in M1 or M2, or other aggregates? Figure 6 suggests that these aggregates display the same behavior as reserves, only on a smaller (so far) scale—they happily crawl up the vertical axis. There is nothing in their behavior so far to suggest that this correspondence could not reach the astonishing level that banks' willingness to hold reserves at the expense of treasuries has reached.

Looking back at an 80-year controversy, one may wonder why the stability of velocity, even at zero interest cost, and the consequent perfect substitutability of treasuries for reserves, was so controversial. One answer may be that for most of that period there was no alternative coherent, simple, economic theory of the price level that could hold in that circumstance. In a monetarist world, strike MV = PY and nothing ties down P. So, it is natural to stick with the idea that velocity must be stable, as otherwise the price level would be indeterminate. To preserve price-level control, monetarists, despite otherwise free-market tendencies, were reluctant to endorse financial innovation, including lots of inside money, electronic transactions, and interest-bearing money. But now we have an equally simple theory—the fiscal theory—that ties down the price level when money and bonds are perfect substitutes, one that requires no monetary or pricing frictions and thus allows arbitrary financial innovation, and we have a long period of apparent empirical validation that inflation is stable at zero rates despite a massive "monetary" expansion.

My conclusion that abundant interest-bearing reserves do not cause inflation does not address many other objections to the Fed's large balance sheet. One may object to the Fed's assets—its purchases of long-term bonds, of mortgage-backed securities, and of other central banks' purchases of corporate bonds (ECB) and even stocks (BOJ)—both on grounds that independent central banks should not try to directly influence risky asset prices, or on political economy grounds that such policies constitute credit allocation better done (if at all) by politically accountable treasuries. This paper is silent on those questions.

III. Fisher

If we grant that inflation is stable at the zero bound, and by implication at an interest rate peg, that observation implies that raising interest rates should sooner or later *raise* inflation, contrary to the usually presumed negative sign. This proposition has become known as the "long-run neo-Fisherian" hypothesis.

This proposition is a form of long-run neutrality under interest rate rules. It basically says that the Fisher equation $i_t = r_t + E_t\pi_{t+1}$ is a stable steady state. "Stable" is a key qualifier. It is a steady state in Old Keynesian models, and interest rates and inflation move together in the long run. But it is an unstable steady state in those models, so pegging the interest rate leads to spiraling inflation. A stable steady state means that inflation will eventually settle down to a fixed nominal interest rate. (I ignore here a long literature that worries whether long-run real interest rates r are affected by steady-state inflation, so the Fisher relationship may not be exactly one-for-one. All that can be trivially added if needed.)

Both flavors of the New Keynesian model have this implication. The fiscal theory addendum only changes how we think about determinacy and equilibrium selection, and thus the immediate, unexpected-inflation response to a shock. Long-run neutrality is a proposition about long-run expectations in any equilibrium.

Stability and long-run neutrality are news to the policy world, however, which is largely based on Old Keynesian adaptive-expectations thinking. If they are true, central banks raising rates will partly cause the inflation they wish to forestall—though in the event will likely congratulate themselves for their prescience. Indeed, inflation will rise before anticipated interest rate increases (figure 12 below gives a good example), and the bank will seem to respond to inflation rather than to cause inflation. Stability and long-run neutrality also imply that low inflation at the zero bound is in part due to pedal misapplication—central banks, by keeping interest rates low, partly caused the low inflation that they were trying, wisely or not, to prevent.

But a long-run positive sign leaves open the possibility that higher interest rates *temporarily* lower inflation, and vice versa. The classic belief need not be wrong and may well reflect short-run experience. We can label the contrary proposition that higher interest rates raise inflation even right away as the "short-run" neo-Fisherian hypothesis.

The quest of this section, then, is to find the minimal simple economic model that produces a temporary negative impact of higher interest rates on inflation, validating at least part of the classic belief. (The qualifiers "simple" and "economic" are important.)

The main result is negative. The basic New Keynesian model produces a uniformly positive sign. One simply cannot say, for example, that sure, the Fisher relation means that raising interest rates raises inflation, but sticky prices overturn that result for a while. They do not. A suite of sensible modifications one might adduce to provide the desired sign do not work. A novel fiscal-theory argument with long-term debt produces the desired negative sign, but it rather deeply changes one's views of just what monetary policy is and how it works.

Just what the core predictions of New Keynesian models for the sign of monetary policy are turns out to be a delicate question, which is the reason for much of this section and its apparent return to basics that one would think were well established, but are not. The short preview: the apparent ability of the New Keynesian model with standard policy rules to deliver a negative response for transitory interest rate shocks is an illusion. In fact the New Keynesian model has an interest-rate policy, which governs expected inflation, and a separate and distinct equilibrium-selection policy, which can induce an unexpected inflation. By engineering an unexpected disinflation via the latter policy (and only by this mechanism), the model can deliver a temporary negative sign for any persistence of the interest rate shock, not just transitory shocks. But that is bad news: There is, therefore, no necessary or logical connection between the Fed's choice to temporarily disinflate and its choice to raise interest rates, which on its own leads uniformly to higher inflation. Such a path remains entirely a Fed choice, not a characterization of how interest rates affect inflation in the economy. Viewed through fiscal theory eyes,

which are observationally equivalent, interest rate rises may historically have coincided with fiscal contractions, which generate an unexpected disinflation. But there is no reason that monetary policy alone—
interest rate changes that do not have contemporaneous changes in fiscal policy—should therefore lower inflation. In either view, monetary
policy—interest rate policy—remains Fisherian.

We are left with three possibilities: (1) The temporary negative sign
is not true. The impression that it is true comes from events that feature
joint monetary-fiscal contractions, and overly aggressive fishing of VAR
specifications. (2) The temporary negative sign is true, but it results from
the simple long-term debt, fiscal-theory mechanism, and has nothing to
do with any of the standard stories. That mechanism also differs sharply
in its implications for policy. (3) The temporary negative sign is true, but
necessarily relies on novel, complex, or noneconomic ingredients. Any
of these possibilities undermines traditional monetary economics.

A.   A Frictionless Benchmark

I start with a simple frictionless model. One may think it obvious that
a frictionless model does not deliver the desired negative sign, and one
may wish to get on to price stickiness and other variations with more
potential to do so. But it turns out those models do not work any better
than the frictionless model, and all the conceptual issues can be shown
in the very simple frictionless model, with much more transparent algebra.

The model consists of a Fisher equation,

$$i_t = r + E_t\pi_{t+1}, \tag{18}$$

the government-debt valuation equation, which implies

$$\frac{B_t}{P_t}(E_{t+1} - E_t)\left(\frac{P_t}{P_{t+1}}\right) = (E_{t+1} - E_t)\sum_{j=0}^{\infty}\beta^j s_{t+1+j}, \tag{19}$$

or, linearizing,

$$(E_{t+1} - E_t)\pi_{t+1} = -(E_{t+1} - E_t)\sum_{j=0}^{\infty}\beta^j s_{t+1+j} / b_t, \tag{20}$$

where b is the real value of debt, and an interest rate policy rule,

$$i_t = (r + E_t\pi_{t+1}^*) + \phi(\pi_t - \pi_t^*) \tag{21}$$

or

$$i_t = r + (1 - \phi)\pi^* + \phi\pi_t + v_t^i. \tag{22}$$

One can derive the first two equations as the two important equilibrium conditions of a complete general equilibrium model with a constant endowment (see Cochrane 2005). The contrast between the two equivalent parameterizations of the interest rate rule, one with a time-varying inflation target π_t^*, and the other with a fixed target π^* and a policy disturbance v_t^i, will turn out to offer important insights. For the purpose of impulse-response functions, the occasionally binding zero bound is not important. This model is "simple," "economic," and consistent with stability at the zero bound.

Response Function

Figure 8 presents responses of inflation to an interest rate rise for this model, as given by equation (18). The model produces a rise in expected inflation starting the period after the rate rise. There is no temporary inflation decline.

This calculation, using equation (18) alone, does not assume a peg, passive monetary policy, or fiscal theory, nor does it deny an underlying policy rule such as equation (22). This is a calculation of equilibrium inflation given a path for the equilibrium interest rate. That interest rate may well be the result of underlying disturbances $\{i_t^*\}$, $\{\pi_t^*\}$ or $\{v_t^i\}$ with any value of ϕ. Indeed, we can and will use equation (22) to back out a sequence of disturbances that produce the desired interest rate path.

The response to a given *interest rate* path is a different object than the response to a given path of *policy disturbances* $\{v_t^i\}$. It is more common to plot the latter. But in the end, we are interested in how changes in inflation correspond to changes in *interest rates*, which we can directly observe. The path of disturbances $\{v_t^i\}$ can be quite different from the interest rate path, as we will see, even having different signs. Solving for the path of inflation given interest rates gives us a more general answer, as the same interest rate path can occur from many different policy disturbance paths, and from both active-fiscal and active-money regimes. It also saves us a reverse-engineering task of finding disturbances that generate the desired path of equilibrium interest rates. Werning (2011) innovated this clever idea of first finding equilibrium inflation given equilibrium interest rate paths, and then, if needed, constructing the underlying policy rule.

Unexpected Disinflation?

By itself, the Fisher equation (18) allows an arbitrary one-period unexpected inflation in the impulse-response function, upward or downward,

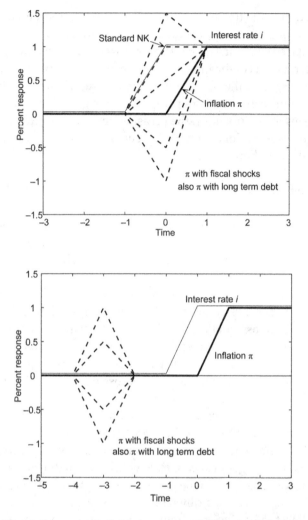

Fig. 8. Response of inflation to a permanent interest rate increase

Note: Frictionless model $i_t = r + E_t\pi_{t+1}$. Top: The rise is announced and implemented at time $t = 0$. Bottom: The rise is announced at $t = -3$. The solid inflation line assumes no unexpected inflation on the date of announcement. The dashed lines add unexpected inflation on the announcement date.

coincident with the announcement of the policy change. The dashed lines in figure 8 plot some possible response functions that pair an unexpected inflation shock with a rise in interest rates.

Perhaps we can deliver the desired negative sign by pairing a negative unexpected-inflation shock with the interest rate rise, choosing, say, the bottom-most dashed line of figure 8?

Equation (20) helps us to think about this issue. Each value of unexpected inflation corresponds to a revision in the present value of future surpluses. Disinflations, by unexpectedly raising the value of government debt, must correspond to a higher present value of future surpluses.

This kind of event may correspond to historical experience. The vast majority of monetary policy changes are reactions to events. It is sensible that fiscal policy reacts to the same events, that the interest rate rises we see historically represent joint monetary-fiscal contractions. One would have to orthogonalize VAR shocks very carefully to measure a monetary policy shock independent of fiscal policy, and no VAR has yet attempted it.

But if that is true, it follows that a pure monetary policy change, consisting of an interest rate rise *without* changes to fiscal policy, would not have a disinflationary effect, and would follow the Fisherian solid line.

This fiscal interpretation and underpinning of a disinflationary surprise is equally valid under "active" as under "passive" monetary policy. Equation (20) holds in classic New Keynesian analysis under active $\phi > 1$ policy just as it does in the fiscal theory with passive monetary policy. If active $\phi > 1$ monetary policy selects the value of unexpected inflation, and fiscal policy "passively" responds by changing surpluses to pay off corresponding changes in the value of the debt, fiscal policy must still change those surpluses, or the disinflation does not happen. Even "passive" fiscal policy must be voted on by Congress and implemented by the Treasury!

More deeply, the induced fiscal reaction is the *mechanism* by which monetary policy affects aggregate demand and thus inflation, even when fiscal policy is passive. The conventional reading of active monetary-passive fiscal policy regards the passive fiscal assumption as wiping out the fiscal equation (19). Then, monetary policy becomes simply a coordination device between multiple equilibria. But that is not the case. The fiscal equation is still present and crucial. When monetary policy selects an equilibrium with lower inflation, and fiscal policy passively raises surpluses, at the original price level, people find government bonds undervalued. They reduce spending on other things to try to buy government bonds, reducing aggregate demand. The price level declines, eventually raising the value of government bonds to their proper level. In a model with no frictions, this is the only way by which a nominal interest rate change affects aggregate demand and hence inflation. If fiscal policy does not cooperate, the aggregate demand does not materialize, and the price level does not change. Monetary policy may be the carrot that leads the fiscal horse that pulls the cart from place to place, but the cart does not just jump from place to place on its own.

Thus, one may index multiple equilibria by their fiscal consequences, even if one does not wish to select equilibria by those consequences.

A Policy Rule with an Inflation Target

Perhaps motivating the same disinflationary equilibria (dashed lines in figure 8) by active monetary policy rules will make them seem more attractive? Here we compute the responses of inflation and interest rates to a monetary policy *disturbance* ($\{\pi_t^*\}$ or $\{v_t^i\}$) rather than to equilibrium interest rates $\{i_t\}$ directly.

Merging the policy rule (21) with the frictionless Fisher equation (18), treating the government-debt valuation equation (20) as passive, determining $\{s_t\}$, and ignoring constants, which drop from the impulse-response function, we have

$$E_t(\pi_{t+1} - \pi_{t+1}^*) = \phi(\pi_t - \pi_t^*). \tag{23}$$

Given the expected sequence of policy disturbances $\{\pi_t^*\}$ then, and $\phi > 1$, any equilibrium $\{\pi_t\}$ will explode going forward other than $\pi_t = \pi_t^*$. Ruling out such forward nominal explosions, we have immediately that monetary policy determines inflation uniquely, on the announcement date as well as dates going forward, with its active policy.

The Fed can achieve any path of inflation it wishes by choice of the process for $\{\pi_t^*\}$. Interest rates will be $i_t = E_t\pi_{t+1}^*$ and unexpected inflation will be $\pi_{t+1}^* - E_t\pi_{t+1}^*$. (King 2000 innovated this insightful parameterization of the model in terms of equilibrium π^* and deviations from equilibrium $\pi - \pi^*$.)

This freedom does little to justify a temporary inflation decline as a characterization of the economy's response to monetary policy, however. An unexpected inflation decline paired with an interest rate increase would be entirely a choice by the Fed. There is no evident reason why the Fed should want to pair an unexpected inflation decline and an interest rate rise, which leads to higher later inflation.

Moreover, this freedom opens the door to open-mouth policy. Suppose at date 0 the Fed announces $\pi_0^* = -1$, $\pi_{1,2,3,...}^* = 0$, rather than $\pi_0^* = -1$, $\pi_{1,2,3,...}^* = 1$ (or the equivalent $v_t^i = E_t\pi_{t+1}^* - \pi_t^*$ disturbances). The latter generates a one-period decline followed by the interest rate and inflation rate rise seen in the lowest dashed line of figure 8. The former generates the one-period decline in inflation by itself, with no change in interest rates at all! All the Fed has to do is to announce the monetary policy disturbance. Then inflation jumps down by just enough that the $\phi\pi_t$ part of the policy rule offsets the disturbance term and interest rates themselves never change.

If the Fed wants disinflation, then, let it just create disinflation by an open-mouth operation, announcing that π_0^* is lower. Why pair an instant disinflation with a subsequent interest rate rise and higher future inflation? If anything, it would be far more sensible to tie a decline in unexpected inflation to a decline in actual inflation via a *lower* interest rate.

The inflation-target expression of the policy rule (21) makes clear that the Fed has two independent and separate policy levers in the New Keynesian active-money world: the Fed has an *interest rate policy* $i_t^* = E_t\pi_{t+1}^*$, which here sets expected inflation, and the Fed has an *equilibrium-selection policy* $\phi(\pi_{t+1}^* - E_t\pi_{t+1}^*)$, enforced by the threat of inflationary or deflationary explosion (23), which selects which of the multiple equilibria left by interest rate policy the economy will jump to. Since one can choose the expected and unexpected components of a stochastic process separately and freely, interest rate policy is completely independent of equilibrium-selection policy. An open-mouth operation is pure equilibrium-selection policy, and it can be paired with any interest rate policy. And a negative response of inflation to interest rates in standard New Keynesian models, here and with sticky prices below, comes entirely from this equilibrium-selection mechanism.

Furthermore, this separation makes it clear that the standard New Keynesian and fiscal theory views are observationally equivalent away from the zero bound. In equilibrium, we never observe $\pi_t \neq \pi_t^*$, so we never observe ϕ. Whether the Fed made an open-mouth operation, and fiscal policy followed passively, or whether $\phi = 0$ and fiscal policy led the unexpected inflation cannot be told apart based on interest rate and inflation data. At the zero bound, however, we know that at least the downward ϕ threat cannot be made.

A Policy Rule with Conventional Disturbances

Perhaps looking at monetary policy via disturbances v_t^i in equation (22) rather than π_t^* in equation (21) will look more reasonable. The former parameterization, though algebraically equivalent, is more common in the literature.

The v_t^i parameterization also helps us to track down a puzzle: I showed above that the Fed can engineer a negative disinflationary response π_0 for *any* path of interest rates $i_{0,1,2\ldots}$. Yet the standard wisdom is that New Keynesian models generate a negative response to transitory monetary policy shocks, and a positive response to persistent monetary policy shocks. As we will see, this standard (false) wisdom comes from specifying a monetary policy disturbance $\{v_t^i\}$ and then limiting the time-series properties of that disturbance.

Repeating the analysis with the v^i paratmerized rule (22), and with $r = \pi^* = 0$ for simplicity, the equilibrium condition is

$$E_t\pi_{t+1} = \phi\pi_t + v_t^i. \tag{24}$$

We solve forward to

$$\pi_t = -\sum_{j=0}^{\infty} \phi^{-(j+1)} E_t v_{t+j}^i.$$

In the AR(1) case

$$v_t^i = \rho v_{t-1}^i + \varepsilon_t^i$$

we have

$$\pi_t = -\frac{1}{\phi - \rho} v_t^i. \tag{25}$$

We also have either from equation (18) or equation (22)

$$i_t = -\frac{\rho}{\phi - \rho} v_t^i. \tag{26}$$

From equation (26), a positive monetary policy shock v^i sends inflation down. That seems like the result we are looking for. But in equation (26), that shock also sends interest rates down. Substituting out v^i from equations (25)–(26), we have

$$\pi_t = \rho i_t. \tag{27}$$

For $\rho > 0$, a higher *interest rate* results entirely in higher inflation. If you have the opposite impression, it comes from confusing the monetary policy disturbance v^i with the interest rate i. They go in opposite directions.

For $\rho = 1$, we recover the permanent interest rate rise of figure 8. In this case, this standard New Keynesian solution method produces a perfectly Fisherian response. Not only does $\pi_{1,2,3\ldots} = 1$, as in the solid line, but inflation jumps up immediately in the period of the shock, $\pi_0 = 1$ as well, shown in the second from the top dashed line, marked "Standard NK" in figure 8. We will see the same behavior with price stickiness.

So, if one hoped that simple or reasonable restrictions such as an AR(1) on $\{v_t^i\}$ produce the desired result, in fact they produce the opposite result. And again, even if it worked, it would reflect the Fed's choice of equilibrium selection via policy disturbance properties, and nothing really about the economy's response to money, interest rates, and so on.

Equation (27) shows a negative effect of interest rates on inflation for $\rho < 0$. Thus we see here a stylized version of the standard false impression that in the New Keynesian model persistent interest rates raise inflation, while temporary rate rises lower inflation. When we add price stickiness below, the cutoff for a positive versus a negative effect is between zero and one, allowing a negative effect for reasonable transitory (low but positive ρ) interest rate movements, but leaving a stubbornly positive effect for persistent (high ρ) interest rate movements.

But this all depends on the AR(1) or similar time-series restrictions on the disturbance process v_t^i. For example, suppose we want to engineer the response of figure 8 with a –1% impact disinflation and a permanent rate rise. We choose $\pi_0^* = -1$, $\pi_{1,2,3,\ldots}^* = 1$. Done. Translated, $v_t^i = E_t\pi_{t+1}^* - \phi\pi_t^*$, that is, $v_0^i = 1 + \phi$, $v_{1,2,3,\ldots}^i = 1 - \phi$ produces this result. It exists, but it is not an AR(1). Likewise, the model can happily generate the other opposite of conventional wisdom—a positive impact inflation with a transitory interest rate. It can generate an open-mouth effect—$v_0^i = 1 + \phi$, $v_{1,2,3\ldots}^i = 0$ produces $\pi_0^* = -1$, $\pi_{1,2,3\ldots}^* = 0$. Nothing about the conventional parameterization other than the artificial AR(1) restriction ties temporary disinflation to the persistence of subsequent interest rate movements.

Anticipated Rate Rises

Many interest rate rises are announced or anticipated long in advance. Both New and Old Keynesian models assign strong effects of anticipated interest rate rises. So, understanding the effect of anticipated interest rate changes is important for policy and understanding episodes.

VARs study unexpected interest rate movements both by historical habit—VARs were developed under the influence of rational expectations models in which only unanticipated monetary policy had real effects—and by econometric necessity—unexpected movements are more likely to be causes of, not responses to, other news about future inflation and output. Announcement shocks not coincident with actual rate movements are also harder to measure.

But for policy and historical analysis, it is important to ask of models what is the effect of an expected policy change.

The bottom panel of figure 8 shows possible impulse-response functions when the rate rise is announced three periods before it occurs. The response function with no inflation innovation and no fiscal policy shock is the same as before. Anticipated monetary policy, or forward guidance, matter.

Here, however, any disinflation must come only on the date of the shock, the date the policy is announced. Unexpected disinflations must be unexpected; equilibrium-selection policy can only select among un-expected movements; fiscal shocks must truly be shocks. This fact raises the bar for interpretation of historical episodes—the model-predicted disinflation will typically start before the actual rate rise. This fact also emphasizes that the disinflation comes from the equilibrium selection part of policy, not the interest rate part, and not at all from the standard channels in which the interest rate itself affects aggregate demand.

B.   Long-Term Debt in the Frictionless Model

Adding long-term debt produces a stable model in which a rise in inter-est rates can produce a temporary decline in inflation, with no change in fiscal surpluses. Sims (2011) makes this point in the context of a de-tailed continuous time model. Cochrane (2018) shows how to solve Sims's model and boils it down to this central point. Cochrane (2001) analyzes the long-term debt case in detail.

Continue with the frictionless model (18), using a constant real inter-est rate r and define $\beta \equiv 1/(1+r)$. In the presence of long-term debt, the government-debt valuation equation becomes

$$\frac{\sum_{j=0}^{\infty} Q_t^{(t+j)} B_{t-1}^{(t+j)}}{P_t} = E_t \sum_{j=0}^{\infty} \beta^j s_{t+j}, \tag{28}$$

where $B_{t-1}^{(t+j)}$ is the amount of zero-coupon debt that matures at time $t + j$, outstanding at the end of time $t - 1$ and thus at the beginning of time t, and $Q_t^{(t+j)} = E_t(\beta^j P_t / P_{t+j})$ is the time t nominal price of a j period dis-count bond.

When the Fed unexpectedly and persistently raises interest rates i_t, it lowers long-term bond prices $Q_t^{(t+j)}$. Debt $B_{t-1}^{(t+j)}$ is predetermined. By as-sumption, primary surpluses do not change. Hence, *the price level P_t*

must jump down by the same proportional amount as the decline in the nominal market value of the debt.

By raising nominal interest rates, the Fed still raises *expected* inflation uniformly; $i_t \approx r_t + E_t\pi_{t+1}$ still applies. Thus, we obtain a downward jump, a one-period disinflation, on the day the higher interest rates are announced and long-term bond prices decline, followed by higher inflation when the higher nominal interest rates occur. The path is exactly the same as the dashed lines figure 8 showed for contractionary fiscal policy, therefore marked "also with long-term debt." Like a shock to surpluses, the mechanism is straightforward "aggregate demand" or wealth effect of government debt. People try to buy or sell undervalued or overvalued government bonds. They drive down or up the price of everything else until the value of government bonds matches the present value of surpluses.

In a model such as Sims (2011) with costs to swiftly changing prices, the downward jump is replaced by a smeared-out period of disinflation. The jump in these simple models is a guide to the cumulative price level decline in the disinflationary period.

Magnitude?

Just how large a disinflation does this mechanism produce? Is it quantitatively significant, and hence a candidate to understand the apparent patterns in the data, or to guide policy?

Suppose the interest rate $i = i_{t+j}$ is expected to last forever. The bond price is then $Q_t^{(t+j)} = 1/(1+i)^j$. Consider a geometric maturity structure, $B_{t-1}^{(t+j)} = \theta^j B_{t-1}$, so $\theta = 1$ is a perpetuity and $\theta = 0$ is one-period debt, and a constant surplus $s_t = s$. Now, the government-debt valuation equation reads

$$\sum_{j=0}^{\infty} \frac{\theta^j}{(1+i)^j} \frac{B_{t-1}}{P_t} = \frac{1+i}{1+i-\theta} \frac{B_{t-1}}{P_t} = \frac{s}{1-\beta}. \tag{29}$$

The continuous time analogue is prettier. With maturity structure $B_t^{(t+j)} = \vartheta e^{-\vartheta j} B_t$,

$$\vartheta \int_{j=0}^{\infty} e^{-ij} e^{-\vartheta j} dj \frac{B_t}{P_t} = \frac{\vartheta}{i+\vartheta} \frac{B_t}{P_t} = \frac{s}{r}. \tag{30}$$

Here $\vartheta = 0$ is the perpetuity and $\vartheta = \infty$ is instantaneous debt. (Algebra in the appendix; see http://www.nber.org/data-appendix/c13911/appendix.pdf.)

Now, suppose interest rates rise permanently and unexpectedly at time t. Denote by i^* the postshock interest rate, and P_t^* the postshock price level. Then, dividing equation (30) for the starred by the nonstarred case,

$$\frac{P_t^*}{P_t} = \frac{i + \vartheta}{i^* + \vartheta}. \tag{31}$$

With this formula, we can get a back-of-the-envelope idea of the size of the disinflation effect and its crucial determinants. The longer the maturity, the stronger the effect. In the most extreme case, pairing this permanent interest rate rise with perpetual debt $\vartheta = 0$, we have $P_t^* / P_t = i / i^*$. A jump in interest rates from 2% to 3% causes the price level to drop to two-thirds of its previous value, a 33% cumulative disinflation!

However, the United States does not issue that much long-term debt. Debt out to a 20-year maturity follows a geometric pattern with $\vartheta \approx 0.2$. In this case, a 1-percentage-point interest rate rise implies $P_t^* / P_t = (0.2 / 0.21) = 0.95$, a 5% drop, or a 5% cumulative disinflation.

Shorter-lived interest rate rises and announcements of future rate rises have less effect still. In the appendix (http://www.nber.org/data-appendix/c13911/appendix.pdf), I show that an interest rate rise from i to i^* that only lasts M years yields in place of equation (31),

$$\frac{P_t^*}{P} - 1 \approx (1 - e^{-\vartheta M})\left(\frac{i + \vartheta}{i^* + \vartheta} - 1\right). \tag{32}$$

An interest rate rise that lasts two years $M = 2$ has only $1 - e^{-\vartheta 2} = 1 - e^{-0.2 \times 2} \approx 1 / 3$ as large an effect as a permanent increase.

An announcement of a future interest rate rise only affects bonds of maturity longer than the announcement delay. An announcement of an interest rate rise from i to i^* that starts in M years yields in place of equation (31),

$$\frac{P_t^*}{P_t} - 1 \approx e^{-\vartheta M}\left(\frac{i + \vartheta}{i^* + \vartheta} - 1\right). \tag{33}$$

Thus, a permanent interest rate rise that is announced two years ahead of time has a $e^{-(0.2 \times 2)}$ or about two-thirds as much effect.

Either mechansim gives us about 2–3% cumulative disinflation for a 1% interest rate change, and less if we combine them. This is at least in the right ballpark—not 0.2% and not 20%.

I pursue more careful calibration of this effect to the actual US maturity structure, in the context of a model with sticky prices and long-term debt, below.

The Answer?

Is this basic mechanism the answer we are looking for to deliver a temporary negative effect of monetary policy on inflation?

In its favor, this basic mechanism unites interest rate policy, forward guidance, and quantitative easing. And all three work in a frictionless model—no monetary frictions, no pricing frictions, and no bond market segmentation. This is an attractive unification and simplification. One later adds frictions for more realistic dynamics, of course.

Interest rate policy works here only by its effect on long-term bond prices, that is, by its implied forward guidance. So, explicit forward guidance has the same effect. For example, paths such as the temporary disinflations at $t = -3$, shown in dashed lines of the bottom panel in figure 8, are achieved here entirely by "forward guidance," that is, an announcement at time $t = -3$ that interest rates will rise at time 0.

To see how this mechanism also encompasses quantitative easing (QE), consider a very simple example. Suppose debt $\{B_{-1}^{(j)}\}$ due at $j = 0, 1, 2, \ldots$ is outstanding at time 0. Suppose further that the government plans neither to sell nor to roll over any more debt. It simply will pay off each coupon $\{B_{-1}^{(j)}\}$ at time j from surpluses at time j.

Now suppose at time 0 the Fed unexpectedly buys back some long-term debt. It announces the plan, then buys debt at new bond prices. The price level at each date $j > 0$ is set by the condition that primary surpluses must soak up maturing debt, since by assumption of this simple example no new debt is issued,

$$\frac{B_0^{(j)}}{P_j} = s_j; \; j = 1, 2, 3\ldots \tag{34}$$

Therefore bond prices at time 0 are

$$Q_0^{(j)} = E_0\left[\beta^j \frac{P_0}{P_j}\right] = P_0 E_0\left[\beta^j \frac{s_j}{B_0^{(j)}}\right]. \tag{35}$$

The price level at time 0 is set by the same condition as equation (34), but on this date bond purchases add some extra cash,

$$B_{-1}^{(0)} - \sum_{j=1}^{\infty}(B_0^{(j)} - B_{-1}^{(j)})Q_0^{(j)} = P_0 s_0. \tag{36}$$

The amounts outstanding are B, so a positive $(B_0^{(j)} - B_{-1}^{(j)})$ corresponds to a debt sale, and a negative value to a purchase.

Substituting the bond price (35) in (36) and rearranging, we have the central result,

$$\frac{B_{-1}^{(0)}}{P_0} = s_0 + \sum_{j=1}^{\infty} \beta^j \frac{B_0^{(j)} - B_{-1}^{(j)}}{B_0^{(j)}} s_j. \tag{37}$$

By buying long-term bonds, the Fed lowers the right-hand side of equation (37), thereby raising P_0, which with price stickiness may stimulate real activity as well. By lowering $B_0^{(j)}$, with P_0 higher, the Fed in equation (35) raises long-term bond prices and lowers long-term interest rates.

Conversely, by selling long-term bonds, the Fed would engineer a rise in long-term rates, and a decrease in the price level today, exactly the downward price-level jump followed by rise in interest rates achieved by the interest rate rise or forward guidance. QE is just the quantity view of the same mechanism.

This model also ties a disinflationary shock to the subsequent interest rate rise, in a way I argued above that standard New Keynesian depictions of Fed equilibrium selection by interest rate policies do not do.

However, there are some important differences between this mechanism and traditional beliefs, and important work on it to be done.

This model is still long-run neutral—persistently higher interest rates eventually raise inflation. This mechanism does not on its own produce the traditional adaptive expectations analysis of the 1980s—doggedly high rates slowly squeeze out inflation. (Figure 10 below illustrates the standard view.) Sims (2011) called this mechanism "stepping on a rake." He views the model as a description of the failed monetary stabilizations of the 1970s, in which interest rate increases produced temporary reductions of inflation that only came back more strongly later.

To produce a successful inflation stabilization, a model of the 1980s, one needs something else. A natural possibility is to view the 1980s as a joint monetary-fiscal stabilization. The interest rate increases of the early 1980s had these temporary effects, but they were paired with fiscal reforms such as the 1982 and 1986 tax act, together with deregulation. Subsequent economic growth was strong, and surpluses surged. The temporary disinflation occasioned by high interest rates turned into a permanent disinflation with fiscal backing.

This mechanism gives a disinflation when the interest rate rise becomes expected, not when it actually happens. This mechanism operates *only* through expected future interest rates and by lowering long-term bond prices. The rise in current interest rates is essentially irrelevant, in sharp contrast with standard investment-savings, liquidity-money (IS-LM) or money supply/demand thinking. Operating in a frictionless model, it has nothing to do with Phillips curves, that is, higher current real rates leading to lower output leading to less pressure on prices and wages. Most deeply, this model does not revive the instability of the Old Keynesian model, which lies behind both traditional activist policy advice and the traditional view of inflation stabilization by doggedly higher interest rates alone. This mechanism offers *nothing* like any story told to undergraduates, Federal Open Market Committee (FOMC) members, or the general public about why higher interest rates lower inflation. The fact that it works in a completely frictionless model, though a feature from the view of clarity and simplicity, is a fatal bug for the purpose of describing traditional beliefs.

Nor does this mechanism easily rationalize traditional short-run policy prescriptions. It is not necessarily possible or wise for the Fed to try to control inflation by exploiting this short-run negative sign. Since the negative sign only appears for *unexpected* policy changes, by unexpectedly devaluing the claims of long-term bondholders, systematic policy has limited effect. And getting the timing and dynamics just right are likely to be a challenge. Since the long-run effect is positive and stable, there is a good case here that the Fed should keep interest rates steady based on its long-run inflation goal and real-rate assessment, and not try to micromanage the path of inflation with activist policy exploiting the transitory negative sign.

Finally, this mechanism rests on important and possibly tenuous fiscal foundations. By raising interest rates, the Fed raises future inflation. This is a gift to the Treasury—the Treasury can reduce surpluses and still pay off the promised nominal value of the debt. By fixing surpluses, I assume the Treasury stubbornly refuses the gift. The size and even sign of the effect revolve crucially on how people think the Treasury will react.

In sum, though this model may well be the answer and may address the data, it is not the answer to every question, and in particular it is not a rationalization of standard beliefs.

To pursue this line, important next steps must follow. First, changes in interest rates with fixed surpluses are a useful textbook, problem-set sort of assumption. But fixed or "exogenous" surpluses are not necessary for the theory, and they are terrible assumptions for policy, econometric, or historical analysis. Just how will the Treasury and Congress respond to inflation? If the Fed, as here, devalues long-term bonds with a promise of future inflation, will the Treasury really take none of that promise and not lower surpluses even a bit? How do people expect the Treasury and Congress to respond to the same events that occasion the Fed's interest rate rise? These are crucial assumptions to understand history and how interest rates and QE operations affect inflation.

In particular, we must face the minor embarrassment that this mechanism seems to predict that QE works to produce inflation, whereas I just argued that QE had no visible impact on inflation. The story is flexible enough to account for this QE failure, of course, as the theory describes an unrealistic partial derivative with fixed surpluses and no future roll-overs. Here, only QE that corresponds to shortening the Treasury maturity structure counts. Mortgage-backed securities (MBS) purchases have no effect. The Treasury issued debt just as fast as the Fed was buying it, so debt in private hands changed less than we think. If the Fed is expected to undo the QE in the future, then the effect vanishes. If the Treasury is expected to roll over the debt when it comes due, then it is at least attenuated. Perhaps QE was accompanied by changes in fiscal expectations—surely true, but what size and sign? Most deeply, this QE was not, in fact, accompanied by visible interest rate changes, as figure 1 makes clear, which are the mark in this model of whether it is effective.

But this smacks of the sort of epicycle argument that I dismissed with Occam's razor. So perhaps these stories of joint fiscal-monetary coordination for excusing the failure of QE also wipe out the disinflationary effects of interest rate rises in other episodes as well, and the negative sign simply is not true.

Second, of course, one must move beyond the extremely simple model presented here to more detailed models capable of matching dynamics. Sims (2011) is a good example, adding a preference for smooth consumption, a monetary policy rule with output and price reactions and inertia, sticky prices, and a fiscal policy rule that raises surpluses in good times. He produces a hump-shaped inflation-response curve in place of my downward jump followed by rise. In a much simpler exercise, I merge this mechanism with a standard simple New Keynesian model below.

More generally, this mechanism generates important ties between the effects of interest rate policy, the maturity structure of outstanding debt, and how fiscal policies react to inflation and output and the maturity structure of the debt that have yet to be faced in a serious quantitative evaluation.

C. A Simple Model of Sticky Prices

The natural response to the failure of the frictionless model with short-term debt is, well, duh, you need sticky prices to get inflation to go down after an interest rate rise. With sticky prices, a higher nominal rate means a higher real rate, a higher real rate means lower aggregate demand, lower output, and via the Phillips curve, lower inflation.

This intuition describes the Old Keynesian adaptive expectations model. But that model is unstable and thus inconsistent with the quiet stable zero bound. We are looking for a model with long-run neutrality on top of a short-run negative sign.

Alas, as we will see here, New Keynesian models do not embody this intuition. They robustly predict higher inflation in response to monetary policy, despite price stickiness.

The points are easiest to see in the very simplified model outlined in Section II.C. The same qualitative results hold in more complex and realistic versions. I verify in particular below that the standard New Keynesian model with an $E_t x_{t+1}$ term works in the same way as the simple model here.

Omitting constants and the zero bound, which are not relevant here, substituting out the output gap x and real rate r from equations (1)–(4), we have the equilibrium condition (5)

$$\sigma \kappa i_t = -\pi_t + (1 + \sigma\kappa)\pi_t^e + \sigma\kappa v_t^r, \tag{38}$$

and the interest rate rule,

$$i_t = \phi\pi_t + v_t^i. \tag{39}$$

Adaptive Expectations

In the adaptive expectations model, $\pi_t^e = \pi_{t-1}$, we solve equation (38) directly for the response of inflation to the path for interest rates as

$$\pi_t = (1 + \sigma\kappa)\pi_{t-1} - \sigma\kappa(i_t - v_t^r). \tag{40}$$

If we wish instead to solve for the response of inflation to a monetary policy disturbance, v^i, we substitute the rule (39) for i_t and solve, leading to equation (9), repeated here:

$$\pi_t = \frac{1 + \sigma\kappa}{1 + \phi\sigma\kappa} \pi_{t-1} - \frac{\sigma\kappa}{1 + \phi\sigma\kappa}(v_t^i - v_t^r). \tag{41}$$

In equation (40), the coefficient on lagged inflation π_{t-1} is greater than one, and the coefficient on the interest rate i_t is negative. Thus, in response

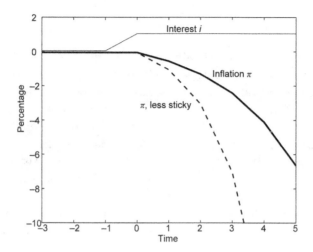

Fig. 9. Simulation of a permanent interest rate rise in the simple Old Keynesian model
Note: The baseline uses $\kappa = 1/2$, $\sigma = 1$. The "less sticky" case uses $\kappa = 1$.

to a sustained rise in interest rates, inflation spirals off negatively. Figure 9 illustrates.

Figure 9 includes the response for less price stickiness, $\kappa = 1$, instead of $\kappa = 1/2$. Sensibly, less sticky prices speed up dynamics. But that just makes the explosion happen faster. The adaptive expectations model does not approach the frictionless limit.

This response to *interest rates* is the same for any value of ϕ, and $\phi < 1$ versus $\phi > 1$ in particular. As in the frictionless model, this response of inflation to interest rates (40) does not assume a time-varying peg $\phi = 0$; it simply assumes that the Fed is following whatever set of shocks is necessary to keep equilibrium interest rates at their assumed value. The rule (41) tells us what path of monetary policy disturbances v_t^i is needed to generate the given path of interest rates; $\phi > 1$ versus $\phi < 1$ does not determine the stability of this response. Here, $\phi > 1$ just means that the Fed would need an ever-increasing set of shocks; v_t^i is necessary to keep interest rates constant.

Why do we not observe this much-feared instability? An Old Keynesian might answer, because governments and central banks are not dumb enough to keep interest rates constant forever in the face of inflation. (Though sometimes it takes them a while to catch on.) Likewise, a deflation spiral eventually spurs fiscal stimulus, helicopter drops, or other extreme measures.

To illustrate, figure 10 plots the response of this simple Old Keynes-

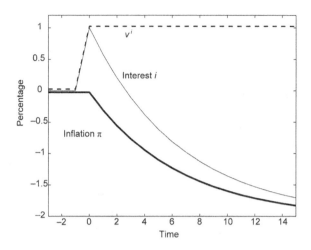

Fig. 10. Response to a step-function monetary policy disturbance in the simple Old Keynesian model.
Note: The figure plots the response to a permanent 1% increase in v_t^i; $\phi = 1.5$, $\kappa = 0.2$, $\sigma = 1$.

ian model to a permanent monetary policy *disturbance*, v_t^i, simulating forward equation (41).

Interest rates rise at first, to get disinflation going, but then quickly follow inflation in order to stop it from going too far. This graph embodies the sequence of events Friedman (1968, p. 6) described of an interest rate change. It also describes the conventional adaptive-expectations view of the 1980s.

In the long run, interest rates move one-for-one with inflation. The model is not Fisherian, however, as the Fisher relationship is an unstable steady state. Interest rates must initially rise to get disinflation going, and then interest rates follow inflation down, not the other way around. At the zero bound, the Fed is unable to lower interest rates and get the negative of this process going.

In equations (40) and (41), the natural rate shock v^r enters along with the interest rate and the monetary policy disturbance, respectively. Thus we can read figure 9 as the response of the economy to a sustained decline in the natural rate when the interest rate does not move, as at the zero bound. The zero bound spiral shown in figure 4 is the same mechanism—and the absence of such a spiral tells us that an interest rate rise is similarly not likely to have the effect shown in figure 9.

Likewise, figure 10 illustrates the reaction of inflation to a permanent decline in the natural rate with no change in the monetary policy *disturbance, v^i,* that is, if the Fed allows (and can allow) the interest rate to follow the usual Taylor rule. A decline in the natural rate would set off a protracted decline in inflation. This is the initial path of inflation in figure 4 before the zero bound binds and the constant interest rate unstable dynamics of figure 10 take over from the constant disturbance dynamics.

The model (41)–(40) makes no distinction between expected and unexpected disturbances, and there are no forward-looking terms. Hence, these responses are the same for anticipated movements as for surprise movements and anywhere in between, that is, policies announced at time $t = -3$, for example. The rational expectations idea that expected and unexpected policy have different effects is not present and announcements of future policies have no effects.

Figure 10 helps to illustrate why it is hard to tell an unstable model, whose central bank is following active policies and not letting instabilities erupt, from a stable model. Equilibrium interest rates and inflation rise and fall together in both cases. Add some noise, and it will be hard to see if the interest rate fall caused the inflation fall or vice versa. That is why the long zero bound is such a telling experiment.

Figure 9 and figure 10 summarize the classic view of the effects of monetary policy. Alas, the underlying model is inconsistent with the observed stability at the zero bound. That stability means we are looking for models with only a temporary negative effect of interest rates on inflation.

Rational Expectations

For the New Keynesian model with rational expectations, $\pi_t^e = E_t \pi_{t+1}$, equation (38) now implies that the response of inflation to equilibrium interest rates is

$$E_t \pi_{t+1} = \frac{1}{1 + \sigma\kappa} \pi_t + \frac{\sigma\kappa}{1 + \sigma\kappa} (i_t - v_t^r). \tag{42}$$

Substituting in the policy rule (39), the response to a monetary policy disturbance is (also previously given in equation [11]),

$$E_t \pi_{t+1} = \frac{1 + \phi\sigma\kappa}{1 + \sigma\kappa} \pi_t + \frac{\sigma\kappa}{1 + \sigma\kappa} (v_t^i - v_t^r). \tag{43}$$

Again, we can calculate the path of inflation corresponding to a given path of equilibrium interest rates in equation (42), without specifying what path of monetary policy disturbances v_t^i and systematic responses

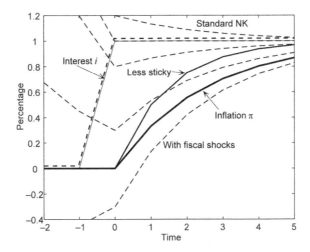

Fig. 11. Simulation of an interest rate rise or natural rate fall in the simple New Keynesian model.

Note: The baseline uses $\kappa = 1/2$, $\sigma = 1$; the "less sticky" case uses $\kappa = 1$. Dashed lines indicate potential multiple equilibria.

$\phi\pi_t$ produced the interest rate path. Again, that inflation path is independent of the policy rule ϕ, and the set of disturbances v^i that generated the interest rate path, neither of which is present in equation (42). Again, equation (42) does *not* necessarily represent the response to a time-varying peg ($\phi = 0$)—though it can.

In equation (42) the coefficient in front of i_t is positive, and the coefficient in front of π_t is less than one. The model has a positive, stable inflation response to an increase in interest rates, rather than a negative, unstable response in the solid line, labeled "Inflation π." Figure 11 presents this response. And the response is Fisherian, both in the short and long run. The whole reason that we are here—the hope that adding price stickiness to the frictionless model illustrated by figure 8 would generate a model with a short-run inflation decline—fails, at least so far.

Already, the New Keynesian model reverses the hallowed doctrine that interest rate pegs are unstable. Now it undoes the widespread presumption that higher interest rates temporarily lower inflation when prices are sticky.

Here too, v_t^r and i_t enter (42) together, so we can read figure 11 as the response of inflation to a natural rate v^r fall, when interest rates do not or cannot move. The natural rate fall *raises* inflation. Higher inflation with a fixed nominal rate produces a lower real rate. Thus, inflation accommodates needed changes in the natural real rate, albeit slowly, all by itself, without the need for active Fed action or announcements. Contrariwise, a rise in the natural rate with no change in interest rates leads to a steady decline in inflation, all on its own, to produce the higher real rate with unchanged nominal rates. One might read the history of slowly decreasing inflation during recovery at the zero bound as an instance of this mechanism.

Figure 11 includes the case of less price stickiness, $\kappa = 1$, in place of $\kappa = 1/2$ in the line labeled "less sticky." Again, dynamics happen more quickly. But in this case, unlike the Old Keynesian adaptive expectations model, dynamics smoothly approach the frictionless limit, in which $i_t = r + E_t \pi_{t+1}$ and expected inflation rises immediately to match the rise in nominal interest rate. This is an attractive property.

(Difficulties with the frictionless limit happen in New Keynesian models when one ties down the equilibria by choices of future inflation and one introduces time—0 jumps. Then small changes in the future inflation imply large jumps in today's inflation, and those changes get bigger as price stickiness is reduced or the horizon increases. Some of these issues are discussed with figure 19 below. Cochrane 2017 discusses the issue at length. *This* calculation smoothly approaches a frictionless limit, in a way the Old Keynesian model above does not. That does not mean that *all* calculations in the New Keynesian literature smoothly approach fricitionless limits. Many do not.)

As in the frictionless model of figure 8, this rational-expectations sticky-price model only ties down expected inflation, so one can add any unpredictable shock δ_{t+1} to the ex post versions of equations (42) and (43), that is, the version with π_{t+1}, not $E_t\pi_{t+1}$, on the left-hand side. One cannot expect unexpected jumps, so for an impulse-response function, multiple equilibria only introduce the possibility of an unexpected jump on the date people learn the new policy.

Unlike the frictionless case, unexpected jumps have lasting effects. To the solutions of equation (42) with $\pi_0 = 0$ we can add

$$\pi_t = \left(\frac{1}{1 + \sigma\kappa}\right)^t \pi_0 \qquad (44)$$

for any value of π_0.

I indicate such multiple equilibria by dashed lines in figure 11. On the date of the announcement, inflation could jump to any of the dashed lines, and would be expected to then continue on that line. For example, in the traditional case that the interest rate rise is a surprise at date 0, inflation at date 0, rather than being 0 (solid line), could jump down to the dashed line at its kink, and then start to rise. In the case of a preannounced rate rise, inflation could jump down to the dashed line at that earlier date. In this way, the graph covers the results of any announcement date.

As in the frictionless case, we might obtain the transitory negative effect with such a downward jump coincident with the announcement of a rate rise.

Again, each such jump has an associated change in fiscal policy, whether "actively" or "passively" achieved, so I label them "with fiscal shocks." Now, such jumps have protracted effects, and begin to look more like a source of smooth temporary disinflation. But adding fiscal shocks to produce a temporary negative response makes no more sense here than in the frictionless case.

(The solid line labeled "inflation π" that does not jump at time 0 corresponds to no change in the present value of surpluses. However, higher nominal rates now imply higher real rates, and therefore a lower present value if surpluses themselves do not change. Thus, the previous definition of monetary policy as a change in interest rates with no change in *surpluses*, rather than one with no change in the present value of surpluses, would include a small upward jump in inflation on the date of announcement. As the sign is not going to help us, I leave quantification of this mechanism to the fuller model below.)

Perhaps transitory interest rate changes naturally produce a negative response—the standard wisdom? If the equilibrium interest rate follows a transitory path,

$$i_t = \rho i_{t-1} + \varepsilon_t,$$

the response of inflation to a time-0 interest rate shock is, from equation (42),

$$\pi_t = \frac{\sigma\kappa}{1 + \sigma\kappa} \frac{\rho^t - [1 / (1 + \sigma\kappa)]^t}{\rho - 1 / (1 + \sigma\kappa)} i_0; \quad t = 1, 2, 3... \tag{45}$$

It is always positive, and typically hump-shaped. The corresponding plot basically just pulls down the right end of figure 11. Again, this result holds for *any* ϕ, and the response is positive for *any* $\rho > 0$. Transitory interest rate movements are not going to give us a temporary disinflation. We really have to add a downward jump.

Policy Disturbances

Perhaps if we specify a policy disturbance sequence rather than an equilibrium interest rate, a downward jump will seem more plausible?

In the New Keynesian model (43), $\phi > 1$ induces instability. The coefficient on π_t is then greater than one. We solve equation (43) forward to

$$\pi_{t+1} = -\frac{\sigma\kappa}{1 + \sigma\kappa} \sum_{j=0}^{\infty} \left(\frac{1 + \sigma\kappa}{1 + \phi\sigma\kappa}\right)^{j+1} E_{t+1}(v_{t+1+j}^i - v_{t+1+j}^r). \tag{46}$$

This solution describes how we pick the multiple equilibrium δ_{t+1}, so it offers hope to pick one of the downward jumps. I dated the equation at $t + 1$ to emphasize this point. (We do not similarly solve equation [41] forward for $\phi < 1$ because there is no jump variable, or undetermined expectation. That unique response just becomes explosive.)

If the disturbance v_t^i follows an AR(1)

$$v_t^i = \rho v_{t-1}^i + \varepsilon_t,$$

we can solve equation (46) at time t to give

$$\pi_t = -\frac{\sigma\kappa}{1 - \rho + (\phi - \rho)\sigma\kappa} v_t^i. \tag{47}$$

From the policy rule (39), the interest rate follows

$$i_t = \frac{1 - \rho(1 + \sigma\kappa)}{1 - \rho + (\phi - \rho)\sigma\kappa} v_t^i. \tag{48}$$

Both i_t and π_t follow AR(1) responses. Using equation (48) to substitute out v_t^i in (48), we can express the relation between inflation and interest rates as

$$\pi_t = \frac{\sigma\kappa}{\rho(1 + \sigma\kappa) - 1} i_t. \tag{49}$$

In the case of a permanent change, $\rho = 1$, these formulas simplify to

$$\pi_{t+1} = -\frac{1}{\phi - 1} v^i; \tag{50}$$

$$i_t = -\frac{1}{\phi - 1} v^i; \tag{51}$$

$$\pi_t = i_t. \tag{52}$$

The negative sign in equations (47) and (50) may lead to some optimism: a positive policy disturbance sends inflation down. But it also sends interest rates down, so the relation between interest rates and inflation remains positive. Again, do not confuse the response to a monetary policy shock with a response to interest rates.

Thus in this standard $\phi > 1$ solution of the New Keynesian model, a permanent ($\rho = 1$) monetary policy shock gives rise to a completely Fisherian response. Inflation rises instantly and follows the interest rate exactly, as shown in the "standard NK" dashed line of figure 11. It is even more Fisherian than the original $\delta = 0$ solution. Despite price stickiness, this instant response is the same as in the frictionless case of figure 8.

Returning to the $\rho < 1$ case, for sufficiently persistent monetary policy, $\rho > 1 / (1 + \sigma\kappa)$, the coefficient on the right-hand side of equation (49) remains positive, so higher interest rates correspond uniformly to higher inflation, just as in the permanent case.

For sufficiently transitory monetary policy, however, $\rho < 1 / (1 + \sigma\kappa)$, equation (49) shows that a higher interest rate with an AR(1) decay at rate ρ results in uniformly lower inflation, also following an AR(1) decay, the long-sought traditional sign. (A reader wishing a graph can look ahead at the bottom-right panel of figure 15. Though the calculations in that figure use the full standard model, the results are visually the same as for this simplified model.) Here, also, the monetary policy disturbance v_t^i acts in the same direction as the interest rate.

This result embodies the conventional wisdom that the New Keynesian model produces a negative response for a transitory policy shock. This sign occurs for $\rho > 0$, unlike the frictionless case in which $\rho < 0$ was necessary for a negative response.

This is not the answer we are looking for, strictly speaking. It generates a negative response to a temporary interest rate rise, but it does not generate a temporary negative response to a sustained interest rate rise. Still perhaps it is good enough?

At the boundary $\rho = 1 / (1 + \sigma\kappa)$, an instructive case reappears—the open-mouth effect. Here, interest rates i_t do not move at all. Inflation simply jumps up or down on the Fed's announcement that a monetary policy shock has occurred. (See the bottom-left panel of figure 15.) With price stickiness, the inflation jump persists with an AR(1) pattern. This case emphasizes how much "monetary policy" in the standard New Keynesian model is about the Fed's equilibrium-selection powers, not about interest rate movements.

The appearance of a link between the persistence and sign of monetary policy is again an artifact of the v_t^i and AR(1) disturbance parameterization. In fact, the Fed can, with a suitable choice of disturbances, select any unexpected inflation consistent with any persistence of equilibrium interest rates.

As in the frictionless case, we can see both facts most easily by parameterizing the policy rule as a time-varying inflation target rather than a v_t^i disturbance,

$$i_t = i_t^* + \phi(\pi_t - \pi_t^*).$$

This parameterization cleanly separates interest rate policy i_t^* from equilibrium-selection policy $\phi(\pi_t - \pi_t^*)$.

While one can calculate responses to arbitrary disturbances $\{i_t^*\}$, $\{\pi_t^*\}$, the equilibrium interest rate may then not come out to $i_t = i_t^*$ and the equilibrium inflation may not come out to $\pi_t = \pi_t^*$. If we parameterize the disturbances so that they obey the first-order conditions of the rest of the model, we have that convenient result. Thus, as the policy rule in the frictionless model satisfied $i_t^* = r + E_t\pi_{t+1}^*$, let the two policy disturbances here satisfy $i_t^* = r_t + E_t\pi_{t+1}^*$. Using equations (2) and (3) and with r*=0 for simplicity, we have

$$r_t = \frac{1}{\sigma\kappa}(E_t\pi_{t+1} - \pi_t) + v_t^r,$$

so write the policy rule

$$i_t = \left[E_t\pi_{t+1}^* + \frac{1}{\sigma\kappa}(E_t\pi_{t+1}^* - \pi_t^*) + v_t^r\right] + \phi(\pi_t - \pi_t^*). \tag{53}$$

Substituting the rule (53) in (42) we obtain, rather than (43),

$$E_t(\pi_{t+1} - \pi_{t+1}^*) = \frac{1 + \sigma\kappa\phi}{1 + \sigma\kappa}(\pi_t - \pi_t^*). \tag{54}$$

Thus, the Fed induces explosive dynamics for any $\pi_t \neq \pi_t^*$, and ruling out such explosions

$$\pi_t = \pi_t^*$$

is the unique equilibrium. Despite sticky prices, the Fed can still achieve any path of inflation it wishes, both expected and unexpected.

Furthermore, the path of unexpected inflation is independent from the path of interest rates. There is no necessary tie between the persistence of interest rates and the sign of the inflation response. Equilibrium interest rates follow

$$i_t = i_t^* = E_t\pi_{t+1}^* + \frac{1}{\sigma\kappa}(E_t\pi_{t+1}^* - \pi_t^*) + v_t^r. \tag{55}$$

Thus, choosing an interest rate path determines $E_t\pi_{t+1}^*$, but the Fed can independently choose $\pi_{t+1}^* - E_t\pi_{t+1}^*$ the next period.

For example, to produce a response function in which interest rates follow an AR(1),

$$i_t = \rho^t i_0; \quad t = 0, 1, 2, \ldots$$

The Fed chooses a disturbance $\{\pi_t^*\}$ that results in this AR(1) for $\{i_t^*\} = \rho^t i_0$. From equation (55),

$$E_0 \pi_{t+1}^* = \frac{\sigma\kappa}{1 + \sigma\kappa} \rho^t i_0 + \frac{1}{1 + \sigma\kappa} E_0 \pi_t^*. \tag{56}$$

Iterating forward,

$$E_0 \pi_t^* = \left(\frac{1}{1 + \sigma\kappa}\right)^t \pi_0^* + \frac{\sigma\kappa}{1 + \sigma\kappa} \left\{ \frac{[1 / (1 + \sigma\kappa)]^{t+1} - \rho^{t+1}}{1 / (1 + \sigma\kappa) - \rho} \right\} i_0. \tag{57}$$

But the choice π_0^* is unconstrained. The Fed can choose whatever instantaneous response of inflation it wishes, for *any* value of ρ, and still produce the AR(1) interest rate response. Equation (57) is no more or less than the full set of solutions indexed by π_0^*, shown by dashed lines for $\rho = 1$ in figure 11. Values of $\pi_0 < 0$ will result in temporary disinflations; values of $\pi_0 > 0$ will speed up the Fisherian response. But there is *no* tie between the persistence of the interest rate response ρ and the sign of the inflation response.

Clearly the i_t^*, π_t^* rule (53) is just a reparameterization of the v_t^i rule (39). For any $\{\pi_t^*\}$ we can construct

$$v_t^i = \frac{1 + \sigma\kappa}{\sigma\kappa} E_t \pi_{t+1}^* + \left(\phi - \frac{1}{\sigma\kappa}\right) \pi_t^* + v_t^r$$

and vice versa. So by choosing a suitable $\{v_t^i\}$, the Fed can similarly produce any sign of the inflation response for any persistence or other property of the interest rate response.

Furthermore, as in the frictionless case, it is even easier in the π_t^* parameterization to construct and interpret an open-mouth operation. The Fed simply announces that its new inflation target will be

$$\pi_t^* = \pi_0^* \left(\frac{1}{1 + \sigma\kappa}\right)^t$$

and it happens. From equation (55), you can verify immediately that the interest rate does not move. (Campbell and Weber 2016 describe similar open-mouth operations.)

Now, perhaps this is our world. Monetary policy at the zero bound has seemed to evolve into central banker statements accompanied by no actual changes in interest rates or asset purchases. Central banks have long moved interest rates, in fact, by simply announcing a change in rate, with actual open-market operations following much later, if at all. (For example, see Brash 2002.) Open-mouth operations in this paper are doubly removed from action, since the central bank can apparently move inflation without even moving interest rates.

Perhaps inflation really has little to do with economics (supply and demand, intertemporal substitution, money, and so forth). Perhaps inflation really is predominantly a multiple equilibrium question. Perhaps "monetary" policy affects inflation entirely by government officials making statements, with implicit never-observed off-equilibrium threats, that cause jumps from one equilibrium to another, validated by passive fiscal policy. Perhaps changes to interest rates, though economically irrelevant and even counterproductive in the long run, evolved as some sort of communication and signaling equilibrium to indicate a policy shock.

If so, again, sufficient becomes necessary. The quest of this paper—a simple, transparent, baseline economic model of the effect of interest rates on inflation—is over, with a negative result and a disquieting implication for the status of monetary policy in the arsenal of robust and well-understood phenomena.

In sum, the sticky-price New Keynesian model works very much like the frictionless model. The intuition that with sticky prices, a higher nominal interest rate produces a higher real interest rate, which depresses aggregate demand, and via the Phillips curve reduces inflation, simply does not describe this model.

D. Full New Keynesian Model

The claim that the frictionless and simplified models capture the behavior of real New Keynesian needs verification. And we need to see how the real model behaves.

I use the standard optimizing sticky-price model,

$$x_t = E_t x_{t+1} - \sigma(i_t - E_t \pi_{t+1}) \tag{58}$$

$$\pi_t = \beta E_t \pi_{t+1} + \kappa x_t \tag{59}$$

$$i_t = \phi \pi_t + v_t^i \tag{60}$$

or

$$i_t = i_t^* + \phi(\pi_t - \pi_t^*) \tag{61}$$

where x_t denotes the output gap, i_t is the nominal interest rate, and π_t is inflation. The last two equations give two equivalent parameterizations of an interest rate policy rule.

The solution of this model for a given interest rate path is derived in the appendix (http://www.nber.org/data-appendix/c13911/appendix .pdf). Inflation and output are two-sided geometrically weighted distributed lags of the interest rate path,

$$\pi_{t+1} = \frac{\sigma\kappa}{\lambda_1 - \lambda_2} \left[i_t + \sum_{j=1}^{\infty} \lambda_1^{-j} i_{t-j} + \sum_{j=1}^{\infty} \lambda_2^{j} E_{t+1} i_{t+j} \right] + \sum_{j=0}^{\infty} \lambda_1^{-j} \delta_{t+1-j} \quad (62)$$

$$\kappa x_{t+1} = \frac{\sigma\kappa}{\lambda_1 - \lambda_2} \left[(1 - \beta\lambda_1^{-1}) \sum_{j=0}^{\infty} \lambda_1^{-j} i_{t-j} + (1 - \beta\lambda_2^{-1}) \sum_{j=1}^{\infty} \lambda_2^{j} E_{t+1} i_{t+j} \right]$$

$$+ (1 - \beta\lambda_1^{-1}) \sum_{j=0}^{\infty} \lambda_1^{-j} \delta_{t+1-j}, \quad (63)$$

where

$$\lambda_{1,2} = \frac{(1 + \beta + \sigma\kappa) \pm \sqrt{(1 + \beta + \sigma\kappa)^2 - 4\beta}}{2}. \quad (64)$$

We have $\lambda_1 > 1$ and $\lambda_2 < 1$. Here, δ_{t+1}, with $E_t \delta_{t+1} = 0$, is an expectational shock indexing multiple equilibria.

Once again, this calculation represents the response of inflation to equilibrium interest rates, that is, to any disturbances that produce the given response of equilibrium interest rates, with any value of ϕ. I do not assume a time-varying peg $\phi = 0$, nor do I assume active fiscal policy, though the calculation is also valid in those cases. One can, and I will later, substitute $i_t = \phi\pi_t + v_t^i$ to derive the response to policy shocks, or to find the policy shock sequence consistent with a given interest rate path.

Interest Rate Response

Figure 12 presents the response of inflation and the output gap to a step-function rise in the interest rate, using equations (62)–(63), and choosing the basic solution $\delta_0 = 0$. I use parameters

$$\beta = 0.97, \kappa = 0.2, \sigma = 1. \quad (65)$$

Inflation rises throughout the episode. Mathematically, that rise is a result of a two-sided moving average with positive weights in equation (62).

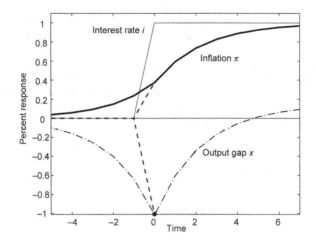

Fig. 12. Response of inflation and output to a step-function interest rate change in the standard IS–Phillips curve New Keynesian model.

Note: The solid and dot-dashed lines show the response to an expected change. The dashed lines show the response to an unexpected change. Parameters $\beta = 0.97$, $\kappa = 0.2$, $\sigma = 1$.

Output declines around the interest rate rise. When the nominal interest rate is higher than the inflation rate, the real rate is high. Output is low when current and future real interest rates are high via intertemporal substitution. Equivalently, the forward-looking Phillips curve (59) says that output is low when inflation is low relative to future inflation, that is, when inflation is rising.

Output eventually rises slightly, as the steady state of the Phillips curve (59) with $\beta < 1$ gives a slight increase in the level of output when inflation increases permanently. Using $\beta = 1$, there is no permanent output effect, and all graphs are otherwise visually indistinguishable. The positive inflation effect does not require a permanent output effect.

The solid and dot-dashed lines of figure 12 plot the responses to a preannounced interest rate rise. The dashed lines plot the responses to an interest rate rise announced on the same date as the rise, date zero. Announced and surprise interest rate paths are the same after the announcement day. The response to an interest rate change announced at any time before zero jumps up to match the anticipated policy reaction on the day of announcement. In this way, the solid and dot-dashed lines capture the response for any announcement day.

In this class of models, expected monetary policy matters—inflation and output move ahead of a pre-announced interest rate rise. Expected and unexpected policy have identical effects after the announcement date because the interest rate shock $i_t - E_{t-1}i_t$ does not appear as a separate right-hand variable in the model's solutions (62)–(63), as money shocks appear in information-based Phillips curves such as Lucas (1972).

"Forward guidance" matters, and outcomes are affected by expectations, even when those expectations are not realized.

In sum, price stickiness smooths the Fisherian response of the frictionless model seen in figure 8, but does not change its character. One might have hoped that price stickiness would deliver the traditional view of a temporary decline in inflation. It does not.

The model does, however, generate the output decline that conventional intuition and most empirical work associates with monetary policy tightening. Raising interest rates to cool off a booming economy, and lowering interest rates to stimulate a slow economy, may still make sense. Doing so just has a different effect on inflation than we might have thought. However, this effect depends on the rather contentious forward-looking Philips curve, which gives lower output when inflation is increasing.

The sign of the responses are not affected, and magnitudes not greatly affected, by changes in the parameters. There is not much you can do to an S shape. The parameters κ and σ enter together in the inflation response. Larger values speed up the dynamics, smoothly approaching the step function of the frictionless model as their product rises. Larger values of β slightly slow down the dynamics. Larger σ on its own gives larger output effects with the same pattern.

Mean Reverting Rates

Perhaps transitory interest rate movements produce a negative sign? Figure 13 plots responses to an AR(1) interest rate shock.

The responses in figure 13 are similar to those of figure 12 in the short run, with a long-run return to zero. The weights in the two-sided moving average (62) are positive, and the same for any interest rate process. They do not give a negative response for any uniformly positive interest rate path, no matter its time-series properties.

Figure 13 serves as an important reminder, however: VARs that estimate transitory interest rate responses do not give us evidence on the long-run Fisher hypothesis. The long zero bound tells us something that we could not observe in the transitory interest rate changes typical of the previous era.

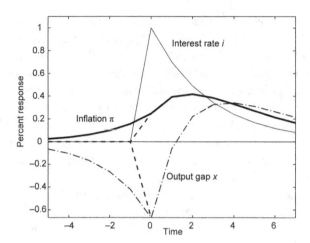

Fig. 13. Response of inflation and output to a mean-reverting interest rate path
Note: Dashed lines are the response to an unexpected change. Solid and dot-dashed lines are the response to an expected change.

Multiple Equilibria

There are multiple equilibria, indexed by the expectational shock $\{\delta_t\}$. As first displayed in figure 8, one might recover a short-run negative inflation response by pairing the announcement of a rate increase with a negative multiple-equilibrium shock δ.

The top panel of figure 14 plots a range of multiple equilibrium responses to the unanticipated step function in interest rates considered in figure 12. Each equilibrium is generated by a different choice of the expectational shock δ_0 that coincides with the interest rate shock at date zero. The bottom panel of figure 14 presents multiple equilibrium responses to an interest rate rise announced at time $t = -3$. These responses are chosen to have the same value of inflation at $t = 0$ as in the top panel. Letters identify equilibrium choices for discussion.

Equilibrium A has a positive additional inflation shock, $\delta_0 = 1\%$. Equilibrium B chooses δ_0 to produce 1% inflation at time 0, $\pi_0 = 1\%$. Equilibrium C chooses δ_0 to have no fiscal consequences, explained below. Between C and D lies the original fundamental equilibrium, with $\delta_0 = 0$, as graphed in figure 12. Equilibrium D chooses δ_0 to produce no inflation at time 0, $\pi_0 = 0$. Equilibrium E chooses $\delta_0 = -1\%$.

The figure shows graphically that the model may have too many equilibria, but all of them are stable, and all of them are Fisherian in the long run, with inflation converging to the higher nominal interest rate.

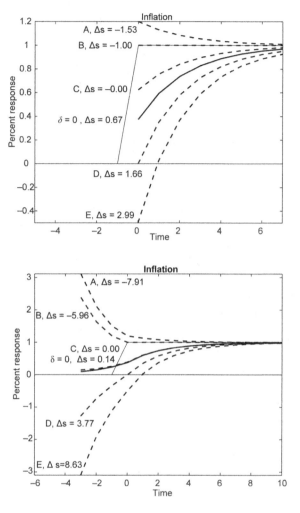

Fig. 14. Multiple equilibrium responses to an interest rate rise, New Keynesian model

Note: Top panel: Unexpected rise. Bottom panel: Expected rise. The solid step function gives the interest rate path. Letters identify different equilibria for discussion. The original case is $\delta = 0$.

In equilibrium B, inflation jumps instantly to the full increase in nominal interest rates, and stays there throughout. Output also jumps immediately to the steady-state value. Thus, despite price stickiness, the model can produce a super-neutral or super-Fisherian response, in which an interest rate rise instantly implies inflation with no output dynamics.

Equilibrium A shows that even more inflation is possible. With a sufficiently large expectational shock, inflation can actually increase by more than the interest rate change, and then settle down, and output can increase as well.

Equilibrium D adds a small negative expectational shock δ_0, so that the initial inflation response is precisely zero. One may be troubled by inflation jumps in the other equilibria, since inflation seems to have inertia in the data. It can be inertial in the model as well, by choosing this equilibrium.

Equilibrium E verifies that the model can produce a temporary decline in inflation coincident with the interest rate rise. Equilibrium E achieves that result by pairing a negative expectational or sunspot shock with the positive interest rate or expected inflation shock. The output responses (not shown) line up with the inflation responses, and equilibrium E produces a jump down in output as well that recovers.

Is there a convincing argument to prefer equilibria such as E, and to view this result as an embodiment of the conventional belief that raising interest rates temporarily lowers inflation?

The issue is not what shock δ_t we will see on a particular date. The question is what shock δ_t we will expect to see *on average*, and *caused by* the Fed's announcement of an interest rate rise.

For that reason, we do not want to fit the correlation of interest rate shocks with unexpected inflation empirically. Our goal is to find economics for an inflation decline, not to fit the most central prediction of monetary economics through a free parameter, the correlation of expected and unexpected inflation shocks. As above, if unexpected disinflation comes from fiscal policy tightening, historically coincident with interest rate increases, that does not mean that future monetary policy, not coincident with fiscal policy, will have the same effect.

Fiscal Index

Each equilibrium choice has a fiscal policy consequence. For each equilibrium choice, then, I calculate the percentage amount by which long-run real primary surpluses must rise or fall for that equilibrium to emerge. Figure 14 presents that number alongside the initial inflation value of each equilibrium.

Again, making this calculation requires no assumption whether fiscal policy is active or passive. We can index equilibria by the passive fiscal policy they require even if we do not select equilibria that way. And, as above, the fiscal expansion or contraction is crucial to producing the aggregate demand that each inflation jump requires.

To make this calculation, I start with the valuation equation for government debt,

$$\frac{B_{t-1}}{P_t} = E_t\left[\sum_{j=0}^{\infty}\beta^j\,\frac{u'(C_{t+j})}{u'(C_t)}\,s_{t+j}\right], \qquad (66)$$

where B_{t-1} denotes the face value of debt outstanding at the end of period $t-1$ and beginning of period t, P_t is the price level, $u'(C)$ is marginal utility, and s_t is the real net primary surplus.

In this case, consumption, equal to output, varies, and real interest rates vary. Higher real interest rates lower the present value of surpluses even when surpluses themselves do not change. Equivalently, higher real interest rates mean higher debt-service costs, which if not met by higher surpluses mean less surplus devoted to repaying debt, and causes inflation. This discount-rate effect is the major change between this model and the frictionless model's analysis of the fiscal consequences of unexpected inflation.

Starting from a steady state with constant surplus s, I calculate the fractional permanent change in surplus Δs, that is, $s_t = S\Delta^s$, which is required of the right-hand side of expression (66) for each response function. The calculation is described in the appendix (http://www.nber.org/data-appendix/c13911/appendix.pdf).

This calculation is simplified in many ways. I specify one-period nominal debt. Here, the objective is to focus on surpluses corresponding to the jumps in the standard model. I study long-term debt in the sticky-price model below. Second, in reality output changes affect primary surpluses, as taxes rise more than spending in booms, and fall more than spending in recessions. We do not need to assume exogenous or fixed surpluses to make these fiscal calculations, or to use the fiscal theory. But some of these effects may represent a change in timing of surpluses—borrowing during recessions that is repaid later during booms—rather than permanent changes that affect the real value of government debt, so adding them in is subtle. Third, inflation also raises revenue due to a poorly indexed tax code. Most of all, perhaps, we could almost as plausibly specify that "monetary policy" changes interest rates without changing the *present value* of the surplus, rather than specify that it does not change surpluses themselves. Realistic monetary-fiscal coordination is not a light topic. A serious calculation of the fiscal impacts of monetary policy requires considerable detail on all these lines. The point here is not quantitative realism, but to capture some of the important effects and to show how one can use fiscal considerations to evaluate different equilibrium possibilities.

The super-neutral equilibrium B in which inflation rises instantly by 1%, also marked $\Delta s = -1.00$ in figure 14, corresponds to a 1% decline in long-run surpluses. The 1% jump in inflation devalues outstanding nominal debt by 1%, and since output is constant after the shock there is no real interest rate change. Equilibrium A, with a larger inflation shock, corresponds to a larger than 1% decline in long-run surpluses.

Equilibrium D has no change in inflation at time 0, and so there is no devaluation of outstanding nominal debt. However, the rise in real interest rates means that the government incurs greater financing costs. These costs require a small permanent rise in surpluses.

In between, at equilibrium C, I find the shock δ_0 that requires no change in surpluses, so $\Delta s = 0$ by construction. Here, the devaluation effect of an inflation shock just matches the higher financing costs imposed by higher real interest rates. The original equilibrium with no expectational shock, $\delta_0 = 0$, implies a small but nonzero change in surpluses to offset the real interest rate effect.

In the frictionless model, with a constant real interest rate, the latter three equilibria are the same and have no inflation shock at time 0. However, at least in this simple calibration, the difference between unexpected inflation C, D, and $\Delta = 0$ is not large. Ignoring real interest rate effects, and discounting surpluses at a constant rate, does not make a first-order difference. One does quite well grafting the simple constant-interest-rate FTPL formulas on to the New Keynesian model.

The difference between equilibria C, $\delta = 0$, and D also punctures one more hope for a negative inflation response. Now, by changing real interest rates, monetary policy has a fiscal effect. Monetary policy changes the present value of surpluses, even if it cannot affect surpluses themselves. And this effect is an important part of current (2017) policy discussions. If the Fed were to raise real interest rates 1%, at 100% debt-to-GDP ratio, that would raise interest costs and the deficit by 1% of GDP, or nearly $200 billion dollars. This interest-expense channel is a possible fiscal-theoretic channel for the impact of monetary policy, stressed most recently by Sims (2016).

Alas, the sign is wrong for our quest. Raising real interest rates lowers the present value of surpluses, and pushes inflation *up*; C and $\delta = 0$ have positive, not negative, inflation.

Equilibrium E, in which inflation temporarily declines half a percentage point after the interest rate shock, requires a 1.54% rise in permanent fiscal net-of-interest surpluses. Disinflation raises the value of nominal debt, which must be paid. To generate a disinflation coincident with the interest rate rise, we must have a contemporaneous fiscal contraction as well, whether arranged actively or passively. Sticky prices make the needed fiscal contraction larger, not smaller. The fiscal contraction required to produce –1% disinflation is now larger than 1%, because it must overcome the inflationary effect of higher real interest rates.

Though it now produces a prettier, more drawn out response, generating a negative effect of monetary policy by pairing an interest rate rise with a contemporaneous fiscal contraction to produce an unexpected disinflation is no more attractive here than in the frictionless case.

Turning to the anticipated shocks in the bottom panel of figure 14, we see the effects of multiple equilibria that are stable forward and hence unstable backward. If we want the same inflation variation on date zero, the multiple equilibria have to jump to larger values on earlier dates. The same-sized jumps at time $t = -3$ will imply smaller variation in inflation when interest rates actually rise at $t = 0$.

Larger inflation shocks at time $t = -3$ mean that the fiscal changes required to support most of the equilibria increase as we move the announcement back in time. For example, the originally super-neutral equilibrium, which required a 1% decline in surpluses in figure 14, now requires a 4.11% surplus decline because of the larger inflation shock. And equilibrium E, selected to generate a 1% decline in inflation when interest rates rise 1%, now requires a 5.6% permanent rise in fiscal surpluses rather than 1.54%.

The exceptions to this rule are the original equilibrium choice $\delta = 0$, the equilibrium choice C or $\Delta s = 0$ with no fiscal impact, and an equilibrium (not shown) that always chooses no inflation on the announcement date, t-3 in this case. All of these equilibria have *smaller* fiscal impacts as interest rates are announced earlier in time, they all converge to the same point, and they are all stable backward. Cochrane (2017) argues these features are useful for equilibrium selection, if one does not want to take a fiscal theory approach. Here, they all lead to Fisherian responses.

Choosing equilibria with no jump in inflation is also an attractive rule. Equilibrium D in figure 14 has this property, and one can construct an equilibrium with no change in inflation upon announcement for the $t = -3$ shock of the bottom panel of figure 14. We do not see inflation jumps in the data, and New Keynesian models are often specified so that inflation must be set one or more periods in advance to reproduce that fact. This choice also is stable, and has limited fiscal impact as the announcement horizon moves backward. And it leads always to positive subsequent inflation.

In sum, the principles of small fiscal requirements, sensible behavior as announcements come earlier than actual rate changes, or limited jumps in inflation all push one to the view that equilibria near the original $\delta = 0$ equilibrium are sensible, and the others less so.

Policy Rules

Perhaps in this full model, spelling out an underlying policy rule can make a disinflationary equilibrium like E more attractive. If monetary policy picks unexpected inflation and fiscal policy is passive, then pairing the announcement of an interest rate rise with a fiscal contraction, as in equilibrium E, might make more sense as a description of monetary policy than does viewing the fiscal contraction as a coincidental action by fiscal authorities. More generally, doesn't the standard New Keynesian model produce a negative sign? That nagging doubt needs to be addressed.

Start with the standard three-equation model, with the standard expression of the policy rule, (58), (59), and (60), with $\phi > 1$, together with an AR(1) policy disturbance,

$$v_{t+1}^i = \rho v_t^i + \varepsilon_{t+1}^i.$$

The government-debt valuation equation (66) is still part of the model, but that equation determines surpluses $\{s_t\}$ by passive fiscal policy.

Figure 15 plots the response of inflation and interest rates to an unexpected monetary policy shock v_t^i for this model.

The top-left panel plots the response to a permanent shock, $\rho = 1$. This shock produces an immediate and permanent rise in the equilibrium interest rate. This is the same response as equilibrium choice B of figure 14. The passive fiscal policy produces the needed 1% fiscal expansion. This standard New Keynesian exercise produces a super-neutral response, inflation rising even faster and sooner than the $\delta = 0$ equilibrium, or the equilibrium C with no fiscal response. This is the same response as in the frictionless model and the simple model of figure 12, which alerts you to the fact that pricing frictions are not central to this model's response.

As in the simpler models, the *disturbance v_t^i* in this parameterization of the policy rule falls though equilibrium interest rates i and inflation π rise. The rule $i_t = \phi \pi_t + v_t^i$ becomes $2 = 1.5(2) - 1$. Inflation has a neg-

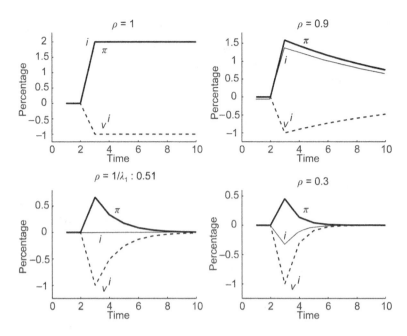

Fig. 15. Response of inflation and interest rates to an AR(1) monetary policy shock v^i with persistence ρ in the standard three-equation New Keynesian model.
Note: $\beta = 0.95$, $\kappa = 1/2$, $\sigma = 1$, $\phi = 1.5$.

ative response to the disturbance, though not to actual interest rates. Confusion between the disturbance, which is not measurable in this model, and the path of interest rates may be one reason for a false impression that this standard model delivers a negative sign.

The top-right panel of figure 15 plots the response of inflation to a persistent $\rho = 0.9$ shock. Interest rates rise, inflation rises, and one still sees a Fisherian result. The unexpected inflation shock is still positive, so it is more Fisherian than the response to an AR(1) interest rate rise with no unexpected inflation, graphed in figure 13. The policy rule is still hurting, not helping, the quest for a negative sign.

The bottom-right panel shows that for a sufficiently short-lived shock, $\rho = 0.3 < 1 / \lambda_1$, interest rates and inflation finally go in opposite directions. The disturbance v^i exceeds the endogenous response $\phi\pi$, so the negative shock produces negative interest rates. This calculation represents the standard wisdom that a sufficiently temporary shock produces a negative inflation response, and this (at last) is the standard result to reference that the standard model can produce a negative response of inflation to interest rates.

This case combines a swiftly mean-reverting process for the interest rate, as graphed in figure 13, with a strong contemporaneous fiscal contraction like case E of figure 14. In equation (62), if interest rates i mean-revert quickly enough, the central terms will be small. Then, if we add a large enough δ shock at time zero, we produce a negative inflation response.

As in the simple models, however, the appearance of a link between the persistence of interest rates and the sign of the response is an artifact of the parameterization of the policy rule and the AR(1) time-series process for its disturbance. The Fed can produce here too *any* sign of the inflation response together with *any* interest rate persistence by a suitable choice of disturbances. Fundamentally, the Fed still has separate and independent interest rate policy and equilibrium-selection policy tools. The negative sign comes entirely from equilibrium-selection policy. Again, this freedom denies our goal—there is no logical link between a rise in interest rates and an unexpected disinflation generating a negative sign.

We get a sense of this result already in the bottom-left panel of figure 15, which plots the inflation response in the knife-edge case $\rho = 1 / \lambda_1$. In this case, naturally lying between positive and negative interest rate responses, the monetary policy shock is a pure open-mouth operation. The endogenous effect $\phi\pi_t$ just offsets the shock v_t^i so inflation moves with no change at all in interest rates. The Fed just announces the policy shock, inflation moves, and the Fed doesn't actually do anything.

As in the simple models, these facts are clearer if we parameterize the policy rule by an interest rate target and an inflation target, equation (61), rather than a conventional disturbance, equation (60), $i_t = i_t^* + \phi(\pi_t - \pi_t^*)$ rather than $i_t = \phi\pi_t + v_t^i$.

Eliminating x_t from equations (58)–(59), we have

$$\sigma\kappa i_t = E_t[-\pi_t + (1 + \beta + \sigma\kappa)\pi_{t+1} - \beta\pi_{t+2}]. \tag{67}$$

It is again convenient to restrict the two disturbances to obey the model first-order conditions. Define i_t^* by

$$\sigma\kappa i_t^* = E_t[-\pi_t^* + (1 + \beta + \sigma\kappa)\pi_{t+1}^* - \beta\pi_{t+2}^*]. \tag{68}$$

Subtract the former from the latter, and use the policy rule $i_t - i_t^* = \phi(\pi_t - \pi_t^*)$,

$$0 = E_t[(1 + \sigma\kappa\phi)(\pi_t - \pi_t^*) - (1 + \beta + \sigma\kappa)(\pi_{t+1} - \pi_{t+1}^*) + \beta(\pi_{t+2} - \pi_{t+2}^*)]. \tag{69}$$

Factoring the lag polynomial, we have

$$0 = E_t(1 - v_1^{-1}L^{-1})(1 - v_2^{-1}L^{-1})(\pi_t - \pi_t^*)$$

with

$$v_i^{-1} = \frac{(1 + \beta + \sigma\kappa) \pm \sqrt{(1 + \beta + \sigma\kappa)^2 - 4\beta(1 + \sigma\kappa\phi)}}{2(1 + \sigma\kappa\phi)}.$$

For $\phi > 1$, we have $\|v_{ii}\| > 1$. The only solution is therefore the forward-looking one,

$$\pi_t = \pi_t^*$$

at every date.

The Fed can, by choice of the monetary policy disturbance, obtain any path of inflation it wishes. Again, with the two instruments, expected inflation $E_t\pi_{t+j}^*$ and unexpected inflation $\pi_t^* - E_{t-1}\pi_t^*$, the Fed can independently choose the interest rate path and the unexpected inflation. *There is no link between unexpected inflation and the path of interest rates.*

Examples with unexpected disinflation and persistent rates, or unexpected inflation and transitory rates, are as straightforward to calculate here as in the simple model or frictionless model. And again, one can construct $v_t^i = i_t^* - \phi\pi_t^*$ shocks to deliver the same results.

An open-mouth policy is just as easy. Suppose the Fed, starting at $i_t^* = 0$, $\pi_t^* = 0$ for $t < 0$, shocks monetary policy for $t \geq 0$ to

$$\pi_t^* = \delta_0 \lambda_1^{-t}. \tag{70}$$

Here, δ_0 is a constant indexing how large the monetary policy shock will be. This is a pure, temporary, change in the Fed's inflation target. Equivalently, suppose the Fed, starting at $v_t^i = 0$ for $t < 0$, shocks monetary policy for $t \geq 0$ to

$$v_t^i = -\delta_0 \phi_\pi \lambda_1^{-t}. \tag{71}$$

This is a pure, temporary, monetary policy disturbance. This shock produces a jump in inflation, which melts away, and no change in interest rates, as graphed in the lower left-hand panel of figure 15.

A disinflation produced by an unexpected inflation shock, preceding a period of rising interest rates, would be entirely a choice by the Fed, having nothing to do with the economy's response to interest rates.

Again, the heart of the argument is equilibrium selection by making the economy unstable. If $\phi < 1$, so $\lambda_2 < 1$, then there is a family of solutions,

$$E_t(\pi_{t+\tau} - \pi^*_{t+\tau}) = \lambda^t_2(\pi_t - \pi^*_t)$$

and any $\pi_t - E_{t-1}\pi_t$ can occur. But if $\phi > 1$ so $\lambda_2 > 1$, then any deviation of $\pi_t - \pi^*_t$ will explode. Ruling out explosions, it won't happen. Many other equilibrium-selection schemes achieve the same purpose (e.g., see Atkeson, Chari, and Kehoe 2010 and the discussion in the online appendix to Cochrane 2011b; www.nber.org/data-appendix/c13911/appendix/pdf).

This construction also verifies that the solution method using equations (62)–(63), solving for inflation given a path of interest rates, does not assume a peg, $\phi = 0$, or fiscal theory. For any ϕ, we can *construct* an active policy rule, a set of i^*_t, π^*_t or a set of v^i_t that generates any of the equilibria displayed in figure 14.

The fact of adding a policy rule, then, does not help us to choose equilibria. It does not link unexpected inflation to interest rates and expected inflation in a useful way. It does not justify the equilibrium with a disinflationary unexpected inflation married to higher interest rates, our one hope for a negative sign in this model.

E.   Long-Term Debt and Sticky Prices

When prices are sticky, nominal interest rate changes imply real interest rate changes, which affect the present value of surpluses. Allowing real interest rate variation and long-term debt, the government-debt-valuation formula becomes

$$\sum_{j=0}^{\infty} Q_t^{(t+j)} \frac{B_{t-1}^{(t+j)}}{P_t} = E_t \sum_{j=0}^{\infty} \beta^j \frac{u'(C_{t+j})}{u'(C_t)} s_{t+j} = E_t \sum_{j=0}^{\infty} \left(\prod_{k=0}^{j-1} \frac{1}{1+r_{t+k}} \right) s_{t+j}. \quad (72)$$

The first equality is the general formula; the second is an approximation reflecting the linearized nature of the New Keynesian model we are working with, in which risk premiums do not vary over time.

As before, the only effect of active fiscal policy is to select an equilibrium, that is, to determine the value of unexpected inflation. Otherwise, the sticky-price dynamics are unaffected.

To review, in the frictionless model with one-period debt, $Q_t^{(t)} = 1$ is the only bond price on the left side of equation (72), and real interest rates r on the right are constant. Hence, a change in nominal interest rates with no change in fiscal surpluses leaves equation (72) unchanged, and there is no jump in the price P_t when the interest rate change is announced.

To a first, expectations-hypothesis, approximation,

$$Q_t^{(t+j)} = E_t \prod_{k=0}^{j-1} \frac{1}{1 + i_{t+k}}.$$

When we add long-term debt in the frictionless model, a rise in expected future nominal rates i lowers bond prices Q. With nothing else changed in equation (72), P_t falls.

With sticky prices, higher nominal interest rates mean higher real interest rates on the right-hand side of equation (72). Higher real rates lower the present value of surpluses, which results in a *positive* shock to the price level P_t, as seen in equilibrium C of figure 14.

Merging long-term debt and sticky prices adds the last two mechanisms. Higher nominal rates lower bond prices, which results in a lower P_t. But to the extent that higher nominal rates mean higher real rates, the present value of surpluses on the right-hand side of equation (72) is also lower, which mutes the disinflationary effect. If prices are perfectly sticky, so that real interest rates equal nominal rates $i_{t+k} = r_{t+k}$, then the right- and left-hand sides of equation (72) move one-for-one, and there is again no effect on the price level P_t.

In sum, we expect that sticky prices will mute the disinflationary effect of an interest rate rise in the presence of long-term bonds. Sticky prices should also provide smoother and more realistic dynamics.

To calculate the response function merging the standard New Keynesian sticky-price model with the fiscal theory and long-term debt, I suppose interest rates start at their 2014 values, and I compute the market value of the debt. I use the 2014 zero-coupon US Treasury debt outstanding provided by Hall and Sargent (2015) for $B_{t-1}^{(t+j)}$, and the 2014 zero coupon yield curve $\{Y^{(t+j)}\}$ from Gürkaynak, Sack, and Wright (2007) for bond prices $Q_t^{(j)} = (1 / Y_t^{(t+j)})^j$. I calculate the nominal market value of the debt as $\Sigma_{j=0}^{\infty} Q_t^{(t+j)} B_{t-1}^{(t+j)}$.

I then suppose forward rates all rise by the interest rate response function, and I calculate the new nominal market value of the debt. I calculate the present value of an unchanged surplus using the government-debt-valuation formula (72), and the model implied path of real interest rates. That consideration chooses a single value of unexpected inflation at the time of the shock, equivalently of the multiple equilibria δ_t, on the announcement date. Equations are in the appendix (http://www.nber.org/data-appendix/c13911/appendix/pdf).

The top-left panel of figure 16 presents the responses of inflation and output to an unexpected and permanent interest rate increase. The

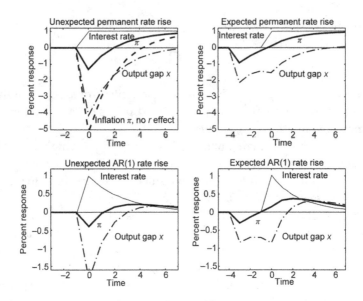

Fig. 16. Response to interest rate rises with long-term debt and sticky prices

Note: I use the 2014 maturity structure of the debt to find the jump in price level that implies no change in primary surpluses. The line "inflation π, no r effect" in the first panel ignores the effect of rising real rates in devaluing future surpluses; $\rho = 0.7$.

devaluation of long-term debt now produces a 1.2% disinflation despite no change in surpluses. Inflation is stable, so eventually rises to meet the long-term interest rate. However, the muliple periods of negative inflation now mean that the *price level* displays a hump-shaped response (not shown). This is the most hopeful graph in this paper for an economically based model that gives the desired response function for monetary policy changes.

In this model, the output gap is related to expected future inflation. After the unexpected downward jump at time 0, the larger expected future inflation produces a sharp –4% output contraction.

Compare to figure 12, with a +0.4% inflation on the date of inflation rise, and a –1% output gap, or compare to the multiple equilibria in figure 14. The devaluation effect of long-term bonds is exactly equivalent to a fiscal contraction past equilibrium E of figure 14—again, dynamics are the same after the initial inflation shock. The longer period of high real interest rates here drives the output gap down to –4% rather than –1% in figure 12. (From the IS curve [58], $x_t = -\sigma E_t \Sigma_{j=0}^{\infty}(i_{t+j} - \pi_{t+j+1})$.)

The dashed line marked "inflation π, no r effect" ignores the change in real interest rates on the right-hand side of equation (72), to show the effect of sticky prices in moderating the long-term-debt disinflationary mechanism. Here, I ignore the effect of rising interest rates in calculating the present value of the surplus, but otherwise leave model dynamics the same. We see that in the original calculation, the solid line, higher real rates substantially lower the present value of surpluses, and make a big moderating difference to the initial disinflation. Models with this long-term debt fiscal mechanism thus produce *less* disinflation from nominal interest rate rises when they have *more* sticky prices. However, this calculation also emphasizes the delicacy of fiscal assumptions. One can read it also as saying that the fiscal authority is partly passive, agreeing to raise surpluses to pay off higher *real interest rates* on the debt, though not agreeing to raise surpluses to pay off the real consequences of price-level jumps. Such behavior induces the larger disinflation.

The top-right panel of figure 16 shows the response when the interest rise is announced three years in advance. Higher interest rates now only affect bonds with three year or higher maturity. Thus, the downward inflation-rate jump is smaller, only 1%. However, there is still a substantial period of negative inflation response, so the price-level response (not shown) continues downward from period –3 to 0, only then starting to rise. Output suffers a less severe contraction, bottoming out at 2% not 4%.

As in the frictionless model, fiscal effects happen only on the day of announcement. This is an important consideration in evaluating this channel. It will not rescue the Old Keynesian view that the interest rate rise itself sets off the disinflation.

The effects get uniformly smaller as the interest rate rise is expected further in the future. When the interest rate rise is expected after the maturity of the longest bond, the disinflationary effect vanishes entirely. Thus, this fiscal channel sensibly predicts smaller effects of expectations further in the future, and does not suffer from the forward-guidance puzzle.

The bottom panels of figure 16 present the response to an unexpected (left) and expected (bottom) AR(1) rate rise, more typical of policy movements identified by VARs. The unexpected transitory rate rise on the left is the (small) slice of interest rate variation that is potentially recovered by VARs. (Though VARs do not attempt to orthogonalize monetary and fiscal policy shocks, $\Delta s = 0$, as I do here.) The disinflation effect is now smaller still, less than 0.5% in both cases. The AR(1) interest rate rise has less effect on longer-term bonds than a permanent rate rise.

In sum, long-lived interest rate rises can produce disinflations on the same order of magnitude as the interest rate rises, and thus have the potential to explain the perceived effects of monetary policy.

F. Money

Perhaps monetary distortions, in addition to pricing distortions, will give us the traditional result. Perhaps when interest rate increases were accomplished by reducing the supply of non-interest-bearing reserves, that reduction in money and liquidity services produced a temporary decline in inflation. Such a finding would explain traditional beliefs, but it would warn us that raising interest rates by raising the rate paid on abundant excess reserves will not have the same temporary disinflationary effect as history suggests.

I introduce money in the utility function, nonseparable from consumption, so that changes in money, induced by interest rate changes, affect the marginal utility of consumption, and thus the intertemporal-substitution equation.

Woodford (2003, p. 111) begins an analysis of this specification. But Woodford quickly abandons money to produce a theory that is independent of monetary frictions, and he does not work out the effects of monetary policy with money. If theory following that choice now does not produce the desired outcome, perhaps we should revisit the decision to drop money from the analysis.

The detailed presentation is in the appendix. The bottom line is a generalization of the intertemporal-substitution condition (58), to:

$$x_t = E_t x_{t+1} + (\sigma - \xi)\left(\frac{m}{c}\right) E_t[(i_{t+1} - i_{t+1}^m) - (i_t - i_t^m)] - \sigma(i_t - E_t \pi_{t+1}). \quad (73)$$

The presence of money in the utility function has no effect on firm pricing decisions and hence on the Phillips curve (59).

Here, $-\xi$ is the interest-elasticity of money demand. Since higher elasticity ξ reduces the size of the effects, I use a deliberately low value $\xi = 0.1$. The value m/c is the steady-state ratio of real money holdings to consumption. The larger this value, the more important monetary distortions. The quantity i_t^m is the interest rate paid on money.

Equation (73) differs from its standard counterpart (58) by the middle, change in interest rate term. Equation (73) reverts to equation (58) if utility is separable between money and consumption $(\sigma - \xi) = 0$, if m/c goes to zero, or if money pays the same interest rate as bonds $i = i^m$.

The expression m / c $(i_t - i_t^m)$ represents the proportional interest costs of holding money. The middle term following $(\sigma - \xi)$ represents the expected increase or decrease in those costs. An expected increase in interest costs of holding money induces the consumer to shift consumption from the future, when holding the money needed to purchase consumption goods will be relatively expensive, toward the present. It acts just like a lower real interest rate to induce an intertemporal reallocation of consumption.

The presence of expected changes in interest rates brings to the model a mechanism that one can detect in verbal commentary: the sense that *changes* in interest rates affect the economy as well as the level of interest rates.

However, monetary distortions only matter in this model if there is an *expected change in future* interest rate differentials. Expected, change, and future are all crucial modifiers. A higher or lower steady-state level of the interest cost of holding money does not raise or depress today's consumption relative to future consumption. An unexpected change in interest costs has no monetary effect, since $E_t(i_{t+1} - i_t) = 0$ throughout.

The model solution is essentially unchanged. The extra term in the intertemporal substitution equation (73) amounts to a slightly more complex forcing process involving expected changes in interest rates as well as the level of interest rates. One simply replaces i_t in equations (62)–(63) with z_t defined by

$$z_t \equiv i_t - \left(\frac{\sigma - \xi}{\sigma}\right)\left(\frac{m}{c}\right) E_t[(i_{t+1} - i_{t+1}^m) - (i_t - i_t^m)].$$

The slight subtlety is that this forcing process is the change in *expected* interest differentials. Lag operators must apply to the E_t as well as what is inside. Inflation depends on past expectations of interest rate changes, not just to past interest rate changes themselves.

I present results for the traditional specification that the interest on money $i_t^m = 0$, so that increases in the nominal interest rate are synonymous with monetary distortions. This case also generates the largest effects. The top panels of figure 17 plot the response functions to our expected and unexpected interest rate step with money distortions $m / c = 0, 2, 4$.

For the unexpected interest rate rise, shown in dashed lines in the top row, the presence of money makes no difference at all. The dashed lines are the same for all values of m / c, and all the same as previously, and the model remains stubbornly Fisherian. This is an important negative

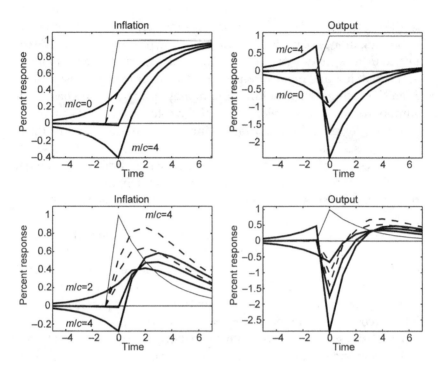

Fig. 17. Responses of inflation and output to an interest rate rise; model with money
Note: The three cases are $m/c = 0, 2, 4$. Solid lines are an expected interest rate rise, and
dashed lines are an unexpected rise.

result. In this model based on forward-looking behavior and thus intertemporal substitution, money can only affect the response to *expected
future* nominal interest rate changes.

The response to an expected interest rate rise, shown in solid lines,
is affected by the monetary distortion. As we increase the size of the
monetary distortion m/c, inflation is lower in the short run. For $m/c =$
4, we get the desired shape of the impulse-response function. The announced interest rate rise produces a temporary decline in inflation,
and then eventually the Fisher effect takes over and inflation increases.

Since interest rates are higher after time 0, the consumer has an incentive to shift consumption to times before 0, that is, to consume when the
interest costs of holding the necessary money are lower. Higher output
corresponds to decreasing inflation, and vice versa, so this pattern of
output corresponds to lower inflation before time 0 and higher inflation
afterward.

The $m/c = 4$ curve seems like a success, until one ponders the size of the monetary distortion—non-interest-bearing money holdings equal, on average, to four years of output. This model is not carefully calibrated, but $m/c = 4$ is still an order of magnitude too large. One may be tempted to look at larger monetary aggregates, but those all pay interest. Interest spreads enter together with m/c in equation (73), so trading larger m/c for a lower interest spread does not help.

Raising σ, which multiplies m/c in equation (73), can substitute for a large m/c, though σ also magnifies the last term, which induces Fisherian dynamics. Also, $\sigma = 4$, $m/c = 2$ produces about the same inflation decline as $\sigma = 1$, $m/c = 4$ produced in figure 17, though it speeds up dynamics as well. Alas, $\sigma = 1$ was already above most estimates and calibrations. A coefficient $\sigma = 4$ implies that a 1-percentage-point increase in the real interest rate induces a 4-percentage-point increase in consumption growth, which is well beyond most estimates. And $m/c = 1$ is already at least twice as big as one can reasonably defend.

Since expected changes in interest rates are the crucial mechanism in this model, perhaps putting in more interest rate dynamics can revive the desired inflation dynamics? The bottom panels of figure 17 shows the response function to an AR(1) interest rate path. In response to an unexpected shock, shown in dashed lines, the presence of money uniformly *raises* inflation. The expected decline in interest costs posed by the AR(1) reversion after the shock shifts consumption from the present to the future. Low output corresponds to an expected rise in inflation. Since the initial rise in interest rates was unexpected, it has no effect on inflation or output.

The response to an expected interest rate increase now has the same pattern, but less disinflation—the $m/c = 4$ case bottoms out at a bit less than –0.2% in the bottom panel of figure 17 rather than –0.4% in the top panel.

In sum, these calculations show what it takes to produce the standard view: for an anticipated interest rate rise only, money in the model can induce lower inflation than a model without monetary frictions produces. If we either have very large money holdings subject to the distortion, or a very large intertemporal substitution elasticity, the effect can be large enough to produce a short-run decline in inflation. Adding money to the model in this way has no effect on responses to an unexpected permanent interest rate rise, and thus does nothing to address typical VAR evidence or the widespread view that unexpected interest rate changes have disinflationary effects.

The mechanism is quantitatively small. Relative to the effects of actual changes in real interest rates, the distortions to intertemporal incentives from greater or lesser costs of holding money are second order.

Also, this mechanism does not give rise to classic intuition. Interest costs of money holdings only affect demand if people *expect* higher or lower interest costs in the future than they experience today. The level of interest costs has no effect.

G.   A Backward-Looking Phillips Curve

Empirically, lags seem important in Phillips curves. The forward-looking Phillips curve (59) specifies that output is higher when inflation is high relative to future inflation, that is, when inflation is declining. Though all Phillips curves fit the data poorly, especially recently, output is better related to high inflation relative to past inflation, that is, when inflation is rising (Mankiw and Reis 2002).

Theoretically, the pure forward-looking Phillips curve is not central. Though it does some violence to the "economic" criterion for the simple baseline theory that we are searching for, we should check if the short- or long-run neo-Fisherian conclusions can be escaped by adding past inflation to the Phillips curve.

The simplest approach is to consider a static Phillips curve. This specification is the $\beta \rightarrow 0$ limit of the three-equation model (58)–(59). Kocherlakota (2016) provides detailed microfoundations for a static Phillips curve.

So consider

$$x_t = E_t x_{t+1} - \sigma(i_t - E_t \pi_{t+1}) \tag{74}$$

$$\pi_t = \kappa x_t. \tag{75}$$

The equilibrium is simply

$$E_t \pi_{t+1} = \frac{1}{1 + \sigma \kappa} \pi_t + \frac{\sigma \kappa}{1 + \sigma \kappa} i_t \tag{76}$$

and hence

$$\pi_t = \sigma \kappa \sum_{j=1}^{\infty} \frac{1}{(1 + \sigma \kappa)^j} i_{t-j} + \sum_{j=0}^{\infty} \frac{1}{(1 + \sigma \kappa)^j} \delta_{t-j}. \tag{77}$$

This is *exactly* the same as the dynamics we found for a static IS curve and forward-looking Phillips curve, $x_t = -\sigma(i_t - E_t \pi_{t+1})$; $\pi_t = E_t \pi_{t+1} + \kappa x_t$ in equation (42). The dynamics are stable, and inflation responds positively to interest rates throughout. Figure 11 already plots the response function for the static Phillips curve case (74)–(75)—and inflation rises smoothly throughout.

We can even include a backward-looking accelerationist Phillips curve, which one may feel more realistic, throwing out forward-looking price setting. Consider a Phillips curve based on firm expectations π_t^e,

$$\pi_t = \pi_{t-1}^e + \kappa x_t$$

and where expectations evolve adaptively as

$$\pi_t^e = (1 - \lambda)\sum_{j=0}^{\infty} \lambda^j \pi_{t-j}.$$

Substituting the output gap from the usual intertemporal IS curve (74),

$$(\pi_t - \pi_{t-1}^e) = (E_t\pi_{t+1} - \pi_t^e) - \sigma\kappa(i_t - E_t\pi_{t+1})$$

$$(1 + \sigma\kappa)E_t\pi_{t+1} = \pi_t + \pi_t^e - \pi_{t-1}^e + \sigma\kappa i_t$$

$$(1 + \sigma\kappa)E_t\pi_{t+1} = \pi_t + (1 - \lambda)\left[\sum_{j=0}^{\infty}\lambda^j\Delta\pi_{t-j}\right] + \sigma\kappa i_t.$$

Figure 18 plots the impulse-response function for this model. It is Fisherian throughout. Unlike the standard model with forward-looking Phillips curve in figure 12, the interest rate rise increases output as well. By giving the "right" positive (Old Keynesian) sign of the relationship between output and inflation, it also gives the "wrong" positive sign of the relationship between interest rates on output, as well as on inflation.

In sum, neither forward-looking IS curves nor forward-looking Phillips curves are essential to producing a short- and long-run Fisherian response.

IV. Policy

To summarize for the purposes of policy implications, the evidence suggests that the zero bound is stable and quiet. There is no deflation spiral and no sunspot volatility. Large interest-paying reserves do not cause inflation. There is a simple economic model, the New Keynesian model with fiscal theory, that is consistent with this interpretation. In that theory, an interest rate peg or passive $\phi < 1$ policy would also be stable and quiet, as long as fiscal policy retains people's confidence. The evidence suggests that contrary classic doctrines were wrong.

The implication of this fact is that persistently higher interest rates will lead to higher inflation in the long run, a form of long-run neutrality. Is there a negative short-run effect? There is as yet no simple economic model for standard beliefs regarding such an effect. There is

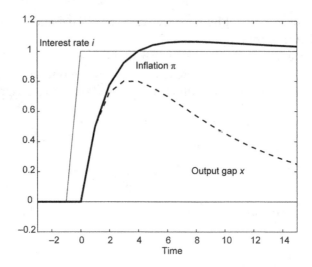

Fig. 18. Impulse response with backward-looking Phillips curve
Note: Model $x_t = E_t x_{t+1} - \sigma(i_t - E_t \pi_{t+1})$, $\pi_t = (1 - \lambda)\Sigma_{j=0}^{\infty}\lambda^j\pi_{t-j} + \kappa x_t$; $\sigma = \kappa = 1$, $\lambda = 0.9$.

as yet only the fiscal theory/long-term debt channel, which is far from the views underlying standard policy beliefs. This excursion should at least reduce one's confidence in a simple view that higher interest rates, when they occur, will lower inflation.

If this is right, what are the consequences for policy going forward?

First, we should not unduly fear the zero bound! Much current policy discussion regards the past zero bound as a narrow scrape with the deflation spiral, and argues for a higher inflation target, or dry powder in the arsenal of unconventional monetary policy and large fiscal stimulus to prevent the spiral from breaking out should we return to the zero bound in the next recession or crisis.

Second, we should not unduly fear the large balance sheet, or at least the large interest-paying reserves that a large balance sheet gives rise to. They do not cause inflation. They also have important financial stability benefits. Deposits backed by reserves are less prone to run.

We have discovered that abundant, safe, government-provided, interest-paying electronic money will not cause inflation. The Treasury could equally well provide "reserves" in the form of abundant fixed-value floating-rate highly liquid debt (see Cochrane 2015, 2014d). The Fed does not need to act as the world's largest money market fund, transforming longer-term government debt into floating-rate government debt. There is no need to keep Treasury debt artificially illiquid for price-level control.

Much current policy discussion, by contrast, sees large reserves as permanently stimulative, in urgent need of reduction, and many commentators wish for a return to a small amount of non-interest-bearing reserves, in order to ensure control of inflation.

Third, we can live the Friedman (1969) rule and enjoy the Friedman-optimal quantity of money. Not only can we have Friedman-optimal interest-bearing reserves, we can have a permanently zero, or very low interest rate, if we wish. Such a rate would not only reduce socially wasteful shoe-leather costs, as Friedman envisaged, it would remove a lot of needless cash management, bill-paying delay and collection hurry, inflation-induced capital income taxation, distortions due to sticky prices under nonzero inflation, and other distortions of inflation and high nominal interest rates.

Policy *can* keep a low nominal rate, insensitive to economic conditions and to inflation. When the real rate rises, inflation will eventually decline to accommodate the real rate, all on its own, and vice versa.

But the policy implications are not so dramatic.

Though the Fed *can* keep a low peg (so long as fiscal policy cooperates), that does not mean that the Fed *should* keep a low peg. In the presence of price stickiness, inflation may take a long time to adjust to the real rate, and output would be affected in the meantime.

The Fed can instead vary the nominal interest rate, raising the nominal rate in good economic times when it thinks the natural rate is higher, and vice versa. Such a policy would result in less inflation variation, and under sticky prices, it would plausibly result in less volatile output as well.

One may distrust the Fed's ability to divine changes in the "natural" rate. Stability opens up an exciting and novel alternative possibility. The Fed could target the spread between indexed and nonindexed debt. It could, for example, decree that one-year, Treasury-inflation-protected securities shall trade at a 1-percentage-point lower yield than one-year Treasury bills, and offer to buy and sell at that price differential, ignoring the overall level of interest rates. This strategy would nail down expected inflation but allow the level of the real interest rate to adjust automatically to market forces. It operates much like an expected Consumer Price Index (CPI) standard, with CPI futures taking the place of gold to define the value of the currency. If an interest peg is unstable, such a standard would not work—the Fisherian steady state would be unstable, and interest and inflation rates would spiral away. But stability implies that expected inflation would have to adjust to the interest-spread target—as always with the fiscal footnote that the Treasury must back the fiscal consequences of large rearrangements of indexed versus nonindexed debt. In sum, $i_t = r_t + E_t \pi_{t+1}$ implies $E_t \pi_{t+1} = i_t - r_t$.

In the other direction, nothing in this analysis denies that the Fed can try to diagnose and offset shocks all over the economy, varying nominal interest rates accordingly, as well as with forward guidance and quantitative easing as analyzed above. It can try to fine-tune the inflation and output path using complex DSGE models, exploiting all the frictions, dynamics, and irrationalities it feels it understands, along with the fiscal/long-term debt channel described above. The rules versus discretion, fine-tune versus leave the hot/cold water shower handles alone debate can continue undeterred.

Thus, observed policy need not change much. We may continue to see Taylorish responses to output and inflation, plus deviations to respond to other concerns such as exchange rates, financial stability, and so forth.

There are some lessons. Most of all, active policy rules are not necessary for inflation stability or determinacy. But the latter were questionable anyway, and unobserved in equilibrium. Writing the rule in the form $i_t = i_t^* + \phi_\pi(\pi_t - \pi_t^*) + \phi_x(x_t - x_t^*)$, where i_t^*, π_t^* and x_t^* represent equilibrium values, the active policy represents only conjectural deviations from equilibrium never seen in equilibrium. *Observed* policy consists of the correlations between i_t^*, π_t^*, and x_t^*. Thus, the lesson that active policy is not important for inflation determination is important for academic papers and deep foundations, but has little impact on actual observed policy making and interest rates. Fed officials think in terms of actual interest rates and not active deviations from equilibrium (see the quote below from Fed Chair Janet Yellen).

More directly relevant to policy, my long and negative search for a simple economic model that delivers one implies that one's faith in the exploitable negative sign of interest rates on inflation should be at least subdued.

We should pay more attention to the fiscal foundations of price stability, but that is not really the Fed's job. If the time comes for a major disinflation, it will have to come from a joint monetary-fiscal stabilization as before. That could look like the 1980s, inaugurated by high interest rates but quickly followed by tax and spending reforms, or it could look like Sargent's ends of inflations, in which fiscal reform ends inflation and high rates together.

The New Keynesian plus fiscal theory framework means that monetary economics is now like regular economics. We can start with a simply supply and demand frictionless benchmark, in which the price level is determinate, and there is a role for interest rate policy, forward guidance, and quantitative easing. Then we can add frictions to taste, to match dynamics. So far, interest-rate-based monetary economics could not be built on a frictionless foundation, and even MV = PY relies on a swiftly vanishing monetary friction.

However, there are some important limits to this analysis and important warnings that must be sounded. It would be simple to interpret these results to say that all a country needs to do to raise inflation is to raise its interest rate, and therefore all a country like Brazil or Turkey needs to do that wishes to lower its inflation rate is to lower its interest rate. That is a dangerous conclusion.

First, such an interest rate move must be persistent and credible. You can't just try the waters. Second, it must wait out a potential move in the other direction, via the long-term debt effect, or if the many complications discussed below can generate an opposite movement via other effects. We have analyzed the simple underlying economic model, but real-world dynamics demand real-world frictions. Third, and most importantly, the fiscal backing and fiscal coordination must be there, especially for disinflation. Lowering nominal rates cannot cure a fundamentally fiscal inflation.

In 2008 the United States and Europe did lower interest rates and lower inflation followed, albeit slowly. But the flight to quality to US and European government debt came first. Just why is a topic for later—lower discount rates rather than high expected surpluses are a likely culprit—but it is undeniable that there was a huge shift in demand toward government debt, and interest rates went down on their own. Contrarywise, many countries have seen monetary stabilization plans of all sorts fall apart when fiscal cooperation was lacking. The government-debt-valuation formula is an integral part of the model, and just lowering interest rates will not work with fiscal trouble brewing.

Likewise, it does not follow from the analysis here that the United States, Europe, and Japan can just peg low interest rates and sleep soundly. The government-debt valuation equation holds, in all models. The question is how it holds, and how it will continue to hold, without requiring a burst of inflation or deflation. A high value of government debt corresponds to high expected surpluses or low discount rates—investors willing to hold government debt despite poor prospective real returns. At the current moment, low discount rates, revealed in part by low real interest rates, seem like a much more likely source of high values than high expected surpluses. But low discount rates can evaporate quickly, especially when debt is largely short term and frequently rolled over. A change in discount rate provokes exactly the same sort of unexpected inflation that a change in fiscal surpluses provokes. And like such a change, there is nothing a central bank can do about it.

Some historic interest rate pegs, like exchange rate pegs and the gold standard, lasted a surprisingly long time. Many pegs fell apart when their fiscal foundations fell apart. With short-term debt that can happen in what feels like "speculative attack," "bubble," or "run" to central bankers. Inflation's resurgence can happen without Phillips curve tightness, and can surprise central bankers of the 2020s just as it did in the 1970s, just as inflation's decline surprised them in the 1980s, and just as its stability surprised them in the 2010s.

V.   Occam

There are many ways one could try to save traditional theories in face of the long quiet zero bound. There are many additional ingredients one could add to try to produce a temporary negative inflation response to interest rates, in a model that is consistent with the long quiet zero bound.

In this section, I take up a number of these possibilities. I argue that some popular ones are implausible. But they are mostly logical possibilities that we cannot disprove with the evidence before us. Most are complex, ex post patches. Sometimes patches turn out to be correct, as did foreshortening of fast-moving objects, and elliptical planetary orbits. Occam's razor reminds us, however, that more often complex patches fail when there is a clear simple alternative, as did epicycles and ether drift.

A.   Offsetting Instabilities?

Perhaps the economy really is unstable as in Old Keynesian/monetarist models, but fiscal stimulus, inflationary quantitative easing, and deftly timed forward guidance just offset a deflationary spiral. If skillfully walked, a tightrope between abysses looks quiet.

Perhaps. Or perhaps stability and quiet are just what they seem to be.

B.   Really Slow Unstable Dynamics?

Perhaps the economy really is unstable at the zero bound as in Old Keynesian/monetarist models, but the dynamics are much slower than we previously thought. If so, the deflation spiral is still waiting to break out any day, even in Japan. Likewise, perhaps the "long-run stability" of velocity, even at low interest differentials, is much longer-run than previously thought. If so, velocity will recover and inflation will finally break out.

Perhaps. But perhaps not. First, this speculation is ex post rationalization. The broad consensus of people using Old Keynesian policy models was and remained throughout that a deflation spiral was a danger. Many monetarists did clearly expect quantitative easing to lead to inflation.

This observation is praise, not criticism. The models clearly made those predictions. People should be commended for offering the advice that their models present. The models were also broadly consistent with prior data. But now the telling experiment has been run, and the models failed. We all understand the dangers of patching a model every time it fails.

Second, patches such as very "sticky" wages are not yet fully worked out and compared more broadly with macroeconomic or microeconomic data. Job churn is a problem for decade-long stickiness. That detailed elaboration is especially missing for Old Keynesian models that dominate policy thinking, but have vanished from academic journals.

Occam suggests, perhaps not: perhaps the economy is stable at the zero bound, and by implication an interest rate peg.

C.   Sunspot Volatility?

Perhaps the New Keynesian prediction of higher inflation volatility under passive policy can be patched. The next few subsections take up this issue.

Sunspots being ephemeral, "there weren't any sunspot shocks" is an irrefutable ex post explanation of quiet.

However, this approach requires a bonfire of previous writing. The New Keynesian literature clearly warned that passive $\phi < 1$ monetary policy causes inflation volatility. That proposition is one of the model's central empirical successes, explaining the greater volatility of the 1970s versus the 1980s. If we throw out the prediction of higher volatility under passive policy in the 2010s, we are hard pressed not also to throw out that central success.

For example, Clarida, Gal, and Gertler (2000, p. 149), who found $\phi < 1$ in the 1970s and $\phi > 1$ in the 1980s, attribute the reduction of inflation volatility to that fact, writing

the pre-Volcker [$\phi < 1$] rule leaves open the possibility of bursts of inflation and output that result from self-fulfilling changes in expectations. . . .On the other hand, self-fulfilling fluctuations cannot occur under the estimated rule for the Volcker-Greenspan [$\phi > 1$] era since, within this regime, the Federal Reserve adjusts interest rates sufficiently to stabilize any changes in expected inflation.

Again, they write

the pre-Volcker rule may have contained the seeds of macroeconomic instability that seemed to characterize the late sixties and seventies. In particular, in the context of a calibrated sticky price model, the pre-Volcker rule leaves open the possibility of bursts of inflation and output that result from self-fulfilling changes in expectations. (Clarida, Gal, and Gertler 2000, 177)

Benhabib, Schmitt-Grohé, and Uribe (2001, 167) likewise write

Perhaps the best-known result in this literature is that if fiscal solvency is preserved under all circumstances, [i.e., passive fiscal policy] . . . a passive monetary policy, that is, a policy that underreacts to inflation by raising the nominal interest rate by less than the observed increase in inflation, destabilizes the economy by giving rise to expectations-driven fluctuations.

They write again in Benhabib et al. (2002), summarizing a "growing body of theoretical work,"

Taylor rules contribute to aggregate stability because they guarantee the uniqueness of the rational expectations equilibrium, whereas interest rate feedback rules with an inflation coefficient of less than unity, also referred to as passive rules, are destabilizing because they render the equilibrium indeterminate, thus allowing for expectations-driven fluctuations.

(Both sets of authors use "stability" to mean "quiet," that is, "low volatility," not as I have used the term.)

Benhabib et al. (2002) survey many other similar opinions, along with policy prescriptions, to avoid the zero interest state, all motivated by the prediction of extra volatility at that state. Indeed, without extra sunspot volatility, low inflation is welfare-improving in this model. It is both Friedman-optimal, and reduces pricing distortions. The fear of sunspot volatility is the main reason these and other authors have made the effort to find policies that avoid the zero bound and return us to permanently higher inflation.

Is there some feature of policy at the long quiet zero bound that eliminated sunspot shocks, but did not eliminate those shocks in the 1970s? There is much opinion that expectations are "anchored." But anchored by what? (If not by fiscal policy!) And why was that force absent in the 1970s? The 1970s did not lack from promises by Federal Reserve and other government officials. We even had those cute little WIN (whip inflation now) buttons. If anchoring was going to work this time, why did economic researchers not know that fact, and opine not to worry about the zero bound?

D. Selection from Future Actions

In much New Keynesian zero-bound literature such as Werning (2011) or Eggertsson and Mehrotra (2014), expectations of future active, destabilizing, policy rules take the place of responses to current inflation to select equilibria while interest rates are stuck at zero. In these models, eventually, either deterministically or stochastically, the economy leaves the zero bound. A destabilizing policy rule selects a unique locally bounded equilibrium in that future state. Modelers then tie equilibria during the zero-rate period to the following equilibria, and thereby eliminate indeterminacies during the zero bound.

One could use this kind of selection scheme to argue that the New Keynesian model does not, after all, predict sunspot volatility at the zero bound. The point of the literature is different, to match data or to study policies such as forward guidance and fiscal stimulus at the zero bound, and selection by future active policies just helps authors not to bother with multiple equilibria. But it is a possibility.

Here is a concrete example, using the simple model (1)–(4) with $r^* = 0$. From time $t = 0$ to $t = T$, there is a negative natural rate shock, $v_t^r = -2\%$. At time $t = T$ the natural rate shock passes so $v_t^r = 0, t > T$, provoking a zero-bound exit. The Fed follows a constrained active Taylor rule (4), so interest rates and inflation follow

$$i_t = \max[\pi^* + \phi_\pi(\pi_t - \pi^*), 0] \tag{78}$$

$$\pi_t = (1 + \sigma\kappa)E_t\pi_{t+1} - \sigma\kappa(i_t - v_t^r). \tag{79}$$

Fiscal policy is passive.

Figure 19 shows possible paths of inflation and interest rate in this

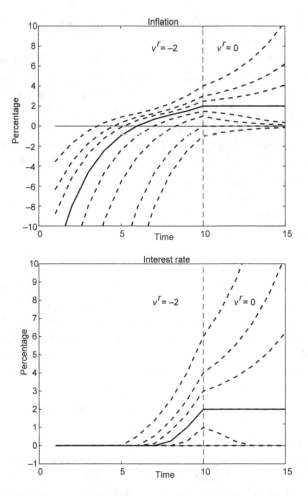

Fig. 19. Selection by future and contingent policy rules

Note: Top: Inflation. Bottom: Interest rates. The solid line is the selected equilibrium. The dashed lines are alternative equilibria. There is a natural rate shock $v^r = -2\%$ from time $t = 0$ to $t = T = 10$. The Fed follows a rule $i_t = \max[\pi^* + \phi_\pi(\pi_t - \pi^*), 0]$. The simple New Keynesian model reduces to $\pi_t = (1 + \sigma\kappa) E_t\pi_{t+1} - \sigma\kappa (i_t - v_t^r); \sigma = 1, \kappa = 1/2, \phi = 2, \pi^* = 2\%$.

model. The thick line in the middle is the selected equilibrium. It fairs in to the inflation target $\pi^* = 2\%$ at $t = T$. The alternative equilibria are deselected even in the stable region, when $i_t = 0$ for $t < T$, by the fact that they diverge from the inflation target π^* for $t > T$.

This equilibrium-selection scheme has many troubles. As in all active monetary policy rules, "anchoring" of inflation expectations does not occur because the Fed is expected to *stabilize* inflation around the inflation target, but because the Fed is expected to *destabilize* inflation should it diverge from the target. Now this threat is removed from current events to the far future—not "eat your spinach or there won't be dessert," but "eat your spinach or there won't be dessert next year."

Furthermore, equilibria in which inflation undershoots the time-T target π^* return back to zero inflation and zero interest rates. They are *locally* unstable around the target π^* and thus $\pi_t = \pi^*$ is the only locally bounded equilibrium, but they are not *globally* unstable, so $\pi_t = \pi^*$ is not the only globally bounded equilibrium. The rationale for ruling them out is tenuous.

Figure 19 also illustrates a predictive failure of this model, highlighted by Werning (2011) and Cochrane (2017). It predicts a jump to deflation at $t = 0$ when the shock hits, which then rapidly improves. This did not happen.

Figure 19 likewise illustrates some of the policy paradoxes of this model, highlighted by Werning (2011), Wieland (2015), and Cochrane (2017). Small changes in expectations of future inflation at time T on the right move initial time 0 inflation around a lot. The further in the future T is, the larger the effect at time 0. And as price stickiness is reduced, the dynamics happen faster, implying larger deflation and greater effect of such promises.

In a stochastic setting, the sensitivity of inflation at time 0 to small changes in expectations at time T might easily produce greater inflation volatility at the zero bound in this model, relative to normal times that active policy picks equilibria immediately. It is not obvious that, were someone to use this argument to quiet inflation at the zero bound relative to $i_t = \phi \pi_t$ policy, that it would work.

Does all concrete action of monetary policy really vanish, leaving only expectations of far-future, off-equilibrium threats behind? Did Japan really avoid deflation in 2001 because people expected some sort of explosive promises around a 2% inflation target to emerge and select equilibria, maybe sometime in 2025 when Japan finally exits zero rates?

Even Fed Chair Janet Yellen (2016) is unsure that promises of future Taylor rules anchor inflation today:

[H]ow does this anchoring process occur? Does a central bank have to keep actual inflation near the target rate for many years before inflation expectations completely conform? . . .Or does . . . a change in expectations requir[e] some combination of clear communications about policymakers' inflation goal, concrete policy actions, . . . and at least some success in moving actual inflation toward its desired level . . . ?

Moreover, she clearly states here that anchoring results because a Taylor rule will, in the future, *stabilize* inflation around the target, in the Old Keynesian tradition, not that it will *destabilize* inflation to produce determinacy as shown in figure 19. If *she* doesn't believe the dynamics of figure 19, why should people in the economy expect such a thing?

Finally, if now, why not in the 1970s? If inflation is quiet now because people know that after we exit the bound active policy will return to select equilibria, why did people in the 1970s not know that sooner or later an era of active policy would return, as, the story goes, it did? Working backward, that expectation should have removed self-confirming fluctuations in the 1970s, and Clarida et al. (2000) should have found nothing.

This search for equilibrium selection might be more attractive if a simpler solution were not at hand. The fiscal theory picks one equilibrium of the zero-bound, New Keynesian model directly. Expectations are anchored by the present value of future surpluses, not by what people believe the Fed might do to select equilibria after a jump to a higher interest rate regime. The fiscal theory plus New Keynesian model does not display policy paradoxes. Each equilibrium corresponds to an innovation in the present value of surpluses, and moving to a larger inflation at time t requires a larger change in the present value of surpluses at time t. The model also has a smooth frictionless limit.

E. *Seven Years of Bad Luck*

Perhaps we weren't really at the zero bound. Perhaps each year people expected interest rates to recover in the very near future. Perhaps time T in the previous graph was always a year or less, addressing the concerns of the last section. Perhaps we were in a stochastic version of the right-hand, "active," unique locally bounded equilbrium of figure 5, one that just briefly touched zero. Perhaps the appearance of a zero bound just represents the proverbial seven years of bad luck, or twenty-five in Japan's case; one bad draw after another.

This view formed the basis of several comments at the conference. As other examples, Swanson and Williams (2014) measure the responsiveness of one- and two-year Treasury bills to macro news, and conclude that they remained responsive from 2008 to 2010, indicating expectations of active policy and a soon-forthcoming exit, only becoming suggestive of a zero bound in late 2011. That still leaves 2011–2017, however. García-Schmidt and Woodford (2015) write similarly no central banks have actually experimented with date-based forward guidance that referred to dates more than about two years in the future; and while the period in which the U.S. federal funds rate target has remained at its lower bound has (as of the time of writing) lasted for more than six years, there was little reason for anyone to expect it to remain at this level for so long when the lower bound was reached at the end of 2008.

(The first sentence is a bit misleading for the questions here. The zero bound is usually thought of as a constraint, not a choice. Forward guidance is only a commitment that should the economy improve the Fed will nonetheless keep rates low, but if the economy does not improve one nonetheless expects zero interest rates even without forward guidance.)

A similar puzzle occurs in matching a standard New Keynesian model such as figure 15, in which only transitory interest rate changes (with an AR[1] response) cause disinflation, to the standard intuition that 1980–1995 represented a disinflation created by a sustained high-interest policy. There, to produce the appearance of high interest rates slowly beating down inflation, one has to argue that 1980 to 1995 represented 15 years of good luck, continual expectations of a return to high interest rates, continually confounded by events.

It is possible that long stretches of data do not represent the impulse-response function of interest rates to inflation, as expectations were always somewhere else. But each year that passes makes a bad luck story harder to maintain, relative to the simple alternative that maybe we are seeing just what we seem to see, stability and at least long-run Fisherian response.

F. Learning and Other Selection Devices

Perhaps multiple zero-bound, New Keynesian equilibria with passive fiscal policy, as illustrated in the left-hand equilibrium of figure 5, can be ruled out by additional equilibrium-selection rules.

Adding some concept of "learnability" to select equilibria is a popular choice. McCallum (2009a, 2009b) claims that applying the e-stability concept in Evans and Honkapohja (2001) to this situation, the active, right-hand equilibrium of figure 5 is learnable, while the left-hand, passive equilibrium and the multiple equilibria leading to it, are not.

Cochrane (2009) disagrees, and argues that learnability leads exactly to the opposite conclusion. The parameter ϕ and monetary policy shock are not identified from macroeconomic data in the active equilibrium.

The policy rule represents an off-equilibrium threat not measurable from data in an equilibrium. There is no way for a child, observing that eating spinach is always followed by dessert, to learn if not eating spinach would be followed by no dessert. However, in the stable passive money equilibrium, $\phi < 1$ is measurable. (See also Cochrane 2011a, pp. 2–6 for an extended discussion of additional learnability concepts and their ability to prune equilibria.)

That debate concerns whether an individual, waking up in a rational expectations equilibrium, can learn the parameters of that equilibrium, enough to form the proper expectations for his or her own behavior. Christiano, Eichenbaum, and Johannsen (2016) explore a different concept of learning, whether if all people in an economy learn, the resulting equilibrium approaches rational expectations, and if so, which rational expectations equilibrium. Like McCallum, they conclude that the active, right-hand equilibrium is learnable, and that the passive, zero-bound equilibrium, and multiple equilibria leading to it, are not. Likewise, García-Schmidt and Woodford (2015) advocate a concept of convergence to rational expectations that they call "reflective" equilibrium, and claim that active-money equilibria are the limits of such reflective equilibria, and passive-money equilibria are not.

This is not the place for a long analysis, but this view has two problems for the point at hand—whether passive-fiscal New Keynesian models predicted more volatile inflation during the long period of near-zero rates. First, the argument is too strong. If the left-most, zero-bound equilibria simply cannot happen, then what do we make of these long stretches at zero interest rates? The only hope, it seems, is to pair this view with the above view that we were not really at the zero bound because everyone expected the economy to jump back to a comfortably active region in no more than a year or so, and the appearance of a zero bound is just a sequence of bad shocks. As above, García-Schmidt and Woodford (2015) are explicit on this point. Second, if multiple equilibria under passive policy cannot occur, that conclusion is true of the 1970s as well as the 2010s. We must again throw out Clarida et al. (2000), Benhabib et al. (2002), and related literature.

More generally, Atkeson et al. (2010) argue that by using "sophisticated policies," the central bank can prune equilibria at any time, zero bound or no zero bound, and thus eliminate indeterminacies. Similarly, Benhabib et al. (2002) and related zero-bound literature crafts policies on top of the policy rule that can, they claim, avoid the zero bound and attendant multiple equilibria. But the question is not so much *can* a central bank or government make equilibrium-selection threats—threats understood, believed, and learned by people—but *did* our central banks and governments make such threats, did people know it, and did economists know it, and did they not worry about sunspot inflation volatility at the zero bound before that volatility failed to materialize.

There are hundreds of other principles one could add to models to select among multiple rational-expectations equilibria. And they will, in general, lead to different results. One might hope that selection will be robust to which principle one uses, a hope expressed by García-Schmidt and Woodford (2015). Yet here my debate with McCallum is instructive. When researchers with different priors approach this question, they come to diametrically opposed answers. Robustness across papers is subject to selection bias.

At this stage in the debate, one can at least say that the view "don't worry about the zero bound and multiple equilibrium volatility at the zero bound because it can't happen," was not commonplace in the New Keynesian literature before 2008.

The other way to select equilibria is to remove the assumption of passive fiscal policy, which restores one simple equation that selects equilibria transparently. It is at least a lot simpler. And if the fiscal theory is not "learnable," then the present value relations underlying all of finance are not learnable either, so economics is in pretty big trouble.

G.   *Irrational Expectations*

Why be so religious about rational expectations? This question reverberated throughout the conference. Bad luck is the same as slow learning, and more generally the analysis in this paper ties stability to rational expectations.

First, it is not so easy. The simple adaptive expectations model gave the traditional sign of the response of inflation to interest rates, but it is unstable at the zero bound. We're looking for a simple model that gives the traditional sign, but is consistent with the quiet lower bound. That is harder to find.

Second, the problems highlighted in this paper stem from the basic sign and stability properties of models. If we had a model with the basic sign and stability properties, then sprinkling in some less than rational expectations to get dynamics right would be more attractive. Putting irrational expectations or other irrationality deeply at the heart of the sign and stability of monetary policy is more worrisome.

Gabaix (2016) is an excellent and concrete example. Gabaix uses a model of rational inattention to argue that people and firms pay less attention to expectations of future income and future prices than they should, modifying the standard three-equation model to

$$x_t = ME_t x_{t+1} - \sigma(i_t - E_t \pi_{t+1}) \tag{80}$$

$$\pi_t = M^f \beta E_t \pi_{t+1} + \kappa x_t \tag{81}$$

$$i_t = \phi \pi_t + v_t^i. \tag{82}$$

where M and M^f are less than one. For sufficiently low M and M^f, Gabaix produces traditional explosive dynamics under a peg, and therefore he produces a negative sign of interest rates on inflation. In this way, Gabaix's model can be seen as a behaviorally microfounded version of the Old Keynesian model studied above.

Kocherlakota (2017) and McKay, Nakamura, and Steinsson (2016) likewise advocate discounting the future consumption in the IS curve (80), though with a less behavioral interpretation.

But to get the traditional sign, Gabaix and Kocherlakota must change the stability properties of the model. As one starts to lower M and M^f, nothing happens at all until the eigenvalues cross one. Cochrane (2016a) finds that one needs quite a lot of irrationality, M less than a half, together with substantial price stickiness $\sigma\kappa$ less than about a half, to cross that boundary. Thus, Gabaix's result is bounded away from rationality and bounded away from the frictionless price limit. A little bit of irrationality or price stickiness will not do.

Gabaix's model also remains unstable, and so does not accommodate the long quiet zero bound without a rather complex patch (section 5.3, and appendix section 9.2). It would be esthetically more pleasing if long-run neutrality were a result of the simple form of a model, and dynamics the result of patches rather than the other way around.

So the model that uses irrational expectations to deliver a temporary negative sign, on top of a frictionless long-run neutral benchmark, has yet to be delivered.

It is certainly not necessary or wise to insist on rational expectations at every data point, and in particular to understand short-run responses to particular events or policies far outside the norm of experience—though economic historians remind us that events "far outside" experience, like financial crises, are in fact common.

But we are looking here for the opposite side of that coin—the fundamental, underlying, long-lasting, simple, and basic economic nature of monetary policy; the central mechanism on which all of policy analysis depends. Are we really satisfied if that foundation relies crucially on noneconomic behavior? Viewed either as introducing irrational expectations or as fundamentally changing our model of intertemporal choice, is it really wise to do such major surgery to economics to accommodate one episode?

The question is not a set of *sufficient* conditions to match dynamics. The question is the minimum *necessary* conditions for the basic mechanism, sign and stability of monetary policy. If irrationality is *necessary* for a negative sign, that verifies my tentative conclusion—that there is no such simple *economic* model. And placing irrational expectations so deeply in the foundations of monetary economics, if that is the answer, paints a revolutionary picture.

Suppose, for example, that a negative effect of interest rates on inflation occurred a few times because people were irrational in their expectations. Lucas's admonition is worth remembering, however, that if policymakers try to exploit this sort of thing, people sooner or later catch on and it stops working. A monetary theory whose basic sign and stability depends on irrational behavior is ephemeral.

Moreover, if this is how monetary policy works then the Federal Reserve should write in its next report to Congress that the sign of the Fed's attempts to control inflation does not rely on simple money supply and money demand rational economics, but instead relies deeply and essentially on a super-rational Federal Reserve offsetting an instability that occurs from people's stupidity, and an interest rate policy that manipulates people's irrationality for their own good. Likewise, if this is the case, economics textbooks need to be rewritten in the same way.

H. More Complex Models

Since the quiet zero bound point depends on the stability and determinacy properties of models, whether eigenvalues are above or below one and how expectations are determined, more complex models do not easily change that result.

It is more likely that one can get a temporary negative sign of interest rates on inflation, without adopting the fiscal-theory plus long-term debt mechanism, out of a model consistent with long-run stability by adding ingredients to the forward-looking, New Keynesian structure.

The models in this paper are also quite simple by the standards of calibrated or estimated New Keynesian models, such as Smets and Wouters (2003), Christiano, Eichenbaum, and Evans (2005), Woodford (2003, sections 5.1–5.2), Rotemberg and Woodford (1997), Del Negro, Giannoni, and Schorfheide (2015), and so forth. (Unfortunately we do not know how these models behave for the experiments of this paper. How do they behave in response to a long-lasting interest rate rise? How sensitive are their predictions to parametric restrictions of the monetary policy shock process?)

So, a natural next step—the sort of thing macroeconomists do all the time when trying to reverse-engineer impulse-response functions— would be to add ingredients such as extensive borrowing or collateral constraints, hand-to-mouth consumers, a lending channel, or other financial frictions, habits, durable goods, housing, multiple goods and other nonseparabilities, novel preferences, labor/leisure choices, production, capital, variable capital utilization, adjustment costs, alternative models of price stickiness, informational frictions, market frictions, payments frictions, more complex monetary frictions, timing lags, individual or firm heterogeneity, and so forth. Going further, perhaps we can add fundamentally different views of expectations and equilibrium, as in Gabaix (2016) and García-Schmidt and Woodford (2015) discussed above, or Angeletos and Lian (2016) (see also the extensive literature review in the latter). I survey a few such models in Section VII below.

But following these paths abandons the qualifier "simple," and with irrational expectations "economic" to our quest for a simple economic model that delivers the basic sign and stability properties of monetary policy. In our quest, this path means that more complex ingredients are *necessary*, not just *sufficient* to deliver the central result. Doing so admits that there is no simple, rational economic model one can put on a blackboard, teach to undergraduates, summarize in a few paragraphs, or refer to in policy discussions to explain at least the signs and rough outlines of the operation of monetary policy—nothing like, say, the stirring and simple description of monetary policy in Friedman (1968).

As with irrationality, if this is the answer, an honest Fed should explain in its next monetary policy report that there is no simple explanation it can give as to why raising interest rates will combat inflation, that this effect is necessarily a big-black-box outcome, and successful policy is dependent on the Fed's technocratic understanding of the above list. It should explain that without these ingredients, if the economy worked by explainable economic mechanisms, the interest rate lever would move inflation positively, not negatively. And honest textbooks should say the same thing. Necessary versus sufficient, dynamic wrinkles versus a basic underlying model, frosting versus cake, are crucial distinctions.

Such an intellectual outcome would also be unusual in macroeconomics. The standard New Keynesian approach views the complex models or even behavioral modifications as refinements, building on equations (58)–(59). The refinements help to match the details of model dynamics with those observed in the data, but the simple model is thought to capture the basic message, signs, stability, and intuition. Except we just found out it does not do so. The standard real business cycle approach views complex models as refinements, building on the stochastic growth model, but that simple model can still capture the basic story. The large multiequation Keynesian models developed in the 1970s built on simple IS-LM models to better match details of the data, but modelers felt that the simple IS-LM model captured the basic signs and mechanisms—indeed, many analysts feel the basic IS-LM model is better than its explicit computerized elaborations.

And this is healthy. Economic models are quantitative parables, and one rightly distrusts macroeconomic predictions that crucially rely on the specific form of poorly understood frictions.

So, I stop here, because if we go down this path, we first agree that no simple economic model delivers the desired sign and stability. We agree that the conclusion of this paper is verified.

The world may well have such a negative sign, due to either irrationality or more complex ingredients. Nothing in this analysis denies that possibility, and let me dispel any impression of an unscientific hostility to adding frictions to macro models.

But if complex frictions are necessary for the basic sign and stability, rather than being used to layer real-world dynamics on top of a simple economic model that gets the simple facts right, that circumstance radically changes the nature of monetary policy. And one must admit that the scientific basis on which we analyze policy, and offer advice to public officials and the public at large, becomes more tenuous.

I. VAR Evidence

If theory and experience point to a positive reaction of inflation to interest rates, perhaps we should revisit the empirical evidence behind the standard contrary view. The main formal evidence we have for the effects of monetary policy comes from vector autoregressions (VARs). There are several problems with this evidence.

First, the VAR literature almost always pairs the announcement of a new policy with the change in the policy instrument, that is, an unexpected shock to interest rates. That habit makes most sense in the context of models following Lucas (1972) in which only unanticipated monetary policy has real effects, and in the context of regressions of output on money, rather than on interest rates, in which VARs developed (Sims 1980).

But in the world, most monetary policy changes are anticipated. VARs may still want to find rare unexpected rate movements, as part of an identification strategy to find changes in policy that are not driven by changes of the Fed's expectations of future output and inflation, but that is a small part of the historical variation. Furthermore, every single interest rate change is described by the Federal Reserve as a reaction *to* some other event in the economy. They never say "and we added a quarter percent for the heck of it," or "so that economists could see what would happen."

Moreover, in the models presented here, anticipated monetary policy has strong effects. In particular, the models with money presented here, as in figure 17, only had a chance of delivering the standard inflation decline if the interest rate rise was anticipated. An empirical technique that isolates unexpected interest rate has great difficulty to find that theoretical prediction.

Second, the analysis of multiple equilibria in figure 14 found that inflation declines occur when an interest rate rise is paired with a fiscal policy tightening. As discussed there, it is plausible that whatever motivates the Fed to raise or lower interest rates also motivates fiscal authorities to change course. It is plausible, therefore, that rate shocks in our data set are like equilibrium E of figure 14. But we want to know what happens if monetary policy moves without coincident fiscal policy changes. VARs have to date made no attempt to orthogonalize monetary policy shocks with respect to fiscal policy, especially expected future fiscal policy, which is what matters here.

Third, VARs typically find that the interest rate responses to an interest rate shock are transitory, as are those of figure 13. As a result, they provide no evidence on the long-run response of inflation to permanent interest rate increases.

Fourth, and most of all, the evidence for a negative sign is not strong, and one can read much of the evidence as supporting a positive sign. From the beginning, VARs produced *increases* in inflation following increases in interest rates, a phenomenon dubbed the "price puzzle" by Eichenbaum (1992). A great deal of effort has been devoted to modifying the specification of VARs so that they can produce the desired result, that a rise in interest rates lowers inflation.

Sims (1992), studying VARs in five countries, notes that "the responses of prices to interest rate shocks show some consistency—they are all initially positive." He also speculates that the central banks may have information about future inflation, so the response represents, in fact, reverse causality. Christiano, Eichenbaum, and Evans (1999, p. 83) take that suggestion. They put shocks in the order output (Y), GDP deflator (P), commodity prices (PCOM), federal funds rate (FF), total reserves (TR), nonborrowed reserves (NBR), and M1 (M). With this specification (their figure 2, top left), positive interest rate shocks reduce output. But even with the carefully chosen ordering, interest rate shocks have no effect on inflation for a year and a half. The price level then gently declines, but remains within the confidence interval of zero throughout. Their figure 5 (p.100), shows nicely how sensitive even this much evidence is to the shock identification assumptions. If the monetary policy shock is ordered first, prices go up uniformly. The inflation response in Christiano et al. (2005) also displays a short-run price puzzle, and is never more than two standard errors from zero.

Even this much success remains controversial. Hanson (2004) points out that commodity prices that solve the price puzzle do not forecast inflation, and vice versa. He also finds that the ability of commodity prices to solve the price puzzle does not work after 1979. Sims (1992) was already troubled that commodities are usually globally traded, so while interest rate increases seem to lower commodity prices, it is hard to see how that could be the effect of domestic monetary policy.

Ramey (2016) surveys and reproduces much of the exhaustive modern literature. She finds that "the pesky price puzzle keeps popping up." Of nine different identification methods, only two present a statistically significant decline in inflation, and those only after four or more years of no effect have passed. Four methods have essentially no effect on inflation at all, and two show strong, statistically significant positive effects, which start without delay. Strong or reliable empirical evidence for a short-term (within four years) negative inflation effect is absent in her survey.

The Christiano et al. (1999) procedure may seem fishy already, in that so much of the identification choice was clearly made in order to produce the desired answer, that higher interest rates lead to lower output and inflation. Nobody spent the same effort seeing if the output decline similarly represented reverse causality or Fed reaction to news of future output, because the output decline fits priors so well. Uhlig (2006) defends this imposition of priors on identification. *If* one has strong theoretical priors that positive interest rate shocks cause inflation to decline, then it makes sense to impose that view as part of shock identification in order to better *measure* that and other responses. (Uhlig's eloquent introduction is worth reading and contains an extensive literature review.)

But imposing the sign only makes sense when one has that strong theoretical prior; when, as when these papers were written, when existing theory uniformly specifies a negative inflation response and nobody is considering the opposite. In the context of this paper, when theory specifies a positive response, when only novel and as yet unwritten theories produce the negative sign, and when we are looking for empirical evidence on the sign, following identification procedures that implicitly or explicitly throw out positive signs does not make sense. And even imposing the sign prior, Uhlig like many others finds that "the GDP price deflator falls only slowly following a contractionary monetary policy shock."

With less strong priors, positive signs are starting to show up. Belaygorod and Dueker (2009) and Castelnuovo and Surico (2010) find that VAR estimates produce positive inflation responses in the periods of estimated indeterminacy. Belaygorod and Dueker (2009) connect estimates to the robust facts one can see in simple plots: through the 1970s and early 1980s, federal funds rates clearly lead inflation movements. Dueker (2006) summarizes.

And even all of this evidence comes from the period in which the Fed kept a small amount of non-interest-bearing reserves, the money multiplier plausibly bound, and the Fed implemented interest rate changes by changing the quantity of reserves. We want to know how inflation will behave in the current regime, in which the Fed will change interest rates by changing the interest it pays on super-abundant reserves, with no open-market operations at all.

VI. Fiscal Theory Objections

I collect here quick answers to some of the most common theoretical and empirical objections to fiscal theory arguments. Many of the these objections came up at the conference. Though each theoretical objection is addressed elsewhere (see, in particular, Cochrane 1998, 2005) since they reappear, it is worth uniting the relevant responses briefly in one place.

The simplest summary: the government-debt valuation equation underlying the fiscal theory is the same as the present value relation underpinning the theory of finance. Any theoretical or empirical objection one has to the fiscal theory is exactly the same objection to price equals present value of dividends. If one is a "budget constraint," so is the other. If one is a knife-edge case that "collapses under the tiniest reasonable perturbation," so is the other. If one is only sustained by strange off-equilibrium promises, so is the other. If one requires "exogenous" surpluses, the other requires "exogenous" dividends. (Neither is the case.) If one is not "learnable" then so is the other. Yes, we do not have an easy independent measure of expected surpluses and discount rates, so we do not have an easy fiscal-theory "test" by calculating an independent prediction for the price level. Yes, we do not have an easy independent measure of expected dividends and discount rates, so we do not have an easy present-value model "test" by calculating a prediction for stock prices. Each equation *holds*, almost trivially—all they need is the absence of arbitrage. One can always discount by expected returns. Thus, neither is testable by itself, and neither allows an easy rejection by looking at time series. No, the fiscal theory cannot be easily invalidated by noting that times of high deficits and debt are not always associated with inflation. No, the present value model cannot be easily invalidated by noting that times of high or low dividends and book values do not always correspond to high or low prices or vice versa. Yes, stock market values are often puzzling given available dividend forecasts, and discount rates are a bit nebulous. Yes, the currently high value of government debt is puzzling given available surplus forecasts, and discount rates are a bit nebulous.

These facts have not kept the present value model from being useful, and at the cornerstone of finance—and its controversies—for decades. Expect of the fiscal theory no less, but also no more. The fiscal theory is, like the present value model, not easily dismissed nonsense. But the fiscal theory, like the present value model, will likely pose challenges to understand the data, and warring and hard-to-test stories. It will not be easy either way.

A. Exogenous Surpluses?

The fiscal theory of the price level does not require that surpluses are "exogenous," just as price = present value of dividends does not require that dividends are "exogenous."

Though it is often useful to think through models and events by thinking of the price level, stock price, or consumption, as determined "given" surpluses, dividends, income, and discount rates, the latter quantities are all economically endogenous and co-determined. Equilibrium conditions do not have a causal structure, as useful as it is to think that way at times.

In particular, the fiscal theory still determines the price level if one models surpluses resulting from proportional taxes. If $P_t s_t = \tau P_t y_t$, then the right-hand side of the government-debt valuation equation becomes τy_{t+j} in place of s_{t+j}. The only P is still on the left-hand side and thus still determined. Including taxes and spending that respond to output and inflation all can leave the basic theory intact. These modifications may well change the quantitative predictions, of course, but those are for another day. Only in the knife-edge case that surplus responses to the price level P_t on the right just cancel those on the left, if the supply and demand curves overlap, then the theory fails.

Like the present value equation, the government-debt valuation equation is not a "budget constraint." The government is not assumed to be a large actor that can "threaten to violate its budget constraint at off equilibrium prices." Nobody can violate budget constraints. The government-debt valuation equation is an equilibrium condition, deriving ultimately from consumer's first-order and transversality conditions. If consumers valued government debt directly, perhaps wishing to wallpaper living rooms with it, then the government would not have to repay debt, and the valuation equation would not hold. It is not a budget constraint of the government any more than the present value equation is a budget constraint on businesses, that forces them to raise dividends in response to prices. For this reason I call the central equation the "government-debt-valuation equation" rather than the common but misleading term "government intertemporal budget constraint."

B. Tests?

The government-debt valuation equation holds in equilibrium in all regimes—active or passive. Therefore, active and passive regimes are observationally equivalent. There is no test for Granger causality, no regression of surpluses on debt or interest rates on inflation, no relationship among time series drawn from the equilibrium of an economy that can distinguish fiscally active and passive, or monetary active and passive, regimes. That fact drives the style of analysis in this paper—only by looking across regimes, or from experiments such as the zero bound episode, can we tell theories apart.

Like price = present value of dividends, the government debt valuation holds under very weak conditions—absence of arbitrage, law of one price. A test necessarily involves auxiliary hypotheses about discount rates, cash flows, information, and so forth.

Therefore, one does not productively address data or distinguish models by "testing" the government-debt valuation equation, any more than one can test price = present value of dividends, or test whether MV = PY describes how money causes inflation or how nominal GDP drives money demand. There is a reason Friedman and Schwartz wrote a whole book, not one definitive Granger-causality test. That is not bad news, it just places fiscal theory exactly in the frustrating but productive realm of the rest of macroeconomics and finance.

C. *Responses to Debt, on and off Equilibria*

In particular, the fiscal theory does not require that fiscal surpluses are set "independently" of outstanding debt, an assumption cited in Christiano's critique at the conference. No. Fiscal theoretic governments borrow money, pay it off, and pay back more when debts are larger, just as one would expect.

In a passive-fiscal regime, the government raises surpluses to pay back debts arising from *any* cause. If a bubble or sunspot causes the price level to decline 50%, the government doubles taxes to repay that windfall to bondholders. An active-fiscal government ignores this kind of debt revaluation. But it does respond to other increases in debt, in particular raising surpluses to pay off debts accumulated from fighting wars and recessions, or rising real interest rates.

This distinction between on-equilibrium and off-equilibrium responses underlies the New Keynesian active-money view, so anyone happy with New Keynesian equilibrium selection should be happy with the fiscal theory as well. Happier, in fact, since the fiscal theory rules out real explosions via the consumer's transversality condition, rather than ruling out purely nominal explosions as some additional principle. Following King (2000), write the policy rule in a New Keynesian model as

$$i_t = i_t^* + \phi_\pi(\pi_t - \pi_t^*) \tag{83}$$

where i_t^*, π_t^* are equilibrium values the Fed desires to select. As before, this is just a convenient rewriting of the usual rule $i_t = \phi\pi_t + v_t^i$. As we have seen, a threat $\phi > 1$ selects $\pi_t = \pi_t^*$, $i_t = i_t^*$ as the unique locally bounded equilibrium. How a central bank's observed interest rate i_t^* responds to observed equilibrium inflation π_t^* is a separate issue from how the central bank responds by off equilibrium $(i_t - i_t^*)$ to off-equilibrium inflation $(\pi_t - \pi_t^*)$. In general—without further restrictions on the policy rule—correlations among equilibrium values are separate from how the central bank responds to a sunspot inflation and one cannot measure off-equilibrium responses with data taken from an equilibrium.

The same argument applies to the fiscal theory. The government can commit to repaying any "on-equilibrium" debt, but to defaulting or inflating away "off-equilibrium" debt. Write

$$\frac{B_{t-1}}{P_t} = E_t \sum_{j=0}^{\infty} \beta^j s_{t+j}. \tag{84}$$

If surpluses respond to *any* change in debt,

$$s_t = \hat{s}_t + \alpha(B_{t-1} / P_t) \tag{85}$$

then, yes, fiscal policy is passive, surpluses adjust on the right-hand side of equation (84) for any price level, and the government-debt valuation equation drops out of equilibrium determination. But if we write the fiscal rule in form analogous to equation (83)

$$s_t = \hat{s}_t + \alpha(B_{t-1} / P_t^*) \tag{86}$$

where * denotes the government's desired equilibrium, then we see exactly the same response in equilibrium—the government pays off its debts—but no response to off-equilibrium price-level bubbles or sunspots. As Taylor-rule off-equilibrium interest rate rises select a unique equilibrium, so fiscal-rule off-equilibrium inaction selects a unique equilibrium. And there is no way to tell apart equation (85) from (86) using data from a given equilibrium, since $P_t = P_t^*$ in equilibrium.

Specification (86) is reasonable. A government following (86) pays off debts it incurs, for example, to finance wars or fight recessions. If the government wants to borrow real resources and keep a stable price level P^*, then such commitment is vital. But a government could and arguably should refuse to accommodate bubbles and sunspots in the price level.

This is also a reasonable model of the gold standard. By following a gold standard, the government announces that it will raise surpluses to pay back debts at the gold value of the currency, no more and no less.

And we have seen cases in which governments do not always rally surpluses to unexpected inflations and deflations. For example, the United States in the 1930s went off the gold standard and defaulted on the gold clause in its bonds after a sharp deflation. It arguably followed (86), not (85).

D. Understanding Data

The second and more interesting category of objections (since it has not been extensively answered in a long literature) is, how can the fiscal theory match data and historical episodes? In this analysis, the obvious unanswered question is, *why* is the present value of surpluses so high, and why is it so quiet (not volatile)? I have been careful to write that the zero bound or an interest rate peg *can* be stable and quiet in the fiscal theory extension of New Keynesian models, not that either *is* stable and quiet. Quiet depends on quiet expectations of fiscal policy.

The short answer is, I don't know. I do not attempt a separate measurement of expected surpluses, and of their discount rate, to produce an independent measure of what the price level or volatility of inflation should be by the fiscal theory.

We know this will not be a trivial exercise. Despite the half century in which the same present value model has dominated finance, attempts to independently measure expected dividends and discount rates, to compute the present value model's prediction for stock prices, and to compare those actual prices have not been productive. And yet the present value model remains the indispensable organizing principle for understanding asset values.

The analysis in this paper stops with the claim that the fiscal theory model *can* account for the quiet zero bound in a way that the other models cannot. I do not claim it is proved, passes additional tests, such as an independent measurement of surpluses and discount rates would provide, or addresses every other event in history. Those would be nice, but not necessary for the claim.

The fiscal theory is at least consistent with the fact that the zero bound does not appear to be a state variable for inflation dynamics. The low volatility of revisions to the present value of surpluses, and low volatility of inflation before and after the zero bound are the same. So there is no particular fiscal theory puzzle about the zero bound. We only need to account for the fact that the volatility of surplus and discount rate expectations did not change much. In fact, there is a glimmer that inflation volatility seems lower at the zero bound than before, so perhaps quiet nominal rates are leading to quieter real rates and therefore quieter present values of debt and inflation. Moreover, quiet present values of surpluses are not the same thing as good present values of surpluses. The puzzle is why markets prize debt so much given surplus forecasts. But this has been a puzzle for two decades. Quiet means only that there is little news on the fiscal front.

E.   What about Japan? And Europe? And the United States?

Since the valuation equation holds, our question is how. Does it require such laughable forecasts and discount rates that it is a useless abstraction? The answer is no.

Japan's debt approaches 200% of GDP, and 20 years of deficit spending have not produced desired inflation. Doesn't the fiscal theory predict hyperinflation for Japan? Europe is north of 100% debt to GDP ratio, and the US is fast approaching. Present value of surpluses? What surpluses? The Congressional Budget Office's (CBO) deficit forecasts have even primary deficits exploding.

The fiscal theory does not predict that high debts or high deficits must correlate with high inflation. The discounted present value of surpluses relative to debt is a far different object than today's raw debt or deficit.

Despite awful projections, it is not unreasonable for bond markets to believe—for now—that the western world's debt problems will be solved successfully. The CBO's deficit forecasts are "if something doesn't change" forecasts, not "conditional mean" forecasts, and they include straightforward policies that can turn surpluses around—mild pro-growth economic policies, mild entitlement reforms. The same angst over debt-fueled inflation emerged in the late 1970s and early 1980s—Sargent and Wallace's (1981) "unpleasant monetarist arithmetic" being only the most famous example. The United States largely repaid greater debts after World War II, and the United Kingdom in the 1800s. A debt crisis leading to inflation will be a self-inflicted wound, not an economic necessity.

More importantly, in my view, the fiscal theory needs to digest the main lesson of asset pricing—discount rates vary a lot, and are vitally important to understand valuations.

Real interest rates are zero or negative throughout the western world, even at very long horizons. From this perspective, the fiscal theory puzzle is not the lack of *inflation*. The fiscal theory puzzle is the lack of *deflation.* Consider a constant discount rate r and an economy growing at rate g, and hence primary surpluses $s_t = \tau y_t$ growing at g. Then,

$$\frac{B_t}{P_t} = E_t \int_{j=0}^{\infty} e^{-rj} s_{t+j} dj = s_t E_t \int_{j=0}^{\infty} e^{(g-r)j} dj = \frac{s_t}{r - g} \qquad (87)$$

or, the ratio of surplus to real value of the debt is $r - g$. The discount rate r matters as much as g. If r declines, the value of the debt rises, so P declines. If r is below g, the absence of past-infinite deflation is the puzzle!

So, to understand low current inflation, the salient fact is the extraordinarily low expected real return on government debt. Debt is valuable despite poor fiscal prospects, not because of great ones. This little calculation also highlights the warning above—$1 / (r - g)$ is very sensitive to r and g. A little higher r not accompanied by g could change our quiet inflation quickly.

F.   What about 2008? And Cyclical Inflation?

Discount-rate variation is likely also to be crucial to understanding episodes such as 2008 and the cyclical correlation of inflation.

Fall 2008. Output falls sharply. Deficits expand into the trillions. The growth slowdown and continuing entitlement problems make future deficits seem even worse. And inflation . . . falls. How is that consistent with the government-debt valuation equation? In every recession, low inflation correlates with large deficits, and vice versa. Isn't the sign wrong?

Again, it is a mistake to confuse current with expected future deficits. A government fighting a war borrows today and simultaneously commits to higher future taxes to pay off the debt—precisely because it does not want to create inflation, and it does want to raise revenue from its bond sales. Our government's fiscal stimulus programs always include at least lip service to future deficit reduction. The surplus should *not* be modeled as an AR(1), but as a series in which a dip today portends a rise in the future. (Cochrane 2001 pursues this point in detail.) Contrariwise, "helicopter drop" plans to deliberately create inflation come with commitments not to repay the debt.

But future surpluses also didn't get a lot *better* in 2008. The answer to a sharp disinflation must then be the discount rate. Both nominal and real interest rates dropped sharply in 2008. A "flight to quality" further lowered the expected return of government bonds relative to corporate bonds. People were trying to hold more government bonds—and to hold less private assets and to spend less to get government bonds.

This mechanism helps as well to understand the general cyclical correlation of inflation. In any recession, output falls, deficits rise, and yet inflation falls. Why? In part, people understand that current deficits correspond to larger future surpluses. But the most important part of the effect is likely that people are willing to hold claims to the same surplus at lower rates of return in a recession than they are in a boom.

G.   What about 1951?

What about all the failed interest rate pegs? The plausible answer and warning: fiscal policy.

For example, Woodford (2001) analyzes the US peg of the 1940s and early 1950s. He credits fiscal-theoretic mechanisms for the surprising stability of the interest rate peg—it did last a decade, and more, if you count zero rates in the Great Depression. In his view, it fell apart when the Korean War undermined fiscal policy. Other countries whose pegs fell apart after World War II, motivating Friedman (1968), were facing difficult fiscal problems. Most historic pegs were enacted along with price controls, exchange controls, and monetary controls as devices to reduce interest payments on the debt (that was explicit in the US case) and to help otherwise difficult fiscal policy. In most historic pegs, central banks were trying to hold down rates that otherwise wanted to rise by lending out money to banks at low rates, and with financial repression to force people to hold government debt they did not want to hold. Our central banks are taking *in* money from banks who can't find better opportunities elsewhere, thus apparently holding interest rates above what they otherwise want to be, in the face of overwhelming demand for government debt. Countries whose pegs fell apart had problems financing current deficits. We have doomsaying forecasts of deficits decades from now. The lessons of historical pegs under vastly different fiscal circumstances do not necessarily apply to all pegs or zero bound episodes.

Interest rate pegs, like exchange-rate pegs, live on top of solvent fiscal policy or not at all. For this reason, too, I have been careful to state the conclusion as "an interest rate peg *can* be stable."

None of this discussion is proof, nor is it intended as such. The point is that *there exists* a vaguely plausible reconciliation of the data with the government-debt valuation equation; that merely citing the episodes does not instantly and easily *disprove* the fiscal theory.

VII. Literature

The doctrines of inflation instability or indeterminacy are longstanding. Milton Friedman (1968, 5) gives the classic statement that an interest rate peg is unstable, and that higher interest rates lead to temporarily lower inflation. Friedman writes that monetary policy "cannot peg interest rates for more than very limited periods." Friedman's (1968, 5–6) prediction also comes clearly from adaptive expectations:

Let the higher rate of monetary growth produce rising prices, and let the public come to expect that prices will continue to rise. Borrowers will then be willing to pay and lenders will then demand higher interest rates—as Irving Fisher pointed out decades ago. This price expectation effect is slow to develop and also slow to disappear.

Friedman stressed the effect of money growth on output rather than interest rates, via IS-LM's IS or modern intertemporal substitution. But the bottom-line dynamics from interest rate to inflation does not depend on this view of the mechanism. The very Keynesian model of figure 9 captures completely Friedman's description of inflation instability and interest rate policy under adaptive expectations.

Friedman was heavily influenced by recent history of his time:

These views [ineffectiveness of monetary policies] produced a widespread adoption of cheap money policies after the war. And they received a rude shock when these policies failed in country after country, when central bank after central bank was forced to give up the pretense that it could indefinitely keep "the" rate of interest at a low level. In this country, the public denouement came with the Federal Reserve-Treasury Accord in 1951, although the policy of pegging government bond prices was not formally abandoned until 1953. Inflation, stimulated by cheap money policies, not the widely heralded postwar depression, turned out to be the order of the day. (Friedman 1968, 5–6)

We do not know how Friedman might have adapted his views with our recent eight years of experience, or Japan's 20 in mind, rather than the inflations of the immediate World War II aftermath.

Taylor (1999) provides a clear statement that Old Keynesian (backward-looking, adaptive expectations) models are unstable, and that Taylor rules induce stability.

The doctrine that inflation is *indeterminate* under an interest rate peg or passive policy, under rational expectations, started with Sargent and Wallace (1975). The basic point: fixing i_t with $i_t = r_t + E_t \pi_{t+1}$ leaves $\pi_{t+1} - E_t \pi_{t+1}$ indeterminate. Their point is quite different from Friedman's instability. Indeterminacy, instability, and volatility are distinct concepts, frequently confused.

The fiscal theory of the price level goes back to Adam Smith:

> A prince who should enact that a certain proportion of his taxes should be paid in a paper money of a certain kind might thereby give a certain value to this paper money. (Smith, *Wealth of Nations*, Book 2, Ch. II.)

Monetary economists have long recognized the importance of monetary-fiscal interactions. The modern resurgence and deep elaboration owes much to Sargent and Wallace (1981) and Sargent (2013). Leeper (1991) shows how the fiscal theory can uniquely determine the price level under passive monetary policy. Sims (1994) clearly states that the fiscal theory and rational expectations overturn Friedman's doctrine of instability, as well as Sargent and Wallace's indeterminacy:

> A monetary policy that fixes the nominal interest rate, even if it holds the interest rate constant regardless of the observed rate of inflation or money growth rate, may deliver a uniquely determined price level.

The observation that interest rate pegs are stable in forward-looking, New Keynesian models also goes back a long way. Woodford (1995) discusses the issue. Woodford (2001) is a clear statement, analyzing interest rate pegs such as the World War II US price support regime, showing they are stable so long as fiscal policy cooperates.

Benhabib et al. (2002) is a classic treatment of the zero-rate liquidity trap. They note that the zero bound means there must be an equilibrium with a locally passive $\phi_\pi < 1$ Taylor rule, with multiple stable equilibria. However, they view this state as a pathology, not a realization of the optimal quantity of money and optimal (low) level of markups, and devote the main point of their paper to escaping the "trap" via fiscal policy.

Schmitt-Grohé and Uribe (2014) realize that inflation stability means the Fed could raise the peg and therefore raise inflation. To them this is another possibility for escaping a liquidity trap. They write

> The paper . . . shows that raising the nominal interest rate to its intended target for an extended period of time, rather than exacerbating the recession as conventional wisdom would have it, can boost inflationary expectations and thereby foster employment.

The standard model here with a forward-looking Phillips curve disagrees that raising inflation raises employment, but that is not a robust feature.

Belaygorod and Dueker (2009) and Castelnuovo and Surico (2010) estimate New Keynesian DSGE models allowing for switches between determinacy and indeterminacy. They find that the model displays the price puzzle—interest rate shocks lead to rising inflation, starting immediately—in the indeterminacy region $\phi_\pi < 1$, as I do.

The possibility that long periods of low rates cause deflation, so raising interest rates will raise inflation, has had a larger recent airing in speeches and the blogosphere. (See Williamson 2013; Cochrane 2013, 2014c; Smith 2014.) Minneapolis Federal Reserve Chairman Narayana Kocherlakota (2010) suggested it in a famous speech:

> Long-run monetary neutrality is an uncontroversial, simple, but nonetheless profound proposition. In particular, it implies that if the FOMC maintains the fed funds rate at its current level of 0–25 basis points for too long, both anticipated and actual inflation have to become negative. Why? It's simple arithmetic. Let's say that the real rate of return on safe investments is 1 percent and we need to add an amount of anticipated inflation that will result in a fed funds rate of 0.25 percent. The only way to get that is to add a negative number—in this case, 0.75 percent.
>
> To sum up, over the long run, a low fed funds rate must lead to consistent—but low—levels of deflation.

To be clear, Friedman (1968) disagrees. Friedman views the Fisher equation as an unstable steady state. Kocherlakota, seeing recent experience, views it as a stable one. Friedman's "long-run neutrality" is that a permanent rise in M gives rise to a permanent rise in P, but a permanent rise in i will lead to explosive P and π. A permanent rise in $\dot{M}$ gives rise to a permanent rise in $\dot{P}$ and therefore of both i and π, but not the other way around. Kocherlakota's "long-run neutrality" is that a permanent rise in i will lead to a permanent rise in π. The difference between a stable and an unstable steady state is key.

Cochrane (2014b) works out a model with fiscal price determination, an interest rate target, and simple k-period price stickiness. Higher interest rates raise inflation in the short and long run, just as in this paper, but the k-period stickiness leads to unrealistic dynamics.

Following Woodford (2003), many authors also tried putting money back into sticky-price models. Benchimol and Fourçans (2012, 2017) study a CES money in the utility function specification as here, in a detailed model applied to the Eurozone. They find that adding money makes small but important differences to the estimated model dynamics. Ireland (2004) also adds money in the utility function. In his model, money also spills over into the Phillips curve (see p. 974). However, he finds that maximum likelihood estimates lead to very small influences of money, a very small if not zero cross partial derivative u_{cm}.

Ireland's Phillips curve comes from quadratic adjustment costs. Andrés, López-Salido, and Vallés (2006) find a similar result from a Calvo-style pricing model. Their estimate also finds no effects of money on model dynamics.

Many authors have noted that the stability, absence of deflation, and subsequent quiet (lack of volatility) of inflation is a puzzle, along with other puzzles in accounting for the great recession. Homburg (2015) points out Japan's "benign liquidity trap" and the puzzle it poses for standard models. He advocates a repair with pervasive credit constraints.

Hall (2011) analyzes many features leading to the large fall in output. As for inflation, he argues for the "near-exogeneity" of the rate of inflation.

Quite a few recent contributions fall in the category of section V.H that adds a long list of ingredients and frictions to match recent experience and address this and related theoretical puzzles.

Eggertsson and Mehrotra (2014) is a good example of the "secular stagnation" view. They select equilibria by expectations of active policy once the zero bound passes, as analyzed in section V.D here. In their model, the stagnation would be cured if the Fed would only commit to a pure peg—expectations of return to active policy are the central problem. (See Cochrane 2014a.)

Christiano, Eichenbaum, and Trabandt (2014) use a detailed nonlinear New Keynesian model, designed to match quantity variables in the slow recovery as well as inflation. They have four big shocks—a "financial wedge," a "consumption wedge," a TFP shock, and changes in government consumption. Their monetary policy includes an active rule with zero bound constraint, forward guidance about keeping interest rates low after the recovery, and, in the taxonomy of this paper, a return to active policy that selects equilibria.

Farhi and Werning (2017) add agent heterogeneity, incomplete markets, uninsurable idiosyncratic risk, occasionally binding borrowing constraints, and bounded rationality in the form of level-k thinking. They are, however, not aimed at explaining the quiet zero bound or reviving the negative sign but to "a powerful mitigation of the effects of monetary policy" and the forward-guidance puzzle.

Del Negro et al. (2015) is an ambitious attempt to account for quiet inflation during the Great Recession, combining more frictions and ingredients than I can compactly summarize here. For their central purpose, understanding why inflation did not fall more, the key assumption is the form of Phillips curve and measurement of marginal costs. For the issues here, they rely on expectations of future active policy to select equilibria at the zero bound, and many years of bad luck.

VIII.   Concluding Comments

The observation that inflation has been stable or gently declining and quiet at the zero bound is important evidence against the classical view that an inflation is unstable at the zero bound, and by implication at an interest rate peg or passive monetary policy, and the New Keynesian view that the zero bound, a peg, or passive monetary policy lead to sunspot volatility. If an interest rate peg is stable, then raising the interest rate should raise inflation, at least eventually.

Conventional New Keynesian models predict that inflation is stable. Adding the fiscal theory of the price level, or related rules for selecting nearby equilibria, removes indeterminacies and sunspots and leads to a very simple monetary model consistent with our recent experience.

Those models also predict that raising interest rates will raise inflation, both in the long and short run. My attempts to escape this prediction by adding money, backward-looking Phillips curves, and multiple equilibria all fail.

The New Keynesian model plus fiscal theory and long-term debt does produce a temporary negative inflation response to unexpected interest rate increases. It is simple and economic, but quite novel relative to standard monetary models. It does not produce the standard, adaptive-expectations view of a permanent disinflation such as the 1980s, nor does it justify policy exploitation of the negative sign, especially in systematic, Taylor-principle form.

It is likely that the negative sign can be found by adding more complex ingredients, including abandoning rational expectations. But that path makes those assumptions necessary, at the foundation of monetary economics, rather than sufficient, small perturbations that get dynamics right.

This paper was also a search for a simple model that captures the effects of monetary policy, but overcomes the critiques of active and instability-inducing Taylor rules in forward-looking models. The New Keynesian plus fiscal theory model in this paper satisfies that criterion.

A review of the empirical evidence finds weak support for the standard theoretical view that raising interest rates lowers inflation, and much of that evidence is colored by the imposition of strong priors of that sign.

I conclude that a positive reaction of inflation to interest rate changes, especially in the long run, is a possibility we, and central bankers, ought to begin to take seriously. At least our faith in a stable exploitable negative relationship coincident with the actual raising of rates ought to be weakened.

The fact of quiet inflation and the theory here rehabilitate interest rate pegs as a possible policy. We can live the Friedman rule of low interest, low inflation, and enormous reserves. Real policies may choose a time-varying peg if central banks think they can offset shocks (v_t^i here may react to v_t^r), and may desire headroom of higher inflation to do that. Such policies may not look that different in practice. But there is no need to fear catastrophic inflation from the former policy configuration.

However, that quiet depends on fiscal foundations. The large demand for government debt, which provides the fiscal foundations of this quiet (under either active or passive views), driven by low discount rates not strong fiscal policies, could evaporate as unexpectedly as it arrived.

Endnotes

Additional author affiliations: SIEPR, Stanford GSB, University of Chicago Booth School of Business and Becker-Friedman Institute, and Cato Institute (http://faculty .chicagobooth.edu/john.cochrane). This paper supersedes a working paper titled "Do Higher Interest Rates Raise or Lower Inflation?" I thank Larry Christiano, Ricardo Reis, Anthony Diercks, Martin Eichenbaum, Xavier Gabaix, Jordi Galí, Edward Nelson, and Mizuki Tsuboi for helpful comments. An algebra appendix and computer programs are on my webpage, http://faculty.chicagobooth.edu/john.cochrane/. For acknowledgments, sources of research support, and disclosure of the author's material financial relationships, if any, please see http://www.nber.org/chapters/c13911.ack.

1. In 1887, Albert A. Michelson and Edward W. Morley set out to measure the speed of Earth through the ether, the substance thought in its day to carry light waves, by measuring the speed of light in various directions. They found nothing: the speed of light is the same in all directions, and the Earth appears to be still. Special relativity follows pretty much from this observation alone.

References

Andrés, J., J. D. López-Salido, and J. Vallés. 2006. "Money in an Estimated Business Cycle Model of the Euro Area. *Economic Journal* 116 (511): 457–77.

Angeletos, G.-M., and C. Lian. 2016. "Forward Guidance without Common Knowledge." NBER Working Paper no. 22785, Cambridge, MA.

Atkeson, A., V. V. Chari, and P. J. Kehoe. 2010. "Sophisticated Monetary Policies." *Quarterly Journal of Economics* 125 (1): 47–89.

Ball, L. 2016. "Ben Bernanke and the Zero Bound." *Contemporary Economic Policy, Western Economic Association International* 34:7–20.

Belaygorod, A., and M. Dueker. 2009. "Indeterminacy, Change Points and the Price Puzzle in an Estimated DSGE Model." *Journal of Economic Dynamics and Control* 33 (3): 624–48.

Benchimol, J., and A. Fourçans. 2012. "Money and Risk in a DSGE Framework: A Bayesian Application to the Eurozone." *Journal of Macroeconomics* 34:95–111.
———. 2017. "Money and Monetary Policy in the Eurozone: An Empirical Analysis during Crises." *Macroeconomic Dynamics* 21 (3): 677–707.
Benhabib, J., S. Schmitt-Grohé, and M. Uribe. 2001. "Monetary Policy and Multiple Equilibria." *American Economic Review* 91 (1) :167–86.
———. 2002. "Avoiding Liquidity Traps." *Journal of Political Economy* 110 (3): 535–63.
Bordo, M. D., C. J. Erceg, A. T. Levin, and R. Michaels. 2017. "Policy Credibility and Alternative Approaches to Disinflation." *Research in Economics* 71 (3): 422–40.
Brash, D. T. 2002. "Inflation Targeting 14 Years On." Speech given at 2002 American Economics Association conference, Atlanta, GA, January 5.
Campbell, J. R., and J. P. Weber. 2016. "Open Mouth Operations." Manuscript, Federal Reserve Bank of Chicago.
Castelnuovo, E., and P. Surico. 2010. "Monetary Policy, Inflation Expectations and the Price Puzzle." *Economic Journal* 120:1262–83.
Christiano, L., M. Eichenbaum, and C. Evans. 1999. "Monetary Policy Shocks: What Have We Learned and to What End?" In *Handbook of Macroeconomics*, ed. M. Woodford and J. B. Taylor, 65–148. Amsterdam: North-Holland.
———. 2005. "Nominal Rigidities and the Dynamic Effects of a Shock to Monetary Policy." *Journal of Political Economy* 113 (1): 1–45.
Christiano, L. J., M. S. Eichenbaum, and B. K. Johannsen. 2016. "Does the New Keynesian Model Have a Uniqueness Problem?" Manuscript.
Christiano, L. J., M. S. Eichenbaum, and M. Trabandt. 2014. "Understanding the Great Recession." Working Paper no. 20040, Cambridge, MA.
Clarida, R., J. Gal, and M. Gertler. 2000. "Monetary Policy Rules and Macroeconomic Stability: Evidence and Some Theory." *Quarterly Journal of Economics* 115:147–80.
Cochrane, J. H. 1998. "A Frictionless View of US Inflation." In *NBER Macroeconomics Annual*, vol. 13, ed. Jonathan A. Parker and Michael Woodford, 323–84. Chicago: University of Chicago Press.
———. 2001. "Long-Term Debt and Optimal Policy in the Fiscal Theory of the Price Level." *Econometrica* 69:69–116.
———. 2005. "Money as Stock." *Journal of Monetary Economics* 52:501–28.
———. 2009. "Can Learnability Save New-Keynesian Models?" *Journal of Monetary Economics* 56 (8): 1109–13.
———. 2011a. Appendix B from John H. Cochrane, "Determinacy and Identification with Taylor Rules." *Journal of Political Economy* 119:565–615.
———. 2011b. "Determinacy and Identification with Taylor Rules." *Journal of Political Economy* 119:565–615.
———. 2013. "What If We Got the Sign Wrong on Monetary Policy?" *Grumpy Economist* (blog), December 19, 2013, https://johnhcochrane.blogspot.com/2013/12/what-if-we-got-sign-wrong-on-monetary.html.
———. 2014a. Comment on Eggertsson and Mehrotra, "A Model of Secular Stagnation." Manuscript.
———. 2014b. "Monetary Policy with Interest on Reserves." *Journal of Economic Dynamics and Control* 49:74–108.
———. 2014c. "The Neo-Fisherian Question." *Grumpy Economist* (blog), November 6, 2014, https://johnhcochrane.blogspot.com/2014/11/the-neo-fisherian-question.html.
———. 2014d. "Toward a Run-Free Financial System." In *Across the Great Divide: New Perspectives on the Financial Crisis*, ed. M. N. Baily and J. B. Taylor, 197–249. Stanford, CA: Hoover Press.

———. 2015. "A New Structure for US Federal Debt." In *The $13 Trillion Question: How America Manages Its Debt*, ed. D. Wessel, 91–146. Washington, DC: Brookings Institution Press.

———. 2016a. Comment on Xavier Gabaix "A Behavioral New-Keynesian Model" Manuscript.

———. 2017. "The New-Keynesian Liquidity Trap." *Journal of Monetary Economics* 92:47–63.

———. 2018. "Stepping on a Rake: the Fiscal Theory of Monetary Policy." *European Economic Review* 101:354–375.

Del Negro, M. D., M. P. Giannoni, and F. Schorfheide. 2015. "Inflation in the Great Recession and New Keynesian Models." *American Economic Journal: Macroeconomics* 7 (1): 168–96.

Dueker, M. J. 2006. "The Price Puzzle: An Update and a Lesson." *Economic Synopses* 4:1.

Eggertsson, G., and N. Mehrotra. 2014. "A Model of Secular Stagnation." NBER Working Paper no. 20574, Cambridge, MA.

Eichenbaum, M. 1992. Comment on "Interpreting the Macroeconomic Time Series Facts: The Effects of Monetary Policy." *European Economic Review* 36 (5): 1001–11.

Evans, G. W., and S. Honkapohja. 2001. *Learning and Expectations in Macroeconomics*. Princeton, NJ: Princeton University Press.

Farhi, E., and I. Werning. 2017. "Monetary Policy, Bounded Rationality, and Incomplete Markets." NBER Working Paper no. 23281, Cambridge, MA.

Friedman, M. 1968. "The Role of Monetary Policy." *American Economic Review* 58:1–17.

———. 1969. "The Optimum Quantity of Money." In *The Optimum Quantity of Money and Other Essays*, ed. Milton Friedman, 1–50. Chicago: Aldine.

Gabaix, X. 2016. "A Behavioral New Keynesian Model." NBER Working Paper no. 22954, Cambridge, MA.

García-Schmidt, M., and M. Woodford. 2015. "Are Low Interest Rates Deflationary? A Paradox of Perfect-Foresight Analysis." NBER Working Paper no. 21614, Cambridge, MA.

Gürkaynak, R. S., B. Sack, and J. H. Wright. 2007. "The US Treasury Yield Curve: 1961 to the Present." *Journal of Monetary Economics* 54 (8): 2291–304. Data at https://www.federalreserve.gov/econresdata/researchdata/feds200628.xls.

Hall, G. J., and T. J. Sargent. 2015. "A History of US Debt Limits." NBER Working Paper no. 21799, Cambridge, MA.

Hall, R. E. 2011. "The Long Slump." *American Economic Review* 101:431–69.

Hanson, M. 2004. "The 'Price Puzzle' Reconsidered." *Journal of Monetary Economics* 51 (7): 1385–413.

Homburg, S. 2015. "Understanding Benign Liquidity Traps: The Case of Japan." *German Economic Review* 18 (3): 267–82.

Ireland, P. 2004. "Money's Role in the Monetary Business Cycle." *Journal of Money, Credit, and Banking* 36 (6): 969–83.

King, R. G. 2000. "The New IS-LM Model: Language, Logic, and Limits." *Federal Reserve Bank of Richmond Economic Quarterly* 86 (3): 45–104.

Kocherlakota, N. 2010. "Inside the FOMC." Speech, Marquette, MI, August 17.

———. 2016. "Fragility of Purely Real Macroeconomic Models." NBER Working Paper no. 21866, Cambridge, MA.

———. 2017. Comment on Cochrane, "Michelson-Morley, Fisher, and Occam: The Radical Implications of Stable Quiet Inflation at the Zero Bound." In *NBER Macroeconomics Annual 2017*, ed. Martin Eichenbaum and Jonathan A. Parker.

Leeper, E. M. 1991. "Equilibria under 'Active' and 'Passive' Monetary and Fiscal Policies." *Journal of Monetary Economics* 27:129–47.

Lucas, R. E. 1972. "Expectations and the Neutrality of Money." *Journal of Economic Theory* 4:103–24.

Mankiw, N. G., and R. Reis. 2002. "Sticky Information versus Sticky Prices: A Proposal to Replace the New Keynesian Phillips Curve." *Quarterly Journal of Economics* 117:1295–328.

McCallum, B. T. 2009a. "Inflation Determination with Taylor Rules: Is New-Keynesian Analysis Critically Flawed?" *Journal of Monetary Economics* 56 (8): 1101–08.

———. 2009b. "Rejoinder to Cochrane." *Journal of Monetary Economics* 56 (8): 1114–15.

McKay, A., E. Nakamura, and J. Steinsson. 2016. "The Power of Forward Guidance Revisited." *American Economic Review* 106:3133–58.

Ramey, V. 2016. "Macroeconomic Shocks and Their Propagation." NBER Working Paper no. 21978, Cambridge, MA.

Rotemberg, J. J., and M. Woodford. 1997. "An Optimization-Based Econometric Framework for the Evaluation of Monetary Policy." In *NBER Macroeconomics Annual*, vol. 12, ed. Jonathan A. Parker and Micael Woodford, 297–346. Chicago: University of Chicago Press.

Sargent, T. J. 2013. *Rational Expectations and Inflation*, 3rd ed. Princeton, NJ: Princeton University Press.

Sargent, T. J., and N. Wallace. 1975. "'Rational' Expectations, the Optimal Monetary Instrument, and the Optimal Money Supply Rule." *Journal of Political Economy* 83:241–54.

———. 1981. "Some Unpleasant Monetarist Arithmetic." *Federal Reserve Bank of Minneapolis Quarterly Review* 5:1–17.

Schmitt-Grohé, S., and M. Uribe. 2014. "Liquidity Traps: An Interest-Rate-Based Exit Strategy." *The Manchester School* 81 (S1): 1–14.

Sims, C. A. 1980. "Macroeconomics and Reality." *Econometrica* 48 (1): 1–48.

———. 1992. "Interpreting the Macroeconomic Time Series Facts: The Effects of Monetary Policy." *European Economic Review* 36 (5): 975–1000.

———. 1994. "A Simple Model for Study of the Determination of the Price Level and the Interaction of Monetary and Fiscal Policy." *Economic Theory* 4 (3): 381–99.

———. 2011. "Stepping on a Rake: The Role of Fiscal Policy in the Inflation of the 1970s." *European Economic Review* 55:48–56.

———. 2016. "Fiscal Policy, Monetary Policy and Central Bank Independence." Lunchtime Talk, Jackson Hole, WY, August 26. http://sims.princeton.edu/yftp/JacksonHole16/JHpaper.pdf.

Smets, F., and R. Wouters. 2003. "An Estimated Dynamic Stochastic General Equilibrium Model of the Euro Area." *Journal of the European Economic Association* 1 (5): 1123–75.

Smith, N. 2014. "The Neo-Fisherite Rebellion." *Noahpinion* (blog), April 23, 2014, http://noahpinionblog.blogspot.com/2014/04/the-neo-fisherite-rebellion.html.

Swanson, E. T., and J. C. Williams. 2014. "Measuring the Effect of the Zero Lower Bound on Medium- and Longer-Term Interest Rates." *American Economic Review* 104:3154–85.

Taylor, J. B. 1993. "Discretion versus Policy Rules in Practice." *Carnegie-Rochester Conference Series on Public Policy* 39:195–214.

———. 1999. "The Robustness and Efficiency of Monetary Policy Rules as Guidelines for Interest Rate Setting by the European Central Bank." *Journal of Monetary Economics* 43:655–79.

Uhlig, H. 2006. "What are the Effects of Monetary Policy? Results from an Agnostic Identification Procedure." *Journal of Monetary Economics* 52:381–419.

Werning, I. 2011. "Managing a Liquidity Trap: Monetary and Fiscal Policy." NBER Working Paper no. 17344, Cambridge, MA.

Wieland, J. 2015. "Are Negative Supply Shocks Expansionary at the Zero Lower Bound?" Manuscript, University of California, San Diego.

Williamson, S. 2013. "Phillips Curves and Fisher Relations." *New Monetarist Economics* (blog), December 15, 2013, http://newmonetarism.blogspot.com /2013/12/phillips-curves-and-fisher-relations.html.

Woodford, M. 1995. "Price-Level Determinacy without Control of a Monetary Aggregate." *Carnegie-Rochester Conference Series on Public Policy* 43:1–46.

———. 2001. "Fiscal Requirements for Price Stability." *Journal of Money Credit and Banking* 33:669–728.

———. 2003. *Interest and Prices*. Princeton, NJ: Princeton University Press.

———. 2012. "Methods of Policy Accommodation at the Interest-Rate Lower Bound." Manuscript. The Changing Policy Landscape: 2012 Jackson Hole Symposium.

Yellen, J. 2016. "Macroeconomic Research after the Crisis." Technical Report, Federal Reserve Board of Governors. Speech given at The Elusive "Great" Recovery: Causes and Implications for Future Business Cycle Dynamics, 60th annual economic conference sponsored by the Federal Reserve Bank of Boston, October, 14.

Comment

Lawrence J. Christiano, Northwestern University and NBER

Introduction

Cochrane's headline argument is straightforward. The US monetary authorities have kept short-term interest rates relatively constant since 2009, suggesting that monetary policy became passive then. The standard New Keynesian model (NK model) predicts that under passive monetary policy, sunspots should have appeared in 2009, raising the volatility of aggregate economic variables. But, Cochrane infers from the observed "stable and quiet inflation" that the predicted sunspots never appeared. In effect, 2009 was a Michelson-Morley moment for the NK model. Cochrane recommends that the nearly universal assumption of active money, passive fiscal policy in the standard NK model be replaced by the reverse: passive money and active fiscal policy. There are other reasons to make this change, according to Cochrane. These include that the standard NK model entangles one in a "menagerie of policy paradoxes" and the standard NK model has many equilibria without any reasonable way to choose between them.

The paper wakes up many old debates that have never been fully settled, some that go back two decades. I respond to many of those challenges in my comment.

The new part of the paper replaces the standard specification of the fiscal theory of the price level, which assumes one-period debt, with an alternative specification in which the government issues debt of all maturities. Cochrane tests the version of the NK model with this adjusted fiscal theory against a common conjecture about what would happen if central banks were to raise the nominal rate of interest permanently. The conjecture is that such an interest rate hike would cause a transitory decline in inflation and output before eventually producing a rise in inflation equal to the rise in the interest rate, and no change in output. The conjecture seems sensible to me, but I do not (yet) see why it requires adopting the fiscal theory of the price level.

The comment proceeds as follows. The next subsection pushes back on Cochrane's claim that the recent data represent a Michelson-Morley moment for the NK model. In the third section, I discuss Cochrane's adjusted fiscal theory and his conjecture about the effects of a permanent interest rate hike. The fourth section responds to Cochrane's remarks on the unique, bounded rational expectations equilibrium in the standard NK model. I also discuss the learnability of that equilibrium, the other equilibria in that model, and the identifiability of the Taylor rule coefficient on inflation. All these are subjects that are raised by Cochrane in his paper, and in each case I push back on the position that he takes.

The fifth section addresses the "menagerie of policy paradoxes" that Cochrane asserts the standard NK model possesses. Finally, the sixth section concludes.

A Michelson-Morley Experiment for the Standard NK Model?

Cochrane's Michelson-Morley argument is based on the premise that US monetary policy became passive, beginning in 2009. By contrast, the conventional view is that monetary policy in fact remained active.[1] Policy only seemed like an interest rate peg because the zero lower bound on the nominal rate of interest had become binding. The NK model predicted that sunspots could not occur during this period because policy was expected to resume an active stance against inflation in the future when the zero lower bound would once again cease to bind. Cochrane scoffs at this view as representing an ex post "rescue by epicycles," presumably by bitter NK-model enthusiasts unhappy about the outcome of the Michelson-Morley experiment.

But, 2009 was no Michelson-Morley experiment. What the economy would look like if something rammed it into the zero lower bound had already been envisioned long ago in Krugman (1998) and Eggertsson and Woodford (2003).[2] For example, the latter paper predicted that inflation and other variables would literally be constant as long as the zero lower bound lasted. Cochrane's suggestion that the relatively small amount of volatility observed after 2009 is an embarrassment requiring a patch to the NK model is a misrepresentation of the literature.

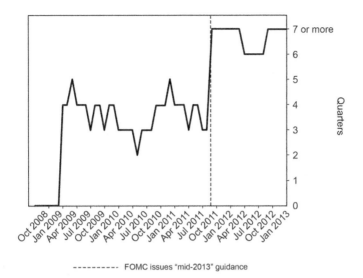

-------- FOMC issues "mid-2013" guidance

Fig. 1. Expected number of quarters until first federal funds rate increase to 25 BP or higher

Source: Swanson and Williams (2014, fig. 4).

Consistent with the conventional view, the level of interest rates were expected to eventually return to normal levels. Consider, for example, figure 1, taken from Swanson and Williams (2014).

Figure 1 shows that throughout 2009–2011, professional forecasters consistently expected the interest rate to lift off from its lower bound within about one year. The forecasts resemble the prediction of Eggertsson and Woodford (2003), according to which the factors that put the economy into the zero lower bound were expected to end according to a Markov chain with constant transition probability.

The results in figure 1 are top coded at seven quarters. So, technically that figure is consistent with the view that 2011 monetary policy had become a peg at zero. In fact, other evidence in the Swanson and Williams paper (see, e.g., their figure 5) suggests that financial market participants continued to expect the interest rate to eventually lift off from its lower bound after 2011.

It is true that it has taken longer than initially expected for rates to come unstuck from zero, but this provides no reason to doubt the conventional narrative.[3] Nor does Cochrane offer any reason to doubt that narrative.

Cochrane argues that there are other reasons, beyond his Michelson-Morley argument, to reject the NK model. I review three here.

The Response to a Permanent Rise in the Nominal Rate of Interest

Cochrane replaces the active monetary policy assumption in the NK model with the assumption that monetary policy is passive. In addition, he introduces an adjusted version of active fiscal policy in the model. In his adjustment, Cochrane replaces the usual assumption of one-period debt with the assumption that the government issues debt of all maturities.

This is an interesting adjustment because it has the effect of causing the time t nominal value of the outstanding debt—which is a state variable in the usual specification—to be a function of time t shocks. The dollar value of the outstanding debt is the dollar price of debt at each maturity times the quantity of that debt. In each case, the price is the inverse of the nominal rate of interest that has the same duration as the associated debt. Thus, a rise in the rate of interest reduces the market value of the debt in dollar terms by reducing the price of debt at each maturity.[4] If the real interest rate does not change, then the real present value of surpluses does not change either. So, the fiscal theory then predicts a drop in the price level to ensure that the real value of all outstanding debt remains unchanged. With sticky prices, the predicted price-level drop in the adjusted theory becomes a slow fall, or a drop in inflation. Note that this implies a rise in the real rate of interest, creating a fall in the present value of government surpluses. This latter effect lessens the need for a fall in the price level. In the numerical simulations, inflation falls.

A substantial part of the paper is devoted to exploring whether, with the proposed adjustment, the fiscal theory can replicate a conjecture that Cochrane says is widespread among central bankers. The conjecture is that an immediate and permanent rise in the interest rate initially leads to a fall in inflation and output, but eventually causes inflation and the interest rate to rise by the same amount, leaving the real interest rate unchanged.

That a permanent rise in the nominal interest rate would ultimately raise the inflation rate by roughly the same amount is a feature shared by most models. So, the challenge is to see if Cochrane's adjusted fiscal theory model can produce a transitory fall in inflation and output in response to a permanent increase in the nominal rate of interest. In view of the results in the previous paragraph, it is perhaps not surprising that Cochrane's model can indeed produce the result. Because his version of the fiscal theory is incorporated into a version of the NK model, the transitory rise in the real interest rate causes output to be low during the transitory period of low inflation.

It would be interesting to explore whether the standard NK model can produce similar effects. Presumably, some version of the Erceg and Levin (2003) imperfect credibility argument would work. Thus, suppose that the monetary authority resolves to increase the inflation target permanently, so that with perfect credibility the standard NK model predicts an immediate and equal permanent jump in both inflation and the nominal rate of interest (see the top-left panel in Cochrane's figure 15). What adjustment would be required to get a transitory fall in inflation? One possibility is that when the monetary authority announces the plan to increase the nominal rate of interest, agents believe the increase is only temporary. In that case, the bottom-right panel of figure 15 suggests inflation would move in the opposite direction from the interest rate, that is, down. The fall in inflation, coupled with the rise in the nominal rate of interest, implies a strong rise in the real rate of interest, which in turn would mean a substantial drop in output.

Why would the announcement of a permanent rise in the interest rate not be credible? One possibility is simply that most interest rate changes are in fact temporary, and permanent shifts are rarely, or never, observed. That such changes in the interest rate are so rarely observed is the reason that it is hard to evaluate the conjecture relative to the data.

But, I agree that Cochrane conducts an interesting model experiment. If someone asked me whether a permanent rise in the interest rate would create a short-term recession while leaving the real rate and output unaffected in the long run, I would probably answer "yes." If there were a follow-up question about which mechanism is more plausible, the fiscal theory or imperfect credibility, I would probably go with the latter. It is hard for me to let go of the skepticism I feel for the fiscal theory.[5]

Equilibrium Selection

Overview

The equilibrium conditions in the standard NK model with active monetary policy have many solutions. There exists a unique bounded solution that is local to steady state, and this is the one that is typically studied in the literature. In part, the reason for focusing on the locally bounded solution is that, being close to steady state, there is a hope that linearization methods for analyzing it provide acceptable accuracy. In addition, the choice to work with the locally bounded equilibrium reflects a perception that equilibrium has the appealing characteristic of being learnable (see, e.g., McCallum 2009).[6] But, Cochrane denies the McCallum result that the unique, locally bounded solution is learnable. If he is right, this would rob the bounded equilibrium of its appeal. The question arises: What is it that keeps the economy in the bounded equilibrium if it cannot be learned? Cochrane's answer is that the equilibrium exists because of a central bank threat to destabilize inflation if the economy should ever diverge from the equilibrium.

I push back against Cochrane's position in the subsection below. I start by explaining why learnability of an equilibrium is appealing. I then summarize the argument for why the unique bounded solution to the NK model *is* learnable and why Cochrane is uncomfortable with that argument. I find Cochrane's position less than compelling. Moreover, if we interpret the bounded solution as the limit of a learning equilibrium, then there exists a very conventional interpretation for how government policy keeps the economy on track, an interpretation that does not involve destabilizing government interventions. In the course of his analysis, Cochrane also makes conjectures about the relationship between what he calls "individual learnability" and learning (see, especially, Cochrane 2009). These conjectures seem incorrect to me, but at the very least they would benefit from further clarification.

Cochrane argues that the nonbounded solutions to the equilibrium conditions of the NK models also deserve attention. I do agree with Cochrane, but only up to a point. Cochrane seems to be suggesting that these other equilibria can be studied by analyzing the explosive paths in linearized equilibrium conditions.[7] This is not a problem in the very simple model that Cochrane sometimes uses (see the Rational Expectations Equilibrium under the Taylor Principle section) because that model is linear. But, in models with sticky prices and nonconstant consumption, not to mention investment, foreign trade, and so forth, the nonlinearities in equilibrium conditions are substantial, away from the steady state.[8] As a rule, linearized equilibrium conditions are a poor guide to understanding equilibrium paths outside of a neighborhood of steady state.[9] Moreover, in many cases models have equilibria that are not local to steady state, and which leave no trace at all in equilibrium conditions that have been linearized about steady state.[10] These possibilities and the need for government policy to select among equilibria are being examined closely in the literature. These studies may well end up supporting the current habit of focusing on the bounded equilibrium in the standard NK model. This is because the socially efficient equilibrium in the NK model is not far from the steady state, so that equilibria far away can be suboptimal. Some of the work on equilibria far from steady state involves the design of "escape strategies" in government policy that act like deposit insurance in the case of bank runs and prevent bad equilibria from forming.[11]

Learning

One motivation for the appeal of learnability is the perspective on rational expectations equilibrium adopted by Lucas (1978, 1437).[12] Lucas notes that rational expectations makes very strong assumptions about how much people know and about their willingness and capacity to perform sophisticated computations. He asserts that for rational expectations equilibrium to be interesting, it must be that "as time passes" it approximates reasonably well the behavior of actual people who behave quite differently, adopting "'sensible' rules of thumb, revising these rules from time to time so as to claim observed rents." This is the perspective that motivates the learning literature, which focuses on whether deviations from rational expectations, coupled with common sense assumptions about learning, lead to convergence to a rational expectations equilibrium. When a rational expectations equilibrium has this convergence property, then we say that equilibrium is *stable under learning*.

Cochrane's sense that the unique, locally bounded equilibrium in the NK model is not learnable greatly reduces the appeal of that equilibrium. It is one of several reasons that motivate his advice that the standard NK model be modified by replacing the assumption of active monetary policy with passive monetary policy and adopting the fiscal theory of the price level. Because the stakes are high and I want to document my claims in the Overview section, I need to review the learning argument, even though it can be found in other places (see, e.g., Evans and McGough 2015). To begin, I first describe the full set of rational expectations solutions to the model. In the second subsection below I turn to learning.

Rational Expectations Equilibrium under the Taylor Principle, $\phi > 1$

I use the model with constant endowment and flexible prices studied in Cochrane (2009, 2011). The equilibrium conditions of the model are:

$$i_t = E_t \pi_{t+1} \tag{1}$$

$$i_t = \phi \pi_t + e_t \tag{2}$$

$$e_t = \rho e_{t-1} + \varepsilon_t, \; E\varepsilon_t^2 = \sigma_\varepsilon^2, 0 < \rho < 1, \tag{3}$$

for $t = 1, 2, \ldots$. Here, i_t denotes the nominal rate of interest, π_t denotes the inflation rate, and e_t denotes a monetary policy shock with given initial condition, e_0. According to equation (1), the nominal rate of interest, adjusted for anticipated inflation, is constant (constant terms are ignored). Equation (2) is the monetary policy rule, where ϕ is the coefficient on inflation. In the standard NK model, the Taylor principle is satisfied:

$$\phi > 1.$$

Equation (3) is the given law of motion of the policy shock.

Applying the argument in Cochrane (2009), I now identify all possible stochastic processes for π_t and i_t that solve equations (1)–(3). Such a stochastic process is a candidate rational expectations equilibrium, and is an actual equilibrium if it satisfies additional equilibrium restrictions such as those implied by nonnegativity of the interest rate or household transversality conditions.

Substituting out for i_t from equation (1) into (2), we obtain a single expression in π_t:

$$\pi_{t+1} = \phi \pi_t + e_t + \delta_{t+1}. \tag{4}$$

for $t = 1, 2, \ldots$. Here, I have used the convenient representation,

$$\pi_{t+1} = E_t \pi_{t+1} + \delta_{t+1},$$

where δ_{t+1} denotes a random variable with the property, $E_t \delta_{t+1} = 0$. Let

$$\psi \equiv \frac{1}{\phi - \rho}. \tag{5}$$

Add ψe_{t+1} to both sides of equation (4), use equation (5) and rearrange to obtain

$$z_{t+1} = \phi z_t + v_{t+1}, \tag{6}$$

where

$$z_t \equiv \pi_t + \psi e_t, \; v_t \equiv \psi \varepsilon_t + \delta_t \tag{7}$$

for $t = 1, 2, \ldots$. Solving equation (6)

$$z_t = \phi^t z_0 + v_t + \phi v_{t-1} + \dots + \phi^{t-1} v_1. \tag{8}$$

A stochastic process that solves the model is defined by a choice of z_0 and of a stochastic process for $\{\delta_t\}$, subject only to $E_t \delta_{t+1} = 0$. A realization of π_t from one of these stochastic processes is constructed in the following way. First, draw a realization of δ_t's from the chosen stochastic process for $\{\delta_t\}$. Then, draw a realization from the stochastic process for the monetary policy innovation, $\{\varepsilon_t\}$. Using equation (8), we can now compute a realization for $\{z_t, e_t\}$, conditional on z_0 and e_0. Using e_t and z_t, for $t \geq 0$, we can compute a sequence of π_t using equation (7). We then obtain i_t using equation (2).

I summarize these observations in the form of a characterization result:

Proposition 1. *A solution to equations (1)–(3) is characterized by a choice of z_0 and of a stochastic process, $\{\delta_t\}$, with $E_t \delta_{t+1} = 0$.*

It is evident from equation (8) that almost all solutions are explosive. If $z_0 \neq 0$, the first term to the right of the equality in equation (8) explodes. If any $v_t \neq 0$, then z_{t+j} also explodes as j increases. We have the following definition:

Definition 2. *A solution is bounded if it has the following properties:*

$$E_0 z_t \to_{t \to \infty} 0$$

$$var_0(z_t) \to_{t \to \infty} < \infty.$$

It is evident that there is only one solution, that is, specification of $(z_0, \{\delta_t\})$, which satisfies boundedness:

Proposition 3. *Suppose $\phi > 1$. The unique bounded solution corresponds to $z_0 = 0$ and $v_t = 0$ for all t and*

$$\delta_t = -\psi \varepsilon_t \tag{9}$$

$$\pi_t = \rho \pi_{t-1} - \psi \varepsilon_t, \tag{10}$$

where $\psi = 1 / (\phi - \rho)$.

We refer to the unique bounded solution as a rational expectations equilibrium on the assumption that the additional equilibrium restrictions like nonnegativity of the interest rate and transversality are satisfied. Many of the explosive solutions are also rational expectations equilibria.

It is easy to see that a person living in the unique bounded rational expectations equilibrium, possessing an infinite amount of data on π_t

and i_t, would have no way to identify the value of ϕ. The autocorrelation of π_t identifies the value of ρ. The variance of the error term, $\psi\varepsilon_t$, in equation (10) involves both ϕ and σ_ε^2, so that neither can be separately identified. This is what Cochrane means when he states that the value of ϕ is not *individually learnable* in the bounded rational expectations equilibrium.

Although the lack of identification of ϕ may at first seem intriguing, it turns out that there is less there than meets the eye, for two reasons. First, lack of individual learnability for ϕ is not a property of NK models generally. An important class of such models adopts a particular recursiveness assumption. In those models it is assumed that the monetary policy shock, e_t, is iid and that the time t values of aggregate variables like output, prices, and wages are determined before the time t realization of e_t.[13] Thus, if monetary policy has the Taylor rule representation adopted by Cochrane, then ϕ can be estimated by an ordinary least squares regression and so it is obviously individually learnable.[14]

Second, Cochrane asserts that there is an important link between individual learnability of ϕ and learnability of a rational expectations equilibrium. But, as I show below, there is in fact no such link (see also Evans and McGough 2015, section 4.2). I turn to learnability in the next subsection.

Is the Bounded Rational Expectations Equilibrium Learnable When $\phi > 1$?

I assume that agents use regression analysis to learn about the stochastic law of motion of the variables in an equilibrium. I suppose that agents begin with an initial set of beliefs about how inflation will be determined in the next period. I index their initial beliefs by $l = 0$. Agents maintain their beliefs during a period of time long enough that sampling uncertainty in regression coefficients can be ignored. Their beliefs affect the actual laws of motion of the economy. Eventually, agents pause and collect all data generated since the last time they updated their beliefs. They then run regressions on the data and use the results to update their beliefs. The updated beliefs are indexed by $l + 1$. This process continues indefinitely. I show that the process converges to the unique bounded rational expectations equilibrium.[15]

Following is a formal definition of the learning mechanism. I describe it constructively, according to how actual data in the learning environment are generated. I refer to data generated in this way as a *learning equilibrium*.

Agents' beliefs are described by two parameters, $(\hat{\rho}_l, \hat{\mu}_l)$, which determine the following perceived law of motion used at time t to forecast π_{t+1}:

$$\pi_{t+1} = (1 - \hat{\rho}_l)\hat{\mu}_l + \hat{\rho}_l\pi_t + \hat{v}_{l,t+1}, \tag{11}$$

where $\hat{v}_{t+1}$ is treated by agents as an iid process.[16] The subscript l takes on values, $l = 0, 1, 2, \ldots$. I assume that agents can start with essentially any initial belief. I impose only the following restriction on $(\hat{\rho}_0, \hat{\mu}_0)$:

$$\hat{\rho}_0 \neq \phi,$$

where $\phi > 1$. Equation (1) implies:

$$i_t = \hat{E}_t^l \pi_{t+1} = (1 - \hat{\rho}_l)\hat{\mu}_l + \hat{\rho}_l\pi_t,$$

where $\hat{E}_t^l$ denotes the expectation, conditional on time t information and beliefs, equation (11), indexed by l. The realized value of current inflation, π_t, adjusts to satisfy the monetary policy rule, equation (2):

$$(1 - \hat{\rho}_l)\hat{\mu}_l + \hat{\rho}_l\pi_t = \phi\pi_t + e_t,$$

or,

$$\pi_t = \frac{(1 - \hat{\rho}_l)\hat{\mu}_l - e_t}{\phi - \hat{\rho}_l}. \tag{12}$$

As I show below, excluding the isolated initial belief, $\hat{\rho}_0 = \phi$, ensures that the division in equation (12) is well defined for all $l = 0, 1, \ldots$.

Agents adhere to their beliefs, $\hat{\rho}_l$ and $\hat{\mu}_l$, for many periods. Then they stop to update their beliefs using all the data generated since the previous update. Their updated beliefs, $\hat{\rho}_{l+1}$ and $\hat{\mu}_{l+1}$ are the parameters of the actual law of motion for π_t induced by their perceived law of motion. The actual law of motion is obtained by multiplying π_t in equation (12) by $(1 - \rho L)$, where L denotes the lag operator:

$$\pi_t = \rho\pi_{t-1} + (1 - \rho)\frac{(1 - \hat{\rho}_l)\hat{\mu}_l}{\phi - \hat{\rho}_l} - \frac{\varepsilon_t}{\phi - \hat{\rho}_l}. \tag{13}$$

The parameters, $(\hat{\mu}_{l+1}, \hat{\rho}_{l+1})$, of the new perceived law of motion are taken from the actual law of motion in equation (13). That is:

$$\hat{\mu}_{l+1} = \frac{1 - \hat{\rho}_l}{\phi - \hat{\rho}_l}\hat{\mu}_l, \, \hat{\rho}_{l+1} = \rho. \tag{14}$$

Evidently, agents' beliefs about ρ converge in one step, with $\hat{\rho}_1 = \rho$. It takes more iterations for beliefs about μ to converge. Still, eventually they learn the true value of μ, which is zero, because, since $\phi > 1$,

$$0 \leq \frac{1-\rho}{\phi-\rho} < 1.$$

We have the following definition:

Definition 4. *Consider a learning equilibrium with* $(\hat{\rho}_0, \hat{\mu}_0)$ *arbitrary, except that* $\hat{\rho}_0 \neq \phi$. *A rational expectations equilibrium is least squares learnable if the actual laws of motion in the learning equilibrium converge, as* $l \to \infty$, *to the laws of motion in the rational expectations equilibrium.*

Since $(\hat{\mu}_l, \hat{\rho}_l) \to (0, \rho)$, where equation (10) is satisfied, we have:

Proposition 5. *The unique bounded solution under the Taylor principle is least squares learnable.*

Evans and McGough (2015) establish a result that is stronger in some respects than the one in Proposition 14. Their results apply when the perceived law of motion is a finite order autoregression, rather than the first-order autoregression considered here. However, their result is "local" in the sense that it assumes the initial perceived law of motion is inside a small neighborhood of the actual rational expectation law of motion. Evans and McGough (2015, Theorem 1) also obtain results for a subset of the nonbounded solutions to equations (1)–(3). The solutions they consider are the ones in which the time series representation of π_t in the actual solution is a second-order autoregression with roots ϕ and ρ. In particular, they allow $z_0 \neq 0$, but they set $v_t = 0$ for all t in (8).[17] For their perceived laws of motion, they consider N^{th} order autoregressions, with $N \geq 2$. Their learning mechanism is the analog of the one used above, and they obtain a local nonstability result: the perceived law of motion diverges from the rational expectations law of motion when it starts in a small neighborhood of that law of motion.

The opening sentence of section 5 in Cochrane (2009) suggests, somewhat surprisingly, that he is aware of the argument underlying Proposition 5. Cochrane states that arriving at Proposition 5 is "easy," but nevertheless concludes that to accept the proposition "is a mistake." Cochrane (2009) reports two reasons why it would be a mistake to accept Proposition 5. First, he says, "Agents must know that alternative equilibria will lead to explosions," but it was not clear to me how this justifies rejecting Proposition 5. Second, Cochrane (2009, bottom 1112) says, "And it deeply begs the question, how does the 'equilibrium' of a new Keynesian model work, in which agents are forecasting based on the same π_t that is being determined?". In effect, the forecasting rule converts the Fisher equation, (1), and the monetary policy rule, (2), into two simultaneous equations in the two unknowns, π_t and i_t. Perhaps I have spent too many years staring at equations of demand and supply, but I have a hard time feeling squeamish about equilibrium objects that are the solution to two simultaneous equations.

Not all the i's have been dotted and t's crossed yet, in the analysis of learning. But, it looks like the bounded rational expectations equilibrium is learnable and the other equilibria are not, when $\phi > 1$. That is, if we require that for an equilibrium to be interesting, it must be learnable, there is only one interesting equilibrium for the model in equations (1)–(3).

Individual Learnability of ϕ When $\phi > 1$

Next, we turn to the individual learnability of ϕ in the learning equilibrium. Learning adds dynamics beyond what occurs in the rational expectations equilibrium, which can be exploited by agents interested in knowing the value of ϕ.

Consider the following definition:

Definition 6. *A parameter is individually learnable in a learning equilibrium if an agent can recover that parameter's value from observations in the learning equilibrium.*

It is easy to see that in the rational expectations equilibrium with learning, the parameter, ϕ, is individually learnable, as in Definition 6. As before, let $\hat{\rho}_l$, $\hat{\mu}_l$, for $l = 0$ correspond to the initial beliefs about ρ and μ. Then, by equation (14) we have $\hat{\rho}_l = \rho$ for $l \geq 1$, and

$$\frac{\hat{\mu}_{l+1}}{\hat{\mu}_l} = \frac{1 - \rho}{\phi - \rho},$$

for $l \geq 1$. Thus, we have, for $l \geq 1$,

$$\phi = \frac{1 - \rho}{\hat{\mu}_{l+1} / \hat{\mu}_l} + \rho.$$

We conclude:

Proposition 7. *Consider a learning equilibrium with $(\hat{\rho}_0, \hat{\mu}_0)$ arbitrary, except that $\hat{\rho}_0 \neq \phi$. The parameter, ϕ, is individually learnable from data in the equilibrium.*

Cochrane argues that underidentification of ϕ in a bounded rational expectations equilibrium inhibits learning. This is not true. In fact, the bounded rational expectations equilibrium is learnable and the value of ϕ is learnable in that equilibrium.

How the Taylor Principle Guides Inflation Expectations When $\phi > 1$

In section V.D, Cochrane discusses his view about how the Taylor principle works to stabilize inflation. He argues that the mechanism is completely different from the way it is described in undergraduate textbooks. There, higher inflation expectations lead to a rise in the interest rate, which then moderates actual inflation by reducing aggregate demand. Cochrane (see, especially, Cochrane 2009, 1113) argues that in the rational expectations equilibrium the Taylor principle works very differently by threatening to destabilize the economy if people choose the "wrong" inflation rate (note the explosion created in equation [8] by $\phi > 1$ if $z_0 \neq 0$). I agree with Cochrane that it is highly improbable that this is the way monetary policy affects a real-world economy. I do not know if Cochrane is right in his characterization of the rational expectations equilibrium.

But, he is definitely not right if we interpret the bounded rational expectations equilibrium as the tail end of a learning equilibrium. The conventional mechanism actually works reasonably well in the learning equilibrium. Suppose, for example, that expected inflation, $\hat{\mu}_l$, jumps in equation (14) for some l. The Taylor principle, $\phi > 1$, means that $\hat{\mu}_{l+1}$ rises by less than $\hat{\mu}_l$ does and subsequent expectations of inflation gradually return down to what they would have been, had $\hat{\mu}_l$ not jumped. The fact, $\phi > 1$, inserts a stationary root in the mechanism, promoting a return to the bounded rational expectations equilibrium if a perturbation to beliefs were to bump it off. No explosion or other drama.

Alleged Implausible Implications of the NK Model When Lower Bound on Nominal Rate of Interest Is Binding

Cochrane suggests that some of the predictions made by the NK model when the lower bound on the nominal rate of interest is binding are probably counterfactual. He is particularly concerned with the model's implications that (a) good technology shocks reduce output, and (b) greater price flexibility imply a larger drop in output.

The proposition that (a) is an implication of the NK model when the lower bound is binding is too simple, to the point of being misleading. That proposition only applies when technology shocks are sufficiently temporary that the wealth effect can be ignored. For example, Christiano, Eichenbaum, and Trabandt (2014) show that when technology shocks are characterized by the degree of persistence assumed in the real business cycle literature, then a positive technology shock raises output. The intuition for this can be found in the interplay between the rate of return and wealth effects triggered by a technology shock. To understand the rate of return effect, recall that, other things the same, a positive technology shock reduces the marginal cost of production, placing downward pressure on inflation. With a binding lower bound on the interest rate, this raises the real rate of interest, reducing consumption and output.

Property (a) would hold if the rate of return effect were the whole story. But, when a positive technology shock is persistent, then there is also a wealth effect. Other things the same, the wealth effect stimulates consumption and output. When the log level of technology in the NK model has a scalar first-order autoregressive representation with autocorrelation, 0.95, as in the real business cycle (RBC) literature, then the wealth effect dominates the rate of return effect in the NK model without capital (see Christiano, Eichenbaum, and Trabandt 2015).

The empirical evidence favors the notion that technology shocks have persistent effects. An early analysis supporting this view appears in Prescott (1986). Updated data on US total factor productivity growth reported in Fernald (2014) has first-order autocorrelation 0.20. This represents even more persistence than is assumed in the RBC literature. The nuclear disaster at Fukushima, Japan, is sometimes viewed as a example of a negative technology shock. That shock is best thought of as persistent because of the deep distrust in nuclear power that it spawned in the Japanese public. Finally, the literature on actual movements of technology reports a great deal of persistence. Technological improvements display a diffusion property, whereby an initial jump is followed by further increases (see .

Christiano, Eichenbaum, and Rebelo (2011) argue that property (b) of the NK model is not as counterintuitive as it may seem at first. They draw attention to the work of De Long and Summers (1986), who argue that the idea is implicit in conventional macroeconomic views dating back at least to the 1920s.

Conclusion

In my discussion, I have pushed back against some of the objections raised by Cochrane against the standard NK model. By doing this, I do not mean to suggest that that model does not require further work. For example, much more work is required to fully understand the equilibrium multiplicity problems. I described some initial steps, but many more are required before we get to the bottom of that issue. Many other model features deserve close attention. For example, it is important to incorporate a structural interpretation of the reduced-form price stickiness assumption. The forward-guidance puzzle also deserves close attention.[18] A full list of important questions to investigate in the NK model is too long to describe here (see Christiano, Eichenbaum, and Trabandt (forthcoming).

The experiment that Cochrane explores in his paper, to study the effects of a permanent rise in the interest rate, is an interesting and important one. It is not an experiment for which we have data, but it is nevertheless relevant for policy discussions at this time. It is exactly the experiments for which we do not have historical evidence that must be done in models.

Endnotes

This comment has benefited from conversations with Marty Eichenbaum, and I am deeply grateful to Yuta Takahashi for extensive discussions and assistance. For acknowledgments, sources of research support, and disclosure of the author's material financial relationships, if any, please see http://www.nber.org/chapters/c13912.ack.

1. For a detailed quantitative analysis, see Christiano et al. (2015).

2. For a discussion of the shocks that caused the Financial Crisis and Great Recession, and why they were not forecast, see Christiano et al. (forthcoming).

3. There is a second reason to doubt Cochrane's Michelson-Morley argument. Even if the United States had adopted a peg in 2009, the NK model would have predicted only that a sunspot equilibrium was *possible*. The model makes not a prediction that a sunspot equilibrium would necessarily have occurred.

4. I would have liked to have seen more discussion of the mechanics by which the interest rate is changed. In particular, I presume the change would have been produced by an open market sale to the private sector of government debt taken from the central bank's holdings. This would increase the quantity of privately held debt, and how can we be sure that the value of that debt would not have increased or stayed the same?

5. I elaborate in Christiano and Fitzgerald (2000).

6. For a more recent analysis, see Evans and McGough (2015).

7. When Cochrane (2009, 1112) makes statements like "the explosive equilibria are learnable," he seems to suggest that the exploding paths predicted by linearized equilibrium conditions should be treated as reasonable approximations to actual equilibria.

8. See, for example, Christiano, Eichenbaum, and Johannsen (2017) for a discussion of the substantial nonlinearities arising from variable consumption, sticky prices, and the lower bound on the interest rate.

9. Stokey and Lucas (1989, exercise 6.7) provide an example of the limits of linearization methods for studying equilibrium trajectories in which the capital stock leaves the steady state. In the example, the linearized equilibrium conditions correctly characterize these trajectories in a neighborhood of steady state, but then become highly misleading as the actual system settles smoothly into a two-period cycle while the linearized system explodes in an oscillatory pattern toward plus and minus infinity. For examples like this

in monetary models, see Christiano and Rostagno (2001) and the references they cite. The point is not that paths that explode away from steady state according to linearized equilibrium conditions are not valid equilibria. The point is that there is nothing to be learned about those equilibria by studying equilibrium conditions that have been linearized around steady state.

10. For two examples, see Christiano and Harrison (1999) and Christiano et al. (2017).

11. See, for example, Atkeson, Chari, and Kehoe (2010), Bassetto (2005), Christiano and Rostagno (2001, and Woodford (2003, sec. 4.3) to name just a few.

12. See also Evans and Honkapohja (2001).

13. The assumption that e_t is iid is not restrictive in terms of observables because in practice Taylor rules include the lagged interest rate as a right-hand variable. For analyses that adopt the recursiveness assumption, see , for example, Sims (1986), Bernanke and Blinder (1992), Rotemberg and Woodford (1997), Christiano, Eichenbaum, and Evans (1999), Giannoni and Woodford (2004), Altig et al. (2011), and Christiano et al. (2015).

14. Cochrane (2011, 601) discusses the recursiveness assumption in his review of Rotemberg and Woodford (1997) and Giannoni and Woodford (2004). However, he asserts that the approach is equivalent to assuming that wages, prices, and output are fixed one period in advance. This is not actually an implication of the procedure because, in principle, it allows nonmonetary shocks to have an immediate impact on these variables. Moreover, these other shocks probably account for the lion's share of the variance in variables like wages, prices, and output so that there is substantial one-step-ahead uncertainty in these variables. Papers that have adopted the recursiveness assumption include Sims (1986), Bernanke and Blinder (1992, Christiano et al. (1999), Christiano, Eichenbaum, and Evans (2005), Altig et al. (2011), and Christiano et al. (2015).

15. The learning mechanism I use is the same as the mapping from perceived to actual laws of motion studied in, for example, Evans and McGough (2015). A difference is that I assume the process proceeds in calendar time, with agents running regressions on observed data. Evans and McGough (2015) assume the learning process proceeds in "notional time," presumably implemented by the agents themselves. The mathematics of the two approaches are the same. However, my calendar time approach allows me to make observations on the individual learnability of ϕ that I could not make if I adopted the Evans and McGough (2015) approach. The latter in effect assume that agents generate the "observed" data in their heads. This requires that agents know the values of all structural parameters, something that my approach does not require.

16. When agents perform regressions (see below) they will never see evidence that contradicts the iid assumption.

17. Allowing for $v_t \neq 0$ complicates the analysis by converting the iid error term in the autoregressive representation of π_t into a first-order moving average.

18. See Farhi and Werning (2017), Angeletos and Lian (20170, and Mckay, Nakamura, and Steinsson (2017) for examples of papers that explore the problem.

References

Altig, D., L. J. Christiano, M. S. Eichenbaum, and J. Lindé. 2011. "Firm-Specific Capital, Nominal Rigidities and the Business Cycle." *Review of Economic Dynamics* 14 (2): 225–47.

Angeletos, G.-M., and C. Lian. 2017. "Forward Guidance without Common Knowledge." Unpublished manuscript.

Atkeson, A., V. V. Chari, and P. J. Kehoe. 2010. "Sophisticated Monetary Policies." *Quarterly Journal of Economics* (February):47–89.

Bassetto, M. 2005. "Equilibrium and Government Commitment." *Journal of Economic Theory* 124 (1): 79–105.

Bernanke, B. S., and A. S. Blinder. 1992. "The Federal Funds Rate and the Channels of Monetary Transmission." *American Economic Review* 82 (4): 901–21.

Christiano, L. J., M. S. Eichenbaum, and C. L. Evans. 1999. "Monetary Policy Shocks: What Have We Learned and to What End?" *Handbook of Macroeconomics* 1 (A): 65–148.

———. 2005. "Nominal Rigidities and the Dynamic Effects of a Shock to Monetary Policy." *Journal of Political Economy* 113 (1): 1–45.

Christiano, L. J., M. S. Eichenbaum, and B. K. Johannsen. 2017. "Does the New Keynesian Model Have a Uniqueness Problem?" Unpublished Manuscript, Northwestern University.

Christiano, L. J., M. S. Eichenbaum, and S. Rebelo. 2011. "When is the Government Spending Multiplier Large?" *Journal of Political Economy* 119 (1): 78–121.

Christiano, L. J., M. S. Eichenbaum, and M. Trabandt. 2014. "Stochastic Simulation of a Nonlinear, Dynamic Stochastic Model." Unpublished manuscript. https://www.dropbox.com/s/bpdhs7d3pxetvyc/analysis.pdf?dl=0.

———. 2015. "Understanding the Great Recession." *American Economic Journal: Macroeconomics* 7 (1): 110–67.

———. Forthcoming. "On DSGE Models." *Journal of Economic Perspectives.*

Christiano, L. J., and T. Fitzgerald. 2000. "Understanding the Fiscal Theory of the Price Level." *Federal Reserve Bank of Cleveland Economic Review* 36 (2): 2–38.

Christiano, L. J., and S. G. Harrison. 1999. "Chaos, Sunspots and Automatic Stabilizers." *Journal of Monetary Economics* 44:3–31.

Christiano, L. J., and M. Rostagno. 2001. "Money Growth Monitoring and the Taylor Rule." NBER Working Paper no. 8539, Cambridge, MA.

Cochrane, J. H. 2009. "Can Learnability Save New-Keynesian Models?" *Journal of Monetary Economics* 56 (8): 1109–13.

———. 2011. "Determinacy and Identification with Taylor Rules." *Journal of Political Economy* 119 (3): 565–615.

De Long, J. B., and L. H. Summers. 1986. "Is Increased Price Flexibility Stabilizing?" *American Economic Review* 76 (5): 1031–44.

Eggertsson, G., and M. Woodford. 2003. "The Zero Bound on Interest Rates and Optimal Monetary Policy." *Brookings Papers on Economic Activity* 2003 (1). https://www.brookings.edu/bpea-articles/the-zero-bound-on-interest-rates-and-optimal-monetary-policy/.

Erceg, C. J., and A. T. Levin. 2003. "Imperfect Credibility and Inflation Persistence." *Journal of Monetary Economics* 50 (4): 915–44.

Evans, G. W., and S. Honkapohja. 2001. *Learning and Expectations in Macroeconomics.* Princeton, NJ: Princeton University Press.

Evans, G. W., and B. McGough. 2015. "Observability and Equilibrium Selection." Technical Report, University of Oregon.

Farhi, E., and I. Werning. 2017. "Monetary Policy, Bounded Rationality and Incomplete Markets." NBER Working Paper no. 23281, Cambridge, MA.

Fernald, J. 2014. "A Quarterly, Utilization-Adjusted Series on Total Factor Productivity." Working Paper no. 2012-19, Federal Reserve Bank of San Francisco. http://www.frbsf.org/economic-research/publications/working-papers/2012/wp12-19bk.pdf.

Giannoni, M., and W. Woodford. 2004. "Optimal Inflation-Targeting Rules. In *The Inflation-Targeting Debate*, ed. B. Bernanke and M. Woodford, 93–172. Chicago: University of Chicago Press.

Krugman, P. R. 1998. "It's Baaack: Japan's Slump and the Return of the Liquidity Trap." *Brookings Papers on Economic Activity* 1999 (2):137–205.

Lucas, R. E. 1978. "Asset Prices in an Exchange Economy." *Econometrica* 46 (6): 1429–45.

McCallum, B. T. 2009. "Inflation Determination with Taylor Rules: Is New-Keynesian Analysis Critically Flawed?" *Journal of Monetary Economics* 56 (8): 1101–08.

Mckay, A., E. Nakamura, and J. Steinsson. 2017. "The Discounted Euler Equation : A Note." *Economica* 84 (336): 820–31.

Prescott, E. C. 1986. "Theory Ahead of Business Cycle Measurement." *Federal Reserve Bank of Minneapolis Quarterly Review* 10 (4): 9–22.

Rotemberg, J. J., and M. Woodford. 1997. "An Optimization-Based Econometric Model for the Evaluation of Monetary Policy." In *NBER Macroeconomics Annual*, vol. 12, ed. B. Bernanke and J. Rotemberg, 297–361. Cambridge, MA: MIT Press.

Sims, C. A. 1986. "Are Forecasting Models Usable for Policy Analysis?" *Federal Reserve Bank of Minneapolis Quarterly Review* 10 (1): 2–16.

Stokey, N., and R. E. Lucas. 1989. *Recursive Methods in Economic Dynamics*. Cambridge, MA: Harvard University Press.

Swanson, E. T., and J. C. Williams. 2014. "Measuring the Effect of the Zero Lower Bound on Medium- and Longer-Term Interest Rates." *American Economic Review* 104 (10): 3154–85.

Woodford, M. 2003. *Interest and Prices: Foundations of a Theory of Monetary Policy*. Princeton, NJ: Princeton University Press.

Comment

Ricardo Reis, *London School of Economics*

Introduction

This is an unusual paper to discuss in a few ways (and I mean this as a compliment) because it leaves my job as a discussant with unusual tasks to perform. Typically, discussants suggest that the authors apply their model to some related question to assess how relevant are the points being made, or they argue that the authors should relax some assumptions to understand the generality of the conclusions, or they point to different data or empirical tests of the validity of the findings. As a result, discussant's suggestions, if followed, would lead to longer papers. This paper is so unusually long, however, more than twice as long as the papers published in the recent past in this publication, that taking on the usual discussant role would do everyone a disservice. The partial derivative of the social welfare function with respect to length here is probably negative.

Moreover, usually discussants take advantage of the fact that fewer people read the discussion than the actual paper to risk being provocative and less guarded than the author. This paper is also unusual in this regard because it makes many bold claims that, purposely or not, try to ruffle feathers and provoke counterarguments. Trying to add more fuel to the fire in my discussion would again probably move us away from the social optimum. The role of this discussion will be instead to be more guarded and tell the reader to seriously consider, but not outright embrace, the stark conclusions that Cochrane reaches.

Because of these two features, this discussion will first try to subtract rather than add to the topics on the table. Because the paper tries to provide an exhaustive and comprehensive review of the theory behind inflation control, it makes many arguments that were already made elsewhere. Much of Sections II and V are spent discussing theoretical points about price-level determinacy when central banks set interest rates. There are, by now, many useful summaries of this literature from Woodford (2003) to Cochrane (2011). Throughout the paper, and especially in Sections II and VI, there is a spirited defense of the fiscal theory of the price level, with arguments similar to those in Sims (2013) and many others. The discussion of how quantitative easing had no impact on inflation because reserves are special provides a compressed version of the points in Reis (2016), and the discussion of the VAR evidence on the effect of monetary shocks summarizes points in Ramey (2017). Finally, the conclusion that including currency in the utility function both has little quantitative effects for realistic parameter values, and is not a promising way to understand monetary nonneutralities, was already in Woodford (2003) or Reis (2007). All of these are useful and important points in the literature, and I understand why the author would like to include them in order to provide readers from outside this literature with a full discussion of all the issues. For those who have seen the topics above before, or who have trouble digesting more than what is in a regular-length paper, then my suggestion is to read Sections I, II.A, III, IV, and VIII.

Given this admittedly narrow perspective on the content of this paper, this discussion is split into three points organized around sections. First, I discuss the empirical puzzle on inflation that this paper starts from, and the author's answer to it. I will argue that his approach has virtues and promise beyond the application in this paper. Second, I reexamine a central point that the author tries to make: that the response of inflation to interest rates shows a deep problem in current standard macroeconomic models. This paper opened my mind to some issues, but I am left not convinced that there is such a deep flaw that must be fixed. My reading of the match between theory and facts is more mixed. Third, and finally, I will argue against the rhetorical approach of this paper of interpreting the recent evidence as either "Michelson-Morley" or "Occam" moments that discredit some theories and support others.

Inflation 2010–2016

Miles et al. (2017) provide a comprehensive review of the developments on inflation across the world so far in the twenty-first century. Figure 1 plots the data series for 2010–2016 US inflation (the percentage annual

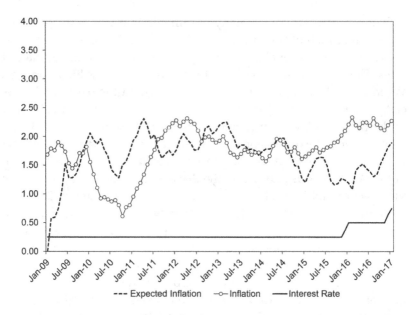

Fig. 1. Annual US inflation (%) at monthly frequency 2009–2017

change in the core CPI), expected inflation (the five-year breakeven from indexed treasuries), and the nominal interest rate (the interest on excess reserves). For the purposes of this paper, five facts are worth highlighting:

1. Nominal interest rates were held by the central bank at a constant level.

2. Expected inflation was quite stable.

3. Forward guidance was heavily used through announcements about future nominal interest rates.

4. Inflation has no clear trend nor any apparent permanent shocks.

5. The variance of inflation has been small.

Why are these five facts interesting from a perspective of monetary theory? The Fisher equation states that:

$$i_t = r_t + \mathbb{E}_t(\pi_{t+1})$$

where i_t is the nominal interest rate, r_t is the real interest rate, and π_t is the inflation rate. If the left-hand side is constant, then expected inflation should move around with shocks to the real interest rate. The period 2010–2016 has seen plenty of signs of changes in productivity, in financial conditions, and in marginal tax rates that should be expected to move real interest rates. There is even some evidence that real interest rates have trended down. That, in spite of these, expected inflation is so constant and inflation shows no trend is quite interesting.

Second, as emphasized by Miles et al. (2017), this was a time of unconventional, and in many cases, unprecedented monetary policies. Focusing solely on interest rates, central banks experimented with different types of forward guidance, different forms of communicating it, and different ways of implementation, all of which likely resulted in different interpretations by the public about the stance of monetary policy. Yet, in spite of all this experimenting, and the many errors that surely came with it, inflation was as stable as it had been in decades. From a practical perspective, one can tally this as a success for central bankers. From an academic perspective, it seems too good to be true, and raises questions instead about whether our theories of inflation are right.

This paper provides a novel explanation for this set of facts. Cochrane starts by assuming an approximately constant safe real interest rate equal to $-\log(\beta)$. As I noted above, this is perhaps not the best assumption for this period, but the main point that follows would remain unchanged, and it simplifies the exposition. It implies that the expected present value of fiscal surpluses, on the right-hand side of the next expression, is independent of monetary policy as long as fiscal surpluses (s_{t+j}) are likewise independent of monetary policy:

$$\frac{\sum_{j=0}^{\infty} Q_t^j B_{t-1}^j}{P_t} = \sum_{j=0}^{\infty} \beta^j \mathbb{E}_t(s_{t+j}).$$

This is the government-debt valuation equation. On the left is the market value of debt. It is the sum of the price at date t of a zero-coupon bond that pays off in j periods (Q_t^j) times the amount outstanding of this bond issued in past periods (B_{t-1}^j). Since these are nominal bonds, the sum must be divided by the price level P_t in order to express it in real units.

Changes in interest rates, which change the nominal yields given by the inverse of Q_t^j, must lead to no changes on the left-hand side since the right-hand side is fixed. But, since the bonds outstanding were set last period, it follows that unexpected changes in monetary policy lead to changes in the price level.

This equation provides a fiscal theory of the price level, but not in the traditional sense according to which exogenous changes in fiscal policy (s_t) affect the price level. Rather, here the focus is on changes in

nominal interest rates and their effect on unexpected inflation, following the work of Cochrane (2001). To see this link, one can use the main
proposition in Hilscher, Raviv, and Reis (2014) to rewrite:

$$\sum_{j=0}^{\infty}\beta^j \left(\frac{B_{t-1}^j}{P_t}\right) \hat{\mathbb{E}}_t \left(\frac{P_t}{P_{t+j}}\right) = \sum_{j=0}^{\infty}\beta^j \hat{\mathbb{E}}_t(s_{t+j}).$$

The new operator, $\hat{\mathbb{E}}_t$, is the risk-neutral expectation that tilts probabilities across states by their relative value as captured by a stochastic discount factor. The exogenous fiscal policy together with the pre-existing
debt obligations pin down the sum of the expected path for inflation,
leaving changes in nominal interest rates to be reflected right away into
different paths for actual inflation. This expression makes clear that this
is true whether the changes are in current nominal interest rates or in
future ones, as in forward guidance. When the news is realized about
nominal interest rates in the present or the future, this has an impact on
the value of the debt, which must be offset by changes in the expected
path of inflation to keep the real value unchanged.

How does this theory account for the last decade? First, as the amount
of outstanding debt is nowadays larger (so a larger B_{t-1}^j), then the effect
of any change in interest rates is smaller on the price level. Second, the
maturity of the US public debt has changed significantly over the last
few decades. With a shorter maturity of privately held debt, then a
shock to future interest rates will have a smaller impact on the current
price level. This theory promises to explain the stability of inflation by
the combination of higher and shorter public debt, together with shocks
to future nominal interest rates.

To gauge the size of both of these effects requires a series for public
debt at different maturities (B_{t-1}^j). Cochrane does very well in avoiding
the use of the series that one can download from the Treasury website:
as Hall and Sargent (2011) document, they do not match the economic
definition of B_{t-1}^j. However, the Hall-Sargent series is also not the right
one to plug into these calculations, since it includes all publicly issued
debt, whether it is privately or publicly held. Holdings of public debt
by social security or local and state pension funds have to be netted out
to match the government-debt constraint. Moreover, the Federal Reserve during this time period bought a large amount of long-term government debt in exchange for short-term central bank reserves. While
these quantitative easing operations do not reduce the total amount of
government debt (reserves are a government debt), they dramatically
reduce the maturity held by the public.

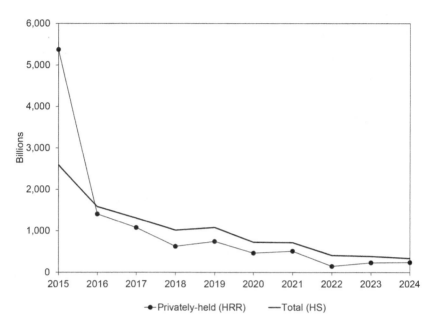

Fig. 2.   US public debt in 2015 by maturity

Figure 2 shows the actual public debt that is privately held, as constructed by Hilscher et al. (2014) and compares it to the Hall-Sargent series. The maturity of debt is considerably shorter as the combination of quantitative easing and the policy of debt issuance over the last 10 years significantly lowered the duration of the debt, as described and emphasized by Hilscher et al. (2014).

Figure 3 plots the impulse responses of inflation to a change in nominal interest rates announced three periods ahead of time in the models discussed in the paper, but using the different calibration for the debt. The top-left panel shows the result of a permanent increase in rates in the flexible price model, while the top-right panel simulates instead a New Keynesian sticky-price model. The bottom-left panel considers instead a three-year increase in nominal interest rates, and the bottom-right panel shows the result of a positive impulse to the AR(1) process for nominal interest rates with serial correlation 0.7.

The effects of the changes in forward guidance about interest rates on inflation are significantly smaller with the right measure of debt. Therefore, the Cochrane explanation is even more credible. In short, perhaps the stability of inflation in response to forward-guidance interest rate

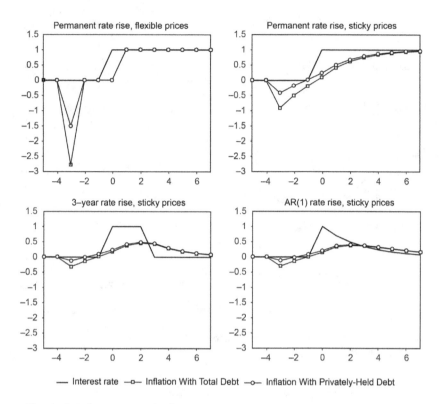

— Interest rate —□— Inflation With Total Debt —○— Inflation With Privately-Held Debt

Fig. 3.   Impulse response of inflation to interest rate shocks: the role of debt maturity

shocks has been due to the large and short maturity of the privately
held government debt.

A related point made in the paper is worth a detour. No matter what
the model of the price level is, the government-debt valuation equation
will hold:

$$\frac{B_{t-1}}{P_t} = \sum_{j=0}^{\infty} \mathbb{E}_t \left[\frac{\beta^j u'(C_{t+j}) s_{t+j}}{u'(c_t)} \right].$$

This makes the very unrealistic assumption that all debt is of one-period
maturity, while allowing for future fiscal surpluses to be discounted
by the marginal utility of consumption. As Cochrane's paper shows,
log-linearizing this around a point where surpluses and consumption
are fixed, and letting x denote the log-deviation of consumption while
$\Delta\mathbb{E}_t = \mathbb{E}_t - \mathbb{E}_{t-1}$, then:

$$\Delta s \approx -\Delta\mathbb{E}_t(\pi_t) + \frac{1-\beta}{\sigma} \sum_{j=0}^{\infty} \beta^j \Delta\mathbb{E}_t(x_{t+j} - x_t).$$

This equation does not get as much attention in the paper or in the literature as it deserves. It links the equivalent change in the fiscal surplus with the surprises to inflation and real interest rates. This equation must hold in any well specified monetary model with a government. Therefore, evaluating the right-hand side after a response to a monetary shock (or any other shock) will give the required change in fiscal surpluses that the government must undertake in order to validate this response in equilibrium. This fiscal index, as Cochrane calls it, can be a very useful object to understand how much fiscal accommodation is needed in monetary models. Moreover, one can potentially construct empirical estimates of each of these variables to shocks, to assess whether they are consistent with the government budget constraint. More generally, evaluating the impulse response of this fiscal index to monetary shocks is an unexplored research area that Cochrane insightfully highlights.

The Nominal Interest Rate Puzzle

A large part of the paper is devoted to the claim that conventional models are unable to generate the result that higher nominal interest rates lower inflation. While it is true that sometimes higher interest rates do lead to higher inflation in simple New Keynesian models, this is far from a universal property of this class of models.

To see this, consider the simplest three-equation New Keynesian model:

$$\pi_t = \mathbb{E}_t\{\pi_{t+1}\} + \kappa y_t$$

$$y_t = -\sigma(i_t - \mathbb{E}_t\{\pi_{t+1}\}) + \mathbb{E}_t\{y_{t+1}\}$$

$$i_t = \phi\pi_t + v_t.$$

All variables are written as log-linear deviations from a steady state and stand for: π_t is inflation, y_t is output, and i_t is the nominal interest rate. There is a single shock, v_t, to interest rates. Finally, κ and σ are both positive parameters, while $\mathbb{E}_t$ is the rational-expectations operator.

Take the simplest possible version of this model that can be solved with pencil and paper. That comes from assuming that v_t is iid. In that case, all expectations are zero in the fundamental solution of the linear expectational system of difference equations. Thus, it follows that inflation and interest rates are equal to:

$$\pi_t = -\left(\frac{\kappa\sigma}{1 + \kappa\sigma\phi}\right)v_t$$

$$i_t = \left(\frac{1}{1 + \kappa\sigma\phi}\right)v_t.$$

Clearly, a positive monetary policy shock raises nominal interest rates and lowers inflation. The intuition is simply that a positive shock leads to higher nominal interest rates, which raise real interest rates, lower current real activity, and so bring down inflation through the Phillips curve. The lower inflation leads to an offsetting fall in the nominal interest rate, but this is smaller than the initial increase, so this second-round effect does not change the prediction that inflation falls and nominal interest rates rise. There is nothing puzzling here.

In the textbook model, the interest rate rule is instead:

$$i_t = \rho + \phi_\pi\pi_t + \phi_y y_t + v_t$$

$$v_t = \psi v_{t-1} + \xi_t.$$

It is true that with this rule and a persistent process for shocks, it is possible for positive monetary policy shocks to lower inflation but also lower nominal interest rates. This happens because the lower inflation and recession both lower interest rates in the policy rule (see, e.g., Sims, Garin, and Lester, forthcoming). Cochrane emphasizes this, and shows that this is true for the paths of interest rates that he feeds into his model, as well as for the parameter values that he chooses. But this model is very standard and has been calibrated numerous times, always generating the conventional result. A standard reference, Gali (2008), has no puzzle: a positive ξ_t shock both raises nominal interest rates and lowers inflation.

This is a textbook example, but one may worry that perhaps the puzzle comes whenever the models are made more complicated by fitting the data. The canonical New Keynesian model of this category is Smets and Wouters (2007). Figure 6 of that paper shows the response to a typical monetary policy shock. Inflation falls, and the nominal interest rates rises for the first six quarters, even if then it becomes slightly negative and converges back to steady date from below the horizontal axis. This is as conventional as it gets for the New Keynesian model, and Cochrane's puzzle is simply not there.

Part of the reason for this puzzling difference on the supposed puzzle comes because Cochrane focuses on what is closer to a permanent change in the inflation target. Instead, now replace the interest rate rule with:

$$i_t = \rho + \pi^* + \phi_\pi(\pi_t - \pi^*) + \phi_y y_t.$$

Now imagine that the inflation target π^* increases unexpectedly and permanently. In this case, the nominal interest rate rises, and so does inflation. This is not puzzling and, I think, is well understood by the economists who use these models. Announcing a permanently higher inflation target will both raise inflation and nominal interest rates. It makes quite a difference whether the reason for higher nominal interest rates is a transitory shock (v_t) or a permanent increase in the target (π^*). These are the conventional cases considered, and there is not much to puzzle about.

Continuing the search for the puzzle, combine the joint assumption that interest rates are zero (or any constant) now and for the next T periods, together with the assumption that afterwards they will follow an interest rate rule like the ones above. Here, yes, one gets the strange result that increasing T, which amounts to keeping interest rates lower for longer, will lead to lower inflation today. This is a reflection of the forward-guidance puzzle of Del Negro, Giannoni, and Patterson (2012): announcements of future policy at zero interest rates leads to several peculiar conclusions in the New Keynesian model. While this is certainly a problem for the sticky-price model, there are already many solutions. One of the first was put forward by Carlstrom, Fuerst, and Paustian (2015), who showed that by replacing the assumption of sticky prices with sticky information, the forward-guidance puzzle disappears. They show that while an announcement of raising interest rates in T periods leads to a positive response of inflation today with sticky prices, it leads to a fall in inflation with sticky information.

In sum, it is only if one considers the interaction of sticky prices with either persistent target-like changes in nominal interest rates, or announcements of future changes in interest rates starting from a peg, that the New Keynesian model leads to higher inflation with higher nominal rates. With regular transitory shocks and standard parameters this does not happen. With forward guidance and sticky information, it does not happen either.

Experiments and Models on Inflation

Cochrane makes strong conclusions from the results of his analysis. Right in the first page of the paper he writes that: "This is a Michelson-Morley moment for monetary policy. We observe a decisive experiment,

in which previously hard-to-distinguish theories clearly predict large outcomes. That experiment yields a null result, which invalidates those theories." In his view: "The observed inflation stability is thus a big feather
in the New Keynesian cap." The concluding comments are that: "The
observation that inflation has been stable or gently declining and quiet at
the zero bound is important evidence against the classical view that an inflation is unstable at the zero bound, and by implication at an interest rate
peg, and the New Keynesian view that these lead to sunspot volatility."

While the stability of inflation since 2010 is noteworthy and poses
interesting challenges to our models of inflation, I do not agree that it is
a Michelson-Morley moment. This is not a decisive experiment; rather,
it is far from satisfying the requisites for being valid. An experiment requires not just a treatment (here zero interest rates) but also a control, a
way to separate the treatment from the reason why it was implemented
in the first place, and a way to control for confounding variables that
may cause differences between treatment and control. In this case, there
is no clear control (other countries, the United State before 2010?), the
treatment clearly came in response to the financial crisis and the recession, which surely have an independent direct effect on inflation, and
there are many confounding variables as productivity, fiscal policy, and
financial conditions all changed during 2010–2016. Staring at the time
series in figure 1 alone is not decisive in any direction.

Moreover, I also was not convinced by the appeals to Occam's razor
to rule out interest rate rules and the New Keynesian model. Cochrane
writes that: "You cannot truthfully explain, say, to an undergraduate
or policymaker, that higher interest rates produce lower inflation because prices are sticky." But, I just did so, at the start of "The Nominal
Interest Rate Puzzle" section of this discussion. Cochrane argues that
"the qualifiers simple and economic are important" for any explanation of the behavior of inflation since 2010. Like beauty, these features
are in the eye of the beholder, but the model in Del Negro, Giannoni,
and Schorfheide (2015) is, to my eyes, not terribly complicated or un-
economic and can fit reasonably well the behavior of inflation. Finally,
Cochrane writes that "now, any theory, especially in economics, invites
rescue by epicycles" acknowledging that there are ways to reverse puzzling predictions, but criticizing them for coming after the fact. However, the ones he discusses in the paper all came *before* the fact, before
the 2010–2016 period. This paper together with Miles et al. (2017) are
the first to emphasize the stability of inflation in this period. There are
no theoretical epicycles, at least yet, because as far I know no one had

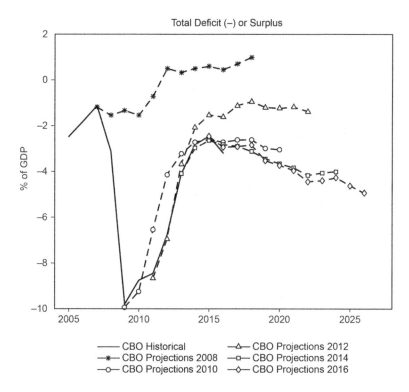

Fig. 4. CBO projections and actual fiscal surpluses
Source: Congressional Budget Office, historical data and 10-year projections.

the time between reading Section II of this paper and getting to Section V to perform such trickery.

Finally, in Section VI, Cochrane concludes that the fiscal theory of the price level can account for this and other movements in inflation. I am certainly open to the possibility, and find the fiscal theory relevant to discuss the behavior of inflation. But looking at the last 10 years, and at the US inflation stability, I do not come out thinking this was a success for the fiscal theory. For starters, from 2008 to 2016, almost every annual number for the deficit came out below what the CBO expected, as seen in figure 4. This was a time of negative fiscal shocks, and a naive fiscal theory of the price level (FTPL) would predict rising, not stable, inflation. Second, this was a time of higher fiscal uncertainty, as reflected in figure 5. Again, a naive FTPL would say that higher uncertainty by rational agents would usually come with more volatile fiscal shocks, and this would lead to volatile inflation.

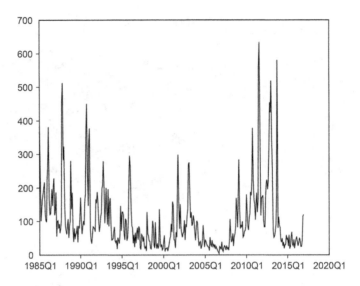

Fig. 5.   Fiscal policy uncertainty index
Source: EPU Index—Baker, Bloom, and Davis (QJE 2016).

I have emphasized that these would be, at best, tests of a naive FTPL. As Section VI of this paper rightly notes, one can rebate them and, in my view, convincingly argue that they are consistent with the FTPL. It does not seem far-fetched to me to argue that the unexpected deficits of the last few years came with improvements in expected future surpluses, or that there have been large changes in the real interest rates at which future surpluses are discounted, helping to stabilize inflation. But, I can see how these explanations could be called epicycles, and some may want to reject the FTPL by applying to Michelson-Morley or Occam. If I raise these points in this discussion, it is to emphasize why, in my view, the episode of the last few years is not a Michelson-Morley or Occam moment for most theories of inflation, including interest-feedback rules or the FTPL. Ultimately, this rhethorical approach does not lead me to strong conclusions.

Conclusion

Because inflation has been low and stable, it does not pose a problem. Thus, it has not drawn too much attention from commentators or policy-makers. From the perspective of researchers though, this stability is surprising, interesting, and worthy of study. Given the shocks, policies, and other circumstances around it, this episode may well be as interesting as the high inflation of the late 1970s. Cochrane provides an important service in this paper in putting a bright light over the behavior of US inflation 2010–2017.

Moreover, Cochrane puts forward a new explanation for this phenomenon that is both intriguing and promising. Privately held US public debt has both increased over the last 20 years, and has become much more concentrated at shorter maturities. These two facts imply that changes in future nominal interest rates now have a smaller impact on inflation because of the smaller debasement effect of inflation on the debt. This provides an intriguing explanation for why forward-guidance shocks have had a moderate impact on inflation. Moreover, the suggestion to measure the fiscal impact of monetary policies deserves more attention from empirical researchers.

Too much of the paper, though, is spent arguing that conventional models of inflation are at odds with the data and that the fiscal theory of the price level is not. In my view, much more has to be put forward to convincingly show that there is indeed some puzzle in the relation between nominal interest rates and inflation, or to use the recent data to dismiss or confirm models in a sweeping way.

Endnote

I am grateful to Andrea Alati, Laura Castillo-Martinez, Chao He, and Nicola Limodio for comments and assistance. Author contact: r.a.reis@lse.ac.uk. For acknowledgments, sources of research support, and disclosure of the author's material financial relationships, if any, please see http://www.nber.org/chapters/c13913.ack.

References

Carlstrom, C. T., T. S. Fuerst, and M. Paustian. 2015. "Inflation and Output in New Keynesian Models with a Transient Interest Rate Peg." *Journal of Monetary Economics* 76 (C): 230–43.
Cochrane, J. H. 2001. "Long-Term Debt and Optimal Policy in the Fiscal Theory of the Price Level." *Econometrica* 69 (1): 69–116.
———. 2011. "Determinacy and Identification with Taylor Rules." *Journal of Political Economy* 119 (3): 565–615.
Del Negro, M., M. P. Giannoni, and C. Patterson. 2012. "The Forward Guidance Puzzle." FRB Staff Report no. 574, Federal Reserve Bank of New York.
Del Negro, M., M. P. Giannoni, and F. Schorfheide. 2015. "Inflation in the Great Recession and New Keynesian Models." *American Economic Journal: Macroeconomics* 7 (1): 168–96.
Gali, J. 2008. *Monetary Policy, Inflation, and the Business Cycle.* Cambridge, MA: MIT Press.

Hall, G. J., and T. J. Sargent. 2011. "Interest Rate Risk and other Determinants of Post-WWII US Government Debt/GDP Dynamics." *American Economic Journal: Macroeconomics* 3 (3): 192–214.

Hilscher, J., A. Raviv, and R. Reis. 2014. "Inflating Away the Public Debt? An Empirical Assessment." NBER Working Paper no. 20339, Cambridge, MA.

Miles, D., U. Panizza, R. Reis, and A. Ubide. 2017. "And Yet It Moves. Inflation and the Great Recession: Good Luck or Good Policies?" Geneva Reports on the World Economy 19, International Center for Monetary and Banking Studies and Centre for Economic Policy Research.

Ramey, V. A. 2017. "Macroeconomic Shocks and Their Propagation." In *Handbook of Macroeconomics*, ed. J. Taylor and H. Uhlig, 71–162. Amsterdam: Elsevier.

Reis, R. 2007. "The Analytics of Monetary Non-Neutrality in the Sidrauski Model. *Economics Letters* 94 (1): 129–35.

———. 2016. "Funding Quantitative Easing to Target Inflation." In *Designing Resilient Monetary Policy Frameworks for the Future*. Paper presented at Federal Reserve Bank of Kansas City, Jackson Hole Symposium, Jackson Hole, WY, August 16.

Sims, C. A. 2013. "Paper Money." *American Economics Review Papers and Proceedings* 103 (3): 563–84.

Sims, E., J. Garin, and R. Lester. Forthcoming. "Raise Rates to Raise Inflation? Neo-Fisherianism in the New Keynesian Model." *Journal of Money Credit and Banking*.

Smets, F., and R. Wouters. 2007. "Shocks and Frictions in US Business Cycles: A Bayesian DSGE Approach." *American Economic Review* 97 (3): 586–606.

Woodford, M. 2003. *Interest and Prices*. Princeton, NJ: Princeton University Press.

Discussion

Early in the discussion, Mark Gertler suggested decomposing the inflation puzzle in the past decade into two distinct questions: (1) why did inflation not drop significantly in response to the output drop during the Great Recession, and (2) why did inflation not increase in response to monetary stimulus and the decline in unemployment during the recovery? Gertler argued that inflation did not decline with output likely due to optimism of market participants, as Larry Christiano and Ricardo Reis pointed out in their presentations, which was evident both in futures markets and in expectation surveys conducted during that time. Gertler said we still do not understand the second part of the puzzle—why it took so long for inflation to finally pick up after the recovery.

Olivier Blanchard said he does not see a puzzle in the fact that inflation was so stable while interest rates were stuck at the zero bound, and that no deflation spiral broke out. He argued that the simple explanation for inflation behavior in the past decade is the responsiveness of consumers' inflation expectations to inflation itself. As evidence, he cited the Michigan Survey of Consumers, in which consumers' reaction to core inflation has been very low in the past decade. Instead, inflation expectations seemed to respond only to headline inflation, which essentially tracks gasoline prices. Blanchard suggested this is easily explained by a salience argument: inflation has been very low for several decades and consumers therefore do not bother thinking about it. Thus it is not surprising that a deflationary spiral did not arise.

Cochrane agreed that inflation expectations did not move, and that this stability explains the lack of a deflation spiral. But he argued this stability of expectations is not about salience, but rather is a simple prediction of the theory in the paper. A large deflation would lead to a large increase in the real debt of the government. To finance the additional debt burden, the government would have to impose subsequent large tax increases. People know such tax increases are politically infeasible and won't happen. Therefore, deflation cannot arise in equilibrium.

Chris Carroll suggested using data on expectations to understand why inflation expectations did not respond to inflation. Carroll agreed with Blanchard, and argued this behavior is likely due to rational inattention. People have not been paying attention to inflation because it was stable in the two decades preceding the crisis. Carroll also noted that rational expectations might not be a suitable assumption to study this period, as the zero lower bound is not an event people have experienced in the past.

Xavier Gabaix and V. V. Chari suggested focusing the paper's empirical analysis on Japan rather than on the United States. While in the United States people expected interest rates to stay at zero for a short time, this is plausibly not the case for Japan, which has experienced nearly two decades at the zero lower bound. Supporting Cochrane's claim, Gabaix argued a standard New Keynesian model implies that inflation in Japan should have been more volatile given that the zero lower bound has been binding for a long period of time.

Larry Kotlikoff shared his draconian view on the US fiscal gap. He argued the fiscal theory of the price level is an unlikely explanation for the US economy because the government has made it almost impossible to understand its intertemporal budget constraint, in particular the true magnitude of the fiscal gap, which he argues is around $250 trillion. If the government withholds the data necessary to calculate its fiscal gap, then a theory that relies on consumers internalizing this gap is not reasonable. Robert Hall agreed with Kotlikoff, raising doubt about the idea that prices are set because people understand the fiscal implications of deflation, specifically that the government could not pay off its nominal debt if prices were lower.

Some participants proposed alternative theories to the fiscal theory of the price level other than consumers' expectations. Xavier Gabaix offered adding behavioral agents into the model. These agents are less forward looking than sophisticated rational expectations agents. In the short run they behave close to myopically, so the predictions of the model would be similar to economic models taught at the undergraduate level where agents are not forward looking. In the long run, these agents behave similarly to rational expectations agents. In response to an interest rate increase, in this case, inflation would drop in the short run and increase in the long run. V. V. Chari noted that the multiplicity of equilibrium in the zero lower bound could also be ruled out by allowing the central bank to commit to off-equilibrium-path actions.

Cochrane raised the concern that whatever the explanation for the behavior of expectations, for example, rational inattention as suggested by Carroll, its impacts on the predictions and policy implications of the standard New Keynesian model need to be taken seriously. For selection among multiple equilibria, he prefers the fiscal theory of the price level to these alternatives, as he finds it simpler and more intuitive. He further commented that agents in the economy do not observe off-equilibrium threats by the monetary authority used to select equilibria in standard New Keynesian models. He finds this explanation implausible, as agents can never learn what these are.

3

Dynamics of Housing Debt in the Recent Boom and Great Recession

Manuel Adelino, *Duke University and NBER*
Antoinette Schoar, *MIT and NBER*
Felipe Severino, *Dartmouth College*

The lasting impact of the mortgage crisis of 2008 on the US economy and international financial markets has spurred an intense debate among economists and policymakers about the origins of the crisis. The collapse of collateral values post-2007 led to a large increase in defaults, which in turn disrupted banks and the shadow banking system and was a leading cause of the deep recession that followed. Even after large government-stabilization programs, low house prices and depressed expectations held back investment and consumption. The rapid increase in household debt over the first decade of the twenty-first century, especially mortgage credit, has been widely documented, but views differ on what drove this expansion in credit. This paper outlines the two major narratives that have been proposed to explain the crisis and lays out the evidence that aims to differentiate them. We call these the *subprime view* and the *expectations view* of the boom and bust. We provide new facts and confirm several prior findings on the evolution of debt, homeownership rates, debt-to-income (DTI) ratios, and loan-to-value (LTV) ratios during both the housing boom and the housing bust.[1] The results support the idea that house prices and house price expectations played a central role in both the expansion of credit and the subsequent housing market bust.

One view of the housing boom and bust is that financial innovation and deregulation in the precrisis period led to increased securitization and delegation in underwriting, which in turn exacerbated agency problems within the mortgage origination chain and led to distortions in underwriting (the *subprime* view). A number of theory papers have laid out particular channels by which these distortions might have affected mortgage lending, such as Parlour and Plantin (2008), Dang, Gorton, and Holmström (2010), and Chemla and Hennessy (2014). Popular narratives (such as Michael Lewis's *The Big Short* in 2015 and the 2010 movie *Inside Job*) put forward the idea that increased misalignment of incentives led financial institutions to provide unsustainable credit to low-income and poor-credit-quality borrowers, so-called subprime borrowers, who previously might have been rationed out of the mortgage market (see, e.g., Mian and Sufi 2015).

The alternative view emphasizes the role of house price expectations in explaining the increased credit supply (the *expectations* view). According to this view, inflated house price expectations led banks to underestimate the potential for losses and the losses given default. Inflated house price expectations might also have led borrowers to increase demand for housing and exploit the expanded credit supply.[2] However, heterogeneous priors about house prices by themselves do not lead to boom-and-bust cycles because prices would immediately adjust, and the impact of optimistic agents in the housing market must vary over time in order to generate those cycles. One channel through which the role of optimistic agents changes endogenously over the business cycle is changes in collateral-lending standards.[3] Looser collateral standards after periods of good performance in the housing market (higher combined loan-to-value ratios [CLTVs]) can allow more optimistic agents to hold a larger fraction of assets and, as a result, drive up house prices.[4] An alternative channel proposes that the *number* of optimistic agents changes with the credit cycle. For example, if house price expectations are extrapolative or adaptive, initial increases in house prices can feed on themselves; see, for example, Barberis et al. (2015), Lo (2004), Gennaioli, Shleifer, and Vishny (2015), or DeFusco, Nathanson, and Zwick (2017). Burnside, Eichenbaum, and Rebelo (forthcoming) provide a different microfoundation via social contagion, where optimistic agents with tighter priors can convince less optimistic agents to change their beliefs.

What might have triggered these initial changes in house prices and expectations? The savings glut that led to increasing capital inflows to the United States and lower interest rates is often seen as a trigger for increasing house prices (see, in particular, Bernanke 2007; Rajan 2011; Bhutta 2015). These might have been exaggerated by demographic trends in mobility (Ferreira and Gyourko 2011) or gentrification trends (Guerrieri, Hartley, and Hurst 2013).

It is important to understand the primary drivers of the recent boom-and-bust cycle in household leverage, since it not only affects the diagnosis but also suggests different policy changes to guard against future crises. If the first view dominates, then regulations that force lenders to have more skin in the game, reduce securitization, and impose stricter screening of (marginal) borrowers are central. Under the second view, the focus needs to be on macroprudential regulation and rules that support the stability of banks, even when asset values change or may be overinflated.[5]

The discussion above illustrates the challenges of differentiating between the subprime view and the expectations view of the crisis. The explanations are not mutually exclusive and may even reinforce each other. If, for example, market participants believe that house prices can only rise, they may not see a need to screen borrowers because higher house prices protect the lender. As a result, changes in house price expectations may themselves trigger changes in lending standards, and the loosening of credit standards might be the *result* of rising house price expectations rather than the cause of those increases.[6] The challenge of cleanly testing these models lies not only in the common problem that economic outcomes are endogenously determined, but also in that expectations are generally not observed.

We show, however, that the expectations view and the subprime view have several defining differences. A central prediction of the subprime view is that a relaxation in credit standards leads to *cross-sectional* dislocations in credit flows toward poorer and subprime borrowers, as Mian and Sufi (2009) point out. As a result, aggregate credit flows, DTI ratios, and even LTV ratios should increase disproportionately for these marginal groups, independent of house price increases. We show that, instead, and in line with the expectations view, areas with rapid house price increases saw the bulk of the credit expansion and similar increases in homeownership rates. In these areas, homeowners also took on more credit by accelerating the speed with which they sell and buy homes (churn) and obtain cash-out refinances. Importantly, though, the credit expansion was not particularly concentrated in low-credit-score or low-income borrowers. At the same time, the distribution of LTV ratios at origination (i.e., the LTV ratios of the new purchases) remained unchanged over the boom period, suggesting that lenders took the higher house prices at face value and lent in *response* to higher house values (higher "Vs")[7]. After the onset of the crisis, however, defaults went up disproportionately in areas where house prices dropped most significantly, and middle-income and average-credit-score borrowers saw a very large increase in their share of total defaults. In what follows, we provide a comprehensive analysis of the credit dynamics of the recent boom-and-bust cycle.

Credit Flows, Stock, and DTI. We first document that there were no significant cross-sectional dislocations in either aggregate credit flows or the stock of household debt across income or FICO bins. Using loan-level data from the Home Mortgage Disclosure Act (HMDA) and Lender Processing Services (LPS), we confirm that the flow of new (purchase) mortgage credit across the income and credit score distribution was stable over the period 2001–2007 (consistent with evidence in Adelino, Schoar, and Severino [2016]). Of course, the dollar amount of purchase mortgage credit grew significantly over this time, but it did so for all income and FICO-score groups. Credit *flows*, however, may tell only an incomplete story of the *stock* of household leverage if households across income groups: (a) differentially retire or refinance existing debt, (b) increase how quickly they buy and sell houses (churn), or (c) change the likelihood of entering into homeownership. Therefore, we first use Survey of Consumer Finances (SCF) data, which track the entire stock of mortgage debt, including purchase mortgages, second liens, and other home equity lines to show that the stock of DTI at the household level increased proportionally across the income distribution. Foote, Loewenstein, and Willen (2016) confirm this finding using Equifax data. We then use data from the American Community Survey (ACS) to create a proxy for the household's debt burden. We look at housing cost as a proportion of income as a measure of the household's mortgage debt burden, including second liens and other home equity lines. We show that housing costs as a share of income moved together for all homeowners in the data with the exception of households at the very top of the income distribution.

The ACS data also allow us to break out the increase in homeownership cost by states with above- and below-median house price appreciation. We find a much higher increase in the cost of ownership for people in high-appreciation areas compared to low-appreciation areas; for example, for the middle 60% of households by income, the cost of owning increases by 6–8 percentage points of income more in these areas than in low-appreciation areas between 2001 and 2006. This increase is entirely reversed by 2011. These results suggest that the changes in the cost of homeownership are fundamentally tied to area house price movements. A very similar picture emerges when we look at house values as a share of income.

While this is separate from the subprime view of the crisis, one might wonder whether DTI ratios and observable characteristics of households capture the full story of the mortgage expansion. For example, did credit flow to households that were "marginal" borrowers on unobservable dimensions (e.g., due to unobserved future income risk)? Testing for unobservable characteristics is difficult by definition, but we can analyze whether mortgage acceptance rates within DTI bins increased during this period. In figure A1 of the appendix, we show that the acceptance rate of mortgage applications within DTI bins did not go up during the boom. In fact, we see a slight downward trend, especially for the higher income groups. Given that approval rates conditional on income bins did not change significantly, it is unlikely that there was a massive change in the selection on unobservables at the same time.

Homeownership Rates. Second, using ACS data on homeownership rates, we show that the boom made homeownership *less* accessible for the lowest-income households. Starting in 2001, low-income households entered homeownership at lower rates than middle- and high-income households, and households above the 20th percentile all saw similar increases in homeownership over the period. When we break out the results by areas with fast and slow house price growth, we find that the results hold similarly in both types of areas. But the steep decline in ownership rates for the lowest-income group already starts in 2001 for areas with low house price appreciation. These results are consistent across three large-scale census surveys (the ACS, the American Housing Survey, and the Consumer Population Survey). The patterns are also consistent with Acolin et al. (2017), who show that subprime lending was not associated with increases in homeownership rates, and with Foote, Loewenstein, and Willen (2016), who use the SCF and find no increases in homeownership for low-income households. These results contradict the view that distortions in credit originations occurred at the extensive margin (Mian and Sufi 2016), and that lax lending standards allowed low-income households, who previously were rationed out of the market, to become homeowners. It also suggests that in the post-2000 period, the Community Reinvestment Act did not achieve its goal of increasing homeownership of lower-income households.

Cost of Renting Relative to the Cost of Owning. Third, using ACS data, we show that the gap in the cost of renting versus that of owning (for recent movers) was relatively close at the beginning of the twenty-first century, but it increases to 4% of income on average at the peak of the boom. After the onset of the crisis, this gap drops by a full 10% of income. For households in the second income quintile, rental costs jump the most and become higher than the cost of owning. These patterns are consistent with the expectations view as in Kaplan, Mitman, and Violante (2016), where future house price appreciation sustains the divergence between costs of renting and owning. The results also suggest that, once the crisis started, large parts of the housing stock were tied up in foreclosures and drove up rental costs, especially for low-income households.

Churn. Another channel through which households can lever up is by increasing how quickly they move into new (potentially larger) homes. Each time a household moves, it typically repays an older (and usually lower LTV and DTI) mortgage and gets a new mortgage, which resets the mortgage to a new and higher level. We show that the rate at which owners moved into new homes peaked in 2006, with approximately 8% of households moving in each year. This rate increased in lockstep across the income distribution. Low-income households had lower levels of churn relative to higher-income ones during the boom, 6% versus 9%, respectively. For all income groups, the rate of movement drops to about 5% during the crisis period and returns to about 6% by 2015. This is in line with the notion that optimistic homeowners exploited increasing house prices by flipping houses more quickly and using the capital gains in one property as a down payment for a larger home (Stein 1995). For example, Piazzesi and Schneider (2009) show that the fraction of homeowners who are very optimistic about house prices doubled between 2004 and 2006 (from 10% to 20% of the population).

LTV. To better understand the role that house prices played in increasing DTI levels during the boom period, we analyze CLTV levels, a central parameter in determining the tightness of collateralized lending.[8] We use data from CoreLogic (formerly DataQuick) for this analysis. A number of theories suggest that increases in house prices play an important role in explaining household leverage via LTV levels (Makarov and Plantin [2013, Landvoigt, Piazessi and Schneider [2015]). Interestingly, the distribution of CLTV levels at origination between 2001 and 2007 was very stable, with almost no changes over time. The median home purchase had a CLTV of 90%, and loans at the 90th percentile of leverage had a CLTV of almost 100%, even at the beginning of the first decade of the twenty-first century. Maybe even more surprisingly, there are no pronounced differences in the evolution of CLTV ratios when we split the data by areas with high and low house price growth or by level of house price. These results are consistent with Ferreira and Gyourko (2015), who use similar data and track CLTVs of households at origination and over time. Taken together, these results do not support a view that lenders relaxed collateral constraints by significantly changing CLTV ratios. Instead, lenders seem to have lent against increased home prices without factoring in the risk that house-price levels could be too high or that there might be a house price downturn. This view is supported by Cheng, Raina, and Xiong (2014), who use personal home transaction data to show that midlevel managers in securitized finance did not seem to anticipate the housing downturn. Also in line with the idea that lenders passively lent against increased house prices but otherwise did not significantly increase access to finance for marginal borrowers, we find that households in all income quintiles who purchase homes have similar (and small) drops terms of the stability of employment over the boom. While higher-income households are more likely to have at least one member of the family employed full time, these differences between income levels did not change over the boom. However, at the onset of the mortgage crisis, we see a sudden spike in the share of households with full-time employment, which most likely reflects the tightening of credit during the Great Recession.

Defaults. Finally, when looking at ex post defaults, Adelino et al. (2016) show that middle-income and prime borrowers all sharply increase their share of total delinquencies in the crisis compared to precrisis patterns. This sharp increase, moreover, is concentrated in prime borrowers in high house appreciation areas in the boom (see also Mayer, Pence and Sherlund [2009], who show that near-prime borrowers had a larger proportional increase in delinquency rates than subprimme ones, Albanesi, De Giorgi, and Nosal [2016] using Equifax data).[9] This set of facts is most consistent with the expectations view, where borrowers took out mortgages against inflated house price values and defaulted when house prices dropped.

In light of the evidence presented above, it is important to understand why some of the earlier empirical literature about the housing crisis arrived at different conclusions to rule out the relevance of the expectations view. The subprime view as proposed in Mian and Sufi (2009) relies on two main findings. First, the authors suggest that there was a disproportionate flow of new mortgage debt to low-income households. This finding seems to be in direct contrast to the findings documented above. The discrepancy stems from the fact that Mian and Sufi (2009) use mortgage and income data aggregated up to the ZIP Code level, and not the household level. At the ZIP Code level, mortgage credit can go up for two reasons: either because there is an increase in average mortgage size (DTI) or because of an increase in originations in a ZIP Code due to quicker selling and buying of houses (churn).[10] As shown in Adelino et al. (2016), the negative correlation between mortgage growth and income growth at the ZIP Code level is entirely driven by the increase in the rate of churn across neighborhoods.[11] Therefore, once we decompose these different margins of credit flows, there is no cross-sectional dislocation in either credit flows or homeownership rates to lower-income or marginal households.

A second major argument to rule out that expectations were the key driver for the credit expansion is that it was instead subprime lending in a ZIP Code (as a proxy for distorted incentives) that drove house price growth. On average, it is the case that neighborhoods with a higher share of subprime lenders (and loans) had quicker credit expansion, since these lenders tend to be in neighborhoods that saw quicker house price growth. However, there is significant heterogeneity in house price growth and the share of subprime loans between neighborhoods. If we do a simple double-sort of ZIP Codes by the market share of subprime lenders and the growth in house prices between 2002 and 2006,[12] we see that growth in mortgage origination sorts strongly with house price growth, independent of the level of subprime lenders in the ZIP Code. This means that credit went up significantly, even in areas with a small fraction of subprime lenders but high house price appreciation. The correlation is much weaker in the other direction: once we control for house price growth in an area, there is only a weak correlation between mortgage growth with the share of subprime lending. This suggests that, even though subprime lenders tend to be located more often in neighborhoods that experienced higher house price growth in the boom, they are unlikely to be driving the growth. While it is, of course, not possible to establish causality with this type of cross-sectional analysis, the results again point to the role of asset prices, even when explaining where subprime lending expanded and where not.

In sum, a careful review of the major trends in mortgage markets leading up to the 2008 crisis casts doubt on a one-sided explanation of the events as a subprime crisis. The results presented here support a view of the boom in which financial institutions and banks bought into increasing house prices because of overly optimistic expectations. This broad-based increase in borrowing and housing prices might have been triggered initially through lower interest rates at the beginning of the twenty-first century. In turn, credit standards may have fallen *as a result* of higher house prices because lenders were too willing to rely on collateral values alone.

Our results also show why it is important to understand the drivers of the crisis. We show that, after 2008, credit to lower-income borrowers dropped dramatically and prompted a significant decline in homeownership rates for low-income households. Seen through the lens of the subprime view, one might have welcomed the change in mortgage markets as a sign that marginal or low-income groups were now successfully being screened out. Under the expectations view, however, these facts raise the concern that regulatory changes that more significantly affected lower-income households prevented them from buying houses when prices were historically low, without improving the stability of the mortgage market.

I. Data Description

We use four main sources of data. First, for all household-level survey data we rely on the American Community Survey (ACS one-year and five-year public use microdata samples [PUMS]), an annual survey conducted by the census of US households. This is the most reliable data source that allows us to jointly analyze a household's homeownership and employment status, financial situation, and demographic situation. We also use census data from 1980, 1990, and 2000 for computing historical homeownership rates in figure 7 (similar to, among others, Acolin, Goodman, and Wachter, forthcoming). Census data is obtained from the Integrated Public Use Microdata Series made available by the Minnesota Population Center at the University of Minnesota (Ruggles et al. 2015).

In the appendix, we also confirm the reported time-series patterns of homeownership using the American Housing Survey (AHS) and the Current Population Survey (CPS)/Housing Vacancy Survey (CPS/HVS), all from the census. The CPS/HVS is a widely cited survey on the aggregate homeownership rate in the United States, but it relies on a much smaller sample than the American Community Survey. As a result, estimates of the homeownership rate in subgroups over time are more reliable using the ACS, which is what we focus on. The appendix shows that, while there are differences in the baseline levels of homeownership between the different samples, our main results hold in all three data sets (ACS, AHS, and CPS/HVS).[13]

Second, we use data from the Home Mortgage Disclosure Act (HMDA) data set, which contains the universe of US mortgage applications in each year. The variables of interest for our purposes are the loan amount, the purpose of the loan (purchase, refinance, or remodel), the action type (granted or denied), the lender identifier, the location of the borrower (state, county, and census tract), and the year of origination. We match census tracts from HMDA to ZIP Codes using the Missouri Census Data Center bridge. This is a many-to-many match, and we rely on population weights to assign tracts to ZIP Codes. We drop ZIP Codes for which census tracts in HMDA cover less than 80% of a ZIP Code's population. With this restriction, we arrive at 27,385 individual ZIP Codes in the data.

Third, we obtain house price data from both the Federal Housing Finance Agency (FHFA) (for state-level house prices) and from Zillow. The ZIP-Code-level house prices are estimated using the median house price for all homes in a ZIP Code as of June of each year. Zillow house prices are available for only 8,619 ZIP Codes in the HMDA sample for this period, representing approximately 77% of the total mortgage origination volume in HMDA.

Fourth, we also use a loan-level data set from LPS that contains detailed information on the loan and borrower characteristics for both purchase mortgages and mortgages used to refinance existing debt. This data set is provided by the mortgage servicers, and we have access to a 5% sample of the data. The LPS data include not only loan characteristics at origination, but also the performance of loans after origination, allowing us to look at ex post delinquency and defaults. One constraint of using the LPS data is that coverage improves over time, so we start the analysis in 2003 when we use this data set. Coverage of the prime market by the LPS data is relatively stable at 60% during this period, but its coverage of the subprime market is lower (at around 30%) at the beginning of the sample and improves to close to 50% at the end of the sample (Amromin and Paulson 2009).

Finally, to look at the role of collateral and loan-to-value in the housing market, we use a data set from CoreLogic (formerly DataQuick) that includes all ownership transfers of residential properties available in deeds and assessors' records over 17 years (from 1996 to 2012) across metropolitan areas in all 50 states. Each observation in the data contains the date of the transaction, the amount for which a house was sold, the size of the first, second, and third mortgages, and an extensive set of characteristics of the property itself.

Table 1
Summary Statistics

	2000	2005	2010	2015
A. *Income (median, 2000 dollars)*	41,900	40,122	39,385	40,161
	Upper Bound of each Quintile:			
Quintile 1 (lowest income)	18,000	19,000	20,200	22,900
Quintile 2	33,300	36,000	39,000	43,400
Quintile 3	51,400	56,800	61,900	70,000
Quintile 4	80,000	90,000	99,800	112,250
B. *Homeowner (%)*	66.2	67.5	65.3	63.1
Quintile 1 (lowest income)	43.1	42.5	39.2	38.8
Quintile 2	56.5	57.3	55.4	53.1
Quintile 3	67.0	68.6	66.6	64.0
Quintile 4	77.7	80.0	77.8	75.0
Quintile 5 (highest income)	86.9	89.6	87.6	85.1
C. *Percent movers (over last 12 months, %)*	7.9	8.2	4.9	5.8
Quintile 1 (lowest income)	6.4	6.6	4.4	4.8
Quintile 2	7.8	7.6	4.6	5.2
Quintile 3	8.4	9.0	5.3	6.0
Quintile 4	8.9	8.7	5.2	6.2
Quintile 5 (highest income)	7.7	8.3	4.7	6.2
D. *Housing cost/income (movers, %)*	26.2	31.0	28.1	24.9
Quintile 1 (lowest income)	52.3	63.9	60.8	59.4
Quintile 2	32.4	39.5	35.1	32.2
Quintile 3	25.7	31.1	27.4	23.9
Quintile 4	21.0	25.3	22.3	20.0
Quintile 5 (highest income)	17.1	19.7	17.5	15.0
Number of observations	5,663,214	1,245,246	1,397,789	1,496,678

Notes: Data from the 2000 Census and the American Community Survey. Panel A shows the income median per year in 2000 dollars in the first row (real income) and then nominal income upper bound for each income quintile. Panel B shows the percentage of homeowners per year and income quintile. Panel C shows the percentage of homeowners than moved within the last 12 months per year and income quintile. Panel D shows the housing cost as a percentage of income shown for homeowners who moved within the last year.

II. Summary Statistics

We show summary statistics for the 2000 Census and the ACS five-year sample in table 1. The first set of statistics refer to real median income in each sample (2000, 2005, 2010, and 2015), as well as the maximum nominal income for quintiles 1 through 4. The income threshold for households in the lowest quintile is $18,000 as of 2000, and about $23,000 as of 2015, both well below half the median income of households in those periods (note, again, that we report real median income; the median nominal income as of 2015 in the ACS was $55,000). This is important to keep in mind when we introduce the results on the share of income spent on housing for each income group.

While we discuss the evolution of homeownership rates in much more detail below, this table shows the level of homeownership for each quintile over time. The main takeaway is that homeownership rates sort strongly with income levels. Households in the lowest quintile hover around 40%, those in the second are about 15 percentage points higher, and households at the very top have a homeownership rate that is above 85% in all years in the data since 2000, and reach close to 90% at the peak of the boom.

We also show summary statistics on the share of homeowners that move in the 12 months prior to the survey year. About 8% of homeowners move in each year during the boom period (2000 and 2005), and this drops significantly during the crisis to about 5%. This pattern is generally visible for all income quintiles.

Finally, table 1 shows the average cost of housing as a proportion of household income for homeowners that moved over the last 12 months. Housing costs include, according to the Census Bureau, "payments for mortgages (. . .) (including payments for the first mortgage, second mortgages, home equity loans, and other junior mortgages); real estate taxes; [all] insurance on the property; utilities (electricity, gas, and water and sewer) (. . .). It also includes, where appropriate, the monthly condominium fee for condominiums and mobile home costs." The average for all homeowners is between 25 and 31% over our sample, with significant variation across income quintiles. Households in the bottom quintile of the income distribution spend over 50% of their income on housing, whereas those at the top are at 20% or below. Variation in the share of income spent on housing tracks the evolution of house prices during this period.

III. Distribution of Purchase Mortgages

We first report a direct measure of the dynamics of purchase mortgage origination between 2001 and 2015. We focus on the 8,619 ZIP Codes for which we have house price information from Zillow, the same sample used in Adelino et al. (2016). We split the sample into quintiles based on the median household income from the IRS in each ZIP Code as of 2002 so that ZIP Codes do not move across quintiles over time.

In 2001, the top quintile of households by income represented approximately 35% of the total purchase mortgage volume originated in the

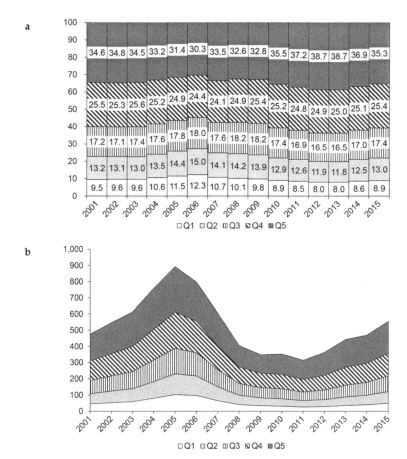

Fig. 1. Distribution of mortgage debt by income quintile

Notes: Panel A shows the fraction of total dollar volume of purchase mortgages by income quintile, and panel B shows the total dollar volume. We use household income from the IRS as of 2002 (i.e., the ZIP Codes in each bin are fixed over time). The cutoff for the bottom quintile corresponds to an average household income in the ZIP Code as of 2002 of $34,000, the second quintile corresponds to $40,000, the third quintile corresponds to $48,000, and the fourth quintile corresponds to $61,000. Sample includes 8,619 ZIP Codes described in the "Data and Summary Statistics" section. Panel A: Share by income quintile (IRS ZIP Code income). Panel B: Total volume by income quintile (in USD billions).

United States (figure 1). The top two quintiles made up 60% of the total, while the bottom quintile accounted for less than 10%. As the housing boom progresses, the share of the bottom three quintiles increases, especially in 2004–2006, to a peak of 47% in 2006 (from 40% at the beginning of the period). This increase is shared across the bottom three quintiles and is not concentrated in the poorest households. This trend reverses in 2006, when the share of the top ZIP Codes by income starts expanding significantly. This is especially pronounced for the top quintile of the distribution, where the share of purchase mortgages goes from 30.3% in 2006 to 38.7% in 2012 and 2013. All bottom three quintiles suffer a reduction in approximately equal proportions. This is consistent with other evidence on the contraction of mortgage credit to low-income households described in the literature (including, among many others, the quarterly Federal Reserve Bank of New York's Household Debt and Credit Reports). Panel B shows the pronounced increase and decrease in overall volume of purchase mortgage origination during this period for the 8,619 ZIP Codes in our data. Figure A2 in the appendix shows that the distribution of purchase mortgage was also stable across the FICO score distribution.[14]

In table 2 we show that the growth in mortgage lending between 2002 and 2006 is strongly driven by house price movements, and much less so by variation in the fraction of loans that were made by subprime lenders as of 2002. To show this, we sort ZIP Codes into quartiles based on the fraction of loans in a ZIP Code that are originated by subprime lenders as of 2002 (based on the US Department of Housing and Urban Development [HUD] subprime lender list), as well as the house price growth in the ZIP Code between 2002 and 2006.[15] This allows us to consider the separate roles of the presence of subprime lenders (as a measure of aggressive supply of mortgages) and house prices in the growth in mortgage origination in the 2002–2006 period. In panel C we show that the house price dimension is much more important for explaining the growth in total mortgage origination than the share of lending done by subprime lenders.

IV. Stock of Debt

The distribution of purchase mortgage could potentially tell us an incomplete story of the *stock* of household leverage if households across income groups (a) differentially retire or refinance existing debt, (b) increase the speed at which they buy and sell houses (churn), or (c) change the likelihood of entering into homeownership. Figure 2 uses data from the Survey of Consumer Finances tracking the entire stock of mortgage debt, including purchase mortgages, second liens, and other home equity lines. It shows that the stock of DTI at the household level increased proportionally across the whole income distribution.

Table 2
Summary Statistics by House Price Growth and Subprime Origination

A. Distribution of ZIP Codes

	Low HP Growth	2	3	High HP Growth
Low subprime	535	651	646	338
2	639	610	522	398
3	583	604	484	483
High subprime	435	351	539	801

B. Fraction of Total Purchase Mortgages Originated by Subprime Lenders (as of 2006)

	Low HP Growth (%)	2 (%)	3 (%)	High HP Growth (%)
Low subprime	3.8	3.8	3.8	4.3
2	8.0	8.0	8.1	8.0
3	12.6	12.4	12.5	12.7
High subprime	22.8	22.1	23.3	26.1

C. Annualized Growth in Total Purchase Mortgage Origination

	Low HP Growth (%)	2 (%)	3 (%)	High HP Growth (%)
Low subprime	7.1	11.3	10.2	14.8
2	7.5	11.0	12.1	15.3
3	7.2	12.1	13.2	17.9
High subprime	8.1	13.6	15.9	18.2

Notes: This table shows descriptive statistics by ZIP Code split by quartiles of the proportion of purchase mortgages originated by subprime lenders (subprime lenders are defined by the HUD subprime lender list), as well as quartiles of house price growth between 2002 and 2006. Panel A shows the number of ZIP Codes associated to each subprime/house price growth cell. Panel B shows the fraction of subprime lenders with respect to all mortgages originated in 2006 in that particular cell. Panel C shows the mortgage growth between 2002 and 2006 within each cell. Data from HMDA, and the sample includes ZIP Codes with nonmissing house price data from Zillow.

V. Housing Costs

We next focus on the sample of movers in the American Community Survey (ACS) and show that the cost of owning a home increases for all quintiles during the housing boom and that it closely tracks the evolution of house prices (figure 3). We use housing costs as a percentage of income for recent movers as our measure of debt burden. We focus on recent movers to proxy for individuals that recently obtained a new mortgage to avoid confounding what happens with the stock of homeowners with the flow of new credit. Housing costs in the ACS include mortgage

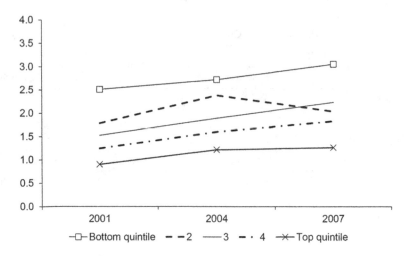

Fig. 2. Mortgage-related DTI by income level

Notes: The figure shows the value-weighted mean DTI of households in the Survey of
Consumer Finances. DTI is defined as the ratio of all mortgage-related debt over an-
nual household income. The sample includes households with positive mortgage debt.
As of 2004, the cutoff for the bottom quintile corresponds to an annual household income
of $25,300, the second quintile corresponds to $44,300, the third quintile corresponds to
$69,700, and the fourth quintile corresponds to $112,700. Mortgage-related debt includes
SCF items *MRTHEL* (Mortgage and Home Equity Loan, Primary Residence) and *RESDBT*
(Other residential debt). This figure appears originally in Adelino et al. (2016).

payments and any other costs associated with owning a home (taxes,
insurance, and utilities, among others). Figure 3 shows the evolution of
housing costs for the top four quintiles[16]. The increase in housing costs is
somewhat higher for the second quintile (at about 6 percentage points)
between 2001 and 2006, and it is about 2–4 percentage points for the
other groups. This cost drops significantly for all income groups starting
in 2006, and in all cases is below the 2001 level by the end of the sample
period (2015). One caveat to this analysis is that we cannot control for
changes in the geographic composition of the sample in each income
quintile. If areas with different housing costs increase or decrease their
weight in the sample of movers over time (which likely happens over
the house price cycle), this can change the interpretation of the results.

For comparison, panel B shows the cost of renting a home for recent
movers. The cost of renting increased consistently throughout the whole
sample period, including during and after the financial crisis, for all income quintiles in the data. Panel C shows the difference between the
costs of owning and renting. The gap in cost for the second income quintile starts at zero, meaning that recent movers spent the same fraction of

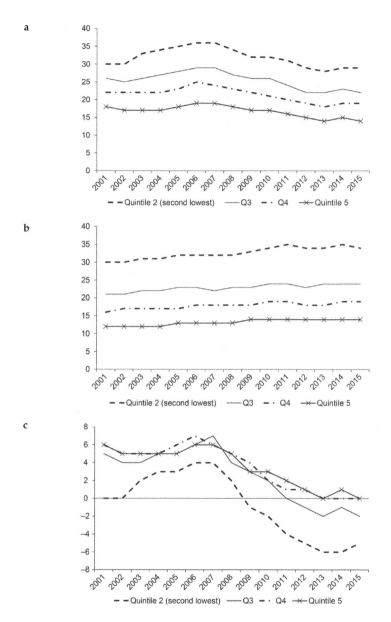

Fig. 3. Annual housing cost as a percentage of income (recent movers)

Source: Data from the American Community Survey.

Notes: Figure shows the evolution of median housing costs by household income quintile. Recent movers are defined as those who bought a home within the last year. Housing costs in the ACS include mortgage payments and any other costs associated with owning a home (taxes, insurance, utilities, among others). Costs are shown as a percentage of household income. The same plots including the first quintile are in figure A3. Panel A: owners; panel B: renters; panel C: difference between the cost of owning and renting.

income on housing irrespective of whether they owned or rented. This gap increases to 4% of income at the peak of the boom, and then drops by a full 10% of income by 2013, consistent with a model in Kaplan, Mitman, and Violante (2016). For the top 60% of households, ownership is associated with a higher cost of housing (by about 4–5 percentage points). This increases slightly by the peak of the boom, and then drops in the bust, to where the cost of owning and renting is the same within each bin.

Figure 4 shows these patterns broken out by states with above and below median house price appreciation. Overall, the message from this figure is that the patterns from the previous figure are significantly more pronounced for areas with a larger boom-bust cycle. Panel A shows that households in quintiles 2 and 3 experience an increase of about 8 percentage points in the cost of housing as a share of income during the housing boom. Quintile 4 has an average increase of 6 points, and the highest quintile of about 4 points. In contrast, panel B shows smaller increases for all groups of households in states with smaller house price increases, as well as smaller reductions in the crisis.

Table 3 shows regressions of the household-level cost of owning a home on a linear time variable ("year"), as well as its square. All regressions control for age and the number of children, as well as state fixed effects. We see a large increase in the burden of housing for all income quintiles, but the results show significantly different patterns for quintiles 3 through 5 during this time period. The difference in the predicted values from this regression amounts to about 1–2 percentage points per quintile at the very peak of the boom. These differences completely disappear at the end of the sample, consistent with the patterns in figures 3 and 4. Columns (2) and (3) split the sample into "boom" and "nonboom" states, and we see that quintiles 1 through 3 are relatively homogeneous in their behavior in boom states, and that quintiles 4 and 5 exhibit statistically different patterns.

VI. Value of Housing as a Proportion of Income

We next consider the evolution of the value of homes as a proportion of household income (the value-to-income ratio). We use value-to-income ration rather than the debt-to-income ratio because data on mortgage balance is not available in the American Community Survey. However, in light of the evidence provided in the next section about the stability of the proportion of housing that was financed with debt, particularly over the boom, and especially for low-priced homes, it is reasonable to

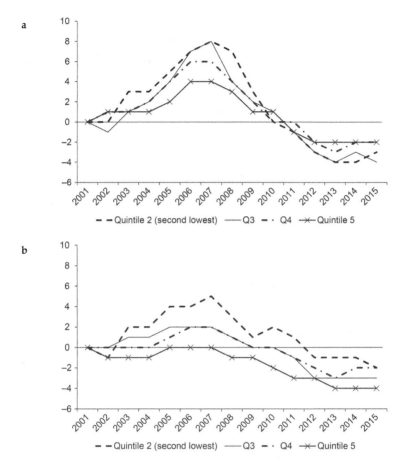

Fig. 4. Change in housing cost as a percentage of income (recent movers, owners only)
Source: Data from the American Community Survey.
Notes: Figure shows the change in median housing costs by household income quintile. Recent movers defined as those who bought a home within the last year. Housing costs in the ACS include mortgage payments and any other costs associated with owning a home (taxes, insurance, utilities, among others). Costs are shown as a percentage of household income. Panel A: "boom" areas (above median state HPA); panel B: "nonboom" areas (below median state HPA).

assume that debt to income followed a similar path to value to income. We calculate the value to income for households that purchased a home in the previous 12 months. This avoids confounding the stock of households with the flow of purchases, and provides a better picture of the availability of credit and the decisions made by both financial institutions and households.

Table 3
Housing Cost as a Percentage of Income (Movers Only)

	All	Boom	Nonboom
Year	2.5186***	3.1746***	2.0464**
	0.4910	0.4513	0.5614
Year^2	-0.1635***	-0.2041***	-0.1343**
	0.0338	0.0322	0.0365
Quintile 2 × year	-0.1164	0.2980	-0.3280
	0.1359	0.1624	0.3460
Quintile 2 × year^2	-0.0116	-0.0476**	0.0091
	0.0090	0.0113	0.0211
Quintile 3 × year	-0.6143*	-0.1687	-0.9643*
	0.2442	0.3375	0.3728
Quintile 3 × year^2	0.0200	-0.0120	0.0450
	0.0167	0.0258	0.0234
Quintile 4 × year	-0.9986**	-0.8833***	-1.1932*
	0.2460	0.1997	0.4325
Quintile 4 × year^2	0.0473**	0.0364*	0.0625*
	0.0154	0.0130	0.0258
Quintile 5 × year	-1.4978***	-1.6875***	-1.5685**
	0.3026	0.2285	0.4044
Quintile 5 × year^2	0.0805**	0.0894***	0.0870**
	0.0192	0.0126	0.0255
Age + children controls	Y	Y	Y
Quintile dummies	Y	Y	Y
State F.E.	Y	Y	Y
Number of obs.	526,480	245,588	280,892
R^2	0.4	0.38	0.42

Note: Data from the American Community Survey. Boom areas defined as states with above median growth in house prices. Weighted OLS regressions using ACS weights.
***Significant at the 1 percent level.
**Significant at the 5 percent level.
*Significant at the 10 percent level.

Value to income increased for households across the whole income distribution (figure 5). The average increase is the same for all households above the 20th percentile up to 2005, and 2006 shows a somewhat larger increase for the second quintile than for the rest of the households. A similar pattern emerges when we focus only on the states with above median increases in house prices, where the 2005–2006 increase is particularly pronounced for the second quintile than for the rest, but where otherwise both the run-up and the fall in the ratio of housing to income is similar for all quintiles. Panel B also shows that the cycle in this ratio is much stronger in high house price appreciation areas, consistent with

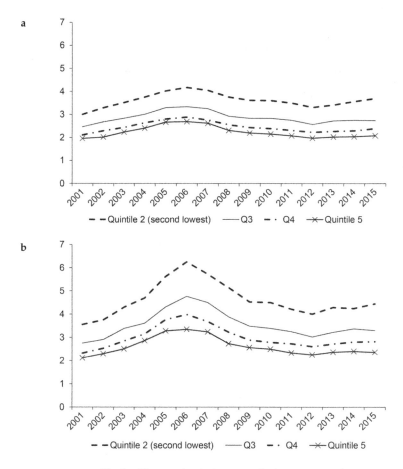

Fig. 5.   House value-to-income ratio (recent movers)

Source: Data from the American Community Survey.

Note: Figure shows the change in median value of homes as a share of household income by income quintile. Recent movers defined as those who bought a home within the last year. Income quintiles 2–5 shown. Panel A: all states; panel B: "boom" areas (above median state HPA).

the evidence in figures 3 and 4 on the cost of owning homes. We show the value-to-income ratio for households in the bottom quintile in figure A4 in the appendix. The burden of housing for the lowest-income households is clearly much higher than that of the top 80%, but the general pattern again closely tracks the variation in house prices.

Table 4 performs a regression analysis that is similar to table 3, but using the value of housing as a proportion of income as the dependent variable. Similar to the regressions in table 3, we again see a strong

Table 4
House Value a Percentage of Income (Movers Only)

	All	Boom	Nonboom
Year	0.5740**	1.0866***	0.3009*
	0.1627	0.2019	0.1094
Year^2	−0.0376**	−0.0705***	−0.0198*
	0.0120	0.0153	0.0080
Quintile 2 × year	−0.0700	0.2094*	−0.0404
	0.0493	0.0707	0.0485
Quintile 2 × year^2	0.0048	0.0130*	0.0033
	0.0033	0.0052	0.0034
Quintile 3 × year	−0.2263**	−0.4606***	−0.1642*
	0.0682	0.0879	0.0609
Quintile 3 × year^2	0.0139**	0.0283***	0.0102
	0.0042	0.0054	0.0048
Quintile 4 × year	−0.2821**	−0.6103***	−0.1710*
	0.0858	0.1137	0.0653
Quintile 4 × year^2	0.0177**	0.0381***	0.0108*
	0.0054	0.0073	0.0049
Quintile 5 × year	−0.3356*	−0.7402***	−0.1898*
	0.1154	0.1532	0.0638
Quintile 5 × year^2	0.0211*	0.0468***	0.0116*
	0.0070	0.0102	0.0048
Age + children controls	Y	Y	Y
Quintile dummies	Y	Y	Y
State F.E.	Y	Y	Y
Number of obs.	515,866	240,279	275,587
R^2	0.25	0.25	0.23

Note: Data from the American Community Survey. Boom areas defined as states with above median growth in house prices. Weighted OLS regressions using ACS weights.
***Significant at the 1 percent level.
**Significant at the 5 percent level.
*Significant at the 10 percent level.

boom and bust cycle that coincides with house price movements. The predicted values from the regression again show that there is a large increase in the multiple of house value over income for all households, with a particularly strong cycle for quintiles 1 and 2. This is especially pronounced for boom states (column [2]).

VII. Homeownership

We next turn to the evolution of homeownership rates during the housing boom and bust. Homeownership rates provide a good measure of the net effect of the expansion of mortgage credit to different house-holds over time (see also Foote, Loewenstein, and Willen 2016). To the extent that credit availability increased for certain groups in the population, we would expect those groups to switch at a higher rate from renting into owning, particularly in the case of groups with lower average homeownership rates. We calculate homeownership rates as the number of households who own their home as a share of all households in each income quintile. The data comes from the American Community Survey one-year surveys, and it covers the 2001 to 2015 period.

Households in the bottom quintile experienced a reduction in homeownership rates during the whole period between 2001 and 2015 (figure 6, panel A, shows the evolution of homeownership for all quintiles of the income distribution). The increase in homeownership rates is almost monotonically increasing in income in the period before the crisis. In fact, households between the 20th and the 40th percentiles experienced a noticeably smaller increase in homeownership rate than all three quintiles above. The cumulative change in the homeownership rate is about 1 percentage point for the second quintile, whereas it peaks at 2–2.5% for quintiles 3 through 5. Panel A includes all states, panel B focuses on states with above median increases in house prices, and panel C restricts the sample to just the four "sand states" (Arizona, California, Florida, and Nevada), where the housing boom was particularly pronounced.

The crisis and recession period is clearly associated with an overall reduction in the rate of homeownership. Our analysis shows that the reduction was widely shared across the income distribution. The lowest-income households experience a very strong reduction that starts in 2006 and flattens out by 2011. All other quintiles experience a steadily lower homeownership rate that undoes the whole increase of the boom and ends up 2–3 percentage points below their level in 2001 by the year 2015.

Panel B shows that states with rapid house price appreciation experienced similar moves in homeownership rates as other states. Specifically, households in the lower two income quintiles seem to have generally smaller increases before the crisis, and a significant reduction in homeownership rates after the crisis. It is notable, however, that the three top quintiles show a fast reduction in the rate of homeownership after the housing bust. In panel C, we find generally similar patterns as before.

In order to verify the robustness of the overall patterns shown in figure 6, we turn to the American Housing Survey (AHS) and the Current

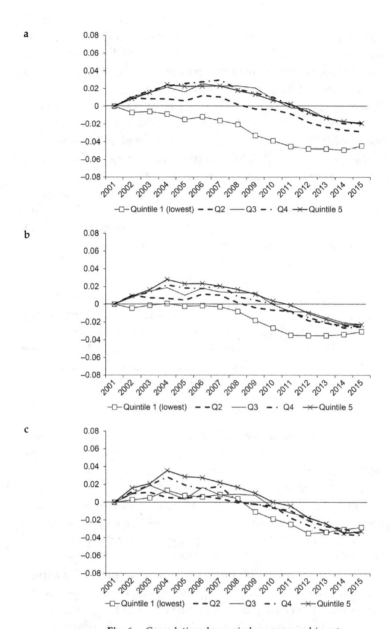

Fig. 6. Cumulative change in homeownership rate

Notes: Figure shows the share of homeowners within each household income quintile in the American Community Survey one-year public use microdata sample. Homeownership rate is calculated as the share of owner-occupied homes over the total number of occupied homes.

House price appreciation is measured between 2001 and 2006. Panel A: all states; panel B: "boom" areas (above median state HPA); panel C: sand states (AZ, CA, FL, NV).

Population Survey/Housing Vacancy Survey (CPS/HVS) and perform the same analysis.[17] We show those results in figure A5 in the appendix. Both the AHS and the CPS/HVS show smaller cumulative increases in the rate of homeownership for households with below median income before the crisis, and large drops after 2007–2008. These results are also consistent with the evidence in Foote, Loewenstein, and Willen (2016), who use the Survey of Consumer Finances and find no evidence that increases in homeownership were concentrated in low-income or marginal borrowers.

Table 5 shows regressions of homeownership status at the individual level on a linear and a quadratic time variable ("year"), as well as interactions of the years with each quintile. Figure A6 shows a plot of the predicted values of this regression for ease of interpretation. These regressions include age of the head of household and the number of children as controls, as well as state fixed effects. The coefficients show that the increase in homeownership rate is significantly higher for quintiles 3 through 5 relative to quintiles 1 and 2. The quadratic term is also significantly different for quintiles 2 through 5 relative to the lowest-income households, which closely mirrors the evidence shown in figure 6. Columns (2) and (3) show that the differences across groups stem mostly from nonboom states. In fact, we find that only quintiles 4 and 5 are significantly different (with larger increases in the boom) in the boom states relative to the lowest income quintile. Panel B reruns the same specification as in the regressions described above, but we form income quintiles within states rather than for the full (pooled) sample. The conclusions are the same as in panel A.

Figure 7 shows a longer time series using data from the decennial census in 1980, 1990, and 2000, combined with American Community Survey five-year PUMS data for 2005–2015. The five-year ACS samples produce more reliable estimates in subgroups than the one-year samples, but they are only available starting in 2005, which is why we use the one-year samples for our year-by-year estimates above.[18] Panel A shows that there was a significant increase in homeownership rates overall in the 1990s, more so than during the 2000–2005 period. The postcrisis period was associated with a large drop in homeownership rates in the United States. Panel B confirms the results using the one-year ACS data in figure 6 for the post-2000 period, and it also shows that households in quintiles 2 through 5 had already experienced a large increase in homeownership during the 1990s.

Table 5
Homeownership Rate by Quintiles over Time

Panel A. Pooled Income Quintiles

	All	Boom	Nonboom
Year	−0.0019	0.0006	−0.0035
	0.0020	0.0030	0.0020
Year^2	−0.0001	−0.0002	0.0000
	0.0001	0.0002	0.0001
Quintile 2 × year	0.0062**	0.0029	0.0087***
	0.0016	0.0025	0.0018
Quintile 2 × year^2	−0.0004***	−0.0002	−0.0005***
	0.0001	0.0002	0.0001
Quintile 3 × year	0.0113***	0.0056	0.0157***
	0.0023	0.0033	0.0023
Quintile 3 × year^2	−0.0007***	−0.0004*	−0.0010***
	0.0001	0.0002	0.0001
Quintile 4 × year	0.0121***	0.0065	0.0169***
	0.0025	0.0039	0.0026
Quintile 4 × year^2	−0.0008***	−0.0005*	−0.0011***
	0.0001	0.0002	0.0001
Quintile 5 × year	0.0109***	0.0082*	0.0129***
	0.0022	0.0036	0.0019
Quintile 5 × year^2	−0.0007***	−0.0006*	−0.0008***
	0.0001	0.0002	0.0001
Age + children controls	Y	Y	Y
Quintile dummies	Y	Y	Y
State F.E.	Y	Y	Y
Number of obs.	13,803,090	6,558,031	7,245,059
R^2	0.19	0.19	0.19

Panel B. Income Quintiles Formed within Each State

	All	Boom	Nonboom
Year	−0.0014	0.0017	−0.0043
	0.0022	0.0034	0.0021
Year^2	−0.0001	−0.0003	0.0000
	0.0001	0.0002	0.0001
Quintile 2 × year	0.0059**	0.0051	0.0067**
	0.0017	0.0026	0.0020
Quintile 2 × year^2	−0.0004**	−0.0003	−0.0004**
	0.0001	0.0002	0.0001
Quintile 3 × year	0.0097**	0.0054	0.0136***
	0.0025	0.0040	0.0031
Quintile 3 × year^2	−0.0007***	−0.0004	−0.0009***
	0.0001	0.0002	0.0002
Quintile 4 × year	0.0119***	0.0075	0.0159***
	0.0027	0.0045	0.0030

(continued)

Table 1
Continued

	All	Boom	Nonboom
Quintile 4 × year²	−0.0008***	−0.0006*	−0.0010***
	0.0001	0.0003	0.0002
Quintile 5 × year	0.0107***	0.0074	0.0137***
	0.0022	0.0042	0.0015
Quintile 5 × year²	−0.0007***	−0.0006*	−0.0008***
	0.0001	0.0003	0.0001
Age + children controls	Y	Y	Y
Quintile dummies	Y	Y	Y
State F.E.	Y	Y	Y
Number of obs.	13,803,090	6,558,031	7,245,059
R²	0.19	0.19	0.19

Source: Data from the American Community Survey.
Note: Boom areas defined as states with above median growth in house prices. Weighted OLS regressions using ACS weights. Figure A6 shows fitted values from the regression.
***Significant at the 1 percent level.
**Significant at the 5 percent level.
*Significant at the 10 percent level.

Table A1 in the appendix uses the five-year ACS PUMS sample for the 2005–2014 period as an additional yearly check on the estimates described for figure 6 (obtained with the one-year ACS sample). The table shows that there is a difference of between 0.5% and 1% for 2005 between the homeownership rates obtained in two samples, but no evidence that this is different for the bottom two quintiles relative to the rest. The difference becomes smaller at 0–0.2% for all other years and income quintiles.

These patterns in homeownership rates may seem surprising given the increase in overall mortgage origination during the boom period, including in the number of purchase mortgages (Adelino et al. 2016). Our results show that the increase in mortgage origination in the aggregate during this time period did not lead to greater access to homeownership by individuals at the bottom of the income distribution, and led to relatively modest increases at the middle and the top of the distribution. These results are consistent with Acolin et al. (2017), who show that subprime mortgage use at the county level was not associated with changes in the homeownership rate, including for low-income and minority households.

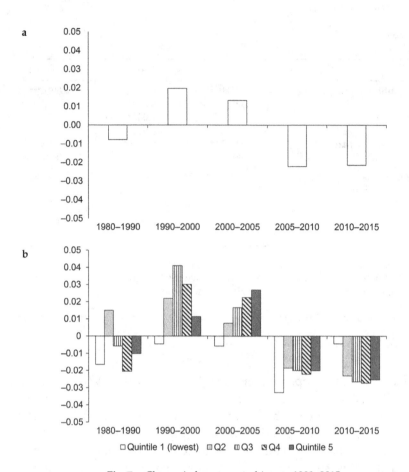

Fig. 7. Change in homeownership rate 1980–2015

Source: Data comes from the Decennial Census for 1980, 1990, and 2000, and from the American Community Survey five-year public use microdata sample for 2005–2015.

Note: Homeownership rate is calculated as the share of owner-occupied homes over the total number of occupied homes. Panel A: all households; panel B: change in homeownership rate by income level.

VIII. Movers and Churn

The evidence on purchase mortgage originations shown in figure 1 is based on ZIP Codes rather than individuals. We use data from the ACS to measure the fraction of homeowners moving homes in each year by income level of households rather than ZIP Codes. We show these results in figure 8. We find that already in 2001 about 8% of households in income quintiles 3 and 4 moved homes in each year. This fig-

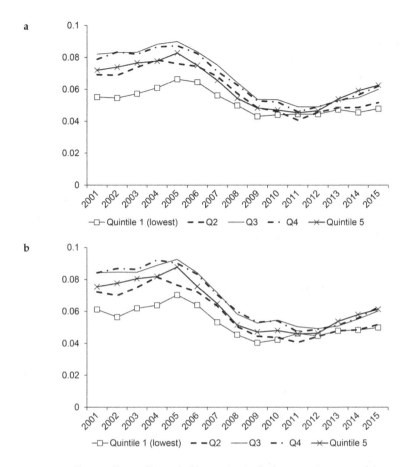

Fig. 8.   Share of households moving in the last year (owners only)

Source: Data from the American Community Survey.

Note: Shares within each household income quintile. Panel A: all states; panel B: "boom" areas (above median state HPA).

ure was closer to 7% for quintiles 2 and 5, and just below 6% for the lowest-income households. We observe an increase in the share of movers during the boom, with a peak in 2005 that is close to 1% higher at all income levels.

The housing crisis is associated with a dramatic reduction in the rate of movers in the data, with all quintiles showing an average of between 4 and 5% share of movers per year, with an increase in this rate starting in 2011. Importantly, all income levels seem to move in lockstep in both the boom and the bust, which again runs counter to the idea that the housing cycle was a phenomenon that was particularly pronounced at the bottom of the distribution. Panel B of figure 8 shows similar evidence for states with above median house price appreciation. Although the shares of movers are slightly higher than those for all states (panel A), all the conclusions hold for high house price appreciation areas and the cycle follows a very similar path.

IX. Loan-to-Value Ratios

We next consider the evolution of combined loan-to-value (LTV) ratios of home purchases using data from deeds records between 2000 and 2012 (from DataQuick, currently CoreLogic). We focus on arm's-length transactions and include first, second, and third liens for computing LTVs.

This analysis means to capture how the debt capacity of housing as an asset class changes over time, and addresses one of the main parameters used in a wide class of models to capture changes in credit constraints. Recent evidence from the Federal Reserve Bank of New York shows the evolution of combined loan-to-value ratios for all households (not just LTVs at origination).[19] We also show the loan-to-value ratio for all households from the Flow of Funds data in figure A7. Both the evidence from the Federal Reserve Bank of New York and the Flow of Funds shows the combined position of US households in terms of home equity and includes the evolution of house prices since a home was purchased, as well as the changes in leverage over time (i.e., the stock of loan-to-value ratios in the economy). These measures include the addition of home equity lines of credit and cash-out refinances, as well as quicker buying and selling of homes (quicker churn) and resetting of mortgages to higher levels. The purpose of the evidence in this section is, instead, to measure the debt capacity of housing over the recent housing cycle.

When we look at the loan-to-value ratios *at origination*, that is, the flow of LTVs of new purchases, we find very small changes over the boom-and-bust cycle across the whole distribution (panel A of figure 9). Panel B shows the evolution of the median LTV for homes at different price levels. Again, as in panel A, these medians are remarkably stable, except for a reduction in LTVs at the peak of the boom for homes between the 25th and 50th percentiles. This evidence is consistent with the work of Justiniano, Primiceri, and Tambalotti (2015) and Ferreira

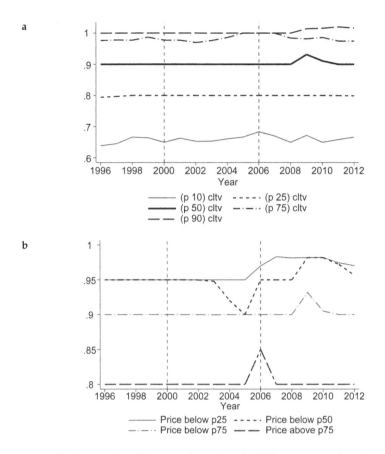

Fig. 9.   Combined loan-to-value ration (CLTV) for home purchase by year

Source: Data comes from CoreLogic (formerly DataQuick).

Note: Sample includes all transactions with positive combined loan to value. Combined loan to value is computed as the sum of the first, second, and third liens taken up to six months after a home purchase transaction. Panel A: all transactions; panel B: median combined loan to value (CLTV) by level of house prices.

and Gyourko (2015), who similarly do not find that LTVs at the time of purchase changed very significantly during the boom. The patterns of CLTV at origination are very similar for states with above and below median house price appreciation during the boom (figure 10). Overall, the evidence on loan-to-value ratios is not consistent with an increase in one of the key parameters associated with a large relaxation of credit constraints, or, put differently, with a significant increase in the debt capacity of homes.

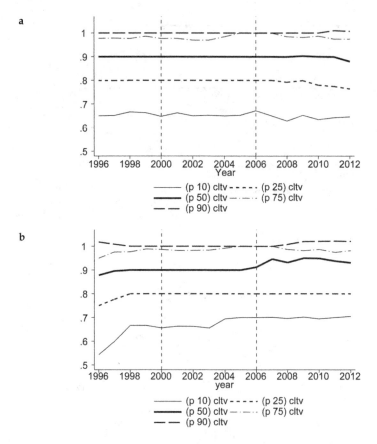

Fig. 10. Combined loan-to-value ratio (CLTV) for boom and nonboom states

Source: Data comes from CoreLogic (formerly DataQuick).

Note: Sample includes all transactions with positive combined loan to value. Combined loan to value is computed as the sum of the first, second, and third liens taken up to six months after a home purchase transaction. Boom states are those with above median house price appreciation. Panel A: "boom" areas (above median state HPA); panel B: "nonboom" areas (above median state HPA).

X. Mortgage Defaults during the Bust

We next show that high-credit-score households and high-income households significantly increase their share of overall delinquencies in the crisis. We show the share of delinquencies by income quintile and FICO scores in figure 11. Delinquency is defined as borrowers missing three or more payments within the first three years after origination. Panel A shows the evolution of the share of delinquent mortgages by

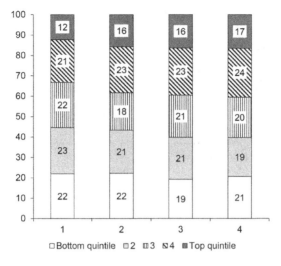

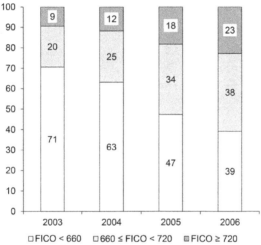

Fig. 11. Mortgage delinquency

Source: Data are from the 5% sample of the LPS (formerly McDash) data set.

Note: Panel A shows the fraction of total dollar volume of delinquent purchase mortgages by cohort, split by ZIP Code income quintile. A mortgage is defined as being delinquent if payments become more than 90 days past due (i.e., 90 days, 120 days, or more in fore-closure or REO) at any point during the three years after origination. We use household income from the IRS as of 2002 (i.e., in all panels ZIP Codes are fixed as of 2002, and cutoffs are the same as those given in figure 1). Panel B shows the fraction of total dollar volume of delinquent purchase mortgages by cohort, split by credit scores. A FICO score of 660 corresponds to a widely used cutoff for subprime borrowers, and 720 is close to the median FICO score of borrowers in the data. This figure appears originally in Adelino et al. (2016). Panel A: IRS 2002 income quintile; panel B: FICO score; panel C: delinquency by house price growth.

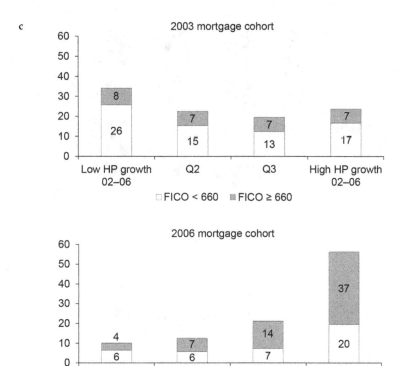

Fig. 11. (continued)

ZIP Code income. Panel B shows the same picture by borrower credit score. Prime borrowers represented 29% of delinquencies over the subsequent three years for the 2003 cohort, but they make up 61% of defaults for loans originated in 2006. Finally, panel C shows that when we split borrowers into areas with high and low house price growth during the boom, we observe that most of the increase in prime delinquencies in 2006 comes from loans originated in areas with high house appreciation, consistent with the important role of house prices for defaults.

XI. Stability of Employment of Recent Movers

As a final test of possible changes in the underwriting standards during the credit boom, we show in figure 12 that households in all quintiles seem to have maintained similar characteristics in terms of the stability

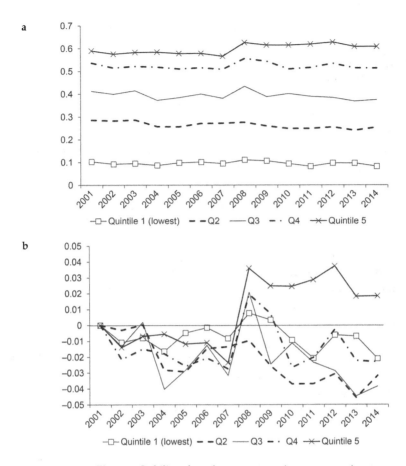

Fig. 12. Stability of employment status (recent movers)

Source: Data from the American Community Survey.

Notes: Figure shows the median share of households who moved in the last 12 months in each income quintile who have stable employment. Stable employment is defined as having at least one full-time employed household member. Panel A: share of recent movers with "stable" employment; panel B: change in share of recent movers with "stable" employment.

of employment over the boom. The boom is associated with a decrease in the number of households that report having at least one household member with full-time employment of about 1–3 percentage points. Importantly, however, this change is common to all income levels, and it is not particularly concentrated in the poorest households. Another way of interpreting these results is that, once we account for household income by binning households into quintiles, this already accounts for many of the common characteristics of moving households. The mortgage crisis is associated with a sudden spike in the share of households with full-time employment, although this change is short-lived for most groups (with the exception of the highest group).

XII. Conclusion

In sum, a careful review of the major trends in mortgage markets leading up to the 2008 crisis calls into question a one-sided explanation of the events as a subprime crisis. The results presented in this paper support a view of the credit boom where financial institutions and banks bought into increasing house prices because of overly optimistic expectations. The catalyst for the initial changes in mortgage demand and house price growth might have been a drop in interest rates in the early twenty-first century that made home purchases more affordable and may have set off the feedback loop between increased house prices and increased expectations. Credit standards may have then fallen *as a result* of higher house prices, since lenders were willing to rely on collateral values alone in making lending decisions. As our results confirm, the distribution of CLTV levels (for purchase mortgages at origination) stayed stable across the boom period, which suggests that lenders almost mechanically lent against increasing house price values.

Our results also show why it is important to understand the drivers of the crisis. We show that post-2008, credit to lower-income and low-FICO borrowers dropped dramatically and prompted a significant decline in homeownership rates for lower-income households. Seen through the lens of the subprime view, this might have been a welcome change in mortgage markets, since marginal or lower-income groups were screened out. Under the expectations view, however, these facts raise the concern that these changes targeted lower-income households and prevented them from buying houses when prices were historically low, without improving the stability of the mortgage market.

Appendix

Table A1

Comparison of ACS One-Year and ACS Five-year Estimates of Homeownership Rate, 2005–2014

A. ACS One-Year

	2005	2006	2007	2008	2009	2010	2011	2012	2013	2014
Q1	41.7	42.0	41.6	41.2	39.9	39.3	38.7	38.4	38.4	38.3
Q2	56.6	57.2	57.0	56.2	55.7	55.6	55.1	54.2	53.6	53.3
Q3	67.6	68.5	68.3	68.3	68.0	66.8	65.8	65.7	64.6	64.2
Q4	79.4	79.6	79.8	78.8	78.4	77.9	77.0	76.0	75.6	74.9
Q5	89.2	89.3	89.3	88.8	88.3	87.7	87.2	86.3	85.7	85.3

B. ACS Five-Year

	2005	2006	2007	2008	2009	2010	2011	2012	2013	2014
Q1	42.5	42.1	41.6	41.2	40.1	39.2	38.6	38.5	38.5	38.4
Q2	57.3	57.2	57.1	56.1	55.7	55.4	54.9	54.1	53.7	53.3
Q3	68.6	68.6	68.3	68.2	68.1	66.6	65.7	65.6	64.6	64.2
Q4	80.0	79.7	80.1	78.8	78.6	77.8	76.9	76.0	75.6	74.9
Q5	89.6	89.2	89.3	88.7	88.3	87.6	87.2	86.3	85.7	85.3

C. ACS Five-Year / ACS One-Year

	2005	2006	2007	2008	2009	2010	2011	2012	2013	2014
Q1	0.8	0.1	0.0	0.0	0.2	−0.1	−0.1	0.1	0.1	0.1
Q2	0.7	0.1	0.1	−0.1	0.1	−0.2	−0.2	0.0	0.1	0.0
Q3	1.0	0.1	0.0	−0.1	0.0	−0.2	−0.1	0.0	0.0	0.0
Q4	0.5	0.0	0.2	−0.1	0.2	−0.1	−0.1	0.0	0.0	0.0
Q5	0.4	0.0	0.0	−0.1	0.0	0.0	−0.1	0.0	0.0	0.0

Note: The table shows homeownership rates across income quintiles computed using the ACS one-year public use microdata sample (panel A) and the ACS five-year sample (panel B). Panel C shows the difference between the two. Panel A uses the same data as figures 3–7. Five-year estimates are not available pre-2005. For a detailed discussion of the differences between the samples, and the advantages and disadvantages of using each data set, please refer to http://www.census.gov/programs-surveys/acs/guidance/estimates.html.

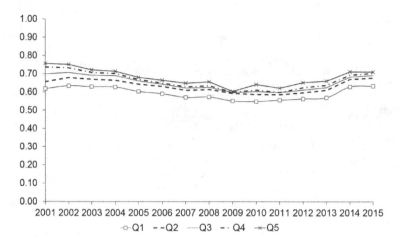

Fig. A1. Mortgage approval rate by income

Notes: This figure shows the fraction of purchase mortgages in the HMDA that are approved each year over the total number of purchase mortgages applications in HMDA split by income quintile. We use household income from the IRS as of 2002 (i.e., the ZIP Codes in each bin are fixed over time). The cutoff for the bottom quintile corresponds to an average household income in the ZIP Code as of 2002 of $34,000, the second quintile corresponds to $40,000, the third quintile corresponds to $48,000, and the fourth quintile corresponds to $61,000. Sample includes 8,619 ZIP Codes described in the "Data and Summary Statistics" section.

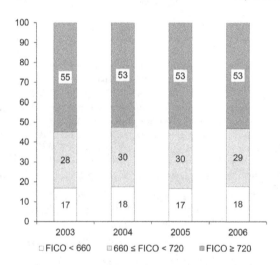

Fig. A2. Mortgage origination by credit score

Notes: This figure shows the fraction of total dollar volume of purchase mortgages in the LPS data split by FICO score. A FICO score of 660 corresponds to a widely used cutoff for subprime borrowers, and 720 is near the median FICO score of borrowers in the LPS data (the median is 721 in 2003, 716 in 2004, 718 in 2005, and 715 in 2006). The sample includes ZIP Codes with nonmissing house price data from Zillow. This figure appears originally in Adelino et al. (2016).

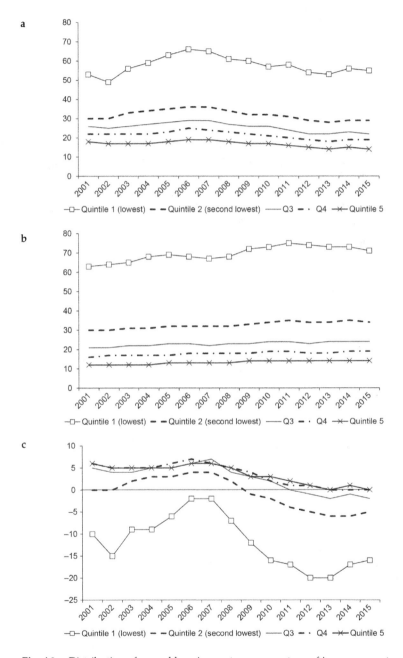

Fig. A3. Distribution of annual housing cost as a percentage of income, recent movers

Source: Data from the American Community Survey.

Note: Medians within each income quintile. Recent movers defined as those who bought a home within the last two years. Income quintiles 1–5 shown. Panel A: owners; panel B: renters; panel C: difference between the cost of owning and renting.

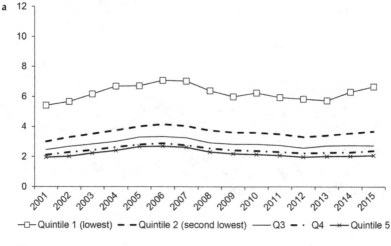

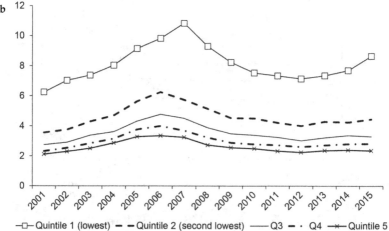

Fig. A4. House value to income

Source: Data from the American Community Survey.

Note: Owners only, recent movers. Medians for each variable. Income quintiles 1–5 shown. Panel A: "boom" areas (above median state HPA); panel B: "nonboom" areas (below median state HPA).

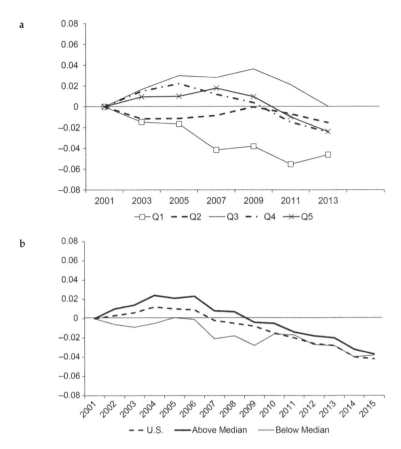

Fig. A5. Change in homeownership rate by income, alternative data sources

Source: Data for CPS/HVS, panels B and C is obtained from https://www.census.gov/housing/hvs/data/histtab17.xlsx, and for panel D from https://cps.ipums.org/cps/.

Note: Share of homeowners within each income quintile for the AHS and CPS/HVS (panels B through D). Panel A: American Housing Survey (AHS); panel B: Community Population Survey/Housing Vacancy Survey (CPS / HVS); panel C: Community Population Survey/Housing Vacancy Survey (CPS/HVS)—adjusted for 2010 change in methodology. Until 2010, householders not responding to the "income" question in the CPS/HVS (panel B) were excluded from the homeownership calculations by family income level (this does not affect the overall US data). According to Census, "this change results in an increase in the homeownership rate of 1.5 percentage points for those at or below the median family income and an increase of 0.3 percentage points for those above the median family income level for the third quarter 2016." This jump is visible in 2010 in panel B and it may help explain the smaller overall postcrisis drop for below-median households in panel B relative to the ACS and the AHS figures (as the cumulative change shown for 2010–2015 is affected by this change). Here we adjust the post-2010 data using the change of 0.3 and 1.5 percentage points reported by the census to construct an "adjusted" 2000–2015 series. Panel D: Community Population Survey/Housing Vacancy Survey (CPS/HVS)—by quintile.

305

c

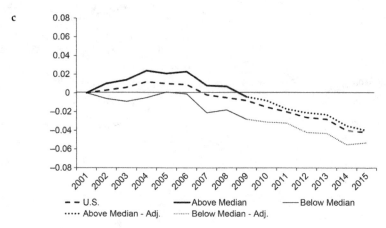

d

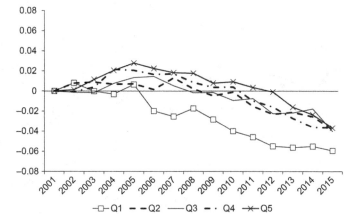

Fig. A5. (continued)

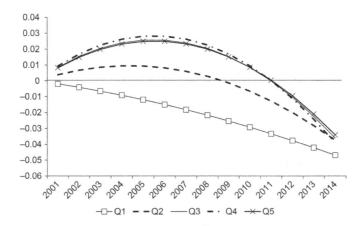

Fig. A6. Fitted values from table 5—homeownership by quintile and year
Source: Data from the American Community Survey.
Note: Coefficient from weighted OLS regressions using ACS weights in table 5.

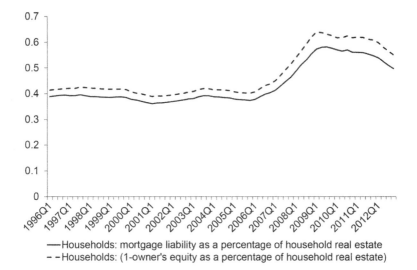

—Households: mortgage liability as a percentage of household real estate
- - Households: (1-owner's equity as a percentage of household real estate)

Fig. A7. Evolution of aggregate combined loan-to-value from Flow of Funds data
Source: Data comes from Financial Accounts of the United States-Z.1. Data from https://www.federalreserve.gov/releases/Z1/current/default.htm.
Note: The dashed line represents one minus the reported owner's equity as a percentage of household real estate assets. The solid line shows the fraction of household mortgage liabilities over household real estate assets. The time period is from 1996 to 2012 with a quarterly frequency.

Endnotes

We thank the editors, Martin Eichenbaum and Jonathan A. Parker, and our discussants, Erik Hurst and Gianluca Violante, for very insightful comments and suggestions. We also benefited from many helpful discussions with participants at the NBER Macro Annual Meeting. All mistakes are, of course, our own. The views expressed herein are those of the authors and do not necessarily reflect the views of the National Bureau of Economic Research. For acknowledgments, sources of research support, and disclosure of the authors' material financial relationships, if any, please see http://www.nber.org /chapters/c13919.ack.

1. Our data come from numerous sources, including the American Community Survey (ACS), the Home Mortgage Disclosure Act (HMDA), the Lender Processing Services (LPS) loan-level data set, and CoreLogic deeds record data.

2. Case and Schiller (2003) analyze how house price expectations form during housing bubbles, and Kaplan, Mitman, and Violante (2016) present a structural model that lays out the implications for consumption, homeownership, and leverage decisions.

3. An earlier literature assumed that credit-constrained borrowers need collateral to borrow because of information asymmetries or limited contract enforcement (see, e.g., Bernanke, Gertler, and Gilchrist 1999; Kiyotaki and Moore 1997; Gertler and Gilchrist 1994; and Rampini and Vishwanathan 2010). If agency problems vary over the business cycle, it can lead to flight to quality and with it reduced collateral values in the bust. These models of the collateral-lending channel assume rational homeowners and banks, and thus would not predict a crash in mortgage markets.

4. See Geanakoplos (2010) for a model of the collateral-lending channel that produces endogenous boom-and-bust dynamics.

5. Several studies also suggest that the housing boom led to broader allocative distortions, for example, on structural labor market imbalances, small business starts, or even students' educational outcomes (see, e.g., Charles, Hurst, and Notowidgo 2015, 2016; and Adelino, Schoar, and Severino 2015).

6. A number of papers present evidence of the loosening of credit standards and increased lending over the boom period (see, e.g., Loutskina and Strahan 2009; Keys et al. 2010; Demyanyk and Van Hemert 2011; Dell'Ariccia, Igan, and Laeven 2012; Nadauld and Sherlund 2013; Agarwal et al. 2014). Although these studies are important in documenting the effects of the crisis, they do not speak directly to its origins.

7. Consistent with this fact, Greenwald (2016) argues that a cap on debt-to-income ratios, not loan-to-value ratios, is the more effective macroprudential policy for limiting boom-bust cycles.

8. This is the combination of all loans taken out on a home divided by the value of the asset.

9. It is a separate (and open) question whether there were "knock-on" effects from early defaults by one type of borrower, particularly subprime borrowers, on higher income and prime borrowers later on. While this could have happened, the aggregate evidence does not show clear lead-lag patterns in the delinquencies by different groups.

10. Take, for example, a situation where the fraction of households that buy homes in a given year increases from 6% to 8%, as we saw happened in the boom. If we sum the total new purchase mortgage debt at the ZIP Code level, it would look as if mortgage debt doubled even if DTIs and LTVs for all households stayed the same.

11. In addition, Mian and Sufi (2009) look at credit flows only between different ZIP Codes *within* the same metropolitan statistical area (MSA) rather than across the country as a whole.

12. Subprime lenders are defined by the Department of Housing and Urban Development, or HUD.

13. The CPS / HVS sample includes approximately 72,000 housing units, versus 500 thousand to 1.5 million households in the ACS, depending on the year. The AHS is approximately the same size as CPS/HVS. For a more detailed comparison of the ACS, AHS, and CPS/ HVS data sets, please refer to https://www.census.gov/housing/homeownershipfactsheet

.html. The CPS/HVS sample is discussed in https://www.census.gov/housing/hvs/methodology/index.html and the ACS sample is described in http://www.census.gov/acs/www/methodology/sample-size-and-data-quality/sample-size/index.php.

14. LPS data is only available to us until 2009, thus we focus on the 2003 to 2006 period.

15. The HUD subprime lender list is available at https://www.huduser.gov/portal/datasets/manu.html.

16. Appendix figure A3 shows the same figure including the bottom quintile. We exclude the bottom quintile for ease of reading the figures, as the housing costs for this group are much higher than for the rest of the distribution. For example, the cost of housing as a percentage of income in 2001 is approximately 50% for the lowest income quintile and only 30% for the second quintile.

17. All three surveys (the ACS, the AHS, and the CPS/HVS) are administered by the census, and there are some differences in the levels of homeownership rates obtained across the three. For a detailed discussion about the pros and cons of each data set, please see https://www.census.gov/housing/homeownershipfactsheet.html.

18. Please see http://www.census.gov/programs-surveys/acs/guidance/estimates.html for a description of the 1-year, 3-year, and 5-year ACS public use microdata samples.

19. http://libertystreeteconomics.newyorkfed.org/2017/02/how-resilient-is-the-us-housing-market-now.html.

References

Acolin, Arthur, Raphael W. Bostic, Xudong An, and Susan M. Wachter. 2017. "Homeownership and the Use of Nontraditional and Subprime Mortgages." *Housing Policy Debate* 27 (3): 393–418.

Acolin, Arthur, Laurie S. Goodman, and Susan M. Wachter. Forthcoming. "A Renter or Homeowner Nation?" *Cityscape*.

Adelino, Manuel, Antoinette Schoar, and Felipe Severino. 2015. "House Prices, Collateral and Self-Employment." *Journal of Financial Economics* 117 (2): 288–306.

———. 2016. "Loan Originations and Defaults in the Mortgage Crisis: The Role of the Middle Class." *Review of Financial Studies* 29 (7): 1635–70.

Agarwal, Sumit, Gene Amromin, Itzhak Ben-David, Souphala Chomsiseng-phet, and Douglas D. Evanoff. 2014. "Predatory Lending and the Subprime Crisis." *Journal of Financial Economics* 113 (1): 29–52.

Albanesi, Stefania, Giacamo DeGiorgi, and Jaromic Nosal. 2016. "Credit Growth and the Financial Crisis: A New Narrative." 2016 Meeting Paper no. 575, Society for Economic Dynamics.

Amromin, Gene, and Anna L. Paulson. 2009. "Comparing Patterns of Default among Prime and Subprime Mortgages." Economic Perspectives 2Q/2009, Federal Reserve Bank of Chicago.

Barberis, Nicholas, Robin Greenwood, Lawrence Jin, and Andrei Shleifer. 2015. "X-CAPM: An Extrapolative Capital Asset Pricing Model." *Journal of Financial Economics* 115 (1): 1–24.

Bernanke, Ben. 2007. "Global Imbalances: Recent Developments and Prospects." Bundesbank Lecture, Berlin, Germany, September 11.

Bernanke, Ben S., Mark Gertler, and Simon Gilchrist. 1999. "The Financial Accelerator in a Quantitative Business Cycle Framework." *Handbook of Macroeconomics* 1 (1999): 1341–93.

Bhutta, Neil. 2015. "The Ins and Outs of Mortgage Debt during the Housing Boom and Bust." *Journal of Monetary Economics* 76:284–98.

Burnside, Craig, Martin Eichenbaum, and Sergio Rebelo. Forthcoming. "Understanding Booms and Busts in Housing Markets." *Journal of Political Economy*.

Case, Karl E., and Robert J. Shiller. 2003. "Is There a Bubble in the Housing Market?" *Brookings Papers on Economic Activity* 2003 (2): 299–342.

Charles, Kerwin, Erik Hurst, and Matthew Notowidigdo. 2015. "Housing Booms and Busts, Labor Market Opportunities and College Attendance." NBER Working Paper no. 21587, Cambridge, MA.

———. 2016. "The Masking of the Decline in Manufacturing Employment by the Housing Bubble." *Journal of Economic Perspectives* 30 (2): 179–200.

Chemla, Gilles, and Christopher Hennessy. 2014. "Skin in the Game and Moral Hazard." *Journal of Finance* 69 (4): 1597–641.

Cheng, Ing-Haw, Sahil Raina, and Wei Xiong. 2014. "Wall Street and the Housing Bubble." *American Economic Review* 104 (9): 2797–829.

Dang, T. V., Gary Gorton, and Bengt Holmström. 2010. "Opacity and the Optimality of Debt in Liquidity Provision." Working Paper, Massachusetts Institute of Technology.

DeFusco, Anthony A., Charles G. Nathanson, and Eric Zwick. 2017. "Speculative Dynamics of Prices and Volume." NBER Working Paper no. 23449, Cambridge, MA.

Dell'Ariccia, G., D. Igan, and L. Laeven. 2012. "Credit Booms and Lending Standards: Evidence from the Subprime Mortgage Market." *Journal of Money, Credit and Banking* 44 (2–3): 367–84.

Demyanyk, Yuliya, and Otto Van Hemert. 2011. "Understanding the Subprime Mortgage Crisis." *Review of Financial Studies* 24 (6): 1848–80.

Ferreira, Fernando, and Joseph Gyourko. 2011. "Anatomy of the Beginning of the Housing Boom: US Neighborhoods and Metropolitan Areas, 1993–2009." NBER Working Paper no. 17374, Cambridge, MA.

———. 2015. "A New Look at the US Foreclosure Crisis: Panel Data Evidence of Prime and Subprime Borrowers from 1997 to 2012." NBER Working Paper no. 21261, Cambridge, MA.

Foote, Christopher L., Lara Loewenstein, and Paul S. Willen. 2016. "Cross-Sectional Patterns of Mortgage Debt during the Housing Boom: Evidence and Implications." NBER Working Paper no. 22985, Cambridge, MA.

Geanakoplos, John. 2010. "The Leverage Cycle." In *NBER Macroeconomics Annual 2009*, vol. 24, ed. D. Acemoglu, K. Rogoff, and M. Woodford, 1–65. Chicago: University of Chicago Press. [plus erratum] [CFP 1304].

Gennaioli, Nicola, Andrei Shleifer, and Robert Vishny. 2015. "Neglected Risks: The Psychology of Financial Crises." *American Economic Review Papers and Proceedings* 105 (5): 310–14.

Gertler, Mark, and Simon Gilchrist. 1994. "Monetary Policy, Business Cycles, and the Behavior of Small Manufacturing Firms." *Quarterly Journal of Economics* 109 (2): 309–40.

Greenwald, Daniel L. 2016. "The Mortgage Credit Channel of Macroeconomic Transmission." MIT Sloan Research Paper no. 5184-16, Massachusetts Institute of Technology, Sloan School of Management.

Guerrieri, Veronica, Daniel Hartley, and Erik Hurst. 2013. "Endogenous Gentrification and Housing Price Dynamics." *Journal of Public Economics* 100:45–60.

Justiniano, Alejandro, Giorgio E. Primiceri, and Andrea Tambalotti. 2015. "Credit Supply and the Housing Boom." NBER Working Paper no. 20874, Cambridge, MA.

Kaplan, Greg, Kurt Mitman, and Gianluca Violante. 2016. "Consumption and House Prices in the Great Recession: Model Meets Evidence." Manuscript, New York University.

Keys, B. J., T. Mukherjee, A. Seru, and V. Vig. 2010. "Did Securitization Lead to Lax Screening? Evidence from Subprime Loans." *Quarterly Journal of Economics* 125 (1): 307–62.

Kiyotaki, Nobuhiro, and John Moore. 1997. "Credit Cycles." *Journal of Political Economy* 105 (2): 211–48.

Landvoigt, Tim, Monika Piazzesi, and Martin Schneider. 2015. "The Housing Market(s) of San Diego." *American Economic Review* 105 (4): 1371–407.

Lewis, Michael. 2015. *The Big Short: Inside the Doomsday Machine (movie tie-in)*. New York: W. W. Norton & Company.

Lo, Andrew. 2004. "The Adaptive Markets Hypothesis: Market Efficiency from an Evolutionary Perspective." *Journal of Portfolio Management* 30:15–29.

Loutskina, E., and P. E. Strahan. 2009. "Securitization and the Declining Impact of Bank Finance on Loan Supply: Evidence from Mortgage Originations." *Journal of Finance* 64 (2): 861–89.

Makarov, Igor, and Guillaume Plantin. 2013. "Equilibrium Subprime Lending." *Journal of Finance* 68 (3): 849–79 .

Mayer, Christopher, Karen Pence, and Shane Sherlund. 2008. "The Rise in Mortgage Defaults: Facts and Myths." *Journal of Economic Perspectives*

Mian, Atif, and Amir Sufi. 2009. "The Consequences of Mortgage Credit Expansion: Evidence from the US Mortgage Default Crisis." *Quarterly Journal of Economics* 124 (4): 1449–96.

———. 2015. *House of Debt: How They (and You) Caused the Great Recession, and How We Can Prevent It From Happening Again*. Chicago: University of Chicago Press.

———. 2016. "Household Debt and Defaults from 2000 to 2010: The Credit Supply View." Kreisman Working Papers Series in Housing Law and Policy no. 28. Available at: https://papers.ssrn.com/sol3/papers.cfm?abstract_id =2606683.

Nadauld, Taylor D., and Shane M. Sherlund. 2013. "The Role of the Securitization Process in the Expansion of Subprime Credit." *Journal of Financial Economics* 107 (2): 454–76.

Parlour, Christine, and Guillaume Plantin. 2008. "Loan Sales and Relationship Banking." *Journal of Finance* 63 (3): 1291–314.

Piazzesi, Monika, and Martin Schneider. 2009. "Momentum Traders in the Housing Market: Survey Evidence and a Search Model." *American Economic Review* 99 (2): 406–11.

Rajan, Raghuram G. 2011. *Fault Lines: How Hidden Fractures Still Threaten the World Economy*. Princeton, NJ: Princeton University Press.

Rampini, Adriano, and S. Viswanathan. 2010. "Collateral, Risk Management, and the Distribution of Debt Capacity." *Journal of Finance* 65:2293–322.

Ruggles, Steven, Katie Genadek, Ronald Goeken, Josiah Grover, and Matthew Sobek. 2015. Integrated Public Use Microdata Series, Minneapolis, University of Minnesota.

Stein, Jeremy C. 1995. "Prices and Trading Volume in the Housing Market: A Model with Down-Payment Effects." *Quarterly Journal of Economics* 110 (2): 379–406.

Comment

Erik Hurst, *University of Chicago and NBER*

There is a large literature suggesting that the recent housing boom-and-bust cycle was partially responsible for macroeconomic conditions during the first decade of the twenty-first century. One goal of this paper is to present a series of new facts to help distinguish between whether a subprime credit expansion and a shift in housing price expectations substantively contributed to the recent housing and mortgage cycles. My own take is it is hard to assess these different stories surrounding the housing boom without additional structure. The reason is that both credit expansions and expectation shifts are endogenous variables. For example, a housing boom due to a credit expansion may cause expectations of borrowers and lenders to change. Likewise, an expectations shock may cause lenders to expand credit to certain types of borrowers. Given the endogeneity, the only way to partition the causes of the housing boom into its various causes is with additional structure.

While this paper does not answer definitely the origins of the recent housing and mortgage cycles, the paper's strength is in marshaling lots of great data to help guide future modeling efforts. My main takeaway from the paper is that the expansion of credit to only subprime borrowers as the primary driver of the housing cycle does not seem to be supported by the data. With respect to the broader questions, I am more mixed. The paper does not rule out the importance of a broad-based credit supply expansion as a potential driver of the housing cycle. Additionally, the paper does not really show convincing evidence that an expectations shock drove the mortgage/housing cycle.

I am going to use the remainder of my comments to do four things. First, I am going to show some additional evidence that reinforces that the expansion of credit was not concentrated among subprime borrowers. Second, I will discuss some recent literature that suggests there was a broad-based expansion of credit supply early in the twenty-first century. I will then show some evidence consistent with a shift in expectations of house price growth during the first decade of the twenty-first century. I end with some concluding thoughts.

Changes in Homeownership Rates during the First Decade of the Twenty-First Century

I very much like the analysis done by the authors exploring homeownership changes over the first decade of the twenty-first century. I, too, believe that changing homeownership rates is a potential indicator for the expansion of mortgage credit. The authors show that the increase in homeownership rates was not concentrated in the bottom part of the income distribution. I was initially worried that the authors split the data by income for the analysis. Income varies over the life cycle. For example, older households may have low income and may not have responded to an expansion of subprime credit. Additionally, income is endogenous to potential changes to credit supply and changes in housing price expectations.

As a solution to this concern, I performed a similar analysis of homeownership rates by splitting households by age-education cells. In particular, I use data from the 2000 Census and the 2005 and 2006 American Community Surveys to explore changes in homeownership rates between 2000 and 2005/2006. I pool the 2005 and 2006 data to increase sample sizes. I make three key sample restrictions. First, I exclude those in group quarters. Second, I exclude those in the military. Finally, I only consider a sample of household heads or spouses of the household head.[1] I split individuals into five education groups based on their highest degree achieved: less than a high school degree, exactly a high school degree, some college but no bachelor's degree, exactly a bachelor's degree, or more than a bachelor's degree. I also split individuals into four age ranges: 21–30, 31–40, 41–55, and 56–65. I compute the homeownership rate in each of the 20 cells in 2000 and then again in 2005/2006. The change in the homeownership rate is just the difference in the cell means between the two periods.

Table C1 shows the results of my analysis. There are a few things to note from table C1. First, the largest increase in homeownership rates were among those with higher levels of education. For all age ranges, the largest increase in homeownership rates were those with some grad-

Table C1
Percentage Point Change in Homeownership Rate between 2000 and 2005/2006

| | Education | | | | |
Age	Ed < 12	Ed = 12	Ed >12 & Ed < 16	Ed = 16	Ed > 16
21–30	–0.034	–0.047	–0.003	0.055	0.095
31–40	–0.023	–0.049	–0.015	0.011	0.051
41–55	–0.004	–0.025	–0.001	0.012	0.016
56–65	–0.024	–0.019	–0.003	0.006	0.014

Notes: Table shows the change in homeownership rate between 2000 and 2005/2006 for different age-education groups. Data from the 2000 Census and 2005 and 2006 American Community Surveys. Sample excludes those in group quarters and those in the military. Sample is restricted to those individuals who report being a household head or the spouse of a household head.

uate school training. The next highest increase in each age range was for those with a bachelor's degree. Second, the increase in the homeownership rate was largest for younger high-educated workers. For example, those between the ages of 21 and 30 increased their homeownership rates by 5.5 percentage points and 9.5 percentage points, respectively, for those with a bachelor's degree and those with some graduate training. Finally, for every age range, there was decrease in homeownership rates for those with only a high school degree.

The results in table C1 reinforce the patterns documented in the Adelino, Schoar, and Severino paper by showing that the increase in homeownership rates was not concentrated among lower-income/lower-education households. If anything, the results suggest that it is the higher-income/higher-educated households that increased homeownership rates the most. To the extent that the patterns are being driven by the young, it is young individuals with a bachelor's degree or more that experienced the biggest shifts in homeownership rates during the housing boom period.

Supporting Evidence for an Increase in Credit Supply

There are two pieces of evidence that I feel are consistent with a broad-based increase in credit supply during the early years of the twenty-first century. First, the increase in the homeownership rate for younger high-educated households occurred in both high house price growth areas and lower house price growth areas. To illustrate that I re-did the analysis in table 1, splitting households by whether they lived in one of the sand states (Florida, Nevada, California, and Arizona) or in any other state. Twenty-one- to thirty-year-old individuals with exactly a bachelors' degree increased their homeownership rate by 5.6 percentage points in the sand states. The comparable number in all other states was 5.5 percentage points. The patterns were broadly similar across other age-education cells. To the extent that homeownership rates are a proxy for changing credit conditions, the increase in credit conditions occurred regardless of house price growth. To me, this is suggestive that there was a broad-based credit expansion during the first decade of the twenty-first century.

More importantly, recent work by Justiniano, Primiceri, and Tambalotti (2017) document that mortgage credit spreads fell sharply during the 2000–2006 period. Simple theory says that an expansion of credit supply is needed to match both the increased level of mortgage credit in the US economy during the 2000 to 2006 period and the falling mortgage credit spreads during the same time period. Additionally, the Justiniano et al. (2017) paper theoretically documents that a credit supply increase can occur without a corresponding change in loan-to-value ratios. The fact that average LTVs only increased slightly during the first decade of the twenty-first century, therefore, is consistent with a broad-based increase in credit supply during the early part of the twenty-first century.[2]

The Adelino et al. paper I am discussing shows convincing evidence that the credit expansion that occurred during the early part of the twenty-first century in the United States was not concentrated among the subprime population. However, there are signals in the data that there was a broader-based credit expansion during the housing boom period. The fact that there was not a disproportionate shift in credit supply for subprime borrowers does not preclude the fact that a broad-based increase in credit supply occurred within the US economy during the early twenty-first century.

Supporting Evidence for a Shift in Household Expectations

The Adelino et al. paper does suggest a shift in expectations as being a potential driver of the recent housing price boom. There is evidence in the literature supporting this hypothesis. Let me briefly highlight three pieces of evidence. First, Case and Shiller (2003) and Case, Shiller, and Thompson (2012) document that homeowners who bought their homes during the early years of the twenty-first century reported expected house price appreciations that were well above long-run average house price appreciations in their respective metropolitan statistical areas (MSAs). Higher house price appreciation in the recent past in the survey respondent's MSA resulted in higher expected housing price growth. Case and Shiller conclude that such patterns are consistent with housing price bubbles in those MSAs. Burnside, Eichenbaum, and Rebelo (forthcoming) use these moments in a theoretical model to show that shifting housing price expectations were an important driver of house price dynamics during the early years of the twenty-first century.

Second, Charles, Hurst, and Notowidigido (2016) build on the work of Ferreira and Gyourko (2011) and show that some MSAs in the early twenty-first century experienced large structural breaks in house price appreciation. The structural breaks were in different time periods in different MSAs, suggesting that aggregate shocks were not underlying the large differential shifts in house price appreciation across locations. The argument that these large structural breaks in house price growth at the local level were consistent with a sharp shift in home purchaser expectations relies on the belief that more traditional housing demand stories evolve smoothly at the local level. The Charles et al. papers document that these large structural breaks in house price growth at the local level are highly correlated with other measures of shifts in expectations. In particular, the estimated local structural breaks in house price growth co-vary strongly both with the fraction of out-of-town homeowners and with shifts in local price-to-rent ratios. Again, movements in price-to-rent ratios are consistent with changing expectations of future house price growth. The fraction of out-of-town buyers is often seen as a proxy for speculative activity within a region.

Finally, Kaplan, Mitman, and Violante (2017) develop a structural model to disentangle different forces driving housing price growth during the early years of the twenty-first century. They conclude that shifting house price expectations are necessary to match salient features of the microdata. Collectively, these papers suggest that changing house price expectations on the part of economic agents were an important driver of house price dynamics during the first decade of the twenty-first century.

Conclusion

In summary, there is a lot of nice data in this paper. The paper provides convincing evidence that the expansion of credit during the early twenty-first century was not concentrated among subprime borrowers. However, the paper says little about the relative importance of whether a broad-based credit expansion or shifts in expectations drove the house price process during the first decade of the twenty-first century. It is really hard to interpret the data without additional structure. The data in this paper will be great for researchers looking to discipline their models with moments from the microdata. In terms of my own beliefs, I conjecture a combination of both credit-supply shocks and shifting house price expectations will be needed to match the data. I look forward to seeing the literature progress.

Endnotes

For acknowledgments, sources of research support, and disclosure of the author's material financial relationships, if any, please see http://www.nber.org/chapters/c13920.ack.

1. In particular, I include only those who have a relationship to head code equal to 1 or 2. The patterns are roughly similar if we include all individuals (not just household heads). However, some of the documented increase in the homeownership rate during the first decade of the twenty-first century was due to the fact that many younger households moved back in with their parents. By focusing on household heads, one can separate trends in homeownership separately from trends in cohabitation.

2. It should be noted that the loan-to-value ratios of subprime borrowers did increase substantially (from something around 0.8 to something close to 1.0) during the early twenty-first century. See, for example, Keys, Seru, and Vig (2012) and Ferreira and Gyourko (2015).

References

Burnside, Craig, Martin Eichenbaum, and Sergio Rebelo. Forthcoming. "Understanding Booms and Busts in Housing Markets." *Journal of Political Economy*.

Case, Karl, and Robert Shiller. 2003. "Is There a Bubble in the Housing Market?" *Brookings Papers on Economic Activity* 2003 (2): 299–342.

Case, Karl, Robert Shiller, and Anne Thompson. 2012. "What Have They Been Thinking? Home Buyer Behavior in Hot and Cold Markets." *Brookings Papers on Economic Activity* 2012:265–98.

Charles, Kerwin, Erik Hurst, and Matt Notowidigido. 2016. "Housing Booms and Busts, Labor Market Opportunities, and College Attendance." NBER Working Paper no. 21587, Cambridge, MA.

Ferreira, Fernando, and Joseph Gyourko. 2011. "Anatomy of the Beginning of the Housing Boom: US Neighborhoods and Metropolitan Areas, 1993–2009." NBER Working Paper no. 17374, Cambridge, MA.

———. 2015. "A New Look at the US Foreclosure Crisis: Panel Data Evidence on Prime and Subprime Borrowers from 1997 to 2012." NBER Working Paper no. 21261, Cambridge, MA.

Justiniano, Alejandro, Giorgio Primiceri, and Andrea Tambalotti. 2017. "The Mortgage Rate Conundrum." Working Paper no. 23784, Cambridge, MA.

Keys, Ben, Amit Seru, and Vikrant Vig. 2012. "Lender Screening and Role of Securitization: Evidence from Prime and Subprime Mortgages." *Review of Financial Studies* 25 (7): 2071–108.

Kaplan, Greg, Kurt Mitman, and Gianluca Violante. 2017. "Consumption and House Prices in the Great Recession: Model Meets Evidence." Working Paper, Princeton University.

Comment

Giovanni L. Violante, *Princeton University, CEPR, IFS, IZA, and NBER*

I will organize my discussion in three parts, each corresponding to a separate section. In the first section, I'll put the question addressed by the authors in the broader context of the literature on the housing crisis. In the second section, I'll reflect on the identity of the *marginal borrowers* whose role in the crisis is key to separate alternative explanations. I'll end this section by arguing that it is very hard to interpret the microdata without some additional theoretical structure. This conclusion motivates the last part of my discussion, the third section, where I will summarize what we can learn from the existing quantitative macro literature that has developed dynamic stochastic equilibrium models to make sense of the recent housing boom and bust.

The Question in Context

This paper belongs to a large, by now, body of work that tries to shed light on the dynamics of the US economy around the Great Recession. In a series of influential articles, Mian and Sufi (see, e.g., Mian and Sufi 2009, 2015) have put forward a compelling housing-driven narrative of the Great Recession that has become the consensus among economists, commentators, and policymakers. We can summarize this narrative as follows:

1. The sharp fall in employment and consumption expenditures in the Great Recession was not driven by a drop in productivity, but it was demand driven.

2. Consumer demand declined because of the collapse in house prices, possibly paired with nominal or real rigidities.

978-0-226-57766-1/2018/2018-0303$10.00

3. The high level of household leverage that existed at the peak of the housing boom amplified the consumption response to the house price shock, what Mian and Sufi have called the household balance sheet effect.

Adelino, Schoar, and Severino agree with this interpretation. In particular, they concur on the key role played by housing and on the household balance sheet as a transmission mechanism of the primitive shock to consumption and employment. It is useful here to recall that other authors have drawn attention to alternative amplification mechanisms, such as firms' balance sheets (e.g., Giroud and Mueller 2015; Gilchrist et al. 2017) and banks' balance sheets (e.g., Gertler and Kiyotaki 2015; Chodorow-Reich 2013).

The disagreement occurs on what can be thought of as the fourth point of the narrative, that is, the origins of the housing boom and bust. According to the Mian and Sufi narrative:

4a. The root of the housing boom-bust was the disproportionate expansion of credit towards marginal borrowers (households previously unable to obtain credit). Following the credit supply expansion, these households levered up and increased their demand for housing which, in turn, pushed up house prices. Later, this excessive debt meant many subprime borrowers found themselves unable to make their mortgage payments. The consequent wave of foreclosures started pulling down house prices and set in motion a vicious circle of low aggregate house prices and unsustainable debt that culminated with the housing bust.

Adelino et al. label this mechanism the *subprime view*. They, instead, favor an alternative interpretation of the origins of the boom and bust—which they call the *expectations view*—that replaces **4a.** with:

4b. The root of the housing boom-bust was an optimistic shift in expectations about future house prices. Households levered up and increased demand for housing which, in turn, pushed up house prices. Later, expectations turned and this led to a fall in demand and house prices.

According to Adelino et al., a central feature of the subprime view is that a credit relaxation leads to a cross-sectional dislocation in credit flows toward marginal borrowers. Instead, the expectations view implies that the credit expansion should be more broad based as all households, including prime borrowers, bought into the belief of fast house appreciation. Given microdata on credit flows, debt, and borrowers' characteristics, one can thus make an attempt to test this prediction.

In their paper, the authors document a set of facts that they interpret as being in contrast with the subprime view. In this respect, this paper

belongs to a growing literature that includes Albanesi, De Giorgi, and
Nosal (2016) and Foote, Loewenstein, and Willen (2016) as well as another recent paper by the same set of authors (Adelino, Schoar, and
Severino 2016) that is challenging some aspects of point **4.a**, which is
the current and more popular narrative of the events.

Before moving to the discussion of how best to separate these two
views in the data, I will point out that, by reading Mian and Sufi, it is
not obvious that their interpretation of the Great Recession is entirely
consistent with what Adelino et al. attribute to them. In their book,
House of Debt, Mian and Sufi (2015, 76) write "The mortgage expansion
to marginal borrowers kicked off an explosion in household debt in the
United States from 2000 to 2007. This is how it all began." However, in
an essay written two years later (Mian and Sufi 2016, 21), their view
seems to have evolved—perhaps thanks to better data not available
at the time of their initial investigation—as they clarify that: "It is crucial to emphasize that the credit supply view of the mortgage boom
does not imply that the lowest income or lowest credit score individuals
were responsible for the aggregate rise in household debt. [This rise in
debt] was driven by home owners borrowing against the rise in home
equity, and [. . .] this was prevalent in most of the distribution [. . .]."

Adelino et al. stick to the first explanation offered by Mian and Sufi.
One could argue that this view—which emphasizes the subprime borrowers as the drivers of the unsustainable growth in mortgage credit—
is a somewhat narrow interpretation of the more general credit-supply
view that Mian and Sufi further articulated in their 2016 piece.

Identity of the Marginal Borrowers

The key distinction between the subprime and the expectations views
is about the role played by marginal borrowers. In order to make this
distinction testable, one has to take a stand on the identity of these marginal borrowers. For much of the paper, Adelino et al. define marginal
borrowers as low-income households. If one accepts this association,
the evidence against the subprime view is quite solid. But, are low-
income borrowers the marginal ones, that is, those previously excluded
from credit in mortgage markets?

Identifying marginal borrowers in the data is notoriously difficult.
The classic approach (Jappelli 1990) uses direct information from survey
or administrative data on individuals whose request for credit has been
rejected by financial intermediaries. I will try to use this approach here,

Table C1
Percent of Applicants Who Were Denied Credit.

| % of MSA Median | HMDA 2000 (Mortgages) | | | | | SCF 1998–2003 (All Credit) | |
	Conventional	FHA Insured	Refi	Home Impr.	Quintile	% Denied	% Discouraged
< 50	43	33	38	50	Q1	42	24
50–79	27	24	32	42	Q2	40	21
80–99	20	22	29	35	Q3	34	20
100–119	16	21	27	30	Q4	23	10
≥ 120	10	21	23	23	Q5	12	6

Note: HMDA: Percent of applicants denied credit by type of loan. Household income measured as percentage of median income of the applicant's MSA. Source: Tables 5-1, 5-2, 5-3, 5-4. SCF: All type of credit (not just mortgages). Household income grouped by quintile of the national income distribution.

exploiting two sources of data. First, the Home Mortgage Disclosure Act (HMDA) data.[1] This database allows one to compute the fraction of loan applications denied by financial institutions by income level of the applicant. Separate tabulations exist for conventional home-purchase mortgages, for FHA, FSA/RHS, and VA-insured home-purchase mortgages, for refinance loans, and home-improvement loans.

Second, the Survey of Consumer Finances (SCF) data has consistently asked over the years two useful questions: (a) *In the past five years, has a particular lender or creditor turned down any request you made for credit?* And, (b) *Was there any time in the past five years that you thought of applying for credit at a particular place, but changed your mind because you thought you might be turned down?* These two questions have been used extensively in the literature to identify individual characteristics of individuals who were denied credit. Since the SCF records household income, we can tabulate the share of applicants denied by income level. The disadvantage of the SCF question is that it applies to all forms of credit, not just mortgages. The advantage is that question (b) allows to overcome the problem—present in the HMDA data—that some households may be discouraged and do not even apply.

Table C1 reports the results for both data sets. I focus on the year 2000, or the period around 2000, since I wish to understand who were the marginal borrowers just before the credit expansion of the first decade of the twenty-first century. In both data sets it appears that there are marginal borrowers, that is, borrowers whose demand for credit was denied, across the entire income distribution. As expected, the denial rate falls with income, but even around the median (i.e., for the middle class) there is a nontrivial fraction of households who got denied credit when applied for it.

These findings suggest that identifying marginal borrowers with low-income households, as done by Adelino et al., can be somewhat problematic. The fact that credit growth increased similarly across all income levels, as convincingly documented by the authors, does not rule out the possibility that much of this credit growth accrued to marginal households who were, until then, excluded from mortgage markets by lenders.

This empirical analysis highlights how hard it can be to interpret the microdata without additional theoretical structure providing some guidance. Luckily, the macro literature has made some progress in this direction. In the next section I will discuss what we can learn from it that can be helpful to understand the separate roles of credit and expectations in the boom and bust.

More Structure Is Useful

I'll begin by illustrating the key economic forces at work in structural models of the credit supply view, and then I'll move on to models of the expectations view.

A.   Models of the Credit Supply View

Prominent examples of this class of models are Favilukis, Ludvigson, and Van Nieuwerburgh (2015), Justiniano, Primiceri, and Tambalotti (2015), and Greenwald (2016). These papers develop dynamic stochastic equilibrium models of the US macroeconomy and show that credit shocks of plausible magnitude *can* induce substantial movements in aggregate house prices. They are important papers because they demonstrate that the Mian and Sufi narrative of the crisis emerges as quantitatively relevant also using a different methodological approach.

The key question is: What does it take for credit booms to generate large house price swings in this class of models? My own reading of these papers is that one needs an economy where, in the equilibrium before the credit shock, there is a very large number of constrained households that would like to consume more housing but they can't. Thus, when more credit becomes available (because maximum loan-to-value or debt-to-income limits are relaxed, as in Favilukis et al. [2015]

and Greenwald [2016], or because the supply of financial assets in the United States increases thanks to foreign inflows of capital, as in Favilukis et al. [2015] and Justiniano et al. [2015]), constraints are relaxed, households demand more housing, and the price goes up.

The main reason why there are many households who are constrained in their housing consumption in these models is that there are *no rental markets*. Everyone must own, but only a small share of the population can afford a large enough downpayment to be at the unconstrained optimal level of housing consumption. Moreover, households close to the constraint are very concerned about potential busts in house prices because in these economies *mortgages are short term and/or there is no option to default*. Therefore, price declines lead to sharp forced drops in consumption in order to quickly repay debt. This tight link between house price and consumption fluctuations makes the housing risk premium a powerful channel for house price dynamics, as explained by Favilukis et al. (2015). Credit relaxations lower the risk premium and push up house prices.[2]

This set of assumptions leading to a large share of constrained individuals is somewhat problematic. In the data, households can always rent a house of their ideal size if they cannot afford its downpayment, and indeed most young households do that: instead of living in an excessively small house they own, they rent a larger one until they have saved enough to afford to buy a house of similar or larger size. Moreover, in the data mortgages are long term and thus, when prices fall, all borrowers need to do to remain in good standing is making the minimum repayment every period, that is, they are not forced to aggressively cut expenditures. Finally, in the United States, households have always the option to default on their mortgage in order to smooth consumption when they end up with negative equity and they are concerned about having to sharply lower consumption in the near future.

It seems clear that relaxing these assumptions and moving toward models with more realistic housing markets and mortgage contracts would significantly dampen the role of credit supply shocks for aggregate house prices.[3]

B. Models of the Expectations View

Kaplan, Mitman, and Violante (2015) develop a structural equilibrium model with a rental market, long-term mortgages, and default.

As expected from the discussion above, in this model looser credit barely affects house prices. However, it does lead to a higher homeownership rate. How can the dynamics of homeownership be disconnected from those in house prices? In the model, renters are unconstrained in their housing *consumption* choice precisely because they have access to a rental stock. However, there are a numbers of renters who are constrained in their housing *tenure* choice because of down payment constraints. When these constraints are relaxed, they opt to buy instead of renting, but they don't demand more housing units: they purchase houses of similar size of the one (already of the optimal size) they rented and, as a result, total housing demand does not rise.[4] Why do these households choose to buy, if they are already consuming the optimal amount of housing services by renting? The reason is that housing is both a consumption good and an asset. For these households, buying housing is the right decision from the point of view of optimizing asset portfolio composition. Put differently, credit limits constrain portfolio allocation not housing consumption, thus relaxing them leads to higher homeownership rate but not higher housing demand.

Finally, in the Kaplan, Mitman, and Violante (2015) model, the credit shock induces a counterfactual rise in leverage during the boom because aggregate mortgage debt rises but prices do not.

Kaplan et al. also study the macroeconomic implications of an optimistic shift in expectations about aggregate house prices shared by both households and lenders.[5] This shift in beliefs induces many current homeowners to upsize in order to realize the expected future capital gain. This push in housing demand fuels house prices.

What happens to rents in the model? Consider the standard user cost condition that links rents ρ and prices p^h (also, let r be the risk-free rate and δ the housing depreciation rate):

$$\rho_t = p_t^h - \frac{1 - \delta}{1 + r} \mathbb{E}_t[p_{t+1}^h].$$

This equation shows that a rise in expected future prices that leads to more housing demand and higher prices today can keep rents roughly constant and pull down the rent-price ratio, exactly as observed in the data over the boom years. So far, so good.

Expectation-Driven Credit Boom

A central feature of the expectation-based narrative is that it can generate, endogenously, a credit expansion toward the subprime borrowers. For

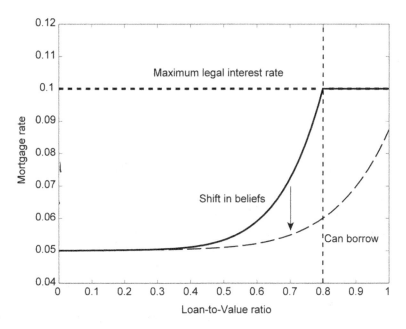

Fig. C1. Example of an endogenous relaxation of credit limits following a shift toward more optimistic expectations about future house price growth that reduces the default probability in the eyes of the lenders.

this to happen, it is crucial that the optimism is also shared by lenders. Figure C1 illustrates the mechanism. Suppose that before the belief shock a certain share of the population is cut off from the mortgage market because, for instance, of a binding cap on interest rates due to antipredatory laws. In the example of figure C1, this cap is set at 10%. Mortgage rates are increasing in the desired loan-to-value ratio because the latter predicts the probability of default which, in turn, raises the risk premium. All households who wish to borrow more than 80% of the value of the house are excluded from credit. When expectations shift, lenders believe house prices will grow. This growth in prices makes defaults less likely and shifts down the mortgage-rate curve. The cap stops binding and a whole set of new marginal borrowers can enter the market.

By pushing subprime borrowers with high leverage into the housing market, this endogenous slackening of credit constraints plants the seed for the spike in foreclosures during the bust.

To sum up, from the Kaplan et al. model we learn that the shift in expectations is capable of generating the boom in house prices and an endogenous inflow of cheaper credit toward the marginal borrowers that is essential to explain the escalation in foreclosures.

Summary

This is an interesting and informative paper that belongs to an important growing empirical literature exploiting rich administrative microdata to shed light on the mechanism that triggered the boom and bust in house prices and transmitted it to employment and household consumption.

The authors reject the subprime view of the crisis because in their data they do not find evidence that marginal borrowers played any special role in the growth of credit, the rise in homeownership, and the spike in foreclosures. For much of the paper they identified marginal borrowers with low-income households, and I argued that is not necessarily correct. I find the mapping between marginal borrowers and low FICO-score individuals more compelling.

I argued that, eventually, one needs more theoretical structure to separate the role of credit supply shocks from expectations. State-of-the-art dynamic stochastic equilibrium models suggest that optimistic lenders' expectations lead to an endogenous credit expansion toward marginal borrowers. This result exemplifies how difficult it is, with data alone without theory, to distinguish between the subprime/credit-supply view and the expectations view of the crisis.

Endnotes

Author contact: glv2@princeton.edu. Prepared for the *NBER Macroeconomics Annual*, 2017. I thank Erik Hurst, Kurt Mitman, and Greg Kaplan for their comments. For acknowledgments, sources of research support, and disclosure of the author's material financial relationships, if any, please see http://www.nber.org/chapters/c13921.ack.

1. HMDA requires lending institutions to make annual disclosures of their home mortgage and home improvement lending activity. Data are publicly available on the Web at: https://www.ffiec.gov/hmdaadwebreport/NatAggWelcome.aspx.

2. To be precise, the economies in Greenwald (2016) and Justiniano et al. (2015) feature a form of long-term mortgages, but they have a representative borrower for whom constraints always bind. The model in Favilukis et al. (2015) is one with heterogeneous households and occasionally binding collateral constraints, but one-period debt. None of these economies features the option to default.

3. For example, in the model of Kiyotaki, Michaelides, and Nikolov (2011), credit-constrained homeowners are relatively few and own a small share of aggregate wealth as a group. As a result, the effect of relaxing the collateral constraint on aggregate prices is small. It is perfectly possible that cheaper credit could lead to very large appreciations in certain segments of the housing market where there are many constrained households. Landvoigt, Piazzesi, and Schneider (2015) document that in the San Diego metropolitan area, during the housing boom of 2000–2005, house prices went up proportionately more (by a factor of three) in the lower segments of the market. Their assignment model implies that a relaxation of loan-to-value limits is consistent with this gradient

in house price growth, since it is the low-income households buying in the bottom segments that tend to be more constrained. However, even the top tiers of the market witnessed appreciation rates of 5–10% per year, and this same shock cannot produce a significant rise in housing demand for those segments because most high-end buyers are unconstrained.

4. This result depends on the ability to convert rental units into owner-occupied units, and vice versa, without severe frictions.

5. In Kaplan et al., households expect house prices to go up because they receive news of a likely future rise in the preference for housing consumption. Burnside, Eichenbaum, and Rebelo (2016) develop a more microfounded model of contagion where waves of optimism and pessimism about future prices can slowly arise in the population.

References

Adelino, M., A. Schoar, and F. Severino. 2016. "Loan Originations and Defaults in the Mortgage Crisis: The Role of the Middle Class." *Review of Financial Studies* 29 (7): 1635–70.

Albanesi, S., G. De Giorgi, and J. Nosal. 2016. "Credit Growth and the Financial Crisis: A New Narrative." Technical Report, Federal Reserve Bank of New York.

Burnside, C., M. Eichenbaum, and S. Rebelo. 2016. "Understanding Booms and Busts in Housing Markets." *Journal of Political Economy* 124 (4): 1088–147.

Chodorow-Reich, G. 2013. "The Employment Effects of Credit Market Disruptions: Firm-Level Evidence from the 2008–9 Financial Crisis." *Quarterly Journal of Economics* 129 (1): 1–59.

Favilukis, J., S. C. Ludvigson, and S. Van Nieuwerburgh. 2015. "The Macroeconomic Effects of Housing Wealth, Housing Finance, and Limited Risk-Sharing in General Equilibrium." NBER Working Paper no. 15988, Cambridge, MA.

Foote, C. L., L. Loewenstein, and P. S. Willen. 2016. "Cross-Sectional Patterns of Mortgage Debt during the Housing Boom: Evidence and Implications." NBER Working Paper no. 22985, Cambridge, MA.

Gertler, M., and N. Kiyotaki. 2015. "Banking, Liquidity, and Bank Runs in an Infinite Horizon Economy." *American Economic Review* 105 (7): 2011–43.

Gilchrist, S., R. Schoenle, J. Sim, and E. Zakrajšek. 2017. "Inflation Dynamics during the Financial Crisis." *American Economic Review* 107 (3): 785–823.

Giroud, X., and H. M. Mueller. 2015. "Firm Leverage and Unemployment during the Great Recession." NBER Working Paper no. 21076, Cambridge, MA.

Greenwald, D. 2016. "The Mortgage Credit Channel of Macroeconomic Transmission." MIT Sloan Research Paper no. 5184-16, Massachusetts Institute of Technology (MIT), Sloan School of Management.

Jappelli, T. 1990. "Who is Credit Constrained in the US Economy?" *Quarterly Journal of Economics* 105 (1): 219–34.

Justiniano, A., G. E. Primiceri, and A. Tambalotti. 2015. "Credit Supply and the Housing Boom." NBER Working Paper no. 20874, Cambridge, MA.

Kaplan, G., K. Mitman, and G. L. Violante. 2015. "The Housing Boom and Bust: Model Meets Evidence" Manuscript, Princeton University.

Kiyotaki, N., A. Michaelides, and K. Nikolov. 2011. "Winners and Losers in Housing Markets." *Journal of Money, Credit and Banking* 43 (2-3): 255–96.

Landvoigt, T., M. Piazzesi, and M. Schneider. 2015. "The Housing Market(s) of San Diego." *American Economic Review* 105 (4): 1371–407.

Mian, A., and A. Sufi. 2009. "The Consequences of Mortgage Credit Expansion: Evidence from the US Mortgage Default Crisis." *Quarterly Journal of Economics* 124 (4): 1449–96.

———. 2015. *House of Debt: How They (and You) Caused the Great Recession, and How We Can Prevent it from Happening Again*. Chicago: University of Chicago Press.

———. 2016. "Household Debt and Defaults from 2000 to 2010: The Credit Supply View." Chicago Booth Research Paper no. 15-17, University of Chicago, Booth School of Business.

Discussion

John Cochrane opened the discussion with three comments. First, he noted the paper's finding that low-income borrowers were not disproportionately favored in the boom implies that government policy at this time to increase homeownership among the poor was relatively unsuccessful. Second, he pointed out that if loan-to-value ratios remained constant through the boom but house prices were rising, then debt-to-income ratios must have risen and thus banks did loosen standards on at least one dimension. Third, he pointed out the fact that people were selling houses, too, so the world is more complex than a uniform belief that house prices will rise. The very large turnover of houses, combined with natural short-sale constraints, and restrictions on housing supply are reminiscent of the Internet stock boom and bust. Antoinette Schoar agreed with Cochrane and pointed out that one of the main results in the paper is that credit (debt-to-income ratios) expanded proportionally across all income groups.

Robert Hall provided several comments about the paper. First, he noted that the subprime market was relatively small at only $250 billion in aggregate, and that this alone could not have caused the crisis. He views this paper as providing further evidence of that assessment. Second, he emphasized that the historical research into underwriting practices provides further evidence of incorrect expectations of house price growth. Underwriting software models in this period assumed prior house levels of house price growth would continue. This, he noted, ignores the finding Cochrane raised in his 2010 AFA Presidential Address that high price-to-dividend ratios empirically forecast not high dividend growth, but lower expected returns. Finally, Hall wondered if the model of housing bubbles and heterogeneous beliefs in the recent paper by Burnside, Eichenbaum, and Rebelo is supported by the results of this paper, or if the model might provide some structure for thinking about expectations more rigorously.

Mark Gertler agreed with the broad message of the paper, but was not ready to completely eliminate the role of increased high-risk mortgages in precipitating the financial crisis. Specifically, he highlighted the importance of the poor performance of Alt-A mortgage originations, which are mortgages issued to borrowers who could qualify for prime mortgages but chose to instead take riskier mortgages, for example, with lower down payment requirements. Gertler explained that increased default in both subprime and Alt-A mortgages caused freezes in money market and asset-backed commercial paper funding markets, which quickly lead to a large drop in credit supply much more broadly. Relatedly, Schoar responded to Gertler's comment by stressing it is important to understand subprime and Alt-A issuance as separate categories. She stressed that typically Alt-A mortgages were taken out by people with high FICO and high income. This suggests that borrowers chose to take up such a mortgage, which again could point to optimistic house price expectations by borrowers as well as lenders. The total size of the subprime market was also very small compared to the Alt-A market and overall mortgage market, so even on this basis alone it would have been difficult for strictly subprime originations to have caused the crisis. In contrast, when Alt-A borrowers started to default, the dollar losses were much higher. She reiterated the conclusion of the paper that the data suggests these borrowers were able to obtain these risky mortgages because banks issuing the mortgages had incorrect expectations of mortgage values.

Chris Carroll took issue with the semantics of the distinction between subprime and Alt-A mortgages. Given that many people refer to these categories together as subprime, rejecting the common narrative that the subprime mortgages caused the housing crisis should require one to show that subprime and Alt-A together did not cause the hypothesis. Carroll stressed that there is really not much controversy if the authors are not willing to rule out the hypothesis that subprime and Alt-A together caused the crisis. Carroll also suggested that the presence of housing market speculators with inflated expectations and easy access to credit could resolve some of the puzzles about house price dynamics.

Manuel Adelino and Schoar responded that this can explain some, but not all, of the variation in house prices. Regarding Carroll's previous points, they noted that even high income and high FICO borrowers who took out GSE loans show the run up in credit and ex post default shown in the crisis. They also disagreed with the contention that there is no controversy, since one view of the crisis suggests that disproportional credit flows to poor and low FICO (subprime) borrowers caused the crisis. While the alternative view suggests that increasing house prices and house price expectations were key to explaining the credit explanation and the subsequent crisis.

Jonathan Parker expanded on Gertler's comment, noting that in fact subprime credit mattered disproportionally because market participants were unsure which of their counterparties were exposed to this risk. However, he cautioned this alone should not be used as evidence that risky subprime mortgages caused the crisis because the same story could also be applied to other small markets. Given these thoughts, Cochrane suggested the paper clarify if it is considering the mortgage default crisis to be the precipitator of a broader crisis or if it was itself the main crisis.

Given the global savings glut preceding the financial crisis lowered interest rates, Parker commented that it would be interesting to look at the distribution of payment-to-income ratios in the data in addition to loan-to-income ratios. If lenders judge credit risk based on the borrower's ability to service their loan, then changes in loan standards are better measured by payment-to-income than debt-to-income in the presence of variation in borrowing rates.

Andrew Caplin stated he was struck by the limited amount of knowledge academics seem to have about the practice of housing finance. Specifically, he mentioned that correspondent lenders routinely reported inflated property values in the documentation they provided to mortgage investors with the express goal of ensuring the loans met loan-to-value requirements of the investors. Caplin suggested that this may be the reason why the authors find loan-to-value ratios remained unchanged through the boom when, in fact, lenders were effectively reducing their underwriting standards. Adelino responded that the data they use in the paper to measure value comes from the actual transaction value of the home, not lenders' private assessments of value, so the paper's results should be robust to this concern.

Ricardo Reis noted that some of the emerging literature on the housing crisis is already affecting policy and policymakers are struggling to figure out what statistics they should target or regulate. He commented that the evidence in this paper seems to suggest targeting loan-to-value ratios is more important than loan-to-income ratios.

Chris Foote offered an alternative framework for the paper to consider. In its current form, the paper creates a dichotomy between two competing hypotheses: a large increase in risky mortgage issuance to poor borrowers versus the belief that home values would continue to rise. Instead, Foote suggested framing the question as whether problems within the financial system lead to the crisis or alternatively whether the financial system was so efficient at intermediating between the demands of borrowers and savers, who may have had inflated expectations. Distinguishing between these two stories generates more testable implications. For example, Foote has found in previous work that financial system insiders lost much more money than outsiders, which is inconsistent with the view of the financial system having poor incentives.

4

Understanding the Great Gatsby Curve

Steven N. Durlauf, *University of Chicago and NBER*
Ananth Seshadri, *University of Wisconsin*

I. Introduction

This paper is designed to provide insights into the relationship between cross-sectional inequality in the United States and the associated level of intergenerational mobility. Miles Corak's (2013) finding that there exists a positive correlation across Organisation for Economic Co-operation and Development (OECD) economies between inequality and mobility, dubbed The Great Gatsby Curve by Krueger (2012) (based on Corak's data), has not only received much scholarly attention, it has entered the realm of political discussions. The Great Gatsby Curve has had political traction in the United States because it has been interpreted as suggesting that high inequality of outcomes is not, in the American experience, offset by higher equality of opportunity or, following Bénabou and Ok (2001), upward mobility. The curve suggests that beliefs in the evitability of this trade-off are illusory.

Substantive interpretation of the international Gatsby Curve is naturally problematic because of the heterogeneity of the countries described, even given their common OECD membership. Cross-country comparisons suffer from the well-understood limits to their ability to identify causal mechanisms because of the high dimensionality of factors that induce this heterogeneity.[1] A focus on a particular country, in principle, allows for understanding of the mechanisms that can produce a Gatsby Curve and hence allows for the assessment of possible government policies. Such a focus, though, changes the nature of the concept of a Gatsby Curve to an intertemporal one: a Gatsby Curve exists if an increase in cross-sectional inequality during one period in time is associated with an increase in the persistence in socioeconomic status between parents whose inequality is measured and their children.

This paper makes the argument that an intertemporal Gatsby Curve is a salient feature of inequality in the United States. We claim that inequality within one generation helps determine the level of mobility of its children and so argue that the Gatsby Curve phenomenon is an equilibrium feature where mechanisms run from inequality to mobility. This claim, which is developed at theoretical and empirical levels, focuses on socioeconomic segregation as the mechanism that generates a Gatsby Curve. We argue that social influences on children create a nonlinear relationship between parental income and offspring income, so increases in inequality, by altering the ways in which family income determines and interacts with social influences, reduce mobility. We focus on the residential community as the locus of human capital and skill formation.

Within economics, theoretical models of social determinants of persistent inequality emerged in the middle 1990s (Bénabou 1996a, 1996b; Durlauf 1996c, 1996b; Fernandez and Rogerson 1996, 1997). These models studied the role of communities in forming human capital and determining member productivity.[2] This work, among other things, represented a good-faith effort to couple substantive sociological ideas with formal economic reasoning.[3] In addition to continuing theoretical work, a substantial body of empirical studies has emerged in the last two decades that has uncovered a plethora of dimensions along which neighborhoods affect socioeconomic outcomes (see Durlauf [2004] and Topa and Zenou [2015] for surveys of the state of empirical findings). Somewhat separately, the last two decades have seen the emergence of a new "social economics" that explores a broad set of contexts in which sociological, social psychological, and cultural mechanisms have been integrated into economic analyses; Benhabib, Bisin, and Jackson (2011) provide a comprehensive overview of the field. Particularly relevant for this paper, much research in social economics has documented the presence of different types of peer influences in education (Epple and Romano [2011] survey the state of the literature).

Our analysis is strongly motivated by and related to these literatures. More generally, the model we develop constitutes an example of what Durlauf (1996a, 2006) titled the "memberships theory of inequality": a perspective that identifies segregation as an essential determinant of inequality within and across generations. We regard this perspective as a potentially important complement to the important developments over the last decade involving the study of cognitive and socioemotional skill formation in childhood and adolescence (see Heckman and Mosso [2014] for a synthesis that focuses on the skills formation/mobility relationship and Lee and Seshadri [2015] for a recent analysis).

Our theoretical model and stylized facts are derived from a specific vision of the nexus between inequality and mobility, one in which segregation represents the fundamental causal mechanism linking inequality and mobility. In our conception, increases in cross-sectional inequality increase the magnitude of the differences in the characteristics of neighborhoods in which children and adolescents develop. This occurs for two reasons. First, increased cross-sectional inequality alters mobility because of interactions between parental input and neighborhood quality relative to an initial income distribution. Second, the degree of income segregation is itself a function of the level of cross-sectional income inequality and so can increase. Greater neighborhood disparities, because of their association with parental income, in turn increase the intergenerational persistence of socioeconomic status.

While we focus on education, the causal chain between greater cross-sectional inequality, greater segregation, and slower mobility may apply to a host of contexts. For example, there is some evidence of increasing assortative matching of workers by skill, which is a prediction of increasing skill heterogeneity or of technical change that increases complementarity between skill types. There is also evidence of increasing assortative matching by ability in colleges. Gary Becker's (1973) demonstration of the efficiency of assortative matching in the presence of complementarity provides an argument for how increasing incentives for segregation are derived from inequality. Separate incentives for segregation exist when agents do not differentially benefit from shared activities. This occurs when more able students do not receive scholarships from schools that match them with less able ones.[4] On the other hand, incentives also exist for diversity, be it through larger groups or intrinsic benefits to differences. For neighborhoods, schools, and firms, there are good reasons to believe that greater inequality of income, of academic ability, of workplace skills increases segregation of types. For example, in their paper Reardon and Bischoff (2011) show that income inequality affects income segregation primarily through its effect on the large-scale spatial segregation of affluence. Once this happens, individuals are decoupled and the mobility of their descendants can take distinct paths.

Section II describes the environment that we study. Section III characterizes income dynamics for the environment. We then turn to empirical evidence that supports our perspective. Section IV describes some broad stylized facts from the empirical literature. Section V presents a set of exercises that complement the broad stylized facts. Section VI presents a calibrated model that links our general theory to some of the empirical patterns we have identified. Section VII provides summary and conclusions.

II.   Neighborhood Formation and Intergenerational Income Dynamics: Model Description

This section outlines an environment in which incomes evolve across generations in response to the social production of education. The purpose of this theoretical exercise is to demonstrate how an intertemporal Gatsby Curve can emerge, as an equilibrium property, from the level of socioeconomic segregation produced by the decentralized choices of individuals. As such, the model captures our general claim that segregation represents a causal explanation for the curve.

One way to understand our argument is to start with a linear model relating parental income Y_{ip} and offspring income Y_{io}

$$Y_{io} = \alpha + \beta Y_{ip} + \varepsilon_{io}. \tag{1}$$

As shown by Solon (2004), this linear relationship can describe the equilibrium of the Becker-Tomes model of intergenerational mobility under suitable functional form assumptions. Note that ε_{io} is an MA (1) process. In this model, changes in the variance of income will not change β, of course, whereas changes in β will change the variance of income. As a statistical object, equation (1) can produce a Gatsby Curve, but only one where causality runs from mobility to inequality.

In contrast, if the equilibrium model mapping of parent to offspring income is

$$Y_{io} = \alpha + \beta (X_i) Y_{ip} + \varepsilon_{io} \tag{2}$$

for some set of variables X_i, a causal mapping from changes in the variance of income to the measure of mobility β, that is, the coefficient produced by estimating equation (1) when equation (2) is the correct intergenerational relationship, can exist. If $X_i = Y_{ip}$ and $\beta(Y_{ip})Y_{ip} = f(Y_{ip})$, then equation (2) becomes a nonlinear family investment income transmission model.

Our theoretical model is taken from Durlauf (1996b, 1996c), which developed a social analogue to the class of family investment models of intergenerational mobility developed by Becker and Tomes (1979) and

Loury (1981); propositions about the model come directly from those papers or derive immediately from results found there. By social analogue, we mean a model in which education and human capital are socially determined and thereby mediate the mapping of parental income into offspring economic attainment. Relative to equation (2), we thus implicitly consider X_i variables that are determined at a community level.

Our model's structure and equilibrium properties can be summarized simply with four propositions.

1. Labor market outcomes for adults are determined by the human capital that they accumulate earlier in life.

2. Human capital accumulation is, along important dimensions, socially determined. Local public finance of education creates dependence between the income distribution of a school district and the per capita expenditure on each student in the community. Social interactions, ranging from peer effects to role models to formation of personal identity, create a distinct relationship between the communities in which children develop and the skills they bring to the labor market.

3. In choosing a neighborhood, incentives exist for parents to prefer more affluent neighbors. Other incentives exist to prefer larger communities. These incentives interact to determine the extent to which communities are segregated by income in equilibrium. Permanent segregation of descendants of the most and least affluent families is possible even though there are no poverty traps or affluence traps, as conventionally defined.

4. Greater cross-sectional inequality of income increases the degree of segregation of neighborhoods. The greater the segregation the greater are the disparities in human capital between children from more and less affluent families, which creates the Great Gatsby Curve.

The model assumptions and properties thus create a causal relationship between cross-sectional (within generation) inequality, levels of segregation, and rates of intergenerational mobility.

Before proceeding, it is important to recognize that our social determination of education approach is only one route to generating equilibrium mobility dynamics of the form (2). Mulligan (1999) showed how credit market constraints, by inducing differing degrees in constraints for families of different incomes, could produce equation (2). In this case, X_i can be thought of as family income. While he did not consider the Gatsby Curve, it clearly could be produced in his model. Becker et al.

(2015) show how the Gatsby Curve behavior can emerge in a family investment model in which the productivity of human capital investment in a child is increasing in the level of parental human capital, which is another choice of X_i in equation (2). Both models, in essence, move beyond the conditions that map the Becker-Tomes model from a constant coefficient autoregressive structure to one in which the autoregressive coefficient varies across families. We will present empirical evidence that is supportive of the way we induce parameter heterogeneity in equation (2), but regard these other approaches as complementary to ours.

A. Demography

The population possesses a standard overlapping generations structure. There is a countable population of family types, indexed by i, which we refer to as dynasties. Each family type consists of many identical "small" families. This is a technical "cheat" to avoid adults considering the effect of their presence in a neighborhood on the income distribution. It can be relaxed without affecting any qualitative results.

Each agent lives for two periods. Agent it is the adult member of dynasty i and so is born at time $t - 1$.[5] In period 1 of life, an agent is born and receives human capital investment from the neighborhood in which she grows up. In period 2, adulthood, the agent receives income, becomes a member of a neighborhood, has one child, consumes, and pays taxes.

B. Preferences

The utility of adult it is determined in adulthood and depends on consumption C_{it} and income of her offspring, Y_{it+1}. Offspring income is not known at t, so each agent is assumed to maximize expected utility that has a Cobb-Douglas specification.

$$EU_{it} = \pi_1 \log(C_{it}) + \pi_2 E(\log(Y_{it+1})|F_t) \qquad (3)$$

where F_t denotes parent's information set.

The assumption that parental utility is a function of the income of their offspring differs from the formulations such as Becker and Tomes (1979), which make offspring human capital the argument in parental utility, as well as those that follow Loury (1981) in assuming that parents are affected by the lifetime utility of offspring. Our formulation retains the analytical convenience of Becker and Tomes, by ruling out the need for a parent to form beliefs about dynasty income beyond

$t + 1$, that is, their immediate offspring. We prefer to directly focus on income as it captures our intuition that parents have preferences over the opportunity sets of their children as opposed to education per se, so in this sense our assumption is more in the spirit of Loury. This all said, we do not believe that there is a principled basis for distinguishing the different preference formulations.

Cobb-Douglas utility plays an important role in our analysis. By eliminating heterogeneity in the desired fraction of income that is spent on consumption, the political economy of the model becomes trivial. More general formulations could be pursued following Durlauf (1996c). The potential problem with more general specifications of preferences is the identification of general conditions that are sufficient for the existence of equilibrium neighborhood configurations. The Cobb-Douglas form is not unique in terms of ensuring existence, but is very convenient.

C. Income and Human Capital

Adult it's income is determined by two factors. First, each adult possesses a level of human capital that is determined in childhood, H_{it-1}. Income is also affected by a shock experienced in adulthood ξ_{it}. These shocks may be regarded as the labor market luck, but their interpretation is inessential conditional on whatever is assumed with respect to their dependence on variables known to the parents. We model the shocks as independent of any parental information, independent and identically distributed across individuals and time with finite variance.

We assume a multiplicative functional form for the income generation process.

$$Y_{it} = \phi H_{it-1}\xi_{it}. \tag{4}$$

This functional form matters as it will allow the model to generate endogenous long-term growth in dynasty-specific income. Equation (4) is an example of the AK technology studied in the growth literature.[6] We employ this technology in order to understand inequality dynamics between dynasties in growing economies.

D. Family Expenditures

Parental income decomposes between consumption and taxes.

$$Y_{it} = C_{it} + T_{it}. \tag{5}$$

The introduction of family-level parental investments, separate from the public provision of education, will be done in the next version of the model. This generalization will be interesting because of the interaction between private investments and neighborhood characteristics. Wodtke, Elwert, and Harding (2016) find complementarity between neighborhood quality and parental investment, suggesting that this extension will exacerbate the potential for segregation to reduce intergenerational mobility, although this intuition does not account for the effects of the complementarity on equilibrium sorting.

E.   Educational Expenditure and Educational Investment in Children

Taxes are linear in income and are neighborhood and time specific

$$\forall i \in nt, \ T_{it} = \tau_{nt} Y_{it}. \tag{6}$$

The total expenditure available for education in neighborhood n at t is

$$TE_{nt} = \sum_{j \in nt} T_{jt} \tag{7}$$

and so constitutes the resources available for educational investment. Figure 7 taken from the NCES shows that there is a lot of spatial variation in per capita public school expenditure. This is due to the fact that spending on public education, the major public program funded by local governments, is funded by local spending. Local spending in turn depends on local property tax rates.

The translation of these resources into per capita educational investment (which will constitute a school's direct contribution to human capital) will depend on the size of the population of children who are educated. Angrist and Krueger (1999) and Card and Krueger (1992) find evidence of small nonconvexities in education in the United States. Thus, we also assume that the education process exhibits nonconvexities with respect to population size, that is, there exists a type of returns to scale (with respect to student population size) in the educational process. Let p_{nt} denote the population size of n at time t. The educational investment provided by the neighborhood to each child, ED_{nt} (equivalent to educational quality), requires total expenditures

$$ED_{nt} = \frac{TE_{nt}}{v(p_{nt})} \tag{8}$$

where $v(p_{nt})$ is increasing such that for some positive parameters λ_1 and λ_2

$$0 < \lambda_1 < \frac{v(p_{nt})}{p_{nt}} < \lambda_2 < 1.$$

One interpretation of this functional form is that there are fixed and variable costs to education quality. For example, Andrews, Duncombe, and Yinger (2002) find evidence of economies of scale at the district level and weaker evidence at the school level. Another is that there are educational benefits to larger communities. The reason for making this assumption is that it allows the number of neighborhoods and their sizes to be endogenously determined without any a priori restrictions on either. Standard models of neighborhood formation and neighborhood effects usually fix the number and size of neighborhoods. These limits, while empirically perfectly reasonable, implicitly build in exogenous constraints on the levels of segregation or integration. Since the core logic of the model is so closely tied to the consequences of inequality for segregation, we do not want any level of integration or segregation to be imposed a priori. In other words, we want the possibilities to exist that all families are combined in a common neighborhood or are completely segregated in separate neighborhoods.

F. Human Capital

The human capital of a child is determined by two factors: the child's skill level s_{it} and the educational-investment level ED_{nt}

$$H_{it} = \theta(s_{it})ED_{nt}, \tag{9}$$

where $\theta(\cdot)$ is positive and increasing. The term "skills" is used as a catchall to capture the class of personality traits, preferences, and beliefs that transform a given level of educational investment into human capital. This formulation is a black box in the sense that the particular mechanisms are not delineated and, for our purposes, modeling them is inessential. The linear structure of equation (9) is extremely important as it will allow dynasty income to grow over time. Together, equations (4), (8), and (9) produce an AK-type growth structure relating educational investment and human capital, which can lead family dynasties to exhibit income growth because of increasing investment over time.

Entry-level skills are determined by an interplay of family and neighborhood characteristics

$$s_{it} = \zeta(Y_i, \bar{Y}_{-i}) \tag{10}$$

where ζ is increasing and exhibits complementarities. Dependence on Y_i is a placeholder for the role of families in skill formation. Dependence on $\bar{Y}_{-i}$ is readily motivated by a range of social interactions models. By this we mean the following. There is a plethora of nonmarket influences that map the characteristics of adults in a community into the process of educational attainment of children. The importance of neighborhood effects on children's test scores was emphasized in Burdick-Will et al. (2011). Some other papers that support the claim that neighborhoods affect child outcomes are Chetty, Hendren, and Katz (2016) and Davis et al. (2017). One example of how neighborhoods affect child outcomes is the role model effects. The aspirations of children and adolescents are influenced by the adults with whom they interact. One form of this is psychological, that is, a basic desire to imitate. Another form is social learning: perceptions of benefits of education are determined by the information that is locally available to the young. For example, Jensen (2010) documents low perceived returns to education among boys in the Dominican Republic and finds that their subsequent education choices respond to information on actual returns. Equations (9) and (10) express the fact that the income distribution in a neighborhood generates distinct political economy and social interaction effects. These dual channels by which neighborhood income affects children combine to determine the properties of the dynastic income processes and hence differences between them, that is, intergenerational inequality dynamics.

G.   *Neighborhood Formation*

Neighborhoods reform every period, that is, there is no housing stock. As such, neighborhoods are like clubs. Neighborhoods are groupings of families, that is, all families who wish to form a common neighborhood and set a minimum income threshold for membership. This is a strong assumption. That said, we would emphasize that zoning restrictions matter in neighborhood stratification, so the core assumption should not be regarded as obviously inferior to a neighborhood formation rule based on prices.

H.   *Political Economy*

The equilibrium tax rate in a neighborhood is one such that there does not exist an alternative one preferred by a majority of adults in the neighborhood. The Cobb-Douglas preference assumption renders existence of a unique majority voting equilibrium trivial because, under these preferences, there is no disagreement on the preferred tax rate. The reason for this is that conditional on neighborhood composition, tax rates determine budget shares, which under private consumption and Cobb-Douglas preferences are, of course, fixed. Families differ in the implicit prices by which offspring income trades off against consumption, because of different influences as embodied in $\phi(\cdot)$, but this is irrelevant with respect to desired budget-share allocation.

I. Borrowing Constraints

Neither families nor neighborhoods can borrow. This extends the standard borrowing constraints in models of this type. With respect to families, we adopt from Loury (1981) the idea that parents cannot borrow against future offspring income. Unlike his case, the borrowing constraint matters for neighborhood membership, not because of direct family investment. In addition, in our analysis, communities cannot entail children who grow up as members to pay off debts accrued for their education. Both assumptions follow legal standards, and so are not controversial.

III. Neighborhood Formation and Intergenerational Income Dynamics: Model Properties

A. Neighborhood Equilibria

What neighborhood equilibria emerge in this environment? Observe that the expected utility of adult it given membership in a neighborhood can be rewritten in terms of neighborhood characteristics as

$$
\begin{aligned}
EU_{it} &= \pi_1 \log((1 - \tau)Y_{it}) + \pi_2 E(\log(\phi H_{nt}(\tau)\xi_{it})|F_t) \\
&= \pi_1 \log((1 - \tau)Y_{it}) + \pi_2 \log(\tau\phi\xi_{it}\theta(\bar{Y}_{nt})\nu(p_{nt})\bar{Y}_{nt}).
\end{aligned}
\tag{11}
$$

Taxes, therefore, determine budget shares for families. The first proposition is immediate from the Cobb-Douglas formulation. A family's preferred tax rate is thus the fraction of income it wishes to spend on education. Under our preference assumption, equilibrium tax rates are unanimously preferred and constant in all neighborhoods $\forall n, t$, that is,

$$\tau_{nt} = \frac{\pi_1}{\pi_1 + \pi_2}.$$

While constant tax rates are empirically unappealing, they simplify the model in useful ways. In particular, Proposition 1 immediately implies a monotonicity property that links the utility of a parent to the income distribution in a neighborhood. Conditional on a given neighborhood population size, p_{nt}, the expected utility of a parent *it* is increasing in monotonic rightward shifts of the empirical income distribution over other families in his neighborhood. This follows from the positive effects of more affluent neighbors on the revenues available for education, as well as the social interactions effects that are built into the model.

The monotonic preference for more affluent neighbors, in turn, allows for a simple construction of equilibrium neighborhoods as well as a characterization of their structure. To see this, consider the highest-income adult at time t. This adult will have the most preferred neighborhood composition. This most preferred neighborhood will consist of all families with incomes above some threshold, since higher-income neighbors are always preferred to lower-income neighbors. All neighbors in that neighborhood will agree on the income threshold since the educational quality of the neighborhood is constant across families[7]. Repeat this procedure until all families are allocated to neighborhoods. This will lead to a stable configuration of neighborhoods.

Proposition 1.   *Equilibrium neighborhood structure.*

i. At each t for every cross-sectional income distribution, there is at least one equilibrium configuration of families across neighborhoods.

ii. In any equilibrium, neighborhoods are segregated.

Proposition 1 does not establish that income segregation will occur. Clearly, it is possible that all families are members of a common neighborhood. If all families have the same income, complete integration into a single neighborhood will occur because of the nonconvexity in the educational-investment process. Income inequality is needed for segregation. Proposition 2 follows immediately from the form of the educational production function nonconvexity we have assumed.

Proposition 2.   *Segregation and inequality.*
There exist income levels $\bar{Y}^{high}$ and $\bar{Y}^{low}$ such that families with $Y_{it} > \bar{Y}^{high}$ will not form neighborhoods with families with incomes $\bar{Y}^{low} > Y_{it}$.

Intuitively, if family incomes are sufficiently different, then more affluent families do not want neighbors whose tax base and social interactions effects are substantially lower than their own. Benefits to agglomeration for the affluent can be reversed when families are sufficiently poorer.

B. Income Dynamics

Along an equilibrium path for neighborhoods, dynasty income dynamics follow the transition process

$$\Pr(Y_{it+1}|F_t) = \Pr(Y_{it+1}|\bar{Y}_{nt}, p_{nt}). \tag{12}$$

This equation illustrates the primary difficulty in analyzing income dynamics in this framework: one has to forecast the neighborhood composition. This leads us to focus on the behavior of families in the tails of the income distribution, in particular the highest and lowest income families at a given point in time.

We first observe that there is a deep relationship between the equilibrium neighborhood configurations in the model and persistent income inequality.

Proposition 3. *Equilibrium income segregation and its effect on the highest- and lowest-income families.*

i. Conditional on the income distribution at t, the expected offspring income for the highest family in the population is maximized relative to any other configuration of families across neighborhoods.

ii. Conditional on the income distribution at t, the expected offspring income of the lowest-income family in the population is minimized relative to any other configuration of families across neighborhoods that does not reduce the size of that family's neighborhood.

The maximization of inequality along an equilibrium path of matches occurs in other contexts. One example is Becker's (1973) marriage model in which complementarities between partners induce assortative matching of types that maximizes differences in the output of marriages. Unlike Becker's case, our equilibria are not necessarily efficient, that is, they do not necessarily lie on the Pareto frontier because borrowing is ruled out.

The maximization of offspring differences by equilibrium neighborhood configurations interacts with the technology structure we have assumed. Higher-income neighborhoods can produce higher expected average growth in offspring income than poorer ones. Formally,

Proposition 4. *Expected average growth rate for children in higher-income neighborhoods higher than for children in lower-income neighborhoods.*

Let g_{nt+1} denote the average expected income growth between parents and offspring in neighborhood n, t. For any two neighborhoods n and n' if $\overline{Y}_{nt} > \overline{Y}_{n't}$ and $p_{nt} \geq p_{nt'}$, then $g_{nt+1} - g_{n't+1} > 0$.

Intuitively, neighbors have three distinct effects on a family. The more neighbors are present in a community (high income or not), the greater is the set of taxpayers to defray fixed costs to educational investment. Higher is the income of a set of neighbors, the greater is the tax base and the more favorable are social interaction effects. The proposition, by ordering neighborhood sizes, formalizes these factors.

Proposition 4 does not speak to the sign of g_{nt}. Under the linear assumptions of this model, there exists a formulation of $\Theta(\cdot)$ and $\xi(\cdot, \cdot, \cdot)$ such that neighborhoods exhibit positive expected growth in all time periods, that is, $\forall nt \, g_{nt} > g_{\min} > 0$. In essence, this will hold when educational investment is sufficiently productive relative to the preference-determined equilibrium tax rates so that investment levels grow (this is the AK growth model requirement as modified by the presence of social interactions). We assume positive growth in what follows.

C. Inequality Dynamics

This model is consistent with extreme forms of income persistence. Our model admits the possibility that the upper and lower tails can decouple from the rest of the population. This possibility is formalized in Proposition 5.

Proposition 5. *Decoupling of upper and lower tails from the rest of the population of family dynasties.*

i. If $\forall nt \, g_{nt} > 0$, then there exists a set of time t income distributions such that the top α% of families in the distribution never experience a reduction in the ratios of their incomes compared to any dynasty outside this group.

ii. If $\forall nt \, g_{nt} > 0$, then there exists a set of time t income distributions such that the bottom β% of families in the distribution never experience an increase in the ratios of their incomes compared to any dynasty outside this group.

The mathematical intuition for this proposition is the following. Differences in the logarithm of income behave in a fashion that is qualitatively equivalent to a random walk with drift. Taking the initial income

difference between two adults as an absorbing barrier, a future reduction of the initial income ratio among descendants is equivalent to asking whether the process ever hits the absorbing barrier. For this environment, the probability is less than one. In our model, disparities between
the neighborhoods experienced by the descendants of the highest- and
lowest-income families can grow and thereby induce disparities in growth
rates across generations. This drift away from the absorbing barrier defined by the initial income difference may be overcome by the shocks
to human capital and income experienced by individual members of a
dynasty. However, because in the absence of shocks disparities would
grow, there is no guarantee that the sample path of shocks will lead
the income disparity to decrease. Local public finance and social interactions can therefore be combined to produce permanent differences
between dynasties.

This proposition does not imply that dynastic income differences can
ever become fixed, that is, that contemporary inequality becomes irreversible. There is no literal poverty or affluence trap in which a dynasty is permanently consigned to absolute or relative income levels.
Permanent differences occur with probabilities bounded between 0 and
1. How can this occur? The key to our results is that the economy is
growing, and so is nonstationary. Specifically, the range of incomes over
which an income takes a probability $1 - \varepsilon$ value changes, for any $\varepsilon > 0$[8].
A growing economy admits forms of intergenerational persistence that
are ruled out in stationary environments. Moreover, the possible (nonzero probability) patterns for dynastic income differences are qualitatively different. Growth, in fact, facilitates the emergence of permanent
inequality.[9]

Our final proposition formalizes one exact sense in which the Gatsby
Curve can be produced by the model.

Proposition 6.   *Intergenerational Great Gatsby Curve.*
*There exists a set of time t income distributions such that the intergenera-
tional elasticity of parent/offspring income will be increased by a mean preserving increase in the variance of logarithm of initial income.*

Underlying the theorem, there are two routes by which Gatsby Curves
can be generated. First, mean-preserving spreads alter the family-specific
intergenerational elasticity of incomes (IGEs), which in this model take the
form $\beta(Y_i, \bar{Y}_t)$. Hence, once can construct cases where the linear approximation, that is, regression coefficient, increases with a mean-preserving

spread. Second, increased inequality can alter segregation. The existence of at least one such income distribution, where inequality increases segregation and so decreases mobility, is trivially proved by an example. Starting with an initial income distribution, in which all families are members of a common neighborhood, an increase in income dispersion that generates multiple neighborhoods will necessarily raise the parent/child income correlation.

Proposition 6 does not logically entail that increases in variance of income increase the intergenerational elasticity of income. The reason is that the model we have set up is nonlinear and the effects of changes in parental income inequality into a scalar measure of mobility such as the IGE will typically not be independent of the shape of the income density, conditional on the variance. Put differently, the construction of a Great Gatsby Curve from our model involves two moments of a nonlinear, multidimensional stochastic process of family dynasties, and so the most one can expect is logical compatibility. The subtleties of producing Gatsby-like behavior in nonlinear models, of course, is not unique to our framework (see discussion in Becker et al. 2015).

IV. Empirical Claims about the Inequality/Segregation/ Mobility Nexus

In this section, we present four broad empirical facts that, collectively, suggest that the generative mechanisms in our theoretical model have empirical salience.

A. Direct Estimates of Gatsby-Like Phenomena

Our first claim is that there is direct evidence of an intertemporal Gatsby Curve: inequality and mobility are negatively associated. This claim might appear to be a nonstarter for the United States, since it is commonly argued that the intergenerational elasticity of income (IGE) between parents and children has not changed much over the last 40 years,[10] despite substantial increases in conventional cross-sectional inequality measures. The invariance of the standard measure may reflect its relative lack of sensitivity to changes in mobility for the offspring of very advantaged and very disadvantaged parents (Kearney and Levine [2016] make this argument). Its parallel previously appeared in the economic growth literature, where evidence of convergence (which is equivalent to 1 minus the IGE) was misinterpreted to argue that there are no nation-level poverty traps (see Bernard and Durlauf [1996] for elaboration). The intuitive point is that if the generative mechanism for the Gatsby Curve involves parameter heterogeneity or nonlinearity, then the empirical Gatsby relationship may not appear in a linear analysis.

There are a number of studies that find a Gatsby relationship once one focuses on the tails of the income distribution. Aaronson and Mazumder (2008), for example, identify covariation between the IGE and two measures of the tail(s) of the income distribution: the 90/10 income ratio and the share of income accrued by the top 10% (see figure 1). In each case, there is a positive relationship between inequality and mobility. Aaronson and Mazumder (2008) also find evidence of a positive relationship between the college wage premium and the IGE (shown in figure 1). This evidence is indirect, but given what is known about the roles of levels of education and inequality, the relationship between the premium and the IGE implicitly links mobility to inequality. This finding is also suggestive of a possible mechanism: the role of inequality in producing educational inequalities that matter in labor force outcomes. Kearney and Levine (2016) also document correlations between different percentile ratios and mobility.

B. Location/Mobility Nexus

Second, there exists a location/mobility nexus. In one interesting recent study, Kearney and Levine (2016) document how at the state level increasing inequality affects mobility-related outcomes. Figure 2 illustrates how variance of state income is positively associated with the high school dropout rate. Note that the dropout rate speaks to the economic prospects of children from less affluent families. It also implies a statistical relationship between income inequality, educational inequality, and implicitly mobility, all consistent with the theoretical framework.

Any discussion of location and inequality must be deeply informed by the seminal work of Chetty, Hendren, Kline, and Saez (2014). This study also finds that high school dropout rates exhibit similar spatial heterogeneity, leading the authors to conclude that "much of the difference in intergenerational mobility across areas emerges when children are teenagers, well before they enter the labor market as adults" (1602). These authors also find a negative relationship between income segregation and mobility as well as between Gini coefficients and upward mobility. Both of these findings are consistent with our theoretical model. (See figure 3.)

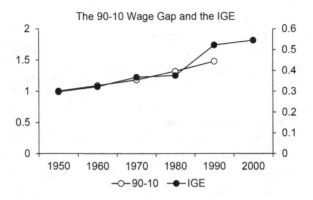

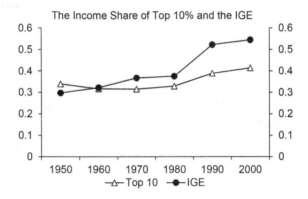

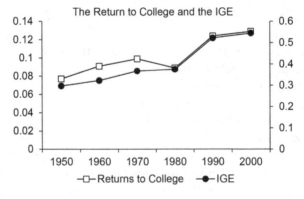

Fig. 1. Rising intergenerational elasticities

Source: Aaronson and Mazumder (2008).

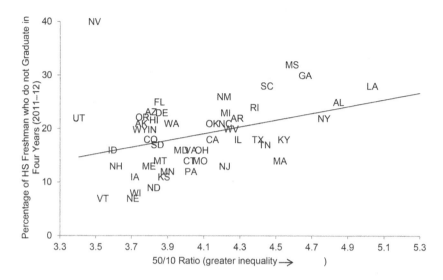

Fig. 2. Relationship between inequality and the rate of high school noncompletion

Source: Kearney and Levine (2016). The graduation data is from Stetser and Stillwell (2014).

Note: The 50/10 ratios are calculated by the authors. The District of Columbia is omitted from this figure because it is an extreme outlier on the X axis (50/10 ratio = 5.66).

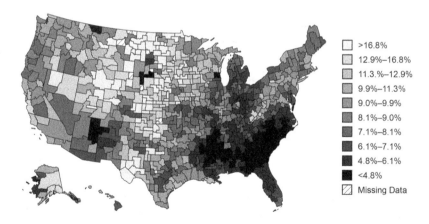

Fig. 3. Chetty, Hendren, Kline, and Saez (2014): Spatial heterogeneity in rates of relative mobility.

Notes: This map shows rates of upward mobility for children born in the 1980s for 741 metro and rural areas ("commuting zones") in the United States. Upward mobility is measured by the fraction of children who reach the top fifth of the national income distribution, conditional on having parents in the bottom fifth. Lighter colors represent areas with higher levels of upward mobility.

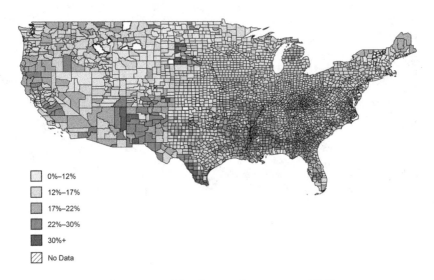

0%–12%

12%–17%

17%–22%

22%–30%

30%+

No Data

Fig. 4. Spatial distribution of poverty rates (2015)
Source: US Census Bureau.

C. Location and Segregation

Our third empirical claim is that there is much evidence of pervasive segregation across locations with respect to factors that matter, at a collective level, education and economic success. The empirical importance of social factors to individual outcomes will not entail anything about mobility unless the social factors lead to differences in community characteristics. We make this claim both with respect to income and to social interactions, the two mechanisms highlighted in our theoretical model.

D. Income

Evidence of economic segregation is straightforward to compile. One dimension of income segregation is the spatial concentration of poverty, which is illustrated in figure 4 at the country level. Similar segregation exists at lower levels of aggregation. Figure 5 reproduces poverty rates across Chicago neighborhoods. Another facet of this stylized fact is the increasing stratification of neighborhoods by income, with some attendant reduction in racial segregation. Reardon and Bischoff (2011) and Reardon, Townsend, and Fox (2015) provide evidence of this phenomenon. Some of these findings are summarized in figure 6 and table 7.

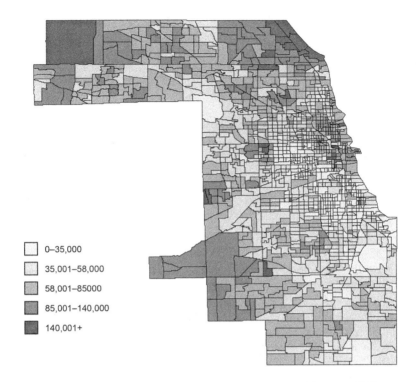

Fig. 5. Income segregation in Chicago (median household income 2007)
Source: US Census Bureau.

These changes matter because of the findings of how the mean and variance of income interact with the IGE coefficient. Leaving aside the variance of census-tract income (which did not prove to have a robust influence on the IGE), all these shifts, via the logic of equation (2), produce the Great Gatsby Curve.

E. Education-Related Mechanisms

Beyond spatial segregation by income, there is substantial spatial variation in factors that matter for education, which represents our fourth stylized fact. One mechanism that produces locational disparity is local public finance in education. Figure 7 illustrates these differences, while figure 8 illustrates these differences in the context of Texas. Of course, differences in per capita student expenditures do not necessarily entail differences in human capital formation, which is the natural object of interest. Many studies of financial resources and cognitive outcomes

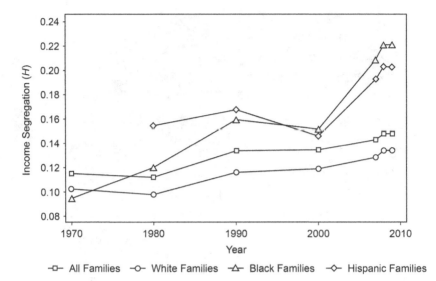

–□– All Families   –○– White Families   –△– Black Families   –◇– Hispanic Families

Fig. 6.   Trends in family income segregation by race

Source: Bischoff and Reardon (2014); authors' tabulations of data from the US Census (1970–2000) and American Community Survey (2005–2011).

Notes: Averages include all metropolitan areas with at least 500,000 residents in 2007 and at least 10,000 families of a given race in each year 1970–2009 (or each year 1980–2009 for Hispanics). This includes 116 metropolitan areas for the trends in total and white income segregation, 65 metropolitan areas for the trends in income segregation among black families, and 37 metropolitan areas for the trends in income segregation among Hispanic families. The averages presented here are unweighted. The trends are very similar if metropolitan areas are weighted by the population of the group of interest.

have failed to identify significant positive covariation (Hanushek 2006). That said, there is a general consensus that certain consequences of expenditures, for example classroom size, have nontrivial influences (see, e.g., Dustmann, Rajah, and van Soest 2003; Krueger 2003). We therefore conclude that this mechanism is important with the obvious caveat that the impact of expenditures depends on what educational inputs are purchased. We also note that the evidence of the effects of expenditures on future outcomes is stronger than it is for cognitive skills. Despite the evidence that the effect of small class size on test scores fades out by eighth grade (Krueger and Whitmore 2001), for example, Chetty et. al. (2011) find that kindergarten classroom quality affects adult earnings.

A distinct mechanism involves social interactions. Conceptually, these can range from primitive psychological tendencies to conform to others, to information-based influences of observed patterns of behaviors

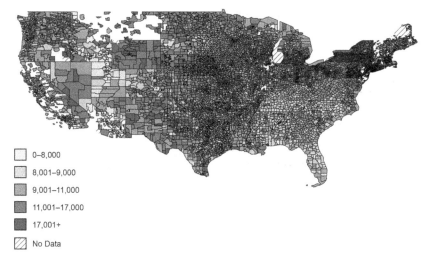

	0–8,000
	8,001–9,000
	9,001–11,000
	11,001–17,000
	17,001+
	No Data

Fig. 7. Spatial variation in per capita public school expenditure
Source: NCES.
Note: Per pupil expenditure in dollars (2014).

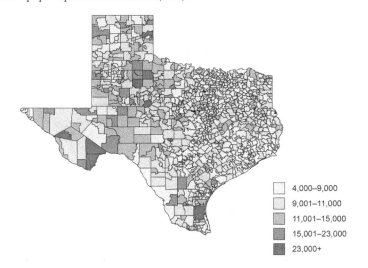

	4,000–9,000
	9,001–11,000
	11,001–15,000
	15,001–23,000
	23,000+

Fig. 8. Spending per student, by school district, Texas
Source: NCES.
Note: Per pupil expenditure in dollars (2014).

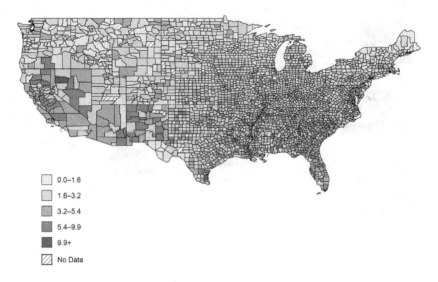

	0.0–1.6
	1.6–3.2
	3.2–5.4
	5.4–9.9
	9.9+
	No Data

Fig. 9.   Exposure to violent crime (violent crimes/1,000)
Source: Uniform Crime Reporting Program.
Note: Violent crimes per thousand people (2012).

and consequences on individual cost-benefit calculations, to more complex notions of culture. There are complex identification problems in the formal identification of social interaction effects because of the endogeneity of social structures such as neighborhoods inducing self-selection issues, as well as social structures inducing correlations in unobservables such as the one that occurs when a teacher influences a classroom (see Blume et al. [2011] for a discussion of identification problems and Durlauf [2004] and Topa and Zenou [2015] for surveys of the evidence on neighborhood effects).

Figure 9 gives one example of a location-determined social interaction effect: exposure to violent crime across the United States. Figure 10 gives a related figure for homicides in Chicago. Exposure to violence has been linked to stress among children and lower educational attainment (e.g., Burdick-Will 2013). One of the robust findings from the Moving to Opportunity demonstration was the positive effect on stress levels among individuals who moved to lower-poverty neighborhoods (e.g., Katz, Kling, and Liebman 2007; Gennetian et al. 2012).

What conclusions do we take from these broad stylized facts? First, there are reasons to believe that the intertemporal Gatsby Curve exists. Second, segregation patterns and associated disparities in social inter-

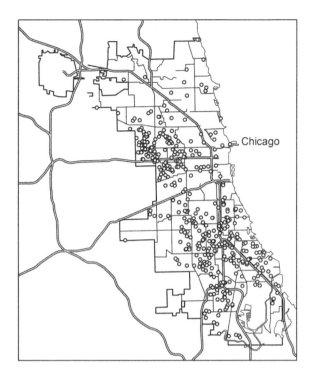

Fig. 10. Distribution of homicides in Chicago
Source: *Chicago Tribune* (accessed May 21, 2016).

actions explain its existence. These constitute the logic and implications of our theoretical framework.

V. Empirical Properties of the Intergenerational Elasticity of Income

In this section, we provide some additional stylized facts on patterns that relate intergenerational mobility to cross-sectional inequality by focusing on some of the statistical properties of the relationship between parent's and offspring's income. The results in this section both complement those provided in section IV and illustrate the statistical relationships that produce the Great Gatsby Curve.

A. Data

We use the parent-child pairs from the Panel Study of Income Dynamics (PSID) with census data on various state, county, and school district characteristics from GeoLytics' Neighborhood Change Database (NCDB). We use the PSID because it includes many birth cohorts, allowing for exploration of how mobility varies along with changes in inequality across time and space. While the PSID's core sample is composed both of the Survey Research Center (SRC) national sample and the Survey of Economic Opportunity (SEO) low-income oversample, given serious sampling irregularities in the SEO sample (Brown 1996) our analysis focuses only on the SRC sample.

In order to compare our results with the results obtained in other papers on the topic, we apply the same set of restrictions that were used in Bloome (2015). To be more specific, we focus on survey years between 1968 and 2007. Given the data, for each parent-child pair we examine permanent family income, defined as a five-year average of total family income. Permanent family income includes income from labor earnings, assets, and transfers such as AFDC accruing to heads, spouses, and other family members. We want to abstract from endogenous family-formation decisions. Thus, our family income measure is not adjusted for family size. We adjust for inflation using the CPI-U-RS. Given the intertemporal nature of our exercise, we focus on permanent family income when the child was 15 and 32 years old as our measures of parental income when the child was growing up and the child's adult income, respectively.

Inequality at the census tract and state level when children were 15 years old is taken from the Decennial Census via GeoLytics' NCDB. The NCDB only provides categorical income data (e.g., the number of families in a certain tract with incomes in the range $5,000–$9,999); therefore, we linearly interpolate the cumulative density function of income. As no maximum income is given for the top category, we assign the remainder of aggregate income (after following the assumption of a piecewise-linear CDF) to this category. When there is no remainder, we assume that all households in the highest category make the lower bound of that category. Inequality measures for intercensus years were linearly interpolated by state. At the family level, for some of the regressions estimated below, we included other control variables such as mother's education and race. To match tracts between census years, we used the tract crosswalk developed by the US2010 Project (see Logan, Xu, and Stults 2014).

Given these restrictions, at the end we have 1,725 parent-child pairs with the average parent income being $22,844 and the child's adulthood income averaging at $19,929 in 1977 dollars. When we include the mother's education level, the number of observations drops to 1,462.

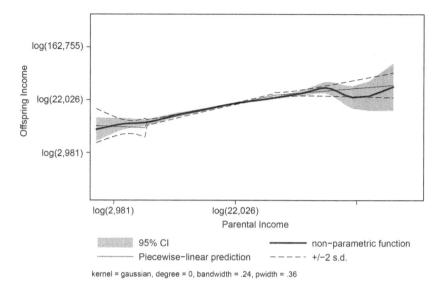

Fig. 11.   Nonparametric estimation of offspring's income given parental income

Note: The figure shows that expected offspring income is nonlinearly dependent on parental income. Offspring income conditional on parental income (solid line) was nonparametrically calculated using a kernel density estimator with a normal density weighting function. All income measures are deflated using CPI-U-RS and expressed in logs. Offspring income is an individual's family income averaged over ages 30–34. Parental income is individual's family income in adolescence (averaged over ages 13–17). The dotted line represents the piece-wise linear prediction of offspring's income given parental income.

On average, 27% of the mothers in the sample were high school dropouts with almost 89% of the sample being white.

B.   Nonlinearity in the Parent/Offspring Income Relationship

Our first exercise considers nonlinearities in the intergenerational mobility process. One explanation of the Gatsby Curve linking the variance of income to mobility is that the linear transmission process is misspecified, that is,

$$y_{io} = f(y_{ip}) + \varepsilon_{io}. \tag{13}$$

It is obvious that, depending on the shape of $f(\ )$, increases in the variance of y_{ip} can increase the variance of y_{io}.

To explore this possibility, we first construct a nonparametric estimate of $f(\ )$. Figure 11 presents the nonparametric function. Figure 12 (panels A and B) presents two ways of measuring local IGE values: $[f(Y_{ip})] \,/\, Y_{ip}$

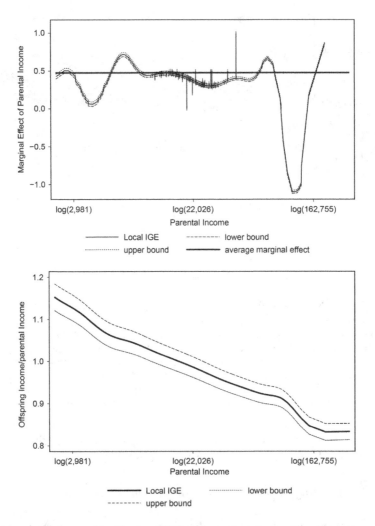

Fig. 12. Local IGE estimates for income

Notes: Panel A: The graph displays local IGE estimates—defined as the marginal effect of parental income at each income level—obtained from nonparametric estimation of off-spring's income conditional on parental income. The dependent variable is the marginal effect of parental income. Lower and upper bounds represent one standard deviation from the local IGE. All income measures are deflated using CPI-U-RS and expressed in logs. Offspring income is an individual's family income averaged over ages 30–34. Parental income is individual's family income in adolescence (averaged over ages 13–17). Panel B: The graph displays local IGE estimates—defined as the ratio of offspring income to parental income level—obtained from nonparametric estimation of offspring's income conditional on parental income. The dependent variable is the ratio of offspring income to parental income. Lower and upper bounds represent one standard deviation from the local IGE. All income measures are deflated using CPI-U-RS and expressed in logs. Off-spring income is an individual's family income averaged over ages 30–34. Parental income is individual's family income in adolescence (averaged over ages 13–17).

Table 1
IGE Regressions for Bottom 10%, Middle 80%, and Top 10% Relative to Nation (Family Income, Ages 30–34)

Variables	(1)	(2)
		6.527***
Low (parents' income below 10th percentile in country)		(1.976)
Mid (parents' income between 10th and 90th percentiles in country)		4.991***
		(0.395)
		8.215***
High (parents' income above 90th percentile in country)		(1.450)
Low * parents' income	0.438***	0.290
	(0.0471)	(0.234)
Mid * parents' income	0.458***	0.487***
	(0.0384)	(0.0399)
High * parents' income	0.456***	0.185
	(0.0353)	(0.134)
Constant	5.271***	
	(0.379)	
Observations	1,617	1,617
R-squared	0.172	0.996

Note: Robust standard errors in parentheses. All income in logs.
***Significant at the 1 percent level.
**Significant at the 5 percent level.
*Significant at the 10 percent level.

and $f'(y_{ip})$, respectively. As the point estimates and associated standard errors indicate, there is some evidence of nonlinearity, particularly in the tails of the income distribution. The decreasing $[f(Y_{ip})] / Y_{ip}$ values are consistent with Chetty, Hendren, Kline and Saez (2014). The derivatives of the transmission function $f'(y_{ip})$, while roughly consistent with the first measure, are too erratic to interpret. Together, we conclude that there is some, but not extremely strong evidence of nonlinearity in the sense of equation (2).

We complement these nonparametric results with some simple regressions that allow for differences in the linear IGE coefficients for parents in the tails of the income distribution as opposed to the middle. Table 1 splits the sample according to whether a family was in the bottom 10%, the middle 80%, or the top 10% of the national income distribution. Table 2 repeats this exercise when income-distribution location is calculated at the state level, while table 3 performs the same exercise at the census-tract level. For each split, we both consider the case where all heterogeneity is consigned to the IGE as well as the case where heterogeneity is allowed in the intercept. The latter heterogeneity is of interest since it speaks to differential growth rates.

Table 2
IGE Regressions for Bottom 10%, Middle 80%, and Top 10% Relative to State (Family Income, Ages 30–34)

Variables	(1)	(2)
Low (parents' income below 10th percentile in state)		6.358***
		(1.831)
Mid (parents' income between 10th and 90th		4.528***
percentiles in state)		(0.395)
High (parents' income above 90th percentile in state)		6.674***
		(1.629)
Low * parents' income	0.518***	0.332
	(0.0474)	(0.217)
Mid * parents' income	0.509***	0.534***
	(0.0384)	(0.0400)
High * parents' income	0.499***	0.323**
	(0.0353)	(0.150)
Constant	4.772***	
	(0.380)	
Observations	1,617	1,617
R-squared	0.172	0.996

Note: Robust standard errors in parentheses. All income in logs.
***Significant at the 1 percent level.
**Significant at the 5 percent level.
*Significant at the 10 percent level.

The national, state, and census-tract level results are similar. In each case, there is relatively little heterogeneity in the IGE coefficients, while there is heterogeneity in the intercepts, with the bottom and top 10% growing more rapidly than the middle 80%. While the precision of the intercept estimates does not allow for very strong statements, these results are suggestive of decoupling of the upper tail of the type that is consistent with the admittedly extreme case of complete immobility that appears as a theoretical possibility. Note that the relatively higher growth of the lower 10% than the middle 80% is evidence of a convergence mechanism that lies outside the linear structure of (1), but nevertheless can generate the Gatsby Curve like behavior.

C. Neighborhood Income and the IGE Levels

Our second exercise considers how the IGE may depend on the mean and variance of neighborhood income. We focus on parametric models that are variations of

Table 3
IGE Regressions for Bottom 10%, Middle 80%, and Top 10% Relative to Census Tract
(Family Income, Ages 30–34)

Variables	(1)	(2)
Low (parents' income below 10th percentile in tract)		5.587***
		(0.532)
Mid (parents' income between 10th and 90th percentiles in tract)		4.826***
		(0.422)
High (parents' income above 90th percentile in tract)		6.067***
		(1.144)
Low * parents' income	0.455***	0.417***
	(0.0334)	(0.0546)
Mid * parents' income	0.467***	0.507***
	(0.0327)	(0.0423)
High * parents' income	0.459***	0.380***
	(0.0307)	(0.106)
Constant	5.216***	
	(0.326)	
Observations	1,617	1,617
R-squared	0.177	0.996

Note: Robust standard errors in parentheses. All income in logs.
***Significant at the 1 percent level.
**Significant at the 5 percent level.
*Significant at the 10 percent level.

$$y_{io} = \alpha + \beta y_{ip} + \gamma_1 \bar{y}_{ig(p)} + \gamma_2 y_{ip}\bar{y}_{ig(p)}$$
$$+ \gamma_3 ineq(y_{ig(p)}) + \gamma_4 y_{ip}ineq(y_{ig(p)}) + \varepsilon_{io}.$$

(14)

The parameters γ_1 and γ_2 capture average group income effects, while γ_3 and γ_4 capture inequality effects. Table 4 presents results where parental income is interacted with census-tract income. Table 5 conducts the same exercise at the state level. Bloome (2015) estimates analogous models for variance at the state level. Table 6 combines census-tract and state variables. We report results using the variance of log income. Models using the Gini coefficient to measure inequality produce extremely similar results.

Table 4, while revealing some fragility in coefficient estimates across specifications, does allow some conclusions to be discerned. There is evidence that census-tract income increases expected offspring income additively (column [2]) and via interaction with parental income (column [3]). Column (4) fails to identify statistically significant effects when both types of average income effects are included, presumably due to collinearity. In contrast, statistically significant evidence is found that census-tract

Table 4
IGE and Interactions with Census-Tract Income Distribution (Family Income, Ages 30–34)

Variables	(1)	(2)	(3)	(4)	(5)	(6)
Family income, ages 13–17	0.471*** (0.0294)	0.361*** (0.0389)	0.363*** (0.0387)	0.363*** (0.0390)	0.450*** (0.0354)	0.370*** (0.0404)
Average income in tract		0.330*** (0.0672)		0.0817 (0.731)		0.571 (0.968)
Income variance in tract		0.0438 (0.0950)			1.081 (1.176)	1.296 (1.504)
Family income * tract avg.			0.0326*** (0.00658)	0.0235 (0.0729)		−0.0244 (0.0953)
Family income * tract var.			0.00266 (0.00959)		−0.134 (0.121)	−0.128 (0.152)
Constant	5.136*** (0.293)	6.261*** (0.389)	6.240*** (0.388)	6.248*** (0.391)	5.374*** (0.356)	6.173*** (0.405)
Observations	1,617	1,153	1,153	1,153	1,153	1,153
R-squared	0.170	0.179	0.179	0.179	0.163	0.180

Notes: For tables 4, 5, and 6: All income deflated using CPI-U-RS. Tract measures are normalized to have zero mean. The dependent variable in the linear regression results of tables 4–6 is an individual's family income averaged over ages 30–34; individual's family income in adolescence is averaged over ages 13–17. Robust standard errors in parentheses.
***Significant at the 1 percent level.
**Significant at the 5 percent level.
*Significant at the 10 percent level.

inequality affects offspring income. With respect to our model, we expected the coefficient on the interaction of family income and variance log income to be negative. This is consistent with the negative signs on family income × log income in columns (5) and (6). Large standard errors make results of these specifications disappointing in terms of corroboration of our ideas. But the positive effect of average census-tract income is supportive of the claim that census-tract membership matters.

The state-level results in table 5 provide clearer evidence that average state income helps predict offspring income. Again, the results for the variance of log income and the Gini coefficient are very similar. Columns (2), (4), and (6) all contain positive and statistically significant estimates of an additive state average effect. Interactions of family income with average state income, which appear in specifications for columns (3), (4), and (6), are statistically significant but exhibit fragile signs as the coefficient in (2) is positive while negative for the others. Income variance is positive and significant in (5), while negative and insignificant in specification (6). This fragility can be understood as a derivative of

Table 5
IGEs and Interaction with State Income Distribution (Family Income, Ages 30–34)

Variables	(1)	(2)	(3)	(4)	(5)	(6)
Family income,	0.471***	0.434***	0.436***	0.426***	0.449***	0.414***
ages 13–17	(0.0294)	(0.0294)	(0.0294)	(0.0287)	(0.0283)	(0.0284)
Average income		0.788***		6.962***		4.871**
in state		(0.145)		(2.132)		(2.462)
Income variance		0.644***			−9.647***	−5.772
in state		(0.177)			(3.189)	(3.625)
Family income *			0.0773***	−0.654***		−0.416*
state avg.			(0.0146)	(0.215)		(0.248)
Family income *			0.0675***		1.002***	0.656*
state var.			(0.0177)		(0.320)	(0.364)
Constant	5.136***	5.502***	5.483***	5.602***	5.363***	5.717***
	(0.293)	(0.292)	(0.293)	(0.285)	(0.282)	(0.282)
Observations	1,617	1,611	1,611	1,611	1,611	1,611
R-squared	0.170	0.184	0.183	0.183	0.178	0.193

Note: Robust standard errors in parentheses. All income in logs; state measures normalized to have zero mean.
***Significant at the 1 percent level.
**Significant at the 5 percent level.
*Significant at the 10 percent level.

collinearity. Finally, income variance, when interacted with family income, affects the IGE positively. This finding is consistent with the logic of our theoretical ideas, which suggests that states with higher income variance will exhibit greater segregation at lower levels.

We complete this discussion by considering regressions that allow for both census-tract and state effects. These appear in table 6. Column (1), which considers census-tract and state-income averages, finds relatively stronger evidence that average census-tract income matters as compared to state income. Column (2) focuses on census-tract and state variances. No variables are statistically significant in isolation, and there is a substantial reduction in goodness of fit relative to the model with average incomes. Column (4) focuses on interactions of means and variances with parental income. Here, average census-tract and state-income interactions are positive and statistically significant as is state-variance interaction. The insignificance of the interactions of census-tract variance and income echoes earlier results. When all variables are combined, average state income survives as being statistically significant.

In summary, with respect to the general ideas of our theoretical framework, we would expect census-tract and state means to enhance

Table 6
IGEs and Census-Tract and State Income Distributions (Family Income, Ages 30–34)

Variables	(1)	(2)	(3)	(4)
Family income,	0.361***	0.442***	0.362***	0.366***
ages 13–17	(0.0391)	(0.0355)	(0.0384)	(0.0407)
Family income *	0.0942		0.0282***	0.0334
tract average	(0.0824)		(0.00604)	(0.104)
Family income *	−0.519*		0.0492***	−0.504
state average	(0.270)		(0.0186)	(0.313)
Average income	−0.633			−0.0627
in tract	(0.826)			(1.050)
Average income	5.329**			5.507*
in state	(2.697)			(3.130)
Family income *		−0.197		−0.116
tract variance		(0.129)		(0.158)
Family income *		0.493	0.0768***	0.0664
state variance		(0.315)	(0.0198)	(0.377)
Income variance		1.638		1.073
in tract		(1.264)		(1.564)
Income variance		−4.357		0.143
in state		(3.155)		(3.777)
Constant	6.257***	5.455***	6.238***	6.208***
	(0.392)	(0.358)	(0.385)	(0.409)
Observations	1,153	1,153	1,153	1,153
R-squared	0.183	0.171	0.190	0.193

Notes: Robust standard errors in parentheses. All income in logs; measures normalized
to have zero mean.
***Significant at the 1 percent level.
**Significant at the 5 percent level.
*Significant at the 10 percent level.

offspring income as well as interact positively with family income. We
would predict the variance of census-tract income to reduce the family
IGE because of increased local integration and state variance to increase
the IGE because of the potential for increased segregation. Thus these
reduced-form findings are qualitatively consistent with our priors, although the lack of robustness to census-tract variance/mobility link
is disappointing, at least with reference to our theoretical model. (See
table 7.)

D. Reduced-Form Great Gatsby Curves

Our final exercises construct some Gatsby Curves from our statistical
models. Figure 13 reports the Great Gatsby Curves that are implied by

Table 7
Increasing Segregation over Time

	1970	1980	1990	2000
Variance of real family income	1.42E8	3.46E8	1.37E9	1.67E9
Variance of log real family income	0.769	0.783	0.907	0.903
Neighborhood sorting index (tract, $ income)	0.378	0.481	0.569	0.756
Neighborhood sorting index (state, $ income)	0.093	0.097	0.173	0.190
Neighborhood sorting index (tract, log income)	0.417	0.429	0.471	0.444
Neighborhood sorting index (state, log income)	0.135	0.101	0.163	0.127
Reardon's H	0.115	0.112	0.134	0.135

Source: Census data from GeoLytics' NCDB, except for Reardon's H (Bischoff and Reardon 2014); the number of metropolitan areas included in the calculations is 117. Reardon's H in the table above is another measure of income segregation used in the literature. To be more specific, it is a rank-order information theory index that compares the variation in family incomes within census tracts to the variation in family incomes in the metropolitan area. It can range from a theoretical minimum of 0 (no segregation) to a theoretical maximum of 1 (total segregation). Even though the magnitude of H does not have a particularly intuitive meaning, differences in H over time are not influenced by the level of income inequality and thus it is a clean measure of the degree of sorting. The interested reader is referred to Bischoff and Reardon (2014) for more details.

equation (13). To generate them, we construct counterfactual values of y_{io} given changes in the variance of y_{io} as produced by scaling the historical y_{io} values. For each counterfactual parental income series, we calculate the implied value of β if (1) is the linear model used to analyze the parent-offspring income relationship.

As indicated by figure 13, the nonparametric family income model does not generate a relationship between inequality and mobility. This is not consistent with the Gatsby Curve idea: greater variance in parental income is associated with higher mobility. Some insight into the reasons for this may be seen in figure 12 (panels A and B). The nonlinearities in our sample suggest high means and lower local IGE coefficients for families in the tails of the income distribution than in the middle. Hence increased spread of parental incomes pushes more families into the lower IGE regions.

Figure 14 reports the implied Gatsby Curve associated with our parametric nonlinear model that is reported in table 1. The unusual shape reflects the fact that spreading income distribution moves families away from the middle linear IGE model toward the models for the upper and lower tails.

For our purposes, there is one important message from figures 13 and 14: nonlinearities in family income dynamics do not provide good

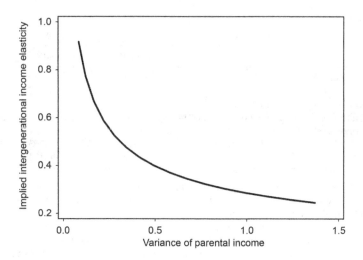

Fig. 13. Great Gatsby Curve implied by nonparametric specification under scaling of parental income.

Notes: The graph depicts how the IGE—the marginal effect of parental income on off-spring's income—responds to scaling of parental income. The initial parental income distribution corresponds to the parental income in the PSID sample. The graph was constructed as follows. We, first, nonparametrically estimated offspring's income given parental income and saved residuals from the estimation. Then for each scaling of log of parental income—that also scaled variance of parental income (horizontal axis)—offspring income is predicted using the nonparametric estimation and residuals from the first step. Afterward, predicted offspring income is regressed on scaled parental income; the regression coefficients—the implied IGEs—are plotted. All income measures are deflated using CPI-U-RS and expressed in logs. Offspring income is an individual's family income averaged over ages 30–34. Parental income is individual's family income in adolescence (averaged over ages 13–17).

reasons to think an intertemporal Great Gatsby Curve exists for the United States.

Our second set of reduced-form Gatsby Curves is generated by parametric models we constructed that included census-tract and state-income distribution characteristics. Since our theoretical mechanism for the Gatsby Curve involves the link between the variance of income and levels of segregation, we need to model the relationship between individual income and census-tract and state analogs. We take two approaches. First, we scale the census-tract, state, and individual incomes proportionately. Second, we explicitly consider segregation. We do so by measuring segregation via the neighborhood sorting index (NSI) due to Jargowsky (1996), defined as

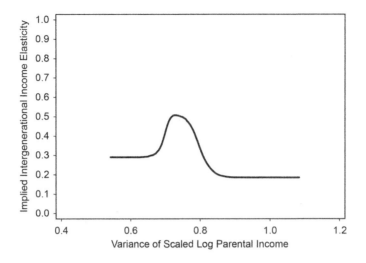

Fig. 14. Great Gatsby Curve implied by parametric specification including parents' percentile in nation.

Notes: This graph depicts how the IGE—the marginal effect of parental income on offspring's income—responds to scaling of parental income. For each scaling of log parental income (from –50% to +100%), offspring incomes are predicted using the estimated coefficients from table 1, specification (2). Then predicted offspring income is regressed on scaled parental income; the regression coefficients are plotted. The horizontal axis displays the variance of the scaled log parental incomes. All income measures are deflated using CPI-U-RS and expressed in logs. Offspring income is an individual's family income averaged over ages 30–34. Parental income is individual's family income in adolescence (averaged over ages 13–17).

$$NSI = \sqrt{\frac{\mathrm{var}(\bar{y}_n)}{\mathrm{var}(y_i)}}$$

where $\mathrm{var}(\bar{y}_n)$ is the variance of average incomes across the neighborhoods under study (census tract or state) and $\mathrm{var}(y_i)$ is the variance of incomes in the population. Using the decomposition

$$y_i = \bar{y}_n + \eta_i$$

and assuming a linear relationship

$$NSI = m \times \mathrm{stdev}(y_i) + \kappa_i$$

we trace out the joint evolution of y_i and $\bar{y}_n$ for different mean preserving changes in the variance of $\mathrm{var}(y_i)$ and use these with our estimated equations to construct implied Gatsby Curves.[11] Figures 15–16 present the Gatsby Curves for census-tract variables, figures 17–18 for state-level variables, while figures 19 and 20 combine both census-tract and state

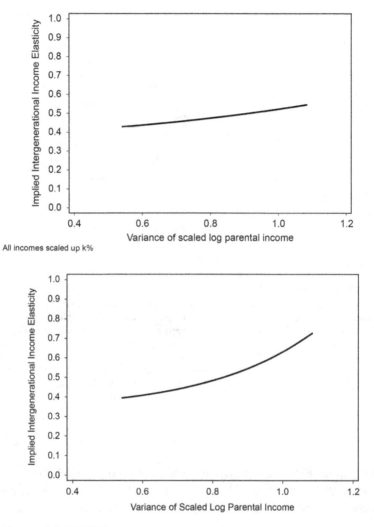

All incomes scaled up k%

Incomes scaled up k%, NSI linear in k

Fig. 15. Great Gatsby Curve implied by parametric specification including tract average, under scaling of parental income.

Notes: This graph depicts how the IGE—the marginal effect of parental income on offspring's income—responds to scaling of parental income. For each scaling of log parental income by k (from –50% to +100%), offspring incomes are predicted using the estimated coefficients from table 4, specification (4). Then predicted offspring income is regressed on scaled parental income; the regression coefficients are plotted. The horizontal axis displays the variance of the scaled log parental incomes. All income measures are deflated using CPI-U-RS and expressed in logs. Offspring income is an individual's family income averaged over ages 30–34. Parental income is individual's family income in adolescence (averaged over ages 13–17).

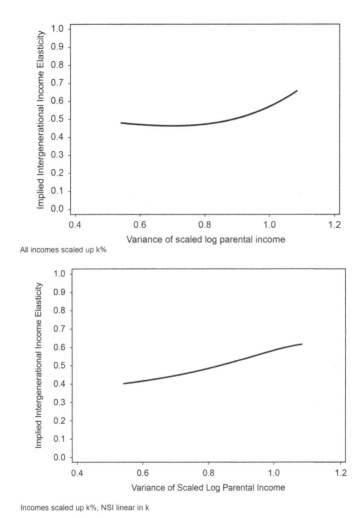

All incomes scaled up k%

Incomes scaled up k%, NSI linear in k

Fig. 16. Great Gatsby Curve implied by parametric specification including tract average and variance, under scaling of parental income.

Notes: This graph depicts how the IGE—the marginal effect of parental income on offspring's income—responds to scaling of parental income. For each scaling of log parental income by k (from –50% to +100%), offspring incomes are predicted using the estimated coefficients from table 4, specification (6). Then predicted offspring income is regressed on scaled parental income; the regression coefficients are plotted. The horizontal axis displays the variance of the scaled log parental incomes. All income measures are deflated using CPI-U-RS and expressed in logs. Offspring income is an individual's family income averaged over ages 30–34. Parental income is individual's family income in adolescence (averaged over ages 13–17).

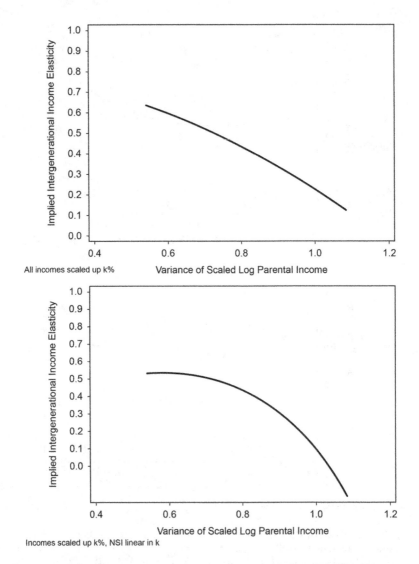

Fig. 17. Great Gatsby Curve implied by parametric specification including state average, under scaling of parental income.

Notes: This graph depicts how the IGE—the marginal effect of parental income on offspring's income—responds to scaling of parental income. For each scaling of log parental income by k (from −50% to +100%), offspring incomes are predicted using the estimated coefficients from table 5, specification (4). Then predicted offspring income is regressed on scaled parental income; the regression coefficients are plotted. The horizontal axis displays the variance of the scaled log parental incomes. All income measures are deflated using CPI-U-RS and expressed in logs. Offspring income is an individual's family income averaged over ages 30–34. Parental income is individual's family income in adolescence (averaged over ages 13–17).

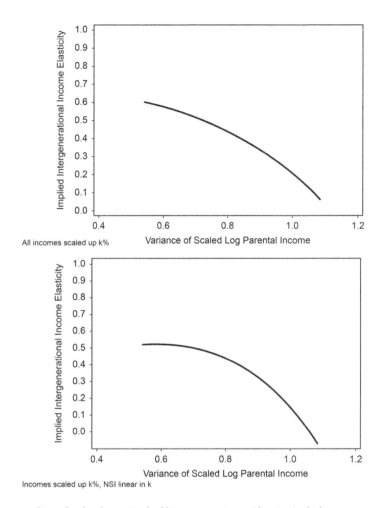

Fig. 18. Great Gatsby Curve implied by parametric specification including state average and variance, under scaling of parental income.

Notes: This graph depicts how the IGE—the marginal effect of parental income on offspring's income—responds to scaling of parental income. For each scaling of log parental income by k (from –50% to +100%), offspring incomes are predicted using the estimated coefficients from table 5, specification (6). Then predicted offspring income is regressed on scaled parental income; the regression coefficients are plotted. The horizontal axis displays the variance of the scaled log parental incomes. All income measures are deflated using CPI-U-RS and expressed in logs. Offspring income is an individual's family income averaged over ages 30–34. Parental income is individual's family income in adolescence (averaged over ages 13–17).

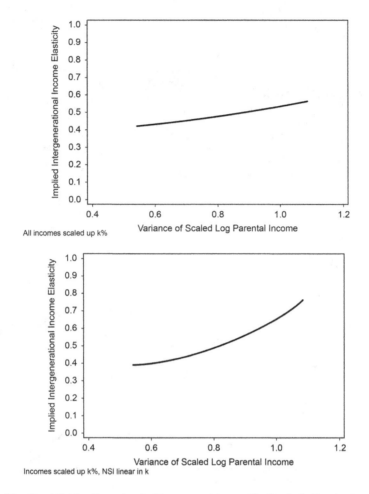

Fig. 19. Great Gatsby Curve implied by parametric specification including tract and state average, under scaling of parental income.

Notes: The graph depicts how the IGE—the marginal effect of parental income on off-spring's income—responds to scaling of parental income. This figure assumes that off-spring income depends linearly on parental income, average tract and state income, and the interaction of parental income with these variables. For each scaling of log parental income by k (from –50% to +100%), offspring incomes are predicted using the estimated coefficients from table 6, specification (1). Then predicted offspring income is regressed on scaled parental income; the regression coefficients are plotted. The horizontal axis displays the variance of the scaled log parental incomes. All income measures are deflated using CPI-U-RS and expressed in logs. Offspring income is an individual's family income averaged over ages 30–34. Parental income is individual's family income in adolescence (averaged over ages 13–17).

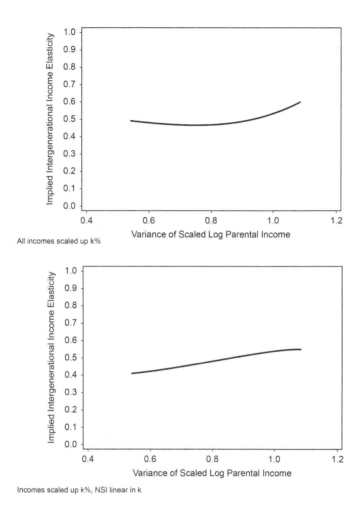

All incomes scaled up k%

Incomes scaled up k%, NSI linear in k

Fig. 20. Great Gatsby Curve implied by parametric specification including tract and state average and variance, under scaling of parental income.

Notes: The graph depicts how the IGE—the marginal effect of parental income on offspring's income—responds to scaling of parental income. This figure assumes that offspring income depends linearly on parental income, average and variance of tract and state income, and the interaction of parental income with these variables. For each scaling of log parental income by k (from –50% to +100%), offspring incomes are predicted using the estimated coefficients from table 6, specification (4). Then predicted offspring income is regressed on scaled parental income; the regression coefficients are plotted. The horizontal axis displays the variance of the scaled log parental incomes. All income measures are deflated using CPI-U-RS and expressed in logs. Offspring income is an individual's family income averaged over ages 30–34. Parental income is individual's family income in adolescence (averaged over ages 13–17).

variables. We consider cases where the results are based on means, as well as the ones where results are based both on means and variances. We choose representative specifications from our tables; results are qualitatively similar for alternative choices.

A consistent picture emerges from these calculations, for both ways of handling the relationship between increases in individual income variation and census-tract and state incomes. At the census-tract level, a Gatsby Curve is implied by our parametric regressions. For state-level variables, a large negative slope occurs. Hence the state-level interactions produce the opposite phenomena from the Gatsby Curve property per se. When census-tract and state variables are combined, a gently sloped positive relationship between income inequality and mobility reemerges. With respect to our two approaches, changes in the NSI produce strong Gatsby effects at the census-tract level while the proportional scaling approach is modest.

We conclude from these exercises that there is some evidence of the Gatsby Curve-like phenomena from the parametric IGE regressions with neighborhood effects. Perhaps unsurprisingly, a necessary condition for stronger evidence is a greater attention to the mechanisms underlying the social interactions/Gatsby relationship. And as argued in Section IV, there is evidence to think the mechanisms that underlie our theoretical model matter in ways that create Gatsby-like outcomes. We thus move from these reduced-form exercises to see whether a calibrated structural model can provide additional insights.

VI. Linking Theory and Empirics: A Calibrated Model

In this section, we integrate the theoretical ideas of Sections II and III with the various facts highlighted in Sections IV and V via a model calibration exercise. The model is a version of Kotera and Seshadri (2017) extended to incorporate heterogeneity at the school-district level.

A. Environment

Households live for four periods, one as an offspring and three as an adult. The first period is 18 years and the next three periods are 6 years each. We keep track of each offspring from birth until the age of 36. Each household i in a school district j maximizes utility given by

$$u(c_{j1}^i) + \theta V(a_j^i, h_{j2}^i, g_j^i) \tag{15}$$

where $u(c_{j1}^i)$ is the utility from consumption c_j^i, $V(a_j^i, h_{j2}^i, g_j^i)$ is the lifetime utility of the offspring at the beginning of the second period, and θ is a measure of parental altruism; g_j^i is a transfer from a parent to his off-spring who can use these resources in the second period. Assume that $g_j^i \geq 0$ so that an offspring cannot be responsible for debts undertaken by his parents on his behalf.

A central feature of the model is the human capital production function—an offspring's human capital depends on his own ability, public and private inputs, parent's human capital, and the average human capital in the neighborhood. Thus, the offspring's human capital varies at the school-district level. Specifically, for household i's offspring in school district j, the stock of offspring's human capital at the beginning of the second period, h_{j2}^i, is given by

$$h_{j2}^i = a_j^i(x_{j1}^i + \bar{x}_j)^{\alpha_1}(h_{j0}^i)^{\alpha_2}(h_j)^{\alpha_3} \qquad (16)$$

where a_j^i is the learning ability, $\bar{x}_j$ represents public inputs, h_{j0}^i is parent's human capital, and h_j is the average parental human capital in a school district, that is, $h_j = (1 / n)\Sigma_i h_{j0}^i$. We assume that $\alpha_1 < 1$, $\alpha_2 < 1$, and $\alpha_3 < 1$. Additionally, $\bar{x}_j$ is collected using local tax rates on income, so $\bar{x}_j = (1 / n)\Sigma_i y_j^i$. We take these rates as given.

An offspring becomes independent at the beginning of the second period. He makes decisions on human capital accumulation and consumption in the second, third, and fourth periods ($\{c_{j2}^i, c_{j3}^i, c_{j4}^i\}$) to maximize his utility

$$V(a_j^i, h_{j2}^i, g_j^i) = \max_{\{c_{j2}^i, c_{j3}^i, c_{j4}^i, g_j^i, n_{j2}^i, n_{j3}^i, x_{j1}^i\}} u(c_{j2}^i) + \beta u(c_{j3}^i) + \beta^2 u(c_{j4}^i) \qquad (17)$$

subject to the budget constraint

$$c_{j2}^i + \frac{c_{j3}^i}{1 + r} + \frac{c_{j4}^i}{(1 + r)^2} = wh_{j2}^i(1 - n_{j2}^i) + \frac{wh_{j3}^i(1 - n_{j3}^i)}{1 + r} + \frac{wh_{j4}^i}{(1 + r)^2} + g_j^i \qquad (18)$$

and the human capital production functions (19)

$$h_{j3}^i = a_j^i(n_{j2}^i h_{j2}^i)^{\gamma_1} + h_{j2}^i$$

$$h_{j4}^i = a_j^i(n_{j3}^i h_{j3}^i)^{\gamma_1} + h_{j3}^i \qquad (19)$$

where β is the discount factor, r is the interest rate, w is the rental rate of human capital, and n_{j2}^i and n_{j3}^i are the time spent on human capital accumulation in the second period. Equation (19) is a standard Ben-Porath human capital accumulation model. It allows individuals to accumulate human capital in the second period in case they received too little education in the first period, either due to the state of birth or by virtue of having poor parents. This extra margin of adjustment leads to a more flexible relationship between first-period investments and earnings at later ages, which we believe is important in understanding the data. With the last three periods, we can relate n^i_{j2} to college education, and wh^i_{j3} and wh^i_{j4} to earnings at ages 24–30 and 30–36, respectively. There are no borrowing constraints in the last three periods.

For simplicity, we assume there is a common wage rate w for all school districts in all states. This will be the case if there is no moving cost so that any spatial difference in the wage rate will be eliminated by migration. Given the large fraction of workers who do not live in their state of birth, we consider this simplification a useful benchmark.

B.   Model Solution

The solution to the model in the last three periods is straightforward. In particular, individuals invest to maximize lifetime income and then allocate consumption across the two periods to maximize discounted utility. Next, the maximization problem in the first period can be written as

$$\max_{c^i_{j1}, x^i_{j1}, g^i_j} u(c^i_{j1}) + \theta V(a^i_j, h^i_{j2}, g^i_j) \tag{20}$$

subject to equation (15), the budget constraint

$$c^i_{j1} + x^i_{j1} + g^i_j = (1 - \tau)y^i_j \tag{21}$$

and a nonnegativity condition $g^i_j \geq 0$.

The first-order conditions for x^i_{j1} and g^i_j are given by

$$\theta V_{h^i_{j2}}(a^i_j, h^i_{j2}, g^i_j)a^i_j\alpha_1(x^i_{j1} + \bar{x}_j)^{\alpha_1-1}(h^i_j)^{\alpha_2}(h_j)^{\alpha_3} = u(c^i_{ji}) \tag{22}$$

and

$$\theta V_{g^i_j}(a^i_j, h^i_{j2}, g^i_j) \leq u(c^i_{ji}) \tag{23}$$

where $V_{h^i_{j2}}(a^i_j, h^i_{j2}, g^i_j)$ and $V_{g^i_j}(a^i_j, h^i_{j2}, g^i_j)$ are the derivatives of $V(a^i_j, h^i_{j2}, g^i_j)$ with respect to h^i_{j2} and g^i_j, respectively, and $u'(c^i_{j1})$ denotes the derivative of $u(c^i_{j1})$ with respect to c^i_{j1}. The first condition implies that private investment would equate the marginal benefits for offspring in the last two periods with the marginal costs incurred by parents in the first period. The second condition holds with equality if $g^i_j > 0$. In this case, the value of a dollar to the parent is the same regardless of whether it is consumed or left to the offspring. Otherwise, if the value of a dollar to the parent is larger when it is consumed, even if $g_j^i = 0$, the inequality in the third condition would be strict.

C. Calibration

Fixed Parameters

We assume a standard CRRA utility function over consumption:

$$u(c) = \frac{c^{1-\alpha}}{1 - \alpha}$$

and

$$V(a_{j1}^i, h_{j2}^i, g_j^i) = \frac{(c_{j2}^i)^{1-\alpha}}{1 - \alpha} + \beta \frac{(c_{j3}^i)^{1-\alpha}}{1 - \alpha} + \beta^2 \frac{(c_{j4}^i)^{1-\alpha}}{1 - \alpha}.$$

We set $\alpha = 2$, $\beta = 0.96^6$, $r = (1 + 0.04)^6 - 1$, where 6 is the number of years in each of the last three periods of our model.

To calibrate the wage rate w, we assume that parental income in school district j is given by

$$y_j = w_j \exp(\varphi \times school_j).$$

In this equation, parental income y_j is decomposed into two components: wage rate w_j and human capital h_{j0}. Since data on y_j and $school_j$ at the school-district level are available from the data, we can pin down w_j if we know h_{j0}. As we do not model parental human capital accumulation, we assume h_{j0} is a function of parental schooling $school_j$ with a coefficient Φ, where $school_j$ is parent's schooling level. We set the return to schooling $\Phi = 0.1$. We calibrate w_j to match y_j. Then, we average them to obtain w appeared in the last three periods. The value of w here is 0.1707.

Lastly, we calibrate τ_j to match public-school spending per pupil in a school district. This data is available from the US Census Bureau. Due to the data availability, we use public-school spending per pupil and average income in 1990 to calibrate τ_j.

Table 8 summarizes the fixed parameters of our model.

Parameters to Be Estimated

We assume that parental human capital h_{j0}^i and an offspring's learning ability a_j^i follow a joint log normal distribution at the national level:

Table 8
Fixed Parameters in the Calibration Exercise

Description	Parameter	Value
CRRA coefficient	α	2.0
Discount factor	β	0.96^6
Return to schooling	ϕ	0.1
Average wage rate in the United States	w	0.1707
Interest rate	r	$(1 + 0.04)^6 - 1$

$$\begin{pmatrix} \log h^i_{j0} \\ \log a_j \end{pmatrix} \sim N \begin{pmatrix} \mu_{h^i_{j0}} & \sigma^2_{h^i_{j0}} & \rho\sigma_{h^i_{j0}}\sigma_{a_j} \\ \mu_{a_j} & \rho\sigma_{h^i_{j0}}\sigma_{a_j} & \sigma^2_{a_j} \end{pmatrix}. \tag{24}$$

Given $school^i_j$ and Φ, parental human capital $h^i_{j0} = \exp(\phi \times school^i_j)$ is available for each school district j. Additionally, the mean ($\mu_{h_{j0}}$) and standard deviation ($\sigma_{h_{j0}}$) of initial human capital at the national level can be calculated. This allows us to focus on the conditional distribution of a^i_j, namely

$$\log a^i_j \mid \log h^i_{j0} \sim N(\mu_{h^i_{j0}} + \rho_{h^i_{j0}a^i_j} \frac{\sigma_{a^i_j}}{\sigma_{h^i_{j0}}} (\log h^i_{j0} - \mu_{h^i_{j0}}), \sigma^2_{a_j}(1 - \rho^2_{h^i_ja^i_j})). \tag{25}$$

In addition to state-specific parameters $\{\mu_{a_j}, \sigma_{a_j}, \rho_{h_{j0}a_j}\}$ that allow the model to match the variation in public-school spending and income across states, we also need to estimate five parameters $\{\alpha^1, \alpha^2, \alpha^3, \eta^1, \theta\}$ that are common to all states; θ is the degree of parental altruism and the rest are parameters governing human capital accumulation in the final three periods. The novel part is to estimate returns to the neighborhood effects, α^3.

Estimation Strategy

We estimate parameters using the Method of Simulated Moments. Let Θ_s be the set of parameters to be estimated. Using data moments M_s, we obtain estimated

$$\hat{\Theta}_s = \arg\min_{\Theta_s}[M_s(\Theta_s) - M_s]'W_s[M_s(\Theta_s) - M_s]'$$

where $M_s(\Theta_s)$ stands for the simulated model moments, and W_s is a weighting matrix. In practice, we use the identity matrix as the weighting matrix W_s.

We use moments largely for child income. This data is available from the PSID. The nice feature of this data is that we are able to use average child income both between 24 and 28 (corresponding to the third period in our model) and between 30 and 34 (corresponding to the fourth period). We exploit them to identify the parameters.

We use average child income in the two periods. The corresponding model moments are $E(wh^i_{j3})$ and $E(wh^i_{j4})$. These moments can identify θ and μ_{a_j}. In particular, μ_{a_j} is sensitive to change in income from the third period to the fourth period because a_j predominantly determines h^i_{j4} given h^i_{j3} in our model. Next, we employ the change in child income between the two periods conditional on parent-schooling level. Here, we create two groups of school districts categorized by parent-schooling level: Group 1 and Group 2 include school districts with parent-schooling levels between 11 and 12 and between 12 and 13, respectively. The corresponding model moments are $E(wh^i_{j4}|Group1)$ / $E(wh^i_{j3}|Group1)$, and $E(wh^i_{j4}|Group2)$ / $E(wh^i_{j3}|Group2)$. These two moments allow us to identify $\{\sigma_{a_j}, \rho_{h_{j0}a_j}\}$. Furthermore, we adopt the three coefficients of variation between 30 and 34. The first one is the overall one and the rest are conditional on parent-schooling level. In the model, we simply compute coefficient of variation of wh^i_{j4}. These moments allow for identification of the return to parent human capital, namely α_2, the return to average human capital in a school district, α_3, and the return to inputs, α_1. Adopting the coefficient of variation conditional on schooling level is effective because variation in parent human capital disappears. Since variation in learning ability can be identified by the change in average child income, we can finally pin down the variation (governed by α_1, α_2, and α_3) in the other elements. Last, return to time for human capital accumulation, η_1, can be identified by average school years in college. This data comes from the 1990 Census. The corresponding moment is $E(6 \times n^i_{j2})$ because the second period represents six years in our model. In total, there are nine moments. Table 9 summarizes the moments.

D. Baseline Results

Targeted Moments

Table 10 and table 11 describe the results of the estimated parameters and the targeted moments. It is worth noting that, with regard to the targeted moments, we do an excellent job in matching the moments for all variables.

Table 9

Data Moments Used in the Calibration Exercise

Moments	Value
Average child income between 24 and 28	$18,788
Average child income between 30 and 34	$24,029
Change in average child income in group 1	1.2744
Change in average child income in group 2	1.3467
Coefficient of variation between 30 and 34	0.4639
Coefficient of variation between 30 and 34 in group 1	0.3807
Coefficient of variation between 30 and 34 in group 2	0.4459
Average school years in college	1.6016

Table 10

Estimated Parameters for the
Calibration Exercise

Parameters	Value
θ	0.3145
	(0.019)
α_1	0.0725
	(0.031)
α_2	0.2912
	(0.1369)
α_3	0.4230
	(0.1174)
η_1	0.4321
	(0.001)
μ_{a_j}	0.3225
	(0.004)
σ_{a_j}	0.3789
	(0.002)
$\rho_{h_j \alpha_j}$	0.1789
	(0.016)

Table 11

Targeted Moments Used in the Calibration Exercise

Moments	Data	Model
Average child income between 24 and 28	$18,788	$18,499
Average child income between 30 and 34	$24,029	$24,295
Change in average child income in group 1	1.2744	1.3068
Change in average child income in group 2	1.3467	1.3099
Coefficient of variation between 30 and 34	0.4639	0.4684
Coefficient of variation between 30 and 34 in group 1	0.3807	0.4089
Coefficient of variation between 30 and 34 in group 2	0.4459	0.4139
Average school years in college	1.6016	1.5952

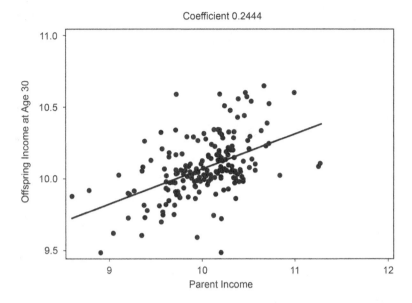

Fig. 21.   Relationship between parental income and offspring income in the model

Nontargeted Moments

First, let us look at relationship between parent income and child income illustrated in figure 21. In this figure, we log-linearize both parent income and child income. We use child income at age 30 (wh^i_{j4} in our model). Notably, there is a positive correlation between parent income and child income. However, the coefficient is smaller than in the data. According to the previous section, the range of the correlation is between 0.36 and 0.44 in the data. By contrast, the correlation in the model is 0.24. One potential reason is that our sample size in our calibration is much smaller. In this exercise, we use only 195 individual data points due to data limitations. This might underestimate the magnitude of the correlation coefficient.

We next turn our attention to local IGE estimates for income. Figure 22 displays local IGE estimates. As in the previous section, the local IGE estimates are defined as the ratio of offspring income to parental income level. Figure 22 shows that the local IGE estimates fall as parent income rises. This exhibits the same pattern qualitatively as in the data. Unlike the data, however, the local IGE estimates fall to 0 in the calibration. Again, this gap between the model and data is due in part to the smaller sample size.

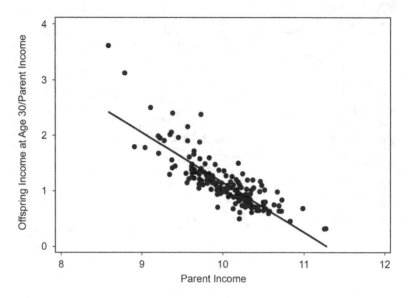

Fig. 22. Relationship between ratio of offspring income to parental income and offspring income.

E. Counterfactual Results

To improve our understanding of the forces at work in our model that help explain the positive correlation between parent income and child income, we use the estimated model to conduct two counterfactual simulations. The first counterfactual simulation examines what would happen if there were no return to the elements for formulating child human capital in the second period. In our model, child human capital contains the three elements: inputs including both public and private ones, parent's human capital, and average human capital in a school district. In this simulation, we study how important each element is to formulate child human capital. The second counterfactual simulation examines the importance of exogenous variables. Here, we change the variation in the following variables: parent income, parent human capital, and average human capital in a school district. This exercise allows us to quantify their roles in explaining intergenerational mobility.

F. Return to Elements for Child Human Capital in the Second Period

Figure 23 summarizes intergenerational mobility in the five cases: (1) baseline, (2) no return to all elements ($\alpha_1 = \alpha_2 = \alpha_3 = 0$), (3) no return to

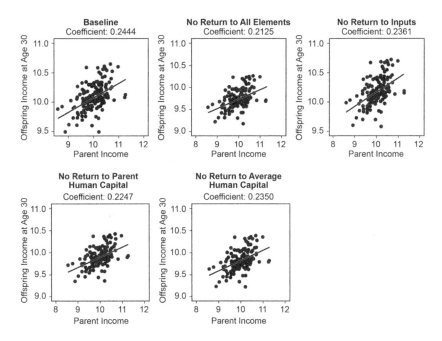

Fig. 23. Counterfactual simulation: Contribution of various elements to intergenerational mobility.

inputs ($\alpha_1 = 0$), (4) no return to parent's human capital ($\alpha_2 = 0$), and (5) no return to average human capital in a school district ($\alpha_3 = 0$). Surprisingly, even if all three elements were eliminated, the correlation coefficient does not fall dramatically. This suggests that the nature part of child human capital (captured by learning ability) plays a significant role. Additionally, when we decompose this effect, we find that the contribution of parent human capital is the largest. More importantly, average human capital makes the same contribution as public-school spending. Therefore, neighborhood effects play a sizable role in our model, as important as the role played by public and private inputs combined.

Impact of Parent Income Distribution

It is interesting to examine the extent to which the distribution of exogenous variables affects intergenerational mobility. In this exercise, we change the variation in parent income, parent human capital, and average human capital in school districts. Specifically, we raise their standard deviations by 20%, holding other variables fixed. Figure 24 presents the

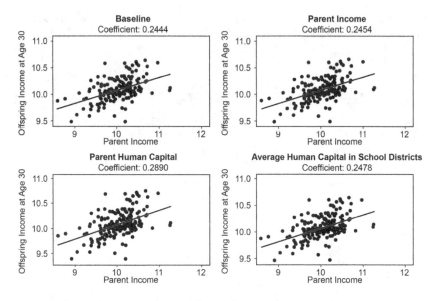

Fig. 24. Counterfactual simulation: Effect of changing dispersion of exogenous variables on offspring income.

result. There are two noteworthy features of these results. First, the impact of greater income dispersion is quite modest, whereas the impact of greater dispersion in parental human capital is salient. In our model, high parent income increases private inputs. However, this does not play as important a role in understanding intergenerational mobility. By contrast, high parent human capital has a direct impact on child human capital and this affects intergenerational mobility. This suggests the importance of the Becker et al. (2015) mechanism for a Gatsby Curve. Second, impact of average human capital is larger than that of parent income. This again suggests a distinct role played by the dispersion in neighborhood effects in understanding patterns of intergenerational mobility. Finally, we note that data limitation prevented the analysis of comovements in dispersion of individual and group variables, so that this exercise likely understates the counterfactual effects of social influences on the Gatsby Curve, which would be consistent with our reduced-form counterfactual.

VII.   Conclusions

In this paper, we have explored some theoretical and empirical aspects of the Great Gatsby Curve. We have argued that the curve may be understood as a causal relationship in which segregation is the mediating variable that converts inequality into lower mobility. We have provided a theoretical model and a set of broad empirical facts that support this view. Our reduced form and structural empirical analyses are consistent with our qualitative claims, but the magnitude of the implied Gatsby slopes is modest. This is so despite the reduced-form evidence that social effects matter for intergenerational mobility and the presence of this property in the structural model we calibrate. We take it as a challenge to better map our theoretical framework into empirical exercises so that the Gatsby-type aspects of inequality and mobility can be better identified.

We conclude this paper with a few comments about policy. There are straightforward routes to justify government interventions in the environment we describe. First, the environment does not correspond to an idealized market economy in which equilibrium outcomes are efficient. The interdependences between individuals created by local public finance and social interactions are classic examples of spillover effects. Markets do not efficiently adjudicate these effects. In particular, in this environment, there is no equalization of the marginal benefits to educational expenditure or of neighborhood quality across individuals. It is possible that Pareto-improving redistribution policies can be implemented. The intuition is simple. The placement of high-ability, low-income children in better educational environments may produce sufficiently higher returns that low-ability, high-income children can be compensated in ways that leave everyone better off. However, it is not clear whether such Pareto-efficient redistributive schemes are empirically meaningful. Other justifications can be derived from the normative argument that motivates equality of opportunity as a social objective.

But what sort of interventions? Here we wish to draw attention to policies that engage in "associational redistribution" (Durlauf 1996a), that is, policies that alter the associations that individuals experience. This form of redistribution is qualitatively different from conventional redistribution policies, which are based on taxes and transfers. While the idea of associational redistribution can abstractly raise unique questions of personal autonomy (obvious for contexts such as the marriage market), here we will note that many policies are in fact chosen in order to engage in associational redistribution: affirmative action is a salient case.

In the context of residential neighborhoods, there are ready mechanisms to alter the degree of socioeconomic segregation. One example of a policy that promotes economic integration of communities is the requirement that a new residential construction should include mixed-income housing. The court-ordered implementation of mixed-housing construction in Mt. Laurel, New Jersey, is a famous example (see Massey et al. [2013] for a discussion of its positive effects on disadvantaged families). Mixed-income housing is closely linked to zoning laws. The common requirement, in affluent communities, that all housing consists of single-family dwellings, is another example of how laws can determine neighborhood composition.

Alternatively, policies can attempt to obviate the effects of neighborhood inequality. In the context of our theoretical model, equalization of school funding across districts is an obvious policy possibility. Another is the redrawing of school district boundaries. Further, once one incorporates distinctions between social influences that occur at the school district and school levels, the rules by which students are assigned to schools become a policy tool.

A key question in thinking about policies of this type is the ability of private choices to cause effects of the policy to unravel. A useful analogy is school busing for racial integration. Court-order school busing was always done within school districts, never across them. As a result, some school districts experienced white flight and became even more segregated than they were previously.

There is an immediate analogy to the school busing case if the policy objective is economic integration of communities: movements from the public-school system to private schools. Note that there is an analogous danger with respect to a policy being counterproductive. Self-interested parents who transfer children to private schools will presumably support lower financial support for public schools than when their children are enrolled in public schools. Hence, in addition to exacerbating economic segregation, as more affluent children are completely isolated, resources could become even scarcer for poor children.

Nothing we have said should be construed as advocating any particular policy. Further, there are complex normative questions involved when one shifts the focus on distribution from income to group memberships. What we do believe is that environments with social influences of the type we have described require consideration of policies that directly focus on how groups, such as neighborhoods, are formed.

Endnotes

We thank Tomokai Kotera, Aiday Sikhova, and Nicholas Tenev for spectacular research assistance and Roland Benabou for enormously helpful comments. Financial support through a research grant from the Institute for New Economic Thinking is gratefully acknowledged. For acknowledgments, sources of research support, and disclosure of the authors' material financial relationships, if any, please see http://www.nber.org/chapters/c13915.ack.

1. Durlauf, Johnson, and Temple (2009) discuss econometric problems specific to cross-country comparisons that justify this general skepticism.

2. Of course, the idea that there are social determinants of behavior had appeared many times previously; see Becker (1974) for a seminal early contribution as well as discussion of social factors in the history of economic thought. Loury (1977) is particularly closely related to the work in the 1990s.

3. The renaissance of neighborhoods research in sociology, for example, Wilson (1987), was very influential in economics.

4. Our point is that, regardless of whether there is complementarity or substitutability between individuals, equal division rules imply that more productive agents will wish to segregate themselves. See Gall, Legros, and Newman (2015) for analysis of environments where inefficient segregation occurs.

5. For variables, the time index t refers to the period in which a variable is realized.

6. See Jones and Manuelli (1992) for infinite horizon growth models and Jones and Manuelli (1990) for overlapping generations models with AK-type structures.

7. Another way to understand the result is to consider the variable $[g(p_{nt})\Theta(\bar{Y}_{nt})] / \bar{Y}_{nt}$, which is the implicit price, in consumption terms, of an additional unit of offspring human capital in a neighborhood. The most affluent family seeks to minimize this price, given the fixed budget share that is implicitly paid for human capital of offspring. The maximization for one family applies to all.

8. This is a technical detail that accounts for the fact that the densities of shocks are not required to have bounded supports.

9. The distinction between the types of persistent inequality found in stationary versus growing environments suggests limitations of conventional forms of inequality measurement such as the intergenerational correlation of income or the Markov transition matrix for relative rankings. Durlauf (2012) discusses some metrics for mobility for environments with growth. If there is a minimum positive average income requirement for the expected growth of income of offspring in a neighborhood, then it is possible for the model to exhibit a conventional poverty trap in the sense that some family dynasties follow a stationary income process, that is, one without growth.

10. See Davis and Mazumder (2017) for a recent important challenge to the conventional claim.

11. If the NSI is linearly related to the standard deviation of income, scaling parental incomes by a factor $(1 + k)$ increases the neighborhood mean by a factor $(1 + k)^2$, and so forth.

References

Aaronson, D., and B. Mazumder. 2008. "Intergenerational Economic Mobility in the United States, 1940–2000." *Journal of Human Resources* 43:139–72.

Andrews, M., W. Duncombe, and J. Yinger. 2002. "Revisiting Economies of Size in American Education: Are We Any Closer to a Consensus?" *Economics of Education Review* 21:245–62.

Angrist, J., and A. Krueger. 1999. "Empirical Strategies in Labor Economics." *Handbook of Labor Economics* 3:1277–366.

Attanasio, O., E. Hurst, and L. Pistaferri. 2015. "The Evolution of Income, Consumption, and Leisure Inequality in the United States, 1980–2010." In *Improving the Measurement of Consumer Expenditures*, ed. C. Carroll, T. Crossley, and J. Sabelhaus. Chicago: University of Chicago Press.

Becker, G. 1973. "A Theory of Marriage, Part I." *Journal of Political Economy* 81: 813–46.

———. 1974. "A Theory of Social Interactions." *Journal of Political Economy* 82: 1063–93.

Becker, G., S. Kominers, K. Murphy, and J. Spenkuch. 2015. "A Theory of Intergenerational Mobility." Working Paper, Northwestern University.

Becker, G., and K. Murphy. 2000. *Social Economics*. Cambridge, MA: Harvard University Press.

Becker, G., and N. Tomes. 1979. "An Equilibrium Theory of the Distribution of Income and Intergenerational Mobility." *Journal of Political Economy* 87:1153–89.

Bénabou, R. 1996a. "Equity and Efficiency in Human Capital Investment: The Local Connection." *Review of Economic Studies* 63:237–64.

———. 1996b. "Heterogeneity, Stratification, and Growth: Macroeconomic Implications of Community Structure and School Finance." *American Economic Review* 86:584–609.

Bénabou, R., and E. Ok. 2001. "Social Mobility and the Demand for Redistribution: The POUM Hypothesis." *Quarterly Journal of Economics* 116:447–87.

Benhabib, J., A. Bisin, and M. Jackson, eds. 2011. *Handbook of Social Economics*, vols. 1 and 2. Amsterdam: Elsevier.

Bernard, A., and S. Durlauf. 1996. "Interpreting Tests of the Convergence Hypothesis." *Journal of Econometrics* 71:161–73.

Bischoff, K., and S. F. Reardon. 2014. "Residential Segregation by Income, 1970–2009." In *Diversity and Disparities: America Enters a New Century*, ed. John Logan. New York: Russell Sage Foundation.

Bloome, D. 2015. "Income Inequality and Intergenerational Income Mobility in the United States." *Social Forces* 93:1047–80.

Blume, L., W. Brock, S. Durlauf, and Y. Ioannides. 2011. "Identification of Social Interactions." In *Handbook of Social Economics*, ed. J. Benhabib, A. Bisin, and M. Jackson. Amsterdam: North Holland.

Blume, L., W. Brock, S. Durlauf, and R. Jayaraman. 2015. "Linear Social Interactions Models." *Journal of Political Economy* 123:444–96.

Brown, C. 1996. "Notes on the SEO or census component of the Panel Study of Income Dynamics." Ann Arbor, MI: Institute for Social Research, Survey Research Center, University of Michigan.

Burdick-Will, J. 2013. "School Violent Crime and Academic Achievement in Chicago." *Sociology of Education* 86:343–61.

Burdick-Will, J., J. Ludwig, S. Raudenbush, and L. Sanbonmatsu. 2011. "Converging Evidence for Neighborhood Effects on Children's Test Scores: An Experimental, Quasi-Experimental, and Observational Comparison." In *Whither Opportunity? Rising Inequality, Schools, and Children's Life Chances*, ed. G. Duncan and R. Murnane, 255–76. New York: Russell Sage.

Calabrese, S., D. Epple, T. Romer, and H. Sieg. 2006. "Local Public Good Provision: Voting, Peer Effects, and Mobility." *Journal of Public Economics* 90: 959–81.

Card, D., and A. Krueger. 1992. "Does School Quality Matter? Returns to Education and the Characteristics of Public Schools in the United States." *Journal of Political Economy* 100 (1): 1–40.

Chetty, R., J. N. Friedman, N. Hilger, E. Saez, D. W. Schanzenbach, and D. Yagan. 2011. "How Does Your Kindergarten Classroom Affect Your Earnings? Evidence from Project Star." *Quarterly Journal of Economics* 126 (4): 1593–660.

Chetty, R., N. Hendren, and L. Katz. 2016. "The Effects of Exposure to Better Neighborhoods on Children: New Evidence from the Moving to Opportunity Experiment." *American Economic Review* 106 (4): 855–902.

Chetty, R., N. Hendren, P. Kline, and E. Saez. 2014. "Where is the Land of Opportunity? The Geography of Intergenerational Mobility in the United States." *Quarterly Journal of Economics* 129:1553–623.
Chetty, R., N. Hendren, P. Kline, E. Saez, and N. Turner. 2014. "Is the United States Still a Land of Opportunity? Recent Trends in Intergenerational Mobility." *American Economic Review* 104:141–47.
Corak, M. 2013. "Income Inequality, Equality of Opportunity, and Intergenerational Mobility." *Journal of Economic Perspectives* 27:79–102.
Davis, J., and B. Mazumder. 2017. "The Decline in Intergenerational Mobility after 1980." Working Paper no. 2017-05, Federal Reserve Bank of Chicago.
Davis, M., J. Gregory, D. Hartley, and K. Tan. 2017. "Neighborhood Choices, Neighborhood Effects and Housing Vouchers." Working Paper, University of Wisconsin.
Durlauf, S. 1996a. "Associational Redistribution: A Defense." *Politics and Society* 24:391–410.
———. 1996b. "Neighborhood Feedbacks, Endogenous Stratification, and Income Inequality." In *Dynamic Disequilibrium Modeling*, ed. W. Barnett, G. Gandolfo, and C. Hillinger. New York: Cambridge University Press.
———. 1996c. "A Theory of Persistent Income Inequality." *Journal of Economic Growth* 1:75–93.
———. 2004. "Neighborhood Effects." In *Handbook of Regional and Urban Economics*, vol. 4, ed. J. V. Henderson and J.-F. Thisse. Amsterdam: North Holland.
———. 2006. "Groups, Social Influences, and Inequality: A Memberships Theory Perspective on Poverty Traps." In *Poverty Traps*, ed. S. Bowles, S. Durlauf, and K. Hoff. Princeton, NJ: Princeton University Press.
———. 2012. "Poverty Traps and Appalachia." In *Appalachian Legacy: Economic Opportunity after the War on Poverty*, ed. J. Ziliak. Washington, DC: Brookings Institution Press.
Durlauf, S., P. Johnson, and J. Temple. 2009. "The Econometrics of Convergence." In *Handbook of Econometrics*, ed. T. Mills and K. Patterson. London: Macmillan.
Dustmann, C., N. Rajah, and A. van Soest. 2003. "Class Size, Education, and Wages." *Economic Journal* 113:F99–120.
Epple, D., M. Peress, and H. Sieg. 2008. "Household Sorting and Neighborhood Formation." Working Paper, Carnegie Mellon University.
Epple, D., and R. Romano. 2011. "Peer Effects in Education: Theory and Evidence." In *Handbook of Social Economics*, ed. J. Benhabib, A. Bisin, and M. Jackson. Amsterdam: Elsevier.
Fernandez, R., and R. Rogerson. 1996. "Income Distribution, Communities, and the Quality of Public Education." *Quarterly Journal of Economics* 111:135–64.
———. 1997. "Keeping People Out: Income Distribution, Zoning, and the Quality of Public Education." *International Economic Review* 38:23–42.
Gall, T., P. Legros, and A. Newman. 2015. "College Diversity and Investment Incentives." CEPR Discussion Paper no. 10337, Center for Economic and Policy Research.
Gennetian, L., M. Sciandra, L. Sanbonmatsu, J. Ludwig, L. F. Katz, G. J. Duncan, J. R. Kling, and R. C. Kessler. 2012. "The Long-Term Effects of Moving to Opportunity on Youth Outcomes." *Cityscape* 14:137–67.
Hanushek, E. 2006. "School Resources." In *Handbook of the Economics of Education*, vol. 2., ed. E. Hanushek and F. Welch. Amsterdam: Elsevier.
Heckman, J., and S. Mosso. 2014. "The Economics of Human Development and Social Mobility." *Annual Review of Economics* 6:689–733.

Jargowsky, P. 1996. "Take the Money and Run: Economic Segregation in US Metropolitan Areas." *American Sociological Review* 61 (6): 984–98.

Jensen, R. 2010. "The (Perceived) Returns to Education and the Demand for Schooling." *Quarterly Journal of Economics* 125:515–48.

Jones, L., and R. Manuelli. 1990. "A Convex Model of Equilibrium Growth: Theory and Policy Implications." *Journal of Political Economy* 98:1008–38.

———. 1992. "Finite Lifetimes and Growth." *Journal of Economic Theory* 58:171–97.

Katz, L., J. Kling, and J. Liebman. 2007. "Experimental Analysis of Neighborhood Effects." *Econometrica* 75:83–119.

Kearney, M., and P. Levine. 2016. "Income Inequality, Social Mobility, and the Decision to Drop Out of High School." *Brookings Papers and Economic Activity.* https://www.brookings.edu/bpea-articles/income-inequality-social-mobility-and-the-decision-to-drop-out-of-high-school/.

Kotera, T., and A. Seshadri. 2017. "Educational Policy and Intergenerational Mobility." *Review of Economic Dynamics* 25 (April): 187–207.

Krueger, A. 2003. "Economic Considerations and Class Size." *Economic Journal* 113:F34–63.

———. 2012. "The Rise and Consequences of Inequality in the United States." Speech given at Center for American Progress, Washington, DC, January 12.

Krueger, A., and D. Whitmore. 2001. "The Effect of Attending a Small Class in the Early Grades on College-Test Taking and Middle School Test Results: Evidence from Project STAR." *Economic Journal* 111:1–28.

Lee, S.-Y., and A. Seshadri. 2015. "On the Intergenerational Transmission of Economic Status." Working Paper, University of Wisconsin.

Logan, John R., Zengwang Xu, and Brian J. Stults. 2014. "Interpolating US Decennial Census Tract Data from as Early as 1970 to 2010: A Longitudinal Tract Database." *Professional Geographer* 66 (3): 412–20.

Loury, G. 1977. "A Dynamic Theory of Racial Income Differences." In *Women, Minorities, and Employment Discrimination,* ed. P. Wallace and A. Lamond. Lexington, MA: Lexington Books.

———. 1981. "Intergenerational Transfers and the Distribution of Earnings." *Econometrica* 49:843–67.

Massey, D., and N. Denton. 1993. *American Apartheid: Segregation and the Making of the Underclass.* Cambridge, MA: Harvard University Press.

Massey, D., E. Derickson, D. N. Kinsey, R. Casciano, and L. Albright. 2013. *Climbing Mt. Laurel: The Struggle for Affordable Housing and Social Mobility in an American Suburb.* Princeton, NJ: Princeton University Press.

Massey, D., and M. Fischer. 2003. "The Geography of Inequality in the United States, 1950–2000 (with commentary)." *Brookings-Wharton Papers on Urban Affairs* 1–40.

Mulligan, C. 1999. "Galton versus the Human Capital Approach to Inheritance," *Journal of Political Economy* 107 (S6): S184–S224.

Reardon, S., and K. Bischoff. 2011. "Income Inequality and Income Segregation." *American Journal of Sociology* 116:1092–153.

Reardon, S., J. Townsend, and L. Fox. 2015. "Characteristics of the Joint Distribution of Race and Income among Neighborhoods." Working Paper, Stanford University.

Roemer, J. 1998. *Equality of Opportunity.* Cambridge, MA: Harvard University Press.

Sharkey, P. 2013. *Stuck in Place: Urban Neighborhoods and the End of Progress toward Racial Inequality.* Chicago: University of Chicago Press.

Solon, G. 2004. "A Model of Intergenerational Mobility Variation over Time and Place." In *Generational Income Mobility in North America and Europe*, ed. M. Corak. Cambridge: Cambridge University Press.

Stetser, M., and R. Stillwell. 2014. "Public High School Four-Year On-Time Graduation Rates and Event Dropout Rates: School Years 2010–11 and 2011–12. First Look. NCES 2014-391." National Center for Education Statistics .

Topa, G., and Y. Zenou. 2015. "Neighborhood and Network Effects." In *Handbook of Regional and Urban Economics*, vol. 5A, ed. G. Duranton, V. Henderson, and W. Strange. Amsterdam: Elsevier.

Wilson, W. J. 1987. *The Truly Disadvantaged*. Chicago: University of Chicago Press.

Wodtke, G., F. Elwert, and D. Harding. 2016. "Neighborhood Effect Heterogeneity by Family Income and Developmental Period." *American Journal of Sociology* 121:1168–222.

Comment

Roland Bénabou, Princeton University and NBER

Theory ahead of Measurement . . .

This is a timely and ambitious paper on an important topic. The phenomenon of social sorting and its role in human capital transmission is one that every parent and homeowner has direct experience with. On the other hand, the economic research tying it to "larger" issues of national inequality, intergenerational mobility, and even aggregate performance may not be immediately familiar to a broad macro audience. For this reason, and to bring out some deeper connections between different types of inequality-mobility mechanisms, I will start with a bit of background.

As the authors explain, between the early 1990s and the early twenty-first century there was a substantial amount of theoretical work on the dynamics of income and wealth inequality, social mobility, and in particular, on their relationships to socioeconomic stratification, which is the topic of this paper. This research, itself following on the pioneering work of Loury (1977, 1981), drew on a few important empirical studies, but the data available at the time was mostly cross-sectional and small-sample. The major trends inspiring it, however, were readily apparent from casual observation: simultaneous increases in income inequality and in the degree of residential segregation by income—best epitomized by the rise of "gated communities"—as well as a host of contentious cases before state supreme courts over wide disparities in school funding.

This mostly theoretical literature led to a general lesson and several specific predictions. The former was part of an even broader message emerging at the time—sadly, the representative agent had died: from growth takeoffs and failures in emerging countries to stagnation and business cycles in industrialized ones, macro outcomes depend on agent heterogeneity and distributional dynamics through a host of channels, both economic and political. Among them, and of primary interest here, is the manner in which a heterogeneous population sorts itself into distinct communities, neighborhoods, and firms, where human capital is accumulated, shared, and used to produce. As to the specific predictions arising consistently from models of this type (e.g., Bénabou 1993, 1996; Durlauf 1996; Fernandez and Rogerson 1996), there were three main ones:

1. More socioeconomically stratified places will tend to have lower social mobility.

2. More unequal places will tend to be, or become, more socioeconomically segregated.

3. Consequently, greater inequality will be associated with lower mobility.

The last implication, in particular, sharply contrasts with the "benign neglect" view, prevalent in much of earlier economics, that social mobility tends to offset cross-sectional inequality, thereby alleviating the need for redistribution.

. . . and Vice Versa

This was before the age of Big Data—and Big Media—so these effects did not yet have fancy names like "Great Gatsby Curve," or get written up and debated by pundits. They were well understood, nonetheless, as were some closely related mechanisms (described below) that also generate a negative relationship between inequality and mobility.

Nowadays, we have massive data sets and amazingly detailed studies (e.g., Chetty et al. 2014), which turn out to strikingly validate the three key predictions. At the same time, relatively little effort is devoted to investigate the exact mechanisms underlying these facts, linking them back to the earlier theories or to newer ones. Thus, after lagging behind theory for some time, measurement has now moved substantially ahead, and a renewed effort at closing the gap is well overdue. This is the endeavor that I see this paper as undertaking, in a manner that is both ambitious in its goals and very open in its assessment of the somewhat mixed nature of the results emerging so far.

I will organize the rest of my discussion in four main parts. First, I will outline some general principles about the types of models that can or cannot account for the major patterns seen in the (national or cross-country) data about what I consider to be an inseparable trinity: inequality, redistribution (whether explicit or implicit), and social mobility. This broader scope will then provide a unified view of a whole class of mechanisms that readily generate a so-called Gatsby Curve, including, of course, the one emphasized in the Durlauf-Sheshadri paper. Next, I will represent these ideas with a simple model and explain how it maps to a reduced form similar to that in the paper. Finally, I will focus on the novel empirical analysis provided by the authors—raising some questions, venturing a few suggestions, and connecting with some other recent evidence.

The Unholy Trinity: Inequality, Redistribution/Mixing, and Mobility

For expositional purposes, I will contrast two main (necessarily simplified) views of this critical politico-social-economic nexus, which I will respectively label "classical" (in the tradition of Becker and Tomes's [1979] seminal work) and "new " (that is, post-1990s).

The most basic case of the traditional view is one in which: (a) pretax inequality is either exogenous (reflecting pure talent, preferences, etc.) or resulting from a smooth process of human and/or physical capital accumulation, occurring under complete asset markets and free of any externalities; (b) consequently, the resulting distributional dynamics are independent of initial conditions, and, in particular, of the initial allocation of individual resources. Conversely, any redistributive policy— whether through taxes and transfers, the education system and its financing, interference in the composition of neighborhoods and communities, and so forth—is only a source of deadweight losses; (d) on the political side, as inequality rises the median (or pivotal) voter becomes poorer and imposes more redistribution, in spite of these costs. This reduces post-tax inequality, but has no effect on pretax inequality nor on social mobility, which are largely exogenous.

An amended, more realistic version of this "classical" view replaces assumption (a) with a recognition that human capital investment, particularly early on in life, is often subject to wealth constraints arising from imperfect markets for credit and insurance. This implies that redistribution and other progressive policies, such as equalizing educational budgets and resources, now dampen the transmission of wealth and income differences, thus increasing social mobility; they can also have potentially positive effects on efficiency and growth. As long as the traditional political-economy view embodied in (d) is maintained, however, two key implications follow. First, the policy response to inequality shocks (international trade, skill-biased technical progress, etc.) is *stabilizing*. Second, and now directly related to our main concern, greater inequality is associated with *higher* mobility.

Clearly, this class of models cannot generate a so-called Gatsby Curve sloping the way we observe in the data (e.g., Corak 2013). They are also counterfactual in another, even more direct way: a number of studies have now established that increased inequality is typically *not* associated with more redistribution (direct or indirect), but with *less*. For instance, De Mello and Tiongson (2006) show that the share of redistributive transfers in gross domestic product (GDP) during 1981–1999 is negatively related, for about 55 countries, to their Gini coefficient during 1970–1980; Ramacharan (2010) shows that, in the United States over 1890–1930, counties with greater land inequality (instrumented by geographical predictors) had lower spending on public education. Of course, contemporary US developments provide perhaps the clearest illustration that assumption (d) goes very much in the wrong direction.

In what follows I will therefore outline a number of channels through which rising equality inequality leads (over some range) to *less* redistribution and equalization of human-capital investment. First among these is the one studied by Durlauf and Sheshadri, namely an exacerbated sorting by income of households across local communities and schools. All of them, however, share the key property of reversing the classical politico-economic mechanism (d). The policy response to inequality shocks will thus now be *destabilizing*: pretax inequality (e.g., in the next generation) becomes further amplified and greater inequality is now associated with *lower* mobility—Gatsby appears.

If the mechanisms involved are strong enough, we even obtain the possibility of *multiple steady states*—across countries, states, cities, and so forth—which, in the cross-section, will display negative relationships between inequality on the one hand, and redistribution (or integration) and social mobility on the other (Bénabou 2000). Thus, in addition to what Durlauf and Sheshadri label a "dynamic" Gatsby Curve, we get the familiar cross-sectional one as well.

Sources of Gatsby Curves: Negative Inequality-Redistribution Mechanisms

1. *Endogenous Socioeconomic Stratification*. This is the channel that Durlauf and Sheshadri emphasize, confronting to modern data some of the key ideas from the literature of the 1990s. There are two key ingredients in the model.

First, some essential inputs into human capital accumulation and transmission are neither privately nor centrally provided, but have the nature of local public goods or externalities. These include property-tax-financed primary and secondary education, but also peer effects, local culture and norms (including crime and safety) that differ widely across towns, neighborhoods, and schools—as amply documented in the paper. I will also note that, whereas local funding of schools is a key feature of the US system, social spillovers and the residential sorting that comes with them remain highly relevant, even in countries with a national education system—probably now more so than ever.

The second key ingredient is that heterogeneous households endogenously sort themselves into communities, school districts, and other "clubs," subject to a trade-off between economies of scale, which favor larger, more integrated groups, and the implicit or explicit sharing of human-capital inputs that occurs within each of them, which the better-off classes seek to avoid. As inequality of resources rises due to exogenous shocks, the trade-off shifts toward the second concern, making richer families less willing to pool resources and externalities. Communities and schools thus become more segregated, material and social inputs more unequal, thereby magnifying the persistence of background differences so that intergenerational mobility declines.

2. *Money (or/and Education) Yields Political Influence*. A second and clearly complementary channel arises from the well-documented fact that wealth, both human and financial, translates into political influence: a person's propensities to turn out at the ballot box, contact their congressman, and, of course, contribute financially to campaigns and causes all rise significantly with their levels of income and education. Moving from inputs to outcomes, research in political science (e.g., Bartels 2008; Gilens 2012) confirms that, across a broad range of domains and time periods, US policy changes are much more responsive to the expressed interests of richer constituents than to those of poorer ones (when the two diverge).

On the theory side, Bénabou (2000) shows that, in such a more realistic political system, the relative wealth (and rank in the distribution) of the pivotal voter will *rise with inequality*, rather than falling as in traditional political-economy models. This means, in turn, that more unequal places and times will be associated with a decline in the extent of redistribution: when incomes start diverging, efficient progressive policies (in education, social or health insurance, urban policy) will increasingly be blocked, and inefficiently regressive ones increasingly promoted. When combined with frictions in human-capital investment, this policy response further amplifies inequality and reduces social mobility.

3. *Inequality Alters Preferences*. The evidence on this channel is still much more limited and tentative than for the previous two, but it is starting to attract interest. The idea is that greater social distance and reduced social contact between different economic classes (compounded by greater physical distance, through the residential and schooling segregation channel) leads to reduced empathy by the better off for the worse off, and thus a reduced willingness to redistribute. Côté, Housea, and Willer (2015) show, using online dictator-game experiments with nationally representative samples, that: (a) controlling for own income, participants from states with greater inequality choose more selfish allocations; (b) when perceptions of inequality in their state are randomly manipulated (by showing them different "pie charts" for the income distribution), participants who now exogenously believe that they live in a more unequal place again behave less altruistically. This kind of "empathic dissociation" mechanism is likely to be even more powerful when income differences correlate with ethnic, national origin, and cultural ones.

4. *Inequality Alters Beliefs*. A related "behavioral" channel concerns the beliefs that people hold concerning the extent of social mobility and its determinants. If, consistent with a lot of experimental evidence, some of the rich "rationalize" (rightly or wrongly) their wealth increases as resulting from meritorious effort, or/and if some of the poor "escape" from their worsening difficulties by focusing on convenient scapegoats and illusory "easy-fix" solutions, then just as in the second mechanism above, redistributive pressure and ultimately social mobility will decline as inequality rises.

A related case is that of a belief in a "just world," maintained through cognitive dissonance to serve both functional and affective needs (Lerner 1982). As shown in Bénabou and Tirole (2006), where the social safety net and redistribution are limited, agents have strong incentives to uphold, and pass on to their children, beliefs that "effort pays," people ultimately get what they deserve and deserve what they get;

where such beliefs predominate, in turn, the majority indeed votes for low taxes. With a generous welfare state, just-world beliefs are much less adaptive, so fewer people maintain them, and a majority votes for high taxes and transfers. This leads to the coexistence of: (a) an "American Dream" equilibrium, with excessively optimistic beliefs about social mobility, high inequality, and little redistribution; (b) a "Europessimistic" equilibrium, with more realistic or even overly pessimistic beliefs about the return to effort, and high redistribution.[1] In a recent study, Alesina, Stantcheva, and Teso (2017) compare perceived versus actual income mobility (from the first to other quintiles) across five OECD countries. A key finding is that, on average, Americans are indeed significantly overly optimistic about the degree of social mobility in their country, while Europeans are overly pessimistic.

A Simple Unifying (But Slightly Cheating) Model

Durlauf and Sheshadri present a model, based on Durlauf (1996), capturing the endogenous-sorting and dynamic-transmission mechanisms described under channel (1) above. That is hard to do, so the analytical results obtained are inevitably limited—for example, characterizing only what happens to the poorest dynasty and the richest one in the economy, and this under appropriately selected ("there exist") current income distributions. I will commit here the opposite sin and outline a bare-bones model that conveys the essence of the idea, brings out the unifying logic discussed above, and yields explicit formulas for income distributions, mobility, and the so-called Gatsby Curve. Nothing comes for free, so the central feature of the Durlauf-Sheshadri framework I will have to give up on is the explicit endogeneization of community formation, which I will instead represent in a very reduced-form manner.

The model, which is a highly stripped-down version of that in Bénabou (2000, 2006), starts with fairly standard production and accumulation equations:

$$y_t^i = \xi h_t^i, \tag{1}$$

$$h_{t+1}^i = \kappa \varepsilon_{t+1}^i (h_t^i)^\alpha (E_t^i)^{\alpha_1} (H_t^i)^{\alpha_2}, \tag{2}$$

$$E_t^i = sY_t^i, \tag{3}$$

leading to

$$h_{t+1}^i = \kappa s^{\alpha_1} \varepsilon_{t+1}^i (h_t^i)^\alpha (H_t^i)^\beta, \text{ where } \beta \equiv \alpha_1 + \alpha_2, \tag{4}$$

In the first two equations, h_t^i and y_t^i are the human capital and pretax income of generation t of dynasty i, coinciding for simplicity; ε_{t+1}^i is child ability (i.i.d. for simplicity), E_t^i is education expenditures, h_t^i captures direct in-home learning, and the average human capital in the community H_t^i represents the influence of peer effects, role models, and other local social spillovers. In the third equation, the constant share of income devoted to educational investment, $E_t^i = sY_t^i$, will result from Cobb-Douglas parental preferences, absent credit markets. Note, finally, the close similarity between equation (4) and the accumulation equation in the Durlauf-Sheshadri model, labeled (16).

Turning now to social-residential structure, and/or education finance policy, I denote by $\tau_t \in 0, 1]$ the economy's degree of socioeconomic integration, mapping into a degree of equalization of investment resources across dynasties (explicit or implicit redistribution). Thus, each individual i lives in a community where average human capital is

$$H_t^i = (h_t^i)^{1-\tau_t}(\tilde{H}_t)^{\tau_t}, \tag{5}$$

where $\tilde{H}_t$ is an economy-wide aggregate (CES index) such that he H_t^i's sum back to the economy-wide average, H_t. A similar relationship naturally holds for incomes, and indeed it is easy to see that the model is quasi-isomorphic to one in which communities are perfectly segregated ($H_t^i = h_t^i$) but incomes, or alternatively educational expenditures, are centrally redistributed according to a progressive scheme of the form $\hat{y}_t^i = (y_t^i)^{1-\tau_t}(\tilde{Y}_t)^{\tau_t}$ or $\hat{E}_t^i = (E_t^i)^{1-\tau_t}(\tilde{E}_t)^{\tau_t}$.

Taking the τ_t's as exogenous for the moment, and assuming lognormal distributions of shocks and initial endowments, yields simple human capital or income dynamics

$$\ln y_{t+1}^i = \ln \varepsilon_{t+1}^i + \ln \kappa + \alpha_1 \ln s + (\alpha + \beta(1 - \tau_t)) \ln y_t^i + \beta\tau_t \ln \tilde{Y}_t, \tag{6}$$

from which we readily see that the *intergenerational elasticity* (IGE),

$$\frac{\partial \ln y_{t+1}^i}{\partial \ln y_t^i} = \alpha + \beta(1 - \tau_t), \tag{7}$$

is increasing in the degree of social sorting τ_t, and more generally declining in the degree τ_t of implicit or explicit redistribution. The dynamics of inequality (variance of log-incomes Δ_t) also readily follow, as does its limit whenever the sequence of τ_t converges to some limit τ_∞:

$$\Delta_{t+1}^2 = (\alpha + \beta\gamma(1 - \tau_t))^2 \Delta_t^2 + \sigma_\varepsilon^2, \tag{8}$$

$$\Delta_\infty^2 = \frac{\sigma_\varepsilon^2}{1 - (\alpha + \beta(1 - \tau_\infty))^2} \equiv D^2(\tau). \qquad (9)$$

Finally, we come to the key question of endogenizing τ_t as a function of the state of the economy at date t. In the classical view described earlier, greater inequality leads to more redistribution, corresponding to an upward-sloping relationship $\tau_t = T(\Delta_t)$; we can now read off from equations (7)–(8) how this *dampens* the transmission of inequality and makes the (dynamic) Gatsby Curve slope the "wrong" way. This also applies to the long run, for example, cross-sectionally: the two curves $\Delta = D(\tau)$ and $\tau = T(\Delta)$ will have a unique intersection, such that an exogenous increase in inequality (σ_ε^2) will result in a higher τ_∞ and consequently a lower intergenerational elasticity.

Suppose now, on the contrary, that the social-structure-or-policy locus $T(\Delta_t)$ slopes up (at least over some range)—for instance, if greater inequality at date t leads households to sort even more assortatively across local communities, as occurs *endogenously* in the Durlauf framework. We then obtain the "new" view lining up much better with the facts: an increase in Δ_t (e.g., from σ_ε^2) leads to a decline in τ_t, and therefore in social mobility (causal and dynamic Gatsby Curve), thereby *amplifying* the transmission of inequality. When the downward-sloping $\Delta = D(\tau)$ and $\tau = T(\Delta)$ curves intersect more than once, moreover, we obtain multiple stable regimes—metropolitan areas, states, countries—all arranged along a very familiar-looking Gatsby Curve.

Empirical Analysis of the Inequality-Segregation-Mobility Nexus

Having emphasized the thread that runs through several mechanisms potentially delivering a Gatsby-type curve, as well as the natural complementarities between them, I now focus again on the one studied by Durlauf and Sheshadri, discussing the new evidence they bring to bear on it. As acknowledged by the authors, the challenges involved are many, so not surprisingly the results of the different empirical exercises are mixed. Overall they do suggest a picture consistent with the theory, but more work will be needed to sharpen it.

A first remark is that the emphasis in the first and theoretical parts of the paper is on the "dynamic" Gatsby Curve—that is, how changes in inequality induce changes in social mobility. Yet the empirical analysis of the intergenerational elasticity of child to parental income (IGE), reported in tables 4–6, appears to use only cross-sectional variations in state or/and census-tract inequality. I thus wonder whether fixed effects could also have been included, or if there is not enough time variation in the relevant series for such estimations to be meaningful? In the latter case, the claims about shifting away from the cross-sectional focus in the preexisting empirical studies should perhaps be tempered somewhat.

A second observation is that some of the results vary a fair amount across specifications —both between tables 4 to 6 and within each of them. When focusing on they key effect of inequality on social mobility (the coefficient on the interaction of parental income with the variance of local incomes), a pattern does emerge that is worth pointing out. Namely, the effect of state-income variance on the IGE (table 5) appears much more stable and robust, in sign and significance, than that of census-tract (about 4,000 people) income variance (table 4). This is consistent with the idea that, at the state level, socioeconomic sorting operates both through unequal school funding across communities and through more localized peer effects, whereas at the census-tract level there is much less flexibility and variation on the school-resources margin, leaving only the peer effects and related local externalities in human capital. In table 6, similarly, when both variances are included, it is that of state incomes that tends to survive.

Where I have more trouble interpreting the empirical exercise is going from tables 4–6 to the inequality-mobility curves plotted in figures 15–20. First, we note again an instability: some of these curves slope down, others up, others yet are relatively flat (perhaps they should also have some kind of error band around them). This naturally reflects their being based on estimates from different tables and different columns in each one, given the variations noted above. It would be useful to discuss some more how a specific column was picked in each table (not always the last one), and especially what difference that makes, if any. More puzzling yet is the way in which the pattern noted above for the IGE's estimated dependence on inequality (which I tend to see as the closest counterpart to the theory) appears to be reversed when an "overall" Gatsby Curve is constructed, from each table, by scaling every family's income by a fixed percentage. Thus, whereas the key coefficient was generally zero in table 4 (census-tract level) and positive in table 5 (state level), in the corresponding figures 16 and 17 the constructed curves respectively slope up and sharply down. This made it a bit difficult for me to understand how these curves map back to the model.

Going forward, one possible way of identifying some of the effects involved, and linking the empirical analysis even more closely to the theory, would be to examine the effects of state-income inequality on the mean and variance of public-education spending across communities. As mentioned earlier (Ramacharan 2010), the historical relationship demonstrated regressive effects of (land) inequality, but what is the picture in recent times, both in levels and in changes?

Lest readers be left with the impression that the evidence provided in these IGE regression is too tentative (perhaps due to the "reflection problem"), let me note first that the paper also provides a calibrated structural model, which the authors use to simulate the effects of increasing (by 20%) the variances of key regressors. The most interesting result, shown in figure 24, is that it is dispersion in parental human capital, more than dispersion in parental income, which has the stronger effect in raising intergenerational persistence. This suggests a greater importance of family and/or local peer effects than of purchased educational inputs. That is certainly plausible, though it would be worth discussing how this fits with the patterns noted above across the regression tables for inequality at different levels.

Second, there is concurrent evidence about the central mechanisms emphasized in the paper and the literature on which it draws. Studying the evolution of US Metropolitan Standard Areas (MSAs), Fogli and Guerrieri (2017) document that: (a) between 1970 and 2000, the United States experienced sharp and parallel increases in the average MSA Gini coefficient and segregation index; (b) during 1980–2000, larger changes in residential income segregation at the MSA level were associated to (significantly) larger changes in MSA income inequality, in line with the theoretical prediction (2) discussed at the start of this comment; (c) the more segregated MSAs display divergence in their trend for income inequality, whereas the less segregated ones display convergence, consistent with prediction (3).

Concluding Thoughts

Naturally, much work remains to be done, both on the social-segregation channel and on the other potential (but highly complementary) sources of a negative inequality-mobility relationship—the so-called Gatsby Curve. This rich paper by Durlauf and Sheshadri is an important and valiant first step in this long overdue reconnection of data with theory.

Endnotes

Financial support for the Canadian Institute for Advanced Research is gratefully acknowledged. For acknowledgments, sources of research support, and disclosure of the author's material financial relationships, if any, please see http://www.nber.org/chapters/c13916.ack.

1. In contrast, the multiple steady states in Alesina and Angeletos's (2005) model based on "fairness preferences" are rational-expectations equilibria: all agents in each country understand exactly the (endogenously country-specific) mobility process they face and the role played in it by effort versus luck.

References

Alesina, A., and G.-M. Angeletos. 2005. "Fairness and Redistribution." *American Economic Review* 95 (4): 960–80.

Alesina, A., S. Stantcheva, and E. Teso. 2017. "Intergenerational Mobility and Preferences for Redistribution." NBER Working Paper no. 23027, Cambridge, MA.

Bartels, L. 2008. *Unequal Democracy: The Political Economy of the New Gilded Age.* Princeton, NJ: Princeton University Press and Russel Sage Foundation.

Becker, G., and N. Tomes. 1979. "An Equilibrium Theory of the Distribution of Income and Intergenerational Mobility." *Journal of Political Economy* 87: 1153–89.

Bénabou, R. 1993. "Workings of a City: Location, Education, and Production." *Quarterly Journal of Economics* 108:619–52.

———. 1996. "Heterogeneity, Stratification and Growth: Macroeconomic Implications of Community Structure and School Finance." *American Economic Review* 86:584–609.

———. 2000. "Unequal Societies: Income Distribution and the Social Contract." *American Economic Review* 90:96–129.

———. 2006. "Inequality, Technology, and the Social Contract." In *Handbook of Economic Growth*, ed. P. Aghion and S. Durlauf. Amsterdam: North-Holland.

Bénabou, R., and J. Tirole. 2006. "Belief in a Just World and Redistributive Politics." *Quarterly Journal of Economics* 121 (2): 699–746.

Chetty, R., N. Hendren, P. Kline, and E. Saez. 2014. "Where is the Land of Opportunity? The Geography of Intergenerational Mobility in the United States." *Quarterly Journal of Economics* 129:1553–623.

Corak, M. 2013. "Income Inequality, Equality of Opportunity, and Intergenerational Mobility." *Journal of Economic Perspectives* 27:79–102.

Côté, S., J. Housea, and R. Willer. 2015. "High Economic Inequality Leads Higher-Income Individuals to Be Less Generous." *Proceedings of the National Academies of Sciences* 112 (52): 15838–43.

De Mello, L., and E. Tiongson. 2006. "Income Inequality and Redistributive Government Spending." *Public Finance Review* 34 (3): 282–305.

Durlauf, S. 1996. "A Theory of Persistent Income Inequality." *Journal of Economic Growth* 1:75–93.

Fernandez, R., and R. Rogerson. 1996. "Income Distribution, Communities, and the Quality of Public Education." *Quarterly Journal of Economics* 111:135–64.

Fogli, A., and V. Guerrieri. 2017. "The End of the American Dream? Inequality and Segregation in US Cities." Manuscript, University of Chicago Booth School of Business.

Gilens, M. 2012. *Affluence and Influence: Economic Inequality and Political Power in America*. Princeton, NJ: Princeton University Press.

Lerner, Melvin J. 1982. *The Belief in a Just World: A Fundamental Delusion*. New York: Plenum Press.

Loury, G. 1977. "A Dynamic Theory of Racial Income Differences." In *Women, Minorities, and Employment Discrimination*, ed. P. Wallace and A. Lamond. Lexington, MA: Lexington Books.

———. 1981. "Intergenerational Transfers and the Distribution of Earnings." *Econometrica* 49:843–67.

Ramacharan, R. 2010. "Inequality and Redistribution: Evidence from US Counties and States, 1890–1930." *Review of Economics and Statistics* 92 (4): 729–44.

Discussion

Charles Manski opened the discussion by saying that in the background of this paper is a normative question about the optimal level of cross-sectional and intergenerational inequality. He suggested using an explicit social welfare function to think about this issue from a social-planning perspective. Laura Veldkamp further encouraged the authors to go in the direction of normative analysis. She said that as a New Yorker the findings in the work are particularly salient, noting that rents change significantly at school district boundaries. Inequality considerations have led cities to put in place policies that ensure low-income housing is available in wealthy areas. She gave as example Manhattan, which incentivizes developers to allocate 20% of the units in newly built luxury buildings to low-income housing. Veldkamp asked the author whether the benefit of placing a low-income family in a wealthy location is linear. For example, is it better to mix some very low-income families in very high-income school districts, or is it better to have many more children moving from the first quintile to the middle quintiles' locations? Steven Durlauf agreed this is a very important question, but said that his model does not tackle this issue.

V. V. Chari noted that in the past 60 years the fraction of spending on education conducted by states has increased dramatically relative to spending conducted by local authorities. He claimed that this force alone suggests intergenerational mobility may have gone up during this period, because this change could potentially decouple the quality of public schools from the wealth of their student populations.

Valerie Ramey asked whether there is evidence on intergenerational mobility going further back in time. She said the authors showed both cross-section inequality and intergenerational immobility has gone up

since the 1970s, but in her view a better test would also include periods in which cross-sectional inequality had declined. She wondered
whether the analysis could be extended to the full postwar period, the
beginning of which marked the beginning of a dramatic decrease in
inequality that lasted for several decades. Durlauf pointed to the work
of Davis and Mazumder (2017), who study this period and show less
intergenerational mobility for cohorts born between 1957 and 1964 than
for cohorts born between 1942 and 1953. Their evidence is in line with
the Great Gatsby Curve, as the former entered the market after the large
rise in inequality that occurred around 1980.

Some participants had questions regarding the measures of inequality and income that the authors use. Gianluca Violante asked whether
the shape of the Great Gatsby Curve depends on the measure of inequality used. Durlauf responded that their results are robust to different measures of inequality. Larry Kotlikoff noted that using pretax
income does not take into account the large increase in transfers that
happened since the 1970s. Durlauf responded that for the purpose of
studying the Great Gatsby Curve the pretax income inequality is a good
measure. However, he agreed that this measure of income might not be
the most suitable for a normative analysis.

Greg Mankiw stated that the original Great Gatsby Curve studied intergenerational mobility and cross-sectional inequality across different
countries. He wondered whether the literature has considered the geographic scope of the analysis, and whether the cross-country relationship is simply spurious. As an example Mankiw compared Europe as a
whole to the United States. Cross-sectional inequality in the Euro area is
higher as countries like Germany are persistently richer than countries
like Greece, and intergenerational immobility is also higher in Europe
as most workers don't leave the country where they were born. These
facts alone imply a negative relation between cross-sectional inequality
and intergenerational mobility, even if there is no causal relationship.
Durlauf agreed that comparing different countries may not be the right
comparison as some countries have more homogeneous population
than others, giving Norway and the United States as an example.

Several participants mentioned related works that study both the
cross-sectional inequality and intergenerational mobility. Antoinette
Schoar brought up the "Moving to Opportunity" experiment. She said
that while the program has no strong effect on first-generation participants (Katz et al. 2001), there does seem to be a big impact on the second generation (Chetty et al. 2016). She suggested the authors try using

the estimates from the "Moving to Opportunity" experiment in their structural model. Mark Gertler mentioned the paper by Chetty and coauthors (Chetty et al. 2017) on the role of colleges in intergenerational mobility. He finds most interesting their finding that mid-tier public universities tend to have the highest rates of bottom-to-top quintile mobility.

Other participants suggested extending the work in several dimensions. Andrew Caplin asked the authors to dig further into the data and channels. He said he would like to understand better the transmission of inequality and beliefs across generations. Martin Eichenbaum wondered whether the findings are robust when controlling for geographic and cultural origins of people in different areas. Relating to Caplin's comment, he noted that if some of this relationship is explained by cultural channels it becomes harder to think about policy designed to improve mobility.

Jonathan Parker suggested the authors use their structural model to understand how a change in intergenerational mobility affects the cross-sectional inequality. In particular, he asked whether, because an initial shock to inequality propagates over generations, its long-run effect could be much larger than its initial effect if left unchecked. Finally, Chris Carroll wondered whether declining rates of entry and exit across firms in the past few decades (Decker et al. 2014) are related to the increase in cross-sectional inequality. He said the two may be related through a political economy channel, and suggested greater inequality may lead political authorities to reduce the degree of competition in the economy.

5

Survey Measurement of Probabilistic Macroeconomic Expectations: Progress and Promise

Charles F. Manski, *Northwestern University and NBER*

I. Introduction

Economists commonly suppose that persons have probabilistic expectations for uncertain events. There are good reasons to think that expectations may vary across persons. Persons forecasting micro events may face different idiosyncratic circumstances. Persons forecasting macroeconomic events may have different knowledge of the state of the economy or different beliefs about how the economy functions.

One might anticipate that economists would regularly use surveys to measure heterogeneous probabilistic expectations. However, collection of expectations data was long rare. Economists have tended to be skeptical of subjective statements. Students have been taught that a good economist believes what people do, not what they say. This perspective inhibited collection of data on expectations. Lacking data, economists have assumed that persons hold particular expectations or have sought to infer expectations from observed choice behavior.

Since about 1990, the historical inhibition of economists against collection of expectations data has progressively lessened, generating a substantial body of modern empirical evidence on the probabilistic expectations of broad populations. Collection and analysis of these data has been performed mainly by microeconomists, and has consequentially been motivated primarily by a desire to inform microeconomic research. An early review article by Manski (2004) described the emergence of this field of empirical study and summarized a range of initial applications. More recent review articles by Hurd (2009), Armantier et al. (2013), Delavande (2014), and Schotter and Trevino (2014) have, respectively, focused on work measuring expectations of older persons,

978-0-226-57766-1/2018/2018-0501$10.00

inflation, populations in developing countries, and subjects making decisions under uncertainty in lab experiments.

The present article begins by describing the history leading to development of the modern literature measuring the probabilistic expectations of broad populations (Sec. II). I first recall the longstanding economic practice of revealed preference analysis, which has studied choice under uncertainty using assumptions about the expectations that persons hold, rather than expectations data. I particularly critique conventional assumptions asserting that persons have rational expectations (RE). I then summarize multiple literatures that have collected various types of expectations data. These include the use of questions seeking verbal responses in attitudinal research and consumer confidence surveys and measurement of probabilistic expectations in cognitive psychology and, more recently, in economics.

Section III overviews the main concerns of the modern economic literature collecting and analyzing data measuring probabilistic expectations. The research of the 1990s and early twenty-first century performed considerable descriptive data analysis, aiming to evaluate how persons respond to the questions posed and to assess the accuracy of elicited expectations. More recent work has increasingly used expectations data to predict choice behavior and to replace expectations assumptions when estimating microeconometric models of decision making under uncertainty. There also has been research aiming to understand processes of expectations formation.

I then describe research on three subjects that should be of direct concern to macroeconomists: expectations of equity returns (Sec. IV), inflation expectations (Sec. V), and professional macroeconomic forecasters (Sec. VI). On the first subject, I first review competing perspectives in finance theory on the existence and importance of heterogeneity of expectations. I then discuss a body of work that elicits probabilistic expectations of equity returns, describes heterogeneity in expectations, and attempts to draw inferences about processes of expectations formation. Some of this work relates elicited expectations to household decisions to include stocks in their portfolios.

Considering inflation expectations, I first mention efforts to measure such expectations nonprobabilistically and then focus attention on the measurement of probabilistic expectations in the recently initiated Survey of Consumer Expectations. I contrast the probabilistic question format used in this survey with the one seeking a point prediction in the venerable Michigan Survey of Consumers. Beyond its specific concern with inflation expectations, this section illustrates the general importance of careful attention to question wording when designing survey questions on expectations and analyzing the responses.

Section VI turns from the expectations of broad populations to those of professional macroeconomic forecasters. I first critique the traditional practice of asking forecasters to make point predictions of future macroeconomic events. While the discussion focuses on macroeconomic forecasting, the cautions I express about interpretation of point predictions apply when asking persons to forecast any uncertain event. I next describe empirical research analyzing the probabilistic expectations data collected in the Survey of Professional Forecasters. Finally, I discuss the practice of central banks in communicating uncertainty and disagreement in their macroeconomic forecasts.

Sections III through VI maintain the assumption that persons have well-defined probabilistic expectations and communicate them accurately in surveys. Section VII questions this assumption in various ways. I first call attention to the prevalence of rounding of probabilistic expectations responses and I summarize research aiming to characterize the extent to which different persons round. I then discuss empirical research on ambiguity (aka Knightian uncertainty) that seeks to elicit expectations that do not have the full structure of precise probability distributions. I also consider the possibility that persons may confound beliefs and preferences, in contrast to the standard assumption of decision theory that beliefs and preferences are distinct concepts.

Section VIII offers my thoughts on the evolution of thinking about expectations formation in macroeconomic policy analysis. I strongly endorse the attention called to expectations formation by Lucas (1976), but not the Lucas assertion that researchers should always assume agents have rational expectations. I favorably observe the increasing willingness of macroeconomic theorists to pose and study alternatives to the RE assumption, but I worry that models of expectations formation will proliferate endlessly in the absence of empirical research to discipline thinking. I caution that little about expectations formation can be learned from empirical research analyzing choice data alone. To make progress, I urge measurement and analysis of the revisions to expectations that agents make following occurrence of unanticipated shocks.

I hope that this paper will be useful to readers of two types. One type is persons who are already undertaking or contemplating initiation of empirical research on expectations. I expect that such persons will want to read the paper more or less in order from beginning to end. A second type is persons who have not yet thought about performing their own empirical research but who are concerned about the assumptions on expectations formation used in macroeconomic policy analysis. Some such persons may want to first do a light read of Sections II through VII, next focus on Section VIII, and then reread parts of Sections II through VII in more depth as it suits them.

II. Development of Research Measuring Probabilistic Expectations

A. Economic Research on Choice under Uncertainty, without Expectations Data

Motivation for economists to measure expectations stems from the long-standing objective of the profession to understand and predict choice under uncertainty. When economists study choice under uncertainty, it has been standard to suppose that utility functions express preferences over outcomes, probabilistic expectations express beliefs about uncertain events, and persons choose actions to maximize expected utility. It has been standard to seek to infer preferences and beliefs from data on observed choices. Empirical research of this type is called revealed-preference analysis, the name given by Samuelson (1938, 1948) in his pioneering work studying choice in deterministic settings.

When considering choice under uncertainty, the actual task of revealed-preference analysis is to learn both preferences and beliefs, not preferences alone. Researchers often confront a severe identification problem: an observed choice made by an agent maximizing expected utility may be consistent with many plausible utility functions and subjective probability distributions. To achieve identification, economists commonly combine choice data with strong assumptions about expectations formation and the structure of preferences.

Assumptions on Income Expectations

To illustrate, consider the assumptions made about personal income expectations in studies of precautionary savings. Economists have regularly assumed that persons have rational expectations regarding future income. That is, they know the actual stochastic process generating their income streams conditional on available private information.

Economists often assume that persons use knowledge of their own past incomes to forecast their future incomes. Perhaps so, but how do persons form expectations of future income conditional on past income? The practice has been to specify the income process up to some parameters and use available data on income realizations to estimate the parameters. Yet researchers differ in their specifications of the stochastic process presumed to generate income. The literature has generated competing models, with no clear way of distinguishing among them in the absence of data measuring expectations. See, for example, Hall and Mishkin (1982), Skinner (1988), Zeldes (1989), Caballero (1990), and Carroll (1992).

The Credibility of Rational Expectations Assumptions

Whether considering income or other expectations, it has been standard practice for economists to assume that decision makers have specified expectations and to suppose that these expectations are "rational" in the sense of being objectively correct conditional on specified information. Imposing such assumptions is enticing because it reduces the task of empirical analysis of choice data to inference on preferences alone. Researchers may also find it self-gratifying to specify their own visions of how the economy works and to assume that the persons who populate the economy share their vision.

Unfortunately, the RE assumptions made in economic research may have little credibility. Early on, Friedman and Savage (1948) argued for the realism of RE by invoking the metaphor of an expert pool player who is able to accurately predict the direction of travel of a billiard ball without knowledge of the relevant physics. However, a pool player operates in a stable environment with ample opportunity for learning-by-doing. RE is far less plausible in realistic economic settings that lack this stability and possibility to learn. Pesaran (1987, 2) phrased the issue well 30 years ago, writing that the RE hypothesis "is based on extreme assumptions and cannot be maintained outside the tranquility of a long-period steady state." More recent discussions appear in Manski (2004) and Gennaioli, Ma, and Shleifer (2016).

For my part, I have repeatedly stressed that economists and ordinary persons face similar inferential problems—identification and induction from finite samples—when they attempt to make sense of the world. Whoever one is, consumer or firm or empirical economist, the inferences that one can logically draw are determined by the available data and the assumptions that one brings to bear. Empirical economists seldom are able to completely learn objective probability distributions of interest, and they often cannot learn much at all. I therefore find it hopelessly optimistic to suppose that, as a rule, the expectations of ordinary persons are even approximately rational.

To illustrate, consider schooling choice, which lacks the stable environment and opportunity for learning-by-doing of the pool game. In Manski (1993), I observed that youth forming personal expectations for the returns to schooling confront inferential problems similar to those that labor economists face when they study the returns to schooling. The research literature in labor economics exhibits much debate on the credibility of assumptions and many disagreements about findings. If experts disagree on the returns to schooling, is it plausible that youth have rational expectations? I think not.

I stressed that decision makers and empirical economists alike must contend with the logical unobservability of counterfactual outcomes. Much as economists attempt to infer the returns to schooling from data on realized schooling choices and outcomes, youth may attempt to learn through observation of the experiences of family, friends, and others who have made their own past schooling decisions. However, youth cannot observe the outcomes that these people would have experienced had they made other decisions.

I used a simple human capital model to show that how youth forecast counterfactual outcomes is consequential. I showed specifically that interpretation of data on schooling choices can depend critically on how youth use ability information to form expectations of the returns to schooling. A particularly striking finding was that, if youth do not possess private information on their ability, a researcher who assumes that they condition expectations on ability may mistakenly conclude from observed choices that youth are unconcerned with the returns to schooling.

I would caution readers who are fond of RE assumptions against thinking that schooling choice is an unusual case. To the contrary, it is the pool game that is atypical of the environments that economic agents face.

B. Survey Elicitation of Expectations

Concern with the credibility of the expectations assumptions made in economic research motivates the idea of asking persons about their expectations. Elicitation of expectations in surveys has a long history in the social sciences, predating measurement of probabilistic expectations by economists. In this section I first briefly describe this precedent research, critiquing the verbal questions posed in attitudinal research and discussing elicitation of probabilistic expectations in cognitive psychology. I then turn to the development of the economic literature.

Attitudinal Research

Attitudinal researchers, primarily sociologists and social psychologists, have long used verbal questions to measure expectations. Respondents may be asked to report whether they "think" or "expect" that a specified event will occur. Sometimes they are asked to report the strength of this belief by reporting whether it is "very likely," "fairly likely," "not too likely," or "not at all likely" that the event will occur. A prominent example is this question on job loss in the General Social Survey, a pivotal sociological survey in the United States (Davis and Smith 1994):

General Social Survey Job-Loss Question: "Thinking about the next twelve months, how likely do you think it is that you will lose your job or be laid off?

    very likely, fairly likely, not too likely, or not at all likely?"

This question illustrates a persistent problem that researchers face in interpreting verbal expectations data—assessment of the interpersonal comparability of responses. Do different respondents to the General Social Survey interpret the phrases "very likely, fairly likely, not too likely, or not at all likely" in the same way? Cognitive research does not give reason to think that responses should be or are comparable. Indeed, the available empirical evidence indicates that interpretation of verbal expectations questions varies substantially between persons (Lichtenstein and Newman 1967; Beyth-Marom 1982; Wallsten et al. 1986). One may also question whether responses are intrapersonally comparable; that is, a given respondent may interpret verbal phrases in different ways when asked about different events.

A second persistent problem is that the coarseness of the response options limits the information contained in the responses to traditional attitudinal questions. Consider, for example, the fertility question asked female respondents in the annual June Supplement to the Current Population Survey (US Census Bureau 1988):

Current Population Survey Fertility Question: "Looking ahead, do you expect to have any (more) children?

    Yes No Uncertain"

The three response options do not enable respondents to express the degree of uncertainty they perceive about their future childbearing.

Consumer Confidence Surveys

A form of attitudinal research long familiar to macroeconomists is the periodic measurement of consumer confidence (or sentiment) in surveys. The monthly Michigan Index of Consumer Sentiment (ICS) is reported regularly in the media, along with commentary on its significance for the economy. So is another measure, the Consumer Confidence Index issued monthly by the Conference Board. The ICS was developed in the late 1940s by George Katona and colleagues at the Survey Research Center of the University of Michigan (Curtin 1982). The Conference Board index has been issued since 1967 (Linden 1982).

Both indices aggregate responses to verbal expectations questions. The ICS is partially based on the coded responses to these questions:

Now turning to business conditions in the country as a whole—do you think that during the next 12 months we'll have good times financially, or bad times, or what?

Good times; Good with qualifications; Pro-con; Bad with qualifications; Bad times

Now looking ahead—do you think that a year from now you (and your family living there) will be better off financially, or worse off, or just about the same as now?

Will be better off; Same; Will be worse off

These questions exemplify the problem that researchers face in interpreting verbal expectations data. How do respondents to the Michigan survey interpret the phrases "business conditions" and "good times financially"? How do respondents answer the questions when they are not certain what will happen in the year ahead?

The idea underlying development of the ICS was that the responses to these and other questions may be useful as "leading indicators" in predicting aggregate consumption and other macroeconomic variables. This proposition was controversial, and the Federal Reserve Board, which funded the Michigan data collection, appointed a committee to assess the value of the SRC data. The Federal Reserve Consultant Committee on Consumer Survey Statistics (1955) issued findings that questioned the predictive power of the Michigan data. The negative findings of the committee were challenged by Michigan researchers, notably Katona (1957).

A contentious conference followed (Universities-National Bureau 1960). Then Juster (1964) reported an intensive study, drawing largely negative conclusions, on the predictive usefulness of verbal approaches to elicitation of consumer expectations. By the mid-1960s, opinion among mainstream economists was firmly negative. However, Michigan continued to perform its consumer survey and to publish aggregated findings in its ICS. Moreover, the Conference Board initiated its own survey and index.

For many years, analyses of the Michigan and Conference Board data mainly examined the time series of aggregate summary statistics, such as the ICS. More recently, some researchers have examined and sought to interpret the underlying microdata. See, for example, Souleles (2004), Piazzesi and Schneider (2009), and Armantier et al. (2013).

Measurement of Probabilistic Expectations in Cognitive Psychology

If persons can express their expectations in probabilistic form, elicitation of subjective probability distributions should have compelling advantages relative to verbal questioning. Perhaps the most basic attraction is that probability provides a well-defined absolute numerical scale for responses; hence, there is reason to think that responses may be interpersonally and intrapersonally comparable. Another attraction is that empirical assessment of the internal consistency of respondents' expectations is possible. A researcher can use the algebra of probability (Bayes Theorem, the Law of Total Probability, etc.) to examine the internal consistency of a respondent's expectations about different events.

When probability has a frequentist interpretation, a researcher can compare elicited subjective probabilities with known event frequencies and reach conclusions about the correspondence between subjective beliefs and frequentist realities. Such *calibration studies* have a long history in cognitive psychology. Lichtenstein, Fischhoff, and Phillips (1982) review findings from 1906 on, and McClelland and Bolger (1994) update the review with findings from 1980 through 1994. Whereas the older studies mostly examined the accuracy of experts (e.g., weather forecasters' reported probabilities of precipitation), much recent research analyzes the expectations of nonexperts, especially students in a cognitive laboratory.

Within cognitive psychology, there has been controversy about the way in which humans internally represent their beliefs, and their ability and willingness to express their beliefs as numerical probabilities. Koriat, Lichtenstein, and Fischhoff (1980) and Ferrell and McGoey (1980)

posed models in which individuals may have some difficulty expressing beliefs as numerical probabilities, but nevertheless concluded that
elicitation of numerical subjective probabilities is feasible. However,
Zimmer (1983, 1984) argued that humans process information using
verbal rather than numerical modes of thinking, and he concluded that
expectations should be elicited in verbal rather than numerical forms.

Erev and Cohen (1990) and Wallsten et al. (1993) have reported that
a majority of respondents prefer to communicate their own beliefs ver-
bally and to receive the beliefs of others in the form of numerical probabilities. This asymmetry is intriguing, but only marginally relevant to
the design of expectations questions. The relevant question is not what
communication mode respondents prefer to use, but rather what modes
they are willing and able to use. Wallsten et al. (1993) report that virtually all of their respondents were willing to communicate their beliefs
numerically, should the situation warrant it.

Another controversy concerns how persons process objective probabilistic information. In an influential article, Tversky and Kahneman
(1974) summarized some experiments in which subjects were presented
with statistics of various forms and were asked for probabilistic predictions of specified events. They interpreted the findings as showing that
persons tend to use certain heuristic rules to process data, rather than
Bayes Theorem.

To the extent that the Tversky and Kahneman experiments shed light
on expectations formation in real life, they cast doubt on the assumption of rational expectations, not on the representation of expectations
through subjective probability distributions. Indeed, Tversky and
Kahneman argued for the psychological realism of subjective probabilities. Considering the propensity of axiomatic decision theorists to view
subjective probabilities as constructs that may be inferred from choices,
they wrote (1130):

It should perhaps be noted that, while subjective probabilities can sometimes
be inferred from preferences among bets, they are normally not formed in this
fashion. A person bets on team A rather than on team B because he believes that
team A is more likely to win; he does not infer this belief from his betting preferences. Thus, in reality, subjective probabilities determine preferences among bets
and are not derived from them, as in the axiomatic theory of rational decision.

The controversy about the Tversky-Kahneman experiments concerns the degree to which they do shed light on subjects' use of Bayes
Theorem to process data. Gigerenzer (1991) argued that the reported

empirical regularities result not from respondents' use of heuristics, but from the manner in which statistical information was presented to them. Here and elsewhere (e.g., Hoffrage et al. 2000), Gigerenzer and his colleagues have reported experimental evidence indicating that respondents perform much better in applying probability theory when statistics are presented in the form of natural frequencies rather than objective probabilities (e.g., "30 out of 10,000 cases" rather than "0.3 percent of cases").

Measurement of Probabilistic Expectations in Economics

Among economists, the idea that survey measurement of probabilistic expectations might improve on the verbal approaches of attitudinal research appears to have originated with Juster (1966). Considering the case in which the behavior of interest is a binary purchase decision (buy or not buy), Juster considered how responses to traditional yes/no buying intentions questions should properly be interpreted. He wrote (Juster 1966, 664): "Consumers reporting that they 'intend to buy A within X months' can be thought of as saying that the probability of their purchasing A within X months is high enough so that some form of 'yes' answer is more accurate than a 'no' answer."

Thus, Juster hypothesized that a consumer facing a yes/no intentions question responds as would a decision maker asked to make a best point prediction of a future random event. Working from this hypothesis, he concluded that it would be more informative to ask consumers for their purchase probabilities than for their buying intentions. In particular, he proposed questions that associate verbal expressions of likelihood with numerical probabilities to elicit purchase expectations for automobiles and other household appliances:

Juster Purchase Probability Questions: "Taking everything into account, what are the prospects that some member of your family will buy a ___ sometime during the next ___ months, between now and ___ ?

Certainly, Practically Certain (99 in 100); Almost Sure (9 in 10); Very Probably (8 in 10); Probably (7 in 10); Good Possibility (6 in 10); Fairly Good Possibility (5 in 10); Fair Possibility (4 in 10); Some Possibility (3 in 10); Slight Possibility (2 in 10); Very Slight Possibility (1 in 10); No Chance, Almost No Chance (1 in 100).

He went on to collect data and concluded that elicited purchase probabilities are better predictors of subsequent individual purchase behavior than are yes/no intentions data.

Market researchers were attracted to Juster's proposal (e.g., Morrison 1979). The idea that expectations might be elicited probabilistically from survey respondents did not, however, draw the immediate attention of economists. When Juster's article was published, economists were preaching that empirical research on decision making should be based on choice data alone. A quarter century passed before economists began to systematically collect and analyze probabilistic expectations data in broad populations.

The conventional economic wisdom finally unraveled in the 1990s. Numerous large-scale surveys now use probabilistic formats to elicit expectations, and a new field of empirical research has emerged. Subjects that have drawn attention include expectations of risks that a person faces (job loss, crime victimization, mortality), future personal income (including returns to schooling and pensions), choices that persons make (durable purchases, voting choices), and macroeconomic events (equity returns, inflation). The modern economic literature measuring probabilistic expectations has developed mainly in isolation from the body of related research in psychology, but there have been occasional notable collaborations of economists and psychologists (see Bruine de Bruin and Fischhoff 2017).

The standard question format has been to seek a response on a [0, 100] percent-chance scale. Thus, the typical question inquiring about a binary event has the structure "What do you think is the percent chance that (a specified event) will occur?"

When inquiring about a continuous random variable, the same format is used to elicit points on the distribution function or the probability that the event will lie in some interval. Thus, a question may have the form "What do you think is the percent chance that (a specified random variable) will have a value less than or equal to (X)" or "What do you think is the percent chance that (a specified random variable) will have a value between (X0) and (X1)?" It is common to ask multiple such questions, varying the threshold X or the interval (X0, X1). The resulting data on the subjective distribution may be analyzed nonparametrically or a specified parametric distribution may be fit to the data. See, for example, Dominitz and Manski (1997b) and Engelberg, Manski, and Williams (2009).

Major repeated surveys in the United States with modules eliciting probabilistic expectations include the Health and Retirement Study (HRS) since 1992 (Juster and Suzman 1995; Hurd and McGarry 1995; Hurd 2009), the Survey of Economic Expectations (SEE) from 1993 to 2002 (Dominitz and Manski 1997a, 1997b), the 1997 cohort of the National Longitudinal Survey of Youth (NLSY97) since 1997 (Fischhoff et al. 2000; Dominitz, Manski, and Fischhoff 2001), the American Life Panel (ALP) since 2006 (Gutsche et al. 2014), and the Survey of Consumer Expectations (SCE) since 2013 (Armantier, Topa et al. 2013, 2016). Further major repeated surveys worldwide include the Bank of Italy Survey of Household Income and Wealth since 1989 (Guiso, Jappelli, and Terlizzese 1992; Guiso, Jappelli, and Pistaferri 2002), analogs of the HRS in many nations, and an analog of the SCE in Canada (Gosselin and Kahn 2015). There also have been many one-time surveys undertaken to provide data for particular research projects.

While there has been an explosion of survey research measuring the probabilistic expectations of households, there exists no similarly large body of research measuring and analyzing the expectations of firms. An early survey that did collect such data was the 1993 Italian Survey of Investment in Manufacturing (see Guiso and Parigi 1999). However, surveys of firm expectations have in the past, and mainly continue to, pose questions seeking verbal responses or point predictions (see Bachmann and Elstner [2015] and the literature cited there).

Regular collection of data on probabilistic expectations of firms is beginning to occur. Two examples are the recent fielding by the Federal Reserve Bank of Atlanta and the US Census Bureau of periodic surveys asking senior managers in firms to provide probabilistic expectations on topics including future product shipments, capital expenditures, employment, and expenditures on materials (see Federal Reserve Bank of Atlanta 2017; US Census Bureau 2016). I have been made aware that similar survey efforts are now in progress in the United States and elsewhere (personal communication from Nicholas Bloom).

III. Concerns of the Modern Microeconomic Literature

The objective of the modern economic literature measuring probabilistic expectations is to shed light on the beliefs that persons hold regarding future events and thereby to help understand and predict their choice behavior. To achieve this, the economists who design survey questions and analyze responses also perform research that aims to learn how respondents interpret the questions posed and to improve question design, so as to enhance the usefulness of the data. In this section I describe the types of research that have been performed.

A. Descriptive Analysis of the Data

Much of the research undertaken in the 1990s and early in the twenty-first century sought to answer basic empirical questions, including these:

A. Are respondents willing and able to reply to questions seeking probabilistic responses? When I began to collect expectations data in the SEE in the early 1990s, I encountered considerable skepticism from researchers who asserted that probabilistic questioning would not "work." A common assertion was that respondents would either refuse to answer the questions or would only give the responses 0, 50, and 100%. It eventually became clear as data accumulated that this assertion was largely incorrect. Response rates to probabilistic expectations questions tend to be as high as or higher than those to traditional attitudinal research questions. Respondents use the full expanse of the 0–100 percent-chance scale, typically rounding to multiples of 5 or 10.[1] See Section VII for discussion of empirical evidence on rounding.

B. In the absence of incentives for honest revelation, do responses reveal the expectations that persons truly hold?[2] Survey researchers cannot directly observe cognition, so this assertion is not answerable definitively. Nevertheless, it is possible to judge the degree to which persons give internally consistent and sensible responses to the questions posed, a criterion called *face validity*. It has been found that responses usually have high face validity when respondents are questioned about well-defined events relevant to their lives. See, for example, Dominitz and Manski (1997a, 1997b) and Bruine de Bruin et al. (2011). There are, however, occasional exceptions. A notable case was that teenagers interviewed in the NLSY97 were found to give highly inaccurate and sometimes logically inconsistent responses when asked to predict their chance of dying in the next year or the next several years (see Fischhoff et al. 2000).

One can also judge the degree to which elicited expectations relate sensibly to observed individual choices. Considerable evidence of this type has accumulated and it has mainly been positive. See the references cited below in Sections III.C and III.D.

C. What expectations do persons hold for their futures? Measurement of respondents' risk perceptions, income and employment expectations, and beliefs about other events has been substantively interesting to economists who heretofore have only been able to speculate about the expectations that people hold. The following section provides an illustration.

Measuring Perceptions of Job Insecurity

Research measuring worker perceptions of job insecurity illustrates the substantive contribution of descriptive analysis. Perceptions of job insecurity have been hypothesized to be determinants of economic outcomes ranging from wages and employment to consumption and savings. Meaningful empirical conclusions about the effects of job insecurity can be drawn only if the concept is defined clearly and measured appropriately. Writers often use the expression *job insecurity* without formal definition, but usage indicates that the expression is commonly intended to convey the chance that a worker will lose his present job and subsequently not obtain a position of comparable value.

To measure job insecurity, SEE posed these questions eliciting probabilistic expectations of job loss and job-search outcomes:

SEE Job-Loss Question: "I would like you to think about your employment prospects over the next 12 months. What do you think is the percent chance that you will lose your job during the next 12 months?"

SEE Search-Outcome Question: "If you were to lose your job during the next 12 months, what is the percent chance that the job you eventually find and accept would be at least as good as your current job, in terms of wages and benefits?"

Manski and Straub (2000) examined 3,561 responses to these questions obtained from 1994 through early 1998. The distribution of responses to the job-loss question was highly skewed, with most respondents perceiving little or no chance of job loss in the year ahead, but some viewing themselves as facing a moderate-to-high risk. The distribution of responses to the search-outcome question had a very different shape, being approximately symmetric and quite dispersed.

The shape of the empirical distribution of search-outcome responses has an interesting interpretation in terms of the theory of job search. Standard models of job search with time-invariant reservation wages imply that the responses to the search-outcome question should be distributed uniformly on [0, 1]. The empirical distribution of responses was reasonably close to uniform.

The responses to the job-loss and search-outcome questions can be combined to yield a composite measure of job insecurity. Let L denote the response to the job-loss question and S the response to the question on search outcome conditional on job loss. Then $L \times (100 - S)/100$ gives the percent chance that a worker will lose his job in the year ahead and subsequently not obtain a position of comparable economic value.

Examination of the cross-sectional and time-series variation across respondents in their perceptions of job insecurity yielded several interesting findings: (a) expectations of job loss tended to decrease markedly with age, but so did expectations of a good outcome should job search become necessary. The net result was that the measure of composite job insecurity tended not to vary at all with age; (b) subjective probabilities of job loss tended to decrease with schooling, and probabilities of good search outcomes tended to increase with schooling. Hence composite job insecurity tended to decrease with schooling; and (c) perceptions of job insecurity varied little by sex but substantially by race. The main differences were in expectations of job loss, with the subjective probabilities of blacks tending to be nearly double those of whites.

B. Analysis of the Accuracy of Elicited Expectations

Researchers have many reasons to be interested in the correspondence between subjective expectations and objective realities. Economists invoking RE assumptions should want to know how well such assumptions describe real decision makers. Social planners contemplating provision of information to the public on the risks associated with detrimental behaviors (e.g., smoking, drug use, school dropout) should want to know how accurately persons perceive such risks.

Perhaps the most direct way to evaluate the accuracy of elicited expectations is to follow respondents over time and compare the events that they experience with the expectations elicited from them. Research of this type has a long history in calibration studies of cognitive psychologists, discussed in the Section II.B. Within economics, the Federal Reserve Consultant Committee on Consumer Survey Statistics (1955) evaluation of the Michigan consumer confidence data argued that interviews provide the only satisfactory way to test the usefulness or relevance of statistics on expectations and intentions. Subsequently, Juster (1966) used data on individual expectations and realizations to evaluate the predictive power of consumer purchase expectations. In the modern literature on probabilistic elicitation, Dominitz (1998) used a one-year follow-up to a preliminary 1993 version of SEE to evaluate the accuracy of respondents' expectations of their weekly earnings. Hurd and McGarry (2002) used mortality realizations to evaluate expectations of survival to ages 75 and 85 elicited from respondents to the HRS in 1992.

Often the longitudinal data necessary to compare expectations with realizations is not available. Then less direct forms of analysis may be informative. When data are collected in repeated cross-sectional surveys, one may compare the expectations elicited from respondents in one wave of the survey with the events realized by respondents in a later wave. Dominitz and Manski (1997a) evaluated the one-year-ahead expectations of SEE respondents interviewed in 1994 in this way, comparing their expectations with the realizations reported by the new sample of respondents interviewed in 1995. A more common way to evaluate accuracy has been to compare mean expectations with historical realizations. Such comparisons assume that successive cohorts of persons have the same distribution of realizations for the event of interest.

In an early study, Hamermesh (1985) used historical mortality data to assess the accuracy of expectations of survival to ages 60 and 80. Hurd and McGarry (1995) used life-table data to evaluate expectations of survival to ages 75 and 85 elicited from HRS respondents of age 51 to 61 in 1992. The NLSY97 elicited the expectations of adolescents for survival one-year-ahead and to age 20. In this case, the expectations were wildly pessimistic relative to the life-table evidence (see Fischhoff et al. 2000).

A further type of analysis considers situations in which persons are asked about future macro events for which it is reasonable to suppose that they have no private information. In these situations, the RE hypothesis predicts that persons should have the same probabilistic expectations. However, expectations have been found to be highly heterogeneous in practice. Research of this type includes Dominitz and Manski (2003, 2004, 2007, 2011) on expectations of equity returns, Delavande and Manski (2012) on expectations of election outcomes, and Armantier et al. (2013) on inflation expectations. See Sections IV and V for further discussion.

C. Using Choice Expectations to Predict Choice Behavior

A long-term objective of economists engaged in research on expectations is to improve our ability to predict choice behavior. Expectations data may be used to predict behavior in two ways. Persons may be questioned about the choices that they would make in specified scenarios, and the responses used directly to predict their behavior. Or, persons may be asked to report their expectations for uncertain states of nature, and these data may be combined with choice data to estimate econometric decision models. I discuss the former approach here and the latter in the next subsection.

A common practice in market research and psychology, and an occasional one in economics, has been to pose choice scenarios and ask respondents to state deterministically what actions they would choose if they were to face these scenarios. However, Manski (1999) cautioned that stated choices may differ from actual ones if researchers provide respondents with different information than they would have when facing actual choice problems. The norm has been to pose *incomplete scenarios*, ones in which respondents are given only a subset of the information they would have in actual choice settings. When scenarios are incomplete, stated choices are point predictions of uncertain actual choices.

Elicitation of probabilistic choice expectations permits respondents to express uncertainty about their choice behavior in incomplete scenarios. The original Juster (1966) proposal was to elicit consumer subjective probabilities for future purchases and use the responses to predict actual purchases. Hurd and Smith (2002) used probabilistic expectations of bequests provided by HRS respondents to predict the bequests that these persons will make. Probabilistic polling questions have been used to elicit voting probabilities and to predict actual voting behavior (see Delavande and Manski 2010; Gutsche et al. 2014).

Use of choice expectations to predict actual choice behavior has two noteworthy features, one advantageous and the other disadvantageous. The advantageous feature is that the approach does not require the researcher to know anything about the decision rules that persons use. The disadvantageous feature is that if this approach is to yield accurate predictions, persons should have rational (or at least unbiased) choice expectations and realized choices should be statistically independent (or at least not strongly dependent) across the population (see Manski 1999).

D. Using Expectations and Choice Data to Estimate Econometric Decision Models

Researchers who employ econometric decision models to predict choice behavior envision using expectations data to relax assumptions about expectations for states of nature. Consider, for example, the situation of labor economists studying schooling behavior. Researchers who observe only the choices that youth make confront a severe identification problem as they seek to infer both preferences and beliefs from data on observed choices. Observation of youths' expectations of the returns to schooling mitigates this problem. Elicitation of entire subjective distributions of life-cycle earnings may be impractical, but a researcher may use whatever expectations data are available to lessen the dependence of inference on assumptions about expectations.

The advantages and disadvantages of this use of expectations data reverse those of the approach discussed in Section III.C. The advantageous feature is that persons need not have rational expectations; it is enough to assume that elicited expectations faithfully describe persons' perceptions of their environments. The disadvantageous feature is that, given expectations and choice data, econometric modeling still requires assumptions about the distribution of preferences in the population of interest.

Research using probabilistic expectations data in econometric analysis of choice behavior has steadily accumulated over time. Early on, Nyarko and Schotter (2002) used a proper scoring rule to elicit expectations of opponent behavior from experimental subjects playing a two-person game and used the expectations to inform their analysis of decision making by subjects. A large experimental literature performing research of this type has developed subsequently. See the review article of Schotter and Trevino (2014).

A similarly large literature has developed using survey data on expectations in econometric choice analysis. Early on, Hurd, Smith, and Zissimopoulos (2004) investigated how the subjective survival probabilities elicited from HRS respondents affect the times when they choose to retire and to begin collecting Social Security benefits. Lochner (2007) combined NLSY97 data on arrest expectations and crime commission to estimate a random utility model of criminal behavior. Van der Klaauw and Wolpin (2008) used HRS data on survival, retirement, and bequest expectations to help estimate a stochastic dynamic model of savings and retirement behavior. Delavande (2008b) surveyed young women regarding their contraceptive choices and elicited expectations for the effectiveness and side effects of alternative methods. She combined expectations and choice data to estimate a random utility model of contraception behavior.

More recently, van der Klaauw (2012) used data on student expectations regarding future occupations to estimate a dynamic model of decisions to have careers in teaching. Zafar (2013) and Wiswall and Zafar (2015) surveyed college students regarding their choice of major, elicited expectations for the monetary and nonmonetary returns to alternative majors, and combined the expectations and choice date to estimate random utility models of choice of major. Giustinelli (2016) surveyed teenagers completing middle school and their parents regarding choice among alternative types of high school and their expectations for successful performance in each type of school and their outcomes thereafter. She used these data to estimate random utility models of choice of high school, recognizing that families may use varying internal household decision processes.

Whereas structural econometric analysis has usually sought to interpret actual choice behavior, researchers have occasionally posed hypothetical choice scenarios, asked respondents to state what actions they would choose in these scenarios, and used the responses as if they are actual choices. As mentioned earlier, stated choices may differ from actual ones if researchers provide respondents with incomplete descriptions of the information that they would have when facing actual choice problems. Given this, Manski (1999) proposed elicitation of choice probabilities rather than deterministic stated choices and showed how the elicited choice probabilities may be used to estimate random utility models. This idea has subsequently been applied by Blass, Lach, and Manski (2010), who analyze consumer willingness to pay for alternative electricity options with differing prices and reliability of supply. It has also been applied by Delavande and Manski (2015), who specified hypothetical election scenarios, elicited subjective probabilities that respondents would choose to vote in these scenarios, and used the expectations data to estimate a random utility of the decision to vote.

E. Analysis of Expectations Formation

Econometric models of decision processes often are used to predict behavior following policy interventions or other events that may alter expectations. When this is so, prediction of behavior requires an understanding of expectations formation. Macroeconomists have long been sensitive to this requirement, it being a central feature of the Lucas (1976) critique of macroeconomic policy evaluation.

Experimental psychologists and economists have studied how persons update objective probabilities following receipt of sample data in highly structured settings like those presented in textbook statistics exercises. A concern has been to test adherence to and characterize departures from application of Bayes Theorem (see, e.g., Tversky and Kahneman 1974; El-Gamal and Grether 1995). It is, however, difficult to draw lessons from this work for expectations formation in real life, where the information that persons receive rarely maps cleanly into a textbook exercise in probability updating. Bayesian updating, which expresses new information through the likelihood function, presumes that data are generated by a well-defined sampling process. Expectations formation in real life requires persons to assimilate government announcements, media reports, personal observations, and other forms of information that may be generated in obscure ways.

One can learn something about updating in real life by eliciting expectations repeatedly from persons, observing how they change over time, and seeking to interpret the observed changes as responses to accumulation of new information. Dominitz (1998) elicited earning expectations at six-month intervals from a spring 1993 cohort of SEE respondents who were re-interviewed in fall 1993. He examined the association between revisions to expectations and the earnings that respondents realized between interviews. Zafar (2011) elicited expectations of the returns to alternative college majors from a cohort of college sophomores who were re-interviewed a year later. He examined how expectations were updated in light of student course experiences during the sophomore year. Dominitz and Manski (2011) elicited expectations of equity returns at six-month intervals from respondents to the Michigan Survey of Consumers. Their analysis of the data suggests that the population may be composed of a mixture of *expectations types*, each updating expectations in a stable but different way; see Section IV.B for further discussion of this work. Such research can in principle be performed with other surveys that elicit expectations repeatedly.

One can also learn from information experiments embedded in surveys, which elicit expectations before and after provision of specified information. Delavande (2008a) explored how women revise their expectations about contraceptive effectiveness following receipt of new information. As part of her survey studying contraceptive expectations and choices, Delavande introduced a hypothetical new contraceptive to her respondents, elicited prior expectations for its effectiveness, and then elicited posterior expectations after providing various forms of further information. To analyze the prior and posterior expectations data, she developed the creative idea of an "equivalent random sample," this being the random sample evidence that would lead a Bayesian statistician to make the same revision to expectations as a given respondent was observed to make.

Wiswall and Zafar (2015) designed and executed a survey of college undergraduates that first elicited expectations about their major choices and the returns to alternative majors. They next provided information to respondents on the empirical distribution of earnings of students who had graduated with different majors. They then again elicited expectations following provision of this information. They used the data on prior and posterior expectations to analyze expectations updating by the respondents.

Armantier, Nelson et al. (2016) first elicited respondent expectations of inflation in the year ahead. They then conducted an information experiment in which they randomly provided some respondents with information about past-year average food price inflation, some with professional economists' median forecast of year-ahead inflation, and others with no information. They subsequently asked all respondents for their expectations of inflation in the year ahead. Their experiment generated an informative panel data set that enabled them to examine how provision of new information induces respondents to update their inflation expectations.

Similarly, Armona, Fuster, and Zafar (2016) used a survey information experiment to examine how consumers revise expectations for home prices. They first elicited respondents' beliefs about past and future local home price changes. They then presented a random subset of the respondents with factual information about past changes and re-elicited expectations.

IV. Expectations of Equity Returns

Having summarized the development and concerns of the literature measuring probabilistic expectations in broad populations, I now discuss in more detail work that collects and analyzes data on expectations for macroeconomic events. Two subjects have drawn particular attention, expectations of equity returns and inflation expectations. I address the former here and the latter in Section V.

A. Competing Perspectives on Heterogeneity of Expectations

Expectations of equity returns are thought to be central determinants of investment in equities and other assets. A motivation for microeconomists to collect data on personal expectations of equity returns has been to assess how expectations vary across the population and how heterogeneity in expectations affects individual portfolio decisions.

In the absence of data on expectations, there long has been disagreement about the extent and nature of heterogeneity in beliefs about returns. Much of the theoretical literature in finance has regarded heterogeneity in beliefs as either nonexistent or unimportant. However, some researchers have argued that heterogeneity in expectations is critical to the functioning of asset markets.

The original formulation of the capital asset pricing model (CAPM) assumed that all investors hold the same expectations for asset returns (Sharpe 1964; Lintner 1965). Subsequent discussions asserted that heterogeneity would not affect the basic CAPM conclusions (Lintner 1969; Sharpe 1970). Adherents of the efficient markets hypothesis contended that prices reveal all privately held information and concluded that expectations must be homogeneous ex post, even if they are heterogeneous ex ante (Fama 1970).

In contrast to the above, theoretical research arguing that heterogeneity of expectations exists and matters includes Keynes (1937), Williams (1938), Miller (1977), Mayshar (1983), Harris and Raviv (1993), Kandel and Pearson (1995), and Morris (1995). These researchers reject the core tenet of the efficient market hypothesis that persons begin with common prior beliefs and develop heterogeneous beliefs only because they receive private signals. They stress that persons may hold divergent opinions even when all information is public. They reason that persons may hold disparate beliefs about how asset markets operate and, hence, they may interpret publicly available information differently. Heterogeneity in interpretation of common knowledge has also been a theme of research in behavioral finance (see Daniel, Hirshleifer, and Teoh 2002).

Theoretical argument alone cannot determine whether and how heterogeneity of expectations affects the operation of asset markets. Nor can a traditional form of empirical research that attempts to infer expectations from asset prices. To accomplish this, researchers often pose representative-agent models, which assume away heterogeneity of expectations.

Even when models of investment behavior permit heterogeneity in expectations, asset prices generally do not reveal the distribution of expectations within the population of investors. My simple study interpreting prices in prediction markets is illustrative (Manski 2006). Prediction markets often ask persons to bet on the occurrence of some event; that is, to take positions on Arrow securities. Various researchers have asserted, without proof, that the observed price on a prediction market is the mean subjective probability of the investors, sometimes called the "market probability" of the event. See, for example, Forsythe et al. (1992) and Wolfers and Zitzewitz (2004). Assuming a population of risk-neutral investors who each bet the same amount, I found that the equilibrium price is not the mean subjective probability but rather is a certain quantile of the cross-sectional distribution of expectations. It was subsequently found by Gjerstad (2005) and Wolfers and Zitzewitz (2006) that price equals the mean subjective probability only if investors are risk averse with utility equal to log(income). In any case, the price on a prediction market does not reveal the degree to which expectations are heterogeneous.

B.   Elicitation of Probabilistic Expectations

To provide an empirical basis for study of heterogeneous expectations of equity returns, Jeff Dominitz and I designed survey questions measuring in probabilistic terms the beliefs that Americans hold about equity returns in the year ahead. We first posed a series of questions on SEE in 1999–2001 and later placed one of these on the Michigan Survey of Consumers in 2002–2004. Similar questions have appeared since 2002 in the biannual administration of the HRS and in some European surveys. Research reporting analysis of these data include Dominitz and Manski (2003, 2004, 2007, 2011), Hurd, van Rooij, and Winter (2011), Hudomiet, Kezdi, and Willis (2011), and Gouret and Hollard (2011). See Ben-David, Graham, and Harvey (2013) for analysis of another panel survey that queried corporate financial executives rather than a general population, eliciting 0.10 and 0.90 quantiles of respondents' subjective distributions of equity returns.

Measurement of probabilistic expectations of equity returns differs sharply from traditional attitudinal surveys that qualitatively classify respondents as "bullish" or "bearish" about the stock market (see, e.g., Fisher and Statman 2000). Other surveys have elicited point expectations of equity returns from various samples of respondents. See Vissing-Jorgenson (2004) and Greenwood and Shleifer (2014) for analyses of these data. I will discuss general problems in interpreting point predictions of uncertain events in Section VI.A.

Cochrane (2011, 1068) has called attention to the difficulty of interpreting responses to questions that use imprecise verbal phrases when asking for point predictions of equity returns, writing: "It does not take long in teaching MBAs to realize that the colloquial meanings of 'expect' and 'risk' are entirely different from conditional mean and variance." Cochrane also conjectured that confounding of beliefs and preferences may occur when surveys elicit point predictions of financial outcomes. He speculated that persons may report so-called *risk-neutral* expectations rather than pure beliefs, writing (1068):

> If people report the *risk-neutral* expectation, then many surveys make sense. An "optimistic" cash flow growth forecast is the same as a "rational" forecast, discounted at a lower rate, and leads to the correct decision, to invest more. And the risk-neutral expectation—the expectation weighted by marginal utility—is the right sufficient statistic for many decisions. Treat painful outcomes as if they were more probable than they are in fact.

Cochrane's definition of risk-neutral expectations as "the expectation weighted by marginal utility" posits a specific form of confounding of beliefs and preferences. As far as I am aware, there does not yet exist empirical research seeking to determine whether persons respond to expectations questions on financial risk in this manner. See Section VII.C for discussion of possible confounding of beliefs and preferences in other contexts.

The basic question in the surveys eliciting probabilistic expectations asks respondents to state the percent chance that a diversified mutual fund will have a positive nominal return in the year ahead. The wording in the Michigan survey was as follows:

> The next question is about investing in the stock market. Please think about the type of mutual fund known as a diversified stock fund. This type of mutual fund holds stock in many different companies engaged in a wide variety of business activities. Suppose that tomorrow someone were to invest one thousand dollars in such a mutual fund. Please think about how much money this investment would be worth one year from now. What do you think is the percent chance that this one-thousand-dollar investment will increase in value in the year ahead, so that it is worth more than one thousand dollars one year from now?

SEE and HRS pose further questions seeking the percent chance that the investment will change in value by more than specified amounts.

The basic descriptive findings are: (a) expectations of a positive nominal return vary substantially across persons and systematically with sex, age, and schooling; (b) the patterns of variation are similar within the Michigan, SEE, and HRS samples; and (c) individual beliefs exhibit considerable stability over time.

Tables 1 and 2 show some of the evidence underlying findings (a) and (b). Table 1, taken from Dominitz and Manski (2011, table 3), provides summary statistics on the Michigan survey data collected from 2002 to 2004 and the SEE data collected from 1999 to 2001. Table 2, taken from

Table 1
Expectations of Positive Nominal Equity Return (by Attribute)

| | Michigan Data | | | | SEE Data | | | |
| | Sample Size | | | | Sample Size | | | |
Attribute	Total	Non-response	Mean	Std. Dev.	Total	Non-response	Mean	Std. Dev.
All persons	7,411	(609)	46.4	29.4	1,212	(439)	68.0	27.5
Male	3,363	(175)	50.2	30.0	625	(149)	68.7	26.9
Female	4,048	(434)	43.2	28.5	587	(290)	67.3	28.1
Non-Hisp. white	5833	(426)	47.3	29.3	993	(348)	68.8	26.8
Non-Hisp. black	610	(76)	41.6	28.9	85	(33)	64.7	30.8
Hispanic	547	(64)	44.9	29.9	—		—	—
American Indian	70	(4)	36.4	28.3	10	(9)	58.5	36.1
Asian	160	(11)	45.4	31.7	29	(6)	60.8	29.7
Age 18–34	1,804	(82)	51.0	26.7	361	(91)	68.9	25.3
Age 35–49	2,520	(132)	48.4	28.4	411	(98)	70.0	26.9
Age 50–64	1,863	(125)	45.9	30.9	265	(114)	67.8	27.6
Age 65+	1,178	(261)	36.1	30.2	152	(122)	62.3	31.8
Schooling 0–12	2,494	(375)	40.1	28.6	151	(140)	59.1	31.6
Schooling 13–15	2,116	(126)	46.9	29.0	382	(139)	68.8	27.8
Schooling 16+	2,745	(92)	51.6	29.2	607	(129)	70.5	25.0

Source: Dominitz and Manski (2011, table 3).

Table 2
Expectations of Positive Nominal Return (PNR) by Attribute (2004 Health and Retirement Study)

| | Male | | | | | | | Female | | | | | | |
| | Number of Respondents to PNR | Mean | Standard Deviation | Quantile 0.25 | 0.50 | 0.75 | Rate of Response to PNR | Number of Respondents to PNR | Mean | Standard Deviation | Quantile 0.25 | 0.50 | 0.75 | Rate of Response to PNR |
Attribute														
All respondents	5,683	53.7	27.0	40	50	75	0.92	7,247	46.0	25.7	25	50	60	0.83
Married or living with a partner														
No	1,080	49.6	28.0	30	50	75	0.87	2,691	43.7	26.4	20	50	60	0.79
Yes	4,603	54.6	26.7	40	50	75	0.93	4,556	47.3	25.3	30	50	60	0.86
Age														
50–59	1,745	55.2	25.8	40	50	75	0.93	2,401	48.1	25.1	30	50	65	0.88
60–69	2,241	54.2	27.0	40	50	75	0.92	2,889	46.8	5.7	25	50	60	0.84
70–80	1,697	51.4	28.2	30	50	75	0.90	1,957	42.1	26.2	20	50	50	0.78
Holds stocks of mutual funds														
No	3,590	50.0	27.9	30	50	70	0.89	4,759	43.1	25.9	20	50	60	0.79
Yes	2,093	60.0	24.3	50	60	80	0.97	2,488	51.6	24.4	40	50	70	0.97

Source: Dominitz and Manski (2007, table 1).

Dominitz and Manski (2007, table 1), gives statistics on the HRS survey data collected in 2004. Finding (c) emerged from analysis of the longitudinal feature of the Michigan survey, which provides two interviews for most respondents, spaced six months apart.

These descriptive findings suggest that individuals use interpersonally variable but intrapersonally stable processes to form their expectations. We proposed (Dominitz and Manski 2011) that the population may be composed of a mixture of *expectations types*, each forming expectations in a stable but different way. We presented an exploratory analysis that uses the Michigan and SEE data to learn about the prevalence of different types, focusing on three types suggested by thinking in orthodox and behavioral finance. These are a *random-walk* (RW) type, who believes that returns are independent and identically distributed over time, a *persistence* (P) type, who believes that recent stock market performance will persist into the near future, and a *mean-reversion* (MR) type, who believes that recent market performance will be reversed in the near future. Using the time series of the S&P 500 to measure recent market performance, we concluded that processes of expectations formation are very heterogeneous. Applying an ordinal criterion to classify types, we found that the fractions of Michigan respondents who express expectations consistent with the RW, P, and MR types are 0.27, 0.41, and 0.32, respectively.

Whether or not one finds persuasive our classification of persons into (RW, P, MR) types, the observed interpersonal heterogeneity of expectations and intrapersonal stability of expectations provides strong empirical evidence against the hypothesis that persons have rational expectations of equity returns. Ordinary persons may have access to substantial common information about the functioning of equity markets, but they rarely have much private information. In the absence of private information, the RE hypothesis predicts that expectations should not vary across persons. Yet respondents to the Michigan, SEE, and HRS surveys expressed large differences in their expectations, which vary systematically across demographic groups and are intrapersonally stable.

C.   Expectations and Stock Holdings

Going beyond measurement of expectations of equity returns, an economist would naturally want to relate expectations to portfolio decisions. Dominitz and Manski (2007) used HRS data to perform an exploratory analysis.

Given some assumptions, a person should hold stocks if his subjective probability of a positive nominal return exceeds his risk-free rate of return. We studied how the fraction of HRS respondents who hold stocks varies with expectations. We found a consistent pattern across groups defined by gender and marital status. In each case, the probability of holding stocks increases substantially as the reported chance of a positive return increases from 0% to roughly 90%. We also found that the fraction holding stocks declines slightly as the reported chance of a positive return increases further from 90 to 100%. We had no ready explanation for this mildly anomalous behavior at the upper tail.

Although our analysis was hardly definitive, we think it suggests that research on portfolio choice would benefit by eliciting expectations of equity returns. Indeed, doing so may help to resolve the famous "equity premium puzzle" that many households hold no risky assets. This behavior is puzzling only to the extent that respondents perceive an equity premium to exist.

Haliassos and Bertaut (1995, 1114) dismissed the notion that subjective expectations explain the low rate of stockholding, writing: "Heterogeneity of opinions is not promising [*as the explanation*], since what is required is the perception that a premium exists, not that it is of a particular magnitude." As more promising explanations, they cited inertia and departures from expected-utility maximization. Our empirical evidence suggests that economic theory can generate the observed phenomenon once we reject the practice of making unwarranted assumptions on expectations and bring to bear expectations data instead.

Our findings from the HRS data are consistent with, but do not prove, the following causal claims: (a) investment portfolios become more conservative as households age because households tend to become less optimistic about equity returns, (b) men invest more aggressively than women because they tend to be more optimistic about equity returns, and (c) many households hold no risky assets because they are not as convinced as economists are about the existence of an equity premium.

V.   Inflation Expectations

Macroeconomists have considered inflation expectations to be a driver of private economic decisions and, hence, to be relevant to formation of monetary policy (e.g., Gali 2008; Sims 2009). A standard way to measure inflation expectations has been to infer them from the observed difference in yields between nominal and real government debt (see, e.g., Haubrich, Pennachi, and Ritchken 2012). However, the difference in yields is easily interpretable only in the context of a representative agent model with strong maintained assumptions about investor risk preferences. Even then it may only provide information on the central tendency of inflation expectations, not about investor uncertainty.

Consumer confidence surveys have long sought to measure inflation expectations within the general population. However, the questions posed have not allowed respondents to express uncertainty. The Michigan Survey of Consumers asks:

During the next 12 months, do you think that prices in general will go up, or go down, or stay where they are now?

Those who respond "go up" or "go down" are then asked to give a specific percent.

A. *Measurement of Inflation Expectations in the Survey of Consumer Expectations*

With the above background, the Federal Reserve Bank of New York in 2006 initiated a major project developing its new Survey of Consumer Expectations (SCE), which since 2013 has elicited a substantial set of probabilistic expectations from its national sample of respondents. The SCE has a rotating-panel design, measuring respondent expectations monthly for up to 12 consecutive months. Improved measurement of inflation expectations was a major motivation for the SCE. Armantier et al. (2013) and Armantier, Topa et al. (2016) discuss the developmental process yielding the SCE and the specifics of the survey design.

Rather than summarize substantive findings obtained to date with the SCE, I call attention here to the differences between the SCE questions eliciting inflation expectations and the questions asked in the Michigan survey. The reason I do so is to emphasize the importance of careful attention to question wording when eliciting expectations.

The team of New York Fed researchers who designed the SCE used an exemplary process to evaluate how persons respond to the Michigan questions and then to formulate the SCE questions. They first used small-scale cognitive interviews to learn how respondents interpret and respond to alternative question wordings. They then scaled up their exploration of respondent behavior by posing alternative questions to respondents of the national American Life Panel and analyzing the responses. Only after this and further cognitive interviewing did they finalize the SCE questions.

The SCE elicits both point and probabilistic predictions of inflation, with randomized ordering of these formats. The survey uses a two-stage format to obtain point predictions. Respondents are first asked:

Over the next 12 months, do you think that there will be inflation or deflation? (Note: deflation is the opposite of inflation).

Depending on their response, they are next asked for a point estimate:

What do you expect the rate of [inflation/deflation] to be over the next 12 months? Please give your best guess.

The question format seeking a probabilistic prediction is as follows:

In your view, what would you say is the percent chance that, over the next 12 months,

the rate of inflation will be 12% or higher	*percent chance*
the rate of inflation will be between 8% and 12%	*percent chance*
the rate of inflation will be between 4% and 8%	*percent chance*
the rate of inflation will be between 2% and 4%	*percent chance*
the rate of inflation will be between 0% and 2%	*percent chance*
the rate of deflation (opposite of inflation) will be between 0% and 2%	*percent chance*
the rate of deflation (opposite of inflation) will be between 2% and 4%	*percent chance*
the rate of deflation (opposite of inflation) will be between 4% and 8%	*percent chance*
the rate of deflation (opposite of inflation) will be between 8% and 12%	*percent chance*
the rate of deflation (opposite of inflation) will be 12% or higher	*percent chance*
	Total

As respondents enter their answers, they can see what the total sums to. Those who give answers that do not add up to 100% receive the notice *Please change the numbers in the table so they add up to 100.*

The SCE questions differ from those of the Michigan survey in various ways. I discuss two important differences here.

Asking about "Inflation" or about "Prices in General"

Prior to the SCE, surveys seeking consumer expectations of inflation posed questions that avoid use of the word "inflation," the presumption being that ordinary persons may not understand the professional economic use of the term. Instead the Michigan and other surveys have asked about expected changes in "prices in general." The NY Fed researchers were concerned that the term "prices in general" is vague. They were aware of research arguing that respondents may interpret this vague term heterogeneously, each thinking about the prices of products that are important to his or her own consumption pattern (see Armantier et al. 2013).

Given this concern, the NY Fed team performed empirical research aiming to understand how respondents interpret the term "prices in general." As recounted in Armantier et al. (2013), they first conducted cognitive interviews with a small sample to identify potential interpretations of the question. After reading the Michigan question out loud, interviewees were instructed to think out loud while generating their answers. They found that some interviewees recognized the question as asking about inflation, whereas others interpreted it as asking about their personal price experiences.

The team then conducted an internet survey with a larger sample recruited through the ALP, thus obtaining sufficient statistical power to examine the association of question interpretations with responses. Respondents first received the Michigan Survey question about "prices in general" and subsequently rated how much they were thinking of different question interpretations taken directly from the cognitive interviews, including "the prices of things you spend money on" and "inflation."

They found that respondents who focused on their personal consumption patterns tended to report higher expectation for the future increase in prices in general than did those who thought about overall inflation. They conjectured that certain psychological theories may explain the observed systematic difference in response. These theories predict that consumers pay more attention to price increases than to price decreases, especially if they are large and frequently experienced. When the NY Fed team probed survey respondents about their understanding of changes to prices in general, they found that a significant fraction believed the intent of the question was to inquire about the prices they recently paid themselves, particularly prices that had increased or decreased markedly, such as those for food or gasoline. They also found that this tendency to think more about prominent price changes in respondents' own price experiences was particularly common among respondents with lower financial literacy.

By contrast, the team found that when they posed questions asking for expectations for the rate of inflation rather than about prices in general, respondents tended to think less about a few salient price changes specific to their own experience and more about price changes across a broader set of items or about changes in the general cost of living, concepts that align more closely to economists' definition of inflation.

They concluded that asking about the rate of inflation directly produces answers more consistent with the concept of inflation expectations of interest to central banks. Based on this experience, the NY Fed team decided that the SCE should inquire directly about inflation rather than about prices in general.

Probability Elicitation in the SCE

A second important difference between the Michigan Survey and the SCE is that the former only asks for point predictions while the latter asks for both point and probabilistic predictions. The probabilistic question format used in the SCE is like that used in the Bank of Italy Survey of Household Income and Wealth and in the Survey of Professional Forecasters, posing a set of intervals and asking respondents to report their subjective probability that inflation will lie in each interval.

When analyzing the respondent-specific data, the NY Fed team has adopted the parametric density estimate that Engelberg, Manski, and Williams (2009, 2011) proposed and utilized in their studies of predictions made by the Survey of Professional Forecasters, which will be discussed in Section VI. When a respondent assigns a positive probability to three or more bins, this estimate assumes an underlying generalized beta distribution, which has four parameters, two to determine its support and two to determine its shape. When a respondent assigns a positive probability to only one or two bins, the underlying distribution is assumed to have the shape of an isosceles triangle.

Armantier et al. (2013) describe the process used by the NY Fed team to explore the properties of the probabilistic question before they finalized its format. They first fielded the question in a special Internet survey and then in an experimental panel survey of consumers that preceded initiation of the SCE. They found that response rates were close to 100% in both surveys. Only about 1% of respondents provided assessments that did not add up to 100%.

They found that, when given the opportunity, most respondents chose to express uncertainty in their probabilistic predictions. The proportion of respondents who put positive probability mass in more than one interval was very high: 96% in the special Internet survey and 89% in the panel surveys. The average number of intervals with positive probability was also high: 4.8 for the special Internet survey and 3.8 for the panel surveys. The fraction of respondents who put positive mass in noncontiguous intervals was very low, ranging from 1.3% in the special survey to 1.6% in the panel surveys. They found that the probabilistic predictions can be approximated reasonably well by the parametric density estimate, which assumes probabilistic beliefs to be unimodal. They also found that respondent point predictions were highly correlated with the means and medians of the parametric density estimates based on the probabilistic predictions. These and other findings are detailed in Armantier et al. (2013).

VI. Expectations of Professional Macroeconomic Forecasters

I now turn from measuring the expectations of broad populations to those of professional macroeconomic forecasters. I begin with the prevailing practice of eliciting point predictions from such forecasters and then discuss probabilistic measurement of their expectations.

A. Problems in Interpreting Point Predictions

Professional forecasters regularly give point predictions of uncertain future events. For example, panel members in the Survey of Professional Forecasters (SPF) give quarterly point predictions of GDP growth and inflation. These point predictions cannot reveal anything about the uncertainty that forecasters perceive. They at most convey some notion of the central tendency of beliefs.

Suppose that forecasters hold subjective probability distributions for future events. Point predictions should somehow be related to the probabilistic expectations that forecasters hold, but how? Forecasters may report the means of their probability distributions for uncertain events or they may report medians or modes. However, forecasters typically are not asked to report means, medians, or modes. They are simply asked to "predict" or "forecast" the outcome. In the absence of explicit guidance, forecasters may report different distributional features as their point predictions. Research calling attention to and analyzing the potential heterogeneity of response practices include Elliott, Komunjer, and Timmermann (2005, 2008), Engelberg et al. (2009), and Clements (2009).

Heterogeneous reporting practices can be consequential for the interpretation of point predictions. Forecasters who hold identical probabilistic beliefs may provide different point predictions, and forecasters with dissimilar beliefs may provide identical point predictions. If so, comparison of point predictions across forecasters is problematic. Variation in predictions need not imply disagreement among forecasters, and homogeneity in predictions need not imply agreement.

Macroeconomic researchers have sometimes interpreted cross-forecaster dispersion in point predictions to indicate disagreement in their beliefs. (See, e.g., Diether, Malloy, and Scherbina 2002; Mankiw, Reis, and Wolfers 2004; Patton and Timmermann 2010; Coibion and Gorodnichenko 2012.) If forecasters vary in the way they transform probability distributions into point predictions, this interpretation confounds variation in forecaster beliefs with variation in the manner that forecasters make point predictions.

A distinct, and more severe, interpretative problem is the longstanding use of cross-sectional dispersion in macroeconomic point predictions to measure forecaster uncertainty about future outcomes. (See, e.g., Cukierman and Wachtel 1979; Levi and Makin 1979, 1980; Makin 1982; Brenner and Landskroner 1983; Hahm and Steigerwald 1999; Hayford 2000; Giordani and Söderlind 2003; Johnson 2004; Barron, Stanford, and Yu 2009; Güntay and Hackbarth 2010; Bachmann, Elstner, and Sims 2013.) This research practice is illogical, even if all forecasters make their point predictions in the same way. Even in the best of circumstances, point predictions provide no information about the uncertainty that forecasters perceive. This point was made forcefully 30 years ago by Zarnowitz and Lambros (1987). Nevertheless, researchers have continued to use the dispersion in point predictions to measure forecaster uncertainty.

Yet another issue is the common practice of aggregating point predictions into a combined forecast. Empirical researchers have long reported that the cross-sectional mean or median of a set of point predictions is more accurate than the individual predictions used to form the mean or median. In a review of this practice in macroeconomic forecasting, Clemen (1989, 559) states:

The results have been virtually unanimous: combining multiple forecasts leads to increased forecast accuracy. This has been the result whether the forecasts are judgmental or statistical, econometric or extrapolation. Furthermore, in many cases one can make dramatic performance improvements by simply averaging the forecasts.

This phenomenon is sometimes colloquially called the "wisdom of crowds." It has only occasionally been recognized that these regularities have algebraic foundations, which do not imply that a combined forecast has any absolute degree of accuracy. The regularity concerning mean predictions holds whenever a convex loss function (or concave welfare function) is used to measure prediction accuracy, by Jensen's inequality. The one concerning median predictions holds whenever a unimodal loss or welfare function is used to measure accuracy. See Manski (2011b, 2016) for discussion of the literature and for analysis.

B.   *Empirical Research on Probabilistic Expectations*

The above suggests that it would be more informative to elicit probabilistic predictions from professional forecasters. Indeed, the SPF asks its panel members to provide both point and probabilistic forecasts of inflation and GDP growth (www.phil.frb.org/econ/spf/). The probabilistic forecasts are subjective probabilities that the outcome will lie in each of 10 intervals. An important feature of the SPF is that the survey has a longitudinal component, with many forecasters providing multiple predictions over the course of several years.[3]

To shed empirical light on the reporting practices of professional forecasters, Engelberg et al. (2009) used data from the SPF to compare point predictions of GDP growth and inflation with the subjective probability distributions held by forecasters. We found that the deviations between point predictions and the central tendencies of forecasters' subjective distributions tend to be asymmetric, with SPF forecasters tending to report point predictions that give a more favorable view of the economy than do their subjective means/medians/modes. We concluded that organizations commissioning forecasts should not ask for point predictions. Instead, they should elicit probabilistic expectations and derive measures of central tendency and uncertainty.

In subsequent research, Engelberg et al. (2011) showed the value of probabilistic expectations data when one seeks to characterize the temporal variation of macroeconomic forecasts. It has been common to aggregate the point predictions reported by SPF panel members at each administration of the survey into a "consensus prediction" and analyze the time series of this aggregate. Summary reports of SPF findings traditionally take this form.

We observed that interpretation of the temporal variation in aggregated predictions can be problematic for multiple reasons: (a) aggregate predictions reveal nothing about the uncertainty that forecasters perceive; (b) they reveal nothing about possible disagreement across the panel of forecasters; and (c) aggregate predictions ignore the fact that the composition of panels of forecasters often change substantially over time. Examining the data on expectations of inflation and GDP growth obtained by the SPF in the period 1992–2006, we concluded that the interpretative problem is always serious in principle and often in practice.

To replace analysis of aggregated predictions, we recommended study of the time series of the probabilistic forecasts made by individual forecasters. Considering each forecaster separately, one may compute parameters that measure the central tendency and spread of elicited subjective probability distributions; we suggested use of the subjective median and interquartile range. This done, a plot showing the subjective (median, IQR) of each forecaster clearly portrays the heterogeneity of forecasts at a point in time. To describe the evolution of expectations across the quarterly administrations of the survey, we recommended enhancing the plot with arrows to indicate how each forecaster changes his beliefs from one quarter to the next.

Figures from our article, reproduced here, illustrate. The top panel of figure 1 displays the subjective medians and IQRs for 2001 GDP growth elicited from forecasters who participated in the SPF in 3Q:2001 and 4Q:2001. Thus, the figure shows GDP growth expectations before and after the terrorist attacks of September 11, 2001. Each forecaster is depicted by an arrow whose tail is his 3Q:2001 prediction and whose tip is his 4Q:2001 prediction. The figure shows that nearly all forecasters revised their subjective medians downward between 3Q:2001 and 4Q:2001. However, forecasters varied in the direction of revisions to their subjective IQRs, some becoming more certain about output growth and others less certain.

The bottom panel of the figure displays the subjective medians and IQRs for 2006 inflation elicited from forecasters who participated in the SPF in both 3Q:2005 and 4Q:2005. Thus, the figure shows inflation expectations before and after Ben Bernanke's nomination to be Chair of the Board of Governors of the Federal Reserve System on October 24, 2005. The figure shows that most forecasters revised their subjective medians upward, but they varied considerably in the magnitude of the revision. Revisions to subjective IQRs were heterogeneous in both direction and magnitude.

C. *Communicating Uncertainty and Disagreement in the Macroeconomic Forecasts of Central Banks*

I find it intriguing to compare the forecasting practice of the Bank of England with that of the US Federal Reserve System. The Bank of England

GDP: Before/After 911

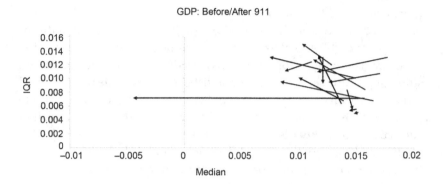

Inflation: Before/After Bernanke Nomination

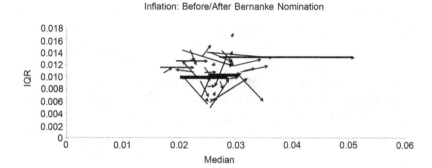

Fig. 1. Change in expectations around events

Source: Engelberg, Manski, and Williams (2011, figure 2).

uses fan charts to visually portray the probabilistic forecasts of inflation and GDP growth made by the Bank's Monetary Policy Committee
(MPC) in its quarterly *Inflation Report*. The Board of Governors of the
Federal Reserve periodically releases a Summary of Economic Projections summarizing forecasts made by the participants in the deliberations of the Federal Open Market Committee (FOMC). Each participant
is asked to make point predictions of GDP growth, inflation, and the
unemployment rate in each of several future years. The Summary of
Economic Projections describes the distribution of the point predictions
across the FOMC participants.

The MPC and the FOMC both present forecasts as distributions. One
may think that these distributions are conceptually similar, but they
are apples and oranges. A fan chart gives a consensus MPC expression
of forecast uncertainty, suppressing possible disagreements among the
MPC members. A distribution presented in the Summary of Economic

Projections describes the diversity of point forecasts made by participants in FOMC deliberations, suppressing whatever uncertainty each person may feel.

To illustrate, suppose that the MPC and the FOMC both forecast that inflation in a future year will lie in the range 1 to 3%. The MPC forecast means that the consensus judgment of MPC members is that there is zero probability that the inflation rate will be less than 1% or more than 3%. The FOMC forecast means that no FOMC member made a point forecast of the inflation rate that was less than 1% or more than 3%.

The SPF and similar European panels have demonstrated the feasibility and usefulness of eliciting probabilistic predictions from panels of macroeconomic forecasters. The members of the MPC and FOMC should similarly be capable of providing informative probabilistic predictions. The MPC and the FOMC could obtain such forecasts and communicate the findings regularly to the public.

VII.   Probabilistic Thinking and Communication

There is by now extensive empirical evidence that survey respondents are willing and able to report expectations in probabilistic form. Given this, empirical economic research analyzing data on probabilistic expectations has increasingly sought to achieve substantive objectives. Researchers usually presume that elicited expectations accurately express the beliefs that persons hold regarding future events. Maintaining this assumption, they aim to learn what expectations persons hold and they use expectations data to help understand and predict choice behavior. Thus, collection and analysis of probabilistic expectations data has become part of normal economic science.

There has, nevertheless, been awareness that the willingness and ability of respondents to report probabilistic expectations does not imply that persons regularly think probabilistically and use subjective probability distributions to make decisions. It has long been known that survey respondents are willing and able to respond to questions seeking point predictions of uncertain events or verbal assessments of likelihood. Yet persons need not use point predictions or verbal assessments of likelihood to make decisions. What the evidence does show is that, however they think and act, people are willing and able to report their beliefs in multiple forms—as point predictions, verbal assessments of likelihood, or probabilistic expectations. See Wallsten et al. (1986, 1993) for analysis of this phenomenon.

This section discusses research that aims to interpret elicited probabilistic expectations, seeking to shed light on how persons respond to the questions posed and how to improve question design, so as to enhance the usefulness of expectations data. Section VII.A considers the common practice of rounding by survey respondents. Section VII.B addresses the possibility that persons may perceive ambiguity (aka Knightian uncertainty) when contemplating uncertain future events. Section VII.C considers the possibility that persons may confound beliefs and preferences.

A.   Rounding

Rounding is the familiar practice of reporting one value whenever a real number lies in an interval. Consider meteorological reports of wind direction. Reports issued to the public commonly delineate eight directions (e.g., north, northeast, east). Those to aircraft pilots delineate 36 directions (e.g., 10, 20, 30 degrees).

Whereas the extent of rounding is common knowledge in standardized communications such as weather reports, recipients of rounded data may be unsure of the extent of rounding in other settings. Uncertainty about the extent of rounding is common when researchers analyze survey responses to numerical questions. Questionnaires do not request that respondents round to a specified degree. There are no firm conventions for rounding responses. Hence, researchers cannot be sure how much rounding there may be in survey data.

Rounding of responses to questions eliciting probabilistic expectations is common and sometimes is substantial enough to warrant attention. Dominitz and Manski (1997a) observed that respondents to SEE tended to report values at 1% intervals at the extremes (i.e., 0, 1, 2 and 98, 99, 100) and at 5 or 10% intervals elsewhere (i.e., 5,10, . . , 90, 95), with responses more bunched at 50% than at adjacent round values (40, 45, 55, 60). These findings have been corroborated repeatedly in other surveys.

It is evident that respondents round their responses to subjective probability questions, but to what extent? When someone states "3%," one might reasonably infer that the person is rounding to the nearest 1%. However, when someone states "30%," one might be uncertain whether the person is rounding to the nearest 1, 5, or 10%. Even more uncertain is how to interpret responses of 0, 50, and 100%. These may sometimes be sharp expressions of beliefs, but some respondents may engage in gross rounding, using 0 to express any relatively small chance of an event,

50 to represent any intermediate chance, and 100 for any relatively large chance.

Moreover, survey data do not reveal why sample members give rounded expectations responses. Some persons may hold precise subjective probabilities for future events but round their responses to simplify communication. Others may perceive the future as partially ambiguous and, hence, not feel able to place precise probabilities on events. Thus, a response of "30%" could mean that a respondent believes that the percent chance of the event is in the range [20, 40] but feels incapable of providing finer resolution.

Considering extreme cases of ambiguity, Fischhoff and Bruine de Bruin (1999) and Bruine de Bruin et al. (2000) suggested that when respondents feel unable to assign any subjective probability to an event, they may report the value 50 to signal epistemic uncertainty, as in the loose statement "It's a 50-50 chance." This idea is formally interpretable as the grossest possible form of rounding, where 50 means that the percent chance lies in the interval [0, 100]. Lillard and Willis (2001) offered an alternative interpretation of rounding for communication, in which respondents first form full subjective distributions for the probability of an event and then report whichever of the three values (0, 50, 100) is closest to the mode of this subjective distribution.

Although survey data do not directly reveal the extent or reasons for rounding in observed responses, analysis of patterns of responses across questions and respondents can be informative. Manski and Molinari (2010) performed such analysis, focusing on the expectations module in the 2006 administration of the HRS. We found that, for each question posed, the great preponderance of the responses are multiples of 5, most responses are multiples of 10, and a moderate minority are multiples of 50. Examining the module as a whole, we found that sample members vary considerably in their response tendencies. A small fraction used only the values (0, 50, 100) throughout the module. Most respondents made fuller use of the 0–100% chance scale. About 0.26 at least once used a multiple of 10 that is not one of the values (0, 50, 100), about 0.51 at least once used a multiple of 5 that is not a multiple of 10, and about 0.12 at least once used a value that is not a multiple of 5. We proposed use of a person's response pattern across questions to infer the person's rounding practice, the result being interpretation of reported numerical values as interval data.

Further analysis of rounding and related reporting behavior in the HRS has been performed by Kleinjans and Van Soest (2014). They develop a panel data model of reporting behavior and estimate it using responses to the HRS from 1994 through 2010. See also Ruud, Schunk, and Winter (2014), who use experimental evidence to conclude that increasing uncertainty makes respondents more likely to round.

B. Ambiguity

Among economists and decision theorists, perhaps the most compelling alternatives to the hypothesis of probabilistic expectations have been put forward in research on decisions under ambiguity. Studies of ambiguity maintain that beliefs have some but not all the structure of a probability distribution. The beginning of modern study of decision making under ambiguity is usually associated with Ellsberg (1961). Early discussions appear in Keynes (1921) and Knight (1921).

A particularly common idea has been that a person may hold a set of subjective distributions for an unknown event, not a single distribution. This idea is a primitive of research on robust Bayes analysis (e.g., Berger 1985), which supposes that persons hold multiple subjective distributions prior to observing data, and it is a conclusion of some work in axiomatic decision theory (e.g., Gilboa and Schmeidler 1989). It is also a conclusion of my research on partial identification of probability distributions, which shows that combining available data with credible assumptions may enable a decision maker to partially but not fully identify an objective probability distribution (e.g., Manski 2000, 2011a). Walley (1991) and Camerer and Weber (1992) review parts of the literature.

Suppose that beliefs take the form of sets of subjective distributions. Then the single distributions that we now elicit from survey respondents are probabilistic summaries of ambiguity, much as point predictions are deterministic summaries of uncertainty. To enable persons to express ambiguity, survey researchers could elicit ranges of probabilities rather than precise probabilities for events of interest. This is straightforward in the case of binary events, for which one can pose questions such as

What do you think is the percent chance that event A will occur? Please respond with a particular value or a range of values, as you see fit.

This format enables respondents to express whatever uncertainty or ambiguity they may feel. A respondent can express complete ignorance by reporting "0 to 100%," bounded ambiguity by reporting "30 to 70%," uncertainty by reporting "60%," or certainty by reporting "100%."

Wallsten, Forsyth, and Budescu (1983) and Manski and Molinari (2010) have reported exploratory research on responses to questions of this type. The objective of the latter work was to probe beneath the evidence of rounding and try to distinguish between rounding for communication and rounding as an expression of ambiguity. I explain here.

We posed a sequence of expectations questions to 552 respondents to the American Life Panel. The first asked an often-studied HRS question about survival expectations, seeking the percent chance that the respondent gives to living to age 75. We then followed up with these questions:

Q1. When you said [X%] just now, did you mean this as an exact number or were you rounding or approximating?

If a person answered "rounding or approximating," we then asked

Q2. What number or range of numbers did you have in mind when you said [X%]?

When the response to Q1 is "an exact number," one can reasonably conclude that rounding was minimal. When the response is "rounding or approximating," one can use the response to Q2 to interpret the data. If a person responds with an exact (nonrounded) number, we think it reasonable to conclude that he was rounding for communication. If he responds with a range, he was rounding to express ambiguity.

All of the respondents answered question Q1. Of the 552 respondents, 264 reported that their response to the survival question was an exact answer and the remaining 288 reported that they had rounded or approximated. Within the group of 288 persons who were asked Q2, all but two responded. Among them, 70 persons reported that they had an exact number in mind and 248 that they had a range in mind. These numbers sum to more than 288 because 31 persons reported that they had both an exact number and a range in mind. Among the 248 who reported a range in response to Q2, the average width of the reported interval was 17.6%.

The results of this exploratory work were encouraging. Respondents to the ALP showed no resistance to being probed about the interpretation of their reported survival probabilities. If questions Q1 and Q2 had been placed on the 2006 HRS, it would have been possible to use the responses to infer rounding rather than the less direct approach we used to assign intervals based on response patterns to standard probabilistic questions.

C. Confounding Beliefs and Preferences

Research on decision making under ambiguity weakens the traditional economic assumption that persons place precise subjective probability distributions on future events, but it maintains the traditional assumption that persons separate their beliefs and preferences. The distinction between beliefs and preferences is expressed in decision theory by supposing that a person choosing an action from a choice set C specifies a state space S that lists all possible states of nature and a state-dependent utility function U(c, s) that values each action c ∈ C in each state s ∈ S. The utility function expresses preferences. The state space expresses a basic form of belief, differentiating between those states that can possibly occur and those that cannot. Placing a precise or a partial subjective distribution on the state space may strengthen the specification of beliefs.

Although separation of beliefs and preferences remains a standard assumption of applied economic analysis, economists have increasingly been willing to theorize about choice behavior with modes of decision making that confound beliefs and preferences. (See, e.g., Akerlof and Dickens 1982; Caplin and Leahy 2001; Brunnermeier and Parker 2005; Gollier and Muermann 2010; Cochrane 2011; Bénabou and Tirole 2016).

Evidence in Research Measuring Probabilistic Expectations

Measuring expectations in a survey is a well-defined task if persons separate their beliefs and preferences. It is less clear how to interpret expectations data if persons confound beliefs and preferences.

There has long been concern that the verbal questions used in attitudinal research may be susceptible to confounding. For example, if one asks a person to state whether it is "likely" or "unlikely" that an event will occur, the concern has been that the person's interpretation of these words may depend on the nature of the event. One of the most basic arguments for elicitation of probabilistic rather than verbal expectations has been that probability provides a well-defined absolute numerical scale for responses. Hence, there is reason to think that responses may be comparable across persons and events.

Accepting the traditional decision theoretic separation of beliefs and preferences, modern research eliciting probabilistic expectations has generally assumed that responses measure beliefs alone, not beliefs confounded with preferences. The empirical evidence has broadly seemed consistent with this assumption. As discussed earlier, survey responses usually have high face validity (Sec. III.A). They often are reasonably accurate when compared with objective frequencies, even if not so much as to warrant being called rational expectations (Sec. III.B). Moreover, there has been considerable success (in the sense of obtaining sensible findings) using elicited probabilistic expectations to replace expectations assumptions when estimating econometric models of expected utility maximization (Sec. III.IV).

The above generalizations notwithstanding, there have been occasional settings in which elicited probabilistic expectations may confound beliefs and preferences. In Section III.A, I noted that teenagers interviewed in the NLSY97 often gave highly inaccurate responses when asked to predict their chance of dying in the next year or the next several years. Their responses tended to wildly overstate the chance of dying, relative to the empirical evidence in life tables (see Fischhoff et al. 2000). One might speculate that their responses conflated the risk of dying with the severity of the event. On the other hand, analysis of HRS data on the expectations of older adults to survive to age 75 has shown these expectations to be reasonably accurate when compared to life tables (see Hurd and McGarry 1995, 2002). It may be that older adults can think separately about the risk of death and its finality, but teenagers are not able to do so.

Measurement of risk of crime victimization may be another setting in which persons confound beliefs with preferences. The attitudinal research literature has long been concerned with confounding of responses to verbal questions in this domain. Numerous surveys ask respondents about their fear of crime (see Warr 1994). Ferraro and LaGrange (1987) argue that such questions confound two concepts—the perceived risk of crime and the emotional response to crime—that need not be strongly associated. In fact, they argue that the empirical evidence suggests these two phenomena are not strongly positively related and, for some criminal activities, may be negatively related.

Dominitz and Manski (1997a) analyzed probabilistic expectations of burglary elicited in the SEE in 1994. We found a pervasive tendency of respondents to overpredict the risk of burglary in the year ahead. Among men, the mean subjective probability of burglary was 0.16, whereas the realized rate at which SEE respondents had been victims of burglary in the previous year was 0.05. Among women, the mean subjective probability was 0.17 and the realized fraction burglarized was 0.03. Our findings on beliefs about risk victimization corroborate the conventional wisdom that Americans perceive crime to be far more prevalent than it actually is (see Bursik and Grasmick 1993, chap. 4). We could not, however, offer a compelling rationale for the phenomenon. In personal communications, some researchers suggested to us that persons tend to be pessimistic about the likelihood of traumatic events. Yet we found no tendency toward pessimism regarding other adverse events—job loss and absence of health insurance—that arguably are as traumatic as burglary.

It is not clear whether confounding of beliefs and preferences explains teenager overstatement of the risk of mortality and adult overstatement of the risk of crime victimization. If confounding does explain these empirical phenomena, one must ask why researchers have not found analogous overstatements when eliciting probabilistic expectations of other personal risks.

VIII. Looking Ahead: Studying Expectations Formation to Inform Macro Policy Analysis

Economists were long hostile to measurement of expectations. In my earlier review of the modern literature (Manski 2004), I wrote that caution is prudent but hostility is not warranted. By the early twenty-first century, we had already learned enough that I felt able to recommend that economists should abandon their antipathy to measurement of expectations. I felt comfortable asserting that persons usually respond informatively to questions eliciting probabilistic expectations for personally significant events. I observed that the unattractive alternative to measurement of expectations is to make unsubstantiated assumptions.

Writing now, I can easily reinforce what I wrote then. We have since the early twenty-first century amassed a very substantial new body of longitudinal data on the probabilistic expectations of the American population through additions to the HRS and through initiation of the ALP and SCE. We have, moreover, learned much through collection of data in special surveys undertaken in many countries to provide data for particular research projects. These new data and the analyses they have enabled strongly corroborate my earlier belief that researchers should measure expectations routinely and use the data to improve our understanding of important features of economic behavior under uncertainty.

While the modern literature has developed mainly with a concern for applications to microeconomics, I see enormous potential for use of probabilistic expectations data in macroeconomics as well. I expect that macroeconomists should find informative much of the data and analysis discussed in this article, particularly the knowledge accumulated of expectations of equity returns (Sec. IV), inflation expectations (Sec V), and the expectations of macroeconomic forecasters (Sec. VI). Moreover, macroeconomists who plan to design and analyze new expectations questions should be able to draw useful lessons about the need for careful attention to question wording (Sec. II.B and Sec. V.A) and how persons respond to probabilistic expectations questions (Sec. VII).

I concluded my earlier review article with a call for study of expectations formation, writing:

> Looking beyond measurement, I see a critical need for basic research on expectations formation. Understanding how persons revise their expectations with receipt of new information often is a prerequisite for credible use of econometric decision models to predict behavior. (Manski 2004, 1371)

Several studies have been performed subsequently (see Sec. III.V and Sec. IV.B), but there remains a critical need for sustained research on expectations formation. Indeed, understanding expectations formation is even more essential to macroeconomics than it is to microeconomics.

Consider, for example, research on the operation of equity markets. A microeconomist may want to learn the distribution of risk and time preferences in a population of potential investors. To achieve this objective, he may obtain a random sample of the population, measure their expectations of returns to equities and other assets, observe their portfolio choices, and use the data to estimate a structural econometric model that assumes each member of the population makes a choice that maximizes expected utility. A macroeconomist may want to use the estimated structural model to predict the dynamics of equity prices that would occur after announcement of an unanticipated change in fiscal or monetary policy. To achieve this objective, one needs to do more than measure the current expectations of equity returns in the population of investors. One needs also to forecast how investors update their expectations after announcement of the policy change and as they observe the subsequent market dynamics.

Similarly, consider research on labor markets. A microeconomist may want to learn the distribution of labor-leisure preferences in a population of potential workers. To achieve this objective, he may obtain a random sample of the population, measure their expectations of life cycle after-tax earnings under alternative labor-supply choices, observe their actual choices, and use the data to estimate a structural model that assumes each person chooses labor supply to maximize expected utility. A macroeconomist may want to use the estimated structural model to predict the dynamics of market wages and aggregate employment after announcement of an unanticipated policy change, such as a change in the income tax schedule. To achieve this objective, one needs to do more than measure current expectations of life-cycle earnings in the population. One needs to forecast how persons would update their expectations after they learn of the new policy and as they observe the subsequent dynamics of the labor market.

A.   *The Dynamics of Macroeconomic Perspectives on Expectations Formation*

Over 40 years ago Lucas (1976) powerfully called attention to the importance of understanding expectations formation when one attempts to predict the outcomes of new macroeconomic policies. Lucas pointed out that optimizing individuals and firms may update their expectations following receipt of new information and revise decisions accordingly. He observed that the econometric models used in the 1970s to predict macro policy outcomes lacked microfoundations. He specifically criticized the failure of these models to distinguish anticipated policy changes, whose enactment should not affect expectations, from unanticipated changes, whose enactment may affect expectations.

Given his critique of the then-prevalent econometric practice, Lucas might have recommended that economists initiate empirical research on expectations formation in order to improve macroeconomic policy analysis. However, he made no such recommendation. Instead, he advocated that macroeconomists should assume that economic agents have rational expectations.

Early in his article, considering Friedman's permanent income model of consumption, Lucas wrote (Lucas 1976, 27) that the model "lacks content" if expectations are viewed as subjective and becomes meaningful only if rational expectations are assumed. Later, considering forecasting in generality, he asserted that assuming rational expectations is a prerequisite for predicting agent behavior, writing:

It is perhaps necessary to emphasize that this point of view towards conditional forecasting, due originally to Knight and, in modern form, to Muth, does not attribute to agents unnatural powers of instantly divining the true structure of policies affecting them. More modestly, it asserts that agents' responses become predictable to outside observers only when there can be some confidence that agents and observers share a common view of the nature of the shocks which must be forecast by both. (Lucas 1976, 41)

Lucas did not explain why he believed that the permanent income model "lacks content" without an RE assumption. Nor did he prove that prediction of agent behavior is possible "only" when rational expectations is assumed. He made these assertions as if they are self-evident. I see no logical reason why RE should be a necessary assumption in macroeconomic analysis. As far as I am aware, neither Lucas nor other macroeconomists have ever provided a logical argument for the necessity of assuming that agents have rational expectations.

Even if the assumption of rational expectations is not necessary for macro policy analysis, it is analytically appealing and has been used because it enables researchers to close their models in a succinct and tidy manner. Woodford put it this way:

The dominant approach for the past several decades of course has made use of the hypothesis of model-consistent or rational expectations (RE): the assumption that people have probability beliefs that coincide with the probabilities predicted by one's model. The RE benchmark is a natural one to consider, and its use has allowed a tremendous increase in the sophistication of the analysis of dynamics in the theoretical literature in macroeconomics. (Woodford 2013, 304)

Yet Woodford and other macroeconomists have increasingly questioned the credibility of the assumption and have entertained alternatives to it. Continuing the passage quoted above, Woodford (2013, 304) wrote:

Nonetheless, the assumption is a strong one, and one may wonder if it should be relaxed, especially when considering relatively short-run responses to disturbances, or the consequences of newly adopted policies that have not been followed in the past—both of which are precisely the types of situations that macroeconomic analysis frequently seeks to address.

Given this motivation, Woodford proceeded to contrast the assumptions and implications of several different ways of relaxing the assumption of rational expectations. Not surprisingly, he showed that the manner in which a model of expectations formation deviates from RE is consequential for prediction of macro outcomes following policy changes.

The large recent literature cited by Woodford makes plain that macroeconomists have increasingly been willing to pose and study models of expectations formation that do not assume RE. See also Sims (2003), Burnside, Eichenbaum, and Rebelo (2016), Eusepi and Preston (forthcoming), and the literatures cited there. However, the new literature being almost entirely theoretical, models of expectations formation have proliferated without evidence on their realism. Woodford (2013, 343) called attention to this in his conclusion, writing:

It may be asked how macroeconomic analysis can be possible with such a wide range of candidate assumptions. One answer would be that empirical studies should be undertaken to determine which of these possible specifications of subjective expectations best describe observed behavior. A few studies of that kind already exist, but the empirical literature remains at a fairly early stage.

Woodford's call for empirical research on expectations formation is welcome. However, I doubt that the theoretical literature developed thus far will provide a satisfactory foundation for empirical research. A potentially large problem is that theorists have typically assumed everyone forms expectations in the same way. For example, Eusepi and Preston (forthcoming, 11) write: "agents are assumed to have identical beliefs, though they do not understand this to be true as they have no knowledge of the tastes and beliefs of other agents." Near the end of their review article, they briefly suggest moving away from this assumption as a direction for future research, writing: "The second dimension where the literature could and should expand is to abandon the assumption of homogeneous expectations" (47).

Assuming homogeneous expectations can greatly simplify theoretical analysis, but this paper has called attention to considerable empirical evidence of substantial heterogeneity in the expectations of households and professional forecasters. Given this, I think it essential to question the robustness of forecasts made with models that assume homogeneous expectations. Where such forecasts are not sufficiently robust, I anticipate that macroeconomists will find it necessary to give up the simplicity of homogeneous expectations and strive to develop tractable models of economies in which agents have flexibly heterogeneous expectations.

When macroeconomists undertake empirical research, I do not expect that it will be possible to learn very much about expectations formation if only data on observed behavior are studied. The problem, as I emphasized in Section II.A, is that revealed-preference analysis of choice under uncertainty requires the researcher to infer from observed behavior both preferences and beliefs, not preferences alone. To reiterate, empirical analysis confronts a severe identification problem: an observed choice made by an agent maximizing expected utility may be consistent with many plausible utility functions and subjective probability distributions.

B.   The Potential Contribution of Expectations Measurement

As described in this paper, measurement of expectations can enable more fruitful study of expectations formation. To make progress, I urge measurement and analysis of the revisions to expectations that agents make following occurrence of unanticipated shocks. Sections III.E and IV.B described some studies that have performed two types of such research. Both types first measure expectations at a specified point in time and then measure revised expectations after provision of new information. They differ in how the new information is provided and when revised expectations are measured.

Some studies re-interview persons at later points in time and examine the revisions to expectations that they make following the occurrence of actual new events. Other studies provide information within the survey and then elicit posterior expectations immediately. Studies of the former type are appealing because they examine real-time revisions to expectations in response to actual informational shocks, but they have the disadvantage that the researcher does not know what new information respondents obtained. Studies of the latter type have opposing advantages and disadvantages: the researcher controls provision of new information, but the setting is artificial.

To give a small sense of what may be learned with data of the first type, consider the expectations of professional macroeconomic forecasters depicted graphically in the top panel of figure 1. The panel displays the subjective medians and IQRs for 2001 GDP growth elicited from 13 forecasters who participated in the SPF in both 3Q:2001 and 4Q:2001. Thus, the figure shows GDP growth expectations before and after the terrorist attacks of September 11, 2001. Each forecaster is depicted by an arrow whose tail is his 3Q:2001 prediction and whose tip is his 4Q:2001 prediction.

Examination of the 3Q:2001 predictions shows moderate heterogeneity in GDP growth expectations prior to the attacks. Across the SPF panel, the subjective median forecast varied from 0.011 to 0.018 and the subjective IQR varied from 0.005 to 0.013. The terrorist attacks and the policy response that followed provide a classic case of an unanticipated shock. The figure shows that nearly all forecasters revised their median forecast downward between 3Q:2001 and 4Q:2001, but the magnitude of the revision varied greatly across forecasters. The median forecast of four forecasters remained essentially unchanged. Eight forecasters reduced their median growth forecast moderately (by about 0.025 to 0.01). One reduced his median forecast substantially, lowering it from 0.015 to −0.005. Forecasters also varied in the direction of revisions to their subjective IQRs, with some becoming more certain about output growth and others becoming less certain.

The evident heterogeneity across forecasters in GDP growth predictions is hard to reconcile with the assumption of rational expectations. It is similarly hard to reconcile with the RE assumption the heterogeneity of forecasts in the bottom panel of figure 1, which shows 3Q:2005 inflation predictions and the revisions that forecasters made to these predictions in 4Q:2005, after Bernanke's nomination to be Chair of the Fed Board. An RE assumption is plainly inconsistent with the observed heterogeneity in the expectations of the SPF panel if forecasters have common knowledge of the state of the economy. To rescue the RE assumption would require that SPF members possess differential private information that makes their prior predictions and revisions to expectations vary as shown in the figure.

I expect that study of revisions to expectations such as in figure 1 will enable macroeconomists to make progress learning about expectations formation. However, I do not think that measurement of revisions to expectations per se will suffice to guide macroeconomic policy analysis. To develop credible models of expectations formation, it will be important to study how persons obtain and interpret new information over time.

To reiterate a point made in Section III.E, economists have generally modeled revision to expectations as a process of Bayesian updating, which expresses new information through the likelihood function. This presumes that data are generated by a well-defined sampling process. However, revision of macroeconomic expectations in real life requires persons to assimilate government announcements, media reports, personal observations, and other forms of information that may be generated in obscure ways.

Introspecting about how I revise my own macroeconomic expectations after receipt of new information, I often find it difficult to conjecture an explicit sampling process. Hence, I am unable to consciously update in the Bayesian manner. Yet I somehow do revise my expectations and find that I can express a posterior subjective probability distribution. If my experience is typical, it will be a challenge to develop realistic models of expectations formation by individuals and firms.

Endnotes

I am grateful for comments on earlier drafts from Nicholas Bloom, Martin Eichenbaum, Pamela Giustinelli, Lawrence Hazelrigg, Jonathan Parker, Wilbert van der Klaauw, and Joachim Winter. For acknowledgments, sources of research support, and disclosure of the author's material financial relationships, if any, please see http://www.nber.org/chapters /c13907.ack.

1. To encourage full use of the percent-chance scale, it helps to familiarize respondents with the scale before commencing substantive questioning. For example, SEE used this introductory statement and opening question about the weather:

Now I will ask you some questions about future, uncertain outcomes. In each case, try to think about the whole range of possible outcomes and think about how likely they are to occur during the next 12 months. In some of the questions, I will ask you about the percent chance of something happening. The percent chance must be a number from 0 to 100. Numbers like 2 or 5 percent may be "almost no chance," 20 percent or so may mean "not much chance," a 45 or 55 percent chance may be a "pretty even chance," 80 percent or so may mean a "very good chance," and a 95 or 98 percent chance may be "almost certain." The percent chance can also be thought of as the number of chances out of 100.

Let's start with the weather where you live. What do you think is the percent chance (what are the chances out of 100) that it will rain tomorrow?

2. An absence of incentives is a common feature of all survey research, not a specific attribute of expectations questions. The literature on *proper scoring rules* develops incentive mechanisms for honest revelation of expectations concerning observable events (e.g., Shuford, Albert, and Massengill 1966; Savage 1971). These mechanisms usually aim to encourage honest revelation under the assumption that respondents maximize expected utility and are risk neutral. Proper scoring rules are regularly used in lab experiments eliciting probabilistic expectations (e.g., Nyarko and Schotter 2002; Schotter and Trevino 2014), but not in survey research. Application of a scoring rule requires the researcher to verify what events do and do not occur. Verification typically is not possible in survey settings. However, Armantier et al. (2015) analyzed whether inflation expectations collected in a survey are informative of decisions the same respondents subsequently make in an incentivized investment experiment.

3. Another panel survey has collected partial probabilistic expectations from professionals. A Duke University survey of senior finance executives at American firms has asked respondents to predict the return to the S&P 500 in the year ahead. The Duke survey used this question format:

Over the next year, I expect the annual S&P 500 return will be:
—There is a 1-in-10 chance the actual return will be less than ___%
—I expect the return to be: ___%
—There is a 1-in-10 chance the actual return will be greater than ___%

See Ben-David et al. (2013) for analysis of these data. The Duke survey also collects point predictions of outcomes in respondents' firms, but not probabilistic predictions. See Gennaioli, Ma, and Shleifer (2016) for analyses of these data.

References

Akerlof, G., and W. Dickens. 1982. "The Economic Consequences of Cognitive Dissonance." *American Economic Review* 72:307–19.

Armantier, O., W. Bruine de Bruin, S. Potter, G. Topa, W. van der Klaauw, and B. Zafar. 2013. "Measuring Inflation Expectations." *Annual Review of Economics* 5:273–301.

Armantier, O., W. Bruine de Bruin, G. Topa, W. van der Klaauw, and B. Zafar. 2015. "Inflation Expectations and Behavior: Do Survey Respondents Act on Their Beliefs?" *International Economic Review* 56:505–36.

Armantier, O., S. Nelson, G. Topa, W. van der Klaauw, and B. Zafar. 2016. "The Price is Right: Updating of Inflation Expectations in a Randomized Price Information Experiment." *Review of Economics and Statistics* 98:503–23.

Armantier, O., W. G. Topa, W. van der Klaauw, and B. Zafar. 2016. "An Overview of the Survey of Consumer Expectations." Staff Report no. 800, Federal Reserve Bank of New York.

Armona, L., A. Fuster, and B. Zafar. 2016. "Home Price Expectations and Behavior: Evidence from a Randomized Information Experiment." Staff Report no. 798, Federal Reserve Bank of New York.

Bachmann, R., and S. Elstner. 2015. "Firm Optimism and Pessimism." *European Economic Review* 79:297–325.

Bachmann, R., S. Elstner, and E. Sims. 2013. "Uncertainty and Economic Activity: Evidence from Business Survey Data." *American Economic Journal: Macroeconomics* 5:217–49.

Barron, O., M. Stanford, and Y. Yu. 2009. "Further Evidence on the Relation between Analysts' Forecast Dispersion and Stock Returns." *Contemporary Accounting Research* 26:329–57.

Bénabou, R., and J. Tirole. 2016. "Mindful Economics: The Production, Consumption, and Value of Beliefs." *Journal of Economic Perspectives* 30:141–64.

Ben-David, I., J. Graham, and C. Harvey. 2013. "Managerial Miscalibration." *Quarterly Journal of Economics* 128:1547–84.

Berger, J. 1985. *Statistical Decision Theory and Bayesian Analysis*. New York: Springer-Verlag.

Beyth-Marom, R. 1982. "How Probable is Probable? A Numerical Translation of Verbal Probability Expressions." *Journal of Forecasting* 1:257–69.

Blass, A., S. Lach, and C. Manski. 2010. "Using Elicited Choice Probabilities to Estimate Random Utility Models: Preferences for Electricity Reliability." *International Economic Review* 51:421–40.

Brenner, M., and Y. Landskroner. 1983. "Inflation Uncertainties and Returns on Bonds." *Economica* 50:463–68.

Bruine de Bruin, W., and B. Fischhoff. 2017. "Eliciting Probabilistic Expectations: Collaborations between Psychologists and Economists." *Proceedings of the National Academy of Sciences* 114 (13): 3297–304.

Bruine de Bruin, W., B. Fischhoff, B. Halpern-Felsher, and S. Millstein. 2000. "Expressing Epistemic Uncertainty: It's a Fifty-Fifty Chance." *Organizational Behavior and Human Decision Processes* 81:115–31.

Bruine de Bruin, W., C. Manski, G. Topa, and W. van der Klaauw. 2011. "Measuring Consumer Uncertainty about Future Inflation." *Journal of Applied Econometrics* 26:454–78.

Brunnermeier, M., and J. Parker. 2005. "Optimal Expectations." *American Economic Review* 95:1092–118.

Burnside, C., M. Eichenbaum, and S. Rebelo. 2016. "Understanding Booms and Busts in Housing Markets." *Journal of Political Economy* 124:1088–147.

Bursik, R., and H. Grasmick. 1993. *Neighborhoods and Crime*. New York: MacMillan.

Caballero, R. 1990. "Consumption Puzzles and Precautionary Savings." *Journal of Monetary Economics* 25:113–36.

Camerer, C., and M. Weber. 1992. "Recent Developments in Modeling Preferences: Uncertainty and Ambiguity." *Journal of Risk and Uncertainty* 5:325–70.

Caplin, A., and J. Leahy. 2001. "Psychological Expected Utility Theory and Anticipatory Feelings." *Quarterly Journal of Economics* 116:55–80.

Carroll, C. 1992. "The Buffer-Stock Theory of Saving: Some Macroeconomic Evidence." *Brookings Papers on Economic Activity* 2:61–156.

Clemen, R. 1989. "Combining Forecasts: A Review and Annotated Bibliography." *International Journal of Forecasting* 5:559–83.

Clements, M. 2009. "'Internal Consistency of Survey Respondents' Forecasts: Evidence Based on the Survey of Professional Forecasters." In *The Methodology and Practice of Econometrics*, ed. J. Castle and N. Shephard. Oxford: Oxford University Press.

Cochrane, J. 2011. "Presidential Address: Discount Rates." *Journal of Finance* 66:1047–108.

Coibion, O., and Y. Gorodnichenko. 2012. "What Can Survey Forecasts Tell Us about Informational Rigidities?" *Journal of Political Economy* 120:116–59.

Cukierman, A., and P. Wachtel. 1979. "Differential Inflationary Expectations and the Variability of the Rate of Inflation: Theory and Evidence." *American Economic Review* 69:595–609.

Curtin, R. 1982. "Indicators of Consumer Behavior: The University of Michigan Surveys of Consumers." *Public Opinion Quarterly* 46:340–52.

Daniel, K., D. Hirshleifer, and S. Teoh. 2002. "Investor Psychology in Capital Markets: Evidence and Policy Implications." *Journal of Monetary Economics* 49:139–209.

Davis J., and T. Smith. 1994. *The General Social Surveys, 1972-1994, Cumulative File*. Chicago: National Opinion Research Center.

Delavande, A. 2008a. "Measuring Revisions to Subjective Expectations." *Journal of Risk and Uncertainty* 36:43–82.

———. 2008b. "Pill, Patch, or Shot? Subjective Expectations and Birth Control Choice." *International Economic Review* 49:999–1042.

———. 2014. "Probabilistic Expectations in Developing Countries." *Annual Review of Economics* 6:1–20.

Delavande, A., and C. Manski. 2010. "Probabilistic Polling and Voting in the 2008 Presidential Election: Evidence from the American Life Panel." *Public Opinion Quarterly* 74:433–59.

———. 2012. "Candidate Preferences and Expectations of Election Outcomes." *Proceedings of the National Academy of Sciences* 109:3711–15.

———. 2015. "Using Elicited Choice Probabilities in Hypothetical Elections to Study Decisions to Vote." *Electoral Studies* 38:28–37.

Diether, K., C. Malloy, and A. Scherbina. 2002. "Differences of Opinion and the Cross Section of Stock Returns." *Journal of Finance* 57:2113–41.

Dominitz, J. 1998. "Earnings Expectations, Revisions, and Realizations." *Review of Economics and Statistics* 80:374–88.

Dominitz, J., and C. Manski. 1997a. "Perceptions of Economic Insecurity: Evidence from the Survey of Economic Expectations." *Public Opinion Quarterly* 61:261–87.

———. 1997b. "Using Expectations Data to Study Subjective Income Expectations." *Journal of the American Statistical Association* 92:855–67.

———. 2003. "How Should We Measure Consumer Confidence (Sentiment)? Evidence from the Michigan Survey of Consumers." NBER Working Paper no. 9926, Cambridge, MA.

———. 2004. "How Should We Measure Consumer Confidence?" *Journal of Economic Perspectives* 18:51–66.

———. 2007. "Expected Equity Returns and Portfolio Choice: Evidence from the Health and Retirement Study." *Journal of the European Economic Association* 5:369–79.

———. 2011. "Measuring and Interpreting Expectations of Equity Returns." *Journal of Applied Econometrics* 26:352–70.

Dominitz, J., C. Manski, and B. Fischhoff. 2001. "Who are Youth At-Risk? Expectations Evidence in the NLSY-97." In *Social Awakenings: Adolescents' Behavior as Adulthood Approaches*, ed. R. Michael, 230–57. New York: Russell Sage Foundation.

El-Gamal, M., and D. Grether. 1995. "Are People Bayesian? Uncovering Behavioral Strategies." *Journal of the American Statistical Association* 90:1137–45.

Elliott, G., I. Komunjer, and A. Timmermann. 2005. "Estimation and Testing of Forecast Rationality under Flexible Loss." *Review of Economic Studies* 72:1107–25.

———. 2008. "Biases in Macroeconomic Forecasts: Irrationality or Asymmetric Loss?" *Journal of European Economic Association* 6:122–57.

Ellsberg, D. 1961. "Risk, Ambiguity, and the Savage Axioms." *Quarterly Journal of Economics* 75:643–69.

Engelberg, J., C. Manski, and J. Williams. 2009. "Comparing the Point Predictions and Subjective Probability Distributions of Professional Forecasters." *Journal of Business and Economic Statistics* 27:30–41.

———. 2011. "Assessing the Temporal Variation of Macroeconomic Forecasts by a Panel of Changing Composition." *Journal of Applied Econometrics* 26:1059–78.

Erev, I., and B. Cohen. 1990. "Verbal versus Numerical Probabilities: Efficiency, Biases, and the Preference Paradox." *Organizational Behavior and Human Decision Processes* 45:1–18.

Eusepi, S., and B. Preston. Forthcoming. "The Science of Monetary Policy: An Imperfect Knowledge Perspective." *Journal of Economic Literature*.

Fama, E. 1970. "Efficient Capital Markets: A Review of Theory and Empirical Work." *Journal of Finance* 25:383–417.

Federal Reserve Bank of Atlanta. 2017. *Decision Maker Survey*. Accessed February 23, 2017. https://www.frbatlanta.org/research/surveys/decision-maker/?panel=1.

Federal Reserve Consultant Committee on Consumer Survey Statistics. 1955. Smithies Committee report in *Reports of the Federal Reserve Consultant Committees on Economic Statistics*. Hearings of the Subcommittee on Economic Statistics of the Joint Committee on the Economic Report, 84th US Congress.

Ferraro, K., and R. LaGrange. 1987. "The Measurement of Fear of Crime." *Sociological Inquiry* 57:70–101.

Ferrell, W., and P. McGoey. 1980. "A Model of Calibration for Subjective Probabilities." *Organizational Behavior and Human Performance* 26:32–53.

Fischhoff, B., and W. Bruine de Bruin. 1999. "Fifty-Fifty = 50%?" *Journal of Behavioral Decision Making* 12:149–63.

Fischhoff, B., A. Parker, W. Bruine de Bruin, J. Downs, C. Palmgren, R. Dawes, and C. Manski. 2000. "Teen Expectations for Significant Life Events." *Public Opinion Quarterly* 64:189–205.

Fisher, K., and M. Statman. 2000. "Investor Sentiment and Stock Returns." *Financial Analysts Journal* 56:16–23.

Forsythe, R., F. Nelson, G. Neumann, and J. Wright. 1992. "Anatomy of an Experimental Political Stock Market." *American Economic Review* 82:1142–61.

Friedman, M., and L. Savage. 1948. "The Utility Analysis of Choices Involving Risk." *Journal of Political Economy* 56:279–304.

Gali J. 2008. *Monetary Policy, Inflation and the Business Cycle: An Introduction to the New Keynesian Framework*. Princeton, NJ: Princeton University Press.

Gennaioli, N., Y. Ma, and A. Shleifer. 2016. "Expectations and Investment." *NBER Macroeconomics Annual 2015*, ed. Martin Eichenbaum and Jonathan Parker. Chicago: University of Chicago Press.

Gigerenzer, G. 1991. "How to Make Cognitive Illusions Disappear: Beyond Heuristics and Biases." *European Review of Social Psychology* 2:83–115.

Gilboa, I., and D. Schmeidler. 1989. "Maxmin Expected Utility with Non-Unique Prior." *Journal of Mathematical Economics* 18:141–53.

Giordani, P., and P. Söderlind. 2003. "Inflation Forecast Uncertainty." *European Economic Review* 47:1037–59.

Giustinelli, P. 2016. "Group Decision Making with Uncertain Outcomes: Unpacking Child-Parent Choice of the High School Track." *International Economic Review* 57:573–602.

Gjerstad, S. 2005. "Risk Aversion, Beliefs, and Prediction Market Equilibrium." Economic Science Laboratory, University of Arizona.

Gollier, C., and A. Muermann. 2010. "Optimal Choice and Beliefs with Ex Ante Savoring and Ex Post Disappointment." *Management Science* 56:1272–84.

Gosselin, M., and M. Kahn. 2015. "A Survey of Consumer Expectations for Canada." *Bank of Canada Review* Autumn:14–23.

Gouret, F., and G. Hollard. 2011. "When Kahneman Meets Manski: Using Dual Systems of Reasoning to Interpret Subjective Expectations of Equity Returns." *Journal of Applied Econometrics* 26:371–92.

Greenwood, R., and A. Shleifer. 2014. "Expectations of Returns and Expected Returns." *Review of Financial Studies* 27:714–46.

Guiso, L., T. Jappelli, and L. Pistaferri. 2002. "An Empirical Analysis of Earnings and Employment Risk." *Journal of Business and Economic Statistics* 20:241–53.

Guiso, L., T. Jappelli, and D. Terlizzese. 1992. "Earnings Uncertainty and Precautionary Saving." *Journal of Monetary Economics* 30:307–37.

Guiso, L., and G. Parigi. 1999. "Investment and Demand Uncertainty." *Quarterly Journal of Economics* 114:185–227.

Güntay, L., and D. Hackbarth. 2010. "Corporate Bond Credit Spreads and Forecast Dispersion." *Journal of Banking & Finance* 34:2328–45.

Gutsche, T., A. Kapteyn, E. Meijer, and B. Weerman. 2014. "The RAND Continuous 2012 Presidential Election Poll." *Public Opinion Quarterly* 78:S233–54.

Hahm, J., and D. Steigerwald. 1999. "Consumption Adjustment under Time—Varying Income Uncertainty." *Review of Economics and Statistics* 81:32–40.

Haliassos, M., and C. C. Bertaut. 1995. "Why Do So Few Hold Stocks?" *Economic Journal* 105:1110–29.

Hall, R., and F. Mishkin. 1982. "The Sensitivity of Consumption to Transitory Income: Estimates from Panel Data on Households." *Econometrica* 50:461–77.

Hamermesh, D. 1985. "Expectations, Life Expectancy, and Economic Behavior." *Quarterly Journal of Economics* 100:389–408.

Harris, M., and A. Raviv. 1993. "Differences of Opinion Make a Horse Race." *Review of Financial Studies* 6:473–506.

Haubrich, J., G. Pennachi, and P. Ritchken. 2012. "Inflation Expectations, Real Rates, and Risk Premia: Evidence from Inflation Swaps." *Review of Financial Studies* 25:1588–629.

Hayford, M. 2000. "Inflation Uncertainty, Unemployment Uncertainty, and Economic Activity." *Journal of Macroeconomics* 22:315–29.

Hoffrage, U., S. Lindsey, R. Hertwig, and G. Gigerenzer. 2000. "Communicating Statistical Information." *Science* 290:2261–62.

Hudomiet, P., G. Kezdi, and R. Willis. 2011. "Stock Market Crash and Expectations of American Households." *Journal of Applied Econometrics* 26:393–415.

Hurd, M. 2009. "Subjective Probabilities in Household Surveys." *Annual Review of Economics* 1:543–64.

Hurd, M., and K. McGarry. 1995. "Evaluation of the Subjective Probabilities of Survival in the Health and Retirement Study." *Journal of Human Resources* 30:S268 92.

———. 2002. "The Predictive Validity of Subjective Probabilities of Survival." *Economic Journal* 112:966–85.

Hurd, M., and J. Smith. 2002. "Expected Bequests and Their Distribution." NBER Working Paper no. 9142, Cambridge, MA.

Hurd, M., J. Smith, and J. Zissimopoulos. 2004. "The Effects of Subjective Survival on Retirement and Social Security Claiming." *Journal of Applied Econometrics* 19:761–75.

Hurd, M., M. van Rooij, and J. Winter. 2011. "Stock Market Expectations of Dutch Households." *Journal of Applied Econometrics* 26:416–36.

Johnson, T. 2004. "Forecast Dispersion and the Cross Section of Expected Returns." *Journal of Finance* 59:1957–78.

Juster, T. 1964. *Anticipations and Purchases*. Princeton, NJ: Princeton University Press.

———. 1966. "Consumer Buying Intentions and Purchase Probability: An Experiment in Survey Design." *Journal of the American Statistical Association* 61:658–96.

Juster, T., and R. Suzman. 1995. "An Overview of the Health and Retirement Study." *Journal of Human Resources* 30:S7–56.

Kandel, E., and N. Pearson. 1995. "Differential Interpretation of Public Signals and Trade in Speculative Markets." *Journal of Political Economy* 103:831–72.

Katona, G. 1957. "Federal Reserve Board Committee Reports on Consumer Expectations and Savings Statistics." *Review of Economics and Statistics* 39:40–46.

Keynes, J. 1921. *A Treatise on Probability*. London: MacMillan.

———. 1937. "The General Theory of Employment." *Quarterly Journal of Economics* 51:209–23.

Kleinjans, K., and A. Van Soest. 2014. "Rounding, Focal Point Answers and Nonresponse to Subjective Probability Questions." *Journal of Applied Econometrics* 29:567–85.

Knight F. 1921. *Risk, Uncertainty, and Profit*. Boston: Houghton-Mifflin.

Koriat, A., S. Lichtenstein, and B. Fischhoff. 1980. "Reasons for Confidence." *Journal of Experimental Psychology: Human Learning and Memory* 6:107–18.

Levi, M., and J. Makin. 1979. "Fisher, Phillips, Friedman and the Measured Impact of Inflation on Interest." *Journal of Finance* 34:35–52.

———. 1980. "Inflation Uncertainty and the Phillips Curve: Some Empirical Evidence." *American Economic Review* 70:1022–27.

Lichtenstein, S., B. Fischhoff, and L. Phillips. 1982. "Calibration of Probabilities: The State of the Art to 1980." In *Judgment under Uncertainty: Heuristics and Biases*, ed. D. Kahneman, P. Slovic, and A. Tversky. New York: Cambridge University Press.

Lichtenstein, S., and R. Newman. 1967. "Empirical Scaling of Common Verbal Phrases Associated with Numerical Probabilities." *Psychonomic Science* 9:563–64.

Lillard, L., and R. Willis. 2001. "Cognition and Wealth: The Importance of Probabilistic Thinking." Michigan Retirement Research Working Paper no. MRRC WP UM00-04, University of Michigan.

Linden, F. 1982. "The Consumer as Forecaster." *Public Opinion Quarterly* 46: 353–60.

Lintner, J. 1965. "The Valuation of Risk Assets and the Selection of Risky Investments in Stock Portfolios and Capital Budgets." *Review of Economics and Statistics* 47:13–37.

———. 1969. "The Aggregation of Investors' Diverse Judgments and Preferences in Purely Competitive Markets." *Journal of Financial and Quantitative Analysis* 4:347–400.

Lochner, L. 2007. "Individual Perceptions of the Criminal Justice System." *American Economic Review* 97:444–60.

Lucas, R. 1976. "Econometric Policy Evaluation: A Critique." *Carnegie-Rochester Conference Series on Public Policy* 1:19–46.

Makin, J. 1982. "Anticipated Money, Inflation Uncertainty, and Real Economic Activity." *Review of Economics and Statistics* 64:126–34.

Mankiw, N. G., R. Reis, and J. Wolfers. 2004. "Disagreement about Inflation Expectations." *NBER Macroeconomics Annual 2003*, ed. Mark Gertler and Kenneth Rogoff, 209–48. Cambridge, MA: MIT Press.

Manski, C. 1993. "Adolescent Econometricians: How Do Youth Infer the Returns to Schooling?" In *Studies of Supply and Demand in Higher Education*, ed. C. Clotfelter and M. Rothschild, 43–57. Chicago: University of Chicago Press.

———. 1999. "Analysis of Choice Expectations in Incomplete Scenarios." *Journal of Risk and Uncertainty* 19:49–66.

———. 2000. "Identification Problems and Decisions under Ambiguity: Empirical Analysis of Treatment Response and Normative Analysis of Treatment Choice." *Journal of Econometrics* 95:415–42.

———. 2004. "Measuring Expectations." *Econometrica* 72:1329–76.

———. 2006. "Interpreting the Predictions of Prediction Markets." *Economic Letters* 91:425–29.

———. 2011a. "Choosing Treatment Policies under Ambiguity." *Annual Review of Economics* 3:25–49.

———. 2011b. "Interpreting and Combining Heterogeneous Survey Forecasts." In *Oxford Handbook on Economic Forecasting*, ed. M. Clements and D. Hendry, 457–72. Oxford: Oxford University Press.

———. 2016. "Interpreting Point Predictions: Some Logical Issues." *Foundations and Trends in Accounting* 10:238–61.

Manski, C., and F. Molinari. 2010. "Rounding Probabilistic Expectations in Surveys." *Journal of Business and Economic Statistics* 28:219–31.

Manski, C., and J. Straub. 2000. "Worker Perceptions of Job Insecurity in the Mid-1990s: Evidence from the Survey of Economic Expectations." *Journal of Human Resources* 35:447–79.

Mayshar, J. 1983. "On Divergence of Opinion and Imperfections in Capital Markets." *American Economic Review* 73:114–28.

McClelland, A., and F. Bolger. 1994. "The Calibration of Subjective Probabilities: Theories and Models 1980–94." In *Subjective Probability*, ed. G. Wright and P. Ayton. New York: Wiley.

Miller, E. 1977. "Risk, Uncertainty, and Divergence of Opinion." *Journal of Finance* 32:1151–68.

Morris, S. 1995. "The Common Prior Assumption in Economic Theory." *Economics and Philosophy* 11:227–53.

Morrison, D. 1979. "Purchase Intentions and Purchase Behavior." *Journal of Marketing* 43:65–74.

Nyarko, Y., and A. Schotter. 2002. "An Experimental Study of Belief Learning Using Elicited Beliefs." *Econometrica* 70:971–1005.

Patton, A., and A. Timmermann. 2010. "Why Do Forecasters Disagree? Lessons from the Term Structure of Cross-Sectional Dispersion." *Journal of Monetary Economics* 57:83–120.

Pesaran, H. 1987. *The Limits to Rational Expectations*. Oxford: Blackwell.

Piazzesi, M., and M. Schneider. 2009. "Momentum Traders in the Housing Market: Survey Evidence and a Search Model." *American Economic Review* 99:406–11.

Ruud, P., D. Schunk, and J. Winter. 2014. "Uncertainty Causes Rounding: An Experimental Study." *Experimental Economics* 17:391–413.

Samuelson, P. 1938. "A Note on the Pure Theory of Consumer Behavior." *Economica* 5:61–71.

———. 1948. "Consumption Theory in Terms of Revealed Preferences." *Economica* 15:243–53.

Savage, L. 1971. "Elicitation of Personal Probabilities and Expectations." *Journal of the American Statistical Association* 66:783–801.

Schotter, A., and I. Trevino. 2014. "Belief Elicitation in the Laboratory." *Annual Review of Economics* 6:103–28.

Sharpe, W. 1964. "Capital Asset Prices: A Theory of Market Equilibrium under Conditions of Risk." *Journal of Finance* 19:425–42.

———. 1970. *Portfolio Theory and Capital Markets*. New York: McGraw-Hill.

Shuford, E., A. Albert, and H. Massengill. 1966. "Admissible Probability Measurement Procedures." *Psychometrika* 31:125–45.

Sims, C. A. 2003. "Implications of Rational Inattention." *Journal of Monetary Economics* 50:665–90.

———. 2009. "Inflation Expectations, Uncertainty and Monetary Policy." Working Paper no. 275, Basel, Switzerland, Bank for International Settlements.

Skinner, J. 1988. "Risky Income, Life Cycle Consumption and Precautionary Savings." *Journal of Monetary Economics* 22:237–55.

Souleles, N. 2004. "Expectations, Heterogeneous Forecast Errors, and Consumption: Micro Evidence from the Michigan Consumer Sentiment Surveys." *Journal of Money, Credit, and Banking* 36:39–72.

Tversky, A., and D. Kahneman. 1974. "Judgement under Uncertainty: Heuristics and Biases." *Science* 185:1124–31.

Universities-National Bureau Committee for Economic Research. 1960. *The Quality and Economic Significance of Anticipations Data*. Princeton, NJ: Princeton University Press.

US Census Bureau. 1988. "Fertility of American Women: June, 1987." Current Population Reports, Series P-20, no. 427, Washington, DC, US Government Printing Office.

———. 2016. *2015 Management and Organizational Practices Survey*. Accessed February 23, 2017. https://www.census.gov/mcd/mops/.

van der Klaauw, W. 2012. "On the Use of Expectations Data in Estimating Structural Dynamic Models." *Journal of Labor Economics* 30:521–54.

van der Klaauw, W., and K. Wolpin. 2008. "Social Security and the Retirement and Savings Behavior of Low-Income Households." *Journal of Econometrics* 145:21–42.

Vissing-Jorgenson, A. 2004. "Perspectives on Behavioral Finance: Does 'Irrationality' Disappear with Wealth? Evidence from Expectations and Actions." *NBER*

Macroeconomics Annual 2003, vol. 18, ed. Mark Gertler and Kenneth Rogoff. Cambridge, MA: MIT Press.

Walley, P. 1991. *Statistical Reasoning with Imprecise Probabilities*. London: Chapman & Hall.

Wallsten, T., D. Budescu, A. Rapoport, R. Zwick, and B. Forsyth. 1986. "Measuring the Vague Meanings of Probability Terms." *Journal of Experimental Psychology: General* 115:348–65.

Wallsten T., D. Budescu, R. Zwick, and S. Kemp. 1993. "Preferences and Reasons for Communicating Probabilistic Information in Verbal or Numerical Terms." *Bulletin of the Psychonomic Society* 31:135–38.

Wallsten, T., B. Forsyth, and D. Budescu. 1983. "Stability and Coherence of Health Experts' Upper and Lower Subjective Probabilities about Dose-Response Functions." *Organizational Behavior and Human Performance* 31:227–302.

Warr, M. 1994. "Public Perceptions and Reactions to Violent Offending and Victimization." In *Understanding and Preventing Violence*, vol. 4, ed. A. Reiss and J. Roth. Washington, DC: National Academy Press.

Williams, J. 1938. *The Theory of Investment Value*. Cambridge, MA: Harvard University Press.

Wiswall, M., and B. Zafar. 2015. "Determinants of College Major Choice: Identification Using an Information Experiment." *Review of Economic Studies* 82: 791–824.

Wolfers, J., and E. Zitzewitz. 2004. "Prediction Markets." *Journal of Economic Perspectives* 18:107–26.

———. 2006. "Interpreting Prediction Market Prices as Probabilities." NBER Working Paper no. 12200, Cambridge, MA.

Woodford, M. 2013. "Macroeconomic Analysis without the Rational Expectations Hypothesis." *Annual Review of Economics* 5:303–46.

Zafar, B. 2011. "How Do College Students Form Expectations?" *Journal of Labor Economics* 29:301–48.

———. 2013. "College Major Choice and the Gender Gap." *Journal of Human Resources* 48:545–95.

Zarnowitz, V., and L. Lambros. 1987. "Consensus and Uncertainty in Economic Prediction." *Journal of Political Economy* 95:591–621.

Zeldes, S. 1989. "Optimal Consumption with Stochastic Income: Deviations from Certainty Equivalence." *Quarterly Journal of Economics* 104:275–98.

Zimmer, A. 1983. "Verbal vs. Numerical Processing of Subjective Probabilities." In *Decision Making under Uncertainty*, ed. R. Scholz. Amsterdam: North-Holland.

———. 1984. "A Model for the Interpretation of Verbal Predictions." *International Journal of Man-Machine Studies*. 20:121–34.

Comment

Andrew Caplin, New York University and NBER

It is a privilege to discuss the vibrant field of survey measurement of probabilistic economic expectations in which Manski has played the essential pioneering role. Validations and other research developments related to these new measurements have been richly presented by Manski (2004), Hurd (2009), and now in Manski's extensive article for the *NBER Macroeconomics Annual*. In my review, I take this material for granted and focus on some interesting facets of the intellectual background to this important field of research, stress the importance of improved measurement of beliefs, and present a very brief "best case" analysis of future developments. I focus on the importance of systematizing our understanding of "errors" in survey responses: I use the quote marks to indicate that this is generally hard to define, let alone to measure. The approach I suggest that has the most promise in this regard takes seriously how attentive survey respondents are to the questions posed.

Origins

Qualitative measurement of subjective beliefs has a long history in psychological research. In a typical survey question in this tradition, respondents place future events in such discrete categories as "possible," "likely," "unlikely," and so forth. For social scientists engaged in quantitative research, these questions are fundamentally unsatisfactory. What do these scales mean to each respondent? If, as is sometimes the case, the respondent has something akin to a subjective probability of 80% in mind, is this possible, likely, very likely, or otherwise? Why would one expect different respondents to have the same subjective scales? Why would one expect these scales to be independent of context? Why not ask for quantitative answers to probability questions rather than insisting that they be boxed and camouflaged in some idiosyncratic and local manner?

Given the ambiguities of the questions in the psychological tradition, it is hardly surprising that there was a move to quantification. Brier (1950) pioneered in the development of probabilistic weather forecasts to get beyond the ambiguity in claiming that it was "quite likely" to rain. In this case, the drive to quantification was statistical. By tracking past conditions and weather outcomes, the forecaster can directly check how often conditions analogous to those currently in force gave rise to rain in the past. This is naturally measured in proportionate terms, making the probabilistic statement a natural summary of the likely implications of current (and past) conditions for the weather tomorrow. Translating this into vague language has few obvious advantages.

While the drive to quantification of probabilities in weather forecasting was pragmatic in nature, the corresponding drive in economics derived more from developments in economic theory. It was associated with advances in the theory of choice under uncertainty, in particular, expected utility theory. In fact, the early literature on belief measurement in experiments was reviewed by Savage (1971) in making his proposal for a "proper" scoring rule. With regard to survey measurement, Haavelmo was among the first to suggest the potential value of responses to quantitative questions on subjective beliefs concerning future values outcomes:

It is my belief that if we can develop more explicit and a priori convincing economic models in terms of these variables . . . then ways and means can and will eventually be found to obtain actual measurements of such data. (Haavelmo 1958, 357)

It is interesting to note that Haavelmo suggested first developing "a priori convincing" models of belief formation before trying to obtain the corresponding measurements. Luckily, the profession has not followed the proposed sequential strategy. Indeed, it is hard to know in what sense and how we could become "convinced" by the a priori theories that we have developed to this point, including the Bayesian hypothesis and rational expectations. Rather than waiting for conviction to arrive, researchers wisely started to diversify their research portfolios by simultaneously developing methods for measuring subjective beliefs. This is the body of research that Manski surveys in his comprehensive paper.

The first to implement quantitative methods of belief measurement was Juster (1966) in the context of future car purchases. Juster considered how responses to traditional yes/no questions on purchase intentions (buy or not buy) were interpreted by respondents. He imagined that the response might reflect which was perceived as more likely. But this limits predictive power. One would expect there to be many who do in the end buy cars who were ex ante less than 50% likely to, and others who do not despite ex ante odds higher than 50%. Juster noted this likely problem with existing measures, and concluded that it would likely be more predictive to let consumers indicate their purchase probabilities in more granular fashion. Even if not everyone has precise subjective beliefs, allowing more refined answers has the potential to reveal more features of the distribution of subjective likelihoods, and thereby improve the quality of the signal that the survey provides the data analyst. So it turned out. Juster conducted a survey to gather just such data on the subjective likelihood of making such a purchase and found that indeed the resulting answers were better predictors of purchase behavior than were the yes/no responses to questions on purchase intentions.

The profession was very slow to internalize the importance of Juster's approach and its broad ramifications. One reason for this was skepticism in the value of such measurement in the broader profession. The traditional viewpoint among economists is that the legitimate subject of our field is choice behavior. In fact, the subjective expected utility theory of Savage even defines beliefs by the properties of idealized choice data. Absent incentives, survey responses are just cheap (and unmodeled) talk. Not having a solid theory of what the answers to unincentivized survey questions mean, what is the point in posing them?

The problem with such a priori arguments against new forms of measurement is that they keep closed research doors that may be important to open. The scientifically correct way to deal with such arguments is therefore to ignore them. That is precisely what the profession in fact did, due to far-sighted leadership of key surveys. The Health and Retirement Survey (HRS) was particularly central. Rather than one funeral at a time, much of the professional resistance to belief measurement was overcome one HRS wave at a time, for which credit is due to its founding fathers, Richard Suzman, Tom Juster, and Bob Willis. The first wave of the HRS was in 1992, and it is no coincidence that this literature took off at approximately the same time. It is only through placement of expectations questions on all waves of the HRS and other panel surveys that their full value is coming to be appreciated. Corresponding questions are now posed in household panel surveys worldwide. As a result of widespread adoption of the quantitative probability measures, the qualitative approach has largely been replaced, even within psychometrics (see Budescu and Wallsten 1995).

Why Measure Beliefs Well, and How?

Manski and associates were key in designing, implementing, and testing the first really custom-designed survey questions on subjective beliefs (Manski 1990; Dominitz and Manski 1997a, 1997b). These questions are designed around the beliefs that subjective expected utility theory places center stage in choice theory. Of equal importance is the fact that they were designed to allow application of estimation methods originally developed for standard random utility models of discrete choice. There is no imposed categorization at all. For a discrete event that may or may not occur, the typical question seeks a percentage chance response on the [0, 100] scale. When the question concerns the future value of some measurable quantity, such as the Dow Jones Index, the same format is used to elicit points on the distribution function or the probability that the event will lie in some interval. By varying the threshold one can, in principle, get very close to recovering the full distribution of beliefs. It is this distribution that can then be used in subsequent analysis of choice behaviors.

Given the backdrop of professional skepticism, it was important in the early days of the literature to validate (in broad terms) both the internal consistency and the external validity of these belief measurements. Many such validation exercises have now been conducted, and (for the most part) the verdict is positive, as detailed in Manski (2004). A few simple and central examples: Hurd and McGarry (1995, 2002) show that individuals and groups with higher subjective survival probabilities live longer, while Hurd and Rohwedder (2012) show that differences in expectations of future stock prices predict the direction of future stock purchases and sales.

While the literature demonstrates clearly the high information content of answers to probabilistic survey questions, their increasing use makes it important to identify sources of error. The best-studied error is apparent overuse of the 50% focal answer. Efforts to model this are producing further innovations in measurement (Bruine de Bruin and Carman 2012; Manski and Molinari 2010). At the same time, there is awareness that details of the response interface impact responses. Numerical probability scales themselves are not universally loved or understood. Visual aids are being developed to present probabilistic constructs in as unambiguous a manner as possible (e.g., the "bins and balls" format of Delavande and Rohwedder [2008]). There are also many fine details to work out in terms of specifying the future variable of interest to an audience that is not trained in the professional jargon of our field and its acceptable ambiguities (GDP?). To reduce the scale of this challenge, cognitive interviews have been employed to great effect to improve the design of survey questions on inflation expectations (Armantier et al. 2013).

As measurement improves, so richer theories can be tested. There is now a virtuous circle setting up in which advances in measurement are liberating researchers to confidently measure changes over time in probabilistic beliefs. This allows critical new questions to be answered related to updating. For example, Wiswall and Zafar (2015a, 2015b) use sequential surveys to understand how provision of objective information on returns to schooling alters beliefs.

The methodological message is more general: the tasks of improving theory and improving measurement are better conducted in parallel than in series. We are at the very earliest days of this virtuous circle, and there is much cause for optimism about our ability to improve understanding of beliefs in coming decades as advances in theory and measurement are increasingly coordinated.

Modeling and Measuring Errors in Probabilistic Survey Responses

In the best case, future research will increasingly systematize our understanding of errors in survey response and how they relate to behavior. In part, this will give us understanding into systematic departures from the standard models of beliefs and updating. The profession (rightly, in my opinion) will not abandon Bayesian updating and rational expectations without solid evidence that alternative models better explain behavior. There are good reasons to doubt that standard behavioral data will be sufficiently compelling to launch alternative models with any confidence. However, if alternative models are supported by complementary data from surveys and from behavior, this will greatly enhance their credibility and likelihood of survival in the intellectual marketplace.

Currently there are two key hurdles to joint use of market and survey data to produce general purpose and better empirically grounded models of beliefs. The first is theoretical and a form of the Lucas critique.

Models of beliefs must be suitable for policy analysis. Even if we infer belief dynamics in a given market from patterns in behavior and in survey responses, we do not know that these patterns will be robust to changes in policy and institutions. As in other fields, the need to understand counterfactual patterns drives a need to model why beliefs evolve as they do in a given setting, and how changes to that setting would impact the resulting pattern of beliefs. The second hurdle is the point noted above: we do not as yet understand patterns of errors in survey responses. We must be very confident in the interpretation of answers before we treat them as strongly suggestive of new models of belief formation. Maybe what we are uncovering is more the pattern in errors in responses to questions about subjective beliefs than actual features of behaviorally relevant belief dynamics.

In the best case that I envisage, we will make progress in both of the above areas in the upcoming years and decades. The reason for this is that economists are finally placing the modeling of attention center stage, in large part inspired by the work of Sims (1998, 2003). The rational inattention model that he introduced, which involves costs based on Shannon entropy, can be generalized in many ways (e.g., Caplin and Dean 2015; Caplin, Dean, and Leahy 2017). All that is really essential to recognize is that thinking is costly, so that we economize on its use. This can be very helpful in understanding patterns in the beliefs that we hold about the outside world: Why bother being well informed about the stock market if one does not have money to invest in it? It can be equally helpful in understanding survey responses, which may result from incomplete consideration of the corresponding reality. In years to come, we will increasingly model and measure patterns of errors in survey response that are revealing of attentional effort. This will teach us a great deal about how to interpret responses, and about how best to use them in fitting models of the evolution of the beliefs that determine market outcomes.

Endnote

For acknowledgments, sources of research support, and disclosure of the author's material financial relationships, if any, please see http://www.nber.org/chapters/c13908.ack.

References

Armantier, O., W. Bruine de Bruin, S. Potter, G. Topa, W. van der Klaauw, and B. Zafar. 2013. "Measuring Inflation Expectations." *Annual Review of Economics* 5:273–301.

Brier, G. W. 1950. "Verification of Forecasts Expressed in Terms of Probability." *Monthly Weather Review* 78:1–3.

Bruine de Bruin, W., and K. G. Carman. 2012. "Measuring Risk Perceptions: What Does the Excessive Use of 50% Mean?" *Medical Decision Making* 32:232–36.

Budescu, D. V., and T. S. Wallsten. 1995. "Processing Linguistic Probabilities: General Principles and Empirical Evidence." In *Decision Making from a Cognitive Perspective*, Psychology of Learning and Motivation: Advances in Research and Theory, vol. 32, ed. J. Busemeyer, R. Hastie, and D. L. Medin, 275–318. Cambridge, MA: Academic Press.

Caplin, A., and M. Dean. 2015. "Revealed Preference, Rational Inattention, and Costly Information Acquisition." *American Economic Review* 105 (7): 2183–203.

Caplin, A., M. Dean, and J. Leahy. 2017. "Rationally Inattentive Behavior: Characterizing and Generalizing Shannon Entropy." NBER Working Paper no. 23652, Cambridge, MA.

Delavande, A., and S. Rohwedder. 2008. "Eliciting Subjective Probabilities in Internet Surveys." *Public Opinion Quarterly* 72 (5): 866–91.

Dominitz, J., and C. Manski. 1997a. "Perceptions of Economic Insecurity: Evidence from the Survey of Economic Expectations." *Public Opinion Quarterly* 61:261–87.

———. 1997b. "Using Expectations Data to Study Subjective Income Expectations." *Journal of the American Statistical Association* 92:855–67.

Haavelmo, T. 1958. "The Role of the Econometrician in the Advancement of Economic Theory." *Econometrica* 35:1–7.

Hurd, M. 2009. "Subjective Probabilities in Household Surveys." *Annual Review of Economics* 1:543–64.

Hurd, M., and K. McGarry. 1995. "Evaluation of the Subjective Probabilities of Survival in the Health and Retirement Study." *Journal of Human Resources* 30: S268–92.

———. 2002. "The Predictive Validity of Subjective Probabilities of Survival." *Economic Journal* 112:966–85.

Hurd, M., and S. Rohwedder. 2012. "Stock Price Expectations and Stock Trading." NBER Working Paper no. 17973, Cambridge, MA.

Juster, T. 1966. "Consumer Buying Intentions and Purchase Probability: An Experiment in Survey Design." *Journal of the American Statistical Association* 61:658–96.

Manski, C. 1990. "The Use of Intentions Data to Predict Behavior: A Best-Case Analysis." *Journal of the American Statistical Association* 85 (412): 934–40.

———. 2004. "Measuring Expectations." *Econometrica* 72:1329–76.

Manski, C., and F. Molinari. 2010. "Rounding Probabilistic Expectations in Surveys." *Journal of Business and Economic Statistics* 28:219–31.

Savage, L. J. 1971. "Elicitation of Personal Probabilities and Expectations." *Journal of the American Statistical Association* 66 (336): 783–801.

Sims, C. A. 1998. "Stickiness." *Carnegie-Rochester Conference Series on Public Policy* 49 (1): 317–56.

———. 2003. "Implications of Rational Inattention." *Journal of Monetary Economics* 50 (3): 665–90.

Wiswall, M., and B. Zafar. 2015a. "Determinants of College Major Choice: Identification Using an Information Experiment." *Review of Economic Studies* 82 (2): 791–824.

———. 2015b. "How Do College Students Respond to Public Information about Earnings?" *Journal of Human Capital* 9 (2): 117–69.

Comment

Lars Peter Hansen, *University of Chicago and NBER*

Introduction

The Manski paper provides much food for thought. Specifically, the paper gives:

- a thoughtful delineation of the challenges and successes of micro probability elicitation;
- a valuable assessment of existing evidence and suggestions for improvements;
- a survey of microeconomic applications; and
- an advocacy and implementation of measuring probabilities of future outcomes instead of just points of central tendency in forecasts.

While the paper has suggestions for a macroeconomic research agenda, it has little to say in terms of specificity of how to embark on this agenda. This is left for others to determine. Survey evidence has long been on the radar screen of macroeconomic research, so I find it valuable to probe what the challenges are to carry out this line of research in a manner that is conceptually appealing and tractable. Were it such an easy and straightforward exercise, this approach arguably would have already had a dominant role in macroeconomic research. In this comment, I explore what the resulting *measurement* and *modeling* tasks are for macroeconomics in order to embrace fully the use of survey evidence on probabilities.

What about Rational Expectations?

Prior to discussing subjective belief models, let me take inventory on rational expectations as an approach to modeling and to econometric practice. In what follows, I draw on discussions from Hansen (2007, 2014). Economic dynamics motivated by applications in macroeconomics and finance have long recognized the need to incorporate beliefs into their analyses. This modeling challenge was well appreciated by economists such as Pigou, Keynes, and Hicks, and their suggestions have had a durable impact on model building. The predominant approach in macroeconomics is to impose rational expectations following Muth (1961), Lucas (1972), and others.

The rational expectations econometrics research program aims to implement these ideas formally. I distinguish between two approaches. The first considers a fully specified stochastic equilibrium model. The dynamic, stochastic equilibrium beliefs inside the model must agree with those implied by the model. The imposition of model-consistent beliefs can be achieved without any formal reference to data. Data come into play in pinning down model parameters by fitting a fully parameterized model to data. A big part of the success of this approach pertains to the analysis of alternative policies or the use of the model to engage in counterfactual analysis. It delivers on a form of structural invariance for a dynamic environment of the type articulated by Hurwicz (1966). The rational expectations approach gives a specific prediction for how beliefs change as one changes specific aspects of the economic environment through changes in the underlying policies. While the rational expectations hypothesis may not capture well some of the transient behavioral responses following policy changes, it eliminates a policy lever that entails systematically fooling people. As we consider backing away from rational expectations, we should keep in mind the underlying aim of structural modeling as a tool to analyze counterfactuals. There are direct extensions that accommodate signal extraction and learning within an equilibrium, including even learning about some unknown parameters governing the evolution of exogenous state variables.

There is a closely related empirical approach that is also used extensively in practice. Applied researchers often use partially specified models. In these settings, the model specification alone does not allow for expectations to be determined by the model. The rational expectations hypothesis is motivated by the existence of sufficiently long time series or other data sets that reveal the actual data evolution. Instead of using the full model specification to determine expectations, rational expectations are enforced through the direct use of data histories as approximations.

One perspective on the survey data is that it provides the opportunity to test the rationality of forecasts. Indeed, a literature has emerged that does precisely this. Examples include Brown and Maital (1981) and Keane and Runkle (1990), but there are many others. An alternative perspective is that the survey evidence opens the door to the study of models in which investors or policymakers have subjective beliefs that could be distinct from the actual data generation.

Disentangling Risk Aversion from Subjective Beliefs

Manski discusses the challenge in distinguishing subjective beliefs from risk aversion. In what follows, I amplify on this discussion and provide my own take on this issue.

Investment decisions are forward looking. When making such decisions, people speculate about the future since the consequences of those decisions play out over time. Thus, models of investment and the resulting pricing implications impose restrictions on beliefs. In this section, I formally make reference to pricing implications, but very similar expressions apply for returns for physical or human capital investments derived from the first-order conditions for optimization.

Pricing restrictions are conveniently represented using so-called stochastic discount factors (see, e.g., Hansen and Richard 1987).[1] The stochastic nature of these discount factors encodes the risk compensation pertinent to investors. These discount factors depend on investor preferences through their implied intertemporal marginal rates of substitution, analogous to a familiar result from price theory. They depend on the market structure because it is the marginal investor who is pertinent in the representation and the identity of the marginal investor could change over time.

There is an empirical challenge in distinguishing beliefs from stochastic discount factors. To address this challenge in a dynamic model, we need a mathematically convenient way to depict subjective beliefs that are distinct from the actual data generation. In what follows, I will take an asset-pricing perspective, but a comparable set of insights apply to investment problems.

Let E denote the expectation operator associated with the actual data generation. To depict subjective beliefs that could be distinct from those implied by the actual data generation, we introduce a positive martingale $M = \{M_t : t = 0, 1, \ldots\}$ with a unit expectation and use this to depict alternative expectations:

$$\tilde{E}(Y_{t+\tau} \mid \mathcal{F}_t) = E\left[\left(\frac{M_{t+\tau}}{M_t}\right) Y_{t+\tau} \mid \mathcal{F}_t\right].$$

This representation is presumed to apply for all $t \geq 0, \tau \geq 0$, and bounded $Y_{t+\tau}$ in the $\mathcal{F}_{t+\tau}$ conditioning information set. Given this holds for bounded $Y_{t+\tau}$, it can be extended to an even larger set of random variables. The martingale ratio $M_{t+\tau} / M_t$ has the interpretation of being a likelihood ratio between subjective belief probability distribution and the actual data generation for data realized between time t and and time $t + \tau$ conditioned on date t information. The use of martingales is a very convenient way to capture a rich family of alternative probabilities, but it is restrictive. Nevertheless, in what follows I will limit attention to subjective probabilities that can be depicted with martingales.

Let $X_{t+\tau}$ denote the payoff to an investment made at date $t + \tau$. A dynamic economic model implies a stochastic discount factor process $\tilde{S} = \{\tilde{S}_t : t = 0, 1, ...\}$ whereby the date t value or shadow value of this investment is:

$$\pi_t(X_{t+\tau}) = \tilde{E}\left[\left(\frac{\tilde{S}_{t+\tau}}{\tilde{S}_t}\right) X_{t+\tau} \mid \mathcal{F}_t\right] = E\left[\left(\frac{\tilde{S}_{t+\tau} M_{t+\tau}}{\tilde{S}_t M_t}\right) X_{t+\tau} \mid \mathcal{F}_t\right].$$

We may equivalently write the date t value as:

$$\pi_t(X_{t+\tau}) = E\left[\left(\frac{S_{t+\tau}}{S_t}\right) X_{t+\tau} \mid \mathcal{F}_t\right]$$

where $S = M\tilde{S}$ is used to represent values under the actual data generation. Given data on values or prices and payoffs, this calculation shows the challenge in disentangling beliefs from other determinants of valuation without imposing further restrictions or incorporating other data.

There are a variety of restrictions that have been used in practice, including rational expectations that restrict $M = 1$, often augmented with parametric restrictions on S (see, e.g., Hansen and Singleton 1982). Expectations data offer a potentially valuable source of information about the subjective beliefs of people inside the economic models of interest. We next consider two possible approaches for introducing subjective beliefs.

Bounds

Consider the perhaps overly ambitious case in which we work explicitly with conditioning information available to agents inside the economic model of interest. Let $X_{t+\tau}$ be a vector of asset payoffs and let $Y_{t+\tau}$

be another vector of variables with observable forecasts. Associated with these two vectors, let

$$\pi(X_{t+\tau}|\mathcal{F}_t) = E\left[\left(\frac{\tilde{S}_{t+\tau}M_{t+\tau}}{\tilde{S}_t M_t}\right)X_{t+\tau}|\mathcal{F}_t\right]\tilde{E}(Y_{t+\tau}|\mathcal{F}_t) = E\left[\left(\frac{M_{t+\tau}}{M_t}\right)Y_{t+\tau}|\mathcal{F}_t\right] \quad (1)$$

where $\pi(X_{t+\tau}|\mathcal{F}_t)$ is a vector of observable prices and $\tilde{E}\,(Y_{t+\tau}|\mathcal{F}_t)$ is a vector of observable forecasts. The observable forecasts can be nonlinear functions of an underlying process. For instance, we allow for forecasts that are conditional probabilities of outcomes that reside in prespecified intervals.

Even given a stochastic discount factor process, $\tilde{S}$, there are typically multiple solutions for the martingale M. Unknown parameters add to this multiplicity. Given the multiplicity, for each candidate stochastic discount factor bounds on properties of the martingales that govern the belief distortions can be constructed. Such bounds could apply, for instance, to the conditional relative entropy, a well-known divergence measure:

$$conditional relative entropy = E\left[\left(\frac{M_{t+\tau}}{M_t}\right)\log\left(\frac{M_{t+\tau}}{M_t}\right)|\mathcal{F}_t\right].$$

In this formula, $\log(M_{t+\tau}/M_t)$ is a log-likelihood ratio between two conditional probability measures, one that governs subjective beliefs and another that governs the actual data generation. Relative entropy computes the conditional expectations of this log-likelihood under the distorted probability distribution. The measure is conditionally convex in the likelihood ratio $M_{t+\tau}/M_t$. Formally, a bound is the minimizing value of relative entropy subjected to the restrictions (1). The minimization problem has a tractable solution for a given a model determined stochastic discount factor $\tilde{S}_{t+\tau}/\tilde{S}_t$.

Computing bounds provides information about how badly distorted beliefs must be from a statistical discrimination perspective in order for the model to be correctly specified. Relative entropy is only one of a wide variety of statistical divergence measures, but it is known to have nice mathematical properties. Interestingly, it has ties to an estimation and inference approach suggested by Kitamura and Stutzer (1997) as an alternative to generalized method of moments (GMM) estimation. While Kitamura and Stutzer sought a refinement for estimation under correct specification, distorted beliefs provide an explicit reason why a rational expectations model might be misspecified and an explicit motivation for computing relative entropy bounds. The Kitamura and

Stutzer approach would then estimate a parameter of interest by minimizing the relative entropy bound, which would be zero under correct specification. Relaxing the rational expectations hypothesis provides an explicit rationale for entertaining the martingale adjustments, and preserving the rational expectations intuition provides motivation for why the bounds should be small. See Hansen (2014), Ghosh, Julliard, and Taylor (2016), and Hansen, Hansen, and Mykland (2017) for further discussion.

While Kitamura and Stutzer (1997) abstract from conditioning information, this information could be snuck in through the back door by imitating the approach of Hansen and Singleton (1982). While this indirect approach is straightforward to implement, explicitly including conditioning information would seem to be an important task to consider as it is the conditional probabilities that are typically relevant for solving models and assessing alternative policies.

More generally, the field of behavioral economics has been captivated by importing ideas from psychology into economics. While this cross-disciplinary activity provides insights, connections to statistical discrimination and complexity also provide valuable inputs. Statistical reasoning informs us when identifying the actual data generation is difficult given historical evidence. In environments that are challenging to infer data generation, there is more scope for both behavioral distortions and belief heterogeneity across different individuals or classes of individuals.

Bounds can be a useful way to organize empirical challenges, but they may limit the scope of quantitative policy assessments. To proceed further requires that more structure be placed on the analysis.

Full Identification

New types of data call for the introduction of new models. For such models to be a valuable tool for quantitative policy analysis, they need to account for the survey responses and allow researchers to map potentially coarse survey responses into well-specified probability models of beliefs.

Just as rational expectations is an equilibrium construct for policy analysis, ideally we would come up with an alternative equilibrium model of beliefs using survey evidence along with forward-looking outcomes and prices to help identify any additional parameters. There are a variety of stabs at filling out the beliefs. For instance, Sargent (1999),

Piazzesi, Schneider, and Benigno (2006), and others use constant gain adaptive learning models to capture beliefs.[2] Adaptive learning is motivated by models with time-varying parameters. Brunnermeier and Parker (2005) provide a game theoretic rationale for why and in what manner the beliefs some people use in making decisions may differ from the actual data generation. Piazzesi, Salomao, and Scneider (2015) and Bhandari, Borovička, and Ho (2016) pose specific models of beliefs matched in part to survey evidence. Bhandari et al. motivate their specification by presuming that decision makers are averse to model misspecification through the consideration of a rich array of alternative probability laws. Adam, Kuang, and Marcet (2012) use misspecified forecasting rules that feedback on endogenous prices to generate novel dynamics in house prices. They purposefully design the misspecifications to be hard to detect via statistical methods. As an alternative belief mechanism for house price dynamics, Burnside, Eichenbaum, and Rebelo (2016) explore the consequences of a particular social learning specification. Finally, Barberis et al. (2015) motivate and explore an "extrapolative expectations" specification of beliefs in an asset-pricing setting. These are alternative examples of fully specified dynamic models that relax rational expectations in particular ways, and some already use survey data for parameter estimation.

Decision theory premised aversion to ambiguity or to potential model misspecification often provides counterpart to a specification of distorted beliefs. (See, for instance, Gilboa and Schmeidler 1989; Petersen, James, and Dupuis 2000; Hansen and Sargent 2001; Epstein and Schneider 2003; Maccheroni, Marinacci, and Rustinchini 2006). As Manski notes, this decision theory provides some additional challenges for elicitation. I now add some of my own views on these. This decision theory presumes decision makers that entertain multiple probability specifications. A common outcome of applying this decision theory are so called "worst-case" probability assessments that support the actual decision making under ambiguity aversion. These worst-case probabilities are linked explicitly to utility consequences of alternative actions. They emerge as a cautious response to the incomplete knowledge of the probabilities. Economic actors behave as if these worst-case beliefs are their actual beliefs and these same beliefs are encoded in prices that clear decentralized security markets. In survey elicitation, respondents may give their best guesses as to the probabilities or they may report worst-case probabilities that justify their actions.[3] Alternatively, survey designers may attempt to elicit probability ranges as discussed by

Manski. It will be hard to elicit full detail of the potential event probabilities, however. As I have already noted, even in the case of purely subjective but unique probabilities, elicitation likely will only be practical for a very limited array of event probabilities. Allowing for probability ranges instead of single probability reports will either widen the bounds I mentioned in the "Bounds" section, or it will accentuate the role of restrictions placed on the full family of potential probabilities.

Parametric specifications, perhaps fit to survey data on probabilities, facilitate the analysis of historical data in a macroeconomic setting. The challenge for some forms of policy analysis is to investigate the systematic consequences of changing economic environments. These changes could be induced by changes in the underlying economic policies. For changes with dynamic implications, holding beliefs fixed except possibly in the very short run is hard to defend. Thus for a model to be predictive in the sense of structural econometrics, we need to know how beliefs change as we change the environment and what aspects of beliefs are invariant. For instance, should we hold fixed the gain parameter in a constant gain algorithm? In environments in which decision makers confront families of probabilities, what are the pertinent families for the new environment? Are parameters that govern ambiguity aversion or concerns about model misspecification invariant when we change policy rules?

Additional ancillary inputs pertaining to beliefs are required for some macroeconomic modeling efforts. For example, in game theoretic models of macroeconomic policy, out-of-equilibrium beliefs become important in determining even equilibrium outcomes. The self-confirming equilibrium formulation of Fudenberg and Levine (1993) gives an extension of rational expectations pertinent to some game theoretic environments with multiple equilibria. Any rationale for retreating from rational expectations may also suggest using some altered notion of a self-confirming equilibrium. Also, it is well known that higher-order beliefs or beliefs about the beliefs of others come into play in some economic environments. For instance, see Townsend (1983), Morris and Shin (2000) and Angeletos, Collard, and Dellas (2017). Should we look to surveys to measure higher-order beliefs? Finally, in dynamic Stackelberg games between policymakers and private agents, the beliefs of both types of players play a role in the equilibrium outcome. Moreover, the Stackelberg leader must speculate as to the private-sector beliefs under alternative policies when acertaining the best course of action.[4]

Conclusions

The research agenda proposed by Manski for macroeconomics is not a new one. It has been on the radar screen of macroeconomists for decades. It has been long recognized that expectations data are of potential value in empirical macroeconomics. As I have described, some important challenges come with implementing this agenda, however. I conjecture that it is the existence of the modeling challenges that accounts for why this agenda has not been fully embraced in quantitative macroeconomic research. Nevertheless, addressing some of these challenges will lead to important advances in the future.

Manski's essay provides valuable insights about the elicitation and use of probabilistic data on beliefs and pushes researchers to measure and use more than medians or best forecasts. Just as with other data sources, however, new evidence requires econometric models for interpreting this evidence. Such models will necessarily include predictions for how people respond to surveys taking account of their incentives to give accurate information.

The information from surveys is typically sparse and incomplete, however. The targets of measurement are often marginal and not joint distributions. Moreover, it is difficult to know what conditioning information is used by economic agents. We may confront the sparseness by exploring bounds on the full set of probabilities of interest or we may fit parametric models to fill in the holes. As I have noted, many parametric approaches already exist in the literature.

Rational expectations is a powerful equilibrium construct and is integrated in the formal construction of a dynamic, stochastic equilibrium suitable for (long-term or well-understood) counterfactual analysis, as in the study of alternative policy rules. As we back off rational expectations, then we are compeled to extend our structural models to encode belief formation in alternative hypothetical environments or confine our use of the resulting models.

Endnotes

I thank Jaroslav Borovička and Peter G. Hansen for helpful comments. Author email: lhansen@uchicago.edu. For acknowledgments, sources of research support, and disclosure of the author's material financial relationships, if any, please see http://www.nber.org/chapters/c13909.ack.
1. This paper in turn builds on the conceptual frameworks of Ross (1978) and Harrison and Kreps (1979).

2. The Sargent analysis aims to learn about an equilibrium via adaptive learning in an environment with multiple self-confirming equilibria.

3. For instance, Bhandari et al. (2016) presume the people report worst-case models.

4. See Woodford (2010) and Hansen and Sargent (2012) for alternative forms of ambiguity that could emerge and influence policy design.

References

Adam, K., P. Kuang, and A. Marcet. 2012. "House Price Booms and the Current Account." *NBER Macroeconomics Annual* 26 (1): 77–122.

Angeletos, G., F. Collard, and H. Dellas. 2017. "Quantifying Confidence." NBER Working Paper no. 20807, Cambridge, MA.

Barberis, N., R. Greenwood, L. Jin, and A. Shleifer. 2015. "X-CAPM: An Extrapolative Capital Asset Pricing Model." *Journal of Financial Economics* 115 (1): 1–24.

Bhandari, A., J. Borovička, and P. Ho. 2016. "Identifying Ambiguity Shocks in Business Cycle Models Using Survey Data." NBER Working Paper no. 22225, Cambridge, MA.

Brown, B. W., and S. Maital. 1981. "What Do Economists Know? An Empirical Study of Experts' Expectations." *Econometrica* 49 (2): 491–504.

Brunnermeier, M. K., and J. A. Parker. 2005. "Optimal Expectations." *American Economic Review* 95 (4): 1092–118.

Burnside, C., M. Eichenbaum, and S. Rebelo. 2016. "Understanding Booms and Busts in Housing Markets." *Journal of Political Economy* 124 (4): 1088–147.

Epstein, L. G., and M. Schneider. 2003. "Recursive Multiple-Priors." *Journal of Economic Theory* 113 (1): 1–31.

Fudenberg, D., and D. K. Levine. 1993. "Self-Confirming Equilibrium." *Econometrica* 61 (3): 523–45.

Ghosh, A., C. Julliard, and A. P. Taylor. 2016. "What is the Consumption-CAPM Missing? An Information-Theoretic Framework for the Analysis of Asset Pricing Models." *Review of Financial Studies* 30 (2): 442–504.

Gilboa, I., and D. Schmeidler. 1989. "Maxmin Expected Utility with Non-Unique Prior." *Journal of Mathematical Economics* 18 (2): 141–53.

Hansen, L. P. 2007. "Beliefs, Doubts and Learning: Valuing Macroeconomic Risk." *American Economic Review* 97 (2): 1–30.

———. 2014. "Uncertainty Outside and Inside Economic Models." *Journal of Political Economy* 122 (5): 945–87.

Hansen, L. P., P. G. Hansen, and P. Mykland. 2017. "Measuring Belief Distortions from Asset Prices." Unpublished Manuscript.

Hansen, L. P., and S. F. Richard. 1987. "The Role of Conditioning Information in Deducing Testable Restrictions Implied by Dynamic Asset Pricing Models." *Econometrica* 55 (3): 587–613.

Hansen, L. P., and T. J. Sargent. 2001. "Robust Control and Model Uncertainty." *American Economic Review* 91 (2): 60–66.

———. 2012. "Three Types of Ambiguity." *Journal of Monetary Economics* 59 (5): 422–45.

Hansen, L. P., and K. J. Singleton. 1982. "Generalized Instrumental Variables Estimation of Nonlinear Rational Expectations Models." *Econometrica* 50 (5): 1269–86.

Harrison, J. M., and D. M. Kreps. 1979. "Martingales and Arbitrage in Multiperiod Securities Markets." *Journal of Economic Theory* 20 (3): 381–408.

Hurwicz, L. 1966. "On the Structural Form of Interdependent Systems." In *Logic, Methodology and Philosophy of Science: Proceeding of the 1960 International Congress*, vol. 44, ed. E. Nagel, P. Suppes, and A. Tarski, 232–39. Amsterdam: Elsevier.

Keane, M., and D. Runkle. 1990. "Testing the Rationality of Price Forecasts: New Evidence from Panel Data." *American Economic Review* 80 (4): 714–35.

Kitamura, Y., and M. Stutzer. 1997. "An Information-Theoretic Alternative to Generalized Method of Moments Estimation." *Econometrica: Journal of the Econometric Society* 65 (4): 861–74.

Lucas, R. 1972. "Expectations and the Neutrality of Money." *Journal of Economic Theory* 4 (2): 103–24.

Maccheroni, F., M. Marinacci, and A. Rustinchini. 2006. "Ambiguity Aversion, Robustness, and the Variational Representation of Preferences." *Econometrica* 74 (6): 1147–498.

Morris, S., and H. S. Shin. 2000. "Rethinking Multiple Equilibria in Macroeconomic Modeling." *NBER Macroeconomics Annual* 15:139–61.

Muth, J. F. 1961. "Rational Expectations and the Theory of Price Movements." *Econometrica: Journal of the Econometric Society* 29 (3): 315–35.

Petersen, I. R., M. R. James, and P. Dupuis. 2000. "Minimax Optimal Control of Stochastic Uncertain Systems with Relative Entropy Constraints." *IEEE Transactions on Automatic Control* 45:398–412.

Piazzesi, M., J. Salomao, and M. Schneider. 2015. "Trend and Cycle in Bond Premia." Working Paper, Stanford University.

Piazzesi, M., M. Schneider, and P. Benigno. 2006. "Equilibrium Yield Curves." *NBER Macroeconomics Annual* 21:389–472.

Ross, S. A. 1978. "A Simple Approach to the Valuation of Risky Streams." *Journal of Business* 51 (3): 453–75.

Sargent, T. 1999. *The Conquest of American Inflation.* Princeton, NJ: Princeton University Press.

Townsend, R. M. 1983. "Forecasting the Forecasts of Others." *Journal of Political Economy* 91 (4): 546–88.

Woodford, M. 2010. "Robustly Optimal Monetary Policy with Near-Rational Expectations." *American Economic Review* 100 (1): 274–303.

Discussion

Chris Carroll opened the discussion by praising Charles Manski for the important contribution his paper will make to the field of macroeconomics. He endorsed Manski's thesis that advances in macroeconomics will require an improved understanding of how expectations are formed and how to correctly elicit expectations and beliefs empirically. Carroll also expressed his view that policymakers tend to evaluate policy through their own personal theories of how agents react to shocks, and called for economists to generate and test alternative theories of how expectations are actually formed.

John Cochrane offered points of praise and "gentle criticism" for the paper. For praise, he commended the paper for highlighting that economists need to be more careful in designing questions to elicit expectations and how to use these expectations in models. For example, economists often fail to recognize that survey respondents may rationally over-report the probability of a high marginal utility event, as marginal utility times probability matters for decisions.

Cochrane pushed back on the paper's criticism of the use of rational expectations in modern economics, arguing two points. First, Robert Lucas's seminal work on the topic never suggested that people immediately update their expectations rationally in a new regime, but instead that their beliefs and rules of thumb slowly converge to reflect the new equilibrium dynamics after a shock or policy change. Second, measuring peoples' expectations today is not informative about how they respond to policy shocks or form expectations in a new regime.

Manski responded to Cochrane's critique by noting that it is not realistic to think of unanticipated shocks as occurring in isolation so that people have time to slowly learn about the new equilibrium dynamics and update their rules of thumb. Instead, it seems more reasonable that the economy is, in fact, facing a constant arrival of new shocks and never settles down into a long-run equilibrium. In this case people do not have time to fully adjust, and the rational expectations argument breaks down.

Several participants gave further comments along these lines. Laura Veldkamp and Robert Hall stressed that rational expectations is no longer the ruling dogma of macroeconomic research. Veldkamp further noted that there has been substantial work examining the aggregate implications of heterogeneous information and informational frictions. The approach she and others have taken has been to model specific informational frictions in the economy and see if their predictions for macroeconomic aggregates are consistent with the data.

Manski argued in response that his point is not that macroeconomists have been ignoring these issues, but that they should be using microeconomic data to learn about how expectations are actually formed. Discussant Andrew Caplin agreed, emphasizing there was no real disagreement between Manski and the discussion participants. Manski's paper stresses that empirical macroeconomic research requires discipline by both the parties collecting data and those using it. While models drive demand for data necessary to test them, survey designers need to be careful in asking questions that actually elicit something meaningful. Similarly, Caplin stressed that macroeconomists using this expectations data need to be careful in understanding what was actually elicited. The fact that participants are already exploring deviations from rational expectations and using data to test their models is not at odds with Manski's points.

Xavier Gabaix commented that his work on behavioral macroeconomics generates different predictions than rational expectations models and that new data on expectation formation is necessary to evaluate these predictions. Survey questions asking about conditional expectations and conditional responses in different scenarios would be particularly valuable.

Ricardo Reis offered three comments. First, he pushed back on the comment by Carroll that economists need more theories of expectations, noting he counted at least 11 theories in the discussion by Lars Hansen. Second, in response to Manski's belief that macroeconomists are not using microdata on expectations, Reis cited his own work presented at the 2004 Macro Annual conference, which used microeconomic data on expectations to study the Phillips curve. He also noted that there have been dozens of subsequent papers written in the same spirit. Finally, he wondered how economists should deal with situations in which a relatively large fraction of respondents report what seem to be very unreasonable expectations. In the context of his own work on inflation expectations, he found more than 30% of the sample provided bizarre responses and thinks future work could benefit from a systematic way of dealing with these data points rather than discarding them.

Manski responded to Reis's final question, saying that rather than simply discarding these observations, a researcher needs to understand why respondents have answered the way they did. Such answers can be due to lack of attention or because respondents actually have the odd beliefs Reis referenced. Only in the first case should these data points be discarded. Manski also noted that one can distinguish between the two cases can be done when longitudinal data is available. Alternatively, some surveys have questions whose purpose is to assess whether respondents are paying attention.

Francis Diebold emphasized the value of financial markets in providing data on real-time expectations formation. In addition to point expectations, markets can also provide estimates of full densities through information in options and other derivative contracts. He further noted that new markets can be designed specifically to elicit information about certain expectations, and called for more work in this direction. Manski embraced this idea cautiously, raising the concern that market expectations reflect consensus and it would thus be difficult to learn about heterogeneous expectations with these methods.

Antoinette Schoar commented that some psychology research suggests peoples' reported beliefs and preferences can easily be manipulated or primed in surveys, and thus it is important to design surveys that filter out this noise to elicit true long-term views. Manski responded that this conclusion is far from a consensus and so this may not be such an important issue.

Robert Hall and Jonathan Parker mentioned the issue of separation of preferences from beliefs discussed in the paper. Hall noted that, at the general level of Arrow and Debreu, beliefs about probabilities are an aspect of preferences. Probabilities become distinct when the specialization to expected utility is made. Parker noted that separating beliefs and preferences may be an overvalued simplification. For example, directly surveying people about well-being may be more insightful than indirectly calculating welfare from a model and separate measures of beliefs and preferences because people may be better at distinguishing and reporting welfare than beliefs.

6

Credit Market Freezes

Efraim Benmelech, *Northwestern University and NBER*
Nittai K. Bergman, *Tel Aviv University*

I. Introduction

Financial market freezes—by which we mean large declines in the volume of transactions in both the primary and the secondary markets that occur over a nontrivial period of time—are typically observed during financial crises. For example, issuance of corporate, mostly railroad, bonds collapsed during the financial crisis of 1873 and did not resume until 1879. Likewise, there was a considerable decline in bond issuances in the financial crises of 1884, 1893, and 1907. Similar patterns can be observed during the Great Depression when issuance of bonds by industrial firms fell dramatically in 1931 and did not recover until 1935.[1] In particular, issuance of real estate bonds, which accounted for 23% of the total corporate bond issuance in the 1920s, came to a halt in 1929 when the market for such bonds dried up. Junk bond issuances that boomed in the first half of the 1980s collapsed in 1990 with the market remaining frozen until 1993. The information technology (IT) revolution led to a boom in issuance of bonds by telecommunication companies, which were in turn purchased and securitized into collateralized bond obligations (CBO). The massive defaults by telecom companies in 2001 and 2002 led to a collapse of the bond securitization market and CBOs have since disappeared. A more recent example of a market freeze took place during the financial crisis of 2008–2009 with the collapse of the structured finance market—the largest and fastest growing financial market in the years leading to the crisis. In particular, not only did the market for mortgage-backed securities such as residential mortgage-backed securities (RMBS) and collaterized debt obligations (CDOs) collapse, but, also, other nonhousing segments of the structured finance markets—ranging from commercial loans securitizations to asset-backed securities—came to a halt, and even the issuance of corporate bonds declined significantly.

Credit freezes and liquidity dry-ups during financial crises affect secondary markets as well. During the financial crisis of 2008-09 illiquidity in the bond market rose dramatically. For example, according to Bao, Pan, and Wang (2011), aggregate illiquidity doubled from its precrisis levels in August 2007, and tripled in March 2008 during the collapse of Bear Stearns. By September 2008, during the Lehman Brothers default and the bailout of AIG, bond illiquidity was five times its precrisis level. As we show in our analysis below, illiquidity in the bond market also rose sharply in the panic of 1873—one of the worst financial crises during the National Bank era. For example, bid-ask spreads doubled from their precrisis levels in August 1873 and remained elevated for more than a year.

This paper analyzes liquidity in bond markets during financial crises with an emphasis on the most recent crisis of 2008–2009. In doing so, we compare two main theories of liquidity in markets: (1) asymmetric information and adverse selection, and (2) heterogenous beliefs.

The classic literature explaining liquidity and frictions in trade between economic agents relies on fundamental insights developed in the information economics literature. As first shown in Akerlof (1970) and Spence (1973), private information held by economic agents generates adverse selection in which buyers demand discounts reflecting their concern about the negative information held by sellers. Dang, Gorton, and Holmström (2012, 2013) and Holmström (2015) apply these insights to develop an asymmetric information theory of liquidity in bond markets. This is the first theory we test to understand the determinants of liquidity in bond markets during financial crises.

The fundamental insight of Dang, Gorton, and Holmström is that the payoff structure of debt contracts generates two regions in which bonds will trade. When bond default risk is relatively low, bond payoffs will be comparatively insensitive to underlying firm value. The value of private information, and hence adverse selection between economic agents, will be relatively low. As a result, when default risk is low, debt is informationally insensitive and liquidity will be high. In contrast, when default risk rises, the sensitivity of bond value to underlying firm value increases as the firm is nearing its default boundary. Private information in this region is valuable, adverse selection is therefore high, and debt liquidity will decline. The main prediction of the Dang et al.

model is thus that bond illiquidity will rise as bond value declines, with the bond moving from the informationally insensitive to the informationally sensitive regions.

The second theory of bond liquidity we analyze stems from the literature on heterogeneous beliefs (see, e.g., Harrison and Kreps 1978; Varian 1989; Harris and Raviv 1993). By assuming that agents hold different fundamental opinions about underlying asset values—some agents are optimistic while others are pessimistic—the literature on heterogeneous beliefs evades the classic no-trade results in the information economics literature (e.g., Rubinstein 1975; Hakansson, Kunkel, and Ohlson 1982; Milgrom and Stokey 1982). Adverse selection is thus mitigated—indeed, dissipated—by agents' high certainty in the correctness of their own opinion of asset value: agents engage in trade for their own *perceived* mutual benefit. Differences of opinion can thus promote trade and increase liquidity. Indeed, if agent A values an asset more than agent B, and believes B's valuation to be simply wrong, then agent A does not fear adverse selection in purchasing the asset from B, nor will she require a discount in doing so. Our empirical tests are aimed, therefore, at analyzing to what extent differences of opinion are positively related to liquidity in debt markets during the financial crisis of 2008–2009.

One caveat about the theoretical prediction that differences of opinion lead to higher liquidity is that the theory relies on assumptions regarding the *joint* distribution of beliefs and endowments. To the extent that opinion dispersion rises in a manner perfectly correlated with the distribution of endowments, it need not be the case that trade and liquidity will rise with the degree of the dispersion. Consider, for example, a scenario with two agents differentiated by their beliefs about asset value—an optimist and a pessimist—where the optimist owns the asset. If, now, opinion dispersion rises in such a way as to make the optimist even more optimistic and the pessimist more pessimistic, there should be no associated increase in trade or market liquidity.[2] Still, if there are numerous agents, and the changes in agents' opinions are not perfectly aligned with current asset holdings, increased dispersion will facilitate trade.

Before turning to testing the ability of the models to explain liquidity of credit markets during financial crises, we begin by providing descriptive evidence on credit issuance dry-ups. We collect data on bond issuance during the period surrounding the 1873, 1929, and 2008–2009 financial crises. The results show that in all three crises there is a substantial decline in bond issuance during and after the onset of the crisis. While the evidence is consistent with liquidity dry-ups and market freezes during downturns in the spirit of Myers and Majluf (1984) and Lucas and McDonald (1990), we cannot rule out that the reduction in issuances is driven by lack of corporate demand for credit stemming from a reduction in investment opportunities. Hence, in our main analysis we focus on liquidity in secondary markets—that is, market liquidity—as opposed to liquidity in primary markets—that is, funding liquidity.[3]

We begin by empirically testing the main prediction of the Dang, Gorton, and Holmström model—namely that during financial crises bond illiquidity rises as bond value declines. To operationalize the empirical tests, we use standard measures of bond illiquidity for the 1873 and 2008–2009 crises. Specifically, we use bid-ask spreads as a measure for bond illiquidity during the 1873 crisis. For the 2008–2009 financial crisis we use γ—the negative covariance of log-price changes in two consecutive periods—that has been proposed by Roll (1984) and has been recently used by Bao et al. (2011) as a measure of bond illiquidity.[4]

Using our hand-collected data from the nineteenth century, as well as TRACE data for the 2007–2009 period, we provide graphical evidence that bond illiquidity rises when bond values deteriorate. For example, the correlation between bid-ask spreads and bond prices during the 1873–1876 period is –0.909. Likewise, the correlation between γ and bond prices during the 2007–2009 period is –0.858. Both correlations are statistically significant at the 1% level. We next test the prediction that bond illiquidity rises as bond price declines in financial crises more formally by estimating a regression model in which the dependent variable is bond illiquidity and the main explanatory variable is lagged bond price. Our results confirm the negative association between illiquidity and bond prices in both the 1873 and 2008–2009 financial crises, even after we control for bond and year-by-month fixed effects. Our evidence confirms the fundamental prediction of the asymmetric information theory of bond liquidity in Dang et al. (2012): bond illiquidity rises as bond price declines during financial crises.[5]

We continue by analyzing the main prediction of the heterogeneous beliefs theory—that is, differences of opinion between economic agents should promote liquidity. Measuring differences of opinion is not trivial as this requires gauging the subjective beliefs of agents engaged in trade. We employ two proxies of differences of opinions in our analysis. The first proxy for differences of opinion in debt markets is the absolute value of the difference between the credit rating of Moody's and S&P in notches.[6] Our second measure of opinion heterogeneity is analyst earnings forecast dispersion. Following the literature on analyst forecast dispersion (see, e.g., Diether, Malloy, and Scherbina 2002), we calculate for each bond-month in our sample the ratio of its firm's standard deviation of analysts' current-fiscal-year annual earnings per share forecasts to the absolute value of the mean analyst forecast.

There are two important caveats to these proxies for opinion dispersion. First, even if the measures accurately capture differences of opinion regarding firm value among rating agencies and among equity analysts, these measures may not accurately reflect differences of opinion among the relevant market participants who are actually trading in the bond markets. Second, it could very well be that incentive structures, career concerns, institutional reputational concerns, and the like are influencing earnings forecasts and credit ratings, implying that the actual beliefs of the analysts and rating agencies are different from those announced to the market. We employ these measures because of their availability, and while they have been used extensively in the literature, we proceed with the analysis with these caveats in mind.

First, we show that the difference of opinion measures rise substantially during the crisis. The S&P-Moody's credit-rating difference, as well as analyst earnings forecast dispersion, spike up post-Lehman collapse—both attaining a maximum in March 2009—before declining. Taken together with the rise in illiquidity during the crisis described above, the fact that mean opinion dispersion *increased* post-Lehman serves as prima facie evidence against the main prediction of the heterogeneous beliefs literature of a positive relation between opinion dispersion and liquidity. A simple means comparison analysis confirms the time-series evidence. Sorting bonds into bins by their degree of bond-rating difference results in a positive and monotonic relation between opinion dispersion and illiquidity. Similarly, sorting bonds by deciles of analyst earnings forecast dispersion uncovers a qualitatively similar result: higher dispersion is associated with increased illiquidity, with the effect being particularly pronounced in the top two deciles of analyst forecast dispersion.

More formally, we estimate a regression model relating bond illiquidity to differences of beliefs using our two measures of opinion dispersion. Regressions are run with year-by-month fixed effects—soaking up common time-series variation—and bond fixed effects that control for non-time-varying bond characteristics. The results show that the Moody's-S&P

bond-rating difference is positively related to bond illiquidity. Similarly, the opinion dispersion measure based on analyst forecast dispersion is also positively related to illiquidity, with the effect concentrated in high levels of forecast dispersion. In contrast to the heterogeneous beliefs theory, increased opinion dispersion does not seem, therefore, to contribute to increased liquidity.

We then run a "horse race" between the Dang, Gorton, and Holmström asymmetric information theory of bond liquidity and the heterogeneous beliefs theory. Estimating regression models relating bond liquidity to bond price, as well as the two measures of opinion dispersion, we show that while the relation between illiquidity and price during the 2008–2009 financial crisis remains negative and statistically significant, the relation between bond illiquidity and opinion dispersion is not statistically significant once bond price is added as a covariate.[7] We continue by estimating the portion of the aggregate increase in bond illiquidity during the financial crisis that can be explained simply by the reduction in bond prices, that is, by the main prediction of the Dang et al. asymmetric information theory of bond liquidity. Using the estimated coefficients from the regression of illiquidity on lagged bond price, and integrating over the full distribution of changes in bond price, we conclude that between a quarter and a third of the increase in bond illiquidity after the collapse of Lehman Brothers in September 2008 can be attributed solely to the concurrent reduction in bond prices.

To summarize, our empirical results are consistent with the information asymmetry theory of liquidity as in Dang et al. (2012). When bond value deteriorates, bond illiquidity increases, as would be predicted by adverse selection stemming from the bond entering a region in which its value is informationally sensitive. The negative relation between bond illiquidity and price explains a large fraction of the rise in illiquidity during the financial crisis, although a sizable fraction remains unexplained.

In contrast, using two proxies for belief dispersion—the Moody's-S&P difference in bond rating and analyst forecast dispersion—we find little support for the hypothesis that liquidity is enhanced as differences of opinion rise. At the aggregate level, as well as using panel data analysis at the individual-bond level, opinion dispersion did not increase liquidity during the crisis period. If anything, the opposite seems to hold, with illiquidity and dispersion positively related, particularly when using the bond-rating difference measure of belief dispersion.

Our results points to a strong link between crises and the dry-ups of market liquidity. We find that asset prices play a crucial role in determining liquidity in debt markets during financial crises. It is precisely when prices decline market-wide that liquidity dries up and issuance of new liabilities becomes difficult, reducing the supply of capital for firms already pushed into distress due to the crisis. Illiquidity in credit markets can have dire consequences for households as well. Precautionary savings in the form of fixed-income securities become hard to sell and households in need of liquid funds may find liquidity difficult to obtain precisely when they need it most.

These results have implications for the efficacy of monetary interventions meant to strengthen the economy during downturns through increased lending by the financial sector. In particular, the asymmetric information theory of liquidity suggests that if these interventions occur when borrower balance sheets are weak, liquidity will not easily flow from the financial sector into the economy. Weak borrower balance sheets will imply that issued liabilities will be informationally sensitive, limiting borrowers' ability to raise debt capital. Monetary interventions meant to inject liquidity from the financial sector into the real economy can thus arrive "too late." In contrast, monetary interventions that occur at an earlier stage—when balance sheets are still sufficiently strong that liabilities issued by borrowers are relatively informationally insensitive—will have a larger effect. As a corollary, if monetary interventions are rendered ineffective because they arrive too late in the cycle, the asymmetric information theory of liquidity suggests that fiscal policy may be effective in complementing monetary policy. In particular, strengthening borrower balance sheets directly through fiscal policy shifts corporate liabilities into a less informationally sensitive region in which monetary interventions meant to increase lending become effective.[8]

The rest of the paper is organized as follows. Section II presents evidence on credit issuance freezes in three financial crises. Section III provides evidence on liquidity and informational sensitivity in financial crises. Section IV evaluates the explanatory power of belief dispersion for liquidity in financial crises. Section V studies the explanatory power of bond prices in explaining illiquidity during the 2008–2009 crisis. Section VI concludes.

II.   Funding Illiquidity during Financial Crises

We define credit market freezes as large declines in the volume of transactions in both primary and secondary credit markets that occur over a

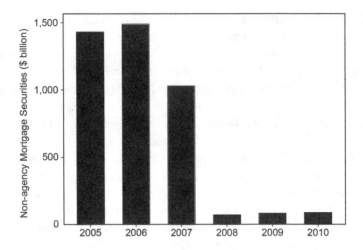

Fig. 1. Nonagency mortgage securities issuance: 2005–2010

nontrivial period of time. This section provides descriptive evidence on credit market issuance freezes during the financial crises of 1873, 1929, and 2008–2009.

A. Credit Issuance Freezes in Three Financial Crises

The most recent example of a credit market freeze took place during the financial crisis of 2008–2009 with the collapse of the structured finance market—the largest and fastest growing credit market in the years leading to the crisis. Issuance of structured finance securities, and especially collateralized debt obligations (CDOs), grew dramatically between 2003 and 2006. While the year 2007 was on track to surpass the record numbers of 2006, the credit crisis that began in summer 2007 brought the market for structured finance to a halt.[9] The collapse of the securitzation market is well illustrated in figure 1, which uses issuance data to illustrate the dramatic decline in issuance of nonagency mortgage securities from 2005 to 2010.[10] Not only did the market for mortgage-backed securities such as RMBS and CDOs collapse, but also other, nonhousing segments of the structured finance markets ranging from commercial loans securitizations (CLO) to asset-backed securities (ABS) came to a halt, and even the issuance of corporate bonds declined significantly. Figure 2 demonstrates that issuance of nonmortgage, asset-backed securities collapsed during the crisis and stayed at a low level in the following years. The decline in the volume of bond issuance was not confined

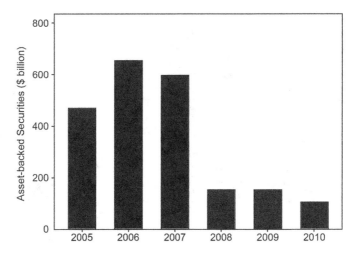

Fig. 2.   Asset-backed securities issuance: 2005–2010

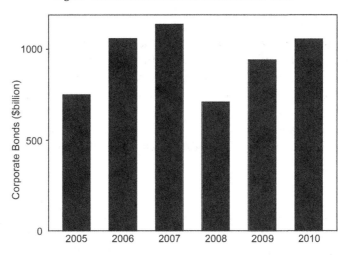

Fig. 3.   Corporate bonds issuance: 2005–2010

only to securitized assets. Figure 3 shows that issuance of corporate bonds also declined considerably in 2008 and returned to its precrisis level only in 2010.[11]

We now turn to another credit market freeze that took place during the financial crisis of 1873. The crisis of 1873 is one of the classic international crises according to Kindleberger (1990). It is also one of Sprague's (1910) four crises of the US National Banking era that eventually led to the creation of the Federal Reserve in 1914. The 1873 crisis is

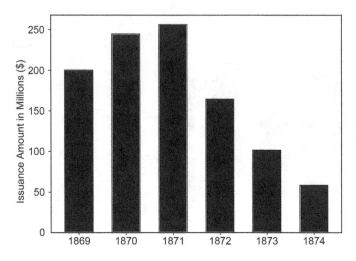

Fig. 4. Corporate bonds issuance: 1869–1874

traditionally viewed as a classic banking panic triggered by the failure
of commercial banks linked to the railroad industry. In turn, the crisis heralded a six-year recession according to the NBER business-cycle
reference dates. We collect information on issuance of bonds, mostly
by railroad companies, for the years 1869–1874 from the Commercial
and Financial Chronicle (CFC)—a weekly business publication that was
first published in 1865 and reported detailed business news, as well as
detailed prices of bonds and stocks. Figure 4 displays the volume of
corporate bonds issuance from 1869 to 1874. As figure 4 demonstrates,
bond issuances declined dramatically in 1873 and 1874 compared to
their level in 1870 and 1871. While we do not have detailed information
on bond issuance after 1874, contemporary observers of the 1873 financial crisis have argued that bond issuance collapsed during the financial
crisis of 1873 and did not resume until 1879.

We provide additional evidence on credit issuance freezes from the
financial crisis of 1929. The crisis began on October 1929 with a crash
of the stock market that marked the beginning of the Great Depression.
According to Mishkin (1991):

The outcome of the panic period starting October 23 and culminating in the
crash on October 29 was a negative return for the month of October of close
to 20%. This was the largest monthly negative return in the stock market up to
that time.[12]

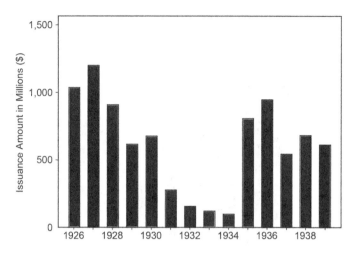

Fig. 5. Industrial bonds issuance: 1926–1939

Figure 5 plots the volume of corporate bond issuance of all industrial firms from 1920 to 1940 in millions of current dollars.[13] As figure 5 demonstrates, issuance of bonds by industrial firms declined in 1929 and then fell dramatically in 1931. The corporate bond market remained frozen until 1935. Benmelech, Frydman, and Papanikolaou (2017) use the collapse of the corporate bond market to identify the effects of funding shortage on firms' employment. They show that bonds were the primary source of debt financing for large firms in the 1920s and that the collapse of the bond market during the Great Depression led firms to layoff many of their employees. Figure 6 provides additional information on credit market freezes during the Great Depression. The figure presents data on issuance of real estate bonds from 1925 to 1934 in millions of current dollars.[14] According to Goetzmann and Newman (2010), total issuance of real estate bonds grew from $57.7 million in 1919 to $695.8 million in 1925. By 1928 new issues of real estate bonds surpassed railroad bond issuance and accounted for 23% of the total corporate bond issuance. As figure 6 illustrates, and consistent with evidence in figure 1 for the 2008–2009 financial crisis, real estate bond issuance collapsed during the crisis with the market for these bonds all but disappearing.

Our results show that in all three crises there is a substantial decline in bond issuance during and after the onset of the crisis. The evidence is consistent with liquidity dry-ups and market freezes during downturns in the spirit of Myers and Majluf (1984) and Lucas and McDonald

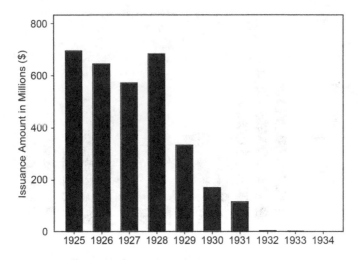

Fig. 6. Real estate bonds issuance: 1925–1939

(1990). Still, we cannot rule out that the reduction in issuances is driven by a lack of corporate demand for credit stemming from a reduction in investment opportunities.

We next turn to provide suggestive evidence on credit market freezes in secondary markets in which market liquidity dries up. Providing such evidence requires information on prices of bonds in secondary markets, which we have collected for two notable financial crises: the 1873 financial crisis and the more recent 2008–2009 crisis.

III. Market Liquidity and Informational Sensitivity

Market liquidity is a notoriously ambiguous concept. By liquidity in secondary markets, we are referring to what is commonly known as "market liquidity"—that is, the ease with which assets are traded (see, e.g., Brunnermeier and Pedersen 2009). In our analysis we employ two measures of market liquidity common in the literature—γ and bid-ask spreads that we define below. In particular, we do not focus on volume of trade as a measure of liquidity, since exogenous variation in the demand for funds is likely to play an important role in determining agents' need to sell their asset holdings—particularly during financial crises—irrespective of the ease with which assets are traded. Put differently, trading volume may be high not because markets are liquid, but because investors require funding.

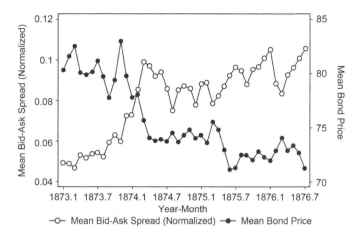

Fig. 7. Bid-ask spreads and bond prices: 1873–1876

A. The Financial Crisis of 1873

We collect weekly information from the CFC on prices of corporate—mostly railroad—bonds from January 1873 up to the end of June 1876. The data include the name of the security, the issuing firm, and the bid and ask prices that prevailed for each security during the week. There are 69,444 bond-week observations in our data set. The CFC reports bid or ask prices for 56,717 bond-week observations, and 12,727 bond-week observations do not have pricing information, suggesting that these bonds were not traded during the week in which the information is not reported. We begin our analysis by calculating an index of bid-ask spreads for bonds that have information on both bid and ask prices. We define the relative bid-ask spread for bond i in week w as:

$$Spread_{i,w} = \frac{Ask_{i,w} - Bid_{i,w}}{Mid\ price_{i,w}}, \qquad (1)$$

where $Mid\ price_{i,w}$ is defined as $(Ask_{i,w} + Bid_{i,w}) / 2$. Next, we calculate $Spread_t$ as an equal-weighed time-series average of $Spread_{i,w}$ across bonds and within a month t.

Figure 7 presents the monthly evolution of bid-ask spreads from January 1873 to June 1876. As the figure shows clearly, bid-ask spreads increased from 0.052 in August 1873 to 0.060 in September 1873 when the crisis started and 0.063 in October 1873. As the financial crisis intensified with more failures of banks and railroad companies, the mean bid-ask spread reached 0.099—almost twice as high as its level before the crisis. Figure 7 also displays the evolution of the mean bond midprice using the data we have collected from the CFC. As figure 7 shows, the decline in bond prices is associated with higher bid-ask spreads—indicating that the bond market became less liquid as bonds' prices declined. The correlation between the mean bid-ask spread and mean bond price is −0.909, and is statistically significant at the 1% level.

We argue that the evidence from the 1873 financial crisis is consistent with the Dang et al. model of the effect of the information-sensitivity of debt on liquidity and liquidity dry-ups in debt markets. The main prediction of the model is that when underlying values deteriorate, debt shifts from being informationally insensitive and becomes informational sensitive, adverse-selection problems rise, and liquidity drops. We now turn to conduct a similar analysis of the relation between bond prices and market liquidity during the financial crisis of 2008–2009.

B.   The Financial Crisis of 2008–2009

We use bond-pricing data from FINRA's TRACE (Transaction Reporting and Compliance Engine). Our initial sample is similar to the one we use in Benmelech and Bergman (2017) and includes all corporate bonds traded in TRACE. We keep bonds with a time to maturity of at least six months and standard coupon intervals (including zero-coupon bonds). Our sample is composed of "plain vanilla" corporate bonds—we do not include securitized assets in the sample and exclude bonds that are issued by financial firms, as well as convertible, putable, and fixed-price callable bonds.

As a measure of illiquidity we use γ, which is defined as the negative covariance of log-price changes in two consecutive periods:[15]

$$\gamma = -Cov(\Delta p_t, \Delta p_{t-1}). \tag{2}$$

Figure 8 presents the evolution of the γ measure of illiquidity over time from January 2006 to December 2010, as well as an index of bond prices that is constructed based on actual bond transactions from TRACE. As the figure demonstrates, and consistent with our findings for the financial crisis of 1873, bond prices and bond illiquidity are negatively correlated. Figure 8 illustrates very clearly the spike in bond illiquidity that coincides exactly with the dramatic decline in corporate bond prices: γ increases from 0.680 in January 2007 to 3.434 in September 2008, the month in which Lehman Brothers filed for bankruptcy,

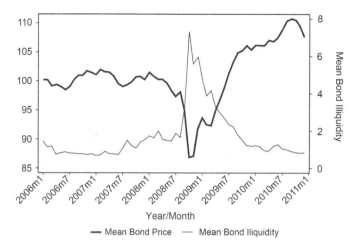

Fig. 8. Illiquidity and bond price: 2007–2009

and to 7.312 in October 2008. The correlation between γ and bond prices during the 2007–2009 period is –0.858 and is statistically significant at the 1% level. Consistent with our findings for the 1873 crisis, we find support for Dang et al. (2013) that when underlying values deteriorate liquidity drops.

Figure 9 refines the analysis in figure 8 by stratifying the time-series evolution of the γ by credit rating. For the ease of graphical representation, we classify bonds into four categories of bond credit ratings where rating category 1 includes the highest quality bonds and category 4 includes the lowest credit-quality bonds. As figure 9 clearly demonstrates, and consistent with Dang et al. (2012), lower credit-rating bonds exhibit higher levels of illiquidity.[16] Moreover, lower quality bonds—especially those in categories 3 and 4—become particularly illiquid during the height of the financial crisis of 2008–2009.

C.   *Regression Analysis of Bond Prices and Liquidity during Financial Crises*

Our graphical evidence for the financial crises of 1873 and 2008–2009 suggests that bond prices and bond liquidity are negatively correlated during financial crises. We next test the prediction that bond illiquidity rises as bond price declines in financial crises more formally by estimating the following baseline specification:

$$Illiquidity_{i,t} = \beta_0 + \beta_1 \times Price_{i,t-1} + b_i\theta + c_i\delta + \varepsilon_{i,t}, \qquad (3)$$

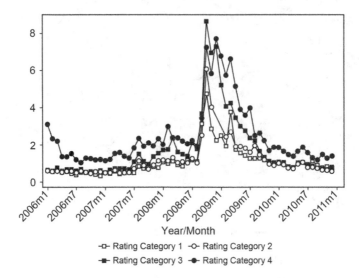

Year/Month

-□- Rating Category 1 -○- Rating Category 2
-■- Rating Category 3 -●- Rating Category 4

Fig. 9.   Average illiquidity by credit rating: 2007–2009

where *Illiquidity* is either γ for the 2007–2009 period or the normalized bid-ask spread $Spread_{i,t}$ for the 1873–1876 period, subscripts indicate bond (i) and either month (for 2007–2009) or week (for 1873–1876) (t), $Price_{i,t-1}$ is bond price, δ_t is a vector of either year or year × month fixed effects, θ_i is a vector of bond fixed effects—and $\varepsilon_{i,t}$ is the regression residual. We report the results from estimating variants of regression 3 in table 1. Tables throughout this paper report regression coefficients and standard errors clustered at the bond level (in parentheses). The main explanatory variable in the table is lagged bond price. Columns (1)–(2) report results for the 2007–2009 period, while columns (3)–(4) report results for the 1873–1876 period.

The results reported in column (1) are based on regression 3, which is estimated with year and bond fixed effects. There is a negative association between illiquidity and bond prices, suggesting that bonds with lower prices are more illiquid (high γ). We obtain very similar results when we include year × month—instead of just year—and bond fixed effects (column [2]). The association between γ and bond price remains negative and significant at the 1% level when we control for bond fixed effects. Likewise, column (3) shows that bid-ask spreads are negatively correlated with bond prices during the 1873–1876 period after controlling for bond and year fixed effects. Column (4) repeats the analysis presented in column (3) and adds year × month fixed effects. The re-

Table 1
Bond Illiquidity and Lagged Prices

	Gamma (1)	Gamma (2)	Bid-Ask Spread (3)	Bid-Ask Spread (4)
$Price_{t-1}$	-0.204***	-0.169***	-0.0033***	-0.0032***
	(0.005)	(0.006)	(0.0005)	(0.0006)
Constant	21.592***	17.768***	0.299***	0.296***
	(0.523)	(0.611)	(0.037)	(0.037)
Bond FE	Yes	Yes	Yes	Yes
Year FE	Yes	No	Yes	No
Year * month FE	No	Yes	No	Yes
Period	2007–2009	2007–2009	1873–1876	1873–1876
Observations	41,672	41,672	27,170	27,170
$Adj - R^2$	0.417	0.458	0.745	0.747

***Significant at the 1 percent level.
**Significant at the 5 percent level.
*Significant at the 10 percent level.

sults are statistically significant at the 1% level, suggesting that bonds that experienced lower prices during the 1873 financial crisis also became less liquid. An important concern regarding the negative relation between bond illiquidity and bond price is one of reverse causality. Rather than declines in bond values causing illiquidity to rise, it could be that bond prices are declining due to an expected (future) reduction in bond liquidity. In Benmelech and Bergman (2017) we conduct detailed analysis to address this endogeneity concern, using instrumental variables and nonlinearities around the default boundary.

IV. Liquidity and Belief Dispersion during the Financial Crisis

A large literature discusses how heterogeneous beliefs can promote trade and liquidity in financial markets (see, e.g., Harrison and Kreps 1978; Varian 1989; Harris and Raviv 1993). This literature provides an alternative theory to trade than that provided by classic asymmetric information and adverse selection theories (Akerlof 1970; Spence 1973). By assuming that agents hold different fundamental opinions about underlying asset values—some agents are optimistic while others are pessimistic—the literature on heterogeneous beliefs evades the classic no-trade results in the information economics literature (e.g., Rubinstein 1975; Hakansson et al. 1982; Milgrom and Stokey 1982). Agents engage in trade for their own perceived mutual benefit. In this section we analyze the relation between differences of opinion and liquidity in the bond market.

Measuring heterogeneous beliefs among market participants is clearly challenging. To test the heterogeneous beliefs theory we use two imperfect measures to proxy for differences of opinion in market participants' assessment of the future value of bonds during the financial crisis. The first measure is the difference between the S&P and Moody's bond credit rating, and is defined as:

$$Rating\ difference_{i,t} = |S\ \&\ P_{i,t} - Moody's_{i,t}|.$$

Since there is a direct correspondence between the Moody's and S&P rating systems, we simply calculate for each bond and month the (absolute value) notch difference between the Moody's credit rating and the S&P credit rating. Credit-rating data are taken from Mergent FISD.

The second measure of differences of opinion employed in our analysis is analyst earnings forecast dispersion. To calculate this dispersion, we match each bond issue to the relevant firm's equity using the six-digit CUSIP. For each month, following Diether et al. (2002), we then calculate the ratio of the standard deviation of analysts' current-fiscal-year annual earnings per share forecasts to the absolute value of the mean forecast.[17] This analyst earnings forecast dispersion measure proxies for differences of opinion regarding firm equity, and so is expected to be a better measure of differences of opinion for bond values with lower credit quality.[18]

$$Forecast\ dispersion_{i,t} = \frac{\sigma(EPS\ forecast_{i,j,t})}{|Mean(EPS\ forecast_{i,j,t})|},$$

where i indicates stock, j indicates analyst, and t indicates month. EPS forecast is the analysts' forecast at each month for current fiscal year annual earning per share.

A.   Liquidity and Belief Dispersion: Descriptive Evidence

Table 2 provides summary statistics of the distribution of the Moody's-S&P bond-rating difference over the sample period 2007–2010. As can be seen, just over 50% of observations exhibit no rating difference. Over a third of bonds exhibit a rating difference of one notch, approximately 9% of bond-months exhibit a rating difference of two notches, and 2% of the sample exhibits a difference of three notches or more. Table 3 provides the distribution of analyst earnings forecast dispersion. As can

Table 2
Bond-Rating Differences: Summary Statistics

Rating Diff.	Frequency	Percent
0	57,117	52.62
1	39,815	36.68
2	9,465	8.72
3	1,298	1.2
4	532	0.49
5	114	0.11
6	163	0.15
7	30	0.03
8	2	0
9	1	0
10	8	0.01
11	1	0
12	1	0
13	2	0
Total	114,572	100

Table 3
Analysts' Forecast Dispersion: Summary Statistics

Mean	0.134
Median	0.030
Std.	0.642
p25	0.013
p75	0.084
Min.	0
Max.	33.3
Observations	46,635

be seen, the median ratio of earnings forecast dispersion—that is, the ratio of standard deviation to mean analyst forecasts—is 0.03, with a 75th percentile of 0.084.

Figures 10 and 11 portray the evolution of dispersion of opinion over the crisis using the two differences of opinion variables. As can be seen in figure 10, analyst earnings forecast dispersion increased greatly following the collapse of Lehman Brothers, with median forecast dispersion more than doubling from 0.024 in September 2008 to its peak of 0.077 in March 2009. The figure clearly shows that earnings forecast dispersion is seasonal, with a yearly frequency. This seasonality arises due to the fact that dispersion is calculated each month with respect to the (fiscal) year-end earnings forecasts. This dispersion will naturally

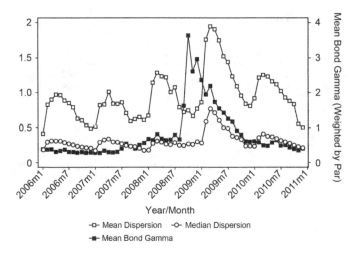

Fig. 10. Mean and median analyst forecast dispersion and bond illiquidity: 2007–2009

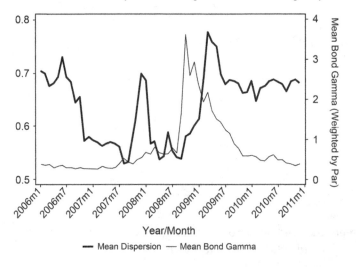

Fig. 11. Mean rating dispersion and bond illiquidity: 2007–2009

decline toward the latter part of the year, as the time until the earnings report shortens. The fact that the dispersion measure is calculated with respect to the end-of-year forecast also explains why the large rise in the measure does not occur immediately after Lehman's collapse in September 2008, but rather early in 2009.

Figure 11 depicts the evolution of the Moody's-S&P bond-rating difference over the crisis. Here we see a spike in the bond-rating difference

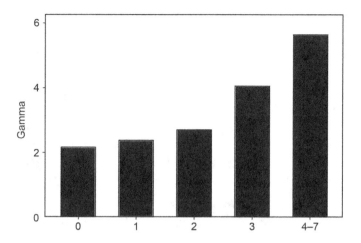

Fig. 12.   Average illiquidity by lagged bond-rating difference: 2007–2009

at the end of 2007, and another larger spike post-Lehman (with a lag as bond ratings take time to adjust). The Moody's-S&P rating difference rises from a mean value of 0.54 in September 2008 to a peak of 0.78 in March 2009.[19] Bond-rating differences decline by August 2009 and remain relatively constant thereafter, but at a level higher than that of early 2007. Indeed, in January 2010, the mean credit-rating difference is 0.67.

Figures 10 and 11 also present the evolution of monthly (par-value-weighted) mean bond illiquidity, as proxied by the γ illiquidity measure. As discussed above, illiquidity sharply rose during the crisis. We note that the concurrent rise of illiquidity and rise of our proxies for differences of opinions during the crisis provides prima facie evidence against the hypothesis that heterogeneous beliefs promote liquidity.

B.   An Empirical Analysis of the Relation between Liquidity and Belief Dispersion

Figure 12 displays average illiquidity calculated over different levels of Moody's-S&P credit-rating difference, while figure 13 depicts average bond illiquidity over the 10 deciles of (lagged) analyst forecast dispersion.[20] Illiquidity in both figures, and throughout the analysis below, is measured by γ. Consistent with the comovement of illiquidity and opinion dispersion depicted in figures 10 and 11, figure 12 shows that illiquidity rises with credit-rating dispersion and particularly so

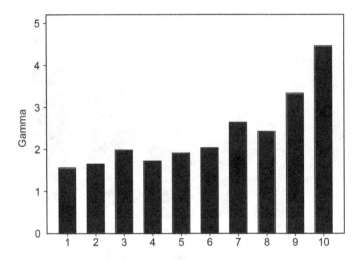

Fig. 13.   Average illiquidity by lagged dispersion of analysts forecast: 2007–2009

for bond-rating differences of three notches or more. Similarly, figure 13 shows that illiquidity rises with higher analyst forecast dispersion. Similar to figure 12, the increase in illiquidity is most pronounced for the top two deciles of forecast dispersion.

Moving to regression analysis, table 4 regresses γ on indicator variables defined over the Moody's-S&P bond-rating differences.[21] Importantly, the regression is run with bond and year-by-month fixed effects to absorb non-time-varying bond determinants of illiquidity, as well as market-wide variation in illiquidity during the crisis. Identification is thus obtained by comparing the illiquidity of two bonds with different measures of the Moody's-S&P spread in the same month and year (as compared to each bond's mean illiquidity).

As can be seen in table 4, increased credit-rating differences between Moody's and S&P are associated with higher bond illiquidity. Difference of opinion, as captured by bond-rating divergence, does not seem to promote liquidity, as would be predicted by the heterogeneous beliefs literature. The economic effect is substantial: controlling for year and month-by-bond fixed effects, as compared to bonds with no disagreement between Moody's and S&P rating, bonds where the respective ratings differ by three notches exhibit a γ illiquidity measure that is higher by 1.26 units, representing approximately 70% of the mean during the crisis. Bonds with a four-notch divergence in ratings exhibit a γ illiquidity measure that is higher by 3.03 units, or 165% of mean γ.

Table 4
Bond Illiquidity and Bond-Rating Differences

	Gamma (1)	Gamma (2)
Rating diff. 1	0.024	0.014
	(0.104)	(0.092)
Rating diff. 2	0.977***	0.658***
	(0.215)	(0.202)
Rating diff. 3	1.615**	1.263**
	(0.705)	(0.636)
Rating diff. 4	3.562***	3.030***
	(0.932)	(0.868)
Constant	0.696***	0.336***
	(0.080)	(0.095)
Bond FE	Yes	Yes
Year FE	Yes	No
Year * month FE	No	Yes
Observations	41,148	41,148
$Adj - R^2$	0.274	0.393

***Significant at the 1 percent level.
**Significant at the 5 percent level.
*Significant at the 10 percent level.

Table 5 runs the analogous regression using indicator variables defined over the quintiles of analyst forecast dispersion. As can be seen, the relation between analyst forecast dispersion and bond illiquidity is generally weak, but the highest quintile of forecast dispersion exhibits substantially larger illiquidity than the lowest quintile of earnings forecast dispersion: with bond and year-by-month fixed effects, the difference between the two quintiles is 0.318, or approximately 250% of the mean level of illiquidity.

Although the positive relation between analyst forecast dispersion and bond illiquidity is not supportive of the heterogeneous beliefs theory, we cannot rule out that endogeneity, and in particular omitted variables, are biasing our results. Indeed, one potential explanation for the positive relation between belief dispersion and illiquidity is that dispersion in beliefs increase when underlying bond values deteriorate. Such a negative relation between belief dispersion and bond price would occur if, for example, heterogeneous beliefs are more likely to arise when bonds become riskier.[22] The positive relation between bond illiquidity and higher bond opinion dispersion in tables 4 and 5 may then simply be reflecting the negative relation between bond price and

Table 5
Bond Illiquidity and Analysts' Forecast Dispersion

	Gamma (1)	Gamma (2)
Forecast dispersion 2	−0.010	0.099
	(0.082)	(0.078)
Forecast dispersion 3	−0.146*	0.030
	(0.089)	(0.092)
Forecast dispersion 4	0.132	0.066
	(0.122)	(0.125)
Forecast dispersion 5	0.382**	0.318*
	(0.174)	(0.174)
Constant	0.650***	0.174
	(0.105)	(0.125)
Bond FE	Yes	Yes
Year FE	Yes	No
Year * month FE	No	Yes
Observations	22,571	22,571
$Adj - R^2$	0.277	0.402

***Significant at the 1 percent level.
**Significant at the 5 percent level.
*Significant at the 10 percent level.

illiquidity combined with the negative relation between bond price and rating dispersion.

Figures 14 and 15 provide initial evidence on the relation between bond risk and opinion dispersion, showing the evolution of the two measures of opinion dispersion during the crisis calculated over four categories of bond credit ratings.[23] Figure 15, which depicts the evolution of average bond-rating differences by bond credit-rating groups, sorts the bonds based on the higher between the Moody's and S&P credit rating. The figures depict the monthly par-value weighted average opinion dispersion measure. As can be seen, lower-rated bonds (rating category 4) exhibit the sharpest rise in opinion dispersion during the crisis. In addition, figure 15 shows a substantial increase in the rating dispersion for the highest credit rating. This is a result of Moody's, but not S&P, downgrading AAA-rated bonds.

To further understand the relation between bond prices and opinion dispersion, table 6 regresses the change in opinion dispersion—either Moody's-S&P credit-rating difference or analyst forecast dispersion—on the change in bond price. As can be seen, difference of opinion, as proxied by bond-rating differences, rise when bond price declines, al-

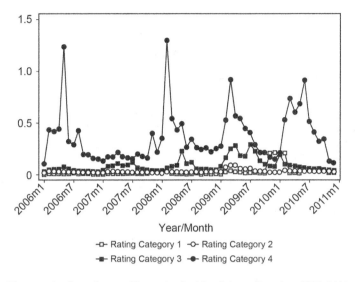

Fig. 14. Analysts forecast dispersion by Moody's credit rating: 2007–2009

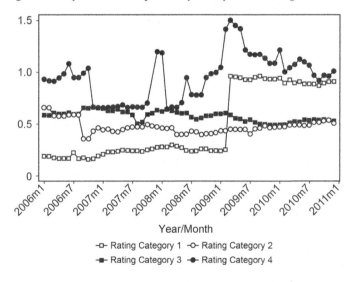

Fig. 15. Mean bond-rating difference by credit rating: 2007–2009

though the effect is not economically large: a one standard deviation decline in bond price increases bond-rating dispersion by approximately
2.5% of the mean rating dispersion (column [1]). However, calculating
the effect over bond-month observations where the γ illiquidity measure is not missing—that is, the sample over which the relation between

Table 6
Changes in Rating Differences and Analyst Dispersion and Price Changes

	Δ Rating Difference	Δ Rating Difference	Δ Analysts Dispersion	Δ Analysts Dispersion
ΔPrice	−0.001***	−0.003***	−0.000	0.004
	(0.000)	(0.001)	(0.001)	(0.002)
Constant	0.004***	0.005***	0.002***	0.000
	(0.001)	(0.001)	(0.000)	(0.002)
Year * month FE	Yes	Yes	Yes	Yes
Gamma not missing	No	Yes	No	Yes
Observations	108,518	41,267	46,363	22,475
Adj − R²	0.00595	0.00593	0.00642	0.00869

***Significant at the 1 percent level.
**Significant at the 5 percent level.
*Significant at the 10 percent level.

illiquidity, bond price, and opinion dispersion is analyzed—triples this economic magnitude, to approximately 7.5% of the mean rating difference. The last two columns of table 6 analyze the relation between analyst forecast dispersion and bond price, showing that it is not statistically significant.

C. Asymmetric Informational and Belief Dispersion: A Horse Race

Table 7 conducts a "horse race" between the two theories of bond illiquidity: the asymmetric information theory, which predicts that illiquidity should decline with bond price, and the heterogeneous beliefs theory, which predicts that differences of opinion promote liquidity. Specifically, the specifications in the table relate the γ measure of bond illiquidity to price as well as to indicator variables defined over the different levels of bond-rating difference. As usual, all regressions are run with bond and year-by-month fixed effects. As can be seen in table 7, illiquidity as measured by γ is still negatively related to bond price— consistent with the asymmetric information theory of liquidity of debt (as in Dang et al. 2012) and the results above. However, as the second column of the table shows, bond-rating dispersion is no longer related to illiquidity in a statistically significant manner once bond price and bond-by-year fixed effects are included.

In a similar manner, table 8 regresses the γ illiquidity measure on both bond price and analyst forecast dispersion. As in table 7, bond price is

Table 7
The Effects of Bond-Rating Differences and Bond Price
on Bond Illiquidity

	Gamma (1)	Gamma (2)
Rating diff. 1	−0.079	−0.062
	(0.083)	(0.079)
Rating diff. 2	−0.009	0.034
	(0.146)	(0.146)
Rating diff. 3	−0.902**	−0.694
	(0.442)	(0.438)
Rating diff. 4	−0.940*	−0.450
	(0.504)	(0.483)
$Price_{t-1}$	−0.210***	−0.174***
	(0.005)	(0.006)
Constant	22.159***	18.314***
	(0.523)	(0.611)
Bond FE	Yes	Yes
Year FE	Yes	No
Year * month FE	No	Yes
Observations	41,148	41,148
$Adj – R^2$	0.421	0.461

***Significant at the 1 percent level.
**Significant at the 5 percent level.
*Significant at the 10 percent level.

still negatively related to bond illiquidity, but differences of opinion, as proxied by analyst forecast dispersion, is not related to γ in a statistically significant manner.

In sum, our results are consistent with the information asymmetry theory of liquidity as in Dang et al. (2012). In contrast, using two proxies for belief dispersion—the Moody's-S&P difference in bond rating and analyst forecast dispersion—we find little support for the hypothesis that liquidity is enhanced as differences of opinion rise. At the aggregate level, as well as using panel data analysis at the individual-bond level, opinion dispersion did not increase liquidity during the crisis period. If anything, the opposite seems to hold, with illiquidity and dispersion positively related, particularly when using the bond-rating difference measure of belief dispersion. However, once we control for bond price movements, belief dispersion is not related in a statistically significant manner to the γ measure of bond-market illiquidity.

Table 8
The Effects of Analyst Dispersion and Bond Price on Bond
Illiquidity

	Gamma (1)	Gamma (2)
Forecast dispersion 2	–0.041	0.073
	(0.070)	(0.070)
Forecast dispersion 3	–0.090	0.141*
	(0.077)	(0.080)
Forecast dispersion 4	–0.114	0.176
	(0.106)	(0.110)
Forecast dispersion 5	–0.370**	0.186
	(0.149)	(0.155)
Price$_{t-1}$	–0.207***	–0.174***
	(0.007)	(0.007)
Constant	21.817***	17.967***
	(0.642)	(0.737)
Bond FE	Yes	Yes
Year FE	Yes	No
Year * month FE	No	Yes
Observations	22,571	22,571
Adj – R^2	0.436	0.479

***Significant at the 1 percent level.
**Significant at the 5 percent level.
*Significant at the 10 percent level.

V. To What Extent Can Bond Price Variation Explain the Rise in Illiquidity during the 2008–2009 Crisis?

We have shown that deteriorations in bond value are associated with rises in bond illiquidity, consistent with the main prediction of the asymmetric information theory of liquidity in debt markets. To what extent can this relation, combined with the market-wide deterioration in bond prices post-Lehman collapse, explain the rise in bond-market illiquidity during the crisis?

To fix ideas, figures 16 and 17 depict the cumulative distribution function and probability density function of bond prices for August and October 2008, as well as January 2009. The figures show the large changes in the distribution of bond prices—with a sharp leftward movement of mass in the distribution of bond prices in October 2008, that is, post-Lehman—which is partially reversed by January 2009.

To understand the role of bond-price deterioration in explaining the behavior of bond-market liquidity during the crisis, we first regress bond

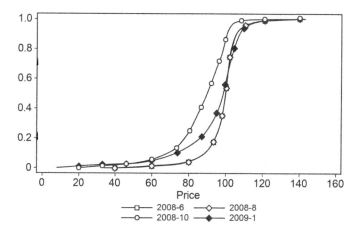

Fig. 16. Bond price cumulative distribution function: 2007–2009

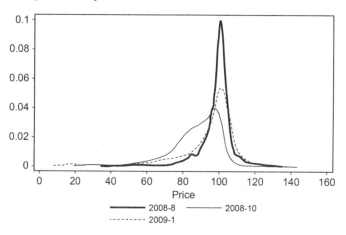

Fig. 17. Bond price probability density function: 2007–2009

illiquidity (proxied by γ) on 20 indicator variables defined over 20 equal-sized bins of lagged bond price, running the following specification:

$$Illiquidity_{i,t} = \beta_0 + \sum_{k=1}^{20} \beta_k \times PriceBin_{i,t-1}^k + b_i\gamma + c_t\delta + \varepsilon_{i,t}, \quad (4)$$

where *Illiquidity* is γ, for bond *i* in month *t*. *PriceBin* is a set of 20 indicator variables based on (within-year) 20 equal-sized bins of bond price—*PriceBin*$_{i,t-1}^k$ equals one if bond *i* is in price bin *k* at month *t* − 1;[24] b_i is a vector of bond fixed effects, and c_t is a vector of either year or year × month fixed effects.[25] Standard errors are clustered at the bond level.

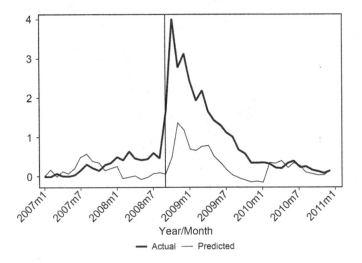

Fig. 18. Predicted illiquidity: 2007–2009 (without bond fixed effects)

Using the regression coefficients, we calculate for each bond in each month in our sample the predicted illiquidity of that bond based on the bond's price. We calculate the market-level predicted illiquidity by calculating the par-value weighted average across all bonds. Figure 18 presents for each month t the change in predicted (weighted-average) bond-market illiquidity from January 2007 to month t, together with the actual change in the weighted average bond-market illiquidity. The figure uses a regression specification that does not include bond fixed effects. Figure 19 displays the analogous predicted change in bond-market illiquidity, but uses the regression specification that includes bond fixed effects.

As can be seen, predicted and actual changes in illiquidity track each other closely up to late 2007 (i.e., precrisis) and from the first quarter of 2010 and on. In the interim period, the increase in actual illiquidity is higher than the predicted increase stemming solely from the decline in bond prices. Still, the leftward shift in the distribution of bond prices, in and of itself, can explain between a quarter and a third of the increase of the rise in actual bond-market illiquidity during the crisis.

VI. Conclusion

This paper analyzes illiquidity in bond markets during financial crises and compares two main theories of liquidity in markets: (1) asymmetric information and adverse selection, and (2) heterogenous beliefs. We find that when bond value deteriorates, bond illiquidity increases, con-

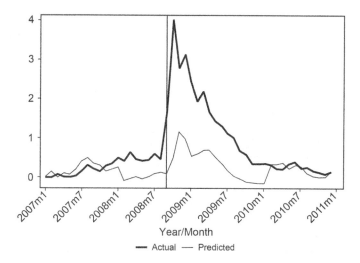

Fig. 19.   Predicted illiquidity: 2007–2009 (with bond fixed effects)

sistent with an adverse-selection model of the information sensitivity of debt contracts as in Dang et al. (2012, 2013) and Holmström (2015). In contrast, we find little support for the hypothesis that opinion dispersion explains illiquidity in financial crises. Our results point to a strong link between crises and the dry-ups of market liquidity and have implications for the efficacy of monetary interventions that are designed to boost lending by the financial sector.

Endnotes

We thank Bengt Holmström for numerous conversations. We also thank Marty Eichanbaum, Ravi Jaganathan, Dimitris Papanikolaou, Jonathan Parker, Sergio Rebelo, Steve Strongin, our NBER Macro Annual discussants V. V. Chari and Raghu Rajan, and seminar participants at the Goldman Sachs Global Markets Institute Academic Fellowship Conference and the NBER's 32nd Annual Conference on Macroeconomics for many comments that have improved the paper. We are grateful to Jack Bao and Kewei Hou for sharing their bond liquidity data. Shoham Benmelech, Zach Mikaya, Khizar Qureshi, Jeremy Trubnick, and Yupeng Wang provided excellent research assistance. Author contacts: e-benmelech@kellogg.northwestern.edu; nbergman@tauex.tau.ac.il. For acknowledgments, sources of research support, and disclosure of the authors' material financial relationships, if any, please see http://www.nber.org/chapters/c13923.ack.

1. See Benmelech, Frydman, and Papanikolaou (2017).

2. In fact, the opposite may hold, as if forced to trade, the optimist will have to sell to the pessimistic agent.

3. For a discussion of the relation between funding liquidity and market liquidity, see Brunnermeier and Pedersen (2009).

4. Our results also hold with alternative measures of illiquidity such as the one proposed in Amihud (2002).

5. In related work, Pérignon, Thesmar, and Vuillemey (forthcoming) empirically examine the market for certificates of deposit in Europe showing that banks experiencing

funding dry-ups subsequently exhibit decreasing performance, consistent with asymmetric information models such as Gorton and Pennacchi (1990), Calomiris and Kahn (1991), and Dang et al. (2012).

6. A one-to-one correspondence exists in the rating system of the two credit-rating agencies, and so this measure is well defined.

7. The fact that the bond-rating difference is no longer positively related to illiquidity once bond price is added as a covariate in the regression analysis likely stems from the fact that price and rating difference are negatively related: decreases in bond price are associated with increases in the Moody's-S&P rating difference. Thus, the positive relation between illiquidity and rating difference may simply be reflecting the negative relation between bond price and illiquidity combined with the negative relation between bond price and rating dispersion.

8. For a model along these lines that relies on an endogenous collateral constraint—rather than on frictions driven by asymmetric information—see Benmelech and Bergman (2012).

9. See Benmelech and Dlugosz (2010).

10. The data used to construct figures 1–3 were obtained from the Securities Industry and Financial Markets Association (SIFMA).

11. Chari, Shourideh, and Zetlin-Jones (2014) provide a dynamic adverse-selection model of secondary loan markets in which reputational considerations give rise to a multiplicity of equilibria. Small reductions in collateral values are shown to bring about collapses in the volume of new issuances.

12. Mishkin (1991, 93).

13. The data is based on table 52 in Hickman (1960).

14. The data is based on Johnson (1936a, 1936b).

15. See Bao et al. (2011) and Benmelech and Bergman (2017) for details about the intuition and the construction of the γ measure.

16. Benmelech and Bergman (2017) provide in-depth analysis of the relation between credit rating and bond liquidity.

17. Data on earnings forecasts are taken from I/B/E/S.

18. For example, consider a firm that has issued a very safe bond trading with a low spread to the maturity-matched Treasury. Even if there exist large differences of opinion regarding firm earnings, these should not be expected to translate into differences of opinion regarding the firm's bond value, which all market participants may agree is very safe, regardless of their position on the firm's equity value.

19. It is interesting to note that the two measures of opinion dispersion, calculated from two different markets (equity and debt) and two differing sets of market participants (rating agencies and equity analysts), attain their maximum value during the crisis in the same month—March 2009. The time-series correlation between the mean forecast dispersion and the mean rating difference is 0.47.

20. Recall that only approximately 1% of the sample has a bond rating of 4 or more.

21. The omitted variable in the regression is a Moody's-S&P credit-rating difference of zero.

22. Thus, one might expect lower belief dispersion regarding the default probability of a AAA-rated bond than for a BB-rated corporate bond.

23. Rating category 1 includes the highest-quality bonds.

24. The first price bin represents bonds with the lowest price.

25. Note that with the inclusion of bond fixed effects, the regression is identified off of changes over time in the level of illiquidity and bond price for each bond.

References

Akerlof, George A. 1970. "The Market for 'Lemons': Quality Uncertainty and the Market Mechanism." *Quarterly Journal of Economics* 84 (3): 488–500.

Amihud, Yakov. 2002. "Illiquidity and Stock Returns: Cross-Section and Time-Series Effects." *Journal of Financial Markets* 5:31–56.

Bao, Jack, Jun Pan, and Jian Wang. 2011. "Liquidity of Corporate Bonds." *Journal of Finance* 66:911–46.

Benmelech, Efraim, and Nittai Bergman. 2012. "Credit Traps." *America Economic Review* 106:3004–32.

———. 2017. "Debt, Information, and Illiquidity." Working paper.

Benmelech, Efraim, and Jennifer Dlugosz. 2010. "The Credit Rating Crisis." *NBER Macroeconomics Annual* 2009:161–207.

Benmelech, Efraim, Carola Frydman, and Dimitris Papanikolaou. 2017. "Financial Frictions and Employment during the Great Depression." NBER Working Paper no. 23216, Cambridge, MA.

Brunnermeier, Markus K., and Lasse H. Pedersen. "Market Liquidity and Funding Liquidity." *Review of Financial Studies* 22:2201–38.

Calomiris, Charles W., and Charles M. Kahn. 1991. "The Role of Demandable Debt in Structuring Optimal Banking Arrangements." *American Economic Review* 81:497–513.

Chari, V. V., Ali Shourideh, and Ariel Zetlin-Jones. 2014. "Reputation and Persistence of Adverse Selection in Secondary Loan Markets." *American Economic Review* 104:4027–70.

Dang Tri Vi, Gary Gorton, and Bengt Holmström. 2012. "Ignorance, Debt and Financial Crises." Working Paper, Columbia University.

———. 2013. "The Information Sensitivity of a Security." Working Paper, Columbia University.

Diether, Karl, Christopher J. Malloy, and Anna Scherbina. 2002. "Differences of Opinions and the Cross Section of Stock Returns." *Journal of Finance* 57:2113–41.

Goetzmann, William N., and Frank Newman. 2010. "Securitization in the 1920s." NBER Working Paper no. 15650, Cambridge, MA.

Gorton, Gary B., and George Pennacchi. 1990. "Financial Intermediaries and Liquidity Creation." *Journal of Finance* 45:49–72.

Hakansson, N., J. Kunkel, and J. Ohlson. 1982. "Sufficient and Necessary Conditions for Information to Have Social Value in Pure Exchange." *Journal of Finance* 37:1169–81.

Harris, Milton, and Artur Raviv. 1993. "Differences of Opinions Make a Horse Race." *Review of Financial Studies* 6:473–506.

Harrison, Michael, and David Kreps. 1978. "Speculative Investor Behavior in a Stock Market with Heterogeneous Expectations." *Quarterly Journal of Economics* 92:323–36.

Hickman, W. Braddock. 1960. *Statistical Measures of Corporate Bond Financing Since 1900.* Princeton, NJ: Princeton University Press.

Holmström, Bengt. 2015. "Understanding the Role of Debt in the Financial System." BIS Working Paper no. 479, Bank for International Settlements.

Johnson, Ernest A. 1936a. "The Record of Long-Term Real Estate Securities." *Journal of Land and Real Estate Economics* 12:44–48.

———. 1936b. "The Record of Long-Term Real Estate Securities: By Cities of Issue." *Journal of Land and Real Estate Economics* 12:195–97.

Kindleberger, Charles. 1990. *Manias, Panics and Crashes,* 4th ed. New York: Basic Books.

Lucas, Deborah, and Robert L. McDonald. 1990. "Equity Issues and Stock Price Dynamic." *Journal of Finance* 45:1019–43.

Milgrom, Paul, and Nancy Stokey. 1982. "Information, Trade and Common Knowledge." *Journal of Economic Theory* 26:17–27.

Mishkin, Frederic S. 1991. "Asymmetric Information and Financial Crises: A Historical Perspective." In *Financial Markets and Financial Crises*, ed. Glenn R. Hubbard, 69–108. Chicago: University of Chicago Press.

Myers, Stewart C., and Nicholas S. Majluf. 1984. "Corporate Financing and Investment Decisions when Firms Have Information That Investors Do Not Have." *Journal of Financial Economics* 13:187–221.

Pérignon, Christophe, David Thesmar, and Guillaume Vuillemey. Forthcoming. "Wholesale Funding Dry-Ups." *Journal of Finance*.

Roll, Richard. 1984. "A Simple Implicit Measure of the Effective Bid-Ask Spread in an Efficient Market." *Journal of Finance* 39 (4): 1127–39.

Rubinstein, M. 1975. "Security Market Efficiency in an Arrow-Debreu Economy." *American Economic Review* 65:812–24.

Spence, Michael. 1973. "Job Market Signaling." *Quarterly Journal of Economics* 87 (3): 355–74.

Sprague, Oliver M. W. 1910. *History of Crises under the National Banking System.* Washington, DC: National Monetary Commission, Government Printing Office.

Varian, H. R. 1989. "Differences of Opinion in Financial Markets." In *Financial Risk: Theory, Evidence and Implications*, ed. Courtenay C. Stone, 3–37. Boston: Kluwer.

Comment

V. V. Chari, *University of Minnesota, Federal Reserve Bank of Minneapolis, and NBER*

Secondary loan markets exhibit a great deal of volatility in the volume of loan issuances. In these markets, originators of loans sell all or part of their loan portfolios to other financial institutions. The market consists of both syndicated loans as well as securitized loans. In August and September of 2008, at the onset of the financial crisis, the volume of syndicated bank loans fell by 37% relative to the previous year (see Ivashina and Scharfstein 2010). New issues in the securitized loan market fell even more dramatically (Chari, Shourideh, and Zetlin-Jones 2014). In the wake of collapses in these markets, policymakers were concerned about the effect of the collapse on broader economic activity and initiated a variety of asset purchase policies intended to restore the volume of new issuances in secondary loan markets. Understanding the nature of these fluctuations and developing models of such collapses is clearly necessary to assess the effects of these policies.

Benmelech and Bergman is a useful empirical contribution to the literature on credit market volatility. The authors analyze data from the 1870s, the 1920s, and the recent financial crisis. They show that in all three episodes, declines in the value of the assets underlying bonds led to sharp declines in the volume of new issuances. They document that measures of illiquidity, such as bid-ask spreads, rise the most for bonds whose market value declines the most relative to face value. A particularly valuable part of the empirical contribution is that they have collected, by hand, data from the 1870s. This data will, I presume, be available to other researchers and will add to our understanding of financial crises.

In a more speculative vein, they argue that they "test" the Dang, Gorton, and Holmström (2013) theory against an alternative theory that traders' beliefs are heterogeneous. A careful reading of their paper shows that they conduct no formal test. Benmelech and Bergman's findings should be interpreted, at best, as providing casual empirical support for the view taken in Dang, Gorton, and Holmström. Indeed, the main contribution of Dang et al. is to argue that debt has desirable properties because it is, in their terminology, "information insensitive," so that issuers who could, in principle, issue a variety of securities optimally choose to issue debt securities. The evidence in Benmelech and Bergman is silent about why issuers of loans choose to issue debt securities. The point of Dang et al. is that debt is valuable because it reduces the likelihood of adverse selection. In my discussion, I will argue that the evidence in Benmelech and Bergman is consistent with the view that adverse selection plays a significant role in accounting for the volatility in credit markets.

In my discussion, I will lay out a theoretical framework, drawn from Chari et al. (2014), which is consistent with the empirical findings Benmelech and Bergman document. This framework is of interest, in part, because for a large range of parameter values, the equilibrium is constrained efficient. Thus, there is no role for policy.

Reputation and Adverse Selection

I will keep the description of the model brief. (See Chari et al. [2014] for a more extended description.) The economy has a large number of loan originators referred to as banks, each endowed with a loan portfolio normalized to 1 and a large number of buyers. All agents are risk neutral. The loan portfolio of each bank yields v with probability π and 0 otherwise. We refer to v as the collateral value of the loan portfolio. The returns are independent across banks. Banks can be of *high quality* in which case $\pi = \bar{\pi}$, or *low quality* in which case $\pi = \underline{\pi}$, with $\underline{\pi} < \bar{\pi}$. We assume that the buyers have a comparative advantage in managing loans, in the sense that the cost to the bank of holding and managing a loan is $c > 0$, and that for the buyers is 0.

Each bank chooses the fraction x of its loan portfolio to sell. Thus, the contract between the banks and buyers can be interpreted as an equity contract. This feature of the model emphasizes that adverse selection can create volatility even with equity contracts. Debt contracts are not essential for adverse selection to play a role. The payoff for a bank of type π that sells a fraction x of its loan portfolio at payment t is

$$t + (1 - x)(\pi v - c),$$

and the profit of a buyer who purchases a fraction of loans x for a payment t from a bank of type π is given by $x\pi v - t$.

If buyers are perfectly informed about the types of banks, it is clearly efficient to have banks sell their entire loan portfolios. We introduce adverse selection by assuming that the bank knows the type of loans in its portfolio and that potential buyers do not. Buyers believe that the bank is high quality with probability μ and low quality with probability $1 - \mu$. We refer to μ as the *reputation* of the bank. We model buyers as engaging in Bertrand-style price competition, so it suffices to restrict the number of potential buyers to two.

Consider the secondary loan market for a given bank with reputation μ. Buyers simultaneously offer contracts to the bank. A *contract*, z, consists of a four-tuple (x_h, t_h, x_l, t_l). Incentive-compatibility requires

$$t_h + (1 - x_h)(\bar\pi v - c) \geq t_l + (1 - x_l)(\bar\pi v - c), \text{ and}$$

$$t_l + (1 - x_l)(\underline\pi v - c) \geq t_h + (1 - x_h)(\underline\pi v - c).$$

A well-known problem with adverse-selection models is that equilibria in pure strategies sometimes do not exist (see, e.g., Rothschild and Stiglitz 1976). Dasgupta and Maskin (1986) show that in many such environments, mixed strategy equilibria do exist. We follow Rosenthal and Weiss (1984) in allowing for mixed strategies on the part of buyers and pure strategies by banks.

A strategy for buyer $j = 1, 2$ is a distribution function $F_j(z)$ over the set $\mathcal{Z}$. A strategy for the bank consists of an action $\delta_j(z_1, z_2; \pi) \in \{0, 1\}$ for $j = 1, 2$, where δ_j denotes the probability that contract j is accepted. Given the mixed strategy by the other buyer, F_{-j}, and the strategy of the bank, δ, the profits earned by a buyer offering contract z are given by

$$\int [\mu \delta_j(z, z_{-j}; \bar\pi)(x_h \bar\pi v - t_h) + (1 - \mu)\delta_j(z, z_{-j}; \underline\pi)(x_l \underline\pi v - t_l)] dF_{-j}(z_{-j}).$$

An *equilibrium* consists of strategies for buyers and a strategy for the bank such that (a) for all z_j in the support of F_j, no alternative contract earns strictly higher profits, and (b) the bank's strategy specifies that its choice maximizes its payoff.

An equilibrium is *separating* if the offers accepted by low- and high-quality banks are different. In such a situation, after trades have occurred, the type of the bank is known. Separating equilibria are of interest when I turn to the dynamic version of the model because future buyers could exploit knowledge of choices by the bank in previous periods and thus affect the behavior of the bank in the current period.

In Chari et al., we characterize the equilibria and show that the equilibrium is unique and separating. Let $d = (\bar{\pi} - \underline{\pi})v / c$ denote the *adverse-selection discount*. This discount captures the extent to which adverse selection reduces trade compared with the full information volume of trade. It turns out that if the bank's reputation $\mu \leq \tilde{\mu}$, the model has a pure strategy equilibrium where

$$\tilde{\mu} = \frac{d}{1 + d},$$

and if $\mu > \tilde{\mu}$, the model has a mixed strategy equilibrium.

In Chari et al., we prove the following proposition.

(The Promise of Adverse-Selection Models in Generating Trade Volume Fluctuations) Decreases in collateral values and increases in the dispersion of bank quality reduce expected trade volumes for banks of all reputational levels and decrease aggregate trade volume.

Although the static adverse-selection model is promising in generating a fall in the expected volume of trade when collateral values fall, all of the decline is due to a decline in the volume of trade of high-quality banks. Low-quality banks always sell their entire loan portfolios. Declines in the volume of trade in secondary markets seem very widespread, suggesting that the volume of trade across banks of varying qualities is highly correlated. Since the static adverse-selection model cannot generate a decline in the volume of trade by all quality types of banks, it faces a correlation challenge when confronted with the data. In Chari et al., we describe a dynamic version of this model and show that it can address the correlation challenge.

The reason the static model cannot address the correlation challenge is that the equilibrium always separates the two types of banks. This separation occurs because buyers have incentives to offer contracts that induce high-quality banks to retain part of their portfolios and offer an attractive price for the rest. Low-quality banks have less of an incentive to accept such contracts because the quality of their portfolios is lower, so retention is less attractive to such banks. That is, buyers have incentive to offer cream-skimming contracts that are more attractive to high-quality banks than to low-quality ones.

Reputation and Adverse Selection in a Dynamic Model

Here I allow for reputational concerns in a dynamic version of the static model. This dynamic model can successfully address the correlation challenge. In the dynamic model it turns out that, with sufficiently little discounting, the equilibrium must necessarily have some pooling. The basic idea is that, with sufficiently little discounting, low-quality banks have strong incentives to mimic the choices of high-quality banks. These incentives imply that cream-skimming contracts are not optimal. With pooling, fluctuations in collateral values induce changes in the behavior of both high-quality and low-quality banks.

Consider, first, a two-period version of the static model. In this version, the quality type of banks is completely persistent in the sense that it is the same in both periods. (In our infinite horizon model, we analyze equilibria with partial persistence.) Loans originated in any period can only be sold in that period, and each bank interacts with a new set of buyers in each period. To allow reputation to play a role, I assume that buyers observe the past contract choices of banks and update their beliefs based on these choices. For simplicity, I assume that buyers do not observe the returns on loans in previous periods, but do observe the contracts chosen. Banks discount future payoffs at rate β.

If banks are sufficiently patient, the equilibrium must display some pooling. The proof of this result is by contradiction. Suppose that an equilibrium exists with complete separation. With such separation, buyers in the last period know the quality level of the bank, so their beliefs are either 1 or 0. The equilibrium in the last period coincides with the static equilibrium with beliefs of 1 or 0, and the associated payoffs of banks can be calculated in a straightforward fashion. If banks are sufficiently patient, in that β is sufficiently large, low-quality banks will mimic the behavior of high-quality banks because the gains in the second period outweigh the losses in the first period.

In Chari et al., we show that this pooling result is particularly strong for banks with sufficiently high reputation levels. In that paper, we prove the following lemma.

Suppose that $\mu \geq \mu^*$ where

$$\mu^* = 1 - \frac{c}{(\bar{\pi} - \underline{\pi})v} = 1 - \frac{1}{d} \tag{C1}$$

and that banks are sufficiently patient. Then full trade by banks of both quality types in the first period is an equilibrium outcome.

In terms of the implications for trade volume, in Chari et al. we prove the following proposition.

(Fluctuations in Trade Volume with Reputational Concerns) If banks are sufficiently patient, a temporary decrease in collateral values weakly reduces expected trade volumes for banks of all reputational levels. Furthermore, if the distribution of reputation has mass below μ^* or in a neighborhood above μ^*, aggregate trade volume strictly falls in the first period.

Recall from the static model that an unanticipated shock to collateral values in the last period reduces volume in that period. These propositions taken together illustrate that if reputational concerns are sufficiently strong, adverse selection can persist and temporary fluctuations in collateral values can induce fluctuations in the volume of trade in both periods. Note also that the volume of trade declines for both high- and low-quality banks so that reputation can help address the correlation challenge.

I turn now to implications for policy in the two-period model. One motivation for such an analysis is that in the wake of the 2007 collapse of secondary loan markets, policymakers proposed a variety of programs intended to restore the volume of trade and to remedy perceived inefficiencies in the market for secondary loans. Under some of these policies, labeled *conventional asset purchase policies*, the government planned to purchase asset-backed securities at prices roughly equal to its perception of the value. In Chari et al., we show that for a large range of parameters, the equilibrium that maximizes the volume of trade is efficient for all reputation levels of banks and that the equilibrium outcomes are inefficient only when the adverse-selection discount is high and reputation levels are low. We show that when equilibrium outcomes are inefficient, unconventional policies that limit private trade can support efficient outcomes.

Another motivation is that policymakers desired to restore the volume of trade because they perceived the collapse as arising from a switch by private agents from one equilibrium to another. Our model has multiple equilibria. We show in Chari et al. that policies in which the government attempts to purchase securities at prices that prevailed before the market collapsed do not by themselves eliminate multiplicity and therefore do not induce an increased volume of trade. In this sense, conventional asset purchase policies are ineffective when reputational concerns are strong. In Chari et al., we describe how unconventional policies can eliminate multiplicity.

In Chari et al., we prove the following proposition. We say that an allocation is ex ante efficient if it maximizes the ex ante expected payoffs of banks subject to incentive constraints and participation constraints of buyers.

Suppose that $\mu \geq \mu^*$. The maximal trade equilibrium is ex ante efficient. Suppose that $\mu \leq \mu^*$ and that banks are sufficiently patient. If $d \leq 2$, the maximal trade equilibrium is ex ante efficient. If $d > 2$, there exists some $\hat{\mu} < \mu^*$ such that for $\mu \geq \hat{\mu}$, the maximal trade equilibrium is efficient, and for $\mu < \hat{\mu}$, the maximal trade equilibrium has inefficiently low levels of volume.

This proposition shows that the mere observation that trade has collapsed does not imply that intervention is desirable.

In Chari et al., we go on to analyze a stochastic infinite-horizon model. The main results from our two-period model turn out to be robust in the infinite horizon. Interestingly, the model is capable of producing a slow buildup of volume in secondary loan markets followed by abrupt collapses. In the model, we introduce stochastic fluctuations in collateral values that are perfectly correlated across banks. We assume that the spread v_t is independently distributed over time and drawn from an identical distribution $G(v_t)$. We allow the quality of the banks to change according to a Markov process. In particular, at the end of each period, with probability λ, each bank draws a new quality level. These draws are independent across banks, and buyers can observe whether a bank has drawn a new quality level. If the bank draws a new quality level, the bank is of high quality with probability μ, where μ is distributed according to the distribution function $\Psi(\mu)$ and $\Psi(\mu)$ is continuous with support on $[0, 1]$. Allowing the quality levels of banks to change ensures that the model has a unique invariant distribution of banks' reputations.

As in the two-period model, if banks are sufficiently patient, then any equilibrium must display some amount of pooling. As in the two-period model, when reputation levels are low, the equilibrium has partial pooling in the sense that high-quality banks use pure strategies and low-quality banks use mixed strategies. In the infinite-horizon model, partial pooling is an equilibrium if current reputation μ_t is below a threshold function $\mu^*(v)$ and below a threshold level μ_h. When reputation levels are high, the equilibrium features complete pooling. Depending on the reputation levels, this complete pooling equilibrium has both high- and low-quality banks selling or holding.

The equilibrium strategy of high-quality banks is to sell their loans if $\mu_t > \mu^*(v)$ and to hold their loans if $\mu_t \leq \mu^*(v)$. The equilibrium strategy of low-quality banks is, in a sense, to mimic the behavior of high-quality banks. These banks sell their loans if $\mu_t > \mu^*(v)$, hold their loans if $\mu_t \leq \mu^*(v)$ and $\mu_t \geq \mu_h$, and mix between selling their loans and holding them if $\mu_t \leq \mu^*(v)$ and $\mu_t < \mu_h$.

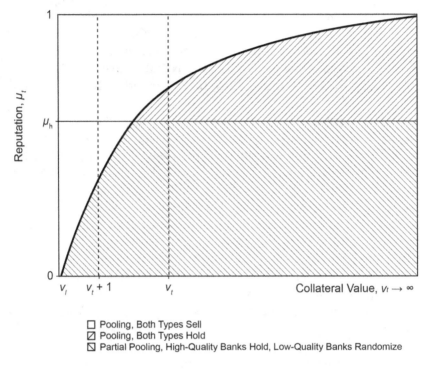

□ Pooling, Both Types Sell
☑ Pooling, Both Types Hold
◩ Partial Pooling, High-Quality Banks Hold, Low-Quality Banks Randomize

Fig. 1.   Strategies of banks and collateral values

In terms of implications for the volume of trade, in Chari et al. we prove the following proposition.

If banks are sufficiently patient and if shocks to collateral values are independent over time, then the aggregate volume of trade is declining in the spread v. Changes in the volume of trade are discontinuous at critical values of the collateral shock.

Figure 1 illustrates the idea behind the proposition. This figure displays the strategies of banks for various values of reputation μ_t in period t. In the partial pooling region, high-quality banks hold their loans and low-quality banks randomize between holding their loans and selling them. The reputation of any bank that holds its loans rises to μ_h in the following period. This feature implies that the equilibrium has a mass point at μ_h. The reputation of any bank that sells its loans falls immediately to 0. In the pooling regions, sellers infer nothing from the bank's actions. Consider an initial collateral value that is at v_t as labeled in the figure. Suppose in period $t + 1$ the economy experiences a fall in collateral values to v_{t+1}. This drop shifts some banks from the partial

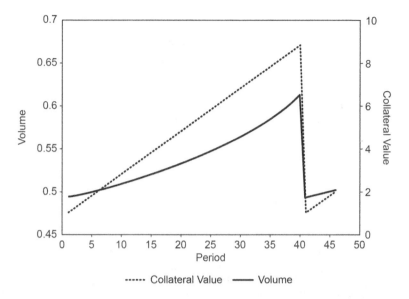

Fig. 2.   Trade volume and collateral values over time

pooling region to the selling region. In particular, because the invariant distribution has a mass point at μ_h, a positive measure of banks change their actions. This feature of the model induces a discontinuous fall in trading volume.

Figure 2 reports results from a numerical example intended to illustrate fluctuations in the trade volume that our model can generate. We have plotted trade volume for a particular simulation of our model. In this simulation, collateral values gradually rise at a linear rate from period 1 to period 40. In period 41, collateral values fall abruptly and then rise at a linear rate from that period onward. The figure shows a sizable increase in volume from period 0 to period 40 and a sharp fall in period 41, after which volume continues to grow. This illustrative simulation captures the idea that the model can generate slow buildups in the volume of trade followed by abrupt collapses.

Conclusion

Benmelech and Bergman are to be commended for their impressive empirical work. In this discussion, I have described a framework with adverse selection and reputation that can account for their empirical findings. The main policy lesson is that, for a large range of parameter values, equilibrium outcomes are efficient. Abrupt collapses in trade volume need not be a sign of poorly functioning markets.

Endnote

For acknowledgments, sources of research support, and disclosure of the author's material financial relationships, if any, please see http://www.nber.org/chapters/c13924.ack.

References

Chari, V. V., Ali Shourideh, and Ariel Zetlin-Jones. 2014. "Reputation and Persistence of Adverse Selection in Secondary Loan Markets." *American Economic Review* 104 (12): 4027–70.

Dang Tri Vi, Gary Gorton, and Bengt Holmström. 2013. "The Information Sensitivity of a Security." Working Paper, Columbia University.

Dasgupta, Partha, and Eric Maskin. 1986. "The Existence of Equilibrium in Discontinuous Economic Games, I: Theory." *Review of Economic Studies* 53 (1): 1–26.

Ivashina, Victoria, and David Scharfstein. 2010. "Bank Lending during the Financial Crisis of 2008." *Journal of Financial Economics* 97 (3): 319–38.

Rosenthal, Robert W., and Andrew Weiss. 1984. "Mixed-Strategy Equilibrium in a Market with Asymmetric Information." *Review of Economic Studies* 51 (2): 333–42.

Rothschild, Michael, and Joseph Stiglitz. 1976. "Equilibrium in Competitive Insurance Markets: An Essay on the Economics of Imperfect Information." *Quarterly Journal of Economics* 90 (4): 629–49.

Comment

Raghuram Rajan, *University of Chicago and NBER*

In the financial crisis of 2008–2009 corporate bond markets became very illiquid, as did a variety of other markets such as structured credit. Why they became so is a very important question for policymakers, especially because policymakers are in the process of creating a framework for liquidity regulation. This paper is therefore very important and timely.

Theories

This paper evaluates two theories of the underpinnings of illiquidity. The first, Dang, Gorton, and Holmström (2012, 2013), argues that bonds are meant to be safe assets, with very little risk. People who buy it do not bother to search for its true value because there is little gain from doing so. The bond trades easily because parties on both sides of the trade are symmetrically informed. However, when the underlying corporate asset values backing corporate bonds fell during the crisis, the bonds fell in price because they were now risky. Not only did prices fall because fundamental values fell, but also because the true fundamental value needed careful assessment and skills to ascertain; some investors would have an advantage over others. Thus bond trading would now be polluted by asymmetric information and bond liquidity would fall significantly. The immediate implication is that a fall in bond prices should be positively correlated with a fall in liquidity.

A second argument is that liquidity relates to differences in beliefs about bond values. If I believe that a bond is undervalued while you believe the same bond is overvalued, we should be willing to trade—so long as we each think the other is misguided and the willingness to trade does not cause either to change beliefs dramatically. The greater the differences in opinion, the more trade should occur. Given that a dramatic change in bond prices could alter beliefs significantly, the authors look to see whether differences in opinion about bond prices could explain the collapse in liquidity. Of course, as the authors acknowledge, some of this depends on endowments. For instance, if before the price drop, the optimists owned bonds, and the dispersion in opinions widened, with the optimism of the optimists falling less than the pessimism of the pessimists, we might see trade fall.

Before getting to the evidence, it may be useful to elaborate a little more on Dang et al. Clearly, equities, even though riskier than corporate bonds, are often more liquid. So the theory cannot be that information-sensitive assets are all illiquid because of the possibility of asymmetric information. It has to be that a change of a bond from being information insensitive to information sensitive disrupts the market and makes the now-risky bond illiquid. If that is so, however, there are other possibilities than asymmetric information disrupting trade.

One possibility is asymmetric skills (Hanson and Sundaram 2013). The bond may initially be held by pension funds with limited analytical ability. As the bond becomes risky, they may simply not understand how to value it. With everyone who holds these bonds in the same boat, they cannot sell to traditional investors in the asset. A few new specialized and skilled buyers who understand the asset, like Blackrock or PIMCO, may come into the market, but given their small numbers they are unlikely to offer competitive prices. So bondholders may be reluctant to sell until more specialists enter the market, and the market price discount from the new lower fundamentals dissipates. The drop in trading then is not because of asymmetric information, but because of limited buyer skills, so that there is what Allen and Gale (2000) call "cash in the market" pricing for the bond. Interestingly, as Diamond and Rajan (2011) argue, the possibility of "cash in the market" pricing in the secondary trading of bonds can also impair primary market loans by institutions. Intuitively, specialized buyers may prefer buying loans at bargain basement prices in the secondary market to tying up their money in low interest loans in the primary market.

One implication of the asymmetric skills theory is that bonds that fall from a higher rating to a lower rating should be illiquid for a while only, until enough skilled bond buyers emerge to push prices up to a level the unskilled bond holders feel reflects fundamentals—the unskilled do not need to know the true value of the bond, they just need to see enough buyers competing to trade. Of course, even the Dang et al. model could explain the increase in liquidity over time for a fallen bond as reflecting the growing presence of skilled and informed buyers on both sides of any trade, as the old uninformed investors sell out and leave. The essential difference in the two models is that trading is hampered in Dang et al. by a fear of getting too low a price from a better informed buyer, while it is hampered in Hanson and Sundaram (2014) by the fear that the price will be low because too few skilled buyers exist (or have too little capital to buy). Unfortunately, it is hard to tell these two models apart.

The policy implications, however, differ. In the Dang et al. model, the fewer the informed, the less the contamination of trades by the possibility of asymmetric information. The aim should then be to depress incentives for information acquisition by pushing up fundamental bond prices, for instance by fiscal transfers to troubled firms that have issued bonds. In the Hanson and Sunderam model, prices would move up to fundamentals and trading would pick up if the skilled buyers had enough capital so that "cash in the market" prices did not prevail, or if enough such buyers were incentivized to investigate these bonds. The policy implication would be not to interfere directly in bond pricing, but instead to offer additional capital to skilled buyers, even while letting the bond discount attract new skilled buyers. Indeed, Hanson and Sunderam argue that an excessive amount of safe bonds may crowd out information gathering altogether, so the government may want to limit how many safe bonds there are (in contrast to Dang et al.).

There is yet another possibility based on the clientele for liquid or money-like instruments. What if high-quality bonds are held primarily for precautionary liquidity purposes, where the bondholder prefers bonds that are not risky so that he can sell them to meet sudden demands for cash (say to make other investments). As soon as they prove to be risky, they lose their moneyness, and the clientele for these bonds diminishes. Over time, new demand emerges for these bonds from those who want higher returns only but before this clientele emerges, there is a decline in price and trading, with causality going both ways.

A final possibility is the aversion to recognizing losses—either for behavioral reasons or for agency reasons. What if investors who lost money on a bond were reluctant to trade it and realize the losses—following the adage that once an investor experience losses, she becomes a long-term investor, hoping the bond will recover. Alternatively, if she holds the bond in a portfolio that does not have to be marked to market, she may decide not to sell for fear of triggering losses and having to raise capital. So, liquidity could dry up for the most impaired bonds.

The point is that there are a number of models that have similar predictions to the ones that Benmelech and Bergman test. It would be nice if they could do more work, perhaps not in this paper, distinguishing between these closely related explanations.

Empirical Findings

The paper finds that a decline in bond prices leads to a decline in bond liquidity, where illiquidity is primarily measured as the transitory component of price changes. By contrast, measures of dispersion in opinion about bond values seem to go the "wrong" way, and are associated with a decline in bond liquidity. Finally, in a horse race, price declines trump differences in opinion in explaining the fall in liquidity.

The authors recognize that there is the possibility of reverse causality—low liquidity could cause low prices. In other work (Benmelech and Bergman 2017), the authors have instrumented bond prices with equity returns, arguing that equity returns affect bond prices directly, but are not correlated with bond liquidity other than through lower bond prices. As with any instrument, one can question this assertion. For instance, lower secondary market liquidity impairs primary market liquidity. Firms that cannot raise money may see returns diminish. So stock returns may be correlated with liquidity other than through bond prices. At any rate, since there are theories (see above) that would argue for reverse causality (changes in liquidity driving bond price changes), and Dang et al. can coexist with reverse causality, I am not sure the authors gain much by asserting it is not at work.

My greater concern on the empirical side is with the measures of dispersion of opinion. One, for example, is the difference between Moody's and S&P ratings. They, however, are acknowledged to measure different things. Moody's rates bonds based on the expected loss to an investor from holding that bond, while S&P measures the probability of default. Could it be possible that these ratings diverge more when a bond suddenly slips closer to default, because the probability of default moves in a different way from the expected loss? One clue could potentially be if, say, Moody's systematically downgrades bonds by less (or more) when bond prices fall a certain amount. That would indicate the increased dispersion of ratings may be caused because rating agencies follow different methodologies rather than because they have differences in opinion—it is hard to imagine that Moody's would be systematically more optimistic (or pessimistic) about bonds.

If my concern is borne out, then the proxy for differences in opinion will track changes in bond prices and may not be measuring anything different. If so, the horse race may not be as discriminating as might otherwise seem.

Analyst forecast dispersion may suffer from a different problem. Analysts are notoriously hesitant to cut ratings, for fear of annoying their clients—often, they stop updating their coverage rather than downgrading the bond. If, following a downturn in a corporation's prospects, some analysts simply leave their forecast stale and unchanged (or drop coverage leaving their old forecasts in place), while others who have fewer business ties to the client change their forecasts immediately, we would see an increase in the dispersion in forecasts soon after adverse events that also moved the bond price. Once again, the dispersion may not really reflect differences in opinion, but differences in the degree to which the analyst feels beholden to the client. One way to check this is to drop stale forecasts, and use only the most recently updated ones. While analysts may not actively lie by shading their forecasts favorably to the client, they may prefer to neglect to update. So the dispersion in fresh forecasts should be lower, if my concerns are borne out.

The broader point is that the measures of differences in opinion need some reexamination, but the relationship between bond prices and liquidity is not affected.

Conclusion

This is a very interesting paper on an important topic with very useful results. Illiquidity and bond price changes are found to be correlated in crises, a feature of credit market freezes. More needs to be done to separate the Dang et al. theory from close alternatives. Distinguishing between theories is necessary because it could affect policy prescriptions. All in all, this is an important contribution.

Endnote

For acknowledgments, sources of research support, and disclosure of the author's material financial relationships, if any, please see http://www.nber.org/chapters/c13925.ack.

References

Allen, Franklin, and Douglas Gale. 2000. "Financial Contagion." *Journal of Political Economy* 108:1–33.
Benmelech, Efraim, and Nittai Bergman. 2017. "Debt, Information, and Illiquidity." Working paper.
Dang, Tri Vi, Gary Gorton, and Bengt Holmström. 2012. "Ignorance, Debt and Financial Crises." Working Paper, Columbia University.
———. 2013. "The Information Sensitivity of a Security." Working Paper, Columbia University.
Diamond, Douglas, and Raghuram Rajan. 2011. "Fear of Fire Sales, Illiquidity Seeking, and Credit Freezes." *Quarterly Journal of Economics* 126 (2): 557–91.
Hanson, Samuel G., and Adi Sunderam. 2013. "Are There Too Many Safe Securities? Securitization and the Incentives for Information Production." *Journal of Financial Economics* 108 (3): 565–584.

Discussion

Chris Carroll opened the discussion by suggesting that if the authors are interested in the determinants of illiquidity in crises they should study the well-known arbitrage opportunities that arose in the recent financial crisis in what were normally very liquid markets. These events cannot be explained by the theories tested in the paper, yet are related to the broader idea that information is especially revealing in extreme times.

John Cochrane cautioned that while the paper studies the impact of price changes on liquidity, many sources of price variation are not related to a change in the informational sensitivity of debt securities. For example, increases in risk-free rates or risk premia will reduce bond prices, but should have no effect on liquidity through an information-sensitivity channel. Further, he raised concern that the informational story of Dang, Gorton, and Holmström (2013) tested in the paper would apply best to short-term debt such as repo and commercial paper, which attract buyers that do not typically pay attention to issuer fundamentals. The paper tests this theory on long-term corporate bond issues, for which liquidity is not as important since most of the investors hold these bonds until maturity.

Several participants promoted the idea that the relationship between price and liquidity during financial crises is more consistent with asymmetric information in secondary markets than it is with the Dang et al. (2013) channel in which illiquidity is related to prices through price declines proxying for increased information sensitivity as default risk increases.

Frederic Mishkin suggested that the empirical results of the paper are consistent with his previous work finding that financial crises are usually precipitated by an event that is associated with a deterioration of information quality. In his view the evidence in the paper is actually consistent with an asymmetric information story.

Larry Christiano and Robert Hall argued that a relationship between price and liquidity in crisis times can be explained by the fact that in a crisis the usual (and informed) buyers and sellers in an asset class all become sellers. Hall remarked that this is especially relevant in the market for long-term corporate debt. Most of this debt is purchased at issuance and held to maturity. The secondary market that does emerge is small relative to total issuance, and large shocks could easily diminish supply of and exacerbate demand for liquidity provision. He further emphasized that in this case, it takes some time for new buyers to emerge or old buyers to recapitalize. Hall cited as an anecdote his own success in exploiting a mispricing in the TIPS market in October 2008. This mispricing emerged because two hedge funds had to rapidly liquidate their TIPS positions because of increased margin requirements on unrelated positions. The mispricing persisted for about six weeks.

Christiano noted the salience of asymmetric information in this story because new buyers have much less experience valuing these assets than the sellers. He then related the dynamics of liquidity in the corporate bond market to those of asset-backed securities held by banks during the 2007–2009 financial crisis. In that case, a run-type situation occurred and banks were forced to try to liquidate large securities positions. But the only potential buyers were uninformed about these assets. Effi Benmelech responded that the run-like dynamics described by Christiano would not apply in his study of the long-term corporate debt of nonfinancial firms.

Related to the discussion of the relationship between liquidity and the identity of buyers, Cochrane added that government policies to prop up bond prices could have adverse consequences for private liquidity creation and for the financial health of corporate debt issuers. He noted that so-called fire sales are also buying opportunities for investors with cash to invest. Propping up prices lowers their buying opportunity and induces them not to keep ready cash around, which makes crises worse.

Further regarding policy, Mishkin noted that the speed and magnitude of government-liquidity provision in response to credit freezes is very important to a policy's success. In the market crash of 1987, Alan Greenspan's announcement that the Federal Reserve would provide backstop liquidity was enough to stem the crisis, and the Fed did not even need to provide the backstop. In 2007 when the interbank market began to freeze, the Fed lowered the discount window rate by 25 basis points, but this was not sufficient.

Jon Steinsson raised the point that liquidity in a market should be related to the degree of belief heterogeneity among participants, since heterogeneous beliefs is among the most salient explanations for why people trade. Benmelech responded that volume and liquidity are not so closely related, and that the modern approach to liquidity measurement is to look at price impact of a given trade.

7

Distortions in Macroeconomics

Olivier Blanchard, *Peterson Institute for International Economics and NBER*

After-dinner talks are the right places to test tentative ideas, hoping for the indulgence of the audience. Mine will be in that spirit, and reflect my thoughts on what I see as a central macroeconomic question: What are the distortions that are central to understanding short-run macroeconomic evolutions?

I shall argue that, over the past 30 years, macroeconomics had, to an unhealthy extent, focused on a one-distortion (nominal rigidities), one-instrument (policy rate) view of the macro economy. As useful as the body of research that came out of this approach was, it was too reductive, and proved inadequate when the Great Financial Crisis came. We need, even in our simplest models, to take into account more distortions. Having stated the general argument, I shall turn to a specific example and show how this richer approach modifies the way we should think about policy responses to the low neutral interest rates we observe in advanced economies today.

Let me develop this theme in more detail.

Back in my student days, that is, the mid-1970s, much of macroeconomic research was focused on building larger and larger macroeconometric models based on the integration of many partial equilibrium parts. Some researchers worked on explaining consumption, others on explaining investment, or asset demands, or price and wage setting. The empirical work was motivated by theoretical models, but these models were taken as guides rather than as tight constraints on the data. The estimated pieces were then put together in larger models. The behavior captured in the estimated equations reflected in some ways both optimization and distortions, but the mapping was left, it was felt by necessity, implicit and somewhat vague. (I do not remember hearing the word "distortions" used in macro until the 1980s.)

These large models were major achievements. But, for various reasons, researchers became disenchanted with them. Part of it was obscurity: the parts were reasonably clear, but the sum of the parts often had strange properties. Part of it was methodology: identification of many equations was doubtful. Part of it was poor performance: the models did not do well during the oil crises of the 1970s. The result of disappointment was a desire to go back to basics.

For my generation of students, three papers played a central role. One was the paper by Robert Lucas (1973) on imperfect information. The other two were the papers by Stanley Fischer (1977) and by John Taylor (1980) on nominal rigidities. While the approaches were different, the methodology was similar: the focus was on the effects of one distortion—imperfect information leading to incomplete nominal adjustment in the case of Lucas, and explicit nominal rigidities, without staggering of decisions in Fischer, with staggering of decisions in Taylor. All other complications were cast aside to focus on the issue at hand, the role of nominal rigidities and the implied nonneutrality of money.

Inspired by these models, further work then clarified the role of monopolistic competition, the role of menu costs, and the role of different staggering structures, showing how each of them shaped the dynamic effects of nominal shocks. The natural next step was the re-integration of these nominal rigidities in a richer, microfounded, general equilibrium model. The real business cycle model, developed by Kydland and Prescott (1982), provided the simplest and most convenient environment. Thus was born the New Keynesian (NK) model, a slightly odd marriage of the most neoclassical model and an ad hoc distortion. But it was a marriage that has held together to this day.

In the hands of researchers like Woodford (2003) or Clarida, Gali, and Gertler (1999), the model provided the basis, or at least the intellectual support, for the development of a new approach to monetary policy, that is, inflation targeting, an approach adopted by most central banks around the world. It had a rich set of implications, with their origin deriving from the basic conceptual structure: one distortion, that is, nominal rigidities in some form (often the convenient Poisson form derived by Calvo), and one instrument, the nominal policy rate. The right use of the instrument could largely undo the distortion. Maintaining constant and low inflation would both minimize distortions and lead to the right level of output, a proposition Jordi Gali and I baptized, tongue in cheek, the Divine Coincidence (Blanchard and Gali 2007).

What I have described is obviously a caricature. First, but this is minor, there had to be at least another distortion: to talk about price setting, firms had to have some pricing power, and this led to a monopoly markup. Under Dixit-Stiglitz constant elasticity assumptions, the markup, however, was constant, and the effects of the distortion were largely irrelevant with respect to the effects of monetary policy. Second, some models had more than one nominal rigidity, for example, rigidities in both wage and price setting as in Erceg, Henderson, and Levin (2000); some models combined real and nominal rigidities, for example, in my work with Gali (Blanchard and Gali 2007). Third, there was important work on credit (e.g., Bernanke and Gertler 1989) and on liquidity (e.g., Diamond and Dybvig 1983; Holmstrom and Tirole 1998). But, while these papers were well known and some of these mechanisms were integrated in DSGE models, they did not become part of the basic model. (I remember telling Bengt that, while I admired his work on liquidity with Jean, I was not sure how central it was to macro.) Stable and low inflation as the target, and the use of the policy rate as the instrument, remained the basic approach to policy.

Even before the Great Financial Crisis, I felt some unease with two characteristics of the basic model and its larger DSGE cousins (Blanchard 2009). The first was that the deep reasons behind nominal rigidities, such as the costs of collecting information or of taking decisions were probably relevant beyond price or wage setting, and thus were relevant for consumption, investment, and portfolio choices, with important but neglected implications for macroeconomic dynamics. The second that the models assumed much too much forward lookingness to agents. When combined with rational expectations, the implications of the Euler equation for consumption, or the interest parity condition for exchange rates, were simply counterfactual.

The financial crisis then made it clear that the basic model, and even its DSGE cousins, had other serious problems, that the financial sector was much more central to macroeconomics than had been assumed. Financial markets were incomplete, raising issues of solvency and liquidity. The role and the importance of debt were central to understanding credit booms and busts. Bank runs were not just a historical footnote, but an essential aspect of maturity transformation. These distortions were at the core of the crisis; nominal rigidities may have made it worse, but even absent nominal rigidities, the financial crisis would likely have led to a large decrease in output.

Since the start of the crisis, DSGE models have been extended to allow for a richer financial sector and integrate some of these distortions (e.g., Gertler and Kiyotaki 2013). But I feel we still do not have the right core model. Put another way, suppose that we were building a small macroeconomic model from scratch. What are, say, the three distortions we would deem essential to have in such a model, and, by implication, to have as the core of any DSGE model? What model should we teach at the start of the first-year graduate course?[1]

I do not have the answer, but I have a few ideas. This is where my talk becomes even more tentative.

My first distortion would remain nominal rigidities. As much as I try, I just cannot interpret macroeconomic evolutions without relying on nominal rigidities. Proof of their relevance is in the ability of central banks to maintain their desired nominal and real interest rates over long periods of time, or in the dramatically different behavior of real exchange rates under fixed and flexible exchange rate systems (Mussa 1986).

My second distortion would be finite horizons. Not so much the finiteness that comes from death and the absence of operative bequest motives, but the finite horizon that comes from bounded rationality, from myopia, from the inability to think too far into the future.

My third distortion would be in the role of own funds in spending decisions, whether it is capital for banks, or capital or collateral for firms or people. While it was only one of many distortions at play in the financial crisis, it can explain much of what happened, and how shocks affect financial intermediation.

How I would actually put them together in a basic model is a much harder question, the difference between a dinner talk and a serious paper. We have off-the-shelf formalizations for nominal rigidities, for myopia, for capital constraints; for example Calvo for the first, Gabaix (2016) for the second, and Holmstrom and Tirole (1997) for the third.[2] Each of them has its strengths and weaknesses, and whether they fit together conceptually is not obvious. (On this, I like the remarks by Cochrane [2016] on the potential misuse of the Gabaix formalization of myopia.) In thinking about how to combine these or other formalizations, I still struggle between keeping strictly to microfoundations or writing plausible characterizations more faithful to the empirical evidence, but more loosely connected to theory (this is the old discussion between the pros and cons of the IS-LM versus the NK model, and whether there is a middle way). But this is a separate set of methodological issues, which I shall leave aside here.

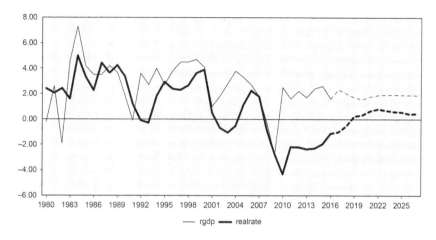

Fig. 1.

The Low Real Safe Rate and Macroeconomic Policy

For better or for worse, simple conceptual frames such as the NK model strongly shape and limit our thinking. With the above discussion in mind, let me take an example, namely the potential policy implications of the very low level of the policy rate needed to maintain output at potential, the so-called neutral rate.[3]

Nearly all the discussion about policy implications has focused on monetary policy. In the one-distortion, one-instrument view of the economy, so long as the policy rate does not hit the zero lower bound, the low neutral rate does not pose a particular problem: the central bank should simply choose a policy rate consistent with this low neutral rate. At the zero lower bound (or, to the extent that we now know that policy rates can be at least slightly negative, the "effective lower bound"), the issue becomes the degree to which financial assets are imperfect substitutes, and how the policy tool kit must be extended to allow for purchases of specific assets. This is indeed how, for the most part, both the policy discussion and policy actions have unfolded.

Figure 1 suggests, however, that the discussion should be more ambitious. It shows the evolution of the one-year real rate (constructed as the difference between the one-year Treasury rate minus the corresponding CBO forecast of inflation) and the real growth rate in the United States since 1980. The one-year real rate has indeed come down since the early 1980s. And, interestingly, it is now substantially below the growth rate, and expected to be below it for the foreseable future. This raises two interesting possibilities:

The first is that the low policy rate reflects a low marginal product of capital, and that the US economy has become dynamically inefficient. This could be the case if, for example, consumers had finite horizons, either for physical reasons as in the overlapping generation model (should we call death a distortion?) or because of bounded rationality. If this were the case, the right policy tool would not be monetary policy, but rather policies aimed at decreasing saving. The right focus should be on fiscal policy. The right policy would be to increase public debt, and such a policy could be Pareto improving.

As exciting as this possibility would be, it does not appear, however, that this is the right explanation for the low safe rate. What matters for dynamic inefficiency is not the relation between the safe rate and the growth rate, but between the marginal product of capital and the growth rate. And the empirical evidence on the marginal product is that it has remained much higher than the growth rate.

This leads to the second hypothesis. That the difference between the marginal product and the safe rate has increased, leading to a low safe rate for a given marginal product. Put another way, it points to a large liquidity or risk premium. This in turn leads to a focus on the factors behind the premium, and the role of distortions in financial markets. Thinking of the premium as a risk premium, it takes us back to the equity premium puzzle identified by Mehra and Prescott (1985), and the various tentative resolutions to the puzzle. Thinking of the premium as a liquidity premium, it takes us to what is behind the demand for safe assets, along the lines of Caballero and Farhi (2014). It leads us to think about the role of financial regulations, and thus the role of regulatory policy. And if the high premium reflects, at least in part, distortions, the focus should then be on both fiscal and financial policies. If, for example, the safe rate is going to remain below the marginal product of capital, this implies that the government can borrow, never repay the debt, and still maintain a stable debt-to-GDP ratio. Should it do it? The fact that it can does not mean that it should. Or, to the extent that various distortions are behind the premium, should it instead remove them, even if this means a higher safer rate, and thus a higher cost of public borrowing?

My intention here was not to give the answers, but to show how much a richer view of the relevant distortions leads to a richer discussion of policy. To repeat and conclude: We must move from a dominant "one distortion/one instrument" to a "many distortions/many instruments" view of the economy. In doing so, the way we think about the economy, and about the appropriate policies, will be much more fertile.

Endnotes

Talk, NBER Macroeconomics Annual Conference, April 2017. I thank Marty Eichenbaum, Jonathan Parker, and Adam Posen for comments. For acknowledgments, sources of research support, and disclosure of the author's material financial relationships, if any, please see http://www.nber.org/chapters/c13955.ack.
    1. This may be a hopeless and misguided search. Maybe even the simplest characterization of fluctuations requires many more distortions. Maybe different distortions are important at different times. Maybe there is no simple model . . . I keep faith that there is.
    2. A fascinating question is why the Euler equation fails. One hypothesis is because of bounded rationality, for example, á la Gabaix. Another is because of borrowing constraints, for example, á la McKay, Nakamura, and Steinsson (2016). The answer is probably both. Interestingly, both lead, at least to a close approximation, to a similar modified Euler equation.
    3. After giving the talk, I was made aware of an article by Davig and Gurkaynak (2015) that has a closely related theme.

References

Bernanke, Ben, and Mark Gertler. 1989. "Agency Costs, Net Worth, and Business Fluctuations." *American Economic Review* 79 (1): 14–31.
Blanchard, Olivier. 2009. "The State of Macro." *Annual Review of Economics* 1:209–28.
Blanchard, Olivier, and Jordi Gali. 2007. "Real Rigidities and the New Keynesian Model." *Journal of Money, Credit, and Banking* 39 (1): 35–66.
Caballero, Ricardo, and Emmanuel Farhi. 2014. "The Safety Trap." NBER Working Paper no. 19927, Cambridge, MA.
Clarida, Richard, Jordi Gali, and Mark Gertler. 1999. "The Science of Monetary Policy: A New Keynesian Perspective." *Journal of Economic Literature* 37:1661–707.
Cochrane, John. 2016. "Comments on a Behavioral New-Keynesian Model by Xavier Gabaix." Working Paper, University of Chicago.
Davig, Troy, and Refet Gurkaynak. 2015. "Is Optimal Monetary Policy Always Optimal?" *International Journal of Central Banking* 11 (S1): 353–82.
Diamond, Douglas, and Philip Dybvig. 1983. "Bank Runs, Deposit Insurance, and Liquidity." *Journal of Political Economy* 91 (3): 401–19.
Erceg, Christopher, Dale Henderson, and Andrew Levin. 2000. "Optimal Monetary Policy with Staggered Wage and Price Contracts." *Journal of Monetary Economics* 46 (2): 281–313.
Fischer, Stanley. 1977. "Long-Term Contracts, Rational Expectations and the Optimal Money Supply Rule." *Journal of Political Economy* 85:191–205.
Gabaix, Xavier. 2016. "A Behavioral New Keynesian Model." NBER Working Paper no. 22954, Cambridge, MA.
Gertler, Mark, and Nobuhiro Kiyotaki. 2013. "Banking, Liquidity, and Bank Runs in an Infinite-Horizon Economy." NBER Working Paper no. 19129, Cambridge, MA.

Holmström, Bengt, and Jean Tirole. 1997. "Financial Intermediation, Loanable Funds, and the Real Sector." *Quarterly Journal of Economics* 112 (3): 663–91.
———. 1998. "Private and Public Supply of Liquidity." *Journal of Political Economy* 106 (1): 1–40.
Kydland, Finn, and Edward Prescott. 1982. "Time to Build and Aggregate Fluctuations." *Econometrica* 50:1345–70.
Lucas, Robert. 1973. "Some International Evidence on the Output-Inflation Trade-Off." *American Economic Review* 63 (3): 326–34.
McKay, Alisdair, Emi Nakamura, and Jon Steinsson. 2016. "The Power of Forward Guidance Revisited." *American Economic Review* 106 (10): 3133–58.
Mehra, Rajnish, and Edward Prescott. 1985. "The Equity Premium." *Journal of Monetary Economics* 15:145–61.
Mussa, Michael. 1986. "Nominal Exchange Rate Regimes and the Behavior of Real Exchange Rates: Evidence and Implications." *Carnegie-Rochester Conference Series on Public Policy* 25:117–214.
Taylor, John. 1980. "Aggregate Dynamics and Staggered Contracts." *Journal of Political Economy* 88 (1): 1–24.
Woodford, Michael. 2003. *Interest and Prices: Foundations of a Theory of Monetary Policy*. Princeton, NJ: Princeton University Press.